D0518455

THE IMPACT OF GOVERNMENT MANPOWER PROGRAMS

In General, and on Minorities and Women

Major Industrial Research Unit Studies

The Wharton School's Industrial Research Unit has been noted for its "relevant research" since its founding in 1921. The IRU is now the largest academic publisher of manpower and collective bargaining studies. ***Major Industrial Research Unit Studies*** **and monographs in special series, such as the Racial Policies of American Industry, the Labor Relations and Public Policy Series, and Manpower and Human Resources Studies, are published as research reports are completed.**

Recent Industrial Research Unit Studies
(Order from Industrial Research Unit, Vance Hall/CS, The Wharton School, University of Pennsylvania, Philadelphia 19174)

No. 44 Herbert R. Northrup and Gordon R. Storholm, *Restrictive Labor Practices in the Supermarket Industry* (1967) $7.50.

No. 45 William N. Chernish, *Coalition Bargaining: A Study of Union Tactics and Public Policy* (1969) $7.95.

No. 46 Herbert R. Northrup, Richard L. Rowan *et al., Negro Employment in Basic Industry: A Study of Racial Policies in Six Industries,* Studies of Negro Employment, Vol. I (1970) $15.00.

No. 47 Armand J. Thieblot, Jr., and Linda P. Fletcher, *Negro Employment in Finance: A Study of Racial Policies in Banking and Insurance*, Studies of Negro Employment, Vol. II (1970) $9.50.

No. 48 Bernard E. Anderson, *Negro Employment in Public Utilities: A Study of the Racial Policies in the Electric Power, Gas, and Telephone Industries,* Studies of Negro Employment. Vol. III (1970) $8.50.

No. 49 Herbert R. Northrup *et. al., Negro Employment in Southern Industry: A Study of the Racial Policies in the Paper, Lumber, Tobacco, Bituminous Coal, and Textile Industries,* Studies of Negro Employment, Vol. IV (1971) $13.50.

No. 50 Herbert R. Northrup *et. al., Negro Employment in Land and Air Transport: A Study of Racial Policies in the Railroad, Airline, Trucking, and Urban Transit Industries,* Studies of Negro Employment, Vol. V (1971) $13.50.

No. 51 Gordon F. Bloom, Charles R. Perry, and F. Marion Fletcher, *Negro Employment in Retail Trade: A Study of Racial Policies in the Department Store, Drugstore, and Supermarket Industries,* Studies of Negro Employment, Vol. VI (1972) $12.00.

No. 52 Lester Rubin, William S. Swift, and Herbert R. Northrup, *Negro Employment in the Maritime Industries: A Study of Racial Policies in the Shipbuilding, Longshore, and Offshore Maritime Industries*, Studies of Negro Employment, Vol. VII (1974) $12.00.

No. 53 Charles R. Perry, Bernard E. Anderson, Richard L. Rowan, Herbert R. Northrup *et. al., The Impact of Government Manpower Programs,* Manpower and Human Resources Studies, No. 4 (1975) $18.50.

THE IMPACT OF GOVERNMENT MANPOWER PROGRAMS

In General, and on Minorities and Women

(Manpower and Human Resources Studies, No. 4)

by

CHARLES R. PERRY
BERNARD E. ANDERSON
RICHARD L. ROWAN
HERBERT R. NORTHRUP

and

PETER P. AMONS
STEPHEN A. SCHNEIDER
MICHAEL E. SPARROUGH
HARRIET GOLDBERG
LARRY R. MATLACK
CORNELIUS A. MCGUINNESS

INDUSTRIAL RESEARCH UNIT
THE WHARTON SCHOOL
VANCE HALL/CS
UNIVERSITY OF PENNSYLVANIA
PHILADELPHIA, PENNSYLVANIA 19174
U.S.A.

Second Printing 1976

This study was prepared for the Manpower Administration, U.S. Department of Labor, under Grant No. 21-42-73-20. Since grantees preparing research under government sponsorship are encouraged to express their own judgments freely, this study does not necessarily represent the Manpower Administration's official opinion or policy. Moreover, the authors are solely responsible for the factual accuracy of all material developed in the study.

Library of Congress Catalog No. 74-13177
MANUFACTURED IN THE UNITED STATES OF AMERICA
ISBN: 0-8122-9087-9

FOREWORD

The study, *The Impact of Government Manpower Programs*, is the first overall attempt to examine the vast evaluative literature and program statistics in order to determine program effectiveness. Because of the significance of these programs to minorities and to women, special attention is devoted to that aspect of impact as well as to overall impact.

This study commenced in October 1972 and required, at first, the identification and location of the evaluative literature, much of which consists of unpublished government or private organization documents. The literature search focused primarily on research and evaluation studies sponsored by the Manpower Administration's Office of Research and Development and conducted by Manpower Administration staff and nongovernment investigators. Excluded from our data base were reports prepared on experimental and demonstration (E and D) projects aimed at investigating the feasibility of new programmatic ideas. Many reports on E and D projects did not attempt to evaluate outcomes of training; instead they focused largely on questions related to program administration. This study concentrates very heavily upon outcome evaluations and field experiments rather than on monitoring or demonstration projects.

The data accumulation task in itself was a massive job, taking many frustrating hours. Professor Rowan supervised this work. He received assistance not only from the project staff but also from our statistician-bibliographer, Miss Elsa Klemp, and from our then editor, Mrs. Ann C. Emerson, in cataloguing the documents. Each researcher compiled his bibliography and then it was integrated by Mr. Peter P. Amons. Mrs. Ellen Sehgal of the Manpower Administration performed wonders in unlocking doors and locating missing studies. We were also assisted by staff members of the Evaluation Office, as well as other staff of the Office of Research and Development, Manpower Administration, especially Mr. Judah Drob. The bibliography testifies to the completeness of this aspect of the project.

The studies were then assigned by program to researchers, and this work was accomplished in the second phase of the project, Part Two—Individual Program Analyses. Individual staff responsibility is noted in each program analysis.

Following this, the integrative analysis was undertaken as phase three of the project. Professors Perry and Anderson undertook the leadership role at this stage. Chapter I in Part One is primarily the work of Dr. Anderson, Chapter II of Drs. Anderson, Perry, and Mr. Stephen A. Schneider, and Chapter III of Dr. Perry. Chapter IV, covering the largely neglected noneconomic impact area, was done under the direction of Professor Rowan, with Miss Harriet Goldberg and Dr. Anderson also making substantial contributions.

Part One includes our analysis of the program statistics. Dr. Anderson supervised this work, with programming and statistical support provided by Mr. Cornelius A. McGuinness and by Mr. Schneider. Dr. Anderson drafted the final chapter, with some assistance by the undersigned.

These accounts of individual credits, although richly deserved, should not obscure the fact that this project was a team one with four faculty members and several graduate students. All chapters of Parts One and Two were read and commented upon by each faculty member and bear the imprint of those comments. In addition, commenters for the Manpower Administration were most helpful. Without in any manner minimizing the assistance of others, some of whom are not known to the Industrial Research Unit staff, we must mention Mrs. Mary Davies, Mrs. Sehgal, and especially Dr. Howard Rosen, Director of the Office of Research and Development, Manpower Administration, who has maintained a lively, direct, and most helpful interest in the project since its inception. His assistance, understanding, and support, as well as his expression of confidence by assigning this study, are all acknowledged with pleasure.

The manuscript and various drafts have been typed by the Industrial Research Unit secretarial staff, Mrs. Veronica M. Kent, Mrs. Toby B. Bridendall, Mrs. Linda S. Ritch, and Miss Mary M. Booker. The difficult editorial tasks were completed by Michael J. McGrath and Miss Klemp. The administrative problems were cared for by our Office Manager, Mrs. Margaret E. Doyle. The senior authors, of course, assume full responsibility for the analyses and opinions expressed, which represent theirs and theirs alone and should in no way be attributed to the Manpower Administration or the University of Pennsylvania.

Philadelphia
May 1975

HERBERT R. NORTHRUP, *Director*
Industrial Research Unit
The Wharton School
University of Pennsylvania

LIST OF AUTHORS

Herbert R. Northrup, Professor of Industry, Director, Industrial Research Unit, Chairman, Labor Relations Council, The Wharton School, University of Pennsylvania.

Richard L. Rowan, Professor of Industry and Co-Director, Industrial Research Unit.

Charles R. Perry, Associate Professor of Management and Industrial Relations and Senior Faculty Research Associate, Industrial Research Unit.

Bernard E. Anderson, Associate Professor of Industry and Senior Faculty Research Associate, Industrial Research Unit.

Stephen A. Schneider, M.B.A., Ph.D. Candidate, Industrial Relations, University of Pennsylvania, and Research Associate, Industrial Research Unit.

Larry R. Matlack, M.B.A., Doctor of Education Candidate, Graduate School of Education, University of Pennsylvania, and Research Associate, Industrial Research Unit.

Harriet Goldberg, Ph.D. Candidate, Industrial Relations, University of Pennsylvania, and Research Associate, Industrial Research Unit.

Peter P. Amons, M.B.A. Candidate, The Wharton School, University of Pennsylvania, and Research Assistant, Industrial Research Unit.

Michael E. Spurrough, M.B.A. Candidate, The Wharton School, University of Pennsylvania, and formerly Research Assistant, Industrial Research Unit.

Cornelius A. McGuinness, M.B.A. Candidate, The Wharton School, University of Pennsylvania, and formerly Research Assistant, Industrial Research Unit.

TABLE OF CONTENTS

Part Two
INDIVIDUAL PROGRAM ANALYSES

LIST OF TABLES

TABLE PAGE

TABLE PAGE

TABLE PAGE

TABLE PAGE

Chapter XV

Chapter XVI

CHAPTER XVII

LIST OF FIGURES

FIGURE PAGE

Part One

INTEGRATED ANALYSIS OF PROGRAMS

CHAPTER I

Manpower Policies and Programs

During the 1960's, concern with the continued presence of serious unemployment and poverty in a prosperous economy led to the development of an active national manpower policy. The policy was expressed in the Manpower Development and Training Act of 1962, as amended, which authorized the U.S. Departments of Labor, and Health, Education and Welfare to promote and financially support work and training programs to upgrade the job skills of unemployed and underemployed workers. An additional legislative mandate was provided through the Economic Opportunity Act of 1964 which created the Office of Economic Opportunity and fostered the emergence of a number of Community Action Agencies dedicated to the provision of a wide range of services to the poor. These services were designed to break down some of the social, political, and institutional barriers to full participation by the poor in the labor market and society at large. Both the MDTA and EOA Acts have been superseded by the Comprehensive Employment and Training Act (CETA) of 1973, a new manpower policy edict designed to increase the role of state and local government and to reduce the role of the federal government in the planning, development, and administration of manpower programs. Under CETA, most categorical programs, except WIN and Job Corps, are to be superseded by local comprehensive manpower programs. The focus of this study, however, will be on the major categorical manpower programs developed under the MDTA and EOA legislation.

OBJECTIVES OF MANPOWER POLICY

A major purpose of national manpower policy is to improve the operation of labor markets by improving the competitive position of individuals facing barriers to employment, such as the lack of job skills, deficiencies in basic education, lack of job market information, social-psychological handicaps, and the inability to obtain supportive services, such as counseling, child care, and transportation. Government expenditures on manpower programs are an investment in human beings designed to increase their income earning ability in either the private or public sector of the economy. The underlying assumption is that barriers to full participation in the labor market are likely to persist for many individuals if they do not receive manpower services through government subsidy and support. This assumption suggests that individuals who receive manpower services should enjoy a more favorable labor market experience than comparable persons who do not participate in manpower programs. Most investigators, who attempt to evaluate the impact of manpower programs, are guided by the expectation that program participation should increase the competitive advantage of the unemployed and underemployed in the labor market. The recent spate of criticism leveled against manpower programs has been based largely upon studies which purport to show that program participants are no better off than similar workers who did not receive government supported manpower services.

Although there is a broad consensus concerning the general goal of manpower programs, there is much less agreement about their specific objectives. There is also no consensus concerning the limitations of manpower activities in relation to other types of social and economic measures designed to improve the general welfare of the population. For example, in assessing the impact of manpower training programs, one prominent manpower economist listed the following objectives: (1) reduce unemployment; (2) reduce poverty; (3) fill labor shortages; (4) improve the trade-off between inflation and unemployment; and (5) reorient major institutions in the labor market.[1] This rather ambitious set of goals may be subsumed within the broad objective of improving the functioning of labor markets, but the range and specificity of the goals would support a wide variety of measures and programs, not all of which would necessarily involve job training or manpower supportive services.

Some economists, viewing manpower programs more narrowly, emphasize their role in achieving economic objectives. For example, in his identification of legitimate goals for manpower programs, Daniel S. Hamermesh focuses upon: (1) increasing the stock of training embodied in disadvantaged workers; (2) removing excessive unemployment in depressed areas; (3) improving the functioning of the aggregate labor market; and (4) fostering more rapid economic growth by increasing the investment in training.[2] This set of goals is not completely different from those identified by Garth L. Mangum, but the different degree of emphasis upon economic as compared with institutional factors would, no doubt, lead Hamermesh to prefer a different set of manpower programs through which government might intervene in the labor market.

1. Garth L. Mangum, *Contributions and Costs of Manpower Development and Training* (Washington, D.C.: National Manpower Policy Task Force, 1967), pp. 7-57.

2. Daniel S. Hamermesh, *Economic Aspects of Manpower Training Programs* (Lexington: D.C. Heath and Company, 1971), pp. 6-7.

A cursory examination of objectives for manpower policy will reveal the inherent conflict which often exists between equally desirable goals. It is clear that the multidimensional objectives of manpower policy cannot be achieved simultaneously. The dilemma often leads to serious differences among special interest groups regarding the priorities that should be attached to alternative goals.

The emphasis of manpower policy has constantly shifted over time in response to changing economic conditions, social awareness, budgetary constraints, and the relative political power of important vested interest groups. The flexibility of manpower programs in response to the changing social and economic environment has, no doubt, contributed to the broad acceptance of government intervention in the labor market. At the same time, however, the constantly shifting focus of manpower policy has reduced the clarity and specificity of goals, thus making it exceedingly difficult to apply a single yardstick in measuring the impact of different manpower programs. Some of the current criticism of manpower programs reflects the failure of evaluators to recognize fully the multiple, and often conflicting, objectives of manpower policy. The clear specification of program goals and objectives is essential to an accurate assessment of the impact of manpower programs upon minorities and women.

FRAMEWORK FOR REVIEWING EVALUATIVE STUDIES

Because of the wide variations among manpower programs, it is necessary to develop a conceptual framework for reviewing the results of the evaluative literature dealing with program impact. The framework developed for this study focuses upon the classification of programs according to their potential for increasing the level and quality of labor force participation among program participants.

The extent of labor force participation among individuals depends upon two major factors: (1) individual productivity and (2) access to the labor market. Individual productivity is important as a determinant of decisions on hiring and upgrading. In the absence of discrimination, the employer will not hire or upgrade an individual if his expected contribution to production is less than the wage rate associated with the job. If wages are not lowered to a level consistent with the productivity of the unemployed worker, then his productivity must be raised to the level of the prevailing wage. Perhaps the most effective way to increase individual productivity is through some form of skill training. The acquisition and development of job skills by increasing individual productivity, should increased the quality of an individual's labor force participation as measured by gains in higher wages, occupational upgrading, and increased employment stability.

Labor market participation is also dependent upon access to available job opportunities. If an individual has limited information about jobs, or faces social, psychological, medical, or institutional barriers to employment in existing jobs, then the individual's participation in the labor market probably will be characterized by a higher degree of unemployment and underemployment and by lower earnings than that experienced by similar workers who do not face such barriers. Consequently, the removal of personal and institutional barriers to labor force participation may be expected to exert an impact upon employment and earnings independent of any change in the relative productivity of the individual through the acquisition of job skills.

Manpower programs differ significantly in the extent to which they focus upon skill training as compared with removing barriers to labor market participation other than lack of skill. Such differences define the range of expectations for short-term economic gains among participants in different manpower programs. Generally, programs which emphasize the acquisition of job skills should be expected to generate greater short-term gains in employment and earnings than programs which emphasize the removal of other types of barriers to participation in the labor market. This expectation flows from the generally observed positive correlation between the level of wages and the skill level of occupations in most labor markets.

Skill acquisition programs may also be expected to generate greater relative earnings gains than job development programs because the latter are disproportionately directed toward disadvantaged workers with few marketable job skills. The job development programs attempt to expand job opportunities for the disadvantaged by removing many of the nonskill barriers to employment. Such programs may generate an increase in the pool of jobs available to disadvantaged workers, but to the extent that the program does not raise individual employee productivity, the jobs obtained are likely to pay relatively low wages.

The tendency for skill development programs to generate greater short-term benefits than programs which emphasize nontraining services may be modified by many factors including, but not limited to, the nature of economic activity, location of the program, characteristics of the enrollees, and period of time during which the post-program economic effect is measured. For example, in an environment of a loose labor market, the hiring patterns of firms may be affected by the presence of excessive unemployment. As a result, variations among individuals in skill training may not be fully reflected by interpersonal differences in earnings. For example, an individual who recently completed a skill training program may be unable to obtain a training-related job and thus may be forced to accept a wage rate lower than experienced workers with similar job skills. Still, to the extent that potential productivity of job applicants, as measured by the acquisition of job skills, may be preferred by employers even during periods of excessive unemployment; individuals who have received job training in a manpower program may enjoy a higher rate of job placement than individuals who have received little job training but much more counseling, outreach, and other types of manpower services. In general, one would expect that the further a manpower program moves from emphasis upon skill acquisition, the lower may be the short-term economic benefits derived by its enrollees from participation in the labor market.

The criteria for measuring the short-term economic benefits of manpower programs to individuals may take different forms: (a) the level of employment, hourly wage rates, and annual earnings after training; and (b) the rate of change in employment, hourly wage rates, and annual earnings after training in comparison with the pre-training period. In addition to the commonly accepted measures of economic benefits, there are factors such as job satisfaction, citizenship, educational attainment, and the quality of health care that may be taken as measures of the noneconomic benefits of training. Several of these measures will be identified and fully discussed later in this study in a section which draws together the major findings of the evaluative literature pertaining to the impact of manpower programs upon minorities and women.

TYPOLOGY OF MAJOR PROGRAMS

The manpower programs developed to implement the national manpower policy resemble a mosaic of goals, administrative structures, and enrollee characteristics. Manpower programs have grown in number and diversity since their origin during the early 1960's, and an accurate appraisal of their impact requires a clear understanding of their service content and enrollee target population.

The programs discussed in this study may be classified into four major categories according to their manpower service mix and expected short-term economic impact. The categories are:

1. Skill training programs
   a. MDTA institutional training
   b. MDTA on-the-job training

2. Job development programs
   a. Job Opportunities in the Business Sector (JOBS)
   b. Public Service Careers (PSC)
   c. Apprenticeship Outreach Program (AOP)
   d. Public Employment Program (PEP)

3. Employability development programs
   a. Opportunities Industrialization Centers (OIC)
   b. Concentrated Employment Program (CEP)
   c. Work Incentive Program (WIN)
   d. Job Corps

4. Work experience programs
   a. Neighborhood Youth Corps (NYC)
   b. Operation Mainstream (OM)

The classification of programs within the above categories is intended only to serve the purposes of this study. It is conceivable that both the classification scheme and the location of separate programs within the classification scheme might differ in a study intended to emphasize issues other than the impact of manpower programs. For example, the job development and employability development categories include programs that differ significantly in their administrative organization, time of origin, enrollee target group, and quality of services provided. In addition, PEP might be considered unique in the sense that it is a job creation rather than a job training program. Still, despite such differences, the classification scheme used in this study combines within each category programs that are more alike in their general approach to manpower service delivery than are programs classified in any of the other categories. A brief description of each program will be presented below, and an attempt will be made to capture the program's uniqueness, as reflected in its skill training content, population target group, administrative organization, and range of supportive services. The same classification scheme will be used below to summarize the evaluative studies that deal with the economic impact of manpower programs.

Skill Training Programs

Manpower Development and Training Act (MDTA).

MDTA programs are authorized by the Manpower Development and Training Act of 1962, which provides for classroom instruction, remedial and skill training, supportive services, and training allowances. MDTA was initially established to meet the need for skill retraining among experienced members of the work force suffering high unemployment. Since its inception, the program has retained an emphasis upon job-oriented goals, i.e., skill training for available jobs in which there is a "reasonable expectation of job placement." A major feature of MDTA has been on-the-job training in which jobless workers are hired and trained at the employer's work site or underemployed workers are upgraded. Wages in such jobs are paid by the employer and training costs by public funds. This approach recognizes and attempts to capitalize on the large role traditionally played by employers in training the work force.

MDTA has been jointly administered by the Departments of Labor and Health, Education and Welfare. State employment security agencies certify eligible applicants and approve the establishment of courses based upon the identification of occupations with future demand in the local labor market, although state vocational education agencies approve curricula and training arrangements. Classroom instruction in the institutional component of MDTA is often provided by local skill centers which sometimes operate in cooperation with the public school system. MDTA was the first federally supported manpower training program developed during the 1960's, and although the target population of the program has included larger proportions of disadvantaged trainees over time, it has continued to emphasize skill acquisition among its manpower service components.

Job Development Programs

1. Job Opportunities in the Business Sector (JOBS).

The JOBS program was created in 1968 as a joint effort of the federal government and private sector employers to hire, train, and retain the seriously disadvantaged. The expectation was that employers would relax entry hiring standards, use government-financed supportive services, and extend employment opportunities to a sector of the labor force unable to compete effectively for many industrial jobs.

JOBS was inaugurated during a period of tight labor markets and increased awareness and concern for the plight of the disadvantaged and the urban poor. The birth of JOBS also coincided with an accelerated effort by the federal government to insure equal job opportunities among government contractors. The increased efforts by the government for equal employment, manifested by Order No. 4 from the Office of Federal Contract Compliance, emphasized the achievement of proportionate goals for minority employment in each firm's work force. Although there was no direct connection between the manpower training and equal employment policies, the common timing of the creation of JOBS and the issue of Order No. 4 may be important in understanding the enrollee characteristics of the program.

The JOBS program is administered by volunteers from the business community working in cooperation with representatives of the U.S. Employment Service. Prospective enrollees are attracted directly from the ranks of the disadvantaged unemployed, and may also be referred to JOBS from numerous community-based manpower and poverty agencies, as well as the employment service. Supportive services for JOBS enrollees may be provided by professional consultants under contract or by community-based organizations.

There has been some criticism that a disproportionate number of enrollees in the JOBS program have been placed in occupations which provide little or no skill training, but are merely unskilled manual jobs certified for government training subsidies. Although the evaluative literature on the JOBS program fails to support a firm judgment on this question, the evidence strongly suggests that the JOBS program is more nearly a short-term employment generating program for the disadvantaged than a program which has significantly increased the investment in the human capital of disadvantaged workers.

2. Public Service Careers (PSC).

The Public Service Careers program was created in 1970 as a modification of the New Careers program established under authority of the Economic Opportunity Act. The purpose of PSC is to provide work experience for the disadvantaged in local, state, and federal government agencies. In pursuit of its objectives, PSC offers on-the-job training and supportive services to new employees and upgrade training for employees at or near the lowest employment levels.

Because they are confined to the public sector, PSC and its predecessor, New Careers, represent a departure from the other manpower programs discussed above. The rationale for the program rests upon two factors: the rapidly growing demand for public services; and the need to open new avenues of career opportunities for disadvantaged workers. In 1971 nearly 12.8 million persons were employed in the government sector. Many of the jobs were located in areas easily accessible to the urban unemployed, and offered wage and fringe benefits equal to or greater than those available in similar private sector jobs.

The goals of PSC are not unlike those of the manpower programs beamed toward private industry. The disadvantaged who are placed in the program are expected to acquire marketable job skills that will lead to a career pattern which minimizes unemployment and poverty. PSC's performance may be evaluated through the application of criteria similar to that used in appraising JOBS and CEP, the two major programs oriented toward the disadvantaged seeking private sector employment. Because of differences in target group focus, degree of skill training, and industry orientation, it would be more difficult to compare PSC with MDTA.

3. Apprenticeship Outreach Program (AOP).

The Apprenticeship Outreach Program is perhaps the most narrowly defined manpower program in terms of a specific occupational objective. The program, financed through MDTA funds, helps young minority recruits qualify for apprenticeships, mainly in the construction industry.

AOP does not offer job training, but merely acts as a recruiting, information disseminating, tutoring, and labor exchange program through which minorities may gain access to established apprenticeship programs administered by trade unions. In some cases, special arrangements between AOP representatives and craft unions allow qualified minorities to obtain journeymen status after a short trial period without completing an apprenticeship program.

AOP is operated by various community-based organizations, civil rights groups, and trade unions under contract with the U. S. Department of Labor. The program has much potential as a vehicle for advancing equal employment opportunity in sectors of the unionized work force which have a record of egregious discrimination against racial minorities. The economic significance of AOP may also be discerned from the fact that the apprenticeable trades are among the highest paid occupations in the labor market. A close examination of AOP reveals its uniqueness as a manpower program. Almost all other programs are much broader in their occupational focus and provide a combination of skill training and other manpower services such as outreach, counseling, and placement. These differences increase the difficulty of applying a uniform criterion for measuring the impact of AOP compared with other types of manpower programs.

4. Public Employment Program (PEP).

National manpower policy veered in a new direction when the Public Employment Program was created in 1971. As a component of the federal government's arsenal of weapons for reducing unemployment and poverty, PEP represented the first major effort toward job creation since the public works program of the 1930's. The program was developed on terms laid down in the Emergency Employment Act of 1971.

Under PEP, the federal government provides funds to state and local governments to hire the unemployed and subsidize their wages in "transitional" public service jobs. The jobs may be found in a wide range of areas in which local government has responsibilities, including education, transportation, environmental quality, health care, and public safety. Supportive services to program participants also may be provided, but less than one percent of federal funds allocated to the program in fiscal year 1972 were spent for such services.

PEP operates with perhaps the least federal government intervention of any manpower program. Broad guidelines are set for the desired population target groups, but the state and local government agencies assume responsibility for recruiting, processing, and hiring the individuals. This administrative feature makes PEP something of a model for the decentralized manpower system authorized by the Comprehensive Employment and Training Act of 1973. For purposes of program evaluation, however, the uniqueness of PEP lies in its focus upon the demand rather than the supply side of the labor market equation.

Employability Development Programs

1. Opportunities Industrialization Centers (OIC).

Organized in Philadelphia in 1964, OIC is a national, grass-roots, community-based manpower program. OIC has obtained most of its operating funds from the federal government through the Departments of Labor, and Health, Education and Welfare, and the Office of Economic Opportunity. OIC stresses a philosophy of self-help in job training, and does not offer training allowances to enrollees.

As a multiservice manpower program, OIC offers outreach, counseling, prevocational training, and job placement. Not all of these services are available at all OICs, and in some communities where OIC operates as a subcontractor to CEP, few services other than prevocational and skill training may be offered.

The term "skill training" may be somewhat deceptive in the case of OIC because the main objective of training is to prepare enrollees for entry-level jobs. This means there is no required length of training in the skill training courses, and different enrollees may complete a specific course in different time intervals. The length of training in OIC skill training courses is closely related to the availability of job opportunities in the local labor market. As a result, when labor markets are tight, it is not unusual for OIC trainees to leave the program after several weeks to accept employment in a training-related job. Further training is expected to be provided by employers on the job. In this respect, OIC differs quite markedly from MDTA which requires enrollment for a fixed number of weeks in a course in order to successfully complete the program.

OIC is almost exclusively located in urban areas and has attracted a significant degree of support from national business leaders. The program is closely identified with the black community and the bulk of all enrollees are members of racial minority groups.

2. Concentrated Employment Program (CEP).

CEP was created in 1967 out of funds drawn from both the MDTA, as amended, and the Economic Opportunity Act of 1964. The program provides one-stop service in manpower and related programs for disadvantaged persons living in areas of high unemployment and poverty. Although both urban and rural communities have CEPs, the program is heavily concentrated in urban poverty areas.

The purpose of CEP was to coordinate the delivery of manpower services from various local organizations, both private and public. The program displays marked differences in structure and administration across localities, but many CEPs were established as the manpower arm of local community action agencies. As a result of Manpower Order 14-69, issued in 1969, the U.S. Employment Service assumed a large role in the delivery of manpower services in CEPs. This arrangement helped to create a more efficient delivery of manpower services than was observed during the first two years of CEP's existence, and enlarged the role of the U. S. Employment Service in providing services similar to those previously performed for the JOBS and MDTA programs.

CEP reflects the view that unemployment rates alone do not measure the full extent of job inadequacy for the disadvantaged poor. The program was created partly because of the failure of tight labor markets during the mid-1960's to lower significantly the unemployment rate in poverty pockets throughout the nation. Manpower planners who created CEP thought the employment problems of the disadvantaged were largely problems of a personal nature and could be solved only by providing a multiple set of remedial manpower services. As a result, most CEPs tend to emphasize such services as outreach, counseling, prevocational training, and job development. There is little emphasis upon skilled job training, and the acquisition of skills by CEP enrollees differs markedly among communities. By focusing upon the disadvantaged and by emphasizing remedial services, CEP attempts to increase the labor force participation of workers concentrated at the very bottom of the income-occupational hierarchy. In this sense, CEP serves much the same target population as the JOBS program.

3. Work Incentive Program (WIN).

WIN was created in 1967 by an amendment to Title IV of the Social Security Act to provide job training and supportive services for employable AFDC recipients so they could become economically independent. Among its major components are orientation, remedial education, vocational training, placement, and follow-up. The revised program (WIN II), effective in July 1972, places first emphasis upon job placement.

In order to encourage their cooperation in hiring WIN enrollees, employers receive a tax credit of up to 20 percent of the first year's wages of WIN hires. In addition, the federal government will finance 90 percent of the training costs. Welfare recipients also have an economic incentive to participate. For those in the program, there is a declining tax on earnings, with participants allowed to keep the first thirty dollars of monthly earnings plus one-third of additional earned income without losing welfare benefits.

The WIN program was created in response to the rapidly growing number of welfare recipients during the mid-1960's. Although welfare recipients also participate in other manpower programs, the seriousness of the welfare problem in the view of many political leaders required a special program geared to the public assistance population. The priority accorded to the WIN objective is revealed in part by the 120 percent increase in expenditures for the program between 1970 and 1972; at the same time, expenditures for CEP decreased by 17 percent and those for the JOBS program also declined.

WIN is administered jointly by local manpower agencies—or local offices of state employment service agencies—and local public welfare agencies. Although these two organizations have a common mandate to facilitate the movement of able-bodied welfare recipients into the regular work force, the U. S. Employment Service and public welfare agencies do not share the same heritage with respect to perceptions of welfare dependency and labor market behavior. Welfare agencies tend to be oriented toward the treatment of personal problems of clients whose dependency is viewed as an unfortunate manifestation of social pathology. Employment Service personnel, on the other hand, tend to emphasize the efficient matching of unemployed workers with existing job vacancies. These separate foci create differences in the professional concerns and competencies of the two organizations, thus generating serious differences at times on questions such as: who should participate in WIN; and what minimum conditions should be met before the individual is introduced into the work force. The differences of perception arising from the different heritages of the administrative organizations have some bearing upon the specific goals by which the performance of WIN might be evaluated.

4. Job Corps.

The uniqueness of the Job Corps is perhaps best reflected in its status as a residential program designed to provide training and education for disadvantaged men and women, 16 through 21 years of age, who are out of work and lack marketable job skills. The Job Corps, created under the Economic Opportunity Act of 1964, concentrates on disadvantaged youth with the most serious problems of employability.

Job Corps centers have been operated by both government agencies and private industry. Among the services available at the centers are counseling, basic education, high school equivalency instruction, skill training, work experience, and placement. The degree of emphasis placed upon different types of manpower services varies across Job Corps centers in response to the special needs of the enrollees and the views of program administrators on how the needs might be met best. As a general rule, however, the Job Corps centers are not distinguished for providing intensive skill training for their enrollees.

In 1969 the structure of the Job Corps was changed when the U. S. Department of Labor assumed responsibility for its administration. The emphasis shifted away from rural and toward urban residential centers. Increased emphasis was also placed upon skill training as compared with nontraining supportive services. This reorientation of the Job Corps narrows the gap between it and other largely urban-based manpower programs like CEP and OIC. At the same time, the heavy concentration of the highly disadvantaged in the Job Corps limits the range of jobs for which skill training is feasible given the length of time (an average of six months) spent by enrollees in the program. Much of the training period must be devoted to remedial education and the removal of many other personal barriers which prevent Job Corps enrollees from enjoying a favorable experience in the larbor market.

Work Experience Programs

1. Neighborhood Youth Corps (NYC).

Measured by expenditures since the beginning of the programs, NYC is second only to MDTA in the galaxy of federally assisted manpower programs. NYC was created in 1964 under authority contained in the Economic Opportunity Act and is designed to keep young people in school, get them back in school, or increase their chance of becoming employable if they are school dropouts. The in-school program emphasizes job market orientation and work experience. Skill training is emphasized for the out-of-school youth.

Among manpower programs, NYC is one of the most ambiguous in regard to short-term labor market criteria. The separate emphases for in- and out-of-school youth and the uncertain direction of the summer program raise serious questions about the compatibility of NYC and some of the economic objectives of manpower policy. The program, like Operation Mainstream, is a major vehicle for income transfer. At the same time, however, there is some question about the extent to which NYC contributes to the investment in the human capital of disadvantaged youth.

This issue is important because the evaluation of NYC depends heavily upon the specification of goals for the program. The services offered in the out-of-school segment of NYC include outreach, orientation, counseling, job training, placement, and some supportive services. These manpower services are also available in other programs in which the NYC target population might participate. For the in-school and summer sectors, however, there are no parallels in other programs. Consequently, an objective appraisal of NYC requires the recognition that the program has multiple objectives, not all of which are intended to enhance individual productivity.

2. Operation Mainstream (OM).

From its inception in 1967 through fiscal year 1972, Operation Mainstream was a rather small manpower program designed to give jobs and work experience to chronically unemployed older persons. Many of the jobs were in local beautification projects and other types of activities intended to improve the quality of life in the community. Because of its special population focus, Mainstream was not intended to be a "training" program, but rather a vehicle for income transfer through job opportunities for the elderly. The jobs available in Mainstream offered an opportunity for the disadvantaged elderly worker to participate in the labor market and to achieve a degree of economic independence that would otherwise not be possible.

U. S. Employment Service (USES)

The programs described above are the major *categorical* manpower programs developed during the 1960's. A much older participant in the manpower field is the U. S. Employment Service. USES was not singled out for separate discussion because it most often acts as an agent of the categorical programs insofar as the manpower service delivery system is concerned. For this reason, it would be difficult, at best, to measure the impact of the employment service upon minorities and women apart from the impact of the categorical programs. Still, the role of the employment service is sufficiently important to warrant independent attention.

The public employment service was organized under the Wagner-Peyser Act of 1933 which authorized the federal government to establish a network of employment offices in the states to provide counseling and placement services for the unemployed, handicapped, veterans, and farm workers. The organization was also authorized to furnish and publish information about employment opportunities and to maintain a system for clearing labor among the states.

During the 1950's, the Employment Service developed special programs related to apprenticeship information, older workers, veterans, ex-prisoners, and Indians. Although there were no special services for racial minorities or women, USES was prohibited from accepting racially discriminatory job orders from firms holding government contracts. Nonetheless, discrimination was almost inevitable in the system operating at the time because state agency performance was evaluated almost exclusively by the placement record. This criterion led state employment officers to develop a close rapport with employers. Indeed many state employment service administrators felt that the best way to help individuals in the labor market was to provide a good placement service which employers could use.

A concerted attempt was made during the early 1960's to expand the services of the Employment Service in major industrial areas in order to expedite the filing of job vacancies and to speed recovery from the 1960-1961 recession. Additional efforts were also undertaken to expand placement programs for youth and to provide more effective services for older workers displaced by automation. Testimony presented by the Director of the Bureau of Employment Security emphasized the new policy goal:

> The labor market experience of the postwar years clearly demonstrates that the objectives and responsibilities of the employment service system broadened and its resources expanded. We intend to make the employment office in each locality a community manpower center. It will work cooperatively with individual workers, employers, education and training institutions, community groups, professional associations and government agen-

cies in the community to meet local manpower problems and achieve the national goals of minimum unemployment of the workforce, and maximum utilization of our manpower resources.[3]

The rather ambitious set of objectives enunciated above were not immediately adopted by employment service personnel at the local level, but over time the organization gradually increased its activity in the delivery of manpower services in cooperation with other manpower organizations. In 1962, USES undertook major responsibilities in the MDTA program for identifying occupations with significant labor demand, certifying and placing eligible candidates, and offering technical assistance. When the poverty program was inaugurated under the Economic Opportunity Act of 1964, the Employment Service was requested to recruit, interview, and refer to the appropriate agencies, young people who would be eligible for or could benefit from the Neighborhood Youth Corps, the Job Corps, and various other work-training programs. Special offices for youth were set up in many low-income areas to make USES accessible to the disadvantaged. By 1966 some 150 Youth Opportunity Centers were in operation throughout the nation, thus reflecting the changing emphasis of the employment service toward the solution of youth employment problems. They have since been discontinued for the most part.

Additional evidence of the Employment Service's expanded outreach activity was found in the cooperation between the Pennsylvania Employment Service and OIC. Shortly after OIC started skill training in 1965, arrangements were made to have an Employment Service representative located in the OIC center to facilitate placement activity. Similar arrangements were made with many of the CEPs organized throughout the nation in 1967 and 1968. In the case of CEP, however, the role of the Employment Service was greatly expanded under Manpower Administration Order 14-69 issued in 1969. Under the order, the employment service acquired the major responsibility for delivering the bulk of all manpower services under the human resource development model adopted by the U.S. Department of Labor. The Employment Service also plays a major role in outreach, counseling, and placement under the JOBS program.

The Manpower Program Mix

The individual descriptions of manpower programs serves only to identify the institutional forms through which manpower policy was implemented during the 1960's. Equally important is the program mix which existed throughout the period.

3. "The Public Employment Service in Transition, 1933-1968," Cornell University, from *Employment Service Review*, Vol. XXVIII, no. 5 (May 1961), p. 3.

In the early 1960's, manpower programs focused upon the bottleneck in labor skills and the serious problem of unemployment among large numbers of experienced workers. Later, as accelerated economic growth reduced the relative unemployment of experienced workers, manpower programs turned to the employment problems of minorities and youth. Table 1 shows the trend of enrollment opportunities and federal obligations in the major programs operating between 1965 and 1972.

The shift of policy emphasis away from programs for skill development and training, and toward those emphasizing work experience and supportive services, may be illustrated by an examination of enrollments and expenditure trends for MDTA and NYC. At the outset, it is important to recognize that the two programs differ sharply in their relative emphasis upon skill training. In 1972, for example, 32 percent of all MDTA institutional funds and 20 percent of the OJT funds were allocated to skill training. In contrast, only 4 percent of the funds spent in post-school work support programs, including NYC, were spent for skill training.[4] Conversely, about 34 percent of the MDTA budget was spent for trainee allowances, compared with nearly 80 percent of the work support program budget.

The sharp difference in program content between MDTA and NYC, together with the enrollment trends of the two programs, brings the nature of manpower policy during the 1960's into clearer focus. In fiscal 1965 45.4 percent of all manpower program enrollment opportunities were allocated to MDTA, whereas 54.6 percent were earmarked for NYC. Between 1965 and 1969, the period of most rapid growth in manpower programs, enrollment opportunities in MDTA declined by 33,000 or 14.4 percent, and the NYC enrollment opportunities increased by 261,000, or 93.9 percent. During the four-year period, federal expenditures for MDTA dropped 14 million dollars, but NYC received additional expenditures of close to 193 million dollars. Largely as a result of these changes, MDTA enrollment dropped to about 22 percent of all manpower program enrollees, but NYC increased to almost 60 percent of all enrollees in 1969. The attrition in the relative level of MDTA enrollment compared with NYC continued through fiscal year 1972.

For a clear perspective of the evolution of manpower programs, it may be well to recall that the shifting focus of manpower policy toward minorities also represented a response of public decision makers to the civil rights revolution. Some of the program changes adopted during the 1960's can be understood only in terms of the concern among political leaders to alleviate the causes of social and economic inequality which breed social unrest.

4. *Budget of the U.S. Government, 1974, Special Analyses* (Washington, D.C.: Government Printing Office, 1973), p. 131.

TABLE I-1. *Manpower Programs*
Enrollment Opportunities and Obligations in Major Programs
Fiscal Years 1965-1972
(In thousands)

Program	Total	1965	1966	1967	1968	1969	1970	1971	1972
Enrollment:									
MDTA	1,866	232	281	271	230	199	211	214	229
Institutional Training	1,138	167	163	126	131	121	147	145	139
JOP-OJT	728	65	118	145	99	78	64	69	91
Neighborhood Youth Corps	4,558	278	528	513	538	540	600	699	863
Operation Mainstream	96	—	—	8	11	14	18	23	22
Public Service Careers	111	—	—	4	3	6	35	42	21
JOBS (federal sector)	302	—	—	8	32	53	60	88	61
Work Incentive Program	385	—	—	—	10	99	66	61	150
Job Corps	68	—	—	—	—	—	22	22	24
Public Employment Program	193	—	—	—	—	—	—	—	193
Total	7,579	510	809	809	824	911	1,011	1,150	1,562
Obligations:									
MDTA									
Institutional Training	$2,101	$249	$282	$216	$222	$214	$287	$275	$356
JOP-OJT	491	37	58	83	75	59	50	60	69
Neighborhood Youth Corps	2,643	128	263	349	282	321	357	426	517
Operation Mainstream	295	—	—	24	22	41	51	72	85
Public Service Careers	281	—	—	16	8	18	89	92	58
Concentrated Employment Program	820	—	25	78	93	114	188	167	155
JOBS (federal sector)	711	—	—	24	90	161	149	169	118
Work Incentive Program	427	—	—	—	9	101	79	64	175
JOB CORPS	532	—	—	—	—	—	170	160	202
Public Employment Program	962	—	—	—	—	—	—	—	962
Total	9,271	414	628	796	802	1,030	1,419	1,485	2,697

Source: U.S. Department of Labor, *Statistics on Manpower*, a reprint from the 1973 *Manpower Report of the President* (Washington, D.C.: Government Printing Office 1973), p. 227.

Note: Totals may not add due to rounding.

This interpretation of the policy makers' motivations is supported by the evidence showing an increase in the NYC enrollment opportunities for the summer months (194.8 percent), almost ten times the rate of growth in NYC enrollment opportunities for the regular school year (20.7 percent) between 1965 and 1968. Furthermore, the organization of the Job Opportunities in the Business Sector program in 1968, under the aegis of the National Alliance of Businessmen, reflected the prevailing view among political decision makers that few gains in the economic and social advancement of the urban disadvantaged unemployed could be expected, if private corporations did not hire first and then train such workers. Social and economic concerns have jointly determined the evolving manpower program mix, and undoubtedly will continue to shape the development of manpower programs in the future.

In summary, manpower policy during the 1960's was heavily oriented toward disadvantaged youth, and was tilted toward income maintenance and supportive service rather than skill training. This is not to say that the funds were not well-spent. The judgment on the value of the expenditures can be made only in relation to the objectives of policy makers who formulated the goals of manpower policy and allocated the funds necessary to achieve the stated goals. From the review of program enrollment patterns, however, it is clear that most program participants were not engaged in a training experience designed to maximize their individual productivity through the acquisition and development of job skills. This conclusion will bear heavily upon any attempt to assess the impact of manpower programs upon minorities and women.

Minority and Female Program Enrollment

The extent to which manpower programs help to alleviate the employment problems of minorities and women depends, in large part, upon the outcomes generated by the programs in which members of the two groups participate. Table 2 summarizes enrollment in the major manpower programs developed since fiscal 1965. The data in Table 2 are drawn primarily from U.S. Department of Labor reports on program operation. Additional data obtained from the Opportunities Industrialization Centers are added to the Labor Department data in order to cover all programs discussed in this study.

Between fiscal years 1965 and 1972, about nine million enrollees participated in the major federally funded manpower programs. Of the total, blacks accounted for 4.1 million enrollees, or 46.3 percent, and women comprised 3.9 million enrollees, or 43.9 percent. Slightly more than seven of every ten trainees (73.2 percent), including minorities and women, were under 22 years of age, and somewhat more than three of every four (78.8 percent) had less than a full high school education.

As indicated in the earlier description of the manpower programs, not all were in operation throughout the period since 1964. MDTA programs had the longest period of continuous operation followed by NYC, Job Corps, Operation Mainstream, and OIC. Each of the remaining programs —including CEP, WIN, JOBS, PEP, and PSC—had been in operation for five years or less at the end of fiscal year 1972.

Throughout the decade, blacks and women did not participate evenly in all programs. Instead, the race-sex composition of enrollment varied significantly across programs, and such variations were closely associated with differences in the content of programs. Unfortunately, the data are not classified in sufficient detail to trace the enrollment trend of black women.

Blacks accounted for 36.4 percent of the enrollees in MDTA, the program emphasizing skill development, but 47.9 percent of the enrollees in the NYC in-school program, which emphasizes work experience and not skill training. Blacks were especially prominent in the employability development programs, accounting for 65.5 percent of the enrollees in CEP, 86.4 percent of those in AOP, and 89.6 percent of those in OIC. In contrast, the black presence was far less prominent in the MDTA-OJT program in which blacks comprised only 27.8 percent of the enrollees, and in PEP in which the black participation rate was 26.0 percent.

Women were well represented in most of the programs but comprised a majority of enrollees only in WIN (63.1 percent), PSC (64.3 percent), and OIC (69.9 percent). Within the skills development programs, women were better represented among the institutional trainees (44.8 percent) than among those engaged in on the-job training (30.4 percent). The work experience jobs of the Neighborhood Youth Corps displayed female participation rates of 45.2 percent in the in-school component, and 47.7 percent for the school dropouts.

Additional insight into the race-sex composition of enrollment may be gained by examining how minorities and women were distributed among different manpower programs. Table 3 shows minority and female enrollment in the major program categories used in this study. Nearly 2.4 million blacks, 57.4 percent of all black program enrollees, participated in the work experience programs which included the Neighborhood Youth Corps as the major component. Slightly more than one-half of the nonminority enrollees (54.5 percent) and more than one-half of the female participants (58.3 percent) were also concentrated in the work experience category.

The widest variations in program participation between blacks and nonminority enrollees occurred in the skill training and employability development programs. Proportionately more blacks than others were concentrated in the employability development programs. This may be a reflection of the high concentration of employability programs such as

TABLE I-2. *Manpower Programs*
Number and Percent by Selected Characteristics of Enrollees in Major Programs
Summary, Fiscal Years 1965-1972
(Numbers in thousands)

Program	All Enrollees	Minorities				Sex		Age Under 22 Years		Education Less Than 12 Years		Received Public Assistance	
		Black		Other		Women							
	Total [a]	Total	Percent	Total	Percent	Total	Percent	Total	Percent	Total	Percent	Total	Percent
MDTA													
Institutional	1,184	466	39.4	48	4.1	530	44.8	494	41.7	668	56.4	162	13.7
OJT	626	174	27.8	19	3.0	190	30.4	221	35.3	299	47.8	32	5.1
Neighborhood Youth Corps													
In-school [b]	4,070	1,948	47.9	216	5.3	1,840	45.2	4,070	100.0	3,966	97.4	1,318	32.4
Out-of-school [b]	917	420	45.8	46	5.0	437	47.7	903	98.5	800	87.2	272	29.7
Concentrated Employment Program	469	307	65.5	35	7.5	199	42.4	193	41.2	307	65.5	64	13.6
Work Incentive Program	406	160	39.4	18	4.4	256	63.1	98	24.1	261	64.3	403	99.3
Job Opportunities in the Business Sector	313	192	61.3	25	8.0	99	31.6	144	46.0	195	62.3	48	15.3
Job Corps [c]	233	140	60.0	23	9.9	63	27.0	233	100.0	213	91.4	79	33.9
Public Employment Program	305	79	26.0	9	3.0	85	27.9	70	23.0	82	26.9	37	12.1
Public Service Careers [d]	112	51	45.5	n.a.	n.a.	72	64.3	23	20.5	40	35.7	22	19.6
Opportunities Industrialization Centers	163	146	89.6	8	5.0	114	69.9	54	33.1	122	74.8	102	62.6
Apprenticeship Outreach Program	22	19	86.4	2	9.1	n.a.	n.a.	20	90.9	2	9.1	n.a.	n.a.
Operation Mainstream [e]	90	20	22.2	12	13.3	23	25.6	3	3.3	69	76.7	18	20.0
Total	8,910	4,122	46.3	461	5.2	3,908	43.9	6,526	73.2	7,024	78.8	2,557	28.7

TABLE I-2, *continued.*

Source: Derived from the following:

U.S. Department of Labor, *Manpower Report of the President* (Washington, D.C.: Government Printing Office)
1968. Table F-8, p. 314.
1969. Tables F-8, p. 244; F-10 and F-11 p. 247; F-12, p. 249, F-15, p. 252.
1970. Tables F-9, p. 312; F-10, p. 313; F-11, p. 314; and F-13 and F-14, p. 316; F-19, p. 321.
1971. Tables F-10, p. 309; F-11, p. 309; F-12, p. 310; F-13 and F-14, p. 311.
1972. Table F-8, p. 268.
1973. Tables F-1, p. 227; F-5, p. 231; F-8, p. 234.
U.S. Department of Labor, Manpower Administration, Public Employment Program statistics.
OIC National Institute, *Annual Report 1971-1972.*

[a] First time enrollees.
[b] Neighborhood Youth Corps total includes September 1965-August 1970 data and fiscal years 1971 and 1972 figures.
[c] Job Corps total includes June 1968, calendar year 1968, and fiscal years 1970, 1971, and 1972 figures.
[d] Public Service Careers total includes data for fiscal years 1970-1972 only, due to absence of socio-economic distributions for previous years.
[e] Operation Mainstream total includes data for fiscal years 1968-1972 only, due to absence of socio-economic distributions for previous year

OIC and CEP in inner-city poverty areas where large numbers of blacks reside. On the other hand, the programs emphasizing skill training (MDTA institutional and OJT) accounted for less than one-fifth of all blacks and women, compared to almost three of every ten nonminority enrollees.

The enrollment patterns show thaι although they were numerically significant in most manpower programs, minority and female trainees were heavily concentrated in programs having a limited emphasis on the acquisition and development of marketable occupational skills. In addition, excluding the Neighborhood Youth Corps, minorities and women were concentrated in programs in operation for five years or less. For these reasons, the assessment of the impact of manpower programs upon the post-training labor market experience of minorities and women will be burdened by a dual problem—the short time frame in which the experience may be measured and the limited expectation of economic gains stemming from the failure of many programs to emphasize skills development. These considerations should be kept in mind in the later discussion of the economic benefits of training.

TABLE I-3. *Manpower Programs Percent Distribution of Enrollment Among Major Program Groups*

Program Group	Nonminority	Blacks	Female
Skill Training[a]	27.2	15.5	18.4
Job Development[b]	8.4	8.3	6.5
Employability Development[c]	11.7	18.3	16.2
Work Experience[d]	54.5	57.4	58.3
Total	100.0	100.0	100.0

Source: Derived from Table 2.

[a] Includes MDTA Institutional and OJT programs
[b] Includes JOBS, PSC, PEP, and AOP programs
[c] Includes OIC, CEP, WIN, and Job Corps programs
[d] Includes NYC-In-School, Summer, and Out-of-School programs

Note: Percents may not add to 100.0 due to rounding.

CHAPTER II

Conceptual and Methodological Problems

There are three basic dimensions to an evaluation of the economic impact of manpower programs. The first centers on the ability of manpower programs to enhance the labor market status and performance of those individuals who participate in them. The second involves program impact upon nonparticipants through changes in labor market institutions and conditions. The third encompasses impact upon broad socio-economic aggregates, such as the incidence of poverty or welfare dependency, the level of unemployment or underemployment, and the extent of labor shortages.

The noneconomic effects of manpower programs may also be divided into several categories, including benefits to the individual participant, to associated individuals, and to society at large. These dimensions of program impact have potential relevance in assessing the effect of manpower services on all enrollees and on minorities and women separately. The task of evaluation, however, is complicated by important conceptual issues surrounding the meaning of "impact," and by serious questions of methodology in measuring impact, however defined. A consideration of the conceptual and methodological issues in program evaluation is a necessary first step toward a full understanding of the impact of manpower programs.

MANPOWER TRAINING PROCESS

The concepts and methodology of program evaluation are based upon a perception of manpower training as a production process. This process is displayed in the schematic diagram illustrated in Figure 1.

The manpower training program begins with a set of human and physical capital inputs which are combined to provide a set of manpower services. Enrollees enter the program, receive a variety of services over a time period, and after leaving the program, are expected to be better equipped to compete effectively in the labor market. Program evaluation, often called "impact" evaluation, is intended to determine if the expected effects of services do indeed occur, and if the enrollees gain benefits that would not have been experienced in the absence of manpower services.

Two types of data dealing with the labor market experience of manpower program participants have been used as the basis for analyses of

FIGURE II-1. *Manpower Training Process.*

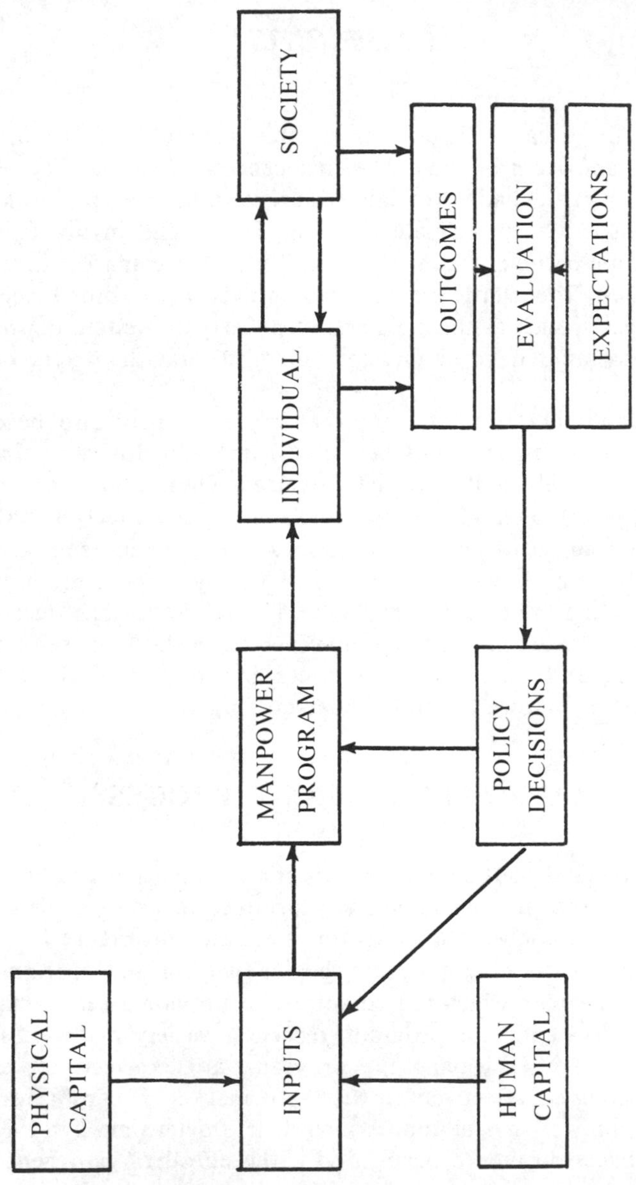

impact: (1) data on post-program levels of earnings, wage rates, and employment; and (2) data on pre-and post-program differences in these variables. The two major techniques utilized to infer impact from earnings and employment data are: comparisons with parallel data for a group of similar individuals not exposed to training; and extrapolation on the basis of trends detected in the pre-program records of participants and/or in the economy as a whole. In general, the longitudinal data would appear to constitute a stronger analytical base because many of the elements associated with the change in an enrollee's status may be isolated and examined for their contribution to the post-program variables. Similarly, the use of comparison groups clearly provides a superior basis for isolating the contribution of manpower programs from the influence of other forces; however, most evaluation studies do not use comparison groups.

The social, political, and economic foundations of federal manpower policies and programs clearly suggest that positive economic benefits for participants are expected from all programs. The magnitude of benefits may vary, however, because of differences among programs in goals, services, and selected target groups. Specifically, systematic differences among programs in short-run labor market impact may be generated by differences in the capability of a program's services to influence enrollee success in the labor market. The expected economic gains from different types of manpower service may be classified as follows:

1. Skill training designed to enhance job skills and productivity and expand the level and/or range of employment opportunities open to individual participants.
2. Job development designed to expand the number and/or range of employment opportunities open to participants through a modification of employment standards, or some reordering of the hiring process.
3. Employability development designed to inculcate those personal attitudes and attributes necessary to satisfy entry-level employment standards where skill requirements are minimal.
4. Work experience designed to provide opportunities to engage in work activities outside the traditional confines of the labor market.

It is also important to note that the magnitude of the labor market benefit to participants from any type of program will vary with changes in labor market conditions and that the extent of such variation is likely to differ dramatically among programs, but in the same order as applies to overall impact. In a loose labor market, for example, improved skills may serve primarily to help trainees compete more successfully for available jobs at low wage rates, rather than help them secure the higher paying jobs that, under normal circumstances, would be available to better trained workers. Improved skills in a loose labor market can make only a modest contribution to facilitating the upgrading of the unemployed.

Finally, it should also be noted that short-run participant labor market benefits are, at best, an imperfect index of true impact upon long-run labor market performance. The long-run economic impact of training is determined more by the qualitative than the quantitative dimensions of the short-run impact of training. Specifically, long-term economic gains will be a function of the nature of the jobs for which trainees can qualify, the quality of the training they receive on those jobs, and the extent of potential for upgrading from those jobs—all of which seem to have the same rank order among programs as do expected short-run labor market benefits.

ECONOMIC AND NONECONOMIC EFFECTS OF TRAINING

Three basic variables have been used to measure the economic impact of manpower programs. These variables, confined to the labor market experience of manpower program participants, are: (1) annual earnings; (2) hourly wage rates; and (3) employment stability, measured by the percent of time employed since training and the frequency of job changes involving some degree of unemployment. Annual earnings provide the most comprehensive measure of labor market performance and clearly constitute the variable of greatest immediate concern to the individual, the family, and society as a whole. Hourly wage rates and employment stability provide insight into relative labor market status and constitute indexes of individual productivity, employability, and economic potential. However, their reliability and validity as measures of manpower program impact are heavily influenced by the state and the structure of labor markets.

In many ways, the assessment of the noneconomic impact of manpower programs poses conceptual and measurement problems far more difficult than those associated with economic impact. First, many of the program impact variables that might be classified as "noneconomic" normally accrue to the individual during the process of training. Such benefits as better health care, improved child-care facilities, and personal counseling are usually classified as supportive services, although they may be among the most significant noneconomic gains received from program participation.

To be consistent in measuring impact, however, only those changes in the individual which are observed or persist after leaving the program should be included in the assessment of noneconomic effects. The dilemma surrounding the time when benefits are observed may bias the measurement of noneconomic effects of training, although the magnitude and direction of the bias are uncertain.

Second, the variables of interest in measuring noneconomic effects include, but are not limited to, psychological well-being, improved feelings of self-worth, greater job satisfaction, and more active and rewarding participation in civic affairs. To these may be added such benefits as improved housing, health care, and general education. A cursory examination of this limited list will show that a number of the potential noneconomic benefits are likely to accrue as much to society as to the individual and may be heavily dependent upon the degree of economic gains from training. Such gains are "noneconomic" only at the second remove; their linkage to changes in earnings and employment is direct and pervasive.

The time span for measuring noneconomic impact is as important as for measuring the economic effects of training. Both short-run and long-run effects are likely to occur, and their full effect may be increasingly difficult to measure over time. The nature of noneconomic benefits is that they may accumulate over time, become reinforced through new perceptions and opportunities, and generate additional gains which multiply the range of short-run benefits initially observed. The cumulative effects of the benefits will depend upon the stability of changes in personal values and opportunities which derive from program participation.

There is no *a priori* basis for suggesting a rank order of noneconomic benefits by type of program as was done for economic impact because it is difficult to distinguish among programs in their capacity to affect values, attitudes, and noneconomic behavior. Some guidance in this area might be obtained if noneconomic and economic benefits were related in a systematic way. The very personalized nature of noneconomic effects, however, casts doubt upon any close relationship between the two types of impact. For example, in a work-oriented, status-conscious society, it is difficult to measure the benefit in self-esteem gained by an individual who becomes self-sufficient, or who experiences a change in occupational status as a result of participating in a manpower program. Such gains can rarely be quantified, and may even be unrelated to the market wage rate.

On the other hand, there are other noneconomic benefits which undoubtedly depend heavily upon the degree of change in earnings experienced by the individual. Benefits of this type are closely related to variations in consumption, and will be related to the different programs in the same order of magnitude as the rank order identified for economic impact.

CONTROL GROUPS

The key to the assessment of program impact is the measurement of change in individual status which is uniquely attributable to participation in the manpower program. The isolation of program effects from all other influences on the individual requires the selection of a control or comparison group. The control group should match the program participants as closely as possible in socio-economic characteristics. Most evaluators of manpower programs agree that without a control group "[i]t is almost impossible to show that improvements experienced by program participants . . . result from participation in the program and not from other causes, e.g., the passage of time and changes in economic conditions."[1]

The pre- and post-training control group approach provides a good potential for measuring differential impact upon minorities and women because changes in impact measures can be compared within sex and race groups. The appropriate control group, however, is a major issue of dispute in the literature of evaluation methodology. At least seven types of control groups can be identified, and each presents problems which limit the availability or reliability of evaluation results.

1. Random selection from applicants to the program. Although this is one of the best for yielding unbiased "estimates of the expected behavior of program participants in the absence of the program,"[2] it requires that the evaluation be built into the program, something which is not commonly done. Also, there is a natural "reluctance of the operating agencies to exclude fully qualified persons from receiving the services of the agencies . . . analogous to a doctor's not treating a patient who has a disease when a drug is available."[3] This is the most serious problem with randomization.

2. Completers who did not use the training.

3. Dropouts from the program prior to completion. The use of these groups as controls is based on the assumption that no benefits can be attributed to the program unless "the job obtained was because the course was completed; [and] . . . the skills learned in the course were needed for the jobs."[4] In some cases these criteria do not hold because real benefits can be derived from program participation, such as personal habits and attitudes, access to information, and evidence of motivation even if the skills learned were not necessary for the job or if the participant dropped out before completion.

---

1. Steven L. Barsby, *Cost-Benefit Analysis and Manpower Programs* (Lexington: D.C. Heath and Company, 1972), p. 16.

2. Michael E. Borus and Charles G. Buntz, "Problems and Issues in the Evaluation of Manpower Programs," *Industrial and Labor Relations Review*, Vol. 25, no. 2 (January 1972), p. 238.

3. Michael E. Borus and William R. Tash, *Measuring the Impact of Manpower Programs—A Primer*, Policy Papers in Human Resources and Industrial Relations 17 (Ann Arbor: Institute of Labor and Industrial Relations, University of Michigan-Wayne State University, 1970), p. 16.

4. Barsby, *op. cit.*, p. 17.

4. Qualified interested nonenrollees. This control group has two potential weaknesses. First, members of the group on their own may have found jobs attractive enough to keep them out of the program or might have been disqualified for allowances or other program support. Second, potential program participants receiving consideration for training come to the attention of counselors and job placement officers more than ordinary job applicants. Such additional informational and psychological services received may help improve their employment and earnings in the labor market.

5. Qualified nonapplicants. The use of qualified nonapplicants is the same as sampling the target population for the control group. This was the procedure used in Gerald G. Somers' study of manpower training in West Virginia and Tennessee and in Richard Solie's study of retraining in Tennessee. Although the controls and participants are matched on labor market conditions and experience, matching personal characteristics is very difficult. In addition, attitude plays an important role in creating a control group.

6. Friends, neighbors and relatives. This source of a control group may be tapped by asking the trainee to refer to a friend, neighbor, or relative who did not participate in a manpower training program. If a sufficient number of eligible control group candidates is not obtained from trainee referrals, the interviewer may canvass the trainee's neighborhood for persons who were unemployed about the time the trainee's course was started.

On its face, this procedure would seem to produce a comparison group virtually free of the biases identified for other types of control groups. A closer examination of the procedure, however, suggests the possibility of at least two types of bias which may be uncertain in measurement. The first is that the trainees and the referrees may differ in psychological bearing and motivation. Such differences might account in part for the failure of the referrees to take advantage of the manpower training opportunity. Second, in cases where the number of referrees is inadequate and some canvassing of the neighborhood is necessary, there may be differences in the control group between those referred by trainees and those selected through the canvassing procedure. In either case, when friends, relatives, and neighbors are selected, differences between the control group and the trainees may be significant in ways that escape the adjustments possible through the use of statistical techniques. The result may be differences—in earnings and employment experience—which are not the result of the training program.

7. Social Security data. The one percent Continuous Work History Sample of the Social Security Administration has often been recommended as a source for the selection of a control group for program eval-

uation purposes. Because of its extensive coverage of individual earnings, the Social Security data would seem to provide an ideal base for control groups. The data provide a long and consistent series about earnings for most workers in the labor force, and have industry, area, race, and sex detail. The major gaps in coverage are for workers whose wages exceed the taxable limit and who were employed in noncovered occupations. These two gaps in coverage are not likely to bias data seriously for evaluative purposes.

Although the comprehensiveness and reliability of the Social Security data are attractive features, the data base has several shortcomings as a source for the selection of control groups. The major problem is the uncertainty about whether those covered by the Social Security system are fully representative of the typical manpower program participant. The data can be standardized by age, sex, industry, and location, but some of the other socio-demographic factors, such as education level, necessary for the selection of a representative control group are not available in Social Security records. A basic question is whether the casually employed low-wage worker who is supposed to typify the manpower program enrollee has enough covered employment to get into the Social Security file. The result is that evaluators cannot be sure a Social Security-based control group is very similar to manpower trainees in values, attitudes, motivation, and other interpersonal characteristics that have such a significant influence upon both pre- and post-training success in the labor market.

In addition, the use of Social Security data for program evaluation raises serious questions of confidentiality that have not yet been resolved between the Social Security Administration and manpower researchers. Several attempts have been made to use the data in manpower program evaluation,[5] but there is only one documented case in which the Social Security data have been made available to a nongovernment research investigator.[6]

Despite their acknowledged limitations, Social Security data offer perhaps the best available source of information for program evaluation purposes. The highly accurate longitudinal earnings history represents a record of post-program labor market performance unmatched by any alternative source of information available at a comparable cost. In fact,

5. Orly Ashenfelter, "Progress Report on the Development of Continuous Performance Information on the Impact of the Manpower Development and Training Act," Technical Analysis Paper No. 12A, prepared for Office of Evaluation, U.S. Department of Labor, 1973; and David J. Farber, "An Analysis of Change in Earnings of Participants in Manpower Training Programs," Department of Labor Internal Report, 1972.

6. Edward C. Prescott and Thomas F. Cooley, "Evaluating the Impact of MDTA Training Programs on Earnings Under Varying Labor Market Conditions," (Philadelphia: University of Pennsylvania, 1972), prepared for Manpower Administration, U.S. Department of Labor.

a panel assembled by the National Academy of Sciences to consider the use of Social Security data in assessing the impact of manpower programs concluded:

> In light of the history of manpower training studies, the SSA data are just as adequate a source of comparison groups as tailor-made sample survey studies. . . . In short, SSA data should be employed in the evaluation of manpower programs—especially those that tend to serve prime-age males, such as the MDTA or NAB-JOBS program. They will be less adequate for evaluating WIN, Job Corps, and the Out-of-School NYC.[7]

COST-BENEFIT ANALYSIS

Cost-benefit analysis is one of the frequently used methodological techniques for summarizing the overall efficiency of manpower programs measured in terms of economic allocative efficiency. Under this method of evaluation, the costs associated with the operation of the program (including the opportunity cost to the trainees for participating) are summarized. An estimate of program benefits is then made and compared to program costs. If the resulting ratio is equal to or greater than one, the program is judged worthwhile; if the ratio is less than one, the conclusion is that economic resources are not being used wisely in continuing the program.

Few aspects of manpower program evaluation have generated as much conflict and controversy as cost-benefit analysis. The technique has been widely criticized, largely because of its emphasis on the monetary benefits and costs of training programs. Many program policy makers and administrators feel that noneconomic considerations deserve at least as much attention as the economic variables in measuring the impact of social action programs, but the noneconomic factors are rarely if ever taken into account by cost-benefit analysts. The result is that some programs, which are especially weak in producing measurable economic benefits but which generate meaningful qualitative effects, may be reduced in size or eliminated because of the limitations of the methods employed in cost-benefit program assessment. As expressed by one leading manpower economist, "The cost-benefit calculus is only one piece of evidence in the appraisal process, and it may not be the most significant piece of evidence."[8]

7. National Academy of Sciences, "Final Report of the Panel on Manpower Training Evaluation—The Use of Social Security Earnings Data for Assessing the Impact of Manpower Training Programs," report prepared for U.S. Department of Labor, Washington, D. C., January 1974, p. 33.

8. Gerald G. Somers, "Criteria for Evaluating Manpower Policies," in *Lessons from a Decade of Manpower Policy* (forthcoming).

The use of cost-benefit analysis in appraising the impact of manpower programs upon minorities and women is especially hazardous. There are numerous private and social benefits and costs associated with training minority and female workers. The changes in the attitudes and values of the trainees, as well as those with whom they interact, can produce unlimited possibilities for post-training gains in both economic and social status. Such changes are likely to prove too diverse and subtle, and too uncertain of direction to warrant accurate measurement on any currently available scale. To appraise program impact upon minorities and women accurately, the noneconomic considerations are highly important.

MEASURING IMPACT ON MINORITIES AND WOMEN

The limitations of evaluative methodology which constrain the accurate measurement of program impact upon all enrollees also reduce the reliability of evaluation studies which measure program impact upon minorities and women. There are conditions peculiar to minorities, however, which further exacerbate the problem of evaluation.

First, minorities have been disproportionately enrolled in work experience, employability development, and job development programs. Many programs of this type are operated by community-based organizations and community action agencies. These organizations, created during the height of the nation's concern with alleviating poverty through increasing the power of the poor, are often staffed by inexperienced administrators. Because they are action oriented, the community action agencies often neglect efficient record keeping. The result is that the statistical data on trainees are often of poor quality and limited quantity. Follow-up studies conducted by such organizations are almost nonexistent. The paucity of good records creates numerous problems for program evaluators interested in selecting a sample of former program participants.

Second, minorities are concentrated in programs which have a narrow range of expected economic benefits. This means a disproportionate number of program participants may have an unfavorable post-training experience in the labor market. These circumstances create difficulty in conducting follow-up studies. As Glen G. Cain and Robinson G. Hollister have observed, "those participants who are easiest to locate are likely to be the most 'successful' . . . because of their apparent stability and . . . those who have 'failed' may well be less responsive to requests to reveal their current status."[9]

9. Glen G. Cain and Robinson G. Hollister, "The Methodology of Evaluating Social Action Programs," in Arnold R. Weber, Frank H. Cassell, and Woodrow L. Ginsburg, eds., *Private-Public Manpower Policies* (Madison: Industrial Relations Research Association, 1969).

Third, most minority group manpower program enrollees are disadvantaged, and a large proportion reside in urban poverty areas. Program evaluators have encountered great difficulty in conducting follow-up studies in such areas because of the high residential mobility of the population and the inherent suspicion and antagonism of the residents toward outsiders.[10] This problem greatly complicates the task of identifying and selecting a representative control group from among disadvantaged nonprogram participants.[11]

Because of these conditions, evaluation studies tend to be very costly and only limited data are available on the differential impact of manpower programs upon minorities and women. A substantial number of the existing evaluation studies, which address the overall question of participant economic impact, do not present data on participant earnings levels, wage rates, or employment experiences by race or sex. Most of the data which are available are confined to post-program labor market experience or pre- and post-program changes in labor market experience in their own right. Only a very few studies have utilized separate control groups by race and/or sex and have provided distinct estimates of the impact of training upon earnings, wages, and/or employment by race or sex.

In addition to the methodological problems associated with an examination of program impact upon minorities and women, other considerations must be kept in mind. Specifically, it is important to recognize that the existence of discriminatory forces and barriers may serve to restrict the range of labor market alternatives and to expand the range of nonmarket alternatives realistically open to minorities and women, with possible implications for the reliability and validity of comparisons between female and minority trainee groups and other groups of trainees or nontrainees. In a word, manpower services of equal quality for men and women or for minorities and nonminorities may be followed by very dissimilar employment and earnings patterns for reasons quite extraneous to the program but related to race and sex discrimination in employment.

The existence of discriminatory barriers in the labor market may influence the character and composition of participant subgroups as well as the post-participation labor market experience of those subgroups. Specifically, systematic differences in the market and nonmarket alternatives open to minorities and women (in contrast to nonminorities and men) may result in minority and female trainee groups which are better qualified and motivated than their white or male counterparts in their own

10. Michael E. Borus, *Evaluating the Impact of Manpower Programs* (Lexington: D.C. Heath and Company, 1972), pp. 143-173.

11. Richard D. Leone *et al., Employability Development Teams and Federal Manpower Programs* (Philadelphia: Temple University, 1972).

right, and in comparison to those similarly situated members of their own race or sex who might be used as controls. Similarly, limitations on the occupational choices and employment opportunities realistically open to female and minority trainees may constrain post-program labor market performance and pre- and post-program changes in earnings and employment in absolute terms, and in relation to the experience of male or white trainees or of the labor force generally, except under exceptionally tight labor market conditions.

The complexity of the forces which shape the economic impact of manpower programs upon their minority and female participants, coupled with the limitations of the data available for assessing such impact, make it difficult to specify a set of expectations for the absolute and relative gains from training for minorities and women. Clearly, one would not expect women and minority trainees to fare as well as other trainees or other workers in the labor market, either before or after training, as long as discriminatory barriers exist; however, this does not constitute evidence that training is without significant benefit to the individual.

THE EVALUATIVE DATA

The evidence discussed in the next chapter about the economic impact of manpower programs upon minorities and women is based on the review of 210 evaluative studies. Table 1 shows the number of studies reviewed for each program. In addition to the evaluative studies, about 90 books, journal articles, and unpublished manuscripts were reviewed as background information on the structure and operation of manpower programs, evaluative methodology, and other issues related to program assessment.

The evaluative studies varied widely in scope, time of enrollee observation, and methodological approach to the evaluative process. A major shortcoming of the available literature is that only 41 of the 210 studies provide post-training data on minorities and women.

In most cases, the studies were little more than descriptive analyses of program operations and enrollment characteristics, with little or no useful information about the post-training labor market experience of enrollees. Slightly less than one of every ten studies used a control group to compare the post-training experience of program participants with comparable individuals who did not receive manpower training services. Very few studies, each of which will be separately identified in Chapter 3, used control groups in assessing the impact of training on minorities and women. In almost every case in which a control group was used, there were valid reasons to question the comparability of the controls and treatment group. The inadequacy of the selection of control groups

TABLE II-1. *Manpower Programs Summary of Evaluative Studies*

Program	Number of Studies Reviewed[a] Total	With Economic Impact Data	With Data on Minorities and/or Women	With Control Group
MDTA (Institutional and OJT)[b]	64	20	14	6
Neighborhood Youth Corps	43	2	2	5
Job Corps	42	2	1	1
Opportunities Industrialization Center	12	6	3	—
Concentrated Employment Program	17	12	7	3
Work Incentive Program	35	14	13	2
JOBS	5	2	1	1
Operation Mainstream	5	1	—	1
Public Service Careers	10	1	—	1
Apprenticeship Outreach Program	4	2	2	1
Public Employment Program	16	1	1	—
Total all programs	252	62	44	20

Source: Data in author's possession.

[a] Studies may be classified in more than one column.

[b] Includes Olympus Research Corp., "The Total Impact of Manpower Programs: A Four-City Case Study," report prepared for Office of Policy, Evaluation and Research, Manpower Administration, U. S. Department of Labor, 1971. The study includes data on four manpower programs in addition to MDTA.

was serious enough to cast doubt on the major conclusions of program impact reported in some studies.

Evaluative studies containing information about the post-training experiences of participants in the job development and employability development programs are virtually nonexistent. The paucity of useful evaluations of such programs greatly reduces the information concerning impact upon minorities since minority trainees were heavily concentrated in the job and employability development programs.

The evaluative studies differ widely in the indices with which post-training economic benefits are measured. Typically, earnings and employment are observed, but the studies display broad variations in the selection of hourly, monthly, and annual earnings as the unit of measurement. In addition, few studies correct for changes in economic variables attributable to circumstances unique to the local labor market in which the evaluation is conducted. In short, although there is a large number of studies available for review, few are very useful as a reliable base of information from which to draw firm conclusions regarding the economic impact of manpower programs in general, and the impact on minorities and women in particular. The next chapter will summarize the results of the evaluative studies and attempt to frame a consensus judgment on the state of knowledge as revealed in the available literature.

CHAPTER III

Economic Impact

There are a limited number of "total impact" studies which have attempted to assess the overall impact of various sets of manpower programs and manpower services upon specific target populations or in specific communities.[1] The most thorough of these studies, and the only one to provide extensive quantitative data on a substantial number and range of programs, is the Olympus Research Corporation study, "The Total Impact of Manpower Programs: A Four-City Case Study."[2] Although this study does not contain comparison groups, the results do provide an interesting and useful overview of the participant economic impact of the multiplicity of manpower programs in operation in most major labor markets.

The Four-City study provides data on levels of and changes in the annual earnings, hourly wage rates, and employment experiences of late 1969 and early 1970 participants in four national manpower programs: MDTA, OIC, CEP, and WIN and in local programs administered by community action agencies in Boston, Denver, San Francisco, and Oakland-Richmond. In the absence of comparison groups, the study relies heavily on general labor market trends and trends in the pre-program labor market experience of participant groups as a basis for inferring impact from these data. In addition, the study contains subjective judgments based on impressions gained from interviews on the labor market impact of several other programs including JOBS, NYC, New Careers, and Operation Mainstream.

The Four-City study is unique in that it attempts to utilize its data on participant labor market experience to assess the relative economic impact of specific types of manpower program services. This assessment encompassed both those programs from which follow-up data on participants had

1. The following reports prepared for the Office of Policy, Evaluation and Research, Manpower Administration, U. S. Department of Labor are illustrative: American Indian Consultants, Inc., "An Evaluation of Manpower Services and Supportive Services to American Indians on Reservations," 1972; Sam Harris Associates, Ltd., "An Evaluation of the Utilization of Manpower and Social Services by Negroes in Eight Southern Cities," 1972; and "A Manpower Program Evaluation Project of All Federally Supported Manpower Programs in the City of Newark, N. J.," 1970; J. A. Reyes Associates, Inc., "An Evaluation of Manpower Systems Services to Mexican-Americans in Four Southwestern States," 1972.

2. Olympus Research Corporation, "The Total Impact of Manpower Programs: A Four-City Case Study," report prepared for Office of Policy, Evaluation and Research, Manpower Administration, U. S. Department of Labor, 1971.

been collected, and those which were evaluated on a subjective basis without the benefit of follow-up data. The results of this assessment may be summarized as follows:

1. "The follow-up data provide a resounding testimonial for skill training. Across the board, those who obtained skill training came through with better employment stability and earnings than those who received only non-skill training."[3]

2. "There is no evidence which leads to the conclusion that placing people in prevocational training makes any difference one way or another." However, although the data were ". . . mixed with respect to orientation and prevocational training," they did provide strong support for the value of basic education and language training—most notably, English as a second language—in enabling individuals to apply existing skills or to learn new ones.[4]

3. Job development programs are desirable and have positive individual impact, but they are too limited in scope to have a major impact. Specifically, the JOBS program was judged to have had a positive influence on individuals and to represent a desirable approach, but "experience in the Four Cities suggests the program will never enroll enough employers or employees to have more than a minor impact." In a more general vein, the study reported that, "despite relatively tight labor markets in all of the cities, there simply were not employers hungrily waiting with attractive jobs in easily accessible locations which they were willing to offer manpower program participants."[5]

4. Work experience programs have been successful in providing needed income and a modest measure of self-esteem for participants, but they have not had and could not reasonably be expected to have had a measurable labor market impact. In general, such programs were characterized as "last resorts" for those "unlikely to make it in the regular labor market" which are justified by the lack of viable alternatives.[6]

The Four-City study also presents data on post-training income, wage rate and employment levels, and pre-/post-training changes in income and wage rate by sex and race, but only on a city-by-city basis. The data on average post-training income levels, wage rates, and employment stability revealed that Anglos generally fared better than any other ethnic group but did not reveal equally clear and consistent differences between male and female participants, except in the case of wage rates.[7]

3. *Ibid.*, Vol. I, p. 81.

4. *Ibid.*, Vol. I, pp. 80-81

5. *Ibid.*, Vol. I, p. 83.

6. *Ibid.*, Vol. I, p. 86.

7. *Ibid.*, Vol. II, Chapter 22, p. 42.

The data on pre-/post-training average changes in income and wage rate revealed no consistent differences among ethnic groups, but consistently greater gains for women than for men were shown. However, this difference was viewed only as supportive of "the more general proposition that low wage rate and low-income groups are more likely to improve than a high wage-income group," and not regarded as sufficient to justify a conclusion that "either sex is better prospect for improvement through manpower training."[8]

Earnings

The Four-City study indicates that, as a group, participants in manpower programs enjoyed higher annual earnings in the year after training than they did in the year or years preceding entry into training, and concludes that "manpower programs had, in general, a substantially positive impact upon the employment and earnings of their enrollees."[9] The magnitude of the gains and impact varied both among cities and among programs, as would be expected given variations in local economic conditions and in specific program services and clientele, but in no case was it sufficient to bring the average income of employed trainees significantly above the basic poverty level. Specifically, the study reported:

> Translated into annual income equivalents, the average enrollee across the four cities [with both pre- and post-training work experience] would have gained $1380 a year over Period I [the 36-month period prior to enrollment] and $1220 a year over Period II [the 12-month period prior to enrollment]. Transformed into percentages, this would have meant a 40-percent increase over Period I and a 30-percent increase in income over Period II. However, the average enrollee who worked following training was still earning only at a rate of $3000 per year. Poverty had been made substantially more comfortable, but not eliminated.[10]

Data on earnings levels and changes by sex revealed that in only two of the four cities was average post-training annual income significantly higher for male than for female participants, and in all four cities female participants recorded greater pre-/post-training gains in income than did male participants (Table 1). Comparable data by ethnic group indicated that, in most cases, Anglos had the highest and Spanish-speaking the lowest post-training incomes; blacks experienced pre-/post-training increases in income similar to whites, and the Spanish-speaking recorded the smallest

8. *Ibid.*

9. *Ibid.*, Vol. I, p. 78.

10. *Ibid.*, Vol. I, p. 7.

TABLE III-1. *Economic Impact of Manpower Programs*
Four-City Study
Annual Earnings Levels and Changes
By Sex and Race

Earnings levels and Changes	Total Average	San Francisco	Oakland	Denver	Boston
Post-training earnings level					
Sex:					
Male	3,150	3,180	3,180	2,660	3,580
Female	2,925	3,260	2,640	2,320	3,480
Race:					
White	3,190	3,300	2,820	2,860	3,780
Negro	2,945	2,940	2,820	2,580	3,440
Spanish-speaking	2,890	3,060	3,020	2,340	3,140
Pre-/post-training earnings gain					
Sex:					
Male	1,250	1,480	1,260	880	380
Female	1,565	2,000	1,440	1,280	1,540
Race:					
White	1,490	1,980	1,360	1,180	1,440
Negro	1,435	1,360	1,400	1,460	1,520
Spanish-speaking	1,180	1,400	1,040	840	1,440

Source: Olympus Research Corporation, "The Total Impact of Manpower Programs: A Four-City Case Study," report prepared for Office of Policy, Evaluation and Research, Manpower Administration, U. S. Department of Labor, 1971, Vol. I, p. 32.

such gains (Table 1). Overall, an unweighted average of individual city data indicated income gains of $1,565 for women as compared with $1,250 for men and of $1,490 for Anglos as compared with $1,435 for blacks and $1,180 for the Spanish-speaking.

Wage Rates

The data on participant wage rates parallel those on earnings and provide an encouraging picture of the earnings potential of participants and of the role of manpower programs in enhancing that potential. In all four cities, the average post-training wage rate for employed trainees exceeded $2.00 per hour—the level required to achieve an income slightly above the poverty line on the basis of full-time, full-year employment. More importantly, trainees in all four cities realized substantial pre-/post-training increases in average wage rates. Specifically, the study reported:

> On the average across the four cities, the average hourly wage rose by $0.50 an hour between Periods I and III and $0.42 an hour between Periods II and III. . . . Of course, wages were rising during the period . . . However, there were no minimum wage increases and little unionization to push up the bottom of the wage structure within slackening labor markets. Since the midpoints of 36 months and 12 months are a year apart, the 12-cents-an-hour difference between the average hourly wage rates of Period I and II may be an indication of the normal wage change in the tighter labor markets which prevailed between 1966 and 1969 and which included a substantial rise in the minimum wage. The normal increase during 1970 should have been no greater.[11]

In all four cities, post-training wage rates were significantly higher for male than for female participants (about $0.45 per hour or 20 to 25 percent); in three of the four cities, female participants experienced greater pre-/post-training gains in wage rates than did their male counterparts (Table 2). Among ethnic groups, Anglos consistently enjoyed the highest post-training wage rates, whereas Spanish-speaking trainees tended to experience the largest pre-/post-training wage rate gains, and black trainees experienced the most limited gains (Table 2). Overall, however, the wage rate gains of women and the Spanish-speaking do not appear to be significantly greater than those of their male or Anglo counterparts, whereas the gains of blacks do appear to be significantly lower, particularly given the proposition that low-wage groups are more likely to outgain the high-wage groups.

---

11. *Ibid.*, Vol. I, pp. 5-6.

TABLE III-2. *Economic Impact of Manpower Programs Four-City Study Hourly Wage Rate Levels and Changes By Sex and Race*

Wage Rate Levels and Changes	Total Average	San Francisco	Oakland	Denver	Boston
Post-training wage rate					
Sex:					
Male	$ 2.48	$ 2.67	$ 2.55	$ 2.28	$ 2.43
Female	2.09	2.25	2.06	1.83	2.21
Race:					
White	2.35	2.53	2.28	2.23	2.38
Negro	2.21	2.48	2.24	1.87	2.27
Spanish-speaking	2.21	2.48	2.15	2.04	2.19
Pre-/post-training wage rate gain					
Sex:					
Male	0.47	0.79	0.34	0.32	0.43
Female	0.51	0.66	0.43	0.38	0.56
Race:					
White	0.49	0.75	0.30	0.35	0.55
Negro	0.38	0.35	0.42	0.30	0.44
Spanish-speaking	0.52	0.78	0.33	0.36	0.60

Source: Olympus Research Corporation, "The Total Impact of Manpower Programs: A Four-City Case Study," report prepared for Office of Policy, Evaluation and Research, Manpower Administration, U. S. Department of Labor, 1971, Vol. I, p. 32.

Employment

The Four-City study focuses on two measures of employment—"employment stability," defined as the percent of available time worked by those reporting employment in a given time period, and "employment intensity," defined as the percent of total potential time worked by the total trainee group, including those not reporting employment in a given time period. Overall, only modest pre-/post-training increases were noted in both employment stability and employment intensity, although in both cases the changes did exceed the change to be expected on the basis of pre-training trends in the employment experience of participants.[12] However, in only one city (Boston) did post-training employment stability exceed 70 percent or post-training employment intensity exceed 50 percent.[13] This somewhat discouraging picture of the employment experience of trainees and the impact of training may have been a reflection of slackening labor markets or the behavior of the substantial number of female WIN trainees in the follow-up sample; it does, however, raise some serious questions regarding the breadth and depth of the true impact of training.

The only employment data available by race or sex relates to post-training levels of employment stability and intensity. In general, these data reveal surprisingly minor differences between male and female or between nonminority and minority participants with respect to either variable. However, they do indicate some consistent, if not significant, differences in favor of male over female and of nonminority over minority participants with respect to both stability and intensity of employment.[14] At least in the case of women, the extent of these differences appears to have been closely related to the nature of the labor market, since they were least noticeable in the heavily white collar and clerical markets in Boston and San Francisco.[15]

SKILL TRAINING—MDTA

There is an ample and highly diverse evaluative literature on MDTA skill training programs, as would be expected given the longevity and breadth of the MDTA training effort. The central focus of much of this literature has been the impact of training upon enrollee employment and earnings, with particular emphasis on determining the cost-effectiveness

12. *Ibid.*, Vol. I, p. 5.

13. *Ibid.*, Vol. I, p. 32.

14. *Ibid.*

15. *Ibid.*

of training. The evaluative studies which comprise this literature, taken individually, are sufficiently narrow in scope and/or open to question on methodological grounds to inhibit generalization; nevertheless, there is a compelling consistency in their findings of economic benefits to enrollees and society which, over time, may be expected to outweigh the costs of training.

Specifically, existing evaluative studies generally indicate pre-/post-program gains in employment, wage rates, and earnings for trainees sufficient to generate favorable benefit-cost ratios ranging from 1.3:1 to 3.5:1, assuming a ten-year service life and 10 percent discount rate.[16] However, these encouraging benefit-cost ratios must be interpreted with caution because they are heavily dependent on the assumption made about the duration of the economic benefits of training.

The available empirical evidence on participant economic benefits from MDTA training by race and sex generally suggests the same patterns that emerged in the Four-City data. Although both women and minorities may do less well in the labor market after training than do their male or white trainee counterparts, at the same time, however, women and minorities do experience substantial improvement in income, wage rates, and employment between pre-and post-training periods.

Earnings

There is a sizable body of data on the earnings of MDTA trainees in the year or years immediately preceding and following training. These data have been drawn from a variety of sources and have been treated in a variety of ways, but a relatively clear and consistent pattern with respect to gross earnings levels and changes is revealed (Table 3). Changes in average annual earnings from pre- to post-training periods ranged from $1,100 to $1,900 with an average of about $1,500, whereas post-training average annual earnings ranged between $2,300 and $4,100 with an average of almost $3,300.

There are only two major studies which provide reasonably comprehensive data on earnings levels and changes of MDTA trainees by sex and by race. The first is David J. Farber's study of 1964 trainees based on Social Security data for the 1958-1962 period and for the year 1965.[17] The second is the "MDTA Outcomes Study" of a nationwide sample of

16. Calculated from: Ernest W. Stromsdorfer, *Review and Synthesis of Cost-Effectiveness Studies of Vocational and Technical Education* (Columbus, Ohio: ERIC Clearing House on Vocational and Technical Education, 1972), pp. 58-59.

17. David J. Farber, "Changes in the Duration of the Post-Training Period and in Relative Earning Credits of Trainees: The 1965-1969 Experience of MDTA Institutional and OJT Trainees, Class of 1964, report, 1971.

TABLE III-3. *Economic Impact of Manpower Programs*
MDTA
Pre- And Post-Training Annual Earnings of Trainees

Study	Training Type	Training Year(s)	Income		Change
			Pre-	Post-	
Hardin and Borus	INST	1960-1963	—	—	1,524
Muir *et al.*	INST		2,296	3,634	1,338
	OJT		2,652	3,860	1,208
Farber	INST	1964	978	2,306	1,328
	OJT	1964	1,500	3,140	1,640
Prescott and Cooley	INST	1967	1,740	3,357	1,617
	OJT	1967	2,157	4,083	1,926
MDTA Outcomes	INST	1969	—	—	1,876
	OJT	1969	—	—	1,614
Four City	INST	1969-1970	2,000	3,100	1,100

Sources: Einar Hardin and Michael E. Borus, *Economic Benefits and Costs of Retraining* (Lexington: D. C. Heath and pany, 1971), p. 47.

Allan H. Muir *et al.*, "Cost-Effectiveness Analysis of On-the-Job and Institutional Training Courses," Planning Research Corporation report prepared for Office of Policy, Evaluation and Research, Manpower Administration, U. S. Department of Labor, 1967, p. 14.

David J. Farber. "Changes in the Duration of the Post-Training Period and in Relative Earning Credits of Trainees: The 1965-1969 Experience of MDTA Institutional and OJT Trainees, Class of 1964," unpublished U. S. Department of Labor report, 1971.

Edward C. Prescott and Thomas F. Cooley, "Evaluating the Impact of MDTA Training Programs on Earnings under Varying Labor Market Conditions," report prepared for Office of Policy, Evaluation and Research, Manpower Administrations, U. S. Department of Labor, 1972, p. 4.

Decision Making Information, "MDTA Outcomes Study," report for Office of Policy, Evaluation and Research, Manpower Administrations, U.S. Department of Labor, 1972, Chapter VII, pp. 7, 10.

Olympus Research Corporation, "The Total Impact of Manpower Programs: A Four-City Case Study," report prepared for Office of Policy, Evaluation and Research, Manpower Administration, U. S. Department of Labor, 1971, Vol. I, pp. 13, 16, 19.

participants who exited training in 1969.[18] Both studies revealed higher pre- and post-training earnings for male than for female trainees in both institutional and on-the-job training programs, but each study showed somewhat different patterns in the structure of pre-/post-training income increases. The Department of Labor study indicated that men outgained women in both institutional and on-the-job programs, whereas the "MDTA Outcomes Study" suggested women outgained men in the institutional program. The "MDTA Outcomes Study" also indicated that whites outgained nonwhites in both institutional and on-the-job training, but the Department of Labor study revealed slightly larger gains for blacks than for whites in the on-the-job program. Taken together, these two studies do not suggest any significant sex or race difference in earnings increases.

There are a number of studies of MDTA trainees which utilize comparison groups and provide estimates of the net earnings impact of training. For the most part, these estimates range from $250 per year to $800 per year and are concentrated between $400 and $500 per year. Einar Hardin and Michael E. Borus, in a study of early programs in Michigan, found a net effect of training of $251 per year, but they also reported wide variations in earnings effects by length of training course, with individuals in the shortest courses (60-200 hours) experiencing net gains of almost $1,000.[19] Earl D. Main, in a nationwide study of 1964 and 1965 institutional trainees, found an earnings impact of $7.87 per week or $409 per year.[20] David O. Sewell, in a study of 1965 and 1966 trainees in North Carolina, detected a net effect of $5.70 per week for institutional training and $11.60 per week for on-the-job training with an overall average equivalent to $433 per year.[21] Ralph E. Smith, in a nationwide simulation study of 1967 institutional trainees, reported a net earnings impact of $416 per year.[22] Finally, Edward C. Prescott and Thomas F. Cooley, in a study based on the Social Security records of 1968 trainees and eligible trainees who failed to appear for training,

18. Decision Making Information, "MDTA Outcomes Study," report prepared for Office of Policy, Evaluation and Research, Manpower Administration, U. S. Department of Labor, Chapter VII, pp. 7-10.

19. Einar Hardin and Michael E. Borus, *Economic Benefits and Costs of Retraining* (Lexington: D.C. Heath and Company, 1971), p. 63.

20. Earl D. Main, *A Nationwide Evaluation of MDTA Institutional Job Training Programs* (Chicago: National Opinion Research Center, University of Chicago, 1966), p. 56.

21. David O. Sewell, *Training the Poor: A Benefit-Cost Analysis of Manpower Programs in the U. S. Anti-Poverty Program* (Kingston, Ontario: Industrial Relations Centre, Queen's University, 1971), p. 85.

22. Ralph E. Smith, "An Analysis of the Efficiency and Equity of Manpower Programs," Ph. D. dissertation, Georgetown University, 1971, p. 85.

reported differentials of about $600 and $800 per year for institutional and on-the-job trainees, respectively.[23]

There are two studies, both utilizing Social Security data, multi-year pre-training income bases, and comparison groups drawn from the Social Security Continuous Work History Sample, which provide far less optimistic estimates of the earnings impact of training. The first of these focuses on 1964 enrollees and found net effects of only $70 per year for institutional training and $310 per year for on-the-job training.[24] The second involves 1968 trainees and reveals substantial negative earnings effects for institutional training and only inconsequential positive effects for on-the-job training.[25] The nature of the results of these studies has led to serious questioning of their methodology and of the usefulness of the Continuous Work History Sample as a source of comparison groups for manpower program participants.[26] In this respect, the following possibilities should be noted:

1. The findings of the 1964 study may reflect a high percentage of displaced workers among trainees for whom multi-year pre-training earnings would overstate their true earnings potential without retraining, both in absolute terms and relative to a comparison group.
2. The findings of the 1968 study may reflect a high percentage of disadvantaged individuals among trainees for whom the range of employment opportunities, even after training, would have been more restricted than for low-income workers generally.

There are five major studies which provide estimates of the net earnings impact of MDTA training by sex and race based on control group or simulation methodology. In general, these estimates indicate that women and minorities did experience substantial gains in income as a result of training, and that these gains, and particularly those realized by black women, compared favorably with the gains of their race and sex counterparts in training (Table 4). The most notable deviations from this pattern appear

23. Edward C. Prescott and Thomas F. Cooley, "Evaluating the Impact of MDTA Training Programs on Earnings Under Varying Labor Market Conditions," report prepared for Office of Policy, Evaluation and Research, Manpower Administration, U.S. Department of Labor, 1971, p. 5.

24. Farber, *op. cit.*

25. David J. Farber, "Highlights: Some Findings From a Follow-Up Study of Pre- and Post-Training Earnings Histories of 215,000 Trainees Participating in Two 1964 and Four 1968 Training Programs," unpublished U. S. Department of Labor study, 1971.

26. A statement of methodology is to found in, David J. Farber, "Methods of Calculating Measures Used in Manpower Training Follow-Up Systems"; a critique of this methodology in Herman P. Miller, "Critique of David Farber's Method of Evaluating the Gains in Earnings of MDTA Trainees"; and a reply to this critique in, David J. Farber, "A Reply to the Miller Critique of the M. A. Method of Evaluating the Gains in Earnings of MDTA Trainees," all are umpublished U. S. Department of Labor documents.

TABLE III-4. *Economic Impact of Manpower Programs*
MDTA
Net Annual Earnings Impact of
Institutional and On-the-Job Programs by Sex and Race

Study	Type of Program	Males		Females	
		White	Nonwhite	White	Nonwhite
Hardin and Borus (60-200 hr. courses)	INST	+557	+1,151	+895	+1,095
Farber	INST	- 48	+ 129	+132	+ 211
(1964)	OJT	+350	+ 551	+291	+ 620
Sewell	INST	—	+ 429	n.a.	n.a.
	OJT	—	+ 384	+756	+ 756
Prescott and	INST	+719	+ 587	+527	+ 624
Cooley	OJT	+842	+ 755	—	—
Farber	INST	-676	- 732	-368	- 364
(1968)	OJT	+ 88	+44	+104	+ 300

Sources: Einar Hardin and Michael E. Borus, *Economic Benefits and Costs of Retraining* (Lexington: D. C. Heath and Company 1971), p. 162.

David J. Farber, "Changes in the Duration of the Post-Training Period and in Relative Earnings Credits of Trainees: The 1965-69 Experience of MDTA Institutional and OJT Trainees, Class of 1964," unpublished U. S. Department of Labor report, 1971.

David O. Sewell, *Training the Poor: A Benefit-Cost Analysis of Manpower Programs in the U. S. Antipoverty Program* (Kingston, Ontario: Industrial Relations Centre, Queen's University, 1971), p. 85.

Edward C. Prescott and Thomas F. Cooley, "Evaluating the Impact of MDTA Programs on Earnings Under Varying Labor Market Conditions." report prepared for Office of Policy, Evaluation and Research, Manpower Administration, U. S. Department of Labor, 1971, p. 11.

David J. Farber, "Highlights: Some Findings From a Follow-up Study of Pre- and Post-Training Earnings Histories of 215,000 Trainees Participating in Two 1964 and Four 1968 Training Programs," unpublished U. S. Department of Labor study. 1971.

in the 1968 Department of Labor study which shows a negative earnings impact for all race and sex groups in institutional training, but a much smaller negative impact for women than men, and in Sewell's findings of zero impact for female institutional trainees in his primarily black sample. The results of the Department of Labor study have been discussed at some length, and Sewell's findings may be traced to the fact that virtually none of the female trainees used their acquired skills in the labor market.[27]

Two of the comparison group studies of MDTA trainees extended their analyses of earnings impact beyond the initial post-training year in an effort to provide insight into the duration of that impact. Prescott and Cooley calculated earnings differences between trainees and controls for a second post-training year and found that such differences declined between the first and second years for all but white female institutional and white male on-the-job trainees, with the overall decline in the earnings advantage of trainees approximately 10 percent.[28] The Department of Labor study of 1964 trainees calculated average differences in earnings gains over a five-year post-training period, as well as for the first post-training year, and found that the five-year average represented only about 60 percent of the first-year impact level; but it also found that the earnings gains of minorities and women were at least as stable and durable as those of nonminorities and men.[29]

Wage Rates

There are numerous reports on wage rate levels and changes for MDTA enrollees at various points over the 1960's and early 1970's. However, such reports must be interpreted with caution, as most are based on the operating statistics maintained by the Manpower Administration and are thus subject to criticism for lack of completeness and possible systematic exclusion of less successful trainees. In general, these reports indicate consistent and sizable pre-/post-training wage rate increases ranging between $0.30 and $0.50 per hour over most of MDTA's history, but also suggest that the gains of minority and female trainees were initially more modest than those of their nonminority or male counterparts (Table 5).

The early evaluations of MDTA institutional training programs reached essentially negative conclusions regarding the impact of training upon wage rates, but they did suggest more positive effects for women than for men. Main, in his study of trainees in courses ending between June 1, 1964, and February 28, 1965, concluded that "the evidence does not indicate that

27. Sewell, *op. cit.*, pp. 72-74.

28. Prescott and Cooley, *op. cit.*

29. Farber. "Changes in the Duration of the Post-Training Period," *op. cit.*

TABLE III-5. *Economic Impact of Manpower Programs MDTA Median Hourly Wage Rates of Trainees Pre- and Post-Training by Sex and Race*

	Institutional			On-the-Job		
Years	Pre-	Post-	Gains	Pre-	Post-	Gains
1965-1966						
Total	$ 1.44	$ 1.73	$ 0.29	n.a.	n.a.	n.a.
Male	1.62	2.06	.44	n.a.	n.a.	n.a.
Female	1.29	1.53	.24	n.a.	n.a.	n.a.
White	1.48	1.81	.33	n.a.	n.a.	n.a.
Nonwhite	1.33	1.59	.26	n.a.	n.a.	n.a.
1967-1968						
Total	1.55	2.04	.49	$ 1.74	$ 2.29	$ 0.55
Male	1.79	2.31	.52	1.97	2.63	.66
Female	1.40	1.81	.41	1.54	1.88	.34
1970-1971						
Total	1.93	2.23	.30	2.13	2.44	.31
Male	2.17	2.49	.32	2.37	2.71	.34
Female	1.77	2.10	.33	1.81	2.01	.20
White	1.96	2.27	.31	2.18	2.53	.35
Black	1.87	2.17	.30	1.96	2.23	.27
1971-1972						
Total	2.07	2.25	.18	2.52	2.68	.16
Male	2.40	2.68	.28	3.05	3.21	.16
Female	1.82	1.97	.15	1.87	2.15	.28
White	2.15	2.37	.22	2.72	2.90	.18
Black	1.90	2.11	.21	2.15	2.36	.21

Sources: "The Influence of MDTA Training on Earnings," Manpower Evaluation Report No. 8. Manpower Administration, U. S. Department of Labor, 1970.

"Earnings Mobility of MDTA Graduates." Manpower Evaluation Report No. 7, Manpower Administration, U. S. Department of Labor, 1969.

U. S. Department of Labor, "Median Earnings of Terminees From The MDTA Institutional and OJT Programs in FY 1971 and FY 1972," unpublished Manpower Administration report, 1972.

MDTA training generally resulted in higher paying jobs. . . . Among women, however, training is associated with higher wages."[30] Gurin, in his comparative study of completers and noncompleters in courses ending between October 1964 and October 1966, found no difference between completers and those who left the program with respect to relative standing on wage rate for their first post-program job; however, he did report that "the findings suggest that training had more impact on the post-program wages of the women than of the men trainees."[31]

This evidence on the wage rate impact of MDTA training clearly conflicts with the theoretical marginal productivity relationship between skill training and wage rates which constituted a basic philosophical underpinning of the MDTA effort. This conflict can be explained, at least in part, by reference to conditions in the labor market. In a loose labor market, such as during the early 1960's and early 1970's, enhanced productivity may serve primarily to enable an individual to compete effectively for available entry-level jobs, rather than to permit him to secure a better job or higher wage rate. However, even in a tight labor market, those barriers which define dual labor markets may so limit the range of opportunities open to individuals that they will effectively preclude either enhanced productivity or higher wage rates.

There are two studies which offer some evidence of a positive wage impact, but both have limited relevance in an overall assessment of the MDTA training effort. Sewell, in his study of North Carolina programs, reported increases in hourly earnings for completers vis-a-vis controls of approximately $0.25.[32] Smith reached a remarkably similar conclusion in his simulation study of 1967 and 1968 completers in attributing $0.25 of a $0.36 increase in hourly wage rates to the effect of training.[33] Sewell's results are methodologically sound, but difficult to generalize given the scope and setting of the study. Smith's results are based on a sufficiently broad sample to be generalizable; however, they are subject to challenge on methodological grounds because they are based on extrapolation over time, during a period of rapid economic growth and extremely tight labor market conditions.

30. Main, *op. cit.*, pp. 47-48.

31. Gerald Gurin, *A National Attitude Survey of Trainees in MDTA Institutional Programs* (Ann Arbor: Institute for Social Research, Survey Research Center, University of Michigan, 1970), p. 222.

32. Sewell, *op. cit.*, p. 71.

33. Smith, *op. cit.*, p. 84.

Employment

Four basic variables have been used to describe the post-program employment experience of MDTA trainees: placement, employment at time of follow-up, percentage of time employed, and employment in a training-related job. The available data on these variables generally suggest that, as a group, those who completed MDTA training fared reasonably well. Specifically, the existing studies tend to reveal the following pattern:

1. between 80 and 90 percent of completers find employment at some point during the year following training;
2. approximately 70 percent of completers are employed at the time of follow-up (six to twelve months after training);
3. about 60 percent of completers find employment in which they believe they utilize skills acquired in training;
4. more than 50 percent of completers are employed at least three-quarters of the time in the post-training period.

The basic studies of MDTA trainees indicate varying differences by sex and race with respect to post-program employment experience which are consistent with the broader pattern of sex and race differences in labor market status and behavior. Somewhat higher percentages of women and minorities report no post-program employment compared to males or nonminorities, and smaller percentages report employment at time of interview for all or most of the post-program period. In addition, these studies also indicate that, in relation to their counterpart groups, women and minorities are:

1. less likely to have a job lined up prior to completion of training or to find their first post-program job soon after completion of training;
2. more likely to utilize the Employment Service in finding their first post-program job and to utilize their training in that job;
3. more likely to express positive attitudes toward their training experience and its role in enabling them to secure employment.

Few attempts have been made to quantify the impact of training on employment, although most studies do suggest that it must be substantial. Mangum compared percentages of trainees working at least 75 percent of the time in the year before and the year after training and found an "apparent 30 percent improvement in employment stability" which he judged "significant, although it is, in part, attributable to general improvements in economic conditions."[34] Main found systematic differences between completers, dropouts, nonenrollees, and control groups with respect to both the percent holding at least one full-time job in the post-training period and the percent employed for all or most of the post-program period; he estimated the employment impact of exposure to training in terms of percent of time employed, as 13 to 23 percent for completers and 7 to 19 percent for dropouts.[35] The relatively small net employment effect of completing training (6 percent or one month out of seventeen) is surprising, but other analyses indicate that it may be because of the favorable experience of those who drop out of training specifically to accept employment.[36]

The "MDTA Outcomes Study" provides a quite different picture of the employment effect of training. That study reported no real change in employment stability between pre- and post-program periods for those trainees who worked in both periods, only minor changes in employment stability for the groups of trainees employed in either or both of the periods, but dramatic change in the number or percent of trainees employed between the two periods. Thus, for institutional trainees, the $1,876 average income gain was composed of the following elements:

1. increased employment—$1,035 or 55 percent;
2. increased employment stability—$489 or 25 percent;
3. increased hourly wage rates—$352 or 20 percent.[37]

The available information on sex and race differences in changes in employment patterns between pre- and post-training periods suggests that women were a primary beneficiary of MDTA training and the data offer some encouragement with respect to the gains of minorities. Much of the success of MDTA training in enhancing the employment prospects of female enrollees can be traced to the nature of the training opportunities afforded them. Specifically, one of the major labor market barriers facing female enrollees appears to have been the lack of a specific salable skill, and one of the strengths of the program was the heavy emphasis on and concentration of female enrollees in courses in the clerical and health fields where demand was strong and specific. This phenomenon received considerable attention in a study of early MDTA training in the Newark labor market which reported "evidence of occupational mobility of women

34. Garth L. Mangum, *MDTA: Foundation of Federal Manpower Policy* (Baltimore: Johns Hopkins Press, 1968), pp. 82-83.

35. Main, *op. cit.*, p. 87.

36. See particularly, Gurin, *op. cit.*, pp. 23-24.

37. Decision Making Information, *op. cit.*, Chapter 1, p. 13.

out of unskilled and semi-skilled occupations and into clerical occupations," and concluded that "MDTA facilitated, in some cases made possible, an occupational shift coinciding with labor market needs."[38] "The Four-City Study" reached the following similar, but stronger, conclusion:

> [T]o meet the "reasonable expectation of employment" requirement while keeping per capita training costs low, MDTA administrators have chosen to train for jobs where openings occur because of high turnover, whether or not they are characterized by rising demand. Two occupational areas happen to be characterized by both high turnover and rising demand: health occupations and clerical occupations. A recent ORC study found these two to comprise 70 percent of all female MDTA skills center enrollments. As a result females are given good employment opportunities, even if they are forced into narrow occupational limits.[39]

JOB DEVELOPMENT—PEP, PSC, JOBS, AOP

The four job development programs have not been subjected to serious scrutiny or systematic evaluation on a significant scale. A number of evaluations of PEP have been initiated, but most have not yet reached the point of final results and conclusions. There has been only one small-scale study of PSC and only three studies of AOP. A considerable body of descriptive material on the JOBS program does exist, but only five studies have been made of the actual operation and impact of the program, and only one of these is either quantitative in nature or broad in scope.

The basic focus of much of the evaluative literature on these job development programs has been their short-run placement record. Primary attention has been given to such basic operational dimensions of the programs as numbers placed, starting wage rates, and percent retained or promoted, in an effort to ascertain whether such programs were meeting their stated quantitative goals. Relatively little attention has been given to assessment of actual participant economic benefits, apparently because such benefits were assumed to flow automatically from the program.

Much of the subjective evaluative literature on these job development programs is pessimistic in tone, but the limited quantitative data which are available generally suggest that they did have a positive impact upon the short-run economic status and labor market experience of their participants, and that such impact was probably more pronounced for minorities and women than for nonminorities and men. The true magnitude and durability of this impact, however, is difficult to estimate because "changes"

38. *Ibid.*, p. 6.

39. Olympus Research Corporation, *op. cit.*, Vol. II, Chapter 24, p. 23.

were extensive and most of these programs have proved highly vulnerable to shifting labor market conditions and shifting programmatic priorities.

Earnings

There are surprisingly few studies which have attempted to measure the earnings gains experienced by participants in job development programs, and the results of a number of the studies which have sought to measure such gains are open to serious question because they are based on simple extrapolations of data on enrollee weekly earnings. Nevertheless, the available data on pre-/post-training changes in enrollees' earnings do present a rather encouraging picture of the potential impact of such programs (Table 6). Changes in estimated annual earnings for all enrollees in these programs ranged from $1,000 to $3,000 and averaged about $2,000, while average post-training annual earnings for enrollees across the programs approximated the $4,000 poverty-level income.

There are two studies of job development programs which provide estimates of the net earnings impact of participation in such programs. One of the Department of Labor studies of 1968 JOBS enrollees included a comparison group drawn from the Social Security Continuous Work History Sample and yielded an estimate of an earnings advantage to participants of about $300 for those in the contract segment of the program and of about $700 for those in the noncontract segment of the program.[40] The study of AOP in Washington, D. C., revealed that completers experienced gains in weekly earnings which exceeded those experienced by dropouts by almost $10 and those recorded by individuals not admitted to the program by about $22.[41]

The study of 1968 JOBS enrollees also provides the only concrete data on the net earnings impact of participation in a job development program by race or sex, other than that provided in the study of the exclusively minority Apprenticeship Outreach Program in the nation's capital. The data from this study of JOBS trainees clearly suggest that the program generated significant gains for its female and minority group participants, gains which generally compared very favorably with those of their male and nonminority counterparts in the program (Table 7). In terms of both gross and net income gains, black women appear to have been the primary beneficiaries of the JOBS program.

The earnings gains of female and black JOBS enrollees are highly en-

40. David J. Farber, "Highlights—First Annual Follow-Up: 1968 JOBS Contract and Non-Contract Program," unpublished U. S. Department of Labor study, 1971, p. 2.

41. Markley Roberts, "Pre-Apprenticeship Training for Disadvantaged Youth: A Cost-Benefit Study of Training by Project Build in Washington, D. C.," report prepared for the Office of Policy, Evaluation and Research, Manpower Administration, U. S. Department of Labor, Ph. D. dissertation, American University, 1970, p. 151.

TABLE III-6. *Economic Impact of Manpower Programs Job Development Programs Pre- and Post-Training Participant Annual Earnings*

Study	Program	Income Pre-	Income Post-	Change
Greenleigh	JOBS	2,300	4,700[a]	2,400
D. O. L.	JOBS	1,500	2,520	1,020
Farber	JOBS-Contract	900	2,800	1,900
	JOBS-Noncontract	1,150	3,600	2,450
RMC	PSC	2,000[a]	5,000[a]	3,000
Roberts	AOP	3,700[a]	5,600[a]	1,900

Sources: Greenleigh Associates, Inc., "The Job Opportunities in the Business Sector Program: An Evaluation of Impact in Ten Standard Metropolitan Statistical Areas," report prepared for Office of Policy, Evaluation and Research, Manpower Administration, U. S. Department of Labor, 1970, p. 91.

Cited in: U. S. Congress, Senate, Committee on Labor and Public Welfare, Subcommittee on Employment, Manpower, and Poverty, *The JOBS Program; Background Information*, 91st Cong., 2d. sess., April 1970, p. 169.

David J. Farber, "Highlights—First Annual Follow-Up: 1968 JOBS Contract and Non-Contract Program," unpublished U. S. Department of Labor study, 1971.

RMC Incorporated, "Evaluation of the PSC Program: Final Report, Vol. I: Findings and Conclusions," report prepared for Office of Policy, Evaluation and Research, Manpower Administration, U. S. Department of Labor, 1972, pp. 13-15, 36.

Markley Roberts, "Pre-Apprenticeship Training for Disadvantaged Youth: A Cost-Benefit Study of Training by Project Build in Washington, D. C.," report prepared for Office of Policy, Evaluation and Research, Manpower Administration, U. S. Department of Labor, Ph. D. dissertation, American University, 1970, p. 151.

[a] Figures based on extrapolations of weekly earnings.

TABLE III-7. *Economic Impact of Manpower Programs JOBS Pre- and Post-Training Annual Earnings Gains 1968 Contract and Noncontract Enrollees By Sex and Race*

Enrollees	Gross Change 1963-1967 to 1969	Net Change Trainees *vs.* Controls
Contract		
Males:	$ 1,911.26	$ 116.24
White	1,959.24	-89.96
Negro	1,895.48	188.04
Females:	1,922.68	620.88
White	1,514.44	207.24
Negro	2,047.36	747.24
Noncontract		
Males:	2,568.36	681.28
White	2,826.84	655.48
Negro	2,457.00	692.44
Females:	2,206.60	867.28
White	1,946.28	623.48
Negro	2.325.00	978.16

Source: David J. Farber, "Highlights—First Annual Follow-Up: 1968 JOBS Contract and Noncontract Programs," unpublished U. S. Department of Labor report, 1971, Tables 1 and 9-14.

couraging but must be interpreted with considerable caution for two reasons. First, data on the educational attainment of the JOBS enrollees included in the Department of Labor study reveal systematic and significant differences by sex, race, and program segment, with respect to percent of enrollees with twelve or more years of schooling, differences which parallel the observed differences in net income gains.[42] Second, given

42. The reported percentages of enrollees with 12 or more years of schooling are as follows:

	Noncontract	Contract
Males:		
White	27.0	23.1
Black	41.7	31.5
Total	37.0	29.3
Females:		
White	37.5	30.0
Black	60.1	43.7
Total	52.9	40.5

the sensitivity of the program to changing economic conditions, it is unlikely that the benefits uncovered in analyzing 1969 incomes would have persisted through the subsequent economic downturn. In this respect, it is less important that enrollees retain specific jobs than that they maintain their attachment to, and standing in, the labor market. In theory, the JOBS program was designed to ensure that such would be the case, but indications of deficiencies in placement and training under the program leave room for serious doubt on this score.

Wage Rates

The starting wage rates received by participants in job development programs have also been regarded as an index of the success of such programs in moving people out of poverty and into meaningful jobs. For example, a Department of Labor study of wages received by JOBS trainees during the latter half of 1969 under the MA-5 portion of the program reported that trainees could expect to receive an average hourly wage of $2.49 after nine months and reasoned that:

> . . . [t] his wage rate further represents an annual wage of $5,200. The average family size for JOBS contract employees is 3.7 and an estimate of the poverty level income for a family of that size is $3,420. Thus the income of the average JOBS employee will be raised considerably above the poverty level. This also indicates that the jobs being offered by employers on the whole cannot be characterized as low wage, deadend jobs.[43]

This line of reasoning is intuitively attractive but can be grossly misleading. The extrapolation of hourly or weekly earnings to annual income figures is questionable, particularly given the high turnover and low retention rates for enrollees during the early years of the program. In this respect, it is interesting to note that if trainees had worked on an average of 50 percent of the time, the income extrapolations cited above would have led to quite different conclusions regarding program impact. Similarly, wage rates are, at best, an imperfect measure of the quality of employment opportunities, as the correlation between wage rates and such factors as skill requirements, training opportunity, and advancement potential is far from perfect. In this respect, it should be noted that the evaluative literature on the JOBS program consistently indicates that a substantial portion of the job opportunities offered through the program required little skill and afforded little opportunity for advancement. One study specifically suggested that:

---

43. Cited in: U. S. Congress, Senate, Committee on Labor and Public Welfare, Subcommittee on Employment, Manpower, and Poverty, *The JOBS Program: Background Information*, 91st Cong., 2d. sess., April 1970, p. 169.

> . . . JOBS hires go into more or less traditional entry level jobs with little opportunity for vertical movement, and such jobs traditionally pay more than those with the potential for advancement.[44]

Available data indicate that most participants in PEP and PSC also were placed in jobs paying more than $2.00 per hour, but comparisons of pre-program wage rates with those received while in the PEP program reveal that participants generally experienced no increase through entry into the program (Table 8). However, these same comparative data on PEP participants do reveal that women experienced consistent wage rate gains and that minorities fared at least as well as nonminorities in terms of wage rate gains. Furthermore, data on wage rates received over the course of participation in PEP suggest that women and minorities experienced larger gains than did men and nonminorities.[45]

The evaluations of AOP reveal relatively favorable wage rate levels and changes among program participants. An evaluation of AOP in Washington, D.C., reported that 60 percent of those who completed the program experienced increases in average hourly earnings as compared to only 20 percent of those in the control group (dropouts or those not selected).[46] A Boise Cascade evaluation of AOP in twelve cities reported an increase in the percentage of program participants holding jobs paying more than $3.00 per hour from 40.5 percent before training to 69.7 percent after training, but also reported parallel increases for dropouts from 15.9 percent to 41.9 percent.[47] However, a study of the program in four cities found that mean starting wages for minorities were consistently lower than those of whites of equal job status.[48]

---

44. System Development Corporation, "Evaluation of the JOBS program in Nine Cities," report prepared for Office of Policy, Evaluation and Research, Manpower Administration, U. S. Department of Labor, 1969, p. 7.

45. WESTAT Research, Inc., "Longitudinal Analysis of the Public Employment Program: Wave I Analysis," report prepared for Office of Policy, Evaluation and Research, Manpower Administration, U. S. Department of Labor, 1972, pp. 3-12.

46. Roberts, *op. cit.*, p. 258.

47. Boise Cascade Center for Community Development, "Report of an Evaluation of the Apprenticeship Outreach Program (AOP)," report prepared for Office of Policy, Evaluation and Research, Manpower Administration, U. S. Department of Labor, 1970, pp. 31, 35.

48. Dennis Derryck, "Improving the Retention Rate of Indentured Apprentices in the Apprenticeship Outreach Program," report prepared for Office of Policy, Evaluation and Research, Manpower Administration, U.S. Department of Labor, 1973.

TABLE III-8. *Economic Impact of Manpower Programs Pre-PEP and PEP Average Hourly Wage Rates Fiscal Years 1972 and 1973 Entrants*

Characteristics	1972			1973		
	Pre-PEP	PEP	Change	Pre-PEP	PEP	Change
Sex:						
Men	$ 3.10	$ 2.98	-$ 0.12	$ 2.87	$ 2.81	-$ 0.06
Women	1.99	2.69	+ .70	2.32	2.44	+ .12
Race:						
Negro	2.59	2.79	+ .20	2.61	2.56	- .05
Spanish	2.64	2.96	+ .32	2.61	2.56	- .05
Indian	2.70	2.75	+ .05	2.74	2.91	+ .17
Total	2.77	2.83	+ .06	2.73	2.70	- .03

Source: U.S. Department of Labor.

Employment

The employment impact of most of these job development programs can only be inferred from data on the basic operational dimensions of the program. To date, 692,000 individuals (excluding JOBS noncontract enrollees) have been served by these programs with many of those reported to have achieved permanent job status and/or to have received promotions or increases in pay.[49] Clearly, some of these individuals would have been unable to find comparable employment in the absence of these programs, but the fact that "creaming" was frequently widespread in the selection of participants raises questions concerning the number of individuals who would have fallen into this category. At the same time, the limited provision for training under most of these programs raises further questions regarding the impact of these programs on the long-run labor market status of those participants who were helped in the short-run.

The true test of the employment impact of these programs lies in the post-placement experience of participants. Unfortunately, there is relatively little data on this aspect of the programs. Studies of PEP provide only fragmentary data on the success of the program in meeting its goal of providing transitional employment in the public sector, but the data that do exist suggest that higher percents of male and white enrollees, than of female or minority participants, have been promoted or transferred to "permanent" positions.[50] The lone study of PSC indicated that a substantial percent of participants in that program achieved permanent status, but provides no data on this point by race or sex.[51] Evaluations of the JOBS program agree that retention rates were low, although not necessarily radically different from those for entry-level employees generally; these evaluations, however, provide no data on retention by race or sex and no data on the experience of those not retained. The studies of AOP provide an unclear picture of the employment experience of participants. The study of the Washington, D. C., program revealed a pre-/post-program increase in the number of weeks worked per year from 34.9 to 38.5 for completers as compared to an increase from 33.2 to 34.0 for controls.[52] However, a study of the program in twelve cities revealed over 10 percent of program participants experienced unemployment in excess of thirteen weeks in the year after their participation in the program;[53]

49. U. S. Department of Labor, *Manpower Report of the President* (Washington, D.C.: Government Printing Office 1973), p. 227.

50. WESTAT Research, Inc., *loc. cit.*

51. RMC Incorporated, "Evaluation of the PSC Program: Final Report, Vol. I: Findings and Conclusions," report prepared for Office of Policy, Evaluation and Research, Manpower Administration, U. S. Department of Labor, 1972, pp. 13-15.

52. Roberts, *op. cit.*, p. 398.

53. Boise Cascade, *op. cit.*, p. 32.

a study of the program in four cities suggested that an industry's retention of AOP participants after leaving the program was lower than that of whites who entered that industry from other sources.[54]

EMPLOYABILITY DEVELOPMENT—OIC, WIN, CEP, JOB CORPS

There are four somewhat disparate manpower programs which offer services designed primarily to enable individuals to meet only entry-level labor market standards—OIC, WIN, CEP, and the Job Corps. Each of these programs offers a range of remedial services, including skill training on a selective basis, in an effort to overcome the most fundamental or obvious barriers to effective participation by specific target groups in the labor market. The evaluative literature on these programs is sparse and composed primarily of relatively narrow studies of program operation and impact in specific locales. The quantity and quality of data on participant labor market benefits which are available from these studies is even more fragmentary and not easily or confidently generalized.

The paucity of data on economic impact makes it difficult to reach any definite conclusions regarding the absolute or relative impact of employability development programs upon the women and minority group members who participated in them. Undoubtedly, individual female and minority group participants in such programs realized substantial gains as a result of their participation. However, there are insufficient data either to justify the conclusion that female or minority participants as a group realized significant economic gains as a result of training or to permit meaningful comparisons of the gains of women and minority group members with those of their male and nonminority counterparts in the programs.

Earnings

There are only four sources of data on the earnings of OIC trainees and none of these includes comparable data for any type of comparison group. OIC follow-up statistics for 1969 show that average trainee earnings increased from $1,900 before training to $2,900 after training; a more intensive review of trainee records in thirteen centers in conjunction with the compilation of these statistics produced 303 cases with complete pre- and post-training income data which indicated far larger earnings gains—in excess of $2,000.[55] Data available from the Four-City study on OIC enrollees in Boston and Oakland suggest that the more modest of the two

54. Derryck, *op. cit.*

55. O.I.C.N.I., *Bi-monthly Progress Report, Report No. 3* (Washington, D. C.: February 1969-March 1969).

estimates of earnings change is the more accurate, since this study shows earnings gains for those employed both before and after participation of $1,400 in Boston and $1,200 in Oakland, and changes in average annual earnings of employed trainees in the pre- and post-training periods of about $1,150 in Boston (from $2,260 to $3,420) and $900 in Oakland (from $1,620 to $2,500).[56] The Four-City study data for Boston conforms surprisingly well to data which emerged from an adequate study of the Roxbury OIC.[57]

OICs generally have served a predominantly minority and female clientele, and a little attention has been given to the race or sex structure of the earnings effects of participation in the program. There is but one study which provides earnings data by race, and only two devote attention to the relative earnings of male and female trainees. A study of the Boston OIC revealed that although the post-training earnings of female graduates were significantly lower than those of male graduates, women experienced slightly greater pre-/post-training earnings increases than did men ($1,300 compared to $1,200).[58] This study also included an attempt to estimate the net earnings impact of OIC training based on projections of "natural wage inflation"; the finding was that training increased mean weekly income by only 2 percent for male graduates and 9 percent for female graduates.[59] A study of fifteen OIC final reports also concluded that women benefited more from OIC training than did men, but supporting data were not provided.[60]

There are only three studies which provide earnings data for CEP enrollees. A 1970 Urban Systems study of almost 1,000 CEP participants in five widely scattered rural areas estimated pre-/post-training changes in average annual earnings of $580 for completers and $815 for noncompleters.[61] A Temple University study of 1969 and 1970 enrollees in the Philadelphia CEP revealed earnings changes of $830 for 1969 enrollees (from $2,030 to $2,860) and $1,120 for 1970 enrollees (from $1,800 to $2,920).[62] Finally, the Four-City study revealed negligible earnings

56. Olympus Research Corporation, *op. cit.*, Vol. I, pp. 13, 23.

57. Francis D. Barry, *The Roxbury OIC: An Economic Case Study of Self-Help Job Training in the Ghetto* (Ithaca: Cornell University, 1973), p. 211.

58. *Ibid.*

59. *Ibid.*

60. Legal Resources, Inc., *Opportunities Industrialization Centers: A Synthesis and Analysis of Fifteen OIC Final Reports* (Washington, D. C.: 1969), p. 79.

61. Urban Systems Research & Engineering, Inc., "Impact of Five Rural Concentrated Employment Programs," report prepared for Office of Policy, Evaluation and Research, Manpower Administration, U. S. Department of Labor, 1971

62. Richard D. Leone *et al., Employability Development Teams and Federal Manpower Programs: A Critical Assessment of the Philadelphia CEP's Experience* (Philadelphia: Temple University Press, 1972), pp. 116-126.

changes for CEP participants in Denver, but substantial gains for those in the Richmond CEP—$1,340 for those employed both before and after training and about $800 for the entire participant group.[63]

There are only two studies of CEP which provide data on participant earnings and employment by sex or race. The study of the rural CEPs estimated that, among completers, male trainees realized annual earnings gains of $608 compared to $538 for female trainees, whereas white trainees gained $724 per year compared to $565 for American Indians, $341 for Chicanos and $197 for blacks.[64] Among noncompleters, however, women were estimated to outgain men, and whites to outgain all groups except Chicanos.[65] The study of 1969 and 1970 enrollees in the Philadelphia CEP revealed somewhat larger pre-/post-training changes in average weekly wages for male trainees than for female trainees, coupled with coincident differences in changes in average weeks worked.[66] Overall, these data suggest pre-/post-training annual earnings gains of $500 to $1,250 for the men compared to negative or negligible gains for the women (Table 9).[67]

There is very little evidence on the economic effects of participation in the WIN program, and the evidence which does exist generally tends to indicate that the program has failed to achieve its goal of reducing welfare dependency. Schiller, in a study of 32 local WIN offices, found that an insignificant number of WIN graduates had been taken off welfare rolls.[68] Unfortunately, Schiller and other evaluators understated the welfare reduction by not including those trainees whose post-program earnings reduced their supplementary welfare payments, yet were not enough to remove them from the AFDC rolls. In a study of the program in nine counties in three states, Fine concluded that "the WIN program, with the possible exception of vocational training, has not resulted in increased employment and earnings."[69] Data from the Four-City study lends some credence to these conclusions, since they indicate that average annual income for all WIN participants across the four cities increased by only about $550 between pre- and post-training periods.[70] However,

63. Olympus Research Corporation, *loc. cit.*

64. Urban Systems Research & Engineering, Inc., *op. cit.*, pp. 109-110.

65. *Ibid.*

66. Leone *et al.*, *op. cit.*, p. 126.

67. *Ibid.*

68. Bradley Schiller, *The Impact of Urban WIN Programs—Phase II: Final Report* (Washington, D.C.: Pacific Training and Technical Assistance Corporation, 1972), pp. 2-5.

69. Ronald A. Fine *et al.*, *Final Report—AFDC Employment and Referral Guidelines* (Minneapolis: Institute for Interdisciplinary Studies, 1972), p. 29.

70. Olympus Research Corporation, *op. cit.*, Vol. I, pp. 13, 16, 19, 23.

TABLE III-9. *Economic Impact of Manpower Programs*
Concentrated Employment Program
Summary of Economic Success of Enrollees by Sex: Philadelphia CEP

Success Measure	1969 Male	1969 Female	1970 Male	1970 Female
Weeks worked:				
Pre-	25.1	25.1	20.6	25.0
Post-	27.7	24.6	33.0	19.0
Difference	+ 2.6	- 0.5	+12.4	- 6.0
Average weekly wages:				
Pre-	$ 86.92	$ 72.25	$ 84.71	$ 73.20
Post-	97.59	81.30	94.33	78.86
Difference	+ 10.67	+ 9.05	+9.62	+ 5.66
Estimated annual income:[a]				
Pre-	$ 2,182.00	$ 1,813.00	$ 1,745.00	$ 1,830.00
Post-	2,703.00	2,000.00	3,113.00	1,503.00
Difference	+ 521.00	+ 187.00	+ 1,268.00	- 327.00

Source: Richard D. Leone *et al.*, *Employability Development Teams and Federal Manpower Programs: The Philadelphia CEP's Experience* (Philadelphia: Temple University Press, 1972), p. 126.

[a] By Industrial Research Unit computation.

if only those participants who were employed both before and after training are considered, a gain of $965 emerges, a gain which is quite comparable to that experienced by MDTA trainees in the four cities. This may suggest that the potential earnings impact of skill training under WIN may not be radically different for skill training under MDTA which has been shown to have a positive impact on the economic status of welfare recipients.[71]

There is no concrete evidence on the impact of WIN upon participant earnings and employment by sex or race. Most studies suggest, however, that the program in the aggregate had a small positive impact upon the economic status of its female and minority participants. Specifically, the available literature indicates that placement rates were lower for women than for men, and that decreases in welfare dependency were more evident for whites than for blacks.

There is no readily available basis for assessing the true significance of these earnings data on participants in OIC, WIN, and CEP. However, the data from the Four-City study provide a useful, if imperfect, framework

71. Edward Prescott, William Tash and William Usdane, "Training and Employability: The Effects of MDTA on AFDC Recipients," *Welfare in Review,* January 1971.

for comparisons of earnings impact (Table 10). Overall, these data suggest that all of the programs had their greatest potential impact upon those with fairly stable labor force attachment (those employed both before and after training), but only a marginal impact upon the average economic and labor market status of their total participant groups. Within this framework, OIC appears to have had the greatest impact, with WIN slightly outdistancing CEP.

These patterns in earnings changes can be traced, at least in part, to differences in trainee characteristics and training services. At best, employability development can be expected to have only a marginal impact upon the relative labor market status of participants. The practical labor market significance of this impact will vary not only with the state of the labor market, but also with the relative pre-training standing of participants in the labor market queue. At the same time, programs may have differential marginal impacts as a function of the extent to which they incorporate skill training in their services. Thus, it is not coincidental that the rank order of programs by apparent economic impact—OIC, WIN, CEP—parallels the rank order of those programs with respect to the extent they provided training with immediate market relevance and the extent to which they served the most disadvantaged segments of the population.

The only available basis for estimating the net annual earnings impact of these employability programs is to be found in the data from the Four-City study on pre-training trends in wage rates and employment stability. On the basis of these data, two sets of estimates were made: (1) based on simple extrapolations of pre-training trends in wage rates and employment stability, except where negative trends were discerned, in which case no further deterioration was assumed; (2) based on substitution of the basic trends in wage rates and employment stability, wherever they exceeded the trends for a specific trainee group, identified in the entire four-city sample. The first extrapolation yielded "unexplained" earnings differences ranging from -$920 to +$1,640 with an unweighted average of +$230; the second yielded a range of unexplained differences of -$920 to +$675 with an unweighted average of +$110. If all negative figures are converted to zeros, the former approach yields an estimate of net effect of about $500, and the latter produces an estimate of approximately $375. Unfortunately, the available data do not permit similar estimates of earnings impact by sex or race across or within these three programs.

There are two 1968 studies of the net earnings impact of Job Corps participation; each study generally suggests only a marginal impact which does not compare favorably with similar estimates for other programs. Cain estimated earnings impact six months after termination from wage rate data on Corpsmen and a comparable group of youth with no Job Corps experiences, and thus computed annual earnings differentials, ranging from

TABLE III-10. *Economic Impact of Manpower Programs*
Four-City Study
Trainee Average Earnings Levels and Changes
Employability Development Programs

Program	Earnings Levels		Gross Earnings Changes		
	Employed Post-	All Trainees	Employed Pre- and Post-	Employed Pre-/ Employed Post-	All Trainees
OIC	$ 2,960	$ 2,115	$ 1.330	$ 1,030	$ 415
WIN	2,650	1,210	965	550	765
CEP	2,570	1,530	900	300	—
All programs	3,025	2,180	1,220	680	800

Source: Olympus Research Corporation. "The Total Impact of Manpower Programs: A Four-City Case Study," report prepared for Office of Policy, Evaluation and Research, Manpower Administration, U.S. Department of Labor, 1971, Vol. I., p. 5-23.

$187.20 to $259.60, in favor of the Corpsmen.[72] Resource Management Corporation conducted a separate analysis of the same national sample eighteen months after termination and concluded that the earnings gains of Corpsmen were not significant.[73]

Wage Rates

The wage rate impact of employability development programs has not been widely probed either theoretically or empirically, and data on wage levels and changes for participants in such programs are limited in quantity and quality. The Four-City study provides the only reasonably consistent set of data in its reports on pre-/post-training wage rate changes for trainees employed both before and after training. Data from the same study on average wages received by trainees employed before entering and after leaving the program are less reliable but more consistent with the limited amount of data available from other studies. Finally, there are a few studies which compare wage rates gains of completers and non-completers and provide the only, albeit imperfect, basis for assessing the true impact of training on wages rates.

The Four-City study data on pre-/post-training wage differences for those employed both before and after training reveal increases of $0.48 per hour for WIN, $0.44 per hour for OIC, and $0.27 for CEP, based on unweighted averages of specific city results.[74] Differences in average wage rates between those trainees with pre-training employment and those trainees with post-training employment were $0.53 for OIC, $0.25 for WIN, and $0.14 for CEP.[75] Thus, in all cases, the observed changes compared favorably with the $0.12 per hour increase to be expected among all participants on the basis of trends in participant pre-training experience.

There are only a few other widely scattered studies of the wage rate changes experienced by participants in employability development programs. An early evaluation of the Seattle OIC revealed a median pre-/post-training wage rate gain for 111 trainees in the $0.40 to $0.49 per hour

72. Glen G. Cain, *Benefit/Cost Estimates for Job Corps* (Madison: Institute for Research on Poverty, University of Wisconsin, 1968), p. 45.

73. Harry R. Woltman and William W. Walton, "Evaluation of the War on Poverty, The Feasibility of Benefit/Cost Analysis for Manpower Programs," Resource Management Corporation report prepared for General Accounting Office, 1968, pp. 87-120.

74. Olympus Research Corporation, Vol. I, pp. 15-19.

75. *Ibid.*

range and also indicated that black trainees, as a group, received slightly higher post-training entry-level salaries than did whites.[76] An unpublished study of WIN participants found pre-/post-training hourly wage rate changes ranging from $0.20 to $0.60 and concluded that ". . . WIN has had a positive impact on the earnings of enrollees, increasing the hourly wage of successful terminees by about 20 percent."[77] This study also revealed substantially greater pre-/post-training wage rate gains for women than for men and parallel, but less dramatic, differences between blacks and whites. The Urban Systems study of rural CEPs reported pre-/post-training changes in hourly wage rates of $0.30[78] and the System Development Corporation study of participants in 19 urban CEPs revealed a change in median hourly wage rates of about $0.10 to $0.20.[79] Neither of these studies provided data by race or sex. Finally, basic data on pre- and post-training wage rates received by Job Corps terminees reveal gains of about $0.20 to $0.30 per hour for the first six months after termination, with relatively little difference between blacks and whites or between males and females.[80]

The few studies which compare pre-/post-training wage rate gains of completers and noncompleters do not provide an optimistic index of the net wage effect of participation in employability development programs. The Urban Systems study of rural CEPs reported not only a pre-/post-training change in average hourly wage of $0.30 for completers, but a change of $0.47 for noncompleters.[81] The data generated by the series of Louis Harris polls of Job Corpsmen and Job Corps "no shows" (i.e., persons selected for training, but who never enrolled) reveal virtually identical pre-/post-program changes in average hourly wage rates; however, the data do suggest that women and black terminees may have fared slightly better vis-à-vis "no shows" than did male or white terminees. A statistical

76. Richard B. Peterson, *An Evaluation of the Seattle OIC* (Seattle: University of Washington, 1968), p. 24.

77. Analytic Systems, Inc., "Incomplete Study Prepared for the Manpower Administration," 1972, pp. IV-4.

78. Urban Systems Research & Engineering, Inc., *op. cit.*, p. 106.

79. System Development Corporation, "Evaluation of the Impact of Selected Urban CEPs," report prepared for Manpower Administration, U. S. Department of Labor, pp. 128-131.

80. These data are cited in *Hearings on the Economic Opportunity Amendments of 1967*, U. S. Congress, Senate, Committee on Education and Labor 90th Cong., 1st sess., 1967, pp. 259, 301, 489, 499.

81. Urban Systems Research & Engineering, Inc., *op. cit.*, p. 106.

analysis of these data resulted in estimates of the wage impact of participation of $0.04 for males and $0.14 for females.[82]

Employment

The available data on the post-program employment experience of participants in employability development programs do not provide a basis for optimism regarding program employment impact. Data from the Four-City study generally suggest that the magnitude and structure of any employment impact of training was heavily influenced by local conditions (Table 11). Given such variability, it is dangerous to calculate averages and difficult to draw general conclusions, but it does appear that, overall, the greatest changes occurred in the percent of time worked by employed trainees—the traditional measure of employment stability. The available data on the labor market activities of Job Corpsmen and "no shows" revealed disappointingly little difference between the two groups with respect to either percent in the labor force or percent employed. Further analyses of these data failed to uncover any significant employment effect of participation for either male or female Corpsmen.[83]

WORK EXPERIENCE—NYC AND OPERATION MAINSTREAM

Operation Mainstream and the Neighborhood Youth Corps are both designed to provide participants with income and work experience outside the labor market context. Neither is directed specifically toward development of the occupational skills of enrollees, and it may be unrealistic to expect significant short-run labor market gains to be associated with participation in either of these programs, particularly in light of the persistently high unemployment rates for youth and the precarious labor market position of the elderly.

The sole extensive evaluation of Operation Mainstream clearly suggests that the program has served almost exclusively as an income transfer device rather than as a manpower program. The study done by Kirschner Associates reported that the earnings provided by the program constituted a major and much needed source of income for participants whose average annual income from other sources was only about $1,000; but, the study also suggested that only an inconsequential number of enrollees find

82. Woltman and Walton, *op. cit.*, p. 20.

83. *Ibid.*

TABLE III-11. *Economic Impact of Manpower Programs Four City Study Pre- and Post-Program Employment of Trainees Employability Development Programs*

Program	Percent Employed Total		Percent of Time Employed			
			Employed		Total	
	Pre-	Post-	Pre-	Post-	Pre-	Post-
OIC-Boston	73	90	60	72	45	65
OIC-Richmond	61	58	54	54	32	31
WIN-Boston	69	48	60	65	41	31
WIN-Denver	36	54	59	48	21	26
WIN-SanFrancisco	29	50	52	52	15	26
WIN-Oakland	35	51	43	61	35	51
WIN-Richmond	39	48	50	61	25	29
CEP-Denver	84	86	59	53	50	46
CEP-Richmond	39	48	50	61	25	29
CEP-Philadelphia	n.a.	n.a.	n.a.	n.a.	46	60

Source: Olympus Research Corporation, "The Total Impact of Manpower Programs: A Four-City Case Study," report prepared for Office of Policy, Evaluation and Research, Manpower Administration, U. S. Department of Labor, Vol. I, pp. 13, 16, 17, 23.

Richard D. Leone *et al., Employability Development Teams and Federal Manpower Programs: The Philadelphia CEP's Experience* (Philadelphia : Temple University Press, 1972).

regular employment as a result of the program.[84] The Four-City study reached a similar but far less flattering judgment, concluding that:

> Operation Mainstream and equivalent work programs are easier to evaluate. In some cases they have been temporary "parking lots" while awaiting entry into other programs. Beyond that, the goal has been some modest self-esteem and income for alcoholics, elderly men, and others unlikely to make it in the regular labor market. It is a last resort but that is where many are at.[85]

84. Dale W. Berry *et al.*, "National Evaluation of Operation Mainstream: A Public Service Employment Program, Phase IV: Comparative Analysis," Kirschner Associates, Inc., 1971, pp. 92-98.

85. Olympus Research Corporation, *op. cit.*, Vol. I, p. 86.

Studies on NYC have reached somewhat similar conclusions. An RMC Incorporated study concluded that ". . . NYC really functions as a combination income-maintenance device and an aging device to help youths [stay] out of trouble until they are old enough to get a sustaining job or to become involved in a training program."[86] The Four-City study assessed NYC as follows:

> The income has been needed and, though some of the experience may have been counterproductive, most of it was probably better than none. The desirability of NYC depends heavily upon the answer to the question, "if there were no NYC, what alternatives would be provided poor youth to earn and to a limited extent to learn?"[87]

Earnings

The nature of the NYC participant population limits the usefulness of pre- and post-program comparisons in evaluating the economic or labor market impact of the program. However, two "control group" studies, based on post-program earnings alone, have been made and both of these reveal negligible differences in earnings between participants and controls. A study of participants and eligible nonparticipants in NYC out-of-school programs in five urban areas in Indiana revealed that, on the average, participants earned $136 more in 1967 than did eligible nonparticipants, but this difference was not found to be statistically significant.[88] Somers and Stromsdorfer conducted an extensive study of a nationwide sample of individuals from the same high schools; the study revealed total before-tax earnings for participants in the post-high school period of $4,159 as compared to $4,247 for controls and parallel differences in average earnings per month since leaving high school.[89]

Both of these studies provide some estimate of the net earnings impact of participation in NYC by sex and/or race. The study of participants in the out-of-school programs in Indiana revealed positive earnings returns for each hour of participation by male enrollees, but only negligible increments in earnings as a result of participation for female enrollees.[90] The study of participants in 60 in-school and summer NYC programs provided

86. Woltman and Walton, *op. cit.*, p. 80.

87. Olympus Research Corporation, *loc. cit.*

88. Michael E. Borus *et al.*, "A Benefit-Cost Analysis of the Neighborhood Youth Corps: The Out-Of-School Program in Indiana," *Journal of Human Resources*, Vol. V, no. 2 (Spring 1970), p. 147.

89. Gerald G. Somers and Ernst W. Stromsdorfer, *A Cost-Effectiveness Study of the In-School and Summer Neighborhood Youth Corps* (Madison: Industrial Relations Research Institute, University of Wisconsin, 1970), p. 64.

90. Borus *et al.*, *op. cit.*, p. 149.

some highly tentative confirmation of this pattern and also suggested that minorities gained more than nonminorities.[91]

Wage Rates

There are relatively few studies dealing with the wage rate impact of participation in NYC. The RMC study estimated the net effect of the program on hourly wages as $0.07 for males and $0.14 for females, but expressed little confidence in the reliability of these estimates.[92] The Somers and Stromsdorfer study of in-school and summer programs revealed the expected sex and race differences among participants with respect to levels of wage rates, but also indicated that only female participants enjoyed higher wage rates than their comparison group, and that black participants showed the greatest disadvantage vis-à-vis their comparison group.[93]

Employment

The available data on the labor market activities of NYC participants in relation to those of comparison groups also fails to generate optimism about the impact of these programs. The Somers and Stromsdorfer study did indicate that participants were employed more, and out of the labor force less, than controls in the post-high school period, but this study also reported that participants had more months of unemployment.[94] A Dunlap and Associates study of the proportion of time spent in various activities by a group of NYC enrollees and matched controls after program participation revealed a similar pattern, with enrollees spending 76 percent of their time at work, looking for work, or in school, as compared with 68 percent of controls.[95] A third study, however, found that higher percents of controls than NYC participants were engaged in labor market activity and were actually employed at the time of two separate follow-up surveys.[96] Finally, the RMC Incorporated study found only minor differences in the percent of participants and of dropouts reporting employment

91. Somers and Stromsdorfer, *op. cit.*, pp. 151-183.

92. Woltman and Walton, *op. cit.*, p. 20.

93. Somers and Stromsdorfer, *op. cit.*, pp. 388-389.

94. *Ibid.*, pp. 151-183.

95. Dunlap and Associates, "Final Report—Survey of Terminees from Out-of-School Neighborhood Youth Corps Projects," report prepared for Office of Policy, Evaluation and Research, Manpower Administration, U.S. Department of Labor p. 53.

96. Regis Walther, Margaret Magnusson, and Shirley Cherkasky, *A Study of the Effectiveness of Selected Out-of-School Neighborhood Youth Corps Programs* (Washington, D. C.: Social Research Group, George Washington University, 1971), Tables 7.7 and 7.8, pp. 288-289.

(2 percent for men and 7 percent for women) and was unable to reach a positive conclusion regarding employment impact.[97]

SUMMARY AND CONCLUSIONS

The existing evaluative literature clearly and uniformly suggests that, as a group, participants in manpower programs have enjoyed higher average annual earnings in the immediate post-training period than they did just prior to their training experience. The magnitude of these earnings gains varied both within and among programs, but it does not appear that the gains were sufficiently large and/or widespread to bring training group average income up to the $4,000 level. However, simple comparisons of pre- and post-training average earnings do not provide the complete index of social and economic impact. The fact that average trainee post-training earnings fell below the poverty level does not mean that no trainee experienced the earnings increase required to move across the poverty line, and it provides no insight into the extent to which even the recorded earnings gains may have been associated with an enhanced sense of personal worth and an altered set of personal values.

The true earnings impact of training is not measured by gross earnings changes over time but by the magnitude of those changes in relation to changes experienced by comparable individuals or groups who were not the beneficiaries of training. The limited number of studies which included such comparison groups clearly indicate that training accounts for only a small portion (generally, 25 to 35 percent) of observed income changes. These studies also suggest substantial variability in net impact across programs. Specifically, the existing evaluative studies suggest the following order of magnitude for the earnings impact attributable to the various types of programs:

1. Skill Training (MDTA)—$400 to $800 per year;
2. Job Development (PEP, PSC, JOBS, AOP)—$300 to $700 per year;
3. Employability Development (OIC, CEP, WIN, Job Corps)— $200 to $400 per year;
4. Work Experience (NYC, Mainstream)—$0 to $200 per year.

The available data on wage rates received by participants in manpower programs before and after training generally indicate increases which compare favorably with basic wage trends in the economy as a whole. Studies conducted between 1965 and 1970 reveal pre-/post-training differences in hourly wage rates of $0.30 to $0.50 which appear to exceed the improve-

97. Woltman and Walton, *op. cit.*, p. ix.

ment in earnings capacity which might have been expected simply on the basis of broad labor market developments even with allowance for institutional factors, such as change in the minimum wage. There is no consistent pattern in the changes in hourly earnings experienced by participants in the various programs. This may reflect common constraints on the range of opportunities open to program participants, most of whom were disadvantaged unemployed after 1966.

There is also strong and consistent evidence that participants in manpower programs, with the possible exception of those in work experience programs for youth and the elderly, experienced substantial improvements in employment, as measured both by increases in aggregate employment rates and changes in the stability of employment between pre- and post-training periods. Overall, these changes were more important than wage rate gains in explaining both the gross and net pre-/post-training earnings increases recorded by program participants, with changes in aggregate employment rates tending to outweigh changes in employment stability, as an explanatory factor in recent years. Thus, it would appear that a primary contribution of manpower programs has been to facilitate entry into the labor force and labor market through varying combinations of outreach, training, and placement, with the more traditional function of fostering upward mobility within the labor force and labor market being less in evidence.

The findings on the relative importance of employment gains in explaining the overall average earnings gains of manpower program participatants has implications for the stability and duration of the economic benefits of training. Specifically, to the extent that the employment effect is dominant, the long-run gains from training will be heavily dependent on the quality of the jobs in which participants are placed in terms of vulnerability to changing economic conditions, transferability of experience and skills acquired on the job, and opportunity for advancement. There is little detailed data on this dimension of the post-program labor market experiences of participants, but the information which is available does not suggest that substantial percents were placed in areas of growing demand, in jobs with substantial skill requirements or training content, or in positions with real potential for advancement.

The available data on the earnings, wages, and employment of manpower program participants by sex and/or race suggest that, overall, such programs have had a limited but positive effect in breaking down labor market barriers confronting women and minorities. Data on pre- and post-program levels of participant earnings, wages, and employment do not contain significant and persistent differentials between men and women and between whites and minorities. Moreover, data on pre-/post-program changes in these variables generally indicate that participation in a manpower program was associated with a narrowing of these differentials in percent and, in some cases, absolute terms.

Overall, the available data tend to indicate that women have benefited more than men, and minorities a substantial amount, from the services provided through the entire range of manpower programs. In general, women, including minority women, experienced larger gains than their male counterparts in a number of programs, and particularly in those programs which had the more significant overall impact upon participant earnings. Although minority males experienced earnings gains, they were generally not comparable or superior to those of their minority counterparts in a similar number of programs.

The pattern of absolute and comparative economic gains of female participants in various manpower programs suggests that they are the beneficiaries of relatively high returns to skill training. The most dramatic evidence of such returns is to be found in the relative earnings and wage rate gains of women in MDTA training programs. Supporting evidence can be found in the superior wage rate gains of female participants in other programs with some skill training components—most notably in OIC, but also to a lesser extent in WIN and Job Corps. The key to these returns lies not entirely in the intrinsic value of skill training, but in the fact of high and rising demand in those fields in which women, including many black women, were trained—the clerical and health-service fields. This clearly distinguishes the female recipients of skill training from many of the white or minority males in the same types of training programs. In this respect, however, it must be noted that low post-program rates of labor force participation among female trainees, particularly among WIN trainees, constituted a major constraint on the overall impact of skill training.

The pattern of comparative economic gains of minority group participants indicates that they have been primary beneficiaries of job development programs such as JOBS and AOP. The strength of these programs in serving minorities may be traced to their impact on discriminatory hiring standards and practices; this interpretation receives some support in the fact that women also fared reasonably well in both JOBS and PEP. The major limitation on the impact of these programs rests on their susceptibility to changing labor market conditions and to shifting programmatic priorities. However, even if the direct economic gains of minority (and female) participants in these programs are only transitory, it is not clear that there are no long-run indirect economic benefits to those participants, although there is little reason to be highly optimistic about the level or incidence of such benefits.

The relative weakness of some of the employability development and work experience programs in improving the labor market status of virtually all the participants is disappointing, but perhaps inevitable. In large measure, the impact of these programs reflects not only the deficiencies in program services vis-à-vis the needs and problems of the old, the young, and the severely disadvantaged, but also the strength of the labor market barriers facing minorities and women. Thus, it may be unfair or unrealistic to judge such programs on the basis of their short-run economic impact alone, and more appropriate to view them as long-run investments in social and human capital.

CHAPTER IV

Noneconomic Impact

The term "noneconomic" is an imprecise one used to denote a wide range of program outcomes which are not measured by short-run changes in employment and earnings. Evaluators have often alluded to the fact that manpower programs may generate changes in the psychological, emotional, and environmental well-being of program participants, although such changes may not be the primary objective of the program. It is conceivable that the noneconomic benefits of training might have long-lasting effects upon trainees who otherwise experience no change, or very small change, in their economic status. Likewise, trainees who derive significant gains in employment and earnings may also experience positive gains in other aspects of personal well-being as a result of the noneconomic benefits of training. More than economic impact, however, the noneconomic effects of training pose numerous conceptual and measurement problems which greatly complicate the task of program evaluation.

The interest in the noneconomic outcome of training is generated, in large part, by the fact that many low-income workers have limited job mobility and high unemployment, not only because of inadequate job skills, but also because of personal attitudes, deficient health care, incomplete societal acculturation, and many personal environmental conditions which restrict the range of opportunity for participation in the labor market. Indeed, a major element in the rationale behind the Economic Opportunity Act of 1964, the legislative declaration of the "War on Poverty," was that the alienation and a sense of powerlessness among the low-income population was a major barrier to government sponsored efforts to raise the income of the poor. Accordingly, the community action agencies, which stood in the vanguard of the war against poverty, concentrated more on enhancing the self-determination and empowerment of the poor than on developing and implementing work and training programs designed to increase the productivity of the low-income population. Specific concern for the noneconomic foundations of poverty and dependency were less obvious, but still evident, in the legislative mandate and subsequent operation of such programs as MDTA, the Concentrated Employment Program, Neighborhood Youth Corps, Operation Mainstream, and the Apprenticeship Outreach Program, several of which are noted for a high proportion of minority group participants.

THE CONCEPT OF NONECONOMIC EFFECTS

The potential scope of noneconomic effects of training is so broad that it almost defies a meaningful definition. Moreover, there is no conceptual framework or body of theory available to suggest a range of expectations in the direction and degree of change in the multiple facets of life which together represent noneconomic benefits. To the extent that any guidelines whatsoever exist in this area, they emerge from middle-class value preferences, concerning social behavior, acculturation, and life style, which characterize the non poor sectors of the community.

For example, the work ethic is one of the major value preferences expressed by the American community. The strong adherence to the work ethic throughout most sectors of society is reflected in the shape and content of social legislation, such as unemployment compensation, Workmen's Compensation, Social Security, and public assistance. Indeed, the shape and content of antipoverty legislation itself, emphasizing the strategy of increasing income through increasing the individual's earning capacity rather than providing a minimum guaranteed income, demonstrates the tenacity of the work ethic. Because of the value preference for work as a rationale for income, manpower programs may be judged a success if one of their noneconomic effects is to increase the willingness of program participants to work. Thus, in evaluating program outcomes, the analyst may begin with the expectation that the program will generate a positive change in the work attitudes of trainees. What is important is that the proclivity to consider positive changes in work attitudes as a benefit of the program flows directly from society's values regarding work, rather than from any *a priori* connection between changes in work attitudes and changes in individual earnings. Further, the devotion to positive changes in work attitudes as a goal of manpower training programs often persists long after the demonstration of empirical evidence that factors other than attitudes toward work explain the wide variation in earnings among members of the work force, especially differences in earnings between the poor and nonpoor.

TYPES OF NONECONOMIC EFFECTS

Although the full range and direction of change in noneconomic benefits may be difficult to specify, it is possible to classify the more common effects. First, it is useful to distinguish between noneconomic benefits, which accrue to the individual during the training process, and those that are experienced subsequent to participation in the program.

Benefits During Training—Supportive Services

The noneconomic benefits experienced during training are commonly known as supportive services. Among the more obvious benefits of this type are health care, child-care services, and basic education. Other program services like counseling, referral, and job placement are sometimes classified as supportive services, but for purposes of this analysis, such services will be classified as "manpower services" because of their direct relationship to job training and job development. The distinction drawn here between supportive and manpower services is arbitrary to some extent, but logical consistency suggests that the manpower services previously identified and discussed in the section on economic impact should not be included in the discussion of noneconomic benefits.

The range and availability of supportive services differs among manpower programs. As a general observation, however, it seems that programs aimed directly toward the disadvantaged—such as CEP, NYC, and Job Corps—provide far more supportive services than programs like MDTA institutional and AOP (now Construction Outreach,) which typically serve a broader clientele. This pattern of supportive service availability is consistent with the view among program planners that disadvantaged workers suffer from relatively greater disabilities than other workers in the labor market, as a result of factors unrelated to the lack of job skills.

Among the questions of importance in assessing supportive services as noneconomic benefits is the persistence of the benefits after leaving the program. To the extent that the benefits are "free goods" to trainees in the process of training, the continued availability of the services will involve some cost after program completion. Whether the individual will incur the cost of purchasing similar services will depend in part upon the increased earnings gained as a result of program participation. Also important here is the availability of comparable services in the community.

Post-Training Benefits

The second major category of noneconomic benefits are those which accrue to the individual after leaving the program. Some benefits, such as job satisfaction, better housing, greater leisure, and a greater sense of security, are based largely on economic gains. Other post-training noneconomic benefits, such as sociability, self-esteem, and enhanced citizenship, are based on socio-psychological factors.

The production of post-training noneconomic gains bears much the same relationship to the training process as post-training economic benefits. More specifically, the impact of the program in generating post-training noneconomic benefits must be based on some element in the training process that provides the foundation for later gains in personal well-being. This might suggest that differences in program content and emphasis generate similar differences in post-training noneconomic benefits. The close connection between program content and post-training noneconomic gains, however, may not be direct except for the noneconomic benefits that are highly correlated with economic gains. Because it is difficult to relate program content to socio-psychological well-being, it would be difficult to predict how different programs might affect the sociability, self-esteem, and similar characteristics of trainees after leaving the program.

Although it is useful to classify noneconomic benefits according to their economic or socio-psychological genesis, it is important to recognize the linkage between the two sets of effects. One example may illustrate the point. Improvements in housing may be defined as the renovation of the existing residence or a move to a more desirable neighborhood. This type of noneconomic gain is heavily dependent upon earnings gains. At the same time, an improvement in housing, especially a move to a better neighborhood, is likely to generate a gain in the individual's self-esteem. Conversely, a gain in self-esteem experienced by the successful completion of a training program is likely to find expression in the desire and motivation to improve one's housing environment. The noneconomic benefits of training may be closely interrelated and mutually reinforcing.

The scope, direction, and linkage of the post-training noneconomic benefits creates serious measurement problems, especially when attempting to assess the extent of noneconomic gains among minority trainees. Much has been written about the life styles, values, and perceptions of urban Negroes and Spanish-speaking poor. The manpower programs of the 1960's were directed toward bringing the attitudes, values, and behavior of these groups closer to the generally accepted standard of the middle class. As will be discussed below, there is little evidence from the evaluative literature to suggest how successful manpower programs were in achieving this objective. The gap in information is attributable, in large part, to the apparent unwillingness of program evaluators to consider noneconomic benefits as important as economic gains in the determination of program success, and the inability of evaluators to design precise concepts and measurement instruments before attempting to assess the noneconomic benefits of training.

STATE OF THE LITERATURE

The voluminous literature on program evaluation reviewed for this study offers very little evidence on the noneconomic effects of training on program participants. Of the more than two hundred studies included in the search for data, only seventeen contained any information pertaining to program effects other than the impact upon employment and earnings.

Among the studies for which data are available, the treatment of noneconomic benefits is uneven and incomplete. Rarely are data available on more than one type of noneconomic effect, and even then the evidence almost invariably pertains only to a small number of program participants at one point in time. There are no time series data on noneconomic effects and very little evidence of any type to permit an analysis of the impact of different types of manpower programs on noneconomic benefits. Data pertaining to the differential impact of the programs on the noneconomic status of minorities and women must be drawn by inference from the race and sex composition of program enrollment.

These limitations in the data place severe constraints on the assessment of noneconomic benefits and reduce the potential for judging the success of manpower programs in terms other than those revealed in program impact upon employment and earnings. Still, where evidence on noneconomic impact is available, although incomplete, additional insight into the effect of manpower programs may be obtained. The following sections of this chapter provide a synthesis and analysis of the evidence relating to the noneconomic effects of training as revealed in the evaluative literature available for review.

SUPPORTIVE SERVICES

Manpower programs, such as CEP, WIN, and the Job Corps, stress the availability of supportive services as an inducement to prospective trainees to enroll. Among the more common supportive services typically offered as part of such programs are medical care, child care, transportation assistance, and legal aid. A major study of the availability and distribution of supportive services was conducted by Camil Associates in 1972. According to the authors:

> Supportive services provision varied considerably among the programs and the individual sites studied, despite the fact that the potential target populations shared many of the same problems. In part, this can be traced to administrative decisions, local options, and community resources. But in large measure it can be traced to the very origins of the programs themselves....
>
> Much of the variation stems from the fact that the enabling legislation is virtually silent on the subject of services .... An examination of the legislation and guidelines of the programs show considerable variation among them in their provision for service delivery.[1]

---

1. Camil Associates, Inc., *Evaluation of Supportive Services Provided for Participants of Manpower Programs, Final Report* (Philadelphia: 1972), p. 9.

The WIN program offers the most comprehensive supportive services, largely because WIN enrollees are AFDC clients and thus entitled to free social services from welfare agencies.[2] Provisions for child care are of particular importance in the WIN program. Most child-care arrangements for manpower trainees are made by the mothers themselves; most are informal babysitting arrangements, as opposed to structured day-care situations.

A physical examination is required before enrollment in most manpower programs. Prospective enrollees with severe medical problems are not accepted in training programs; some applicants have been referred to other agencies after failing the medical test. Data are available on the number and variety of medical services provided for Job Corps enrollees. Analyses of medical care, including the sickle-cell anemia identification program and dental care provisions, however, have not been thorough. Rather meager evidence on the impact of the programs upon the health of participants is available, and no attempt is made to determine whether manpower programs provide the best means of detecting medical problems and caring for them once identified.

TRAINEE ATTITUDES AND JOB SATISFACTION

Information obtained through interviews provides the primary basis for analysis of the enrollees' assessments of the programs in which they were enrolled and changes in work attitudes and self-esteem. For the most part, the programs were rated highly. Not surprisingly, completers thought the programs were more helpful than those who dropped out. Findings by race and sex are sometimes supplied.

Trainee attitudes toward the program might be expected to exert some impact upon the trainee's probability of remaining in the program until satisfactory completion of training. Evidence of the relationship between attitudes toward the program and trainee completion rates is absent in the literature. Moreover, even where data are available by race and sex, there is no information to suggest how race/sex differences in attitudes toward the program affect trainee performance in the program and post-training experience. Thus, there is no way to judge the relative significance of attitudes toward the program in an evaluation of trainee success.

Although attitudes toward the program might be expected to affect in-program performance, attitudes toward work should exert their greatest impact upon post-training job stability. To the extent that such a relationship exists, the noneconomic gain in positive work attitudes should be related to post-training economic gains in earnings. Again, however, the available data do not allow an examination of this important relationship;

2. *Ibid.*, p.12.

thus, there is no basis for judging the importance of attitudinal change as an element in the improvement of trainee socio-economic status.

Manpower Development and Training Act

MDTA training stresses labor market oriented goals, in contrast to some of the newer manpower programs which focus on general noneconomic gains, as well as enhanced employability. Thus, it is not surprising that the literature's discussion of the secondary objectives of MDTA is restricted to its impact on job satisfaction and self-esteem.

In general, studies report relatively favorable responses from participants on: (1) attitudes toward the training experience; (2) feelings regarding the role of training in preparing them to compete in the labor market; and (3) satisfaction with post-training jobs. Females and, to a lesser extent, minority participants indicate somewhat more positive views than their male or nonminority counterparts who participated in the program.

In an evaluation of the institutional component, Earl D. Main notes the following responses:

> Two-thirds (66 percent) of "completers" and one-fourth (26 percent) of "dropouts" said that the MDTA training they received helped them obtain employment (53 percent for both respondent types combined). The proportion who said "yes" was larger for women (59 percent) than for men (49 percent). Among "completers," women found training helpful more often (73 percent, compared to 62 percent of men), but among "dropouts," men were a little more likely than women to say training helped them get a job (28 *vs.* 21 percent).
>
> While only 46 percent of "completers" had "a lot" of confidence before training, 79 percent expressed "a lot" when interviewed—an increase of 33 percent. For "dropouts" the corresponding increase was only 14 percent (from 58 to 72 percent). Though "dropouts" had more confidence than "completers" had before training, "completers" held a slight advantage afterward. Women and men expressed roughly similar levels of confidence when interviewed, which means that women gained more since before training—when men had a definite advantage. Female "completers" gained the most—their proportion with "a lot" of confidence rose from 39 percent before training to 79 percent "now"—a rise of 40 percent (male "completers" rose from 51 to 79 percent—a gain of 28 percent).[3]

A U.S. Department of Labor study compared the effectiveness of the institutional and OJT components of MDTA. Participants were asked to respond to the question, "All things considered, how well did you like the training?" Seventy-two percent of those in the institutional program compared with 53 percent of OJT enrollees answered "very well." Seventy-seven

3. Earl D. Main, "A Nationwide Evaluation of MDTA Institutional Job Training Programs" National Opinion Research Center, University of Chicago, 1966, pp. 35, 39.

percent of the blacks, 67 percent of whites, and 60 percent of the Spanish-speaking groups replied in the affirmative.[4]

Job Opportunities in the Business Sector

Job Opportunities in the Business Sector (JOBS) was aimed at helping the disadvantaged in a hire now-train later program. Only one study of the program attempted to evaluate the noneconomic gains of enrollment in JOBS. The Greenleigh Associates study does not present evidence by race or sex. It is noted, however, that "thirty percent of respondents felt that their own estimation of themselves had improved."[5]

Neighborhood Youth Corps and Job Corps

Both the Neighborhood Youth Corps and Job Corps programs are aimed at helping youth overcome barriers to effective participation in the labor market. Enrollee views on the value of their training experience and changes in work attitudes have been discussed in the literature on both programs. Reports of job satisfaction, work attitudes, and increased self-esteem of NYC participants generally deal with the out-of-school component.

In a study directed by Regis H. Walther, enrollees rated the NYC out-of-school program in four cities on a five-point scale ranging from "not at all useful" (1) to "very useful" (5). The mean rating of overall usefulness was generally over "4," with female subjects indicating a more positive response to this question.[6] Enrollees' estimates of their chances of achieving their ten-year occupational goals were also noted. Most of the study subjects had employment objectives that were perhaps beyond their capacities to achieve, in that they required new job and training experience. Approximately three-fourths of the respondents, however, rated their chances of goal achievement as "very good" or "fairly good."[7]

William C. Eckerman, Eva K. Gerstel, and Richard B. Williams studied the characteristics of NYC enrollees in North Carolina and found a relationship between academic achievement and work attitudes:

4. National Analysts, "The Effectiveness of the Training Program Under MDTA," report prepared for Manpower Administration, U.S. Department of Labor, 1965, Appendix II.

5. Greenleigh Associates, Inc., *The Job Opportunities in the Business Sector Program—An Evaluation of Impact in Ten Standard Metropolitan Statistical Areas* (New York: 1970), p. 30.

6. Regis H. Walther, Margaret L. Magnusson, and Shirley E. Cherkasky, *A Study of the Effectiveness of Selected Out-of-School Neighborhood Youth Corps Programs (A Study of Selected NYC-1 Projects)* (Washington, D.C.: Social Research Group, George Washington University, 1971), p. 229.

7. *Ibid.*, p. 325.

> . . . [E]nrollees who have proceeded further in formal education and score more highly on aptitude and achievement tests also seem to subscribe to a philosophy of life which may be highly instrumental to upward mobility in our society today.[8]

Another review of NYC participants six months after enrollment concluded that there was an initial shift in self-esteem and work attitudes, as a result of participation in NYC, which thereafter tended to remain stable.[9]

A study comparing enrollees in the NYC in-school program and a carefully chosen control group concluded that enrollment in

> . . . the program had no discernible impact on the youths' conception of work, their willingness to relinquish the security of steady training that would prepare them for better jobs, their perception of conditions which may interfere with obtaining suitable employment, their professed job characteristic preferences or their occupational expectations.[10]

More than one-half of those interviewed by Louis Harris and Associates six months after they left the Job Corps felt that they were better off than before enrollment. When queried about the usefulness of Job Corps training, 75 percent of the women and 64 percent of the male participants responded positively. More graduates than dropouts found their instruction helpful. On the whole, a larger percent of blacks than whites, and women than men found their training useful. Two-thirds of the Corpsmembers considered their instruction valuable, but only one-quarter felt that they were given enough training to get a job.[11]

Work Incentive Program

Leonard Goodwin conducted a major study of the work orientation of welfare recipients enrolled in WIN. Based on questionnaire responses, this report indicated that enrollees on welfare have the same dedication to the

---

8. William C. Eckerman, Eva K. Gerstel, and Richard B. Williams, "A Comprehensive Assessment of the Problems and Characteristics of the Neighborhood Youth Corps Enrollees: A Pilot Investigation" Research Triangle Institute, 1969, p. 134.

9. Melvin Herman and Stanley Sadofsky, *Study of the Meaning, Experience and Effects of the Neighborhood Youth Corps on Negro Youth Who Are Seeking Work, Part V: Neighborhood Youth Corps Six Months After Enrollment—A Follow-Up Study* (New York: New York University, 1968).

10. Gerald D. Robin, *An Assesment of the In-School Neighborhood Youth Corps Projects in Cincinnati and Detroit with Special Reference to Summer-Only and Year-Round Enrollees— Final Report* (Philadelphia: National Analysts, Inc., 1969), p. 90.

11. Louis Harris and Associates, "A Study of August 1966 Terminations From the Job Corps," in U. S. Congress, Senate, Committee on Education and Labor, Part I, *Hearings on the Economic Opportunity Amendments of 1967,* 90th Cong., 1st sess., 1967, pp. 434, 387, 389.

work ethic as persons from families whose members work regularly. It was found that the poor of both races and sexes identify their self-esteem with work to the same extent as nonpoor persons do. Goodwin also found that black WIN trainees exhibit relatively low self-confidence, but he modified this finding with the statement that nonpoor blacks exhibited the same characteristic. He concluded that the distinguishing factor between the employed and the unemployed poor is not the work ethic, but a combination of poor job opportunities and environmental barriers to employment.[12]

The evaluative literature suggests that trainees have a high regard for the WIN program. A longitudinal study of WIN dropouts compared the views of those in the program with noncompleters.[13] The most frequently reported reasons for satisfaction were the chance for advancement and content of training, with completers citing them more often than dropouts.

POST-TRAINING NONECONOMIC EFFECTS

The evaluative literature provides limited data on three types of post-training noneconomic benefits: (1) job satisfaction; (2) more formal schooling; and (3) better citizenship. A dissertation by Darrell Jones evaluated the socio-psychological and socio-economic effects of MDTA on trainees in four Michigan labor markets.[14] Based on a comparison of 151 MDTA enrollees in the program between August 1963 and July 1965, and a control group of equal size consisting of individuals who were interested in MDTA, but who did not enroll, Jones indicated that trainees expressed significantly greater job satisfaction. Differences between trainees and controls were found on only one socio-psychological scale; trainees ranked significantly higher in sociability, but not in the rate of change in sociability, in comparison with the control group.[15]

A comparison of participant pre- and post-training status showed no difference in job satisfaction between the last full-time jobs held before training and jobs held after training. It seems, then, that job satisfaction was not influenced by training. Additional data were provided on the status of enrollees before and after training by race and sex. Males earned more than females after training, but females were much happier in their

12. Leonard Goodwin, *A Study of the Work Orientations of Welfare Recipients Participating in the Work Incentive Program* (Washington, D.C.: The Brookings Institution, 1971).

13. David S. Franklin, *A Longitudinal Study of WIN Dropouts: Program and Policy Implications* (Los Angeles: Regional Research Institute in Social Welfare, School of Social Work, University of Southern California, 1972), p. 154.

14. Darrell G. Jones, "An Evaluation of the Socio-Psychological and Socio-Economic Effects of MDTA Training on Trainees in Selected Michigan Programs," Ph. D. dissertation, Michigan State University, 1966.

15. *Ibid.*, pp. 103, 109.

post-training jobs. Indeed, there is a highly significant difference in the degree of job satisfaction expressed by males and females.[16]

Operation Mainstream

The primary impact of Operation Mainstream has been to supplement the income of enrollees. The work activity involved in the program, however, has had remarkable secondary impact.

Kirschner Associates interviewed 850 Operation Mainstream enrollees to determine their perceptions of the program's impact upon their lives. Ninety-seven percent were satisfied with their Operation Mainstream jobs. When asked which aspect of their jobs they enjoyed the most, the enrollees' responses, in order of frequency, were: (1) the specific work they were doing, indeed their pleasure in having a job; (2) the association with the other enrollees; and (3) the financial gain (mentioned only 11.6 percent of the time). Overall, 63 percent said there was nothing they disliked about the program.[17]

Public Employment Program

Enrollees in the Public Employment Program were generally satisfied with their jobs. When asked how the PEP job compared with the characteristics sought in an ideal job, 85 percent of the respondents indicated that the PEP job had all or some of them. Of those interviewed, 83 percent felt that their PEP assignment was useful, rather than just a job.[18]

An attempt was made to determine differential job satisfaction in PEP by sex and ethnic group.[19] Measurements of job satisfaction were based on the proportion of enrollees of a given characteristic who were terminating their employment in PEP—the Likelihood of Termination (L.O.T.) ratio. The basic assumption was that individuals of a specific group found to have the lowest L.O.T. ratios are more satisfied with their jobs.

---

16. *Ibid.*, p. 143.

17. Dale W. Berry *et al., Final Report*, "National Evaluation of Operation Mainstream, A Public Service Employment Program—Phase IV: Comparative Analysis," Kirschner Associates, Inc., 1971, pp. 194-202.

18. National Planning Association, "A Preliminary Analysis of the Impact of the Public Employment Program on its Participants," U.S. Department of Labor, 1972, pp. 37, 39.

19. Marjorie S. Turner, *The First Year Experience with Public Emergency Employment: San Diego City and County* (San Diego: California State University, 1971).

Better Citizenship and Impact on Crime

Some students of manpower programs have tested the presumed goal of assisting enrollees in becoming better citizens. Among the factors that have been used to ascertain the impact of manpower programs on the citizenship of participants are: (1) contact with police; (2) religous service attendance; (3) membership in a social club; and (4) voter registration. The reduction in criminal activity is discussed in the literature on Job Corps and Neighborhood Youth Corps.

It is often suggested that the purpose of the summer component of the Neighborhood Youth Corps is to prevent riots from occurring in city ghettos. One analysis of the NYC summer project in Washington, D.C., found an inverse relationship between the number of NYC slots and the incidence of crime. This study concluded that NYC had a slightly beneficial impact upon aggregate juvenile delinquency statistics, [20] but this alleged relationship did not appear to be statistically conclusive.

The objective of the Gerald D. Robin study of the NYC in-school and summer program was to ascertain what behavioral changes could be attributed to participation in NYC. The delinquency profile for the experimental youth was delineated for the periods before they enrolled in NYC, while they were working in the program, and from the point of enrollment to the date of offense check. Robin concluded that " . . . NYC participation, among both males and females, is unrelated to delinquency prevention or reduction."[21]

Of those polled six months after termination from Job Corps, 15 percent of the enrollees answered that they had had contact with police; Negro graduates and women comprised the smallest groups.[22] A before and after Job Corps comparison is not possible because of the absence of crime data prior to enrollment.

Ex-Corpsmembers categorized their religious attendance, both before and after the Job Corps experience, as regular, occasional, or never; almost all Job Corps participants indicated a decrease in such activities. Only 12 percent of those interviewed stated that they belonged to a club or social group; more males than females, and more graduates than dropouts, denoted membership in an organization. Of the 20 percent interviewed who were eligible to vote, a larger percent of blacks than whites, and men than women, were involved in the electoral process.[23] Unfortunately, data are not available to permit a comparison of the pre- and post-training experience.

---

20. U.S. Department of Labor, "Analysis of the NYC Summer Project," 1972, mimeographed, p. 34.

21. Robin, *op. cit.*, p. 151.

22. Harris, "A Study of the August 1966 Terminations," *op. cit.*, p. 453

23. *Ibid.*, pp. 443, 445, 447.

INCREASED SCHOOLING

Three variables have been used to measure the improvement in schooling associated with participating in a manpower program: (1) the number of enrollees who were school dropouts when they entered the program, but who returned to school during their program enrollment; (2) the number of enrollees who received a high school diploma or its equivalent during program enrollment; and (3) the improvement in basic education, generally measured by increases in reading ability and mathematical skills. Although many of the major manpower programs might produce one or more of these favorable impacts on schooling, the evaluative literature provides evidence only on the increased schooling experienced by participants in the Neighborhood Youth Corps and the Job Corps. A few studies of the Apprenticeship Outreach and the MDTA programs provide vague references to the role of schooling in supporting the potential for success in training. The evaluative reports on these programs, however, provide no empirical evidence on changes in schooling experienced by program participants.

NYC Out-of-School Program

A study conducted by Walther, Magnusson, and Cherkasky inquired into the impact of NYC on the high school dropout problem.[24] The investigators found that females were more likely to return to school and to complete high school when they did return, than were males. The study also revealed, however, that a greater percent of those in the control group than of those in NYC returned to school. The implication of this finding is that the impact of NYC on school enrollment was either nonexistent or very limited.

The extent to which participation in manpower programs has resulted in increased schooling is difficult to document. Difficulties arise in measuring school achievement because many of the enrollees do not have the attitudes toward testing associated with middle class society. Many tests used in defining academic gains have been found to be culturally biased. In addition, comparisons of groups in terms of grades completed and educational attainment are inconclusive. In many cases, the act of formally withdrawing from school may have occurred years after the individual had lost interest in attending class. Graduation from high school is not necessarily synonymous with educational skills; even those who

24. Walther, Magnusson, and Cherkasky, *op. cit.*, p. 254.

have a high school diploma have been found deficient in reading and arithmetic skills.

Some evidence on the educational impact of the original NYC out-of-school program (NYC-1) is supplied by the Accelerated Learning Experiment (ALE) of programmed instruction.[25]

Five percent of the males who left ALE did so because they received a high school diploma or an equivalent. It was concluded that this program achieved significantly better results than conventional programs, especially with male enrollees; attendance records were considered the major criteria for this conclusion. Progress in reading and arithmetic, as measured by the California Achievement Tests, however, showed that the scores of a sizable percent of the subjects were lower after six months than initially. Thus, ALE cannot be considered an unequivocal success.

A New Education Program (NEP) was designed to provide more effective education for the revised NYC-2 program:[26]

> In general, the ALE students participated about the same length of time as NEP students, but ALE students showed far less gain on measures of academic achievement. In the ALE, 36 percent of the initial students were in the program at least six months while the comparable NEP proportion was 31 percent; but, only about 55 percent of ALE students tested after six-months' participation showed academic improvement as compared with 90 percent of the comparable NEP students.[27]

It was thus concluded that NEP is a more effective program than ALE. The improvements in the academic skills were not associated with the sex of NEP students.[28] Because many trainees were in the program for only a few months, there is some question about how much of their gain in schooling should be attributed to participation in ALE or NEP.

---

25. Regis H. Walther, Margaret L. Magnusson, and Shirley E. Cherkasky, *The Accelerated Learning Experiment: An Approach to the Remedial Education of Out-of-School Youth: Final Report* (Washington, D.C.: Social Research Group, George Washington University, 1969).

26. Regis H. Walther, Margaret L. Magnusson, and Shirley E. Cherkasky, *A Study of the Effectiveness of the Graham Associates' Demonstration Project on NYC-2 Education Programming* (Washington, D.C.: George Washington University, Manpower Research Projects, 1973).

27. *Ibid.*, p. 56

28. *Ibid.*, p. 40

NYC In-School Program

The effect that the in-school component could have on the dropout rate appears to be limited by the manner in which youths are selected for enrollment. Because of the lack of evaluative data, the General Accounting Office (GAO) was unable to determine the extent to which the NYC program may have influenced the high school dropout rate.[29] The GAO found that there were no significant efforts made by project sponsors to select youth who were potential dropouts and who were likely to be dissuaded from this course by what the NYC program has to offer.

There was an attempt to use a control group in Robin's assessment of the in-school Neighborhood Youth Corps projects.[30] Analysis was restricted to black youth since too few white youths were interviewed in Phase I to provide statistically meaningful information. Based on data collected through school files, the general findings of this study of the in-school program revealed no evidence that NYC had a favorable effect upon the scholastic achievement of its enrollees. In fact, since enrollees spent time working instead of at their studies, participation in NYC actually impaired grades of enrollees who had previously performed adequately in their studies (at least a C average prior to enrollment).[31]

Somers and Stromsdorfer analyzed the educational benefits of the in-school and summer components of NYC. For the total sample, it was concluded that the NYC program had no statistically significant effect on the probability of high school graduation or on the years of school completed. There is no difference in the probability of high school graduation between NYC females and their control group counterparts.[32]

White NYC participants are no more likely to graduate from high school than their control group, whereas black NYC participants are 8.2 percent more likely to graduate. American Indian NYC participants are about 14.6 percent more likely to graduate, but Mexican American NYC enrollees are about 21.2 percent less likely to graduate than their control group. The positive effect of the NYC program on Negroes is attributable to the fact that Negro female NYC participants are about 12.5 percent more likely to graduate than their control group counterparts.[33]

---

29. Comptroller General of the United States, *Effectiveness and Administrative Efficiency of the Neighborhood Youth Corps Under Title I-B of the Economic Opportunity Act of 1964* (Washington, D.C.: Government Printing Office, 1969).

30. Robin, *op. cit.*

31. *Ibid.*, p. 161.

32. Gerald G. Somers and Ernst W. Stromsdorfer, *A Cost-Effectiveness Study of the In-School and Summer Neighborhood Youth Corps* (Madison: Industrial Relations Research Institute, Center for Studies in Vocational and Technical Education, University of Wisconsin, 1970), pp. 213, 227.

33. *Ibid.*, p. 228.

Job Corps

Although increased schooling was an apparent goal of the Job Corps, there is little evidence to indicate the impact of the program upon the schooling and academic achievement of minorities and women. For example, in its evaluation of the Civilian Conservation Centers, the General Accounting Office noted that various required educational programs were being made available to Corpsmen and that participants were achieving a reasonable rate of progress in the reading program. In light of the short time that Corpsmen were in the program and their generally low academic level at the time of entry, few could have been expected to meet the academic program minimum goal of a seventh grade reading level.[34] A general lack of emphasis on the academic training program reduced the opportunity for Corpsmen to achieve their maximum potential. Enrollees were often assigned to projects without regard to their vocational needs and were excused from educational classes to ensure completion of their projects. Similar results were also evident at Job Corps centers besides Acadia.

Louis Harris and Associates questioned terminees on their pre- and post-program school attendance. Enrollees were asked to indicate if they thought the program helped in preparation for school. There was little difference in the percent of enrollees attending school before and six months after participation in Job Corps. Of the 11 percent of Job Corps enrollees in school at the time of their first interview, six months after leaving the program, 71 percent replied that Job Corps helped them prepare for their return; of those who graduated and were continuing their education, 70 percent indicated that Job Corps "helped a lot."[35]

In his doctoral dissertation, Stephen R. Engleman based his analysis of educational achievement on the Paragraph Meaning and Arithmetic Computation subtests of the Stanford Achievement tests.[36] In assessing the relationship between length of stay in the program and educational achievement, Engleman carefully notes that the time spent in Job Corps is not synonymous with time spent in the general education program. Formal academic classes did not necessarily begin within the first thirty days, nor did the Corpsmen necessarily attend these classes until the time of the terminal test. Engleman also indicates the possible cultural bias of the tests. Engleman's study further reveals that Job Corps was

34. Comptroller General of the United States, *Effectiveness and Administration Of The Acadia Job Corps Civilian Conservation Center Under The Economic Opportunity Act Of 1964— Bar Harbor, Maine* (Washington, D.C.: Government Printing Office, 1969), p. 29.

35. Louis Harris and Associates, "A Study of August 1966 Terminations," *op. cit.*, p. 428.

36. Stephen R. Engleman, "An Economic Analysis of the Job Corps," Ph. D. dissertation, University of California, Berkeley, 1971, pp. 43-44.

more successful in improving basic academic skills of trainees who entered with achievement levels below sixth grade than those having higher achievement levels at entry.

OTHER PROGRAMS

Reference to the relationship between manpower program participation and both school attendance and academic achievement also appears in the literature on the Apprenticeship Outreach and MDTA programs. AOP attempts to help its trainees overcome educational barriers that obstruct entry into apprenticeship programs. Information on the educational component of AOP, however, is confined to descriptions in government pamphlets used by AOP for recruiting purposes. Such data are not empirical in content, and thus cannot be used for evaluative purposes.

> Those who need basic education and language training need them badly. It is no surprise that the follow-up data . . . came through so strongly in support of such programs . . . . There seem to be many among the Spanish and Chinese-speaking immigrants who have substantial skills which can be applied only after language competence has been achieved. The returns to this effect have been great despite considerable weaknesses in the techniques in use.[37]

The implication of the author's conclusion is that basic education was a major noneconomic benefit of training. Again, however, there are no empirical data to quantify the number of enrollees who obtained the benefit, or how the benefits were distributed among trainees classified by race and sex.

DATA SEARCH AMONG PROGRAM ADMINISTRATORS

The paucity of data on the noneconomic effects of manpower training does not allay the widespread belief among many program administrators that such benefits are pervasive and worthwhile. In an effort to find additional evidence on noneconomic effects, a search was undertaken among program administrators who might be in a position to know about program impact data that were unpublished, or otherwise unknown to nongovernment program evaluators.

The search for data focused on program officers in the Washington headquarters of the Manpower Administration, MDTA, JOBS, WIN, Job Corps, NYC, and CEP. In addition, contact was also made with

37. Olympus Research Corporation, "Total Impact of Manpower Programs: A Four-City Case Study" (Washington, D.C.: 1971), Vol. I, p. 81.

administrators of the OIC program at its headquarters office in Philadelphia. Both research and development, and program operations officers were interviewed, although most contacts were confined to the former group.

Two basic questions were explored:

1. Did the program administrator know of any hard data pertaining to the noneconomic impact of the training program?
2. Did the program administrator know of any anecdotal or impressionistic evidence on noneconomic effects?

Unfortunately, the search process failed to uncover substantially more information than was already known to the investigators. No additional data were obtained for CEP or the MDTA, JOBS, and OIC programs. Some research reports with usable information on the WIN program were discovered, and their results were included in the analysis presented above. Much the same may be said of the few additional reports and other relevant data obtained on the Job Corps and NYC.

Several major conclusions regarding the availability of data on noneconomic effects may be drawn from the special search undertaken by the investigators. First, manpower administrators at the headquarters offices have strong opinions about the noneconomic benefits of training, but have little hard data that can be used to substantiate their views. In this regard, the Director of the Women's Job Corps may be typical of many program operating officers.

From the vantage point of Washington, D.C., the program director has gained the impression that among the noneconomic benefits received by participants in the Women's Job Corps are greater self-esteem, better child-care facilities, and substantially improved health care. In addition, there was some reason to believe that many female Job Corps participants improved their basic education and experienced a decline in the incidence of anti-social behavior as a result of being in the program. Although some Job Corps enrollees undoubtedly experienced gains of this type, the headquarters office had no data to quantify the number of persons so affected, or the type of benefits received.

Second, a data search undertaken by the Manpower Administration's Office of Research uncovered some quantitative data on the impact of the Job Corps upon health services.[38] The search revealed that a study is currently underway to discover the type of health services received by Job Corps enrollees as a result of their participation in the program. Some preliminary findings of the study were provided, and are discussed above in the section on noneconomic benefits from the Job Corps. The nature of the data on Job Corps related to health care, however, suggests

38. Memorandum from Ellen Sehgal to Dr. Howard Rosen, "Information on the Job Corps," dated October 9, 1973.

that program administrators in the field may have reports or other in-house information that can be organized and summarized in a way that would make it possible to measure, even imperfectly, the incidence of this type of noneconomic benefit. At the present time, reporting systems do not require program administrators to collect and maintain information on noneconomic benefits; thus, such data are not available on a systematic basis.

In conclusion, noneconomic benefits may be among the most important effects of manpower programs. In an isolated study which attempted to measure both economic and noneconomic benefits simultaneously, the statistical results suggested that the effect of the Oak Ridge, Tennessee, training program on reducing personal alienation, increasing reading ability, increasing community involvement, and increasing church attendance of the enrollees, exceeded the measured impact of the program on trainee employment and earnings.[39] Although reported evidence on such outcomes is limited, the basic data may be available in the files of program administrators. However, it is not collected and organized in a way that would lend itself to analysis for program evaluation purposes.

In view of the state of knowledge in this area, several comments on future research may be in order. The study of noneconomic benefits of manpower programs is both feasible and highly desirable. Conceptual and measurement problems would make the task difficult, but not impossible. Some noneconomic benefits are heavily dependent upon economic status. For these, the conceptual problems would be minimal and the measurement problems clearly manageable. For noneconomic effects more psychologically or emotionally based, measurement scales are available, though imperfect, in the fields of psychology and sociology. It might be useful to require some psychological and attitudinal pretesting for all manpower program participants, or for a scientifically based sample. This would provide very useful base line data for a later comparison with post-training measures. Even with cross section data, however, potentially useful evidence might be obtained from a carefully drawn experimental design for research. In any case, the assessment of noneconomic gains is value-laden and depends largely upon societal norms of behavior. To the extent that such behavior is closely related to labor market success, and to the extent that manpower policy is directed toward producing such behavior, then systematic data on the noneconomic outcomes of training should be made an essential part of regularly collected data on manpower enrollees.

---

39. Training and Technology Project, *The Effects of a Training Program on the Personal Lives of Its Graduates* (Oak Ridge: U.S. Atomic Energy Commission, 1970).

CHAPTER V

Program Operating Statistics

Thus far, our source of information on the impact of manpower programs has been confined to the evaluative studies conducted primarily by investigators under contract with the U.S. Department of Labor, Manpower Administration. The evaluative studies focused almost exclusively on sample data collected by investigators in the field. Another source of information pertaining to program operations, but not yet discussed is the Manpower Administration's files on the characteristics of program participants. These data, drawn from a national reporting program and assembled by the Office of Administration and Management, will be reviewed and analyzed in this chapter for additional evidence on the impact of manpower programs on minorities and women.

Program Coverage

The records of 1,454,314 enrollees who participated in the major manpower programs at some time during fiscal years 1969 through 1972 were obtained from the Office of Administration and Management. Of the total number of records reviewed, race and sex identity were available for 1,297,156 enrollees. Individual program data were available for MDTA institutional and OJT, WIN, and NYC out-of-school programs, and for CEP. Data on the Job Corps, separately compiled by the Labor Department, were also included to make the program coverage in this chapter as complete as possible in comparison with the earlier discussion. Although other categorical programs were required to send periodic reports on the characteristics of enrollees to the Manpower Administration, no consistent series of operating statistics were available for programs other than those listed above.

Focus of the Analysis

In reviewing the operating statistics, the focus of the analysis will be the same as that followed in previous chapters—to search for evidence on the differential impact of manpower programs on minorities and women. The operating statistics, however, contain several major deficiencies which complicate the task of assessing program outcomes. First, the data do not include a comparison or control group that can be used as a standard of measurement for outcomes observed among man-

TABLE V-1. *Manpower Program Statistics Percent of Records with Unreported Data for Selected Trainee Characteristics Fiscal Years 1969-1972*

Characteristics	Weighted Average All Programs	MDTA Institutional	MDTA OJT	WIN	CEP	NYC Out-of-School	Job Corps
Collected at time of entry:							
Trainee's annual income before training	48	27	18	50	28	98	100
Family income	23	26	18	14	29	9	44
Pre-training wage	26	17	15	21	18	47	60
Race	6	4	4	4	2	9	17
Marital status	18	—	—	—	1	1	12
Pre-training years employed	21	2	3	5	4	57	100
Education in years	3	1	1	1	1	2	14
Enrollment date	—	—	—	—	—	—	—
Number in family	9	13	8	4	7	10	14
Weeks unemployed pre-training last year	26	27	28	11	15	62	28
Weeks unemployed pre-training 'current spell'	32	27	42	21	19	85	28
Unemployment Insurance claimant	17	1	2	2	3	30	100
Military service	18	5	7	11	16	10	76
Disadvantaged	16	1	3	1	2	22	100
Poverty	16	3	7	3	6	5	100
Head of family	13	1	—	—	1	2	100
Public assistance	2	1	1	—	1	2	14

TABLE V-1, *continued*

Sex	—	—	—	—	—	—	—
Rural-urban	40	26	43	41	49	95	12
Pre-training labor force status	3	1	1	1	2	5	12
Age	0.5	—	—	—	—	—	4
Collected at termination:							
Nature of termination	47	38	49	62	56	64	13
Termination date	39	31	38	36	43	28	69
Collected in follow-up survey:							
Post-training wage	35	85	86	89	78	100	72
Post-training employment status	78	74	81	88	76	100	55
Post-training hours	93	91	91	100	100	100	72

Source: U. S. Department of Labor, Manpower Administration, Office of Administration and Management.

power program participants. As a result, it will not be possible to estimate the change in enrollee status uniquely attributable to participation in specific manpower programs. Several investigators have used the operating statistics as a source from which small samples of enrollees have been drawn for comparison with other groups, such as the Continuous Work History Sample of the Social Security Administration. The results of such comparisons were discussed in Chapter III and will not be repeated here.

When the operating statistics are reviewed separately from other sources of data, the program impact evaluation must necessarily proceed in broad terms and focus on such characteristics as the composition of the enrollee population and the level and rate of change in outcome variables, such as the rate of completion, rate of placement, and pre-/post-training change in the wage rate and employment status of program participants. By comparing these variables across programs, and between different race/sex groups within programs, some evidence on differential impact might be obtained.

A second major deficiency is that the possibilities for investigating program outcome variables are reduced even more by the incomplete reporting of data in the manpower information file. Much of the information an analyst might want for purposes of program evaluation is not available in sufficient quantity to permit a reliable assessment of program impact across large numbers of enrollees. For example, the MA-101 reporting form, the basic source of data on the characteristics of program enrollees, contains 39 items of demographic and economic information potentially useful for program evaluation. The information includes items, such as race, sex, disadvantaged status, family income, and employment status upon entering the program. There are broad differences, however, in the rate of reporting for different enrollee characteristics (Table 1).

In the data reviewed for this study, all records identified sex and 94 percent of all records identified the enrollee's race, but only 59 percent identified the enrollee's termination date, and 30 percent, the nature of the termination. Most discouraging, for purposes of economic impact evaluation, is that only 15 percent of all records recorded the enrollee's post-training wage rate, only 7 percent had post-training hours worked, and only 22 percent had post-training employment status. In general, the frequency of records having full information on trainee characteristics varied according to the stage of the training process in which the records were completed. Information collected at the time of entry into the program was most complete, whereas information obtained at program termination and follow-up had the lowest rate of completion. This pattern of reporting reflects a pervasive problem of record-keeping that is well-known to manpower program administrators. Still, if data on post-program follow-up are not available in the Manpower Administration national reporting files, the information system cannot be very useful for program impact evaluation.

One advantage of the operating statistics is that they included all enrollees in specific categorical programs in all geographic areas in which the program was in operation. This produced a body of aggregate data that can be used as base line information for comparison with the results of *ad hoc* evaluative studies which were almost always limited to either one or a small number of labor markets.

Within the limitations imposed by the operating statistics, the following analysis will attempt to shed light on several questions important for this study specifically, and for program evaluation in general:

1. Who was served by the programs? How many minorities and women participated in each program, and how did their participation vary during fiscal years 1969 through 1972?
2. What was the quality of program participation during the years of interest, as measured by program completion rates?
3. What economic outcomes did program participants experience? How do such outcomes differ, with respect to the levels of post-training wages and the rates of change in the pre-/post-training wages? What variations in these patterns are evident by race and sex?
4. How do the results of the comparisons obtained in (1) through (3) compare with the results derived from the analysis of the evaluative studies?

In order to answer these questions, the analysis will focus on two types of data drawn from the operating statistics files. One part of the analysis will focus on "population data," or the 1,297,156 records for which both race and sex status were available. The other part of the analysis will deal with a subset of 49,400 records selected from the total number of records. The subset consists of all records that show both race and sex status, and both pre- and post-training wage rate.

POPULATION DATA

According to the available information, the black enrollees were most prevalent among all enrollees in CEP and WIN during fiscal years 1969 through 1972 (Table 2). White males clearly dominated the enrollment in MDTA institutional and OJT skill training programs. Slightly more than two-fifths (40.8 percent) to one-half (50.8 percent) of all enrollees in these programs were white males, compared to participation rates of less than one-fifth among blacks and women.

The imbalance in enrollment by race and sex may also be seen by

TABLE V-2. *Manpower Program Statistics*
Number and Percent Distribution of Enrollees by Race and Sex
Fiscal Years 1969-1972

	MDTA													
	Institutional		OJT		WIN		CEP		NYC		Job Corps	
Characteristics	Total	Percent	Total	Percent	Total	Percent	Total	Percent	Total	Percent	Total	Percent
White:												
Male	162,203	40.8	66,389	50.8	80,945	28.8	42,089	20.8	41,091	30.3	39,545	26.4
Female	87,649	22.0	22,631	17.3	83,045	29.5	25,428	12.6	33,402	24.6	12,799	8.5
Negro:												
Male	77,649	19.5	25,691	19.7	24,077	8.6	75,797	37.4	25,621	18.9	71,627	47.8
Female	70,154	17.6	15,795	12.1	93,037	33.1	59,128	29.2	35,522	26.2	25,842	17.2
Total	397,655	100.0	130,506	100.0	281,104	100.0	202,442	100.0	135,636	100.0	149,813	100.0

Source: Manpower Administration, Office of Financial and Management Information Systems.

Note: Percents may not add to 100.0 due to rounding.

comparing the distribution of each group across the different programs. Viewed from this perspective, the 162,203 white males far exceeded the enrollment of the group in any other program. In contrast, no other race or sex group was so disproportionately concentrated in a single program. Black males were almost equally distributed across MDTA institutional, CEP, and the Job Corps, whereas black females showed a heavy concentration in WIN, CEP, and MDTA. This race/sex pattern is very much like that discussed in Chapter I where aggregate enrollment data for fiscal years 1965 through 1972 were discussed.

The trend in the number of enrollees served by the different manpower programs between fiscal years 1969 and 1972 showed a reasonably consistent pattern across race and sex groups (Table 3). In general, the enrollment in MDTA institutional training programs rose sharply for all race/sex groups in 1971, but at the expense of enrollment in the OJT programs. During the same period, there was evidence of expanding enrollment among both white males and females in CEP, whereas the number of blacks in that program remained reasonably stable.

Throughout the period, men dominated the enrollment in the Job Corps, but sharp gains in the enrollment of both black and white females were observed in 1972. Another distinction in the trends by sex, but not by race, was the relatively greater decline of women than men in the NYC out-of-school program over the entire time period.

Enrollee Characteristics

The socio economic characteristics of enrollees during fiscal years 1969 through 1972 are summarized in Appendix Tables A-1 and A-2. Twenty-five variables are listed in the tables to provide a broad overview of the type of enrollees served by the six selected manpower programs. Overall, the race and sex composition of enrollment revealed by the data corresponds closely to the general patterns described above and in Chapter I.

An examination of the pre-training income status shows that enrollees in each of the programs were drawn heavily from economically deprived families. Enrollees in OJT, however, were relatively better off in both individual and family income than were enrollees in the other programs. In fact, the family income distribution of OJT enrollees shows that, although on the average the program served a low-income group, a sizable proportion of enrollees (18.7 percent) were drawn from families on the margin of the middle class. Much of this pattern may be attributed to the relatively longer pre-training employment experience and relatively lower pre-training unemployment rate among OJT enrollees in comparison with all others.

The appendix tables show very clearly the limited quantity of data on post-training economic variables. Each of the programs showed a propor-

TABLE V-3. *Manpower Program Statistics*
Number of Enrollees by Race, Sex, and Year of Enrollment
Fiscal Years 1969-1972

Characteristics	MDTA Institutional	MDTA OJT	WIN	CEP	NYC Out-of-School	Job Corps
1969						
White:						
Male	29,366	9,563	17,633	—	13,666	1,493
Female	19,481	4,555	16,284	—	12,166	455
Negro:						
Male	15,729	3,703	5,875	—	9,632	2,581
Female	16,097	2,554	19,322	—	15,358	942
1970						
White:						
Male	26,113	23,409	15,427	11,842	10,636	8,574
Female	15,753	9,960	23,337	6,670	8,956	2,534
Negro:						
Male	14,478	9,353	4,960	26,571	7,612	15,712
Female	14,095	6,851	29,197	21,578	9,731	5,386
1971						
White:						
Male	52,332	22,803	32,675	14,773	9,535	10,220
Female	27,753	6,451	32,092	9,494	6,833	3,410
Negro:						
Male	24,108	8,792	9,801	26,458	4,997	18,501
Female	21,430	4,711	36,623	20,049	5,914	6,887

TABLE V-3, *continued.*

1972						
White:						
Male	54,392	10,614	15,110	15,474	7,254	19,258
Female	24,662	1,565	11,332	9,264	5,447	6,400
Negro:						
Male	23,334	3,843	3,441	22,768	3,380	34,833
Female	18,532	1,679	7,895	17,501	4,519	12,627
All years:						
White	249,852	89,020	163,890	67,517	74,493	52,344
Negro	147,803	41,486	117,114	134,925	61,143	97,469
Total[a]	397,655	130,506	281,004	202,442	135,636	139,813

Source: Manpower Administration, Office of Administration and Management.

[a] The total of all enrollees does not include minority groups other than Negro, nor does it include enrollees for whom race and/or sex characteristics were unreported.

tion of 70 percent or more in records with unreported data on post-training hourly wages. Data on post-training employment status and hours worked were also frequently unavailable in each of the programs. Thus, although the enrollee characteristics data may be useful for describing who participated in the manpower programs, only limited data on the post-training status of enrollees may be drawn from the records.

A close examination of the data shows that the MDTA skill training programs served disadvantaged blacks to a markedly greater degree than disadvantaged whites (Table 4). In fact, with the exception of the NYC out-of-school program, nearly two-thirds or more of the blacks in each of the programs was disadvantaged. In comparison, disadvantaged whites were heavily concentrated only in WIN and CEP. This pattern of enrollment suggests that the manpower programs were reaching their minority group target population during fiscal years 1969 through 1972, although the number of participants was small in relation to the probable universe of need.

Completion Status

The enrollee characteristics records were not complete in information pertaining to program completion (Table 5). Less than one-half of all records reported whether enrollees completed the program, and information on this question was available more frequently for white males in MDTA than for any other race or sex group in the various programs.

On the basis of the limited data available, several observations can be made regarding the completion status of enrollees. First, program completion rates were uniformly higher among both blacks and whites of both sexes in the skill training programs than in WIN, CEP, NYC, and the Job Corps. Second, although small differences in completion rates were observed between male and female enrollees, the proportion of enrollees of both races completing WIN was about one-third and the proportion completing CEP, one-half. Across both race and sex groups, the Job Corps reflected the lowest completion rates of any of the programs included in the analysis. The position of the Job Corps, however, may be influenced by that program's slightly different definition of "completion," in comparison with the concept used by other programs.

ANALYSIS OF SUBSET DATA

In order to gain a sharper view of the impact of manpower programs on enrollees as revealed in the operating statistics, a sample of 49,400 records was drawn from the 1.3 million records showing race and sex identity. Each record included in the sample has information on both pre- and post-training wage rate, and information on the enrollee's edu-

TABLE V-4. *Manpower Program Statistics Number and Percent of Enrollees by Disadvantaged Status and Race Fiscal Years 1969-1972*
(Numbers in thousands)

Characteristics	MDTA Institutional Total	MDTA Institutional Percent	MDTA OJT Total	MDTA OJT Percent	WIN Total	WIN Percent	CEP Total	CEP Percent	NYC Out-of-School Total	NYC Out-of-School Percent
Disadvantaged:										
White	139.3	35.4	36.1	28.5	138.9	49.9	64.4	32.4	21.8	22.4
Negro	112.5	28.6	26.0	20.6	113.5	40.8	128.9	65.0	21.2	21.8
Not disadvantaged:										
White	108.7	27.6	50.9	40.3	23.4	8.4	1.8	0.9	35.9	36.9
Negro	32.7	8.3	13.5	10.6	2.6	0.9	3.3	1.7	28.1	28.9
Total	393.2	100.0	126.6	100.0	278.4	100.0	198.4	100.0	97.3	100.0

Source: Manpower Administration, Office of Financial and Management Information Systems.

Note: Percents are calculated using the total number of whites and Negroes for whom disadvantaged data were available and may not add to 100.0 due to rounding.

TABLE V-5. *Manpower Program Statistics*
Percent of Enrollees with Termination Status Reported
and with a Completion Status
Fiscal Years 1969-1972

Race and Sex	MDTA Institutional Reported	MDTA Institutional Completed	MDTA OJT Reported	MDTA OJT Completed	WIN Reported	WIN Completed	CEP Reported	CEP Completed	NYC Out-of-School Reported	NYC Out-of-School Completed	Job Corps Reported	Job Corps Completed
White:												
Male	80.1	71.9	36.0	76.7	40.2	28.3	19.5	56.4	8.0	65.0	35.2	17.8
Female	59.6	80.5	11.3	79.7	31.9	32.0	11.5	59.6	12.6	32.1	11.4	19.1
Negro:												
Male	43.0	68.7	12.0	72.9	9.4	31.3	32.2	53.5	9.0	33.4	62.8	25.2
Female	43.0	76.8	7.1	81.4	34.7	37.2	25.2	57.9	12.5	31.4	22.4	29.8

Source: Manpower Administration, Office of Administration and Management.

cational status, household status, enrollment termination date, and nature of program termination. Because follow-up data are not available for noncompleters, all individuals in the sample are program completers for whom there was information on the selected personal characteristics. Thus, the selected subset of records may be skewed with respect to outcomes, but there is no way to determine the direction or extent of this, except to say that it reflects not only differences in program completion rates across race/sex groups, but also incomplete reporting.

Some comparisons between the composition of the population and the subset are shown in Table 6. The record selection criteria produced a slightly larger proportion of men than women in each program in comparison with the population. The most dramatic change in the male-female composition of enrollment occurred in WIN where the proportion of all male enrollees increased from 37 percent of the population to 62 percent of the sample. This means that the sample for WIN is a distorted facsimile of the program, as far as the sex composition of enrollment is concerned.

In addition, the black presence is slightly lower in the sample for the MDTA institutional and OJT programs than in the population, but sharply lower in the WIN and CEP samples. The differences shown for the latter two programs reflect the tendency of the sample selection criteria to produce a lower representation of black female than of black male enrollees.

The difference between the race and sex composition of the sample and the population will probably bias the results of the race and sex comparison of changes in wage rates experienced by the enrollees. Neither the direction nor the magnitude of the bias, however, can be predicted from the available evidence. The sample was not drawn with an intention to analyze the data according to the rules of statistical inference. Instead, this study will show only the differences in economic outcomes, measured by hourly wage rates, between a relatively small number of black and white enrollees for whom comparable wage rate data were available.

COMPARISON OF POST-TRAINING WAGE RATES

The differences among the four race and sex groups in post-training hourly wage rates, and in the change in hourly wages before and after training, are shown in Figures 1 through 9.

MDTA Institutional and OJT Programs

There were 16,191 enrollees included in the sample of persons enrolled in the MDTA institutional program. Of that number, 11,519 were white and 4,672 were black. A comparison of post-training hourly wages shows

TABLE V-6. *Manpower Program Statistics*
Percent Distribution of All Enrollees and a Sample
By Race and Sex

Characteristics	MDTA Institutional Total	MDTA Institutional Sample	MDTA OJT Total	MDTA OJT Sample	WIN Total	WIN Sample	CEP Total	CEP Sample	Job Corps Total	Job Corps Sample
Sex:										
Male	61.0	55.0	70.0	72.0	37.0	62.0	58.0	64.0	74.0	83.0
Female	39.0	45.0	29.0	27.0	62.0	38.0	41.0	36.0	25.0	17.0
Race:										
White	69.0	71.1	68.0	72.0	42.0	69.0	33.0	42.0	35.0	24.0
Negro	31.0	28.8	32.0	28.0	58.0	31.0	66.0	58.0	65.0	75.0
Race and sex:										
White										
Male	40.8	42.6	50.8	55.7	28.8	50.0	20.8	28.7	26.4	20.2
Female	22.0	28.5	17.3	16.2	29.5	18.6	12.6	13.4	8.5	4.2
Negro										
Male	19.5	12.5	19.7	16.7	8.6	12.1	37.4	35.2	47.8	62.6
Female	17.6	16.4	12.1	11.3	33.1	19.2	29.2	22.5	17.2	12.9
Total	100.0	100.0	100.0	100.0	100.0	100.0	100.0	100.0	100.0	100.0
Sample as a percent of all enrollees[a]	4.1		3.1		3.7		7.8		2.0	

Source: Manpower Administration, Office of Administration and Management.

Note: Percents may not add to 100.0 due to rounding.

[a]Program population figure used was the total of white and Negro enrollees, both sexes.

FIGURE V-1. *MDTA Institutional Training Program Mean Post-Training Hourly Wage ($\bar{x}$) and Difference in Mean Hourly Wage (Δ) Before and After Enrollment*[a] *by Race, Sex and Education Fiscal Years 1969-1972*

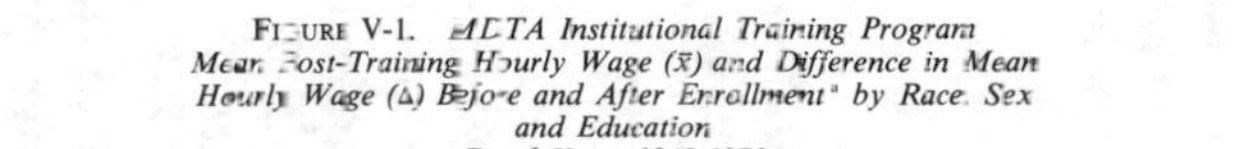

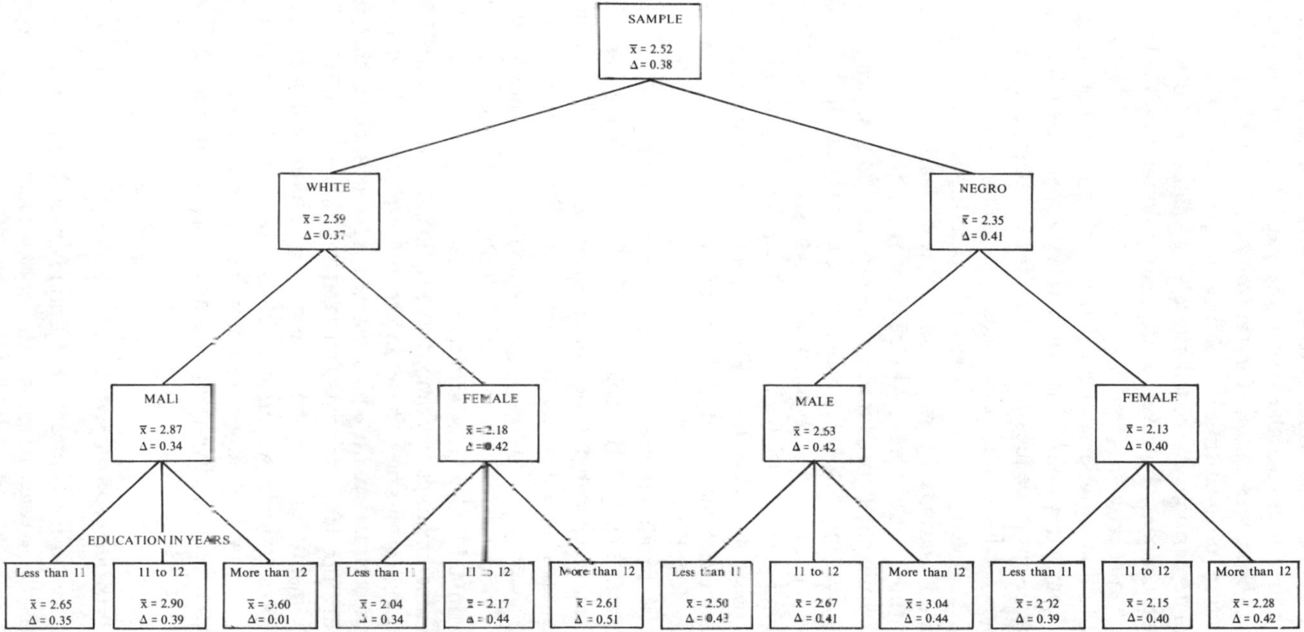

Source: Office of Administration and Management, Manpower Administration, U. S. Department of Labor.

Note: Sample of 16,191 trainees from a population of 435,975.
$\bar{x}$ = mean post-training hourly wage.
Δ = mean difference between pre- and post-training wage.

[a] After enrollment refers to six month follow-up survey.

that, on the average, white enrollees enjoyed slightly higher post-training wages than blacks, but the size of the gain in hourly wages measured by cents per hour was higher for the minority group. A review of the sex composition of post-training hourly wages shows that both black and white male earnings exceeded those of females of both races. The cents per hour changes, however, were nearly equal for blacks of both sexes and for white females.

An additional dimension on the post-training wage gains may be obtained from a review of the wage rates experienced by individuals with different levels of educational attainment. The data show very clearly that higher educational attainment, measured by years of school completed, is systematically associated with higher post-training earnings, although variations by race and sex are clearly evident. For example, among those who were in MDTA institutional high school graduation or the equivalent produced post-training hourly wages of $3.60 for white males and $3.04 for black males, but less than $3.00 for females of both races. In fact, black male high school dropouts earned higher post-training wages than either black or white females with more than twelve years of schooling. These results for the MDTA institutional program reflect the continuing obstacles facing women in the labor market, even when they obtain training in specific job skills.

The post-training hourly wages for white male OJT enrollees were 14.3 percent higher and black male OJT enrollees 8.4 percent higher than wages for comparable males in institutional training programs. Women of both races, however, fared worse in OJT than in institutional training when measured by hourly wages. Moreover, not only were post-training wages lower for women in OJT than in institutional programs, but women in OJT also experienced smaller net gains in hourly wages over pre-training earnings in comparison with gains experienced by women in institutional programs. These differences are probably attributable to the different occupations in which women were trained in the two programs. There are no data, however, to confirm this expectation. In OJT as in MDTA institutional, higher educational attainment was associated with higher post-training wage rates, but women were at a relative disadvantage in the level of wages in comparison with men. It should be noted that there were relatively few women included in the OJT records summarized in Figure 2.

Concentrated Employment Program

Enrollees in the Concentrated Employment Program did not experience gains in wage rates equal to those observed among enrollees in either MDTA institutional or OJT programs. CEP enrollees gained only $0.25 per hour over pre-training hourly wages, compared to a gain of $0.38

FIGURE V-2 MDTA On-the-Job Training Program
Mean Post-Training Hourly Wage (X̄) and Difference in Mean Hourly Wage (Δ) Before and After Enrollment by Race, Sex, and Education
Fiscal Years 1969-1972

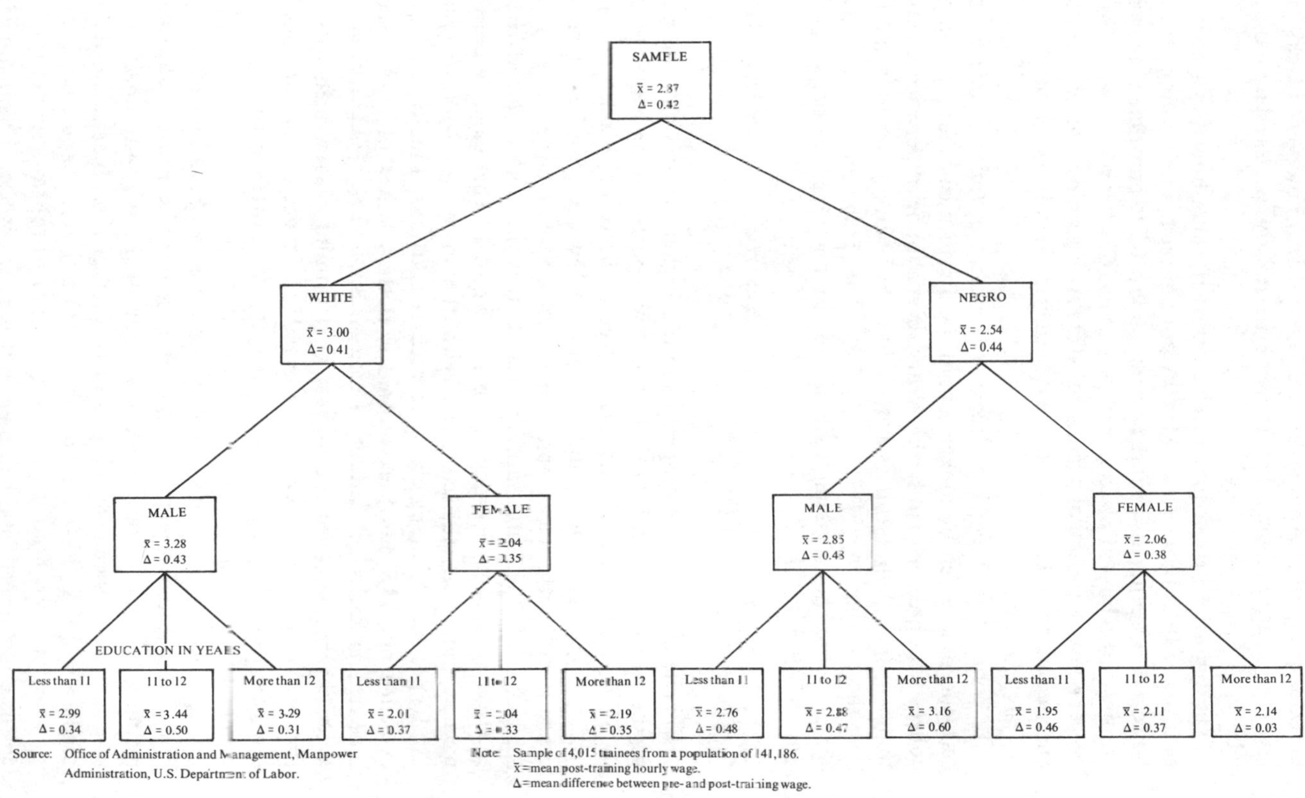

Source: Office of Administration and Management, Manpower Administration, U.S. Department of Labor.

Note: Sample of 4,015 trainees from a population of 141,186.
X̄=mean post-training hourly wage.
Δ=mean difference between pre- and post-training wage.

per hour for MDTA institutional trainees, and $0.42 per hour for those in OJT programs. Among all CEP enrollees, however, blacks of both sexes registered slightly larger gains in hourly wages than comparable whites.

The typical CEP enrollee received post-training hourly wages 13.5 percent lower than those of his MDTA counterpart. The earnings for blacks, however, were not discounted as much by CEP enrollment as were the earnings of whites. For example, the black CEP enrollee earned only 4.9 percent less than similar blacks in MDTA programs, whereas white CEP enrollees earned 17.7 percent less than similar whites in MDTA institutional programs.

In contrast to MDTA enrollees, the wages of CEP enrollees were not influenced as much by longer schooling. In no race or sex group did enrollees with greater than twelve years of schooling experience significantly higher wages than enrollees with eleven to twelve years of schooling, as was the case among MDTA enrollees. This result may reflect the labor market constraints facing the highly disadvantaged workers, typical of most CEP enrollees.

Work Incentive Program and Job Corps

Enrollees in the WIN program showed higher post-training wages ($2.58 per hour) than enrollees in CEP, but lower post-training wages than those in MDTA institutional and OJT. Again, however, black enrollees had lower wages than whites, and women had lower wages than men. On the other hand, both blacks and women experienced larger gains in hourly earnings over their pre-training level than white males; indeed, the largest relative gain was recorded by black women. The gains among black women, however, still left them with the lowest post-training earnings ($2.10 per hour) among the four race/sex groups. Finally, the follow-up evidence on WIN enrollees showed a positive effect of higher schooling on earnings for black and white women but not for men. Although male WIN enrollees enjoyed the highest post-training wages, men with greater than 12 years of schooling experienced a net decline in earnings during the post-training period in comparison with wages earned prior to entering the program.

The lowest post-training wages were earned by Job Corps enrollees. The 2,325 Job Corps participants included in the sample showed post-training earnings of only $2.00 per hour. Although only small differences in wages were evident between the two race groups, blacks showed slightly higher earnings ($2.03) than whites ($1.92) and experienced relatively greater gains in hourly wage rates over the pre-training period. Women consistently earned less than men, but whereas white women showed post-training earnings ($1.61) no higher than the federal minimum wage, black

FIGURE V-3. *Concentrated Employment Program*
Mean Post-Training Hourly Wage ($\bar{x}$) and Difference in Mean Hourly Wage (Δ) Before and After Enrollment by Race, Sex, and Education
Fiscal Years 1969-1972

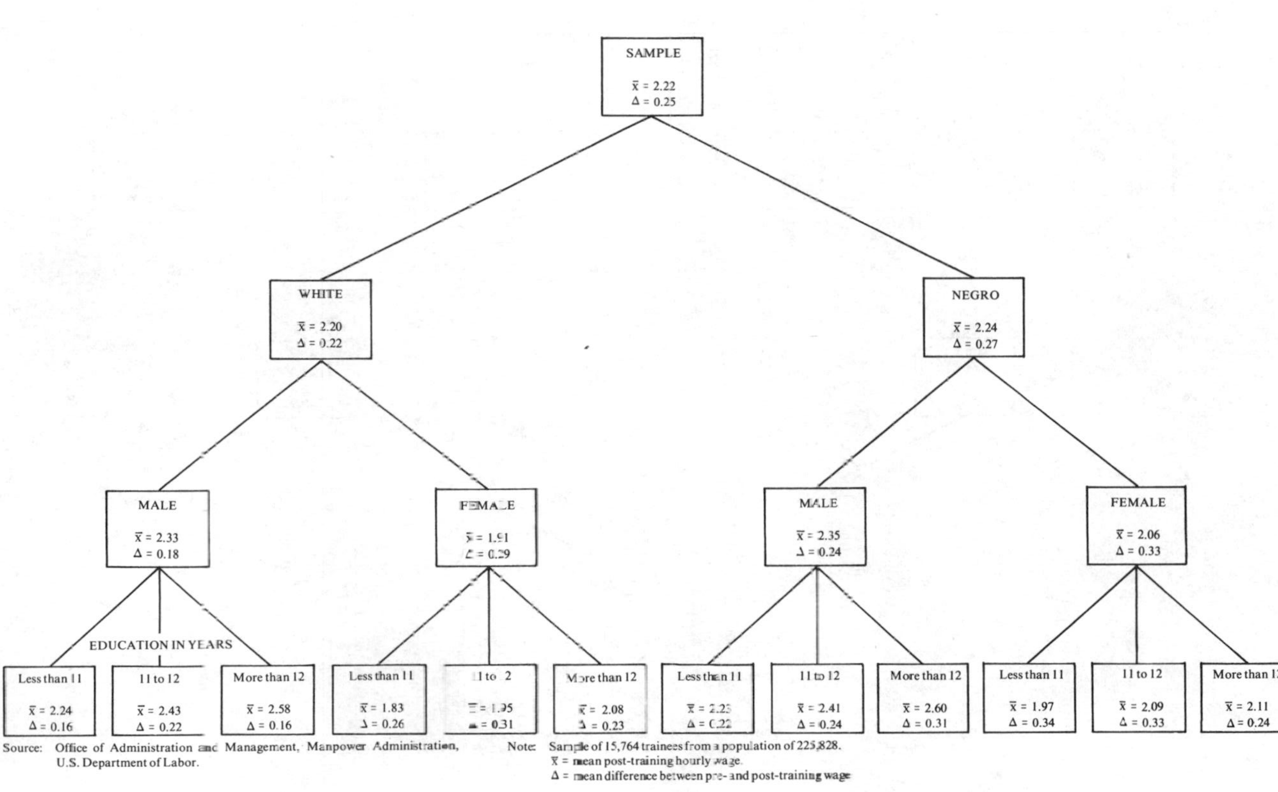

Source: Office of Administration and Management, Manpower Administration, U.S. Department of Labor.

Note: Sample of 15,764 trainees from a population of 225,828.
$\bar{x}$ = mean post-training hourly wage.
Δ = mean difference between pre- and post-training wage

FIGURE V-4. *Work Incentive Program*
Mean Post-Training Hourly Wage (X̄) and Difference in Mean Hourly Wage (Δ) Before and After Enrollment by Race, Sex, and Education
Fiscal Years 1969-1972

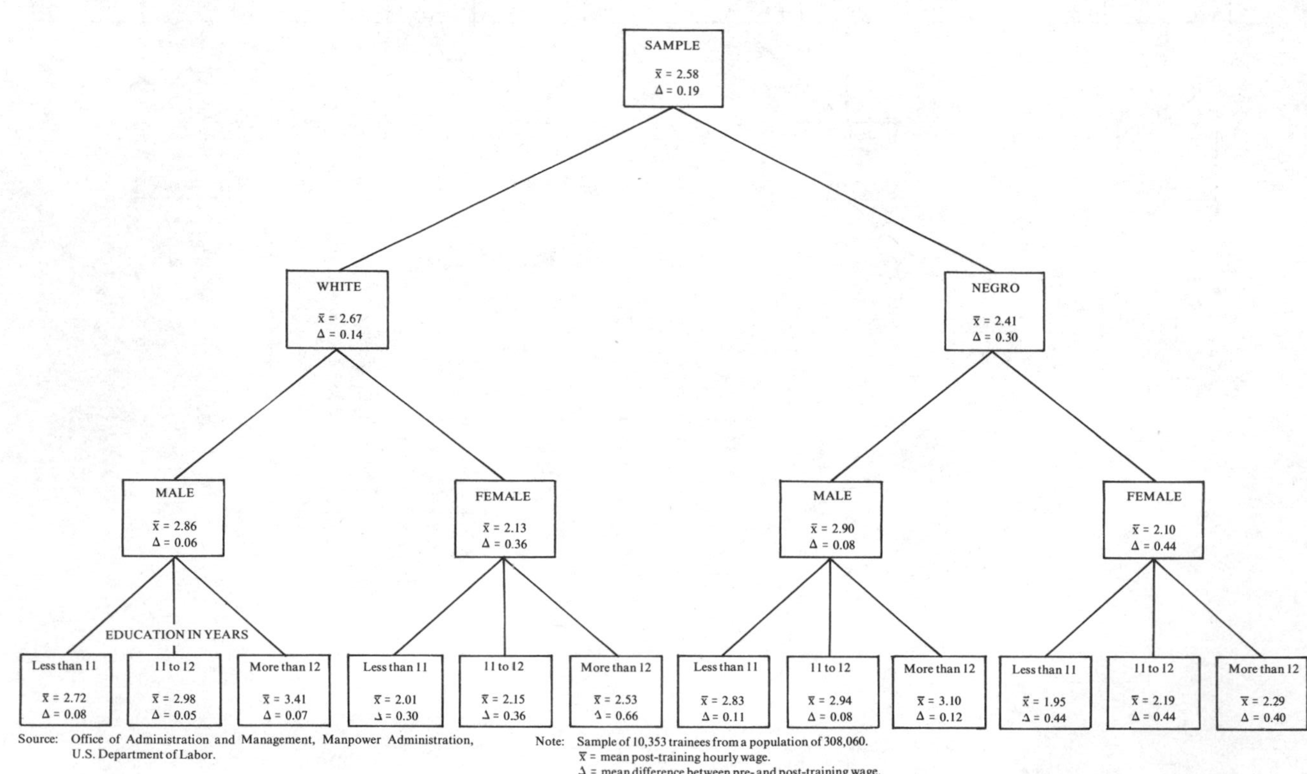

Source: Office of Administration and Management, Manpower Administration, U.S. Department of Labor.

Note: Sample of 10,353 trainees from a population of 308,060.
X̄ = mean post-training hourly wage.
Δ = mean difference between pre- and post-training wage.

female hourly wages were markedly higher ($1.88). Overall, the typical Job Corps enrollee in the sample earned more the greater his years of schooling, but post-training wages were relatively low even for those who completed twelve years of school.

Post-Training Earnings by Household Status

Of all persons included in the sample, 32,722, or 70.5 percent, were heads of households and might be assumed to have greater economic needs. Almost three of every four whites (73.8 percent) had primary household responsibilities, compared with nearly two of every three blacks (65.3 percent).

The post-training wages of heads of households were uniformly higher than wages of other enrollees across both race and sex groups. In addition, the differences by program in the level of post-training wages for primary household earners followed closely the pattern discussed above for all enrollees. Male MDTA institutional enrollees earned slightly less than those in OJT, and slightly more than those in CEP, whereas females in the institutional programs reported higher post-training wages than enrollees of the same sex in either OJT, WIN, or CEP. Black women who were heads of households showed higher post-training wages than similar white females in OJT and CEP. In WIN, female heads of households of both races showed similar hourly earnings ($2.14 for whites compared to $2.12 for blacks). In CEP and in the OJT and WIN programs, however, female primary earners had lower wages ($2.07) than similar women enrollees in the MDTA institutional programs ($2.20). Overall, then, although heads of households of both races were in a slightly better wage position than others, the wages of female heads of households failed to show as wide a margin over the wages earned by other women as did the wages of male heads of households to other men.

Significance of Mean Wage Differences

The post-training hourly wages discussed above merely denote the differences in level and rate of change classified by race, sex, and household status. It is a matter of interest to inquire into the statistical significance of such differences in order to gain some perspective on the meaning of wage rate adjustments following participation in manpower programs. The significance of differences in post-training mean hourly earnings and of changes in hourly earnings before and after training is measured by the chi square test (Table 7).

The data show that differences in post-training mean hourly earnings between black and white males were highly significant in each of the programs. Post-training wage differences between black and white fe-

TABLE V-7. *Manpower Program Statistics*
Cross-tabulation Results Between Races by Hourly Post-Training Wages and Difference in Hourly Wages Pre- and Post-Training

	MDTA							
	Institutional		OJT		WIN		CEP	
Results	Male	Female	Male	Female	Male	Female	Male	Female
Post-training wage:								
Mean for white (in dollars)	2.59	2.18	3.28	2.04	2.86	2.13	2.33	1.91
Mean for Negro (in dollars)	2.63	2.13	2.85	2.06	2.90	2.10	2.35	2.06
x^2 between races	60.94[a]	8.68[b]	29.59[a]	2.87[c]	48.75[a]	12.70[a]	15.90[a]	183.34[a]
d.f.	3	3	3	3	3	3	4	4
Difference in wage pre-training and post-training:								
Mean for white (in dollars)	0.34	0.42	0.43	0.35	0.06	0.36	0.18	0.29
Mean for Negro (in dollars)	0.42	0.40	0.48	0.38	0.08	0.44	0.24	0.33
x^2 between races	19.00[a]	13.97[b]	4.44[c]	11.73[b]	5.81[c]	30.96[a]	29.08[a]	19.40[a]
d.f.	5	5	5	5	5	5	5	5

Source: U.S. Department of Labor, Manpower Administration, Office of Administration and Management.

[a] Denotes significance at less than the 0.01 level.
[b] Denotes significance at less than the 0.05 level.
[c] Denotes significance at greater than the 0.10 level, therefore not significant.

FIGURE V-5. *Job Corps*
Mean Post-Training Hourly Wage ($\bar{X}$) and Difference in Mean Hourly Wage (Δ) Before and After Enrollment by Race, Sex, and Education
Fiscal Years 1969-1972

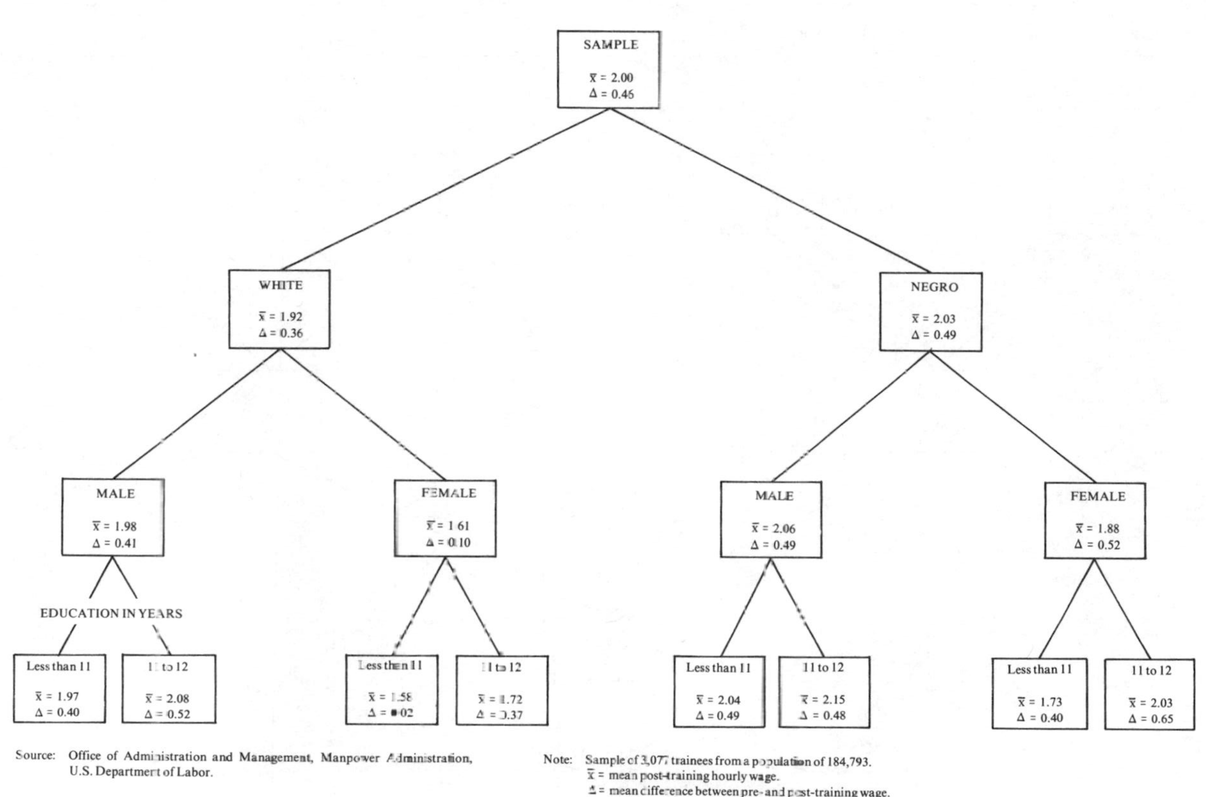

Source: Office of Administration and Management, Manpower Administration, U.S. Department of Labor.

Note: Sample of 3,077 trainees from a population of 184,793.
$\bar{X}$ = mean post-training hourly wage.
Δ = mean difference between pre- and post-training wage.

FIGURE V-6. *MDTA Institutional Training Program*
Mean Post-Training Hourly Wage (x̄) After Enrollment by Race, Sex, and Head of Household
Fiscal Years 1969-1972

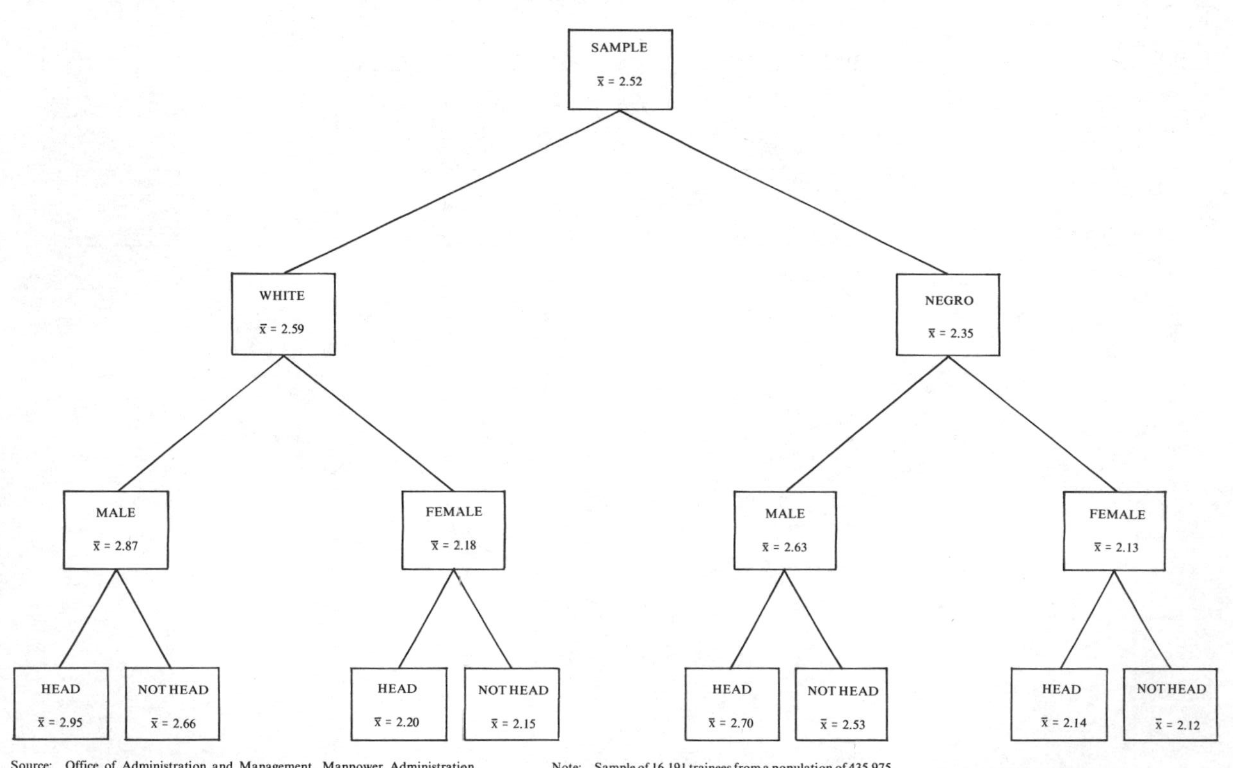

Source: Office of Administration and Management, Manpower Administration, U.S. Department of Labor.

Note: Sample of 16,191 trainees from a population of 435,975.
x̄ = mean post-training hourly wage.

FIGURE V-7. *MDTA On-the-Job Training Program*
Mean Post-Training Hourly Wage ($\bar{x}$) After Enrollment by Race, Sex, and Head of Household
Fiscal Years 1969-1972

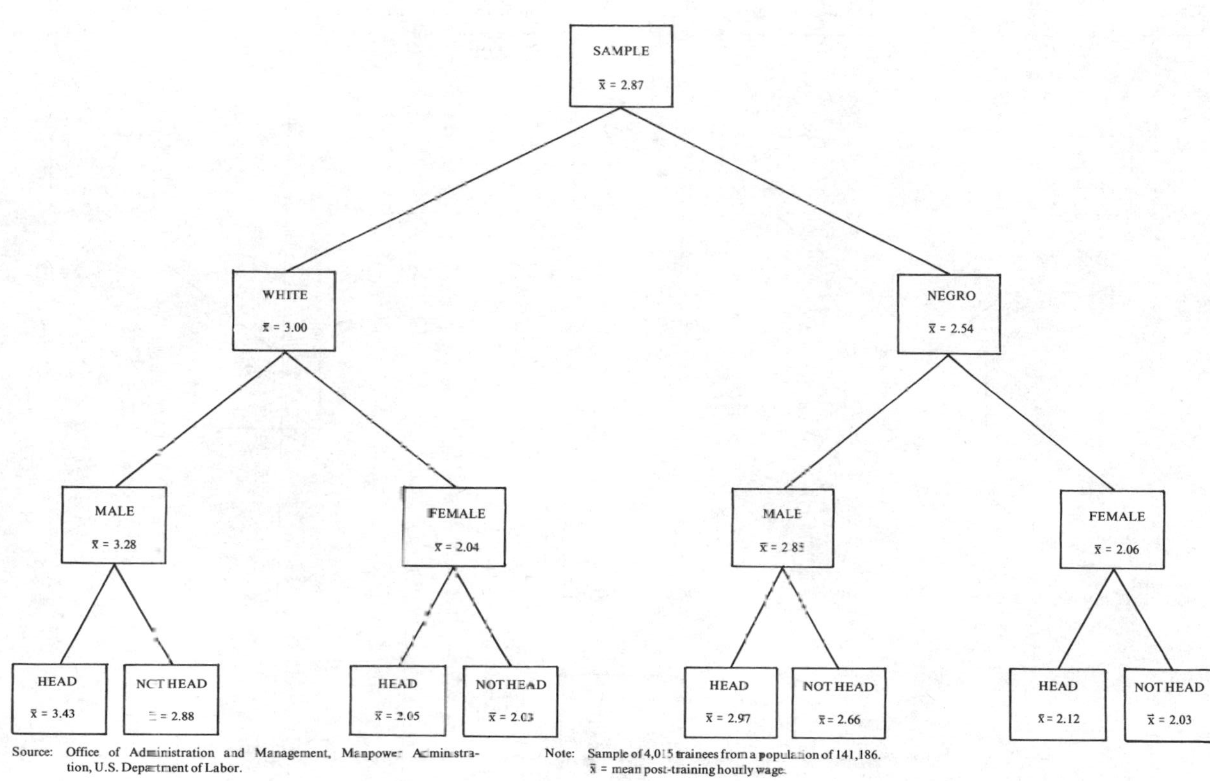

Source: Office of Administration and Management, Manpower Administration, U.S. Department of Labor.

Note: Sample of 4,015 trainees from a population of 141,186.
$\bar{x}$ = mean post-training hourly wage.

FIGURE V-8. *Concentrated Employment Program*
Mean Post-Training Hourly Wage ($\bar{x}$) After Enrollment by Race, Sex, and Head of Household
Fiscal Years 1969-1972

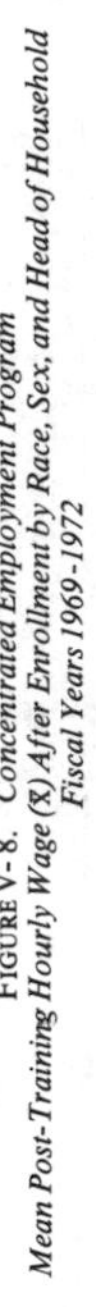

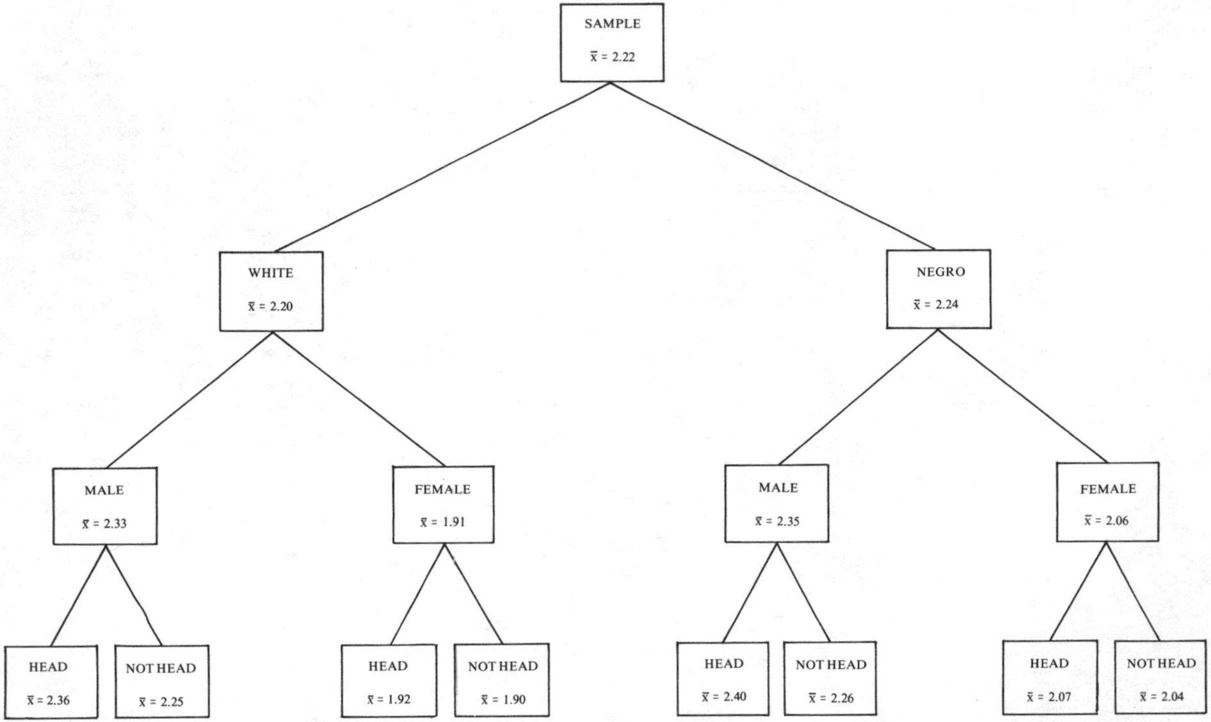

Source: Office of Administration and Management, Manpower Administration, U. S. Department of Labor.

Note: Sample of 15,764 trainees from a population of 225,828.
$\bar{x}$ = mean post-training hourly wage.

FIGURE V-9. *Work Incentive Program*
Mean Post-Training Hourly Wage ($\bar{x}$) *After Enrollment by Race, Sex, and Head of Household*
Fiscal Years 1969-1972

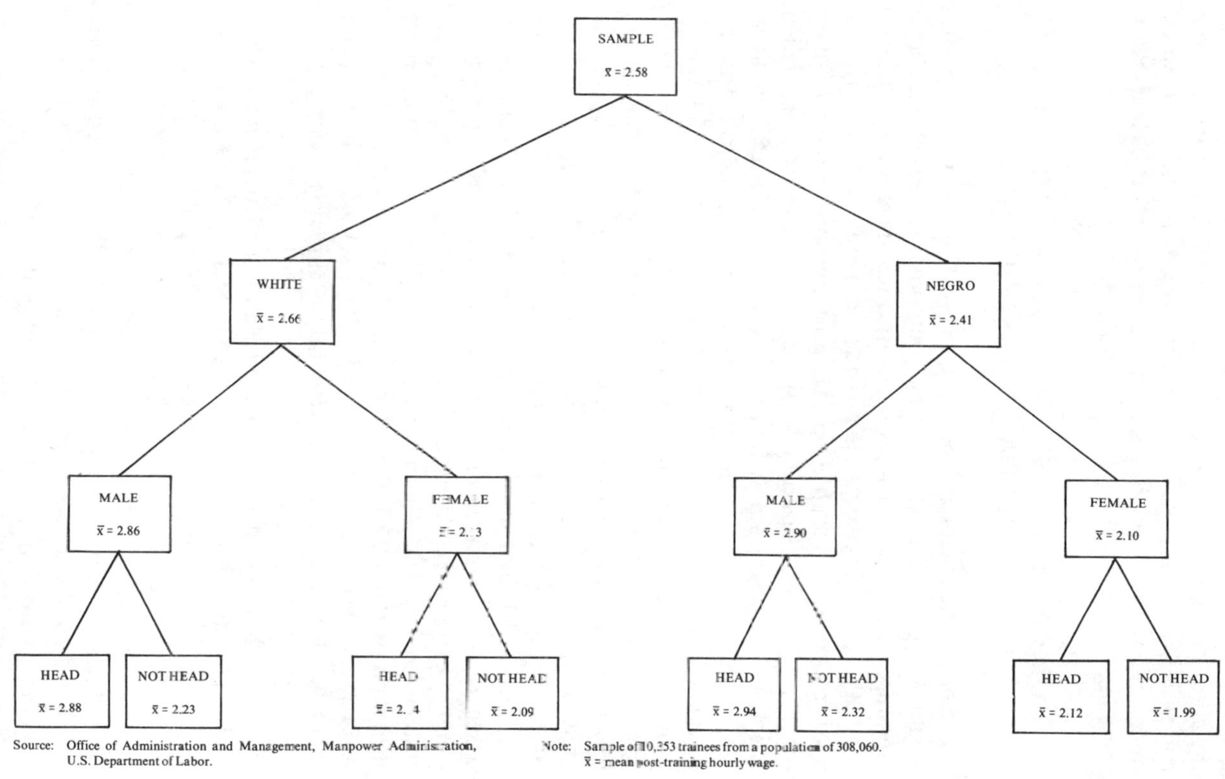

Source: Office of Administration and Management, Manpower Administration, U.S. Department of Labor.

Note: Sample of 10,353 trainees from a population of 308,060.
$\bar{x}$ = mean post-training hourly wage.

males, however, were significant in each of the programs, but significant at the .01 level for only WIN and CEP. These results suggest that although the absolute value of the difference in post-training wages between blacks and whites was not large in any of the programs, the observed differences were greater than might be expected because of chance variations in sampling.

COMPARISON OF EVALUATIVE STUDIES AND OPERATING STATISTICS

Serious deficiencies in the data prevent a useful comparison of the results of post-training economic outcomes revealed in the evaluative literature with outcomes revealed in the program operating statistics. First, the operating statistics provide data only on wage rates and labor market status as variables in the post-training economic status of enrollees. For this reason, only those evaluative studies which provide estimates on post-training wage rates would be useful in a comparison of outcomes revealed in the two data sources. As indicated in the previous discussion, however, relatively few studies contained estimates of post-training wage rates. The limited number of studies with comparable outcome measures reduces significantly the value of a comparison of research results between the evaluative studies and the program operating statistics.

Second, the comparison of research results must be constrained also by noncomparability in the scope of coverage in the evaluative studies compared with that in the operating statistics. The evaluative studies are based on the investigation of economic outcomes experienced by small samples of enrollees in selected labor markets. In contrast, the operating statistics represent the accumulation of follow-up reports drawn from all programs without regard to location. Thus, differences in post-training wage rates observed in the separate data sources will be strongly influenced by local labor market conditions in areas where the evaluative studies were conducted.

Finally, because of the limited availability of data, only MDTA, CEP, and WIN can be included in the comparison of research results. In the case of MDTA, however, the comparison would not be meaningful because the evaluative studies of MDTA, which provide data on post-training wage rates, were based on an analysis of Manpower Administration data! The evaluative studies of WIN and CEP are based on independently developed follow-up data, but the outcome measures were obtained from interviews with only a relatively small number of enrollees.

Such data comparability problems suggest that any comparison of research results obtained from the evaluative studies with results obtained from the analysis of the program operating statistics would be highly speculative, inconclusive, and almost meaningless. There are simply not enough evaluative studies with follow-up information even reasonably similar in time and place to offer a foundation for comparing research results.

TABLE V-A1. *Manpower Program Statistics*
Number of Enrollees with Selected Characteristics
Fiscal Years 1969-1972
(In thousands)

Characteristics	MDTA Institutional	MDTA OJT	WIN	CEP	NYC Out-of-School	Job Corps
Fiscal year:						
1969	90.9	22.7	65.8	—	58.7	8.3
1970	77.6	53.3	81.8	74.1	42.6	44.3
1971	136.5	46.3	120.0	79.3	32.5	46.3
1972	131.0	19.0	40.5	72.5	24.7	85.9
Race:						
White	251.0	89.1	164.0	67.6	74.7	52.3
Negro	147.9	41.5	117.2	135.1	61.3	97.5
Other[a]	21.2	5.6	14.0	17.5	8.5	3.0
Sex:						
Male	264.6	99.5	115.1	131.7	77.7	137.1
Female	170.9	41.4	192.6	93.8	80.3	47.5
Age:						
Under 19	57.5	18.3	29.3	37.8	129.6	140.0
19-21	116.5	32.9	46.4	64.4	20.3	37.9
22-34	173.6	56.8	159.4	88.1	3.4	0.1
35-44	51.4	17.4	52.6	20.9	1.0	—
Over 44	36.7	15.7	20.3	14.6	3.9	—

TABLE V-A 1. *Manpower Program Statistics (continued)*

Characteristics	MDTA Institutional	MDTA OJT	WIN	CEP	NYC Out-of-School	Job Corps
Education:						
Less than 8 years	24.6	10.0	36.8	19.2	16.7	20.3
8-10 years	38.6	42.0	119.7	73.4	109.1	111.8
11-12 years	242.3	77.6	134.3	117.4	29.3	27.7
More than 12 years	26.0	9.4	13.8	8.1	0.3	0.1
Marital status:						
Single	196.9	55.4	74.5	115.4	130.3	160.0
Married	161.4	71.2	133.4	74.3	19.0	1.6
Divorced	8.3	2.1	4.4	3.6	1.0	2.3
Widowed	68.1	12.0	94.3	31.0	6.1	—
Trainee annual income:						
Less than $1,001	95.3	24.8	60.6	64.5	1.9	n.a.
1,001-3,000	135.5	43.1	63.4	80.0	1.0	n.a.
3,001-5,000	57.3	26.6	22.9	15.5	0.2	n.a.
5,001-7,000	17.3	11.0	5.6	2.0	—	n.a.
More than 7,000	10.9	10.3	2.4	0.9	—	n.a.
Annual family income:						
Less than $1,001	43.5	9.7	34.8	29.9	31.7	4.8
1,001-3,000	128.6	35.8	13.3	83.3	58.0	36.2
3,001-5,000	81.1	29.8	71.9	37.6	50.7	44.3
5,001-7,000	24.9	16.4	17.2	7.8	3.5	14.5
More than 7,000	36.0	23.1	6.3	2.3	0.2	4.8
Pre-training labor force status:[b]						
Employed	25.0	24.8	2.9	3.3	4.1	2.3
Underemployed	60.6	22.6	15.9	10.5	1.5	10.3
Unemployed	316.8	87.2	252.7	203.1	143.3	137.6
School	3.1	1.2	6.2	1.3	0.4	13.1
Not in labor force	24.3	3.0	25.9	2.3	1.2	—

TABLE V-A 1. *Manpower Program Statistics (continued)*

Characteristics	MDTA		WIN	CEP	NYC	Job Corps
	Institutional	OJT			Out-of-School	
Weeks unemployed pre-training last year:						
Less than 10	59.6	32.9	22.6	33.4	22.2	23.5
11-25	95.1	30.5	49.7	49.8	17.2	16.1
More than 26	163.8	38.0	201.9	109.7	21.2	93.8
Weeks unemployed pre-training 'current spell':						
Less than 10	123.5	41.9	40.2	69.7	6.8	23.5
11-25	85.2	19.1	51.6	43.6	6.1	16.1
More than 26	106.0	20.9	151.3	69.5	10.4	93.8
Years pre-training employment:						
Less than 1	57.1	25.6	77.3	56.6	67.0	n.a.
1-2	134.2	29.9	56.0	62.4	1.0	n.a.
3-9	156.2	47.3	99.9	66.9	0.3	n.a.
More than 9	79.8	34.0	60.4	30.8	0.1	n.a.
Pre-training hourly wage:						
Less than $1.50	82.8	20.1	72.0	39.5	48.4	36.5
1.50-2.00	143.9	46.3	87.0	87.7	30.4	31.9
2.01-2.50	57.7	19.8	33.6	29.1	3.6	3.5
2.51-3.50	53.4	19.1	34.2	22.6	1.8	1.4
More than 3.50	22.7	14.6	17.1	6.7	0.5	1.5
Post-training hourly wage:						
Less than $1.50	2.3	0.2	1.6	0.9	—	8.6
1.50-2.00	22.3	5.7	12.2	23.9	0.1	29.9
2.01-2.50	16.3	4.8	8.9	12.8	—	7.2
2.51-3.50	16.1	4.8	8.2	9.3	—	4.5
More than 3.50	6.9	3.8	3.0	2.6	—	1.5
Unreported	372.0	121.9	27.4	176.2	158.2	133.1

TABLE V-A 1. *Manpower Program Statistics (continued)*

Characteristics	MDTA Institutional	MDTA OJT	WIN	CEP	NYC Out-of-School	Job Corps
Post-training employment status:[c]						
Employed	74.2	21.2	37.4	53.9	0.3	48.3
Not employed or seeking	15.7	1.9	0.1	0.1	—	24.4
Armed forces	1.2	0.2	0.4	0.5	—	4.7
Looking for work	21.7	2.6	0.2	0.1	—	5.3
Unreported	321.8	114.8	270.2	171.2	158.0	102.1
Post-training hours worked weekly:						
Less than 15	0.4	0.1	—	—	—	0.3
15-34	2.7	0.5	—	—	—	4.4
35-40	30.1	9.9	0.1	—	—	42.2
More than 40	5.4	2.2	—	—	—	4.7
Unreported	397.2	128.5	307.9	225.8	158.4	133.2
Length of time in program:[d]						
Less than 3 months	71.4	29.9	16.7	34.6	26.3	10.8
3	29.7	11.2	11.3	14.1	10.7	5.5
4-5	56.0	14.9	25.4	23.4	18.1	9.4
6-12	109.0	22.0	77.9	39.8	38.5	21.7
13-18	22.4	6.5	36.2	11.6	13.1	6.6
More than 18	9.5	2.6	27.9	4.7	7.3	2.5
Nature of termination:						
Completed	209.2	54.6	38.4	55.2	18.5	36.7
Dropped	50.9	16.2	79.2	41.5	38.5	123.9
Transferred	11.3	0.2	0.2	1.8	0.3	24.1
Military:						
Veteran	100.1	33.5	32.9	29.7	2.1	1.9
Rejectee	16.7	7.1	8.2	8.0	2.2	23.2
Other	298.1	91.5	233.0	152.0	137.8	18.1

TABLE V-A 1. *Manpower Program Statistics (continued)*

Characteristics	MDTA Institutional	MDTA OJT	WIN	CEP	NYC Out-of-School	Job Corps
Head of family:						
Yes	254.0	83.5	263.9	129.8	12.3	n.a.
No	178.8	56.9	42.6	94.3	143.7	n.a.
Number in family:						
Less than 5	315.5	107.7	223.8	167.2	69.7	71.5
5-10	57.6	20.6	66.4	38.9	59.9	75.0
More than 10	5.0	1.4	5.3	4.4	12.9	12.3
Unemployment insurance:						
Yes	43.0	9.4	7.5	8.0	0.4	n.a.
No	386.1	128.2	293.8	210.3	111.3	n.a.
Poverty:						
Yes	243.1	62.0	278.9	205.2	149.9	n.a.
No	139.0	69.0	19.5	7.5	0.3	n.a.
Disadvantaged:						
Yes	287.2	68.5	278.0	215.0	48.9	n.a.
No	151.1	68.0	26.9	5.7	73.2	n.a.
Public assistance:						
Yes	62.6	7.7	302.2	31.0	51.4	56.3
No	370.6	131.5	5.0	192.8	104.0	103.6
Rural-urban:						
Urban	237.8	55.7	161.1	89.6	5.0	137.7
Rural	86.9	23.6	22.6	24.7	3.8	26.1
Total program trainees [f]	435,975	141,186	308,060	225,828	158,472	184,793

Source: Manpower Administration, Office of Financial and Management Information Systems (upublished data).

[a] "Other category" includes Manpower classifications of American Indian, Oriental, and other.

[b] Family farm worker classification is omitted due to neglible percentage.

[c] Waiting for work category is omitted due to negligible numbers.

[d] Computation of length of time in the program is based on the enrollment date and the termination date.

[e] Exhaustee classification is recoded to "no."

Total figure in actual numbers

TABLE V-A2. *Manpower Program Statistics*
Percent Distribution of Selected Trainee Characteristics
Fiscal Years 1969-1972

Characteristics	MDTA Institutional	MDTA OJT	WIN	CEP	NYC Out-of-School	Job Corps
Fiscal year:						
1969	20.8	16.0	21.4	—	37.0	4.5
1970	17.8	37.7	26.5	32.8	26.9	24.0
1971	31.3	32.8	38.9	35.1	20.5	25.0
1972	30.1	13.4	13.1	32.0	15.6	46.5
Race:						
White	57.6	63.1	53.2	29.9	47.1	28.3
Negro	33.9	29.4	38.1	59.8	38.6	52.8
Other [a]	4.8	5.5	4.5	5.1	5.4	1.7
Sex:						
Male	60.1	70.5	37.4	58.3	49.0	74.2
Female	39.2	29.4	62.5	41.5	50.6	25.7
Age:						
Under 19	13.2	12.9	9.5	16.7	81.8	75.8
19-21	26.7	23.3	15.1	28.5	12.8	20.5
22-34	39.8	41.2	51.7	39.0	2.2	—
35-44	11.8	12.3	17.0	9.2	0.6	—
Over 44	8.4	11.1	6.6	6.5	2.4	—
Mean age		28.2	28.6	25.8	18.5	17.4

TABLE V-A 2. *Manpower Program Statistics (continued)*

Characteristics	MDTA Institutional	MDTA OJT	WIN	CEP	NYC Out-of-School	Job Corps
Education:						
Less than 9 years	5.6	7.1	11.5	8.5	10.5	11.0
8-10 years	31.8	29.8	38.9	34.7	68.9	60.5
11-12 years	55.8	55.0	43.6	52.0	18.5	15.0
More than 12 years	6.0	6.6	4.5	3.6	0.2	—
Mean years	10.8	10.7	10.0	10.4	9.2	9.1
Marital status:						
Single	45.2	39.2	24.2	51.1	82.2	86.6
Married	37.0	50.4	43.3	32.9	12.0	0.9
Divorced	1.9	1.5	1.4	1.6	0.7	1.3
Widowed	15.6	8.5	30.6	13.7	3.8	—
Trainee annual income:						
Less than $1,001	22.1	17.6	19.7	28.6	1.2	n.a.
1,001-3,000	31.1	30.5	20.6	35.4	0.6	n.a.
3,001-5,000	13.1	18.9	7.4	6.9	—	n.a.
5,001-7,000	4.0	7.8	1.8	0.9	—	n.a.
More than 7,000	2.5	7.3	0.8	0.4	—	n.a.
Mean annual income	$2,423.54	$3,334.87	$1,988.10	$1,691.94	$1,392.47	n.a.
Annual family income:						
Less than $1,001	10.0	6.9	11.3	13.3	20.0	2.6
1,001-3,000	29.5	25.3	43.2	36.9	36.6	19.6
3,001-5,000	18.6	21.1	23.3	16.7	32.0	24.0
5,001-7,000	8.0	11.6	5.6	3.4	2.2	7.9
More than 7,000	8.3	18.7	2.1	1.0	0.2	2.6
Mean family income	$3,743.55	$4,808.30	$2,848.88	$2,548.65	$2,672.71	$3,815.73
Pre-training labor force status:[b]						
Employed	5.7	17.5	0.9	1.5	2.6	1.2
Underemployed	13.9	16.0	5.2	4.6	0.9	5.6
Unemployed	72.7	61.8	82.0	89.9	90.0	74.4
School	0.7	0.8	2.0	0.6	0.2	7.1
Not in labor force	5.6	2.1	8.4	1.0	0.8	—

TABLE V-A 2. *Manpower Program Statistics (continued)*

Characteristics	MDTA Institutional	MDTA OJT	WIN	CEP	NYC Out-of-School	Job Corps
Weeks unemployed pre-training last year:						
Less than 10	13.7	23.3	7.3	14.8	14.0	12.7
11-25	21.8	21.6	16.1	22.1	10.8	8.7
More than 26	37.6	26.9	65.5	48.6	13.3	50.8
Mean	27.4	21.8	38.0	29.8	24.0	38.3
Weeks unemployed pre-training 'current spell:'						
Less than 10	28.3	29.6	13.1	30.9	4.3	12.7
11-25	19.5	13.5	16.7	19.3	3.9	8.7
More than 26	24.3	14.8	49.1	30.8	6.6	50.8
Mean	21.6	17.2	37.6	23.2	28.1	66.6
Years pre-training employment:						
Less than 1	13.1	18.1	25.1	25.0	42.2	n.a.
1-2	30.8	21.2	18.2	27.6	0.7	n.a.
3-9	35.8	33.5	32.4	29.3	0.2	n.a.
More than 9	18.3	24.1	19.6	13.6	—	n.a.
Pre-training hourly wage:						
Less than $1.50	19.0	14.2	23.4	17.5	30.6	19.8
1.50-2.00	33.0	32.8	28.3	38.8	19.2	17.2
2.01-2.50	13.2	14.0	10.9	12.9	2.2	1.9
2.51-3.50	12.2	13.5	11.1	10.0	1.1	0.7
More than 3.50	5.2	10.3	5.6	2.9	0.3	0.8
Mean pre-training wage	$2.07	$2.39	$2.03	$1.96	$1.49	$1.63
Post-training hourly wage:						
Less than $1.50	0.5	0.2	0.5	0.4	—	4.6
1.50-2.00	5.1	4.0	4.0	10.6	—	16.2
2.01-2.50	3.7	3.4	2.9	5.7	—	3.9
2.51-3.50	3.7	3.4	2.6	4.1	—	2.4
More than 3.50	1.6	2.7	1.0	1.2	—	0.8
Unreported	85.0	86.0	89.0	78.0	100.0	72.0
Mean post-training wage	$2.49	$2.91	$2.42	$2.25	$2.64	$1.92

TABLE V - A 2. *Manpower Program Statistics (continued)*

Characteristics	MDTA Institutional	MDTA OJT	WIN	CEP	NYC Out-of-School	Job Corps
Post-training employment status:						
Employed	17.0	15.0	12.1	23.8	0.2	26.1
Not employed or seeking	3.6	1.4	—	—	—	13.2
Armed forces	0.3	0.1	0.1	0.2	—	2.6
Looking for work	5.0	1.9	—	—	—	2.9
Unreported	74.0	81.0	87.6	76.0	99.8	55.0
Post-training hours worked weekly:						
Less than 15	0.1	—	—	—	—	0.1
15-34	0.6	0.4	—	—	—	2.4
35-40	6.9	6.7	—	—	—	22.8
More than 40	1.2	1.5	—	—	—	2.5
Unreported	91.1	91.0	100.0	100.0	100.0	72.0
Length of time in program: [c]						
Less than 3 months	16.0	21.2	5.4	15.3	16.6	5.8
3 months	6.8	7.9	3.7	6.2	6.8	3.0
4-5 months	12.8	10.6	8.2	10.3	11.4	5.1
6-12 months	25.0	15.6	25.3	17.6	24.3	11.7
13-18 months	5.1	4.6	11.7	5.1	8.3	3.6
More than 18 months	2.2	1.9	9.1	2.1	4.6	1.3
Mean weeks	6.5	5.5	10.6	6.3	7.2	7.3
Nature of termination:						
Completed	48.0	38.7	12.4	24.4	11.7	19.9
Dropped	11.7	11.4	25.7	18.3	24.3	67.1
Transferred	2.6	—	—	0.8	—	—
Military:						
Veteran	22.9	23.7	10.7	13.1	1.3	1.0
Rejectee	3.8	5.0	2.6	3.6	1.4	12.6
Other	68.4	64.8	75.6	67.3	87.0	9.8

TABLE V-A 2. *Manpower Program Statistics (continued)*

Characteristics	MDTA Institutional	MDTA OJT	WIN	CEP	NYC Out-of-School	Job Corps
Head of family:						
Yes	58.3	59.1	85.7	57.4	7.7	n.a.
No	41.0	40.3	13.8	41.7	90.7	n.a.
Number in family:						
Less than 5	72.4	76.3	72.6	74.0	44.0	38.7
5-10	13.2	14.6	21.6	17.2	37.8	40.6
More than 10	1.2	1.0	1.7	1.0	8.2	6.6
Unemployment insurance:[c]						
Yes	9.9	6.6	2.4	3.5	0.2	n.a.
No	88.6	90.8	95.4	93.1	70.2	n.a.
Poverty:						
Yes	55.8	43.9	90.5	90.9	94.6	n.a.
No	31.9	48.9	6.3	3.3	0.2	n.a.
Disadvantaged:						
Yes	53.8	48.5	90.2	95.2	31.5	n.a.
No	34.7	48.2	8.7	2.5	46.2	n.a.
Public assistance:						
Yes	14.3	5.4	98.1	13.7	32.4	30.4
No	85.0	93.1	1.6	85.4	65.6	56.0
Rural-urban:						
Urban	70.8	39.5	52.3	39.7	3.2	74.5
Rural	25.9	16.7	7.3	10.9	2.4	14.1
Total	100.0	100.0	100.0	100.0	100.0	100.0
Total program trainees	435,975	141,186	308,060	225,828	158,472	184,793

Source: Manpower Administration, Office of Administration and Management.

Note: Percents are calculated by using the total number of trainees for the program but may not add to 100.0 due to unreported data for certain characteristics.

[a] "Other category" includes Manpower classifications of American Indian, Oriental, and other.
[b] Family farm worker classification is omitted due to negligible percent.
[c] Computation of length of time in the program is based on the enrollment date and the termination date.
[d] Exhaustee classification is recoded to "no."

CHAPTER VI

Summary and Conclusions

For more than a decade, the U.S. Department of Labor has supported a program of research designed in part to evaluate the impact of manpower programs. The research effort, authorized by the Manpower Development and Training Act of 1962, as amended, and the Economic Opportunity Act of 1964, as amended, produced a large body of information pertaining to the planning, operation, and effectiveness of manpower programs; however, this research has not produced a consensus on how well manpower programs have achieved their stated objectives, or whether the programs accomplished any worthwhile objectives at all. Some of the confusion rests on the failure of legislators and program administrators to define objectives clearly. Much of it rests on the failure of investigators to define clearly the scope of inquiry and to ask the right questions when attempting to judge the significance of manpower research. Very often conclusions have been drawn from incomplete data or the misinterpretation of research results.

OBJECTIVES OF THE STUDY

This study was designed to focus on the impact of manpower training programs on minorities by race and sex, as revealed in evaluative studies sponsored by the Department of Labor. The study is a comparative examination of whether manpower training programs have been more effective for minorities and women than for the majority population. The study may be useful as a source of base line data and information against which future changes in the status of minority and female manpower program participants can be measured.

Research Design

The research objectives were approached by examining 252 evaluative studies of manpower programs conducted by investigators within and under contract to the Office of Research and Evaluation of the Manpower Administration. Data were obtained on thirteen separate manpower programs which comprised the core of the nation's active manpower training effort under the Manpower Development and Training Act of 1962, as amended, and the Economic Opportunity Act of 1964, as amended. The study focused primarily on research and evaluation studies and did not include the results of program assessments prepared for the evaluation of experimental and demonstration projects. Moreover, the study was designed to identify and to document the impact of manpower programs on their participants. No attempt was made to measure the cost of training or to assess the effectiveness of training activities in relation to their costs and benefits.

The evaluative studies varied widely in scope, time of enrollee observation, and methodological approach to the evaluative process. In most cases, the studies were little more than descriptive analyses of program operations and enrollment characteristics, with little or no useful information on the post-training labor market experience of enrollees. Evaluative studies containing information on the post-training experiences of participants in the job development and employability development programs are virtually nonexistent. The paucity of useful evaluations of such programs greatly reduces the information concerning program impact on minorities since they were heavily concentrated in the job and employability development programs.

Less than one of every four studies provided post-training data on minorities and women, and slightly less than one of every ten used a control group to compare the post-training experience of program participants with comparable individuals who did not receive manpower training services. In almost every case in which a control group was used, there were valid reasons to question the comparability of the controls and the treatment group. The inadequacy of the selection of control groups was serious enough to cast doubt on the major conclusions of program impact reported in some studies. In short, although there is a large number of studies available for review, few are very useful as a reliable base of information from which to draw firm conclusions regarding the economic impact of manpower programs in general, and the impact on minorities and women in particular.

In addition to the review of evaluative studies, the investigators also examined many background materials on the planning, development, and operation of manpower programs, and on the state of the art in the methodology of program evaluation. Data on manpower program participants from 1969 through 1972 were obtained from records assembled in the Manpower Administration management information system. These data were reviewed and analyzed to determine whether the program operating statistics represent a source of information consistent with the evaluative studies. Finally, an *ad hoc* survey was conducted among a sample of program administrators whom the investigators had reason to believe had unpublished information on the noneconomic impact of training activities. The information available from the survey was more limited than expected, but did provide additional support for some of the observations obtained from the review of the evaluative studies.

SUMMARY OF FINDINGS

As might be expected from a study of the size undertaken here, the research results are numerous and difficult to synthesize without a major cost in clarity, specificity, and objectivity. Careful judgment must be applied in selecting the most representative results of the investigation and, in the process, much important detail will be left out and many necessary qualifications will not receive the emphasis they deserve. The following summary of findings represents an attempt to present the highlights of the investigatory results with the hope that the reader will carefully examine the main chapters of the study for further elaboration, explanation, and understanding.

Typology of Manpower Programs

The categorical manpower programs developed during the 1960's resemble a mosaic of goals, organization structures, and enrollee characteristics. Yet, an examination of the programs will reveal some similarities in the functional mix of manpower services among broad groups of programs. When viewed from the perspective of the service mix, the programs may be classified in the following categories: skill training, employability development, job development, and work experience. Although this classification scheme may not be meaningful for all discussions of manpower training programs, it is quite useful for purposes of this study, primarily because the value of economic benefits generated by the different programs declines as the program moves from a relative emphasis on skill training toward an emphasis on work experience. In addition, a classification scheme focusing on variations among programs in their manpower service mix would seem highly consistent with the information needs of manpower planners under the Comprehensive Employment and Training Act of 1973. Although the findings of this study are not complete with respect to program impact on the state and local level, there is sufficient evidence to suggest the direction, if not the magnitude, of program impact associated with programs emphasizing one package of services as compared with another.

Of course, the declining impact of programs on economic benefits as one moves from skill training to work experience programs may be a function of enrollee characteristics, program objectives, or other factors that have little to do with the mix of services offered. Thus, although the results of this study suggest a relatively greater economic impact of skill training compared to other types of programs, it would be incorrect to conclude that skill training is the *sine qua non* for successful manpower programs developed for all types of enrollees.

Minority and Female Participation

Evidence contained in this study confirms the conclusion that minorities and women were very prominent among participants in manpower training programs. In all programs combined, and for fiscal years 1965 through 1971, minorities accounted for about 51 percent, and women for 43.4 percent of all enrollees. An examination of the enrollment data shows that blacks represented by far the bulk of all minorities in manpower programs, and although the aggregate data are less precise on the sex distribution of the racial groups, a review of individual program enrollment data supports the conclusion that black women were among the major recipients of manpower services.

Although the aggregate enrollment data suggest that about one-half of all enrollees were minorities, and two of every five were women, these proportions varied significantly across individual programs. The minorities, and especially blacks, were heavily concentrated in CEP, OIC, JOBS, and the Job Corps. More than 60 percent of the enrollees in each of these programs were black. Minorities also were the exclusive participants in the Apprenticeship Outreach Program which was designed specifically to increase the minority presence in apprenticeable trades. There was substantial participation of minorities in the Neighborhood Youth Corps also, but as a proportion of all enrollees, minorities were less prominent in NYC than in the programs identified above.

Female manpower participants were most prominent in WIN, Public Service Careers, and OIC. As with minorities, females were also found in large numbers in NYC and CEP, although they represented less than one-half of all enrollees in both programs. It is most important to note that minorities and women were disproportionately concentrated in programs, which according to the classification scheme identified above, were limited in their emphasis on skill training.

Economic Impact

The impact of manpower programs has been most pronounced in those programs which have focused on skill training and job development, and it has been least significant in those programs which have been confined to pre-vocational training or work experience—the very programs which have served the highest concentrations of youth, minorities, and women.

Evidence obtained from an analysis of program operating statistics shows that, on the average, blacks earned less than whites, and women less than men, when post-training hourly wages are considered. On the other hand, both blacks and women experienced larger gains in hourly earnings over their pre-training level than white males, with the largest relative gain recorded by black women participants in CEP and in the WIN and Job Corps programs. The gains among black women, however, still left them with the lowest post-training earnings among the four race/ sex groups in these programs.

The limited data, which are available in the evaluative studies on economic impact by race or sex, generally indicate that manpower programs have had a limited, but positive, effect in breaking down the labor market barriers confronting minorities and women. Further, those data suggest that women have gained significantly from manpower training, and also offer encouragement regarding the gains of minorities. Women have experienced larger gains than their male counterparts in a number of programs, particularly those which had the more significant overall impact on participant earnings. Minorities, on the other hand, do appear to have experienced earnings gains of varying comparability to those of their nonminority counterparts in a similarly substantial number or favorable range of programs.

The pattern of absolute and relative economic gains of female participants in various manpower programs indicates that they have been the beneficiaries of relatively high returns to skill training. The most dramatic evidence of such returns is to be found in the net earnings and wage rate gains of women in MDTA training programs. Supporting evidence can be found in the superior wage rate gains of female participants in other programs with some skill training components—most notably OIC and, to a lesser extent, WIN and Job Corps. The key to these returns, however, lies not entirely in the intrinsic value of skill training but in the fact of high and rising demand in those fields in which most women were trained—the clerical and health-service fields. In this respect, it must be noted that low rates of labor force participation among female trainees, particularly among WIN trainees, represent and are likely to continue to represent a major constraint on the overall impact of skill training.

The pattern of absolute and relative economic gains of minority group participants indicates that they have benefited most from job development programs such as JOBS and AOP. In fact, the one program in which minorities, but not women of either race, were concentrated and which had a high potential for generating post-program economic gains was the Apprenticeship Outreach Program. If there is one conclusion that may be drawn clearly from the vast evidence examined in this study, it is that AOP has been the single most successful manpower program beamed toward minorities, as far as short-term economic benefits are concerned.

The strength of these programs in serving minorities may be traced to their impact on discriminatory hiring standards and practices; this is an interpretation which receives some support in the fact that women, particularly black women, fared quite well in both JOBS and PEP. The major limitation on the impact of these programs rests on their limited scope and sensitivity to changing labor market conditions and shifting programmatic priorities. Even if the direct economic gains of minority (and female) participants in these programs are only transitory, it is not clear that there are no long-run benefits to those participants in terms of enhanced access to and standing in the primary labor market.

The relative weakness of employability development and work experience programs in improving the labor market status of virtually all participants is disappointing, but perhaps inevitable. In large measure, the impact of these programs is constrained not only by the weakness of program services in relation to the needs and problems of the old, the young, and the severely disadvantaged, but also by the greater strength of the labor market barriers confronting minorities and women. Thus, it may be unfair or unrealistic to judge such programs on the basis of their short-run economic impact alone and more appropriate to view them as long-run investments in social and human capital.

Many of the gains in earnings among minorities and women are attributable to the higher frequency of employment, rather than higher hourly wage rates earned during the post-training period. The relative importance of employment gains in explaining the earnings gains of manpower program participants has potential implications for the stability and duration of the economic benefits of training. Specifically, to the extent that the employment affect is dominant, the long-run gains from training will be heavily dependent on the quality of the jobs in which participants are placed, in terms of vulnerability to changing economic conditions, transferability of experience and skills acquired on the job, and opportunity for advancement. There is little detailed data on this dimension of the post-program labor market experience of participants, but the information which is available does not suggest that substantial percents were placed in areas of growing demand continued with substantial skill requirements or training content, or in positions with real potential for advancement.

Noneconomic Impact

Noneconomic benefits may be among the most important effects of manpower programs. Unfortunately, because few investigators included the search for noneconomic benefits in their evaluative research designs, the available data on the noneconomic effects of training programs are exceedingly limited.

The paucity of data on noneconomic effects may be attributed in part to the failure of program administrators to keep a record of the distribution of supportive services during the training process. In addition, the limited incidence of psychological testing prior to and after training has greatly reduced the body of evidence that might have been available to measure the changes in attitudes, motivation, and job satisfaction that are normally considered indexes of noneconomic effects. This study represents probably the most exhaustive search for information on noneconomic benefits yet undertaken by manpower researchers under contract to assess the impact of manpower programs. The results of the effort may be measured by the limited evidence gleaned from the numerous studies reviewed and from a survey conducted among a selected group of manpower administrators. The conclusion that must be drawn on the basis of the evidence is that, although manpower programs have undoubtedly generated benefits to trainees in noneconomic well-being, the magnitude and incidence of such changes are virtually impossible to measure on the basis of manpower research currently available.

Summary of Operating Statistics

An examination and analysis of the OFMIS data covering 1,454,314 enrollees in manpower programs in fiscal years 1969 through 1972 yield results in short-term economic gains similar to those discovered in the review of the evaluative literature. Although the order of magnitude and direction of change displayed in the operating statistics is generally consistent with the other findings, it would be unreasonable to suggest that the OFMIS files might serve as a source of data useful for measuring the impact of manpower programs. The operating data cannot be used for this purpose mainly because they are incomplete in reporting economic data, and they do not provide a comparison group against which the gains of manpower participants might be measured. Some preliminary work has been done with Social Security records, but the results have contradicted the assessment of economic gains achieved by participants in such disparate programs as MDTA and the Job Corps. The conclusion that emerges from this evidence is that much additional work remains to be done in designing a management information system supported by the Manpower Administration and capable of generating the type of data required to measure the impact of training programs on their participants.

SUGGESTIONS FOR FUTURE RESEARCH

On the basis of the evidence contained in this study, several comments can be made regarding future research on manpower program evaluation.

First, in the assessment of program impact on individual participants, much more attention should be devoted to the noneconomic benefits of training. This is especially important in measuring the effectiveness of manpower training for minorities since the limited job mobility and high unemployment of such groups are attributable not only to inadequate job skills, but also to personal attitudes, deficient health care, incomplete societal acculturation, and many personal environmental conditions which limit the range of opportunity for full participation in the labor market. If minority group status can be improved by participation in work and training programs, the changes in noneconomic conditions, such as work attitudes, health care, and physical environment, are likely to represent a major component in the overall advancement of the group. Such program effects should be identified and measured by research investigators more systematically than is the current practice.

Second, future research on impact evaluation might be more valuable to program planners and administrators if greater attention were devoted to the link between specific combinations of manpower services and observed economic and noneconomic outcomes. Despite the large volume of evaluative research reviewed for this study, there is little evidence to suggest how alternative combinations of services affect the post-training experiences of program participants. In the discussion above, this question was approached very broadly by attempting to group together programs whose manpower service mixes were similar. Such a procedure, however, is not very satisfactory for purposes of program planning because the variation in the content and quality of manpower services within specific categorical programs tends to be very wide. As manpower policy moves toward greater decentralization under the Comprehensive Employment and Training Act of 1973[1], one of the major tasks confronting program evaluators will be to determine which kinds of services "work" best in achieving predetermined goals of increased earnings and employment for the disadvantaged unemployed.

A third consideration is that the difficulty of reconciling the results of research conducted by separate investigators suggests the need for clearer standards for evaluative research. Research studies on the impact of manpower programs almost invariably focus on different labor markets, population target groups, and time periods. More significantly, the studies often differ sharply in their definition and methodology for measuring program outcomes. As a result, instead of adding to the cumulative storehouse of knowledge regarding the effectiveness of work and training programs, the studies provide only isolated evidence of program outcomes observed among a small sample of participants who are likely to be unrepresentative of any larger group.

1. Public Law 93-203, 93rd Congress, 5.1559, December 28, 1973.

The move toward greater comparability in research results can be stimulated mainly by research sponsors, such as the research funding offices of the U.S. Department of Labor, Manpower Administration, and the National Science Foundation. Of course, one cost of greater comparability in research will be a reduction in the almost unlimited flexibility currently available to investigators to design research projects according to their personal preferences. This cost would probably be small in relation to the benefits gained in planning and developing more effective manpower programs.

The manpower research community has enjoyed a decade of support under the Manpower Development and Training Act of 1962. During that time, major developments were achieved in the design and use of new analytical concepts and tools applied to the impact evaluation of social action programs. In the next decade, more emphasis should be placed on applying the most useful tools of analysis more uniformly in research on human resource policy, and at the same time progress should be made toward developing even better tools of analysis. Finally, the difficulties associated with conducting evaluative research might be mitigated substantially by including evaluative research planning in the program development process. The evaluative research reviewed for this study revealed the unfortunate consequences associated with investigators attempting to reconstruct data in the field while conducting impact evaluations. The lack of systematically collected follow-up data presents a major barrier to the process of evaluation and will continue to limit the value of program impact assessment if measures are not taken to modify current practices in record-keeping in manpower service delivery agencies.

This problem may be alleviated somewhat by current plans to develop a Continuous Manpower Participant Survey as part of the evaluative effort undertaken in response to CETA. The results of this study strongly support the need for such time series or longitudinal kind of data on participant earnings and employment status. If the collection of such information can be incorporated in the early planning for the implementation of CETA, perhaps future evaluators will have a far more reliable data base on which to make judgments regarding the impact of manpower programs on the post-training status of enrollees.

Part Two

INDIVIDUAL PROGRAM ANALYSES

CHAPTER VII

Manpower Development and Training Act

by
Charles R. Perry

The Manpower Development and Training Act of 1962 is the longest living legislative expression of the "active manpower policy" which captivated society throughout much of the 1960's. The longevity of the Act is in no small measure attributable to the adaptability of MDTA training programs to changing economic conditions and political priorities. Throughout their ten-year history, however, MDTA training programs have been characterized by relatively conservative labor market oriented goals in comparison with some of the newer manpower programs which have tended to focus on general social and economic uplift, as well as on enhanced employability.

The scope and structure of the MDTA training effort ensures a high degree of diversity and variability in actual training opportunities and services. In general, MDTA programs have been operated under a wide range of social and economic conditions on both a cross-sectional and a longitudinal basis. The administrative structure for MDTA programs was designed to accommodate such variations in basic social and economic conditions and, perhaps incidentally, to provide latitude for the play of shifting political and institutional forces. As a result, such variables as nature, scope, location, and timing of training opportunities and services have been determined as much by short-run expendiency as by long-run grand administrative design.

Program History

The roots of the Manpower Development and Training Act can be traced to the "great automation scare" of the late 1950's and to the related concern over the plight of the displaced worker.[1]

MDTA represented a merger of the established concern for the displaced worker with the emerging consensus that there were as many vacant jobs as unemployed persons, the problem being one of "square pegs and round holes." This automation-structuralist diagnosis of the unemployment problem was clearly reflected in the preamble to the Act which found: (1) there is a demand for trained personnel; (2) there is a

1. An excellent account of the MDTA program history is found in Garth L. Mangum, *MDTA: Foundation of Federal Manpower Policy* (Baltimore: Johns Hopkins Press, 1968), pp. 9-42.

shortage of workers even during periods of high unemployment; and (3) it is in the national interest to identify and train workers for these openings. This rather modest philosophical underpinning was undoubtedly dictated in part by the need to secure acceptance of a large-scale government venture into the manpower training field; it would also account for the fact that the program was clearly focused on adult workers with long labor force attachment.

By the time MDTA became operational in late 1962, it had been overtaken by economic developments and soon thereafter underwent its first major reorientation—a shift in program focus from older established workers to youthful members of the labor force. The impetus for this change came from two sources: (1) a decline in overall employment rates and a sharp drop in the rates for married men at the same time that youth unemployment rates remained disturbingly high; and (2) a late 1962 report of the National Commission on Technology, Automation and Economic Progress which played down the threat of technological unemployment. The result of these economic and political developments was a set of amendments to MDTA in 1963 which gave greater priority to youth through expanded occupational training opportunities, liberalized eligibility standards, and training allowances, and made provision for prevocational training as part of MDTA programs.

Between 1963 and 1966, MDTA programs underwent a second major reorientation in response to shifting political and social priorities and changing pressures from the supply side of the labor market. This time the reorientation was designed to make MDTA programs more accessible to minorities and to the disadvantaged. These changes were presaged by passage of the Civil Rights Act and the Economic Opportunity Act and reflected in liberalizing amendments to MDTA in 1965 and 1966. The process was completed in 1966 when, by administrative action, a distinction was made between training for shortage occupations and training tailored to the needs of the disadvantaged. Two-thirds of available training resources were committed to the latter endeavor.

The 1966 program reorientation also involved a shift in emphasis from institutional to on-the-job training with the establishment of the goal to place 50 percent of all MDTA trainees in OJT. This shift in emphasis exerted pressure on the administrative machinery for MDTA-OJT programs to which it could not respond. The responsibility for MDTA-OJT programs had been given to the Bureau of Apprenticeship and Training on the assumption that its long-standing contacts with employers and unions would give it an advantage in negotiating contracts for MDTA-OJT opportunities. In fact, the Bureau had neither the staff nor the inclination to justify this assumption. It was even less enthusiastic and effective in placing minority or disadvantaged individuals in OJT slots, because it was unwilling to strain long-standing relationships with employers and unions who were reluctant to take on "less desirable" workers, particularly in the face of loose labor market conditions and minimal allowances for training costs. This problem had been recognized as early as 1964 and had led to the negotiation of national contracts for OJT slots as a supplement to and substitute for local agreements, but could no longer be ignored or circumvented after the 1966 program reorientation. The result was a series of administrative changes and experiments during 1967 which culminated in the announcement of the NAB-JOBS program and the termination of the MDTA-OJT program except for national contracts. Finally, MDTA-OJT programs were formally merged with the JOBS program in the creation of the JOBS-Optional program in 1971.

PROGRAM SCOPE AND OPERATION

A total of almost 1.9 million persons have been enrolled in basic MDTA programs over the first ten years of their existence (fiscal year 1963 through fiscal year 1972). MDTA institutional training accounted for slightly more than two-thirds of total enrollments and MDTA on-the-job training for just under one-third. In recent years, institutional training has served between 130,000 and 150,000 enrollees per year and on-the-job training between 80,000 and 100,000 per year.

Overall, MDTA training programs, and particularly OJT programs, have served a population composed primarily of males, whites, and high school graduates. Women accounted for 41.6 percent of total enrollment in institutional programs between fiscal year 1963 and fiscal year 1972 and only 28.6 percent of total enrollment in OJT programs over the same period. The comparable figures for blacks and other minorities are 39.5 percent and 28 percent, respectively. Almost 50 percent (48.1) of all institutional enrollees had twelve or more years of schooling as did 53.4 percent of all OJT enrollees over the ten-year period.

An analysis of demographic data on enrollees by fiscal year over the ten-year period reveals the expected increases in percentages of total enrollments in both programs accounted for by women, minorities, and individuals with less than twelve years of schooling during the latter part of the 1960's (Table 1). However, the data also show that this trend did not persist and, indeed, was reversed after 1969. This fluctuation is consistent with the general pattern of program orientation over the period, but also conforms closely to changes in basic labor market conditions and strongly suggests the existence of "creaming" in referral and selection of trainees when labor market conditions permit.

Meaningful data on occupations for which training was conducted are not available for the entire ten-year history of MDTA. Some data, however, are available for the early years of the program and for fiscal years

TABLE VII-1. *MDTA*
Percent Distribution of Enrollee Characteristics
Fiscal Years 1963-1972

Characteristics	Total	1963	1964	1965	1966	1967	1968	1969	1970	1971	1972
Sex:											
Male											
Institutional	58.8	63.8	59.7	60.9	58.3	56.8	55.4	55.6	59.4	58.5	63.2
OJT	71.4	80.8	70.9	71.9	72.0	67.0	68.4	65.1	65.9	74.3	77.5
Female											
Institutional	41.2	36.2	40.3	39.1	41.7	43.2	44.6	44.4	40.6	41.5	36.8
OJT	28.6	19.2	29.1	28.1	28.0	33.0	31.6	34.9	34.1	25.7	22.5
Age:											
Under 22											
Institutional	38.0	25.4	35.3	42.6	38.1	40.0	38.5	37.5	37.1	39.9	37.9
OJT	34.6	31.1	27.6	38.5	39.6	34.8	35.8	36.1	35.1	34.8	32.2
22-44											
Institutional	52.0	64.2	53.9	47.3	50.9	49.0	50.7	52.2	54.2	51.6	54.4
OJT	55.5	59.1	63.6	51.0	50.8	55.2	53.6	53.8	54.0	55.2	59.0
45 and over											
Institutional	10.0	10.4	10.8	10.1	11.0	11.0	10.8	10.3	8.8	8.5	7.7
OJT	9.9	9.8	8.8	10.5	9.6	10.0	10.6	10.1	11.0	10.0	8.8
Race:											
White											
Institutional	60.5	76.5	69.9	67.7	62.5	59.1	50.8	55.9	59.2	55.6	61.2
OJT	72.0	83.0	76.2	77.1	76.2	73.1	64.2	61.1	66.8	68.7	73.4

TABLE VII-1 *continued*

Characteristics	Total	1963	1964	1965	1966	1967	1968	1969	1970	1971	1972
Negro											
Institutional	35.9	21.4	28.3	30.1	35.2	38.0	45.4	39.7	36.0	39.3	33.1
OJT	25.1	13.1	22.9	20.9	22.1	24.5	33.1	35.4	30.3	26.4	22.7
Other											
Institutional	3.6	2.1	1.8	2.2	2.3	2.9	3.8	4.4	4.8	5.1	5.7
OJT	2.9	3.9	0.9	2.0	1.7	2.4	2.7	3.5	3.0	4.9	3.9
Education:											
8 years or less											
Institutional	15.7	10.7	14.1	18.3	16.3	18.2	19.2	18.8	14.6	12.4	9.7
OJT	14.9	15.6	14.2	14.0	14.2	14.1	15.5	16.5	17.3	15.2	12.4
9-11 years											
Institutional	36.2	30.0	33.3	34.1	35.7	38.9	40.6	38.8	38.1	36.2	32.0
OJT	31.7	28.7	29.0	30.6	28.7	30.7	34.2	35.0	36.5	33.1	30.0
12 years or more											
Institutional	48.1	59.3	52.6	47.6	48.0	42.9	40.2	42.4	47.2	51.4	58.3
OJT	53.4	55.7	56.8	55.4	57.1	55.2	50.3	48.5	46.2	51.7	57.6
Totals:											
Institutional											
(In thousands)	1,284.6	32.0	68.6	145.3	177.5	150.0	140.0	135.0	130.0	155.6	150.6
Percent	100.0	100.0	100.0	100.0	100.0	100.0	100.0	100.0	100.0	100.0	100.0
OJT											
(In thousands)	626.8	2.1	9.0	11.6	58.3	115.0	101.0	85.0	91.0	71.7	82.1
Percent	100.0	100.0	100.0	100.0	100.0	100.0	100.0	100.0	100.0	100.0	100.0

Source: U.S. Department of Labor, *Manpower Report of the President* (Washington, D.C.: Government Printing Office)
1971, Table 7, p. 305;
1972, Table F-5, p. 268;
1973, Table F-5, p. 231 and Table F-8, p. 234.

Note: Percents may not add to 100.0 due to rounding.

1970 through 1972. On the basis of this limited data, it appears that about two-thirds of OJT enrollees and one-third of institutional enrollees were trained for skilled or semiskilled operative positions. Service occupations accounted for between 10 and 15 percent of trainees in both programs. White collar occupations accounted for about 30 percent of all institutional trainees and 10 percent of all OJT trainees. Most training for white collar occupations under both programs was concentrated in two categories—clerical and health services.

Overall, approximately two-thirds of all MDTA enrollees complete training and about three-quarters of those who do complete training have reported being employed at the time of the last post-training follow-up which normally occurs six months after completion of training. As would be expected, completion rates are slightly higher and short-run post-training employment rates significantly higher for OJT than for institutional training. Unfortunately, published data on completion rates and post-training employment rates do not include breakdowns by race or sex.

REVIEW OF EVALUATIVE LITERATURE

There is an ample and highly diverse evaluative literature on MDTA sponsored and MDTA-related training programs, as would be expected given the longevity and breadth of the MDTA training effort. Unfortunately, however, much of this literature is not directly relevant to an assessment of the basic impact of MDTA on the labor force or the labor market; even within the relevant literature, there is a surprising paucity of hard data on the impact of MDTA training programs.

The early studies of federal manpower programs were heavily influenced by pressure to provide evidence to justify the principle of an active manpower policy, but constrained by the novelty of those programs in developing the requisite data. The result was a series of studies, characterized by concern with relatively explicit and concrete indicators of program effectiveness and reliance on the most readily available or accessible sources of data. These constitute the basic literature on the effectiveness of federal programs to "retrain the displaced."

This literature is composed of two distinct types of studies. The first encompasses the early studies of MDTA which, of necessity, tended to be more descriptive than analytical, to be based on data available from or through the program, and to be focused primarily on such variables as enrollee characteristics, attitudes, and immediate post-training employment and wages as indexes of program effectiveness. The second includes the more rigorous empirical studies designed to isolate the impact of training on enrollee earnings and to estimate the social return on the federal investment in manpower training which was made during the mid-1960's. The majority of these early cost-benefit studies were necessarily based on ARA rather than MDTA programs and confined to relatively narrow retraining programs in specific social, cultural, and economic settings which limit their relevance in an overall assessment of MDTA training.

Acceptance of the principle of an active federal role in manpower training brought a basic change in the scope and focus of manpower programs and manpower program evaluation. Within the MDTA framework, these changes were reflected in the 1966 program reorientation which formalized the shift from "retraining the displaced worker" to training the "disadvantaged individual" and in the commitment of programmatic and evaluative resources to innovation and experimentation in the provision of training services. The result was a marked increase in attention to the social impact and implications of existing and experimental service structures and a sharp drop in the quantity and quality of analysis of the impact of basic programs on the economic status and labor market performance of enrollees.

There are three widely disparate sources which can be drawn upon in an assessment of the effectiveness of basic MDTA training programs in serving the disadvantaged in the tight labor markets of the late 1960's. There are a few studies of enrollee earnings based on program data or Social Security records which provide aggregate measures of impact. More detailed information on the source, structure, and probable stability of observed earnings impact can be drawn from the single comprehensive study of basic MDTA programs made in the past five years and from a limited number of the "total impact" studies of manpower programs made over the same period. Finally, inferential information can be drawn from some of the evaluations of experimental and demonstration (E and D) projects, although most are too limited in scope or depth to provide much insight into the actual or probable impact of MDTA programs.

The central focus of most evaluations of basic MDTA training programs has been enrollee employment and earnings. Relatively little attention has been given to the nature and structure of training inputs, either in their own right or as factors influencing the short-run and long-run economic status of trainees. This concentration on short-run economic output is consistent with the relatively conservative goals of the original MDTA training effort and the relatively stringent cost-effectiveness test applied to that effort. However, it does not necessarily provide good insight into the various social, economic, and institutional forces which may have influenced the short-run labor market behavior and performance of trainees or into the probable long-run effects of training on enrollee earnings. Such insight may be crucial to an understanding of the comparative impact of retraining the displaced in a loose labor market context and of training the disadvantaged in a tight labor market, in general, and to an assessment of the relative gains of women and minorities, in particular.

Three types of sources of data have been used in evaluating MDTA training programs—program operating statistics, independent field interviews, and Social Security records. Each of these provides data by race and sex, but most studies have not exploited fully the potential for race-sex cross-classification inherent in the data. Furthermore, each of these types of data has its own advantages and deficiencies; no study has made serious use of more than one type of data, and cross-checking has been confined to the validation of trainee samples. The relative strengths and weaknesses of each of these types of data are worth noting as background to any discussion of research findings.

1. Program operating statistics provide an extensive body of data on program enrollees, but are of questionable reliability and validity, given the low priority attached to data collection and recording at the field level and the lack of complete follow-up data for substantial numbers of trainees; they are confined to simple indexes of labor market status for only limited periods of time both pre- and post-training.
2. Field interview data generally appear to be more reliable and have provided more intensive information on labor market performance before and after training than is available from program statistics; however, these data have been subject to somewhat the same limitations as program data in terms of time span and completeness of follow-up.
3. Social Security data have been utilized to study the earnings of a large body of MDTA trainees over a protracted period of time with relatively little sample attrition, but these data provide no detailed information on employment, wage rates, or occupation and exclude earnings from noncovered employment—an exclusion which may be particularly significant for minorities and women.

Both cross-sectional and longitudinal analysis have been used in evaluations of MDTA training programs. A number of the early studies of MDTA focused primarily or exclusively on the post-training labor market experience of enrollees, either in absolute terms or relative to the experience of dropouts, applicants who did not enroll, or friends of trainees. The early cost-benefit studies and most of the recent evaluations of MDTA programs focus on differences between pre- and post-training labor market experience as the measure of the impact of training. These studies, however, differ significantly in regard to the sophistication of their approach to controlling the influence of nontraining variables in translating observed inter-period differences into changes attributable to training. In this respect, the studies fall into three categories:

1. those which use no formal controls, but rely implicity or explicitly on general labor market conditions and trends as a basis for "discounting" observed pre-/post-training differences;
2. those which trace pre-training labor market experience over a sufficiently long period of time to permit construction of a "trend line" so that trainees can be used as their own controls;
3. those which identify or construct independent comparison groups as a basis for control of nontraining variables.

MDTA training can be expected to have only a marginal impact on trainee labor market behavior and performance, and primary emphasis should be placed on those research findings which are based directly on the measurement of changes between pre- and post-training periods, rather than those based solely on differences in post-training status. In this context, greater weight must be given to those studies which attempt comparison group analysis, because uncontrolled studies cannot adequately distinguish the contribution of training to observed changes or differences in labor market performance. The use of comparison groups mitigates this problem, but only to the extent that the group approximates a true control group. Unfortunately, the preferred approach to control group construction, random assignment, has not been feasible in this area for political reasons; thus, researchers have had to rely on other, less desirable devices.

These same methodological considerations apply to assessment of the impact of MDTA training on minorities and women. However, few studies have attempted to develop separate control groups by race and sex or to compute separate sex or race coefficients for training variables in multivariate regression analyses of earnings changes. Thus, assessment of the relative gains from training for minorities and women must be undertaken primarily on the basis of the gains to whites and males. Such comparisons, however, do not provide a true picture of the impact of training as long as discriminatory barriers exist in the labor market, unless one is willing to assume or assert that MDTA training should eliminate such barriers.

PROGRAM IMPACT

The existing evaluative studies of MDTA institutional and/or on-the-job training generally indicate post-program employment, wage rates, and earnings for trainees, as a group, which compare favorably to their pre-program experience and, in most cases, to the experience of similarly situated individuals who were not exposed to or did not complete training. In general, these benefits have been sufficient to generate favorable benefit-cost ratios ranging from 1.3:1 to 3.5:1, assuming a ten-year service life and a 10 percent discount rate. However, these encouraging benefit-cost ratios must be interpreted with caution because they are heavily dependent on the assumption made regarding the duration of the economic benefits of training. There is at least suggestive evidence that the assumption of a ten-year service life may be overly optimistic.

The cost-benefit studies of early ARA training programs revealed annual economic benefits per trainee ranging between $335 and $735 and benefit-cost ratios of between 4:1 and 6:1, assuming a ten-year service life and a 10 percent discount rate.[2] Studies of MDTA training programs have revealed similar annual benefits ($400-$800) but more moderate benefit-cost ratios (1.3:1-3.5:1) using the same service life and discount rate assumptions.[3] These differences between ARA and MDTA may reflect little more than differences in program scale and context, and thus indicate only that the returns to training are greater in small-scale programs in relatively depressed labor markets where the employment advantage of trainees might be most marked. In this respect, it is significant that virtually all of these studies make reference to the importance of employment gains in the observed economic benefits.

The available cost-benefit studies of MDTA training programs suggest that on-the-job training is far more cost-effective than is institutional training. Two of the five leading cost-benefit studies of MDTA deal explicitly with OJT and both show benefit-cost ratios in excess of 3:1.[4] In contrast, four of the five studies reported benefit-cost ratios for institutional training below 2:1.[5] This difference can be traced primarily to differences in federal training costs which may or may not accurately reflect true differences in the cost of training. Specifically, the costs of on-the-job training will be understated to the extent that private employers absorb a portion of the cost of training above and beyond the amount reflected in training allowances and/or above and beyond the training costs which would have been incurred without the program.

These benefit-cost ratios are encouraging, but highly dependent on the assumption made as to the duration of the economic benefits of training. Specifically, if a five-year rather than a ten-year service life is assumed, the above ratios are reduced by about 40 percent and the cost-effectiveness of MDTA institutional training is open to serious challenge. There

---

2. Einar Hardin, "Benefit-Cost Analyses of Occupational Training Programs: A Comparison of Recent Studies," in Somers and Wood (eds.), *Cost-Benefit Analysis of Manpower Policies* (Kingston, Ontario: Queen's University, 1969), p. 113.

3. Calculated from: Ernst W. Stromsdorfer, *Review and Synthesis of Cost-Effectiveness Studies of Vocational and Technical Education* (Columbus: ERIC Clearing House on Vocational and Technical Education, 1972), pp. 58-59.

4. *Ibid.*

5. *Ibid.*

is little definitive data on the duration of the benefits of training, but there is some suggestive evidence that the assumption of a ten-year service life may be optimistic. One study of time trends in the benefits of retraining found rapid erosion of the post-training employment gains of trainees.[6] A second study of time trends in relative earnings of 1964 MDTA trainees found a similar erosion and indicated about a five-year half life for post-training earnings gains.[7]

The available cost-benefit studies of MDTA training provide little information on the "non-earnings" benefits of training. Many of the studies allude to such benefits, but only two have attempted to specify and quantify them. One study measured the savings in unemployment compensation and welfare assistance associated with training, and consequently reported average savings of $38 per trainee in the year after training.[8] A second study attempted to estimate fiscal benefits in a variety of areas such as welfare, health service, food and housing programs, and crime loss and prevention by ingenious, but highly questionable, means; this study concluded that savings in these areas may have run as high as 15 percent of total federal training costs.[9]

Available cost-benefit studies also provide only limited insight into the relative effectiveness of training by race or sex. Two studies of early ARA training in West Virginia and one study of MDTA training in rural North Carolina show significantly higher benefit-cost ratios for men than women.[10] However, the results of a cost-benefit analysis of early MDTA training courses in Michigan indicated that for short courses (60-200 hours) training was far more cost/effective for women than for men; also indicated by the results were significantly higher benefit-cost ratios for

6. Richard Solie, "Employment Effects of Retraining the Unemployed," *Industrial and Labor Relations Review*, Vol. 21, no. 2 (January 1968), p. 225.

7. David J. Farber, "Changes in the Duration of the Post-Training Period and in Relative Earning Credits of Trainees: The 1965-1969 Experience of MDTA Institutional and OJT Trainees, Class of 1964," unpublished U.S. Department of Labor report, 1971.

8. Einar Hardin and Michael E. Borus, *The Economic Benefits and Costs of Retraining* (Lexington: D.C. Heath, 1971), pp. 76, 90.

9. Allan H. Muir *et al.*, "Cost/Effectiveness Analysis of On-the-Job and Institutional Training Courses," Planning Research Corporation report prepared for Office of Policy, Evaluation and Research, Manpower Administration, U.S. Department of Labor, 1967, pp. 15-21.

10. Glen G. Cain and Ernst W. Stromsdorfer, "An Economic Evaluation of Government Retraining Programs in West Virginia," in Somers (ed.), *Retraining the Unemployed* (Madison: University of Wisconsin, 1968), p. 326; Ernst W. Stromsdorfer, "Determinants of Economic Success in Retraining the Unemployed," *Journal of Human Resources*, Vol. III, no. 2 (Spring 1968), p. 157; and David O. Sewell, *Training the Poor: A Benefit-Cost Analysis of Manpower Programs in the U. S. Anti-Poverty Program* (Kingston, Ontario: Industrial Relations Centre, Queen's University, 1971), p. 85.

TABLE VII-2. *MDTA*
Pre-and Post-Training Annual Earnings of Trainees

Study	Training Type	Training Year(s)	Income		Change
			Pre-	Post-	
Hardin and Borus	INST	1960-1963	—	—	$ 1,524
Muir *et al.*	INST		$ 2,296	$ 3,634	1,338
	OJT		2,652	3,860	1,208
Farber	INST	1964	978	2,306	1,328
	OJT	1964	1,500	3,140	1,640
Prescott and Cooley	INST	1967	1,740	3,357	1,617
	OJT	1967	2,157	4,083	1,926
MDTA Outcomes	INST	1969	—	—	1,876
	OJT	1969	—	—	1,614
Four-City	INST	1969-1970	2,000	3,100	1,100

Sources: Einar Hardin and Michael E. Borus, *The Economic Benefits and Costs of Retraining* (Lexington, Massachusetts: D.C. Heath, 1971), p. 47.

Allan H. Muir *et al.*, "Cost/Effectiveness Analysis of On-the-Job and Institutional Training Courses," Planning Research Corporation report prepared for Office of Policy, Evaluation and Research, Manpower Administration, U.S. Department of Labor, 1967, p. 14.

David J. Farber, "Changes in the Duration of the Post-Training Period and in Relative Earning Credits of Trainees: The 1965-69 Experience of MDTA Institutional and OJT Trainees, Class of 1964," unpublished U.S. Department of Labor report, 1971.

Edward C. Prescott and Thomas F. Cooley, "Evaluating the Impact of MDTA Training Programs on Earnings Under Varying Labor Market Conditions," report prepared for Office of Policy, Evaluation and Research, Manpower Administration, U.S. Department of Labor, 1972, p. 4.

Decision Making Information, "MDTA Outcomes Study," report prepared for the Office of Policy, Evaluation and Research, Manpower Administration, U.S. Department of Labor, 1971, Chapter VII, pp. 7, 10.

Olympus Research Corporation, "The Total Impact of Manpower Programs: A Four-City Case Study," report prepared for Office of Policy, Evaluation and Research, Manpower Administration, U.S. Department of Labor, 1971, Vol. I, pp. 13, 16, 19.

blacks than for whites, with the highest sub-group ratio being for black females.[11]

Earnings

There is a sizable body of data on the earnings of MDTA trainees in the year or years immediately preceding and following training. These data have been drawn from a variety of sources and have been treated in a variety of ways, but do reveal a relatively clear and consistent pattern in regard to gross earnings levels and changes (Table 2). Changes in average annual earnings from pre-training to post-training periods ranged from $1,100 to $1,900 with an average of about $1,500, whereas post-training average annual earnings ranged between $2,300 and $4,100 with an average of almost $3,300.

The data on income levels and changes by race and sex, which are available from existing studies, are less extensive and consistent. The most comprehensive of such data are contained in a Department of Labor study of 1964 MDTA trainees based on a comparison of 1965 Social Security earnings credits with average credits for the 1958-1962 period.[12] This study revealed the expected higher earnings levels of men, whites, and on-the-job trainees both before and after training, and also showed larger absolute gains for men than for women in both institutional and on-the-job training. The study, however, did reveal larger gains for blacks than for whites among all but female institutional trainees, although the differences were small (Table 3). A study of 1967-1968 MDTA graduates also based on Social Security data provides partial confirmation of these findings in reporting larger income gains for men ($1,617) than for women ($1,418) in institutional training, but does not include comparable data by race.[13]

The "MDTA Outcomes Study" of 1969 trainees provides the only other source of data on gross earnings levels and changes by race and sex. This study reveals the same basic pattern of earnings levels by sex, race, and type of training, but also suggests that women experienced larger average income gains than men in institutional training and that whites outgained nonwhites in both on-the-job and institutional train-

11. Hardin and Borus, *op. cit.*, p. 146.

12. Farber, *op. cit.*

13. Edward C. Prescott and Thomas F. Cooley, "Evaluating the Impact of MDTA Training Programs on Earnings Under Varying Labor Market Conditions," report prepared for Office of Policy, Evaluation and Research, Manpower Administration, U.S. Department of Labor, 1972, p. 4.

TABLE VII-3. *MDTA*
Earnings of 1964 Completers by Race, Sex, and Program Pre-and Post-Training

Race and Sex	Pre-Training 1958-1962		Post-Training 1965		Change	
	INST	OJT	INST	OJT	INST	OJT
Males:	$ 1,351	$ 1,956	$ 2,798	$ 3,699	$ 1,447	$ 1,743
White	1,489	2,058	2,934	3,782	1,445	1,724
Negro	944	1,481	2,398	3,308	1,454	1,827
Females:	525	597	1,707	2,023	1,182	1,426
White	595	590	1,816	1,993	1,221	1,403
Negro	399	623	1,512	2,137	1,113	1,514

Source: David J. Farber, "Changes in the Duration of the Post-Training Period and in Relative Earning Credits of Trainees: The 1965-69 Experience of MDTA Institutional and OJT Trainees, Class of 1964," unpublished U.S. Department of Labor report, 1971, Tables 10-13.

ing.[14] The superior earnings gains of women in institutional training, however, appear to arise in large measure from the substantial number of female institutional trainees who were not active participants in the labor market prior to training. Comparisons of either average earnings of those employed before training with average earnings of those employed after training, or average pre- and post-training earnings of those employed before and after training, indicate that men clearly outgain women in both institutional and on-the-job programs. These comparisons also tend to reveal a somewhat more dismal picture of the relative gains of minorities vis-à-vis whites.

The ultimate test of the earnings impact of training rests not on measurement of gross changes in average trainee income, but on assessment of the significance of those changes in relation to incomes gains experienced by similar groups of individuals who were not exposed to training. Fortunately, a number of comparison group studies of MDTA trainees do exist to provide the basis for such an assessment of impact. These studies, as would be expected, provide far more conservative estimates of the overall impact of MDTA training on earnings than are

14. Decision Making Information, "MDTA Outcomes Study," report prepared for Office of Policy, Evaluation and Research, Manpower Administration, U. S. Department of Labor, 1971, Chapter VII, pp. 7, 10.

suggested by simple changes in income, and confirm the superior earnings gains of on-the-job trainees. However, they also suggest far more optimistic conclusions regarding the relative earnings impact of MDTA training for women and minorities.

There are four major studies which provide estimates of the net earnings impact of MDTA training on the basis of data gathered through field interviews. These estimates range from about $200 per year to over $400 per year, but are concentrated at the upper end of that range. Main, in a nationwide study of 1964 and early 1965 institutional trainees, found a training effect of $7.87 per week or $409 per year.[15] Sewell, in a study of 1965 and 1966 institutional and on-the-job trainees in North Carolina, found net earnings effects of $5.70 per week for institutional training and $11.60 per week for on-the-job training, with an overall average equivalent to $433 per year.[16] Similarly, Smith's nationwide study of 1967 institutional trainees reported a net effect of $416 per year.[17] Finally, Hardin and Borus, in a study of early programs in Michigan, found a net effect of training of $251 per year, but also found wide variations in earnings effects by length of course ranging from $976 per year for the shortest courses (60-200 hours) to $136 per year for the longest courses (1,201-1,920 hours).[18] The authors offer no explanation for this phenomenon, which has not been found in other studies.

Three studies have attempted to estimate the net earnings effects of MDTA training based on data obtained from Social Security records. These studies provide a far less consistent and more controversial set of estimates of earnings impact of training. Prescott, in a study of 1968 trainees and a control group of eligible enrollees who chose not to enter training, found positive earnings effects ranging from about $600 per year for institutional training to about $800 per year for on-the-job training.[19] However, two Department of Labor studies utilizing a comparison group drawn from the Social Security Continuous Work History Sample resulted in far less optimistic conclusions. The first of these studies focused on 1964 enrollees and found net effects of only $70 per year for institutional training and $310 per year for on-the-job training.[20]

15. Earl D. Main, *A Nationwide Evaluation of MDTA Institutional Job Training Programs* (Chicago: National Opinion Research Center, University of Chicago, 1966), p. 56.

16. Sewell, *op. cit.*, p. 85

17. Ralph E. Smith, "An Analysis of Efficiency and Equity in Manpower Programs," Ph.D. dissertation, Georgetown University, 1971, p. 85.

18. Hardin and Borus, *op. cit.*, p. 63.

19. Prescott and Cooley, *op. cit.*, p. 5.

20. Farber, *op. cit.*

The second involved 1968 trainees and found substantial negative earnings effects for all groups of institutional trainees and only very slight positive effects for most groups of on-the-job trainees.[21]

The nature of the results of these latter two studies has led to serious questioning of their methodology and of the usefulness of the Continuous Work History Sample as a source of comparison groups for manpower program participants.[22] In this respect, the following possibilities should be noted:

1. The findings of the 1964 study may reflect a high percentage of displaced workers among trainees for whom multi-year pre-training earnings would overstate their true earnings potential without retraining, both in absolute terms and relative to a comparison group.
2. The findings of the 1968 study may reflect a high percentage of disadvantaged individuals among trainees for whom the range of employment opportunities, even after training, would have been more restricted than for low income workers generally.

There are five major studies which provide data on the net earnings effect of MDTA training by sex and race. With few exceptions, the data from these studies indicate that, relative to other similarly situated members of their sex or race not exposed to training, women and minorities experienced greater income gains (or, at least in the case of women, smaller income losses) as a result of training than did their male or white counterparts in MDTA training, with minority women appearing to have been the group most benefited by training (Table 4). The most notable deviation from this pattern appears in Sewell's findings on the gains of female institutional trainees in his primarily black sample, but these findings can be traced to the specific labor market and training program studied.[23]

The duration of any earnings impact of training should be a major factor in assessing the overall effectiveness of manpower programs and may be a crucial factor in assessing relative program impact on women and minorities who face discriminatory barriers in the labor market.

21. David J. Farber, "Highlights: Some Findings From a Follow-up Study of Pre- and Post-Training Earnings Histories of 215,000 Trainees Participating in Two 1964 and Four 1968 Training Programs," unpublished U.S. Department of Labor report, 1971.

22. A statement of methodology is to be found in David J. Farber, "Methods of Calculating Measure Used in Manpower Training Follow-Up Systems"; a critique of this methodology in Herman P. Miller, "Critique of David Farber's Method of Evaluating the Gains in Earnings of MDTA Trainees"; and a reply to this critique in David J. Farber, "A Reply to the Miller Critique of the M.A. Method of Evaluating the Gains in Earnings of MDTA Trainees," all are U. S. Department of Labor unpublished documents.

23. Sewell's results reflect the fact that virtually none of the female institutional trainees in his sample elected to utilize their skills in the labor market. Sewell, *op. cit.*, pp. 72-74.

TABLE VII-4. *MDTA*
Effect of Training on Net Annual Earnings
By Race and Sex

Study	Type of Training	Males		Females	
		White	Nonwhite	White	Nonwhite
Hardin and Borus (60-200 hr. courses)	INST	+557	+1,151	+895	+1,095
Farber (1964)	INST	-48	+129	+132	+211
	OJT	+350	+551	+291	+620
Sewell	INST	—	+429	n.a.	n.a.
	OJT	—	+384	+756	+756
Prescott and Cooley	INST	+719	+587	+527	+624
	OJT	+842	+755	—	—
Farber (1968)	INST	-676	-732	-368	-364
	OJT	+88	+44	+104	+300

Sources: Einar Hardin and Michael E. Borus, *The Economic Benefits and Costs of Retraining* (Lexington: D. C. Heath, 1971), p. 162.

David J. Farber, "Changes in the Duration of the Post-Training Period and in Relative Earning Credits of Trainees: The 1965-69 Experience of MDTA Institutional and OJT Trainees, Class of 1964," unpublished U.S. Department of Labor report, 1971.

David O. Sewell, *Training the Poor: A Benefit-Cost Analysis of Manpower Programs in the U.S. Anti-Poverty Program* (Kingston, Ontario: Industrial Relations Centre, Queen's University, 1971), p. 85.

Edward C. Prescott and Thomas F. Cooley, "Evaluating the Impact of MDTA Training Programs on Earnings Under Varying Labor Market Conditions," mimeographed report prepared for Office of Policy, Evaluation and Research, Manpower Administration, U.S. Department of Labor, 1972, p. 11.

David J. Farber, "Highlights: Some Findings From a Follow-up Study of Pre- and Post-Training Earnings Histories of 215,000 Trainees Participating in Two 1964 and Four 1968 Training Programs," unpublished U.S. Department of Labor study, 1971.

The literature of manpower program evaluation has recognized this fact, but contains little concrete information on the actual duration of training benefits. However, two of the studies of MDTA trainees which utilize Social Security data have extended their analysis of earnings impact beyond the first post-training year and provided data on earnings impact over time by sex and race. In general, these studies suggest a far more rapid deterioration of earnings benefits than has been assumed in most cost-benefit analyses, but do not suggest major changes over time in the relative benefits of women and minorities (Table 5).

Prescott and Cooley, in their study of 1968 trainees, calculated earnings differences between trainees and controls for two post-training years and found that such differences declined between the first and second years for all but white female institutional trainees and white male on-the-job trainees.[24] For institutional trainees the largest declines (over 25 percent) were found among those groups—white males and black females—which had shown the largest first-year net gains. Overall, the pattern of changes and second-year earnings effects suggests that, in the long run, whites may benefit considerably more than blacks, but that women may continue to enjoy net benefits in excess of their male counterparts.

TABLE VII-5. *MDTA*
Effects of Training on Net Annual Earnings Over Time by Sex and Race

Characteristics	1964 Trainees		1968 Trainees	
	1st Year	1st 5 Years	1st Year	1st 2 Years
Institutional:				
Males				
White	-48	-142	+719	+620
Nonwhite	+129	+102	+587	+527
Females				
White	+132	+148	+527	+593
Nonwhite	+211	+247	+624	+545
On-the-job:				
Males				
White	+350	+202	+842	+869
Nonwhite	+551	+472	+755	+718
Females				
White	+291	+170	n.a.	n.a.
Nonwhite	+620	+573	n.a.	n.a.

Sources: David J. Farber, "Changes in the Duration of the Post-Training Period and in Relative Earning Credits of Trainees: The 1965-69 Experience of MDTA Institutional and OJT Trainees, Class of 1964," unpublished U.S. Department of Labor report, 1971, Tables 10-13.

Edward C. Prescott and Thomas F. Cooley, "Evaluating the Impact of MDTA Training Programs on Earnings Under Varying Labor Market Conditions," report prepared for Office of Policy, Evaluation and Research, Manpower Administration, U.S. Department of Labor, 1972, p. 11.

24. Prescott and Cooley, *loc. cit.*

The Department of Labor study of 1964 MDTA graduates also contains data on earnings differences between trainees and controls over a five-year post-training period.[25] These data on average earnings differences over the full period also show considerable erosion of earnings benefits for all but women in institutional training, but the pattern of such erosion generally reinforces the sex/race structure of earnings benefits observed in the first post-training year. Specifically, these data suggest that, in the long run, women benefit more than their male counterparts, particularly in institutional training, and that blacks continue to realize relatively greater earnings benefits than whites.

Wage Rates

The function of skill training, such as that carried out under MDTA, is to enhance or expand the labor market skills of trainees in an effort to increase their employability and productivity. To the extent that the MDTA training effort was successful in the endeavor, it is reasonable to expect that trainees would have commanded a higher wage rate after training than before and that any such change would have exceeded basic wage increases over the training period.

The theoretical relationship between skill training and wage rates is clear, but there are two sets of forces which can be expected to condition the observed wage rate impact of training—the state of the labor market and the character of the trainee group. In a loose labor market, enhanced employability and productivity may serve primarily to enable an individual to compete effectively for available jobs rather than to enable him to command a higher wage rate. This is particularly likely to be the case in highly structured labor markets characterized by downward wage inflexibility. In any labor market, the nature of a trainee group may vary with respect to the relative balance between those who utilize the program for lateral mobility and those for whom the program is designed to foster upward mobility. This distinction has general relevance, but is particularly significant in light of the basic shift in MDTA program emphasis from the displaced to the disadvantaged over the 1960's.

There are numerous reports on and analyses of pre- and post-training wage rates for MDTA enrollees. Virtually all of these, however, are based on the program statistics maintained by the Department of Labor, which are incomplete and subject to criticism for possible systematic exclusion of the least successful trainees. Overall, however, these data on wage rates reveal consistent and sizable pre-/post-training gains ranging from about $0.30 per hour during the early years of the program to almost $0.50 per hour in the late 1960's, but with a marked drop thereafter

25. Farber, "The 1965-69 Experience of MDTA Institutional and OJT Trainees," *op. cit.*

(Table 6). The available data on wage rates also reveal both lower absolute wage levels and lower absolute changes in wage rates for women than for men and for minorities than for whites (Tables 7 and 8).

Few studies explicitly apply control or comparison group methodology to wage rate changes. The studies of early ARA training programs were unable to detect any significant wage rate effect of training, although all found highly significant increases in annual earnings. A review of the findings of the cost-benefit studies of ARA training programs led one author to the following conclusion:

> No previous analysis demonstrates unambiguously that the increase in the earnings of workers which were found to be associated with training were attributable to increases in the hourly wage rates of trainees. On the contrary, the evidence available in these studies seems to indicate that the increases in earnings associated with training were entirely attributable to increases in the employment of workers.[26]

The early evaluations of MDTA institutional training programs reached essentially the same negative conclusion regarding the overall impact of training on wage rates, but did suggest more positive effects for women and/or minorities. In a descriptive study of training programs completed between September 1, 1963, and August 31, 1964, National Analysts found only wage rate changes which "roughly paralleled general increases in wage levels during this period," but did report that Negroes experienced greater gains than other groups.[27] Gurin, in a comparative study of completers and noncompleters in classes ending between October 1964 and October 1966, found no difference between completers and those who left the program in regard to relative standing on wage rate for first post-program job; however, Gurin did report that the findings suggest that training had more impact on the post-program wages of women than of men trainees.[28] Finally, Main concluded in his comparison group study of trainees in courses ending between June 1, 1964, and February 28, 1965:

> The evidence does not indicate that MDTA training generally resulted in higher paying jobs. "Completers" and "controls" reported about the same wages on their last full-time job since training . . . . Among women, however, training is associated with higher wages . . . .[29]

26. Sewell, *op. cit.*, p. 43.

27. National Analysts, "The Effectiveness of the Training Programs Under MDTA," report prepared for Manpower Administration, U.S. Department of Labor, 1965.

28. Gerald Gurin, *A National Attitude Study of Trainees in MDTA Institutional Programs* (Ann Arbor: Survey Research Center, Institute for Social Research, University of Michigan, 1970), p. 222.

29. Main, *op. cit.*, pp. 47-48.

TABLE VII-6. *MDTA*
Median Hourly Rate of Trainees
Pre- and Post-Training

Termination Time Span	Enrollee Wage Rates					
	Institutional			On-the-Job		
	Pre-	Post-	Change	Pre-	Post-	Change
1962-1965	$ 1.44	$ 1.74	$ 0.30	—	—	—
1965-1966	1.44	1.73	.29	—	—	—
1967-1968	1.55	2.04	.49	$ 1.74	$ 2.29	$ 0.55
1969	1.77	2.15	.38	1.82	2.19	.37
1969-1971	—	—	.48	—	—	.36
1971	1.93	2.23	.30	2.13	2.44	.31
1972	2.07	2.25	.18	2.52	2.68	.16

Sources: Garth L. Mangum, *MDTA: Foundation of Federal Manpower Policy* (Baltimore: Johns Hopkins Press, 1968), p. 102.

"The Influence of MDTA Training on Earnings," Manpower Evaluation Report No. 8, Manpower Administration, U.S. Department of Labor, 1970.

"Earnings Mobility of MDTA Graduates," Manpower Evaluation Report No. 7, Manpower Administration, U.S. Department of Labor, 1969.

Decision Making Information, "MDTA Outcomes Study," report prepared for Office of Policy, Evaluation and Research, Manpower Administration, U.S. Department of Labor, 1971, Chapter V, p. 3.

Unpublished study based on program operating statistics for fiscal year 1969, fiscal year 1970, Manpower Administration U.S. Department of Labor.

"Median Earnings of Terminees from the MDTA Institutional and OJT Programs in FY 1971 and FY 1972," unpublished report, Manpower Administration, U.S. Department of Labor, 1972.

TABLE VII-7. *MDTA*
Median Hourly Wage Rates of Trainees
Pre-and Post-Training by Sex

Termination Time Span	Institutional				On-the-Job			
	Pre-	Post-	Change	Percent Change	Pre-	Post-	Change	Percent Change
1963-1965								
Male	n.a.	n.a.	$ 0.38	—	n.a.	n.a.	$ 0.57	—
Female	n.a.	n.a.	.32	—	n.a.	n.a.	.31	—
1965-1966								
Male	$ 1.62	$ 2.06	.44	27.2	n.a.	n.a.	—	—
Female	1.29	1.53	.24	18.6	n.a.	n.a.	—	—
1967-1968								
Male	1.79	2.31	.52	29.0	$ 1.97	$ 2.63	.66	28.2
Female	1.40	1.81	.41	29.0	1.54	1.88	.34	22.1
1969								
Male	2.02	2.47	.45	22.0	2.03	2.44	.42	21.0
Female	1.57	1.95	.38	24.0	1.67	1.98	.31	19.0
1969-1971								
Male	n.a.	n.a.	.44	—	n.a.	n.a.	.37	—
Female	n.a.	n.a.	.49	—	n.a.	n.a.	.35	—
1971								
Male	2.17	2.49	.32	14.7	2.37	2.71	.34	14.3
Female	1.77	2.10	.33	18.6	1.81	2.01	.20	11.0
1972								
Male	2.40	2.68	.28	11.7	3.05	3.21	.16	5.2
Female	1.82	1.97	.15	8.2	1.87	2.15	.28	15.0

TABLE VII-7 *continued*

Sources: Allan H. Muir *et al.*, "Cost/Effectiveness Analysis of On-the-Job and Institutional Training Courses," Planning Research Corporation report prepared for Office of Policy, Evaluation and Research, Manpower Administration, U.S. Department of Labor, 1967, p. 28.

"The Influence of MDTA Training on Earnings," Manpower Evaluation Report No. 8, Manpower Administration, U.S. Department of Labor, 1970.

"Earnings Mobility of MDTA Graduates," Manpower Evaluation Report No. 7, Manpower Administration, U.S. Department of Labor, 1969.

Decision Making Information, "MDTA Outcomes Study," report prepared for Office of Policy, Evaluation and Research, Manpower Administration, U.S. Department of Labor, 1971, Chapter V, pp. 5, 8.

Unpublished study based on program operating statistics for fiscal year 1969, fiscal year 1970, Manpower Administration, U.S. Department of Labor.

U.S. Department of Labor, "Median Earnings of Terminees From the MDTA Institutional and OJT Programs in FY 1971 and FY 1972," unpublished report, Manpower Administration, U.S. Department of Labor, 1972.

TABLE VII-8. *MDTA*
Median Hourly Wage Rates of Trainees
Pre- and Post-Training by Race

Termination Time Span	Institutional				On-the-Job			
	Pre-	Post-	Change	Percent Change	Pre-	Post-	Change	Percent Change
1962-1965								
White	$ 1.48	$ 1.80	$ 0.32	21.6	n.a.	n.a.	n.a.	—
Nonwhite	1.32	1.60	.28	21.2	n.a.	n.a.	n.a.	—
1963-1965								
White	n.a.	n.a.	.32	—	n.a.	n.a.	$ 0.48	—
Nonwhite	n.a.	n.a.	.53	—	n.a.	n.a.	.42	—
1965-1966								
White	1.48	1.81	.33	22.2	n.a.	n.a.	n.a.	—
Nonwhite	1.33	1.59	.26	19.5	n.a.	n.a.	n.a.	—
1969								
White	1.85	2.22	.37	20.0	$ 1.87	$ 2.24	.37	20.0
Negro	1.63	2.02	.39	24.0	1.77	2.11	.34	20.0
1971								
White	1.96	2.27	.31	15.8	2.18	2.53	.35	16.1
Negro	1.87	2.17	.30	16.0	1.96	2.23	.27	13.8
1972								
White	2.15	2.37	.22	10.2	2.72	2.90	.18	6.6
Negro	1.90	2.11	.21	11.1	2.15	2.36	.21	9.8

TABLE VII-8 *continued*

Sources: Garth L. Mangum, *MDTA: Foundation of Federal Manpower Policy* (Baltimore, Maryland: Johns Hopkins Press, 1968), p. 102.

Allan H. Muir *et al.*, "Cost/Effectiveness Analysis of On-the-Job and Institutional Training Courses," Planning Research Corporation report prepared for Office of Policy, Evaluation and Research, Manpower Administration, U.S. Department of Labor, 1967, p. 28.

"The Influence of MDTA Training on Earnings," Manpower Evaluation Report No. 8, Manpower Administration, U.S. Department of Labor, 1970.

Decision Making Information, "MDTA Outcomes Study," report prepared for Office of Policy, Evaluation and Research, Manpower Administration, U.S. Department of Labor, 1971, Chapter V, pp. 5, 8.

"Median Earnings of Terminees From the MDTA Institutional and OJT Programs in FY 1971 and FY 1972," unpublished report, Manpower Administration, U.S. Department of Labor, 1972.

Studies of later MDTA training programs do show positive wage effects. The first such study and the one with the soundest control group methodology was Sewell's study of institutional and on-the-job training programs in North Carolina in which he reported increases in hourly earnings for "completers" vis-à-vis "controls" ranging from about $0.22 for females in on-the-job training to $0.25 for males in both the on-the-job and the institutional programs.[30] In Smith's study of 1967-1968 MDTA graduates nationwide, he concluded that, on the basis of a simulation model, about two-thirds ($0.25 out of $0.36) of observed pre-/post-training difference in trainee average hourly wage rate could be attributed to training.[31] Finally, the Olympus Research Corporation study of the total impact of manpower programs in four cities reached a remarkably similar conclusion for trainees in a variety of programs in late 1969 and early 1970 on the basis of simple extrapolation of aggregate trainee pre-training wage rate experience.[32] Unfortunately, none of these studies provide generalizable data on the relative wage rate impact of training by race and sex.

Employment

The basic goal of MDTA training is to provide enrollees with those skills required to compete successfully for existing employment opportunities, and one fundamental index of program effectiveness is the post-training employment experience of trainees. In this context, it is important to note that the true impact of training can be expected to vary with the state of the labor market and to take somewhat different forms for various enrollee groups. Specifically, the employment advantage of MDTA trainees vis-à-vis nontrainees should be greater in a relatively loose labor market where the potential for displacement is more significant; in addition, the employment impact of training should differ between the "displaced" and the "disadvantaged" in regard to the relative importance of gains in employment stability, as opposed to changes in employment rates.

Four basic variables have been utilized to describe the post-program employment experience of trainees: placement, employment at the time of follow-up, employment stability, and employment in a training-related job. Placement generally is measured in terms of the percentage of enrollees reporting employment at some time during the post-program period

30. Sewell, *op. cit.*, p. 71.

31. Smith, *op. cit.*, p. 84.

32. Olympus Research Corporation, "The Total Impact of Manpower Programs: A Four-City Case Study," report prepared for Office of Policy, Evaluation and Research, Manpower Administration, U.S. Department of Labor, 1971, Vol. I, pp. 5-6.

under consideration (normally about one year) and provides the most favorable index of employment impact. Employment at the time of the interview takes account of any deterioration in the labor market status or labor force attachment of trainees over time and provides a more realistic basis for assessing the extensive impact of training in terms of employment or unemployment rates. Employment stability refers to the percentage of time worked by those reporting employment in the post-program period and provides insight into the quality and/or depth of the employment impact of training. The percentage of trainees who utilize their training in post-program employment provides further insight into the strength of the impact of training.

The available data on these four variables generally suggest that, as a group, those who completed MDTA training did fare reasonably well in terms of their post-training employment experience. Specifically, existing studies tend to reveal the following pattern:

1. between 80 and 90 percent of completers find employment at some point during the year following training;
2. approximately 70 percent of completers are employed at the time of follow-up (six to twelve months after training);
3. about 60 percent of completers find employment in which they believe they utilize skills acquired in training;
4. more than 50 percent of completers are employed at least three-quarters of the time in the post-training period.

These same studies point out significant differences in post-program employment experience which are consistent with the larger pattern of race and sex differences in labor market status and performance. In general, higher percentages of women and minorities report no post-program employment than do males or nonminorities, whereas smaller percentages report employment at the time of the interview or for all or most of the post-program period. In addition, these studies also indicate that, in relation to their counterpart groups, women and minorities are:

1. less likely to have a job lined up prior to completion of training or to find their first post-program job soon after completion of training;
2. more likely to utilize the Employment Service in finding their first post-program job and to utilize their training in that job;
3. more likely to express positive attitudes toward their training experience and its role in enabling them to secure employment.

Few attempts have been made to quantify the impact of training on employment stability, but most studies suggest that it must have been substantial. Mangum compared percentages of trainees working at least 75 percent of the time in the year before and the year after training and found an "apparent 30 percent improvement in employment stability," which he judged "significant, though it is in part attributable to general improvements in economic conditions."[33] Main found systematic differences between completers, dropouts, nonenrollees, and noncontacts in regard to both percentages holding at least one full-time job in the post-training period and percentages employed for all or most of the post-program period. Main estimated the employment impact of exposure to training, in terms of percent of time employed, as 13 to 23 percent for completers and 7 to 19 percent for dropouts.[34] The relatively small net employment effect of completing training (6 percent or one month out of seventeen) is surprising, but other analyses indicate that it may be because of the favorable experience of those who drop out of training specifically to accept employment.[35]

The "MDTA Outcomes Study" provides quite a different picture of the employment effect of training. That study reported no real change in employment stability between pre- and post-program periods for those trainees who worked during both periods, only minor changes in employment stability for the groups of trainees employed in either or both of the periods, but dramatic change in the number or percent of trainees employed as between the two periods. Thus, for institutional trainees, the $1,876 average income gain was composed of the following elements:

1. increased employment rates—$1,035 or 55 percent;
2. increased employment stability—$489 or 25 percent;
3. increased hourly wage rates—$352 or 20 percent.[36]

The overall importance of employment in explaining the earnings gains of MDTA trainees coupled with the structure of the employment effect identified in the "MDTA Outcomes Study" raises questions about whether the program is merely an elaborate placement device. The answer to this question rests on a determination of the extent to which the program enables its trainees to gain access to jobs in industries or occupations, otherwise closed to them, which offer greater and/or more stable earnings in either the short run or the long run. The available data on employment stability provide a basis for limited optimism in regard to the short run, but there is no comparable body of data on the quality of the jobs opened to trainees to permit any judgment on long-run potential.

The limited information on sex and race differences in employment patterns available from these and other studies suggests that women were a primary beneficiary of MDTA training, but offers less encouragement

33. Mangum, *op. cit.*, pp. 82-83.

34. Main, *op. cit.*, p. 87.

35. See particularly, Gurin, *op. cit.*, pp. 23-24.

36. Decision Making Information, *op. cit.*, Chapter 1, p. 13.

about the gains of minorities (Table 9). In all cases where comparative data on the post-program employment experience of completers and noncompleters or nonenrollees eligible for training are available by sex, females completers display greater advantage vis-à-vis female dropouts and nonenrollees than male completers vis-à-vis dropouts or nonenrollees; the same pattern was noted in the test of an earlier study of the program in Newark.[37] The magnitude of the differences may be overstated by the greater propensity of men to drop out or fail to enroll in order to accept employment, but the consistency of the pattern lends credence to the direction of the difference. The same comparisons yield a less consistent and encouraging picture of the relative employment effect of exposure to or completion of training for minorities which tends to suggest, given the inherent weakness and potential biases in the data, that minorities did gain as a result of training, but less than whites. The key to this pattern appears to rest on the role of training in inducing or facilitating enhanced labor force participation. This is suggested by data from the "MDTA Outcomes Study" which revealed little pre-/post-program change in employment stability, but significant increases in employment intensity (defined as percent of total potential working time actually worked by all trainees) for all groups, with women experiencing greater gains than men, and whites greater gains than blacks.[38] In this context, the following conclusions of the study of early MDTA training in the Newark labor market deserves note:

> The present study suggests that MDTA was helpful in solving the employment problem of those without a firmly fixed occupation, but capable of meeting the demands of training in occupations which, for them, represented a measure of progress and stable employment. . . .
> . . . training offered some persons an opportunity to acquire the skills necessary to shift from intermittent employment, seasonal work or odd jobs to a stable job with some security . . . . [A]mong those who completed training this was relatively more true of the women than of the men.[39]

Much of the success of MDTA training in enhancing the employment prospects of female enrollees can be traced to the nature of the training opportunities afforded them. Specifically, one of the major labor market barriers facing female enrollees appears to have been lack of a specific salable skill, and one of the strengths of the program was the heavy emphasis on the concentration of female enrollees in courses in the clerical

37. Jack Chernick, Bernard P. Indik and Roger Craig, *The Selection of Trainees under MDTA* (New Brunswick, New Jersey: Rutgers University, 1965), p. 106.

38. Decision Making Information, *op. cit.*, Chapter VI, pp. 3-4.

39. Chernick *et al.*, *op. cit.*, p. 58.

TABLE VII-9. *MDTA*
Post-Program Employment Experience
Of Completers, Dropouts, Nonenrollees:
Results of Selected Studies

Study	Variable	Race and Sex	Completers Percent	Dropouts Percent	Nonenrollees Percent	Controls Percent
Main	Percent employed post-program	Male	93	91	90	79
		Female	84	64	72	54
Chernik	Percent employed at follow-up	White	75	53	56	n.a.
		Negro	68	60	52	n.a.
Gurin	Percent employed at follow-up	Male	84	79	n.a.	n.a.
		Female	72	48	n.a.	n.a.
Main	Percent employed 80 percent of time	Male	60	59	60	28
		Female	41	19	21	6
Gurin	Percent employed total period	Male	64	65	n.a.	n.a.
		Female	54	38	n.a.	n.a.
		White	63	57	n.a.	n.a.
		Negro	54	40	n.a.	n.a.

TABLE VII-9 *continued*

Sources: Earl D. Main, *A Nationwide Evaluation of MDTA Institutional Training Programs* (Chicago: National Opinion Research Center, University of Chicago, 1966), pp. 40, 62.

Jack Chernik *et al.*, *The Selection of Trainees Under MDTA* (New Brunswick, New Jersey: Rutgers University, 1965), p. 107.

Gerald Gurin, *A National Attitude Survey of Trainees in MDTA Institutional Programs* (Ann Arbor: Survey Research Center, Institute for Social Research, University of Michigan, 1970), pp. 23-24, 26.

and health fields where demand was strong and specific.[40] This phenomenon received considerable attention in the Newark study which found "evidence of occupational mobility of women out of unskilled and semi-skilled occupations and into clerical occupations," and concluded that "MDTA training facilitated, in some cases made possible, an occupational shift coinciding with labor market needs."[41] The Four-City study reached the following similar, but strong conclusion:

> To meet the "reasonable expectation of employment" requirement while keeping per capita training costs low, MDTA administrators have chosen to train for jobs where openings occur because of high turnover, whether or not they are characterized by rising demand. Two occupational areas happen to be characterized by both high turnover and rising demand: health occupations and clerical occupations. A recent ORC study found these two to comprise 70 percent of all female MDTA skills center enrollments. As a result females are given good employment opportunities, even if they are forced into narrow occupational limits.[42]

Noneconomic Impact

The MDTA training effort has been, from its inception, characterized by relatively conservative goals and narrow emphasis on improving the labor market status of its trainees. Thus, it is not surprising that program administrators and program evaluators alike have done little to gather data on the noneconomic benefits of training to participants or society. In this respect, the following statement from the most recent major study of MDTA is illustrative:

> The first question of evaluation methodology is, "What criteria should be used to measure success?". MDTA might generate a number of positive outcomes. The skills of the labor force might be upgraded, thus contributing to both productivity and adaptability. Skill shortages might be alleviated, thus removing bottlenecks and lessening inflationary pressures. Attitudes toward society and government might be improved, thus curbing social unrest and disorganization. Welfare and other dependency costs might be cut. But all of these are secondary to MDTA's primary purpose: to improve the employability, the employment, and the earnings of those persons Congress and the administering agencies have declared eligible for the program.
>
> Hence, a proper evaluation of MDTA's outcomes must answer the important question, "To what extent do eligible enrollees enjoy more satisfactory employment and higher earnings than would have been theirs had they never become involved in such a program?". A total impact evaluation

40. For a case where training in the health occupations did not prove to enhance the employment of female trainees see Sewell, *op. cit.*

41. Chernick *et al.*, *op. cit.*, p. 6.

42. Olympus Research Corporation, *op. cit.*, Vol II, p. 24-23.

would go beyond the outcomes for the program enrollees to deduct negative impacts, if any, on nonenrollees. But that is not encompassed in the scope of the current assignment.[43]

The few studies that have sought to assess the broad economic and social impact of the MDTA training effort generally suggest that such impact has been slight, at best. Specifically, these studies indicate that MDTA training programs:

1. had only a very weak marginal impact on national unemployment rates even under very favorable labor market conditions;[44]
2. had a negligible impact on the supply of labor in skill shortage occupations;[45]
3. had little real or lasting impact on community institutions such as the local employment service and the educational system, except in isolated cases.[46]

The lone exception to this pattern is found in the Planning Research Corporation study of the program which estimated significant social benefits from training in such areas as health care, housing and crime loss.[47] However, the estimate of such benefits was based on a set of assumptions regarding the impact of training on aggregate unemployment rates which had no empirical foundation and is difficult to reconcile with the results of the above cited study of the overall impact of MDTA training on unemployment rates.

A number of studies have extended their analyses to encompass the attitudes of participants toward the training experience, their feelings regarding the role of training in preparing them to function effectively in the labor market, and their satisfaction with post-training jobs. In general, these studies report relatively positive responses from participants, with female and, to a lesser extent, minority participants expressing somewhat more favorable views than their male or nonminority counterparts in training. In this respect, the following findings of the Main study of 1964 institutional trainees are worthy of note.

43. Decision Making Information, *op. cit.*, pp. 1-8, 1-9.

44. Malcolm Cohen, "The Direct Effects of Federal Manpower Programs in Reducing Unemployment," *Journal of Human Resources*, Vol. IV, no. 4 (Fall 1969).

45. Olympus Research Corporation, "Evaluation of the Effectiveness of Institutional Manpower Training in Meeting Employers' Needs and Skills Shortages Occupations," report prepared for Office of Policy, Evaluation and Research, Manpower Administration, U.S. Department of Labor, 1972, p. 3-5.

46. Olympus Research Corporation, "The Total Impact of Manpower Programs," *op. cit.*, Vol. II, pp. 24-5 to 24-23.

47. Muir *et al., loc. cit.*

In addition to the general types of skills discussed above and the more specific job skills which are particularly useful in the various occupations for which the training was given, the following "skills" were learned, according to open-ended responses of the trainees: (1) personal relationship or getting along with other people—9 percent; (2) psychological well being or feelings of confidence or independence—4 percent; (3) personal appearance grooming or posture—3 percent; and (4) how to look for or apply for a job—2 percent. Personal relationships were named slightly more often by "completers" (11 percent) than by "dropouts" (5 percent). Women were a little more likely than men to mention personal relationships (12 percent *vs.* 7 percent) and personal appearance (7 percent *vs.* 1 percent).[48]

Two-thirds (66 percent) of "completers" and one-fourth (26 percent) of "dropouts" said that the MDTA training they received helped them obtain employment (53 percent for both respondent types combined). The proportion who said "yes" was larger for women (59 percent) than for men (49 percent). Among "completers," women found training helpful more often (73 percent, compared to 62 percent of men), but among "dropouts," men were a little more likely than women to say training helped them get a job (28 *vs.* 21 percent).[49]

While only 46 percent of "completers" had "a lot" of confidence before training, 79 percent expressed "a lot" when interviewed—an increase of 33 percent. For "dropouts" the corresponding increase was only 14 percent (from 58 to 72 percent). Though "dropouts" had more confidence than "completers" had before training, "completers" held a slight advantage afterward. Women and men expressed roughly similar levels of confidence when interviewed, which means that women gained more since before training—when men had a definite advantage. Female "completers" gained the most—their proportion with "a lot" of confidence rose from 39 percent before training to 79 percent "now"—a rise of 40 percent (male "completers" rose from 51 to 79 percent—a gain of 28 percent).[50]

Of those who had one or more full-time jobs since training, most claimed that they liked their latest job: 54 percent said "very well," and another 32 percent said "fairly well." Only 6 percent said "not well at all," and 8 percent said "not so well." Men and women had similar response patterns, but there was a large difference related to respondent type. Only 42 percent of "controls" liked their most recent jobs "very well," compared to 62 percent of "completers," 59 percent of "dropouts," and 55 percent of "didn't enrolls". Not only did fewer "controls" find full-time work—they didn't like the jobs they did find as well as trainees did.[51]

The single most comprehensive study of the noneconomic participant benefits of MDTA training is an unpublished doctoral dissertation completed in 1966 which focused considerable attention on the socio-psychological status of a group of trainees and a group of eligible and interested

48. Main, *op. cit.*, p. 34.

49. *Ibid.*, p. 35.

50. *Ibid.*, p. 39.

51. *Ibid.*, p. 41.

nonenrollees both before and after training.[52] Socio-psychological status was determined by the use of six scales: responsibility, self-acceptance, well-being, sociability, security, and rigidity. Trainees generally tended to show positive pre-/post-training movement on each of these scales, with the possible exception of well-being.[53] However, significant differences between completers and dropouts and between completers and controls were found only on the sociability scale.[54]

CONCLUSIONS

The available data on the post-program labor market performance of MDTA trainees strongly suggests that the program has had a positive impact on the economic status of those trainees. Existing evaluative studies generally indicate post-program employment, wage rate, and earnings levels for trainees as a group which compare favorably to their pre-program experience and, in most cases, to the experience of similarly situated individuals who were not exposed to or did not complete training. The nature, extent, and probable duration of the economic impact of training has tended to vary over time with changes in the state of the labor market and the composition of the training group; and to differ among various groups of trainees and types of training. But overall, women and minorities do appear to have realized substantial benefits from training.

The basic contribution of MDTA training has been to provide trainees with specific skills, personal confidence, and institutional contact required to facilitate entry or reentry into the primary labor market, rather than to serve as a vehicle for upward mobility within that market or as a force for change in the institutional structure of that market. The primary source of the economic gains of trainees, as measured by gains in annual earnings, has been enhanced employment levels and stability rather than increased wage rates or favorable occupational changes. There is little evidence that the program had any widespread impact on the basic institutional dimensions of labor markets, such as employer hiring standards or practices, the role or mission of employment services, and the structure or scope of other training services which might have had favorable implications for the long-run status of women and minorities in the labor market.

52. Darrell G. Jones, "An Evaluation of the Socio-Psychological and Socio-Economic Effects of MDTA Training on Trainees in Selected Michigan Programs," Ph.D. dissertation, Michigan State University, 1966.

53. *Ibid.*, p. 191.

54. *Ibid.*, p. 187.

The importance of the employment variable, and particularly employment levels, in trainee group earnings gains raises serious questions concerning the true value of the MDTA training program. To the extent that the employment impact of the program rests primarily on the placement effort, there are other, less expensive means to the same end. Even if the employment impact comes from some combination of increased confidence and enhanced job-specific skill, the effects of training may be short-lived because time may erode the employment advantage of trainees vis-à-vis nontrainees, particularly during periods of economic expansion when tightening labor markets force employers to assume an increasing share of the costs of training. There is some evidence in data on long-run trainee earnings gains which indicates such erosion and brings into question the conclusions of early cost-benefit studies based on what appears to be unrealistic assumptions regarding the duration of the benefits of training. However, the data also suggest that the erosion of benefits is weakest for those trainees who are able to utilize training to move into occupations or jobs which might not have been open to them in the absence of training—specifically, among female institutional trainees where movement into clerical occupations was prevalent and among black on-the-job trainees where placement in skilled jobs was significant.

MDTA training programs have served substantial numbers of women and minorities over their ten-year history and have served them reasonably well. Women in particular have utilized the program to facilitate entry or reentry into the labor market and to gain access to jobs in the growing clerical and health fields. Minorities and particularly minority males, however, have enjoyed only limited gains from MDTA training, although this may be as much or more a function of forces in the labor market as a result of any deficiency in the program.

The evidence on the benefits of training by race and sex is severely limited and provides an unclear and uncertain picture. In absolute terms, both women and minorities may do less well in the labor market after training than their male or white trainee counterparts, as might be expected, given discriminatory barriers and differences in attachment to the labor force. At the same time, however, women and minorities do experience substantial improvement in labor market experience between pre- and post-training periods—improvement which compares favorably with that of their counterparts in training. Only in the case of women however, did these gains compare favorably with the experience of similar individuals who did not complete or were not exposed to training.

The apparent advantage of women in terms of gains from training can be traced to several forces. Women who enter and complete training undoubtedly have stronger attachment to the labor force and greater economic motivation than do similarly situated women who did not enter or do not complete training. At the same time, women are more likely to be dependent on training to secure employment and less likely to drop out of training to take a job than men, thereby distorting the motivational comparability of male and female completers. Above and beyond these essentially methodological problems, however, the occupational structure of training opportunities for women did generate highly favorable short- and long-run benefits for the female trainee population. The fact that large numbers of women were trained in the clerical and health fields where demand was not only high in the short run, but growing in the long run, appears to have been a major factor in the relative level, structure, and durability of the earnings gains for women.

Minorities appear to have gained from training, but less than their white counterparts, although the difference between the two groups is not substantial. Minority males, in particular, showed only limited gains from training and it is not clear whether this was the result of constrained choice in training occupations or barriers in the labor market. Minority females, however, realized substantial gains which approached and, in some cases, exceeded those of their white trainee counterparts. However, it is not possible to determine the extent to which the relative gains of minority women reflect the positive occupational change noted generally among women as opposed to simply higher levels of employment and labor force attachment.

CHAPTER VIII

Job Opportunities in the Business Sector

by
Charles R. Perry

The objective of the JOBS program is to place "disadvantaged" individuals into meaningful jobs in the private sector on a "hire now-train later" basis. The philosophical foundation of the program rested on the judgment that "instant jobs" for the disadvantaged on a large scale constituted one means of alleviating the social and economic pressures underlying the urban riots of the mid-1960's. The practical elements of this instant-job approach to social unrest were disarmingly simple:

1. Voluntary business commitments to reserve some existing and prospective job openings for disadvantaged persons (as defined by established Department of Labor criteria) on a "hire now-train later" basis.
2. Structuring or restructuring of private training programs to provide the full range of supportive services, pre-vocational education, and job training required to integrate the disadvantaged individual into the work force fully and on a meaningful long-run basis.
3. Availability of federal subsidies to cover the marginal costs of hiring, training, and integrating the disadvantaged.

The JOBS program is administered by the Manpower Administration of the Department of Labor in conjunction with the National Alliance of Businessmen (NAB), a nonprofit organization created to encourage participation in the program and to provide assistance to participating firms in developing and implementing training programs. The JOBS program has two components—contract (federally subsidized) and noncontract (privately financed). In theory, the only difference between the two is utilization of available federal subsidies, but, in fact, noncontract participants enjoy considerably greater flexibility and freedom regarding the following program elements:

1. The extent to which they are required to keep records regarding the number and characteristics of those hired under the program;
2. The extent to which they are expected to utilize the Employment Service and Concentrated Employment Program as a source of disadvantaged workers;
3. The extent to which they are required to secure Employment Service certification of hires as disadvantaged;
4. The extent to which they are required to develop formal programs

of supportive services and job training for the disadvantaged and to submit to scrutiny concerning the scope and quality of those programs.

Program History

The JOBS program was announced with great fanfare in President Johnson's January 1968 manpower message and was eagerly espoused by the Nixon administration in 1969. As originally proposed, the program was to be concentrated in 50 major cities, although this number was subsequently expanded to over 150. The initial goal was to place 500,000 disadvantaged persons in meaningful jobs by June 1971.

The JOBS program met an unexpectedly enthusiastic response from the business community. The combination of social responsibility, the sense of social urgency growing out of the earlier riots, the desire for favorable publicity, and shortage of labor in the extremely tight labor market of 1968 induced a high percentage of firms contacted by the local NAB offices to pledge jobs. By July 1968, some 165,000 permanent jobs had been pledged, far surpassing the original interim goal of 100,000 jobs by July 1969. Of those pledged, only one-third were linked to federal subsidies with the remaining two-thirds being noncontract "freebies."[1]

The early operational problems of the JOBS program in converting pledges into placements have been widely discussed in the literature. Some early pledges never materialized into actual job orders and new pledges became more difficult to secure. Referrals were slow in coming in at the outset, the ratio of placements to referrals was well below expectations, and turnover among those placed was far higher than anticipated. Despite these difficulties, the program was an apparent success; by the end of June 1970, NAB and the Department of Labor were able to report a total of 494,710 trainees hired (about three-quarters of which were noncontract) with a retention rate of 47 percent.[2]

The economic slowdown which began in 1970 had a strong and immediate impact on the JOBS program. Workers placed through the programs were, in many cases, the first to be laid off in the face of slackening demand, and employers generally became reluctant to meet their outstanding commitments and resistant to any pressure to make further pledges. As a result, the program has faded from public prominence, although NAB has continued to function both in the area of employment for the disadvantaged and in the Jobs for Veterans campaign.

1. Arnold L. Nemore and Garth L. Mangum, "Private Involvement in Federal Manpower Programs" in Arnold R. Weber *et al.* (eds.), *Public-Private Manpower Policies* (Madison: Industrial Relations Research Association, 1969), p. 69.

2. Comptroller General of the United States, *Evaluation of Results and Administration of the Job Opportunities in the Business Sector (JOBS) Program in Five Cities* (Washington, D.C.: General Accounting Office, 1971), p. 13.

PROGRAM SCOPE

Comprehensive data on the number and nature of persons served by the JOBS program are virtually nonexistent and the data which are available are of questionable reliability and validity. The Department of Labor does maintain operating statistics on the contract portion of the program, but fear of inhibiting employer participation in the program has made it reluctant to establish and enforce the rigorous reporting requirements necessary to ensure the integrity of these statistics. The National Alliance of Businessmen did make some attempt to compile statistics on the noncontract portion of the program during its early years, but the validity of these data is highly suspect because they were based on unverified and, in many cases, unverifiable company reports submitted in the context of strong political and social pressure to show results.

The JOBS program was credited with the placement of almost 500,000 persons by the end of June 1970, with the contract segment of the program accounting for only about one-quarter of this total. By the end of 1971, the total had grown to approximately 825,000, and by the end of 1972, to some 1.1 million, with the contract segment of the program accounting for about 40 percent of the placements after June 1970 and one-third of the overall program total.[3]

Basic demographic data are available for only 217,000 of the almost 500,000 placements claimed for the JOBS program through the end of June 1970.[4] These data clearly indicate that the JOBS program served a predominantly male (71 percent) and black (71 percent) clientele during its first two years and lend credence to suggestions that "black" and "disadvantaged" were regarded as synonymous by participating firms in the early stages of the program. The data also indicate that the program did reach the disadvantaged or near-disadvantaged, as some 60 percent of the reported hires had less than twelve years of schooling with almost 85 percent from families with incomes of $4,000 or less.

Data on demographic characteristics of JOBS trainees by program segment are available for about 169,000 persons hired under the program through February 28, 1970.[5] Overall, these data are consistent with the data from the larger and later sample cited above, but they do reveal some interesting and significant differences between the contract and noncontract segments of the program. Specifically, the data indicate that non-

3. U.S. Department of Labor, Manpower Administration, *Manpower Technical Exchange*, Vol. V, no. 9 (May 18, 1973), p. 3.

4. Comptroller General of the United States, *op. cit.*, Appendix I, p. 1.

5. U.S. Senate, Committee on Labor and Public Welfare, Subcommittee on Employment, Manpower, and Poverty. *The JOBS Program: Background Information* (Washington, D.C.: Government Printing Office, 1970), pp.176-177.

contract firms did exploit their greater potential flexibility in recruiting "disadvantaged" workers and suggest that the result was a somewhat "superior" group of trainees in the noncontract segment of the program. A full 95 percent of those hired under the contract portion of the program were certified as disadvantaged by state employment services, community action agencies, or Concentrated Employment Programs as compared with only about 25 percent of those hired through the noncontract program where employer certifications accounted for almost 70 percent of the total. Coincidentally, higher percentages of noncontract than contract trainees were male, white, with twelve or more years of schooling, and with family incomes in excess of $4,000 (Table 1).

Demographic data are available for fragmentary samples of JOBS contract trainees for fiscal years 1970 and 1971 and fiscal year 1972 through March 31, 1972. These data provide a clear indication of the nature and extent of the impact of slackening demand for labor on program service to its original target group. Specifically, the data suggest an upward trend in the percentages of women, whites, and those with at least a high school education among JOBS trainees after 1970 (Table 1).

PROGRAM OPERATION

The JOBS program initially was touted as a job-creation program designed to provide meaningful work experience for the disadvantaged. However, there was little in the basic structure of operation of the program to foster such action, and there is little evidence that the program resulted in either the creation of new jobs or the modification of existing jobs on a significant scale for the benefit of the disadvantaged. In practice, job pledges typically were sought and secured on the basis of existing or prospective openings due to normal turnover, and the resulting employment opportunities were confined primarily, but not exclusively, to entry-level blue collar and service jobs. A Conference Board study of the program provided the following picture of the nature of the employment opportunities made available as a result of the NAB-JOBS effort:

> There is evidence, too, that companies opened new jobs to the disadvantaged, especially in the clerical group. Companies also experimented—often experiencing better than average success—with the use of disadvantaged individuals as scientific and engineering technicians, computer console operators. . . . Most of the companies, however, did their hiring for unskilled laborer jobs, unskilled clerical jobs such as mailboys and file clerks, and semi-skilled operator jobs such as machine operators.[6]

6. National Industrial Conference Board, *Employing the Disadvantaged: A Company Perspective* (New York: The Conference Board, Inc., 1972), p. 11.

TABLE VIII-1. *Job Opportunities in the Business Sector*
Percent Distribution of Characteristics of Persons Hired

	1968-2/28/70			7/1/69-6/30/70	7/1/70-6/30/71	7/1/71-3/28/72
	Total	Noncontract	Contract	Contract	Contract	Contract
Sex:						
Male	73	74	70	69.2	66.3	69.0
Female	27	26	30	30.7	33.7	31.0
Race:						
Black	73	70	77	74.0	56.3	44.9
White	21	23	16	19.0	35.7	46.4
Other	7	6	7	7.0	8.0	8.7
Education:						
8 years or less	13	12	15	14.8	18.2	16.7
9-11 years	48	46	52	51.0	44.1	40.0
12 years and over	40	43	33	33.6	37.7	43.2
Family income:						
$0-2,000	49	48	50	51.4	55.1	45.6
$2,001-4,000	36	36	37	35.9	33.7	40.7
Over $4,000	15	16	13	12.6	11.1	13.8
Total	100	100	100	100.0	100.0	100.0
Total number	169,161	113,049	56,112	79,508	58,001	31,180

Source: U.S. Senate, Committee on Labor and Public Welfare, Subcommittee on Employment, Manpower and Poverty, *The JOBS Program: Background Information* (Washington, D.C.: U.S. Government Printing Office, 1970), pp. 176-177; and U.S. Department of Labor, Manpower Administration computer runs dated 9-5-70, 11-23-71 and 3-31-72. Percents may not add to 100.0 due to rounding.

The structure of the job opportunities made available through the JOBS program explains why women, in the aggregate, were not well represented in the program. The nature of those opportunities raises serious questions concerning the extent to which the minorities who constituted the overwhelming majority of enrollees were truly well served, particularly in the long run. Specifically, the program may have offered immediate employment and wages to some who would not otherwise have had access to them, but it does not appear to have provided the prospect for economic advancement necessary to ensure stable and lasting enrollee participation in the primary labor market. The General Accounting Office study noted that " [a] significant number of the jobs provided by contractors paid low wages and appeared to afford little or no opportunity for advancement."[7] A study by Greenleigh Associates concluded that "most jobs offered through the JOBS program are dead end and are likely to be vulnerable to technological change."[8]

Basic to the JOBS program concept of "hire now-train later" was recognition that the disadvantaged would require a greater investment in training and a broader range of supportive services than did "normal" hires; provision for such training and services was an integral part of the program. Specifically, participating employers were encouraged to provide not only on-the-job training, but such services as orientation, counseling, basic education, medical and dental examinations and services, subsidies for transportation and child-care costs, and sensitivity training for supervisors, with the cost of such services covered under the contracts.

All evaluations of the JOBS program point out great variability among firms in the range and quality of training and supportive services. Furthermore, it is clear that the JOBS program was not uniformly successful in eliciting those training inputs which could be expected to facilitate best the integration of the disadvantaged into the work force in the short run and into the labor force in the long run. Overall, the quantity and quality of training and other services appears to have been superior in the contract segment of the program, but the record of contract participants in providing services contracted and compensated for was far from good. The GAO study reported that for 17 of the 31 contracts reviewed, the contractors were providing substantially fewer services than were required by the contracts.[9] The Greenleigh Associates study indicated that trainees were virtually unanimous in finding such support services as medical and dental care helpful, but also reported that:

7. Comptroller General of the United States, *op. cit.*, p. 47.

8. Greenleigh Associates, Inc., "The Job Opportunities in the Business Sector Program—An Evaluation of Impact in Ten Standard Metropolitan Statistical Areas," report prepared for Office of Policy, Evaluation and Research, Manpower Administration, U.S. Department of Labor, 1970.

9. Comptroller General of the United States, *op.cit.*, pp. 126-135.

> Trainees were asked to rate the extent to which the individual supportive services provided had been helpful to them. Numerous respondents were unable to answer these inquiries because they had not received many of the services although a review of MA contracts indicated that most contracts called for a complete support services program.[10]

Retention rates have been regarded as a central measure of the effectiveness of the JOBS program and considerable concern has been expressed over the apparently high turnover rate among JOBS trainees during the early years of the program. The report on activity under the program through June 30, 1972, acknowledged a retention rate of only 47 percent, but indicated that this did not represent a level of turnover significantly higher than that generally experienced for new employees in entry-level positions. Analysis of available records on terminations under the contract segment of the program for fiscal years 1970-1972 reveals a very encouraging improvement in retention rates—from about 52 percent in 1970 to almost 65 percent by March 1972—although there is no way to determine the extent to which this trend reflected increases in program effectiveness rather than changes in the quality of trainees and/or in the availability of alternative employment opportunities. Interestingly, these data reveal no significant racial differences in termination rates and only a relatively limited difference between men and women.

REVIEW OF EVALUATIVE LITERATURE

The JOBS program has not been subjected to serious scrutiny or systematic evaluation on a significant scale. A considerable body of descriptive material on the concept and structure of the program does exist, as do a number of theoretical analyses of the possible or probable economic effects of the program. However, only five studies have been made of the actual operation and impact of the program, and only one of these is either quantitative in its nature or broad in its scope. In addition, a few other studies have touched on the JOBS program in the course of evaluating overall effectiveness or total impact of manpower programs in specific settings or on specific target groups, but these contribute only impressionistic information on the economic impact of the program. In this respect, the following conclusion of the Four-City study is illustrative:

> It is most difficult of all to assess the impact on enrollee employment and earnings of NAB-JOBS. Hiring standards were changed somewhat. Substantial numbers of jobs were made available to persons, many of whom would have been unable to find access to them. Changed attitudes on the part of the relatively few employers involved probably improved access for

10. Greenleigh Associates, Inc., *op. cit.*, p. 93.

> some not counted in the totals. The impact could not be positive, even if there is no way to measure its magnitude.[11]

The basic focus of most of the evaluative literature on JOBS has been the short-run employment effects of the program. Primary attention has been given to such basic operational dimensions of the program as the nature of employment opportunities made available, the characteristics of those hired, the retention rate for those hired under the program, and the quantity and quality of training services made available to participants in an effort to document claims that the program was meeting its goal of providing meaningful jobs for the disadvantaged on a "hire now-train later" basis. Relatively little attention has been given to measurement of actual participant benefits, apparently because such benefits were assumed to flow automatically from the program in proportion to its ability to meet its stated goals.

The lack of complete and accurate data on enrollees has been, and remains, a major barrier to meaningful evaluation of the JOBS program. The fragmentary nature of national program operating statistics, particularly for the noncontract portion of the program, has precluded all but speculative judgments regarding the overall effectiveness of the program in meeting even its basic employment/employability goals. In the absence of sound national data, evaluations have been forced to rely on "unscientific" sampling procedures and "nonstatistical" methods of analysis and have been handicapped in even these efforts by the lack of adequate company records on trainees in both contract and noncontract participating firms. Thus, most evaluations of the program have been restricted to qualitative appraisal of program operations rather than quantitative analysis of program impact and have had to rely on anecdotal material rather than true statistical evidence.

Much of the subjective evaluative literature on the JOBS program is pessimistic in tone, but the lone quantitative study of its impact suggests that it did have a definite positive impact on the short-run economic status and labor market experience of a significant number of disadvantaged and near-disadvantaged individuals during its early years. Although its short-run economic impact on participants appears to have been significant, the scope and durability of this impact is much in doubt. The scope of employer participation was limited. And even within that employer population, the hire now-train later principle of the program, was seriously undermined by the economic slowdown of 1970-1971. Unfortunately, there is no basis for an accurate assessment of the extent to which the program and its participants were able to withstand these pressures

11. Olympus Research Corporation, "The Total Impact of Manpower Programs: A Four-City Case Study," report prepared for Office of Policy, Evaluation and Research, Manpower Administration, U.S. Department of Labor, 1971, Vol. I, p. 43.

in the short run, or recover from their effects in the long run, as the economy returned to full employment.

IMPACT ASSESSMENT

The JOBS program was the beneficiary of a great deal of highly favorable publicity during its early years and strong claims were made for its success in opening employment opportunities for large numbers of disadvantaged persons and effectuating basic changes in industry recruiting patterns, hiring standards, and training programs. The existing evaluations of the program provide only heavily qualified subjective evidence to support these claims, although most reach relatively favorable conclusions regarding the overall employment impact of the program.

There is a general consensus in the literature that the tight labor market conditions which prevailed in the late 1960's were a major factor in the apparent numerical success of the program. A System Development Corporation (SDC) study of the program in nine cities was most explicit on this point:

> The JOBS program has been operating in a period of high employment. Even among disadvantaged and minorities unemployment levels have been, until very recently, at unprecedented lows. So in a sense, one ingredient for the success of the JOBS program was a given: Employers needed people to fill their entry level jobs, and people were increasingly in short supply. JOBS, and particularly MA contracts, offered the prospect of opening up a "new" resource of manpower and many employers turned to it.[12]

The literature is less clear and consistent in regard to the question of the relative roles of the program and the tight labor market in explaining the apparent expansion in employment opportunities for the disadvantaged. In this respect, the following conclusion of the Four-City study is illustrative:

> NAB-JOBS must be declared a positive influence on the individual, the labor market and the employers. At worst the enrollee gets a job he could have obtained without the program, but probably stays in it longer than he might otherwise have done. At best he gets upgraded into a regular job and continues to progress upward in the employing system.[13]

---

12. System Development Corporation, "Evaluation of the JOBS Program in Nine Cities," report prepared for U. S. Department of Labor, 1969, p. 3.

13. Olympus Research Corporation, *op. cit.*, Vol. I, p. 86.

The GAO study of the program in five cities reported that "many JOBS enrollees were not perceptibly different from normal hires, were being offered jobs that they could ordinarily get without the JOBS program" and concluded that the programs had been effective only "in focusing the attention of businessmen on the employment problems of disadvantaged persons."[14] The Greenleigh study acknowledged that "many self-motivated persons, applying on their own initiative, were referred by employers . . . for certification as NAB trainees," but concluded that the program had helped "to reduce employer prejudices and discriminatory hiring practices."[15] Finally, the SDC study found "evidence that the program may have begun a process leading to lasting change in the hiring practices of employers, and concluded that:

> One consequence of JOBS, probably in combination with other programs, forces and trends, has been a heightened awareness among employers that there is a potential talent resource that they have been traditionally and steadfastly overlooking, and that the extra effort required to exploit it is affordable.[16]

There is general agreement that whatever impact the program had on employer attitudes, standards, or practices was confined to a limited number of employers and differed between contract and noncontract participating employers. An NICB evaluation of the program clearly indicated that NAB-JOBS had little or no impact on firms that had no prior experience in employing the disadvantaged, but that it was successful in getting companies with prior experience to increase the number of disadvantaged they employed; it was concluded that "[p]ossibly the most significant impact of NAB's first three years has been not so much on whether a company employed the disadvantaged as upon what companies did with the disadvantaged after they were hired."[17] The 'SDC study reached the following similar but more detailed conclusion:

> Substantial numbers of disadvantaged individuals would doubtless have been hired during the past year if there had been no JOBS Program, owing to the generally tight job market. However, one result of JOBS has been to enlarge the pool of available manpower. . . . Another result has been to improve the opportunities for, and retention of, employees who would have been hired in any case, but for whom little in the way of pre-job training or supportive services would have been provided.

14. Comptroller General of the United States, *op. cit.*, p. 24.

15. Greenleigh Associates, Inc., *op. cit.*, p. 42.

16. System Development Corporation, *op. cit.*, p. 8.

17. National Industrial Conference Board, *op cit.*, p. 11.

> The first impact—enlarging the manpower pool—has been felt primarily in the non-contract portion of the program. Employers who traditionally hire disadvantaged individuals for jobs characterized by low wages, limited opportunity, minimum training requirements and undesirable working conditions have continued doing so while participating in JOBS....
> The second impact—on the opportunities for trainees—has been almost entirely in the contract portion of the JOBS Program. Among MA contractors there are also many employers who have traditionally hired disadvantaged applicants for entry jobs. Participation in the program under contract has enabled them to invest more in training and retention, and has required them . . . to accept candidates they might otherwise have considered unacceptable.[18]

Economic Impact

Considerable attention has been devoted to the hourly and weekly earnings of JOBS enrollees as an index of the success of the program in moving disadvantaged individuals into meaningful employment and out of poverty, with highly favorable results. For example, one study reported average weekly earnings among its sample of 1969 trainees of $91, which it extrapolated to an annual income of about $4,700, and compared very favorably to the $2,300 average family income of trainees over the previous twelve months.[19] Similarly, a Department of Labor study of wages received by JOBS trainees during the latter half of 1969 under the MA-5 portion of the program reported that trainees could expect to receive an average hourly wage of $2.49 after nine months and reasoned that:

> This wage rate further represents an annual wage of $5,200. The average family size for JOBS contract employees is 3.7 and an estimate of the poverty level income for a family of that size is $3,420. Thus the income of the average JOBS employee will be raised considerably above the poverty level. This also indicates that the jobs being offered by employers on the whole cannot be characterized as low wage, deadend jobs.[20]

This line of reasoning, although intuitively attractive, can be grossly misleading. The extrapolation of hourly or weekly earnings to annual income figures is questionable, particularly given the high turnover and low retention rates for enrollees during the early years of the program. Specifically, it is interesting to note that, if trainees had worked on an average of only 50 percent of the time, the income extrapolations cited above would have led to quite different conclusions regarding program

18. System Development Corporation, *op. cit.*, p. 37.

19. Greenleigh Associates, Inc., *op. cit.*, p. 91.

20. U.S. Senate, *op. cit.*, p. 169.

impact. Similarly, wage rates are, at best, an imperfect measure of the quality of employment opportunities, as the correlation between wage rates and such factors as skill requirements, training opportunity, and advancement potential is far from perfect. In this respect, it should be noted that the evaluative literature on the JOBS program consistently indicates that a substantial portion of the jobs offered through the program required little skill and afforded little opportunity for advancement. One study specifically suggested that:

> . . . JOBS hires go into more or less traditional entry-level jobs with little opportunity for vertical movement, and such jobs traditionally pay more than those with the potential for advancement.[21]

Evaluations of the JOBS program generally appear to have taken for granted the existence of significant earnings benefits to enrollees and have not sought to verify such benefits or to measure their magnitude in a rigorous sense. However, some data on annual earnings of JOBS program participants are available from two separate Department of Labor studies of 1968 JOBS enrollees based on Social Security records. Both of these studies reveal significant increases in earnings associated with participation in the program, but do not indicate the hoped for wholesale movement across the poverty line. The first of these studies was based on a comparison of 1966 and 1968 earnings for a random sample of enrollees and found a pre-/post-enrollment change in mean earnings from $1,499 to $2,522—an increase of almost $1,100.[22] The second of these studies was based on a comparison of average earnings for the 1963-1967 period with 1969 earnings for a sample of more than 60,000 participants, in both the contract and noncontract portions of the JOBS program in 1968, and found changes in average annual earnings of about $1,900 for contract enrollees and $2,450 for noncontract enrollees, which brought their average post-program earnings to approximately $2,800 and $3,600, respectively.[23]

This latter study includes a comparison group drawn from the Social Security Continuous Work History Sample and provides a basis for estimating the net earnings impact of participation in the JOBS program. The approach used to construct the comparison group was identical to that used in the case of MDTA trainees and may suffer from the same weaknesses. However, the results it yielded were markedly different. Specifically, a comparison of earnings gains for participants

21. System Development Corporation, *op. cit.*, p. 7.

22. Cited in: U.S. Senate, *op. cit.*, p. 168.

23. David J. Farber, "Highlights—First Annual Follow-up: 1968 JOBS Contract and Non Contract Program," unpublished U.S. Department of Labor report, 1971, p. 2.

and nonparticipants between the 1963-1967 base period and 1969 revealed an advantage to participants of about $300 for those in the contract segment of the program and over $700 for those in the noncontract segment of the program, with the difference between the two segments attributable, at least in part, to differences in the race/sex structure and educational attainment of the participant populations.

This latter study also contains the only concrete data on the labor market performance of JOBS enrollees by race and sex currently available. These data clearly indicate that the program did generate significant short-run earnings gains for its female and minority group participants—gains which generally compared favorably with those of their male and nonminority counterparts in the program (Table 2). The

TABLE VIII-2. *Job Opportunities in the Business Sector Pre- and Post-Training Annual Earnings Gains 1968 Contract and Noncontract Enrollees By Sex and Race*

Sex and Race	Gross Change 1963-1967 to 1969	Net Change Trainees *v.* Controls
Contract:		
Males	1,911.26	116.24
White	1,959.24	89.96
Negro	1,895.48	188.04
Females	1,922.68	620.88
White	1,514.44	207.24
Negro	2,047.36	747.24
Noncontract:		
Males	2,568.36	681.28
White	2,826.84	655.48
Negro	2,470.00	692.44
Females	2,206.60	867.28
White	1,946.28	623.48
Negro	2,325.00	978.16

Source: David J. Farber, "Highlights—First Annual Follow-up: 1968 Jobs Contract and Noncontract Programs," unpublished U.S. Department of Labor report, 1971, Tables 1 and 9-14.

data on gross pre-/post-training income changes fail to conform consistently with the expected pattern of sex and race differences, as males outgained females only in the noncontract segment of the program, and whites outgained blacks only in the case of male trainees. The data on the net earnings effect of participation consistently fail to conform to the expected pattern, as women outgained men, and blacks outgained whites in virtually every race/sex category in both program segments. In terms of both gross and net income gains, black women appear to have been the primary beneficiaries of the JOBS program.

The superior earnings gains of female and black JOBS enrollees are highly encouraging, but they must be interpreted with considerable caution for two reasons. First, data on the educational attainment of the JOBS enrollees included in the Department of Labor study reveal systematic and significant differences by sex, race, and program segment in regard to percent of enrollees with twelve or more years of schooling, differences which parallel the observed differences in net income gains.[24] Second, given the obvious sensitivity of the program to changing economic conditions, it is far from certain that the benefits uncovered in analyzing 1969 incomes would have persisted through the subsequent economic downturn. In this respect, it is less important that enrollees retain specific jobs than that they maintain their attachment to, and standing in, the labor market. In theory, the JOBS program was designed to ensure that such would be the case, but indications of deficiencies in placement and training under the program leave room for serious doubt on this score.

Noneconomic Impact

Only one study of the JOBS program dealt directly with noneconomic benefits to participants. The Greenleigh study attempted to assess the derivative benefits of employment in terms of individual self-esteem and life style, with relatively favorable results. That study reported that most trainees "described life style changes in terms of more leisure time and more adequate income with which to meet family expenses" and that "thirty percent of respondents felt that their own estimation of themselves had improved."[25] The study also indicated that a substantial proportion of trainees felt that their family relationships had been

24. The reported percentages of enrollees with twelve or more years of schooling are as follows:

	Noncontract	Contract
Males:		
White	27.0	23.1
Negro	41.7	31.5
Total	37.0	29.3
Females:		
White	37.5	30.0
Negro	60.1	43.7
Total	52.9	40.5

25. Greenleigh Associates, Inc., *op. cit.*, pp. 29-30.

strengthened and reported that many trainees who remained in the program spoke of new or renewed feelings of usefulness and status among their neighbors.[26]

CONCLUSIONS

The available data regarding the operation and outcome of the JOBS program indicates that it did have a definite positive impact on the economic status of a significant number of disadvantaged and near-disadvantaged individuals during its early years. There is also reason to believe that the program generated broader social and economic benefits in facilitating an expansion in the total effective supply of labor in the face of high and rising demand for labor. Although the short-run effects of the program are clear, its long-run impact is much in doubt. The program and its basic principle, hire now-train later, were seriously undermined by the loosening of the labor market. And there is no basis on which to estimate the extent to which either would be revived, once full employment is again approached. In addition to the question of employer attitudes and commitment in the long run, there is a question as to the "staying power" of those already served by the program, both in terms of specific jobs in the short run, and participation in the labor force and primary labor market in the long run.

There is no general consensus or clear evidence about the process of the mechanism by which the JOBS program achieved its results. However, the available information suggests that the labor market impact of the program was "extensive" rather than "intensive", in that it served more to expand the scope of the supply of labor for existing jobs than to foster new types of training and/or employment opportunities. In effect, the program appears to have operated to support basic market forces in breaking down barriers, which had served to inhibit or preclude meaningful employment for the disadvantaged or near-disadvantaged, on both sides of the labor market. Specifically, the program, and its attendant publicity, added social and institutional pressure to that exerted by the tight labor market to lower hiring standards. Program publicity coupled with outreach efforts and promises of jobs, expedited the entry into the primary job market of previously isolated individuals. This entire process may well have been facilitated by the fact that the greatest shortage of labor was at entry levels and that some substantial portion of the individuals drawn into the primary labor markets were equal or superior to those already there.

The nature of the jobs offered through the JOBS program limited the number of women who could be served by the program. However, the

26. *Ibid.*, p. 2.

short-run benefits to those women, and particularly those black women who were brought into the primary labor market through the program, were significant and significantly greater than was the case for their male counterparts. To some extent, the superior earnings gains of women may reflect superior employability, as is suggested by the data on percentage of enrollees with twelve or more years of schooling. In this case it would appear that the primary function of the program was to eliminate barriers on the supply side of the market. If this were the case, there is hope that the effects of the program on the individual enrollees will be more than transitory.

Minority groups have been well served by the JOBS program in terms of both numbers and short-run earnings impact. However, there is strong suggestive evidence that the economic downturn may have eroded the gains of male enrollees, the overwhelming percentage of whom were black. There is no way to estimate the extent to which minority enrollees who were adversely affected by changing economic conditions will remain and be competitive in the primary labor market, but one must suspect that discriminatory forces will take their toll.

Overall, it can be said that the JOBS program did generate real and significant short-run economic benefits for its female and minority group participants—benefits which exceeded those for other participant groups. Unfortunately, such benefits were probably transitory for what may be a substantial number of those involved because of a change in basic economic conditions. However, the true long-run test of the impact of the program rests on the extent to which it was successful in inducing permanent changes in the labor market behavior of both disadvantaged workers and participating employers—changes which would have the effect of enhancing the speed and magnitude of the impact of economic expansion on the disadvantaged and near-disadvantaged. It is, as yet, unclear whether the JOBS program had such an impact.

CHAPTER IX

Public Service Careers and New Careers

by
Larry R. Matlack
Research Associate
Under the Direction of
Bernard E. Anderson

The Public Service Careers and New Careers programs were developed to provide employment opportunities for disadvantaged workers in the public sector. The policy initiative on which the two programs were based grew out of the observation that there were many unemployed and underemployed workers in need of better jobs, and at the same time, there were increasing needs for public services.[1] The two programs reflected the attempt of manpower planners to achieve two worthwhile objectives simultaneously. This report will review the background and development of the programs and will analyze the results of evaluative studies which provide evidence of the impact of the two programs on minorities and women.

Program History

The continuous growth of the service sector has given a measure of stability to the labor market. Not only do the service industries continually provide new jobs for the increasing labor market, but they also act as magnets attracting into the labor force those groups within the population, such as youth and housewives, whose labor force participation is highly elastic with respect to job opportunities.

Recognizing that the public service area provides an opportunity for work-experience programs to help the disadvantaged find permanent employment, several different strategies for the definition of new public service jobs were developed. One model involved "breaking down existing professional or skilled jobs and generally separating out the simpler tasks."[2] This approach, labeled the "job spinoff" approach by Bennett Harrison, was institutionalized in 1966 through an amendment to the Economic Opportunity Act which created the New Careers Program.[3] The concept of the New Careers Program first achieved widespread

1. Harold L. Sheppard, *The Nature of the Job Problem and the Role of New Public Service Employment* (Kalamazoo: W. E. Upjohn Institute, 1969), pp. 19-20.

2. Sidney A. Fine, *Guidelines for the Design of New Careers* (Kalamazoo: W. E. Upjohn Institute, 1967), p. 13.

3. Bennett Harrison, *Public Service Jobs for Urban Ghetto Residents* (Washington, D.C.: National Civil Service League, Fall 1969), p. 12.

notice in 1965 with Arthur Pearl and Frank Riessman's book, *New Careers for the Poor*.[4] Their New Careers concept was an antipoverty strategy based on the premise that a career implies permanence and the opportunity for upward mobility and is, therefore, different from a job.[5] The design of the New Careers legislation incorporated these ideas in an effort to:

> . . . Relieve shortages of professional personnel in human service activities and . . . to meet the need of the unemployed and underemployed for meaningful jobs with career-ladder possibilities.[6]

The program was designed to prepare disadvantaged adults and out-of-school youth for careers in public service areas such as health, education, welfare, neighborhood redevelopment, and public safety. To a greater extent than other manpower programs, New Careers emphasized classroom training before or along with on-the-job training. Enrollees who completed the program were guaranteed full-time jobs by the agencies which provided the training.

During fiscal year 1967, the New Careers program was funded at $15,537,000 and provided 4,400 enrollment opportunities. In 1968, a national contract was signed with the Planned Parenthood Federation of America to train family-planning aides in family-planning clinics and other agencies in four regions.[7] Before it was subsumed within the Public Service Careers program in 1970, New Careers provided 13,000 enrollment opportunities for the disadvantaged worker.[8]

In 1970 the concept of using the service sector to upgrade unemployed or underemployed workers was expanded. The new program, called Public Service Careers (PSC), was not initiated by an act of Congress but was established under the legislative authority of the Economic Opportunity Act (EOA) of 1964, Title I-B as amended in 1966, and the Manpower Development and Training Act of 1962, Title II. New Careers was designed to prepare disadvantaged adults for careers in human service fields such as health and education, but PSC was designed to secure, within merit principles, permanent employment for the dis-

4. Arthur Pearl and Frank Riessman, *New Careers for the Poor* (New York. The Free Press, 1965).

5. Floyd Decker *et al., Municipal Government Efforts to Provide Career Employment Opportunities for the Disadvantaged* (Washington, D.C.: National League of Cities, 1969), p. 4.

6. U.S. Department of Labor, *Manpower Report of the President* (Washington, D.C.: Government Printing Office, 1969), p. 102.

7. *Ibid.*, p. 103.

8. U.S. Department of Labor, *Manpower Report of the President* (Washington, D.C.: Government Printing Office, 1973), Table F-1, p. 227.

advantaged worker in public service agencies in state and local governments.

In 1969 the more than 80,000 units of state and local government in the United States employed more than nine million workers. By 1975 the various governmental units may employ more than eleven million workers.[9] To help meet these growing manpower needs and also to open new career opportunities for the disadvantaged, the PSC program was designed to pay part of the cost of on-the-job training and intensive supportive services required for disadvantaged workers hired by public agencies. PSC also will help finance upgrading activities.

At the start of 1970, enrollments were exclusively in the New Careers segment of the larger PSC program. However, after July 1970, two factors influenced the buildup of PSC enrollments—a decline in business activity and the addition of a new program segment. Known as STEP (Supplemental Training and Employment Program), the new program segment was designed for workers who had completed training courses, were unemployed, and would benefit from additional training and work experience while waiting for regular opportunities. By November 1970, PSC was in full operation and by December, enrollment had reached 12,000. The upward trend in enrollment continued and reached 34,000 by November 1971.

Two factors contributed to a downturn in PSC enrollments to 20,000 by July 1972. First, the STEP component, which had been a temporary response to the 1970 economic downturn, was phased out. In addition, some of the twenty-one-month contracts and grants that initiated the program with state and local agencies expired in May 1972 and were not renewed.[10] Between 1967 and 1972, the PSC program, including New Careers, had more than 111,000 enrollees.[11]

PROGRAM STRUCTURE AND GOALS

The overall objectives of the Public Service Careers program are to "help secure, within merit principles, permanent employment for disadvantaged persons in governmental agencies at all levels, and to stimulate the upgrading of current employees" with the aim of satisfying

9. U.S. Department of Labor, *Manpower Report of the President* (1969), *op. cit.*, p. 73.

10. *Ibid.*, p. 53.

11. U.S. Department of Labor, *Manpower Report of the President* (1973), *op. cit.*, Table F-1, p. 227.

public sector manpower needs.[12] As part of its effort to achieve the above aims, PSC also strives to eliminate or overcome institutional skill deficiency and environmental barriers which prevent the most effective and efficient use of human resources in the public sector.

Institutional barriers are characteristics of an organization's structure and operation which restrict the range of job opportunity for many employees. Among such barriers are job families with little promotion potential and preselection standards which bear little relevancy to job performance, and discriminatory hiring practices.

Individual barriers are personal characteristics of disadvantaged workers which limit their competitive potential in the labor market. Generally these barriers include inadequate education, poor health, lack of training or skills, and often poor work attitudes.

Environmental barriers consist of the lack of services within a community. These barriers, which include poor transportation facilities, poor health care services, or lack of day care centers, hinder the disadvantaged worker in seeking or retaining employment.

Although at first glance PSC's design may appear to compete with the Civil Service system, such competition is not intended. PSC's goal is to work with the Civil Service system to perform the public's business most efficiently and effectively by assisting "public personnel on all levels of government to increase their capabilities, [and] to structure their merit systems to meet present program goals and needs."[13] This work may involve job restructuring, task analysis, test redesign, and supervisory training.

To achieve this goal, PSC has a four-part program based on the concept of "hire now-train later." Each part of PSC concentrates on one segment of the public sector as follows:

PSC Program Plans

Plan A: Employment and upgrading in state, county, and local governments.

Plan B: Employment and upgrading in agencies receiving federal grant-in-aid such as public hospitals and schools.

Plan C: Incorporates all existing New Careers programs.

12. U.S. Department of Labor, *Public Service Careers Plan "A" Handbook* (Washington, D.C.: Manpower Administration, 1971), p. 1-2.

13. *Ibid.*, p. 1-3

Plan D: Employment and upgrading in the federal service. Under this system a worker may be hired on the basis of an interview rather than through an examination. Upon completing probationary requirements, he becomes a regular employee of the agency for which he works without having to meet other qualifying standards.

Each plan has two components:

Entry—involves hiring and training persons who will be making their entry into public service positions.

Upgrade—involves persons currently employed in public service who will be training to upgrade or improve their skills.

In any project there can be Entry without Upgrade, but not the reverse.

Each PSC project has two phases:

Phase I: Program Refinement—a thirteen-week period beginning when an administrator and a sponsor sign a contract. There is no training during this period, only planning and staffing.

Phase II: Program Implementation—includes enrollee recruiting, selection, and training. Phase I and Phase II should not exceed twenty-one months.

The Department of Labor reimburses sponsors of Plan A and Plan B projects for the "extraordinary" costs involved in hiring and training PSC enrollees.[14]

The Public Service Careers program is designed to operate at all levels of government service. To make the program responsive to local needs, it is intentionally flexible and allows innovation in each sponsoring agency to meet the specific needs of the community, jurisdiction, or project design for grant-in-aid programs.

PSC is also structured both to benefit from and to complement the activities and services of other manpower programs. For example, CEP, WIN, Job Corps, and NYC may direct individuals to PSC if that program is the most appropriate for them. In addition, CEP often provides PSC trainees with supportive services.[15]

---

14. U.S. Department of Labor, *Plan "A" Handbook, op. cit.*, pp. 1-4 to 1-5.

15. U.S. Department of Labor, *Manpower Report of the President* (Washington, D.C.: Government Printing Office, 1970), p. 74.

TABLE IX-1. *Public Service Careers*
Percent Distribution of Enrollee Characteristics
By RMC Entry Enrollee Data and OMMDS Data [a]

Characteristics	Plan A		Plan B	
	OMMDS [a]	RMC	OMMDS [a]	RMC
Age:				
Under 22	27.1	30.9	20.6	14.9
22-44	55.6	61.8	59.9	68.3
Over 44	17.4	7.3	19.4	16.8
Sex:				
Male	43.8	51.0	40.0	41.6
Female	56.2	49.0	60.0	58.4
Race:				
Black	50.6	64.7	39.7	54.0
White	38.4	16.9	48.1	34.8
American Indian	7.1	2.9	7.9	5.6
Oriental	0.3	0.3	0.9	0.6
Other	3.6	15.2	3.4	5.0
Highest grade completed:				
Less than 12 years	42.7	48.4	48.5	42.2
High school graduate	48.6	42.6	41.8	44.1
Post-high school	8.7	9.0	9.8	13.7
Marital status:				
Single	31.7	41.1	24.8	18.6
Married	48.5	31.5	56.5	43.5
Divorced/separated	16.9	25.0	15.9	36.0
Widowed	2.9	2.0	2.8	1.9
Individual annual income:				
Less than $2,500	75.5	57.7	52.5	42.9
2,500 - 3,499	10.4	17.2	17.0	23.6
3,500 - 4,499	5.5	10.8	11.1	11.8
4,500 - 5,499	2.6	5.8	6.7	7.5
5,000 - 6,499	1.9	3.8	4.9	5.6
More than 6,500	4.0	2.3	7.9	6.8
Refused/do not know	—	2.3	—	1.2
Total	100.0	100.0	100.0	100.0

Source: RMC Incorporated, "Evaluation of the PSC Program—Final Report, Volume I: Findings and Conclusions," report prepared for Office of Policy, Evaluation and Research, Manpower Administration, U.S. Department of Labor, 1972, p. 14.

Note: Figures may not add to 100.0 percent due to rounding.

[a] Office of Manpower Management Data Systems superseded by Office of Financial and Management Information Systems.

Target Group

The target population for the PSC program varies slightly between program sectors. In the Entry component of the program, enrollees must be disadvantaged and at least eighteen years old. In the Upgrade component of the program, eligible enrollees must be employed by the sponsoring agency at the time the contract with PSC is awarded. The eligibility standards are flexible, but selection favors low-income employees who have been employed by the sponsor for an extended period.

Plan A and New Careers (Plan C) enroll more females than males and more minorities than whites (Tables 1 and 2). While Plan B also enrolls a majority of women, it is the only program segment in which there is a greater percentage of white than black enrollees (48.1 percent to 39.7 percent). In most other demographic areas, the program segments are very similar. The majority of enrollees are between 22 and 44 years old and about one-half have at least completed high school.

The characteristics of enrollees are consistent with the objectives of PSC. In many cases the enrollees already hold jobs and would therefore be expected to be older. Also, because government jobs require a high school diploma, one may expect a high incidence of PSC enrollees with that amount of formal education.

REVIEW OF EVALUATIVE LITERATURE

The only comprehensive study of the PSC program is a three-part evaluation conducted between March 1970 and March 1972 by RMC Incorporated of Bethesda, Maryland.[16] The study examines Plans A and B, the two segments of PSC that are under the jurisdiction of the Department of Labor.

RMC selected 40 project sites and interviewed more than 300 program and public officials, approximately 600 enrollees, and about 200 supervisors. During 1971, interviews were conducted in two rounds about nine months apart. In most cases each individual was interviewed during both the first and second visits.

The RMC sample shows a slightly higher proportion of nonwhites, a lower proportion of unmarried enrollees, and a higher pre-program median income than U. S. Department of Labor data on PSC enrollees (Table 1). The two data sources differ in part because the RMC survey was conducted several months before the national data were collected. Between the two time periods, PSC grew more than sixfold in enroll-

16. RMC Incorporated, "Evaluation of the PSC Program—Final Report," report prepared for Office of Policy, Evaluation and Research, Manpower Administration, U.S. Department of Labor,1972.

ment. RMC interviewed 329 Entry enrollees and 136 Upgrade enrollees, but these samples represent only 9 percent of the Plan A enrollees and 3 percent of the Plan B enrollees listed in Table 1. The RMC sample is, therefore, representative of early PSC enrollees located primarily in urban areas where nonwhites comprise a significant proportion of the population, and wages are somewhat higher than the national average.[17]

Studies of the New Careers program in the nation at large were not available. Several studies, however, did focus on the impact of local programs. A 1969 study conducted by the National League of Cities, *Municipal Government Efforts to Provide Career Employment Opportunities for the Disadvantaged*, examined municipal programs in six cities (Dayton, Detroit, El Paso, New York, San Francisco, and Washington, D.C.).[18] All the cities had federally sponsored programs, usually of the New Careers type. Although there was no cost-benefit study of the programs, some favorable subjective impact on the delivery of governmental services and on the enrollee was found.

The Olympus Research Corporation conducted a study of the impact of various manpower programs in Boston, Denver, San Francisco, and Oakland.[19] Also, an in-depth study of the Minneapolis New Careers project was conducted by General College and Minnesota Center for Sociological Research during 1968-1969.[20] Data were collected by questionnaire from all 281 enrollees in the two-year program and more than 200 were interviewed. In addition extensive efforts were made to follow up 105 candidates who dropped out of the program.

PROGRAM IMPACT

The study conducted by RMC Incorporated did not specifically analyze the impact of PSC on minorities and women. The PSC program enrolled more women than men. Depending on the program component, PSC consisted of about 50 percent minorities. Therefore, to the extent that the program had an impact on its enrollees in general, it is probable

17. RMC Incorporated, "Final Report, Volume I: Findings and Conclusions," *op. cit.*, pp. 13-15.

18. Decker *et al., loc. cit.*

19. Olympus Research Corporation, "The Total Impact of Manpower Programs: A Four-City Case Study," report prepared for Office of Policy, Evaluation and Research, Manpower Administration, U.S. Department of Labor, 1971.

20. Frank R. Falk, *The Frontier of Action: New Careers for the Poor—A Viable Concept* (Minneapolis: General College and Minnesota Center for Sociological Research, n.d.).

TABLE IX-2. *New Careers*
Percent Distribution of Trainee Characteristics
1968-1969

Characteristics	1968[a]	1969
Sex:		
Male	36.8	29.9
Female	63.2	70.1
Age:		
Under 22	0.5	8.4
22-34	65.2	59.5
35-44	20.1	19.6
45-54	10.9	10.2
55 or over	3.2	2.2
Median	31.5	30.7
Race:		
White	24.8	33.0
Negro	73.9	61.1
American Indian	0.1	2.7
Oriental	—	0.8
Other	1.2	2.3
School years completed:		
6 years or less	3.2	1.9
7-9 years	22.9	16.7
10-11 years	35.8	31.7
12 years or more	38.0	49.7
Median years	11.4	12.0
Marital status:		
Single	23.4	28.7
Married	38.3	31.2
Widowed, divorced, separated	38.3	40.1
Estimated family income:		
Below $1,000	—	—
1,000 - 1,999	53.5	21.7
2,000 - 2,999	27.9	2.1
3,000 - 3,999	12.9	1.7
4,000 - 4,999	4.1	58.5
5,000 - 5,999	1.5	15.9
Median wage	1,934	4,418
Total	100.0	100.0
Total sample	953	2,148

Source: U.S. Department of Labor, *Manpower Report of the President* (Washington, D.C.: Government Printing Office), 1969, Table F-12, p. 249; 1970, Table F-10, p. 313.

Note: Percents may not add to 100.0 percent due to rounding.
[a] Data for August 1967 to September 1968.

that the program also had an impact on minorities and women. A special section of this report will discuss the impact of PSC on minorities and women.

Of most direct interest in assessing the impact of PSC is the economic impact the program has on enrollee income and employment status. However, in terms of the broad goals of PSC—to break down the institutional barriers to careers in the public sector—a judgement of program success can also be made by determining whether the enrollees continued to work satisfactorily in public service employment in sufficient numbers to warrant the program effort.

The major conclusions reached by RMC are as follows: (1) short-run enrollee economic impact associated with PSC participation is favorable from both the career and income perspectives; (2) skill training and basic education are the most valuable services offered to enrollees; and (3) limited institutional change was accomplished through PSC.

Employment

Of the 600 participants surveyed by RMC, 70 percent of the Entry enrollees were employed about 42 percent of the year prior to joining PSC. Using the maximum average salary of sampled enrollees of $85 per week, the estimated average enrollee earnings were less than $2,000 per year for the weeks employed.[21] This is substantially below the "near-poverty" indicator of $4,500 (nonfarm) for a family of four used by the program.

The direct economic benefits of the program are realized by enrollees through the "hire now-train later" philosophy of PSC. Entry enrollees are offered full employment as well as education and training. This fact alone ensures an improvement in the financial situation of the enrollee. While assigned to the program, workers earned average weekly wages of $97, which extends to about $5,000 per year, an increase of $3,000 above pre-program income.[22]

As a direct benefit of their guaranteed jobs, 68 percent of the Entry enrollees reported receiving a pay raise during their tenure in the program and 25 percent received a promotion.[23] In addition, Upgrade enrollees averaged a 9.6 percent annual increase in salary while participating in PSC. The national average salary progress of all noneducation state and local government employees was 7 percent in 1969 and 9 percent in 1970.[24] The Olympus study did not contain an in-depth analysis of the employ-

21. RMC Incorporated, "Final Report, Volume I," *op. cit.*, p. 35.

22. *Ibid.*, p. 37.

23. *Ibid.*, p. 38.

24. *Ibid.*, p. 36.

ment status of PSC enrollees, but did suggest that New Careers provided opportunities for entry-level white collar jobs and for further education for enrollees with the ability and ambition to be upgraded.[25]

Job Stability

Enrollees generally were placed on a probationary or training status, which lasted from six months to a year. Following completion of this period their position in the agency would be protected by merit system status achieved either by satisfactory job performance or by passing a test. RMC's survey indicated that 59 percent of Plan A and 51 percent of Plan B enrollees achieved this permanent status (see Table 3).

In terms of pre-/post-wage levels and job stability, PSC program completers appear to have benefited from the program. In terms of employment, PSC has been successful because 93 percent of its Entry enrollees achieved permanent or probationary status in their public service jobs. Measured by gains in social welfare, the results of the RMC study are mixed. In general, all Entry enrollees, completers as well as noncompleters, benefited from the program through increased weekly salaries. Although the noncompleters did benefit from increased salaries on jobs found after leaving PSC, they seem to have experienced problems in finding those jobs; only 42 percent of the noncompleters were employed when RMC conducted their second round of interviews.

Attitude

Eighty-seven percent of all Entry enrollees and 96 percent of Upgrade enrollees surveyed liked their jobs with PSC, and enrollees were optimistic about holding a job a year from the first interview. Although less optimistic at the second interview, an overwhelming majority of enrollees (77 percent of Entry and 79 percent of Upgrade) still felt that they would be employed a year from the survey. This optimism is not surprising considering that 60 percent of all enrollees felt that the training and education they received was the most favorable aspect of the program.[26]

Both Entry and Upgrade components of Plan A programs emphasize training in three job categories (Table 4): managerial occupations, clerical and sales work, and service occupations. About 78 percent of Entry and Upgrade enrollees fell into these three training areas. Of the 337 participants who completed the PSC program, 80.9 percent received training in these occupations, most of them in the clerical and sales area.[27] Plan B programs emphasized similar occupational training. Approximately 70.3 percent of the 859 Entry enrollees and 44.7 percent of the 398 Upgrade enrollees participated in these occupations. Of the 177

25. Olympus Research Corp., *op cit.*, pp. 41-42.

26. RMC Incorporated, "Final Report, Volume I," *op. cit.*, p. 45.

27. RMC Incorporated, "Final Report, Volume II," *op. cit.*, Tables 5-1 to 5-4, pp. 55-58.

individuals who completed the Plan B program, 147 received training in these three service categories.[28]

TABLE IX-3. *Public Service Careers*
Work Experiences and Work Attitudes of Program Participants

Experiences and Attitudes	Total	Plan A	Plan B
Percent of enrollees employed at all during previous year	70	71	66
Percent of year employed	42	39	49
Average highest salary per week in previous year	$85	$86	$83
Gross PSC salary per week (Entry enrollees)	$97	$98	$94
Percent of enrollees receiving pay raise	68	70	63
Percent of enrollees receiving promotion for which a test was required	22	25	17
Upgrade:			
Pre-PSC salary, per week	$99	$102	$97
Salary at start of program, per week	$119	$114	$122
Salary at follow-up, per week	$128	$123	$130
Average yearly raise (percent)	9.6	13.2	8.4
Percent of enrollees achieving permanent job status	56	59	51
Percent achieving probationary status	37	40	28
No merit system (percent)	7	1	21
Terminees:			
Percent employed	42	35	54
Average weekly earnings	$96	$94	$98
Liked job (Entry—percent)	87	85	93
Liked job (Upgrade—percent)	96	90	99
Percent of enrollees expecting to be in a job one year later:			
Entry:			
First interview	80	81	78
Second interview	77	72	88
Upgrade:			
First interview	87	82	90
Second interview	79	59	90

Source: RMC Incorporated, "Evaluation of the PSC Program—Final Report, Volume I: Findings and Conclusions," report prepared for Office of Policy, Evaluation and Research, Manpower Administration, U.S. Department of Labor, 1972, pp. 35-52.

28. *Ibid.*

TABLE IX-4. *Public Service Careers*
Areas of Training of Enrollees in Program

Occupational Group	Plan A				Plan B			
	Entry		Upgrade		Entry		Upgrade	
	No.	Percent	No.	Percent	No.	Percent	No.	Percent
Professionals and technicians	49	3.3	26	4.3	114	13.3	64	16.1
Managers	175	11.7	117	19.4	153	17.8	102	25.6
Clerical and sales workers	517	34.7	209	34.7	132	15.4	43	10.8
Service workers	475	31.8	141	23.4	320	37.2	33	8.3
Farming, fishing, forestry, and related areas	13	0.9	3	0.5	9	1.0	—	—
Processing operatives	2	0.1	—	—	—	—	—	—
Machine trade	13	0.9	38	6.3	—	—	—	—
Bench work	—	—	—	—	—	—	—	—
Structural work	96	6.4	37	6.1	16	1.9	24	6.0
Miscellaneous	43	2.9	17	2.8	109	12.7	132	33.2
Unknown	109	7.3	15	2.5	6	0.7	—	—
Total	1,492	100.0	603	100.0	859	100.0	398	100.0

Source: RMC, Incorporated, "Evaluation of the PSC Program Final Report Volume II: Second Round Site Visit Results," report prepared for Office of Policy, Evaluation and Research, Manpower Administration, U.S. Department of Labor, 1973, Tables 5-1 to 5-4, pp. 55-58.

Program Services

In an attempt to remove some of the barriers disadvantaged workers face in gaining employment, PSC provides extensive supportive services, including transportation subsidies for one month, child-care service (either through other manpower programs or through direct cost reimbursement to the enrollee for a maximum of thirteen weeks), medical services, basic education, and training.

Although all of the above contribute to enrollee success, some are more effective than others. Transportation subsidies are a benefit; however, it is lack of convenient transportation facilities that hinders participation in PSC, not distance of commuting or expense. Twenty-seven percent of RMC's sample Entry enrollees reported commuting difficulties, and about 14 percent of the sample used PSC subsidies for their commuting.[29]

At first interview 23 percent of the women with children at home asserted that caring for their children prevented them from getting or keeping jobs. By the second round of interviews, only 10 percent of these women still cited child care as a problem. Only two of 67 terminees cited this as the primary reason for leaving the program.[30]

The education and training services of the program as viewed by the majority of enrollees as the most beneficial services offered by PSC. More than 50 percent of Entry enrollees reported limited education, limited skills, or lack of experience as a barrier to obtaining jobs they desired. Ninety-six percent of the participants said that classes were helpful.[31] This satisfaction probably results from the flexibility of the education and training programs which could be altered to meet individual needs of enrollees.

Minorities and Women

RMC did not attempt to analyze the differential impact of PSC on minorities and women, nor did RMC collect data from which such analyses could be performed. However, since PSC has been beneficial for the average enrollee in increasing job stability and post-program salary levels, the program probably also benefited minorities and women.

An alternative evaluation of the impact of PSC on minorities and women may be obtained by examining the program's effectiveness in lowering barriers which have hindered these groups in obtaining employment. It is often the disadvantaged and poorly educated who are most affected by unrealistic job requirements, testing procedures, and discri-

---

29. RMC Incorporated, "Final Report, Volume I," *op. cit.*, pp. 22-23.

30. *Ibid.*, p. 27.

31. *Ibid.*, pp. 18, 30.

minatory hiring practices. To the extent that PSC has been successful in changing hiring procedures to facilitate promotions and hiring of the disadvantaged, it has benefited minorities and women. RMC concludes that it is "clear that PSC participants are not only in most cases certifiably disadvantaged. . . .They are usually not less disadvantaged and in many cases are more so than individuals hired or advanced in similar jobs under 'regular' standards."[32]

Since 99 percent of the Plan A enrollees and 79 percent of the Plan B enrollees surveyed had achieved at least probationary status on their jobs while PSC participants, it is reasonable to conclude that PSC has been effective in opening career channels to minority and female participants.

As another indication of the overall impact of PSC, 72 percent of the Entry and 56 percent of the Upgrade enrollees surveyed felt better prepared for a job because of participation in the program.[33] In addition, 68.3 percent of the Entry and 54.6 percent of the Upgrade enrollees surveyed had received a raise since joining PSC, and almost 30 percent in both components had received promotions.[34]

Of the 38 projects surveyed by RMC, substantial data about enrollee perceptions of the program were available for 26 individual programs. Of these 26 projects, 19 had a majority of nonwhite enrollees. In all but two cases, income while enrolled in PSC was higher than income before participation. In addition, in all of these 26 programs, at least one-half of the enrollees interviewed stated that PSC had helped them find a better job.[35]

NEW CAREERS PROGRAM

The evaluative literature on the New Careers program is subjective in nature, often emphasizing the impact the program has on the delivery of services rather than the impact of the program on enrollees. In addition, little information is available on the differential impact of New Careers on minorities and women. In general, the available studies indicate that New Careers has been successful in establishing some career employment opportunities for the disadvantaged, particularly for the disadvantaged female.

32. *Ibid.*, p. 142.

33. RMC Incorporated, "Final Report, Volume III: Second Round Interivew Results," *op. cit.*, p. 7 and Table 3-8.

34. *Ibid.*

35. *Ibid.*, pp. 73-140

Employment and Job Stability

Although empirical evidence is very limited, the six-city survey conducted in 1969 by the National League of Cities suggested that the New Careers program was successful in placing enrollees in career-ladder positions in the municipal services area. The project in New York City is an outstanding example of the program's success. Of the 960 jobs available, 825 were filled by the time of the survey, and all enrollees were expected to become permanent city employees.[36] No post-program records of employment were analyzed by the study.

The Olympus study indicated similar success for the New Careers projects in the four cities surveyed. The Boston New Careers project was part of the local CEP organization. Between 1967 and 1970, the program had 741 enrollees. Little information was available for program completers since the first group had just completed the two-year training schedule at the time of the survey. Approximately one-half of the program enrollees completed training. Those who remained in their jobs following program completion experienced some financial benefit from their training, as their average hourly wages increased from about $2.00 per hour to between $2.70 and $3.00 per hour.[37]

The Denver project had mixed success. Although it was relatively successful in terms of hourly wage increases for enrollees, the program was poorly designed and program planners miscalculated the community willingness to invest in jobs which corresponded to the aspirations of the New Career enrollees. The program expired in the fall of 1968 after one year of operation. Nevertheless, 42 of the 78 enrollees in the program had achieved permanent career employment and had shown an average post-program wage improvement of $0.51 to $2.27 per hour.[38]

The Bay Area (San Francisco, Oakland, Richmond) programs surveyed by Olympus also showed mixed success. Of the 669 people who had enrolled in the New Career programs by the spring of 1970, 184 had found permanent employment. On the other hand, 238 graduated or dropped out of the program without finding a job.[39] This project was a particularly rigorous one because enrollees were required to attend a community college on a full-time basis while working 20 hours a week. The project, then, was an elite one, limited to a select group which could handle school and work at the same time.

36. Decker *et al., op. cit.*, p. 104.

37. Olympus Research Corporation, "Volume II," *op. cit.*, pp. 6-11 to 6-12.

38. *Ibid.*, p. 14-30.

39. *Ibid.*, p. 20-23.

In general, the Olympus study concluded that the New Careers projects in the four selected cities enrolled a minority of trainees with above average education whose expectations exceeded the program's ability to deliver. Despite some success in placement, the program did not achieve its goals of breaking down the customary barriers to employment of the disadvantaged and restructuring jobs. It did manage, however, to open access to many entry-level white collar jobs.[40]

The study of the Minneapolis New Careers program undertaken by the University of Minnesota between 1967 and 1968 does not touch upon job placement rates or pre-/post-wage increases.

Program Services

Virtually all the New Career projects surveyed in the various studies provided comprehensive services to the enrollees. In some cases, the New Careers projects were not able to supply all the needed services and therefore other manpower programs or public agencies assumed the tasks. In general, all projects provided enrollees with medical and dental examinations, job and family counseling, legal aid, remedial education, and day care facilities. Some projects also offered transportation subsidies to enrollees.

The extensive supply of services available to help the enrollee is probably one factor which influenced enrollee attitudes concerning the New Careers program. All three program evaluations cited above reported that program participation had a positive influence on enrollee self-perception and general outlook on life. The National League of Cities study concluded that the program "raised the hopes and ambitions of enrollees and provided them with an opportunity to play a meaningful role in society and, at the same time, many now have expectations of financial independence they never before thought possible."[41]

Impact on Minorities and Women

The great majority of New Careerists are female. This can be attributed primarily to the program's emphasis on employment in human services, an area which tends to attract women rather than men. In addition, the use of social workers and clergymen for recruiters, combined with the establishment of relatively high educational requirements, reinforces the tendency toward a high female-male enrollee ratio. Therefore, although program data may not be classified in a way that permits analysis of the impact on women, any general program benefits will, in all probability, be indicative of benefits to women. The same conclu-

40. Olympus Research Corporation, "Volume I," *op. cit.*, p. 42.

41. Decker *et al.*, *op. cit.*, p. 24.

sion may be reached with respect to minorities since, according to the figures in Table 2, the New Careers program enrolls significantly more nonwhites than whites.

Although the National League of Cities study does not analyze the impact of the New Careers program by race or sex, its conclusion that the program has raised enrollee aspirations and helped them to secure jobs implies that there have been benefits for women and minority groups.[42] Similarly, the Minneapolis study did not classify the data by race or sex. Nonetheless, because 172 of the 280 enrollees surveyed were female, and 160 enrollees were nonwhite, program-derived benefits were most likely benefits for minorities and women.[43] The data revealed some significant improvements in the self-concept of enrollees, maintenance of fairly high aspirations for mobility, and a slight trend toward entry into subprofessional careers.[44]

Of the studies cited, only the Olympus Research Corporation analysis delineates program success by sex and race. Of the 741 people enrolled in the Boston New Careers project, about one-half completed training. Of those who finished the program, about 50 percent were women and between 75 and 85 percent were black.[45] No measure of placement rate for completers was made. Despite the absence of this statistic, the post-program hourly wage increase from $2.00 to between $2.70 and $3.00 indicates that some benefit must have accrued to minorities and women through program participation.[46]

The demise of the Denver New Careers project was probably caused by overexpectation on the part of enrollees. According to the survey, the enrollees were disillusioned because their "promised new careers remained entry-level white collar jobs."[47] Despite this, the program still managed to place 42 of its 78 enrollees, of whom 39 were either black or Spanish American. The average hourly wage rate improvement for all placements was $0.51 to $2.27. Females benefited the most, showing an improvement of $0.62 per hour, while blacks and enrollees of Spanish American descent showed an increase of $0.46 and $0.56, respectively.[48] No statistics of this type were available for the Bay Area programs.

42. *Ibid.*

43. Margaret Thompson, "The New Careerist: A Description," in Falk, *op. cit.,* Appendix G, pp. 3-5.

44. Frank R. Falk, "Social-Psychological Changes in New Careerists," in Falk, *op. cit.,* Appendix I, p. 21.

45. Olympus Research Corporation, "Volume II," *op cit.,* p. 6-12.

46. *Ibid.*

47. Olympus Research Corporation, "Volume I," *op. cit.,* p. 42.

48. Olympus Research Corporation, "Volume II," *op. cit.,* p. 12-29.

CONCLUSIONS

Public Service Careers (PSC) and New Careers (which was subsumed into PSC in 1970) were pioneer projects in the development of public sector employment for the disadvantaged. The objectives of PSC are to secure employment for disadvantaged persons in all areas of public service and to stimulate the upgrading of current employees with the aim of satisfying public sector manpower needs.

In general, PSC has facilitated career placement in public service areas. PSC has placed enrollees who are doing as well as similar non-PSC workers, and it has been particularly beneficial to disadvantaged enrollees. When viewed in terms of its income effect, PSC has had a positive impact on enrollees. In particular, since wages in the public sector for nonskilled work are generally higher than wages for similar work in the private sector, participation in the program has benefited enrollees.

The PSC program enrolls more women than men and, depending on the program component, about 50 percent minorities. Therefore, to the extent that the program had an impact on its target group as a whole, it is probable that it also had an impact on minorities and women. The program has been somewhat effective in altering institutional requirements for promotion, from reliance on testing to more reliance on satisfactory job performance. This change had the effect of opening new career channels to minority and female participants.

Although there have not been extensive follow-up studies to measure the long-range impact of PSC, the findings of the evaluative literature indicate that the program had a favorable impact from both a career and an income perspective for enrollees.

The New Careers component of PSC has been particularly successful in terms of its impact on the attitudes of its enrollees. In general, it has raised enrollee hopes and ambitions and enabled them to play a meaningful role in society. In many cases enrollees can look forward to an economic independence which they never before felt capable of achieving.

Still, the New Careers program has fallen short of several of its goals. Principally because of its small size and limited funds, the program has not had a great impact on the services rendered by municipal governments. These same limitations also make it impossible for a program such as New Careers to have any significant impact upon unemployment. Although the program has been relatively successful in placing enrollees who finish the training, for many the program title, "New Careers," is a misnomer. The title promises what the program is incapable, for the most part, of delivering. The average educational achievement for New Careers enrollees is considerably above that of participants in other manpower programs. To such enrollees a new career means a position with career potential, not a clerical, stenographic, or subprofessional job.

Many problems arise to thwart a program which promises a new career to the disadvantaged worker. Among these problems are institutional hindrances such as unions, professional and societal rules for membership, and legal barriers such as Civil Service and licensing requirements. Faced with the lack of resources to break down these traditional barriers or to restructure jobs, the New Careers program was doomed to be less than the success hoped for, at the time it was designed.

CHAPTER X

Apprenticeship Outreach Program

by
Stephen A. Schneider
Research Associate
Under the Direction of
Herbert R. Northrup

The purpose of this study is to examine in depth the Apprenticeship Outreach Program. This examination encompasses a review of the general nature of the program, including background and brief history, the program's structure and operation, a review of the existing program evaluations and their findings, and an analysis of program statistics.

Program Purpose and Background

The Apprenticeship Outreach Program (AOP) is designed to increase the proportion of minority group members in the apprenticeable skilled trades, especially those in building construction. The clear assumption inherent in the program is that blacks and other minorities are not able to obtain the necessary skills, either informally or formally, to qualify them for craft jobs. In fact, a majority of craftsmen probably achieve their status by informal training methods, rather than by formal apprenticeship programs.[1]

To a certain extent, informal entry is possible for Negroes in some trades, especially the "trowel" ones (bricklaying, plastering, cement work), and to a lesser extent in carpentry and painting. There is a long tradition of blacks in the "trowel trades," particularly dating back to slavery in the South, hence, there is some black representation in these crafts. The young Negro desiring informal instruction can sometimes gain it from relatives and friends in a manner similar to whites. Moreover, these crafts, except perhaps in some finishing work, do not require the technical knowledge and stringent requirements of some others. The observant laborer or helper can sometimes learn the rudiments of the trade. Nevertheless, the opportunities to "pick up" skills in these trades remain much greater for whites than for minorities.

For the electrical, plumbing, and mechanical trades, the problems for minorities are more severe. Developed not long before the beginning of the twentieth century, these crafts had no tradition of Negro utilization. Traditionally the black has been systematically excluded from such work, from the training for such work, and from the building and metal trades

1. See Howard G. Foster, "Nonapprenticeship Sources of Training Construction," *Monthly Labor Review*, Vol. XCIII, no. 2 (February 1970), pp. 21-26.

unions therein.[2] With his relatives and friends excluded, the opportunity for a young black to gain informal instruction in these trades has been minimal.

Formal instruction, moreover, is more important in the electrical, plumbing, and mechanical trades than in many others. Greater technical knowledge and detailed standards are required for these crafts which result in formal training for a higher portion of craftsmen. Not only has discrimination kept minorities out of apprentice programs, but for these crafts in particular, the qualifications have tended to exclude minorities who might have entered.[3] As Mangum has noted:

> Members of minority groups have little knowledge of apprenticeship opportunities, and few know craftsmen or union officials who can act as their advocates. Deficiencies in their education preclude their passing the increasingly technical entry exams, even when they surmount other barriers.[4]

It was to overcome the entry difficulties that the Apprenticeship Outreach Program was created.

NATURE OF THE PROGRAM

The Apprenticeship Outreach Program (AOP) is authorized by the Manpower Development and Training Act of 1962 to assist minority groups in entering apprenticeship programs.[5] The program is designed to create equal opportunity for minorities by providing intensive tutoring programs up to ten weeks to prepare youths for entrance examinations in a particular apprenticeable trade mainly in the construction industry.

History

The AOP is an outgrowth of efforts by Recruitment Training Programs (formerly the Workers' Defense League) in 1964 to assist minority applicants desiring entrance into apprenticeship programs in the con-

2. For a general background on the subject of the Negro craftsman and his exclusion from trades, see Herbert R. Northrup, *Organized Labor and the Negro* (New York: Kraus Reprint edition, 1971), pp. 17-47.

3. See F. Ray Marshall and Vernon M. Briggs, Jr., *The Negro and Apprenticeship* (Baltimore: Johns Hopkins Press, 1967).

4. Garth L. Mangum, *MDTA Foundation of Federal Manpower Policy* (Baltimore: Johns Hopkins Press, 1968), p. 115.

5. *Daily Labor Report*, No. 242 (Washington, D.C.: Bureau of National Affairs, December 14, 1972), p. E-1.

struction industry. The Workers' Defense League (WDL), founded in the 1930's as a civil rights organization, turned to the apprenticeship problem in 1963. With a grant from the A. Philip Randolph Foundation in 1964, WDL established a successful program in the Bedford-Stuyvesant area of New York City.[6] In 1967 the Department of Labor provided funds for the expansion of its program to the WDL in a number of cities. Additional grants were made to the National Urban League, local Building Trades Councils, and other community-based organizations.

Scope of AOP

There are four basic methods of support for outreach programs: (1) by contractual agreement, the Joint Apprenticeship Program of the WDL has been provided with funds to operate programs in cities under national centralized direction; (2) the National Urban League has been provided with funds by contractual agreements which, in turn, are subcontracted to individual Urban Leagues in different cities to operate Labor Education and Advancement Programs (LEAP); (3) individual contracts are made with local AFL-CIO Building Trades Councils (BTC) in different areas; and (4) individual contracts are made with other nonprofit, local sponsors. At the present time the national administration of the BTC programs is being transferred to the AFL-CIO Human Resources Development Institute (HRDI) as local contracts expire and are refunded by the Department of Labor.

Program sponsor, number of locations, and cumulative number of indentures as of August 1973 since program inception are summarized in Table 1.

AOP can be considered as one large service process. The primary objective is to move qualified minorities into apprenticeship programs. As such, services focus on preparation for the entrance process. Applicants are generally tested to determine their qualifications. Counseling is provided, with emphasis on what to expect from the industry and what to expect during apprenticeship. Some formal training is furnished, although limited to language arts, mathematics, and trade-related subjects. Practice is provided in taking written and oral examinations. Assistance is given in traveling to examination sites, filling out required forms, securing proof of high school education, and in other related matters. Project staffs attempt to keep in touch with participants after they have been placed in apprenticeship programs to aid in problem solving. Attempts are also made to maintain close contacts with the Joint Apprenticeship

6. See F. Ray Marshall and Vernon M. Briggs, Jr., *Equal Apprenticeship Opportunities—The Nature of the Issue and the New York Experience* (Ann Arbor: The Institute of Labor and Industrial Relations, University of Michigan and Wayne State University, 1968).

TABLE X-1. *Apprenticeship Outreach Program Locations and Indentures by Sponsor August 1973*

Sponsor	Locations	Indentures
National Urban League	37	9,187
Workers' Defense League	25	5,825
AFL-CIO	32	7,950
Local Independent Sponsors	24	3,808
Total	118	26,770

Source: U.S. Department of Labor, Bureau of Apprenticeship and Training.

Councils (JAC) to determine when programs are accepting applicants and how previous placements are performing. Staffs also try to stay alert to discriminatory practices.

Local project staffs are provided with technical assistance by the national staffs of the WDL, National Urban League, and Building Trades Councils and Human Resources Development Institute of the AFL-CIO. In addition, support is provided by the Bureau of Apprenticeship and Training (BAT), and the U.S. Training and Employment Service, a branch of the Department of Labor that serves as a job referral service and works in conjunction with the various state employment services. Local projects may seek assistance from local public employment service offices and from Apprenticeship Information Centers. BAT monitors the local projects.

The distinguishing feature of AOP is that acceptance into AOP is constrained by the qualifications for apprenticeship programs set by the unions, unionized construction employers, and the JAC. In other words, the objective is to work within the system rather than against the establishment, which is represented by the building trades unions and the unionized construction employers. From the possible target population, the target group referred and accepted must meet the qualifications for acceptance into the apprenticeship programs. In effect, AOP is a process by which target group referrals are prepared for the selection criteria of apprenticeship. The emphasis is on working with the qualifications set by the apprenticeship programs and not on attempting to alter those qualifications. As an example, if a high school diploma is a requirement for entrance, and it is in most cases, AOP does not prepare participants for GED exams but only accepts those with the diplomas. In some cases, however, the system and the establishment are circumvented. Dennis A. Derryck has noted a case involving a local union in New York City that had a specific high school average as requirement for admission to its apprenticeship program. "Rather than challenge the basis of this requirement, WDL sought the cooperation of the local teachers union and got them to change the grades on the minority applicants' transcripts."[7] Figure 1 illustrates how the AOP process operates. Outreach activities begin in the minority target population. Interested potential minority group members are referred to AOP for further screening. The screening component is based on the qualifications for the apprenticeship programs. These qualifications include age, education, lack of criminal records, etc. Those screened and accepted into AOP are processed and prepared for apprenticeship by practice in written and oral tests and by the variety of services offered by AOP. As can be seen in the diagram, the people flow from the left to the right whereas information flows from the right to the left. Qualifications for apprenticeship programs are determined by the Joint Apprenticeship Committee composed of representatives of the BAT, the employers, and unions. This qualification information flows through the AOP process to the referred minority target population. In essence, candidates for the AOP program are constrained by the apprenticeship qualifications established by the JAC.

PROGRAM STRUCTURE AND OPERATION

The characteristics of enrollees, more than anything else, set the outreach program apart from other manpower programs. Since AOP is small compared to other manpower programs, separate tabulations of participant characteristics are not reported in the more conventional sources of information such as the *Manpower Report of the President*. The characteristics of participants were taken from a comprehensive cross-sectional evaluation of AOP.[8]

As would be expected, approximately 88 percent of the participants were Negro and some 3.5 percent were nonminority, indicating the inclusion of other minority groups such as the Mexican Americans who usually participate in the southwestern and western regions of the country. No females have ever been reported in the program. Differentiation from other programs is provided by the relatively stable backgrounds of the participants. Indicators of stable background are the fact

7. Dennis A. Derryck, "Retention of Minorities in Apprenticeship: The Nature of the Issue," paper presented at a Conference on Apprenticeship Research and Development, Manpower Administration, U.S. Department of Labor, Washington,D.C., May 30, 1973, p. 3, note 2. Proceedings forthcoming.

8. Boise Cascade Center for Community Development, "Report of an Evaluation of the Apprenticeship Outreach Program (AOP)," report prepared for Manpower Administration, U.S. Department of Labor, 1970, p. 7.

FIGURE X-1. *Apprenticeship Outreach Program Process Model*

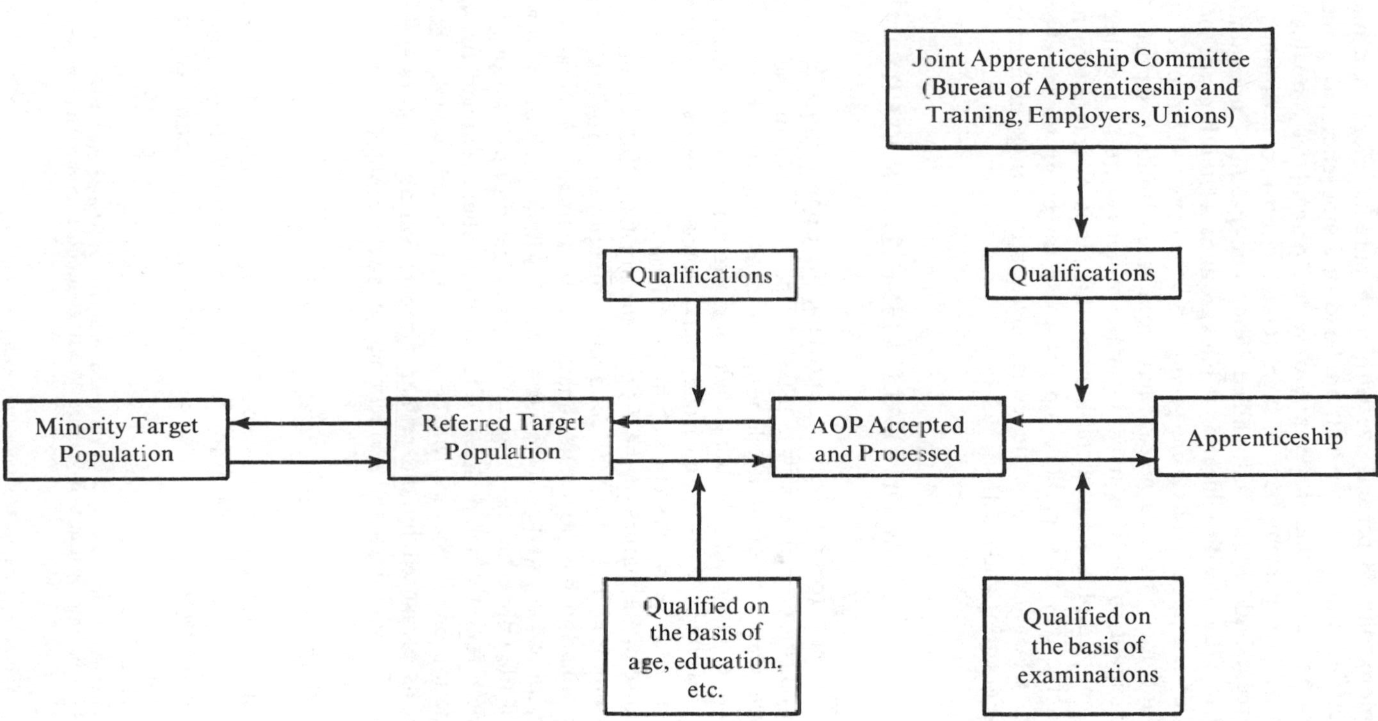

Note: People flow from left to right, data and information flow from right to left.

that more than 43 percent live with both parents, more than one-fourth are married, more than one-half are head of a household, 67 percent lived in the area more than ten years, only ten percent have no high school diploma, 12.4 percent have a high school equivalency diploma, almost 25 percent had fathers with skilled labor backgrounds, and almost one-half had fathers with educational backgrounds of tenth grade or higher. Most of the participants were young—8.5 percent were over 25 years of age—and more than 25 percent had completed military service. Overall, a participant in AOP is a young male minority group member with a high school diploma and a stable home life. It is of interest to note that the alternatives to apprenticeship for these target group members are a college education or a white collar occupation, thus indicating rather high goal setting and ideals.

REVIEW OF EVALUATIVE LITERATURE

The major forces involved in improving the opportunities for minorities in the construction industry consist of: the pressures of the civil rights movement and resultant legislation, union efforts, training programs in the private sector, and the hometown plans resulting in part from government pressures. As one researcher has noted recently, "[T]here have been only a few research studies of this experience."[9]

Because of the nature of the Apprenticeship Outreach Program, a publicly supported but privately conducted manpower program, a nationwide evaluation has not been conducted. In actuality, after an extensive search, only two studies have been found which deal directly with the issue of the impact of the program on its target group. Two other studies have been found which address AOP in an ancillary manner. Background information on the studies will be given. This is followed by the project impact as measured by the primary impact variables of retention, employment and earnings, and the secondary impact variables.

Evaluation Background

The study by the Boise Cascade Center for Community Development is as close to a nationwide evaluation as is available.[10] Four programs in twelve cities were reviewed and assessed: National Urban League in At-

9. Charles A. Myers, *The Role of the Private Sector in Manpower Development*, Public Studies in Employment and Welfare No. 10 (Baltimore: Johns Hopkins Press, 1971), p. 43.

10. Boise Cascade Center for Community Development, *op. cit.*

lanta, Baltimore, Chicago, and Columbus; Workers' Defense League in Brooklyn, Buffalo, and Cleveland; Building and Trades Councils in Dallas, Houston, Knoxville, and Oakland; and Trade Union Leadership Council in Detroit. The cities were not chosen on a probability basis and, therefore, conclusions could not be generalized to the entire AOP. The study period was from December 1969 to March 1970. The principal sources of information were data reported to the Department of Labor on each person placed in an apprenticeship slot, in depth interviews with 404 randomly selected participants in the twelve cities, and interviews with 299 program-related individuals. At the end of 1969, approximately 5,000 individuals were placed as apprentices, with approximately 52 percent still in apprenticeship programs. Particular emphasis was placed on the distribution of placements among the various trades, i.e., mechanical *vs.* nonmechanical, retention rates, differential earnings and employment rates, and minority acceptance into construction apprenticeship programs as a percentage of all apprentices.

An evaluation of Project Build—an experimental and demonstration pre-apprenticeship program sponsored by the Greater Washington Central Labor Council and designed to bring more inner-city blacks into the building trades through apprenticeship—was undertaken by Markley Roberts.[11] The program began in early 1968. At the time of the study, 521 individuals had been referred to the program, 215 were accepted, 143 had completed the program, and 79 were retained after one year. The study was an interview survey of 110 placed completers, 20 dropouts, and 65 nonselected applicants. Choosing dropouts and nonselected applicants for the control group may be of questionable validity. Although these groups are matched on demographic variables, there may be psychological variables, such as attitude toward work, which contribute to vast differences. This can jeopardize the results of the study.

Theresa R. Shapiro looked at the New Orleans AOP, a program which began in November 1968 as the Labor Education Advancement Program (LEAP) under the joint sponsorship of the Urban League and the Building and Trades Council of Southeast Louisiana.[12] Starting with 668 referrals to LEAP, 229 were acceptable; however, this was many more than could be placed immediately in light of the reduced construction activity in 1969 and 1970. Over the life of the program, there were 231 applicants, 108 placements, 90 indentures, and 22 dropouts.

---

11. Markley Roberts, "Pre-Apprenticeship Training for Disadvantaged Youth: A Cost-Benefit Study of Training by Project Build in Washington, D.C.," report prepared for Manpower Administration, U.S. Department of Labor, Ph.D. dissertation, American University, 1970.

12. Theresa R. Shapiro, *Negro Construction Craftsmen in a Southern Labor Market* (New Orleans: Louisiana State University, 1972).

The purpose of another study, "Improving the Retention Rate of Indentured Apprentices in the Apprenticeship Outreach Program" by Dennis A. Derryck, was to specify both the needs of indentured apprentices and the institutional arrangements that currently exist to facilitate the retention of apprentices placed by AOP.[13] The interview schedule consisted of choosing four cities representative of 82 AOP locations at the time of the study. The cities had to satisfy the requirements of placing at least 100 minority apprentices, operating at least two years, placing a significant number of apprentices in at least three mechanical crafts, and maintaining a staff with reasonable stability. The programs and cities chosen were the Workers' Defense League in Cleveland, the Urban League in Denver, the Building and Trades Council in Dallas, and the Negro Trades Union Leadership Council and other independent sponsors in Philadelphia. Forty apprentices, one-half AOP-placed minority and one-half white, were interviewed in each city; ten of each group of twenty were on an active basis, ten were not. The white apprentices were from the four crafts which had the highest dropout rate in AOP. Other program-related personnel were interviewed.

PROGRAM IMPACT

The effects of the outreach program are measured by their impact in three broad areas: retention rates, employment, and earnings. First, the studies disclosed a range of retention rates, all greater than 50 percent; 50 percent is considered the average and was adopted as the bench mark. These retention rates are shown in Table 2. The retention rates in the New Orleans and the Derryck studies were calculated as retentions per indentured apprentice; consequently, these were higher than those found in other studies since most dropouts occur before indenture.

Second, two of the studies examined the employment variable in depth. The Boise Cascade evaluation studied measures of employment stability (Table 3), and the Project Build study compiled data comparing AOP completers to a matched control group on the basis of the number of weeks employed in the twelve-month periods before and after program participation (Table 4). In addition, the New Orleans study cited a 10 percent unemployment rate, whereas the Derryck study indicated that the percentage of minorities laid off was twice as much as the layoffs for whites, although the amount of overtime was the same. The data show

13. Dennis A. Derryck, "Improving the Retention Rate of Indentured Apprentices in the Apprenticeship Outreach Program," report prepared for Manpower Administration, U.S. Department of Labor, Florence Heller Graduate School for Advanced Studies in Social Welfare, Brandeis University, Waltham, Massachusetts, 1973.

TABLE X-2. *Apprenticeship Outreach Program Retention Rates by Evaluation Report*

Report	Retention Rate
Boise Cascade	51.8
Project Build	64.0
New Orleans	69.7
Derryck	80.5

Sources: Boise Cascade Center for Community Development, "Report of an Evaluation of the Apprenticeship Outreach Program (AOP)," report prepared for Manpower Administration, U.S. Department of Labor, 1970, Table 4, p. 30.

Markley Roberts, "Pre-Apprenticeship Training for Disadvantaged Youth: A Cost-Benefit Study of Training by Project Build in Washington, D.C.," prepared for Manpower Administration, U.S. Department of Labor, Ph. D. dissertation, American University, 1970, p. 106.

Theresa R. Shapiro, *Negro Construction Craftsmen in a Southern Labor Market* (New Orleans: Louisiana State University, 1972), Table III, p. 33.

Dennis A. Derryck, "Improving the Retention Rate of Indentured Apprentices in the Apprenticeship Outreach Program," report prepared for Manpower Administration, U.S. Department of Labor, Florence Heller Graduate School for Advanced Studies in Social Welfare, Brandeis University, Waltham, Massachusetts, 1973, p. 10.

TABLE X-3. *Apprenticeship Outreach Program Measures of Employment Stability Boise Cascade Evaluation*

Measure	Percent
Previous full-time employment	73.5
Full-time employment in year prior to program	49.7
Full-time in school in year prior to program	21.2
Currently employed	81.1
Post-program unemployment less than 4 weeks	70.2
Post-program unemployment greater than 13 weeks	11.2
Employment with less than 30 hours per week average	7.4

Source: Boise Cascade Center for Community Development, "Report of an Evaluation of the Apprenticeship Outreach Program (AOP)," report prepared for Manpower Administration, U.S. Department of Labor, 1970, p. 32.

TABLE X-4. *Apprenticeship Outreach Program Employment Measures for Completers and Controls Project Build Analysis*

Measure	Completers	Controls
Yearly mean number of weeks in pre-program employment	34.9	33.2
Yearly mean number of weeks in post-program employment	38.5	34.0
Change in employment	+3.6	+0.8
Percent change	+10.4	+2.3

Source: Markley Roberts, "Pre-Apprenticeship Training for Disadvantaged Youth: A Cost-Benefit Study of Training by Project Build in Washington, D.C.," prepared for Manpower Administration, U.S. Department of Labor, Ph.D. dissertation, American University, 1970, p. 398.

that AOP has had significant impact on the employment status of its participants.

Third, as with the employment variable, earnings were addressed primarily by the Boise Cascade and Project Build studies. The Boise Cascade study found that the percentage of all participants earning more than $3.00 per hour increased from 40.5 percent before the program to 69.7 percent after participation in the program. Dropouts had comparable increases in earnings, with 15.9 percent earning $3.00 per hour before the program and 41.9 percent earning $3.00 per hour or more after dropping out. This phenomenon is attributed to the improvement in attitudes of dropouts and job-getting skills obtained while participating in the program. Project Build compiled the pre- and post-earnings data, expressed as percentage increases in earnings, shown in Table X-5.

The New Orleans study indicated that monthly and/or yearly income was generally higher than before the onset of apprenticeship. Moreover, the Derryck study found that minority group members earn consistently less than whites of equal status when mean starting wages of apprentices are comparable; on the average, white craftsmen continued to earn more than minorities of the same status ($5.12 per hour *vs.* $4.75 per hour). It is important to note that although whites earn more than minorities, the average hourly wage for minorities, $4.75, was consistent with the Boise Cascade evaluation. In regard to the earnings variable, the evaluations concluded that AOP has had significant impact in improving the earnings of its participants, but that minority earnings may lag behind those of nonminority group members.

TABLE X-5. *Apprenticeship Outreach Program Percent Increases in Post-Program Over Pre-Program Earnings*

Earnings Measure	Percent Increase for Completers	Percent Increase for Controls
Average hourly earnings	60	20
Weekly earnings	55	15
After tax weekly earnings	60	14

Source: Markley Roberts, "Pre-Apprenticeship Training for Disadvantaged Youth: A Cost-Benefit Study of Training by Project Build in Washington, D.C.," prepared for Manpower Administration, U.S. Department of Labor, Ph. D. dissertation, American University, 1970, pp. 258-259.

Secondary Impact

The Boise Cascade study examined the external impact of AOP, whereas the Derryck study sought out the factors that contributed to the retention of indentured apprentices. It is worthwhile to highlight both of these findings.

There are four areas of external impact of AOP: (1) impact on unions in regard to the admittance of minority individuals in apprentice classes; (2) relationship between the project staffs and union officials; (3) extent to which the community perceived the program as being effective; and (4) quality and extent of the relationships worked out with other manpower agencies.

The desired impact on unions was to increase the percentage of minorities in the apprenticeship classes of the "harder-to-qualify-for" trades. In some cities, minorities gained entrance into trades which had not admitted them in the past. There are two explanations for increases in minority apprentices—the relaxation of formal and informal entrance requirements and better qualified candidates. The AOP concept is to work with the participants; this is the most likely explanation for the observed increases. Informal practices might have been relaxed, although this was not a sought after goal. These increases in minority apprentices imply a positive external impact of the unions.

The relationship between project staffs and union officials served only to create a favorable climate for project effectiveness but did not have any positive influence on changing union attitudes. Considering community impact, it was found that the participants' attitudes toward AOP were a function of how the community perceived the program. A rather surprising outcome was that, in most cases, relationships between AOP and other manpower agencies, such as Apprenticeship Information Centers, were strained, thus indicating competition rather than coordination and cooperation. Of additional interest is the outlining of eight factors which affect program effectiveness. Within the local environment, the factors are: project leadership, union attitudes, level of construction activity, effective use of project staff, community attitude, and quality of local education. The global factors are: government influence from the Equal Employment Opportunity Commission and the Office of Federal Contract Compliance and the amount of technical assistance provided by the projects' offices at the national level.

The Derryck study noted several variables which contributed to the retention of indentured apprentices—ability of the apprentice to perceive and resolve his personal problems, participation in the informal structures associated with the job, such as attending union meetings, and situations where the apprentice is head of a household. The study also concluded that many minority individuals, given a decent wage and mobility, will adjust to a particular job despite lack of knowledge even of the nature of the work or despite previous work history. This conclusion follows from the common condition of underemployment among minorities and the disadvantaged. One of the explanations for this phenomenon is that an underemployed individual will increase his productivity upon upgrading.

PROGRAM STATISTICS

The evaluations reviewed and assessed in the previous section provide some insight into the impact of Apprenticeship Outreach on its target group and its effectiveness in meeting its objectives. In assessing the outreach program, earnings and usual employment measures are of questionable importance. The outreach program is a job development program with emphasis on entrance to and retention in apprenticeship programs from which minorities have previously been excluded. This emphasis is expressed in three objectives: (1) to provide assistance to minority youths in securing entrance to all construction trades; (2) to help minority youths gain entrance to apprenticeship programs of trades which have traditionally excluded minorities, namely the electrical, pipe, and mechanical crafts; and (3) to achieve retention rates comparable to the previous nationwide experience. The operating statistics of AOP can be used as measures of program effectiveness indicating progress toward the achievement of the stated objectives. This section describes and analyzes the operating statistics in an effort to show the effectiveness of the outreach program.

Description of Program Statistics

Statistics on the operation of the Apprenticeship Outreach Program consist of activity summary reports completed on a monthly basis since June 1968. Because of program start-up problems and time lags in reporting, consistent data are available only since October 1968.

The activity reports show the number of AOP placements in the month of the report and the total cumulative indentured placements from the beginning of the program through the reporting month. The placements, current and cumulative, are classified into seventeen crafts and a miscellaneous trades category. The total number of dropped indentures, voluntary and dismissed, are also reported. In addition, the placements are classified by sponsoring agency and the local project within each agency.

Since the inception of the program, the activity reports have been prepared by three different offices within the Department of Labor. Initially, the reports were prepared by the Equal Employment Opportunity (EEO) staff of the Bureau of Apprenticeship and Training (BAT). The responsibility for preparation was passed on to the BAT Field Service Office. The EEO staff again prepared the reports from July 1971 through January 1972. Beginning in February 1972, the reports have been the responsibility of the Office of National Projects Administration with the data compiled and prepared by the Office of Financial and Management Information Systems.

There have been a few changes in the makeup of these reports since they were first produced. Initially dropped indentures were reported on a cumulative basis until August 1969. From August 1969 through January 1972, both monthly and cumulative dropped indentures were reported. Since June 1972 only monthly dropouts have been maintained. Unfortunately, no reports were prepared between February and May 1972. At the end of 1973, the most recent report available for this analysis was the activity summary for August 1973.

Analysis of Program Statistics

The analysis of the program statistics follows the lines of the three explicit objectives of the outreach program—entrance to the construction trades, entrance to trades previously excluded from, and retention. Each part of the analysis is discussed separately.

Entrance to Construction Trades. It is apparent that one objective—to provide assistance to minority youths in securing entrance to all construction trades—is basic to and takes precedence over the other two program objectives. Gaining entrance to all crafts, for minorities, is paramount to the placement of these individuals in a particular set of crafts, and interest in the retention of these apprentices cannot exist before their placement in these programs occurs.

The effectiveness of the outreach program in meeting this entrance goal can be measured by determining the contribution of the outreach program to the level of minority participation in apprenticeship programs. A proxy measure for total apprenticeship programs is the federally serviced workload. The federal workload represents "federally registered apprenticeship programs in 21 states, which covers two-thirds of all apprentices. The remainder are registered with state councils in 29 states."[14]

The contribution of the outreach program is determined by a comparison between AOP placements and minority accessions to the federal workload. This comparison is made with two sets of crafts. The first set includes the twleve crafts which represent the construction industry: electricians, pipe trades, iron workers, sheet metal workers, carpenters, glaziers, painters, roofers, brick-stone-tile masons, [15] cement masons, lathers, and plasterers. AOP placements in these twelve crafts are compared to minority accessions to apprenticeship programs in the construction industry. The second set involves the addition of five other crafts: asbestos workers, elevator constructors, machinists, operating engineers, and miscellaneous. These seventeen crafts are compared to minority accessions to apprenticeship programs for total industry, consisting of the following six industries: construction, metal manufacturing, nonmetal manufacturing, public utilities transportation, trade and services, and mining.

Table 6 shows the comparison for the twelve construction crafts. AOP placements and minority accessions to the federal workload are provided for six-month intervals from the period ending June 1969 to the period ending June 1973.

The ratio of AOP placements to minority accessions shows that the outreach program provides a substantial and increasing contribution to the numbers of minority members in the apprenticeship programs of these crafts. Figure 2 is a graphic display of the information in Table 6.

Table 7 provides the same comparison for the seventeen crafts in which AOP makes placements and the minority accessions to apprenticeship programs in six industries. This comparison suggests the same interpretation as the data concerning only twelve of the crafts—a substantial and increasing contribution to minority group participation in apprenticeship programs. Figure 3 is a graphic display of the information in Table 7.

Table 8 shows the number of total and minority accessions to appren-

14. *Construction Labor Report*, No. 863 (Washington, D.C.: Bureau of National Affairs, April 12, 1972), p. A-6.

15. This combines the two crafts, bricklayers and tile setters.

TABLE X-6. *Apprenticeship Outreach Program Comparison of Placements and Minority Accessions To the Federal Workload in the Construction Industry (12 Crafts)*

Date	AOP[a]	Construction Federal Workload	Contribution Ratio
6-69	1,306	2,289	57.1
12-69	1,515	3,036	49.9
6-70	1,024	2,329	44.0
12-70	1,533	2,883	53.2
6-71	1,616	2,293	70.5
12-71	2,739	4,009	68.3
6-72	2,613	2,951	88.5
12-72	3,836	5,148	74.5
6-73	2,552	n.a.[b]	—

Source: U.S. Department of Labor, Bureau of Apprenticeship and Training.

[a] Derived from Table 10.

[b] Accessions to the federally serviced workload are not available at this time because the responsibility for the data computation has shifted to the Office of Financial and Management Information Systems.

ticeship programs in the federal workload for all industries and the construction industry alone. Minority accessions, as a percentage of the total, are also shown. This information indicates that not only the absolute numbers but also the proportion of minority accessions to apprenticeship programs have increased. It should be noted that the federally serviced workload series is not available for the current six-month interval ending June 1973 because the responsibility for the preparation of this data has shifted from the Bureau of Apprenticeship and Training to the Office of Financial and Management Information Systems (recently renamed Office of Administration and Management) since the reorganization of the Manpower Administration.

The information in Table 8, combined with the information in the two previous tables, indicates that the outreach program has become a major source of minority apprentices in federally registered apprenticeship programs. The outreach program has provided a substantial and increasing share of the minority accessions to apprenticeship programs; at the same time, the numbers and proportion of minority accessions to

FIGURE X-2. *Apprenticeship Outreach Program Placements as a Percent of Total Minority Accessions In Federally Registered Apprenticeship Programs (FWL) For 12 Construction Crafts January 1969— December 1972*

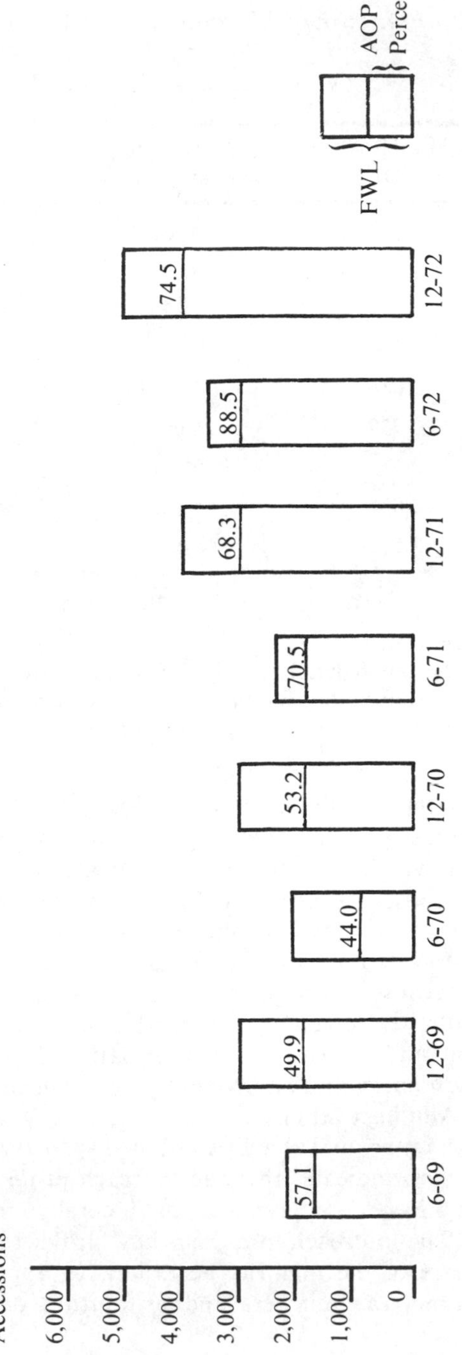

Source: U.S. Department of Labor, Bureau of Apprenticeship and Training.

TABLE X-7. *Apprenticeship Outreach Program Comparison of Placements and Minority Accessions To the Federal Workload in Total Industry (17 Crafts)*

Date	AOP	Total Federal Workload	Contribution Ratio
6-69	1,537	4,169	36.9
12-69	1,771	4,559	38.8
6-70	1,281	3,834	33.4
12-70	1,779	4,089	43.5
6-71	1,987	3,538	56.2
12-71	3,536	5,427	65.2
6-72	2,827	4,187	67.5
12-72	4,733	6,735	70.3
6-73	3,442	n.a.[a]	—

Source: U.S. Department of Labor, Bureau of Apprenticeship and Training.

[a] Accessions to the federally serviced workload are not available at this time because the responsibility for the data computation has shifted to the Office of Financial and Management Information Systems.

these programs have increased since the inception of the outreach program. This is a clear indication that AOP has been effective in providing entrance opportunities for minority youths to the apprenticeship programs of the skilled trades.

Entrance to Low Utilization Trades. The set of twelve construction trades can be segmented into three categories based on the type of work performed: electro-mechanical trades, intermediate trades, and trowel trades. The electro-mechanical trades are the electricians, pipe trades, iron workers, and sheet metal workers. These crafts are characterized historically as affording severely limited opportunities to minority group members. The intermediate crafts are the carpenters, glaziers, painters, and roofers. These trades have traditionally admitted blacks on a moderately limited basis. The trowel trades, consisting of the cement masons, brick-stone-tile masons, lathers, and plasterers, are crafts in which black representation has been historically strong. Increasing the minority representation in the electro-mechanical crafts is a second objective at which AOP is directed.

The effectiveness of the outreach program in meeting this objective can be determined by viewing the distribution of AOP placements in the

FIGURE X-3. *Apprenticeship Outreach Program Placements as a Percent of Total Minority Accessions In Federally Registered Apprenticeship Programs (FWL) For 17 Crafts in 6 Industries January-December 1972*

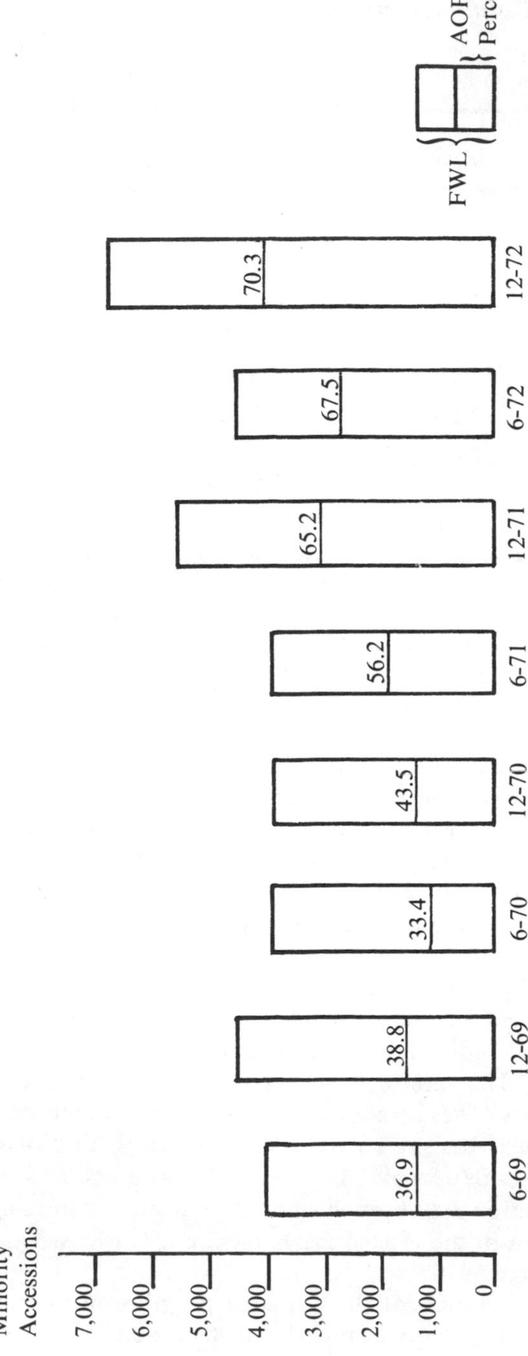

Source: U.S. Department of Labor, Bureau of Apprenticeship and Training.

TABLE X-8. *Apprenticeship Outreach Program*
Ethnic Composition of Registered Apprentices in Training[a]

Total Industry				Construction Industry			
	Accessions in Period				Accessions in Period		
Date	Total	Minority	Percent	Date	Total	Minority	Percent
6-69	36,447	4,169	11.4	6-69	18,529	2,289	12.4
12-69	53,025	4,559	8.6	12-69	27,773	3,036	10.9
6-70	31,784	3,834	12.1	6-70	16,593	2,329	14.0
12-70	35,079	4,089	11.7	12-70	20,977	2,883	13.7
6-71	25,243	3,538	14.0	6-71	14,954	2,293	15.3
12-71	33,631	5,427	16.1	12-71	22,279	4,009	18.0
6-72	24,804	4,187	16.9	6-72	14,520	2,951	20.3
12-72	39,066	6,735	17.2	12-72	26,720	5,148	19.3

Source: U.S. Department of Labor, Bureau of Apprenticeship and Training.

[a] Federally serviced workload.

trades. The twelve construction trades are used, rather than the seventeen crafts in which AOP makes placements, because the construction trades are the crafts of primary interest, and these placements account for almost 84 percent of all placements made by the outreach program.

Table 9 presents AOP cumulative placements in the twelve crafts, category subtotals, and total for all crafts. These numbers of placements are taken at six-month consecutive time intervals from December 1968 to June 1973.

In Table 10, AOP placements for six-month intervals for crafts, categories, and totals are shown. These entries are calculated by taking the difference between column figures for two consecutive time intervals from Table 9.

Table 11 displays the vertical percentage breakdown for the crafts and categories in Table 12. Each entry in this table is calculated by taking the corresponding entry in Table 10 and dividing by its column total. The columns of Table 11 add up to 100 percent or unity. These semi-annual breakdowns indicate that, since the beginning of the program, there have been gains in the placement of outreach participants in the electro-mechanical crafts, with compensating decreases in the percent placement of individuals in the intermediate and trowel trades. This demonstrates the effectiveness of the program to place minority group members in skilled trades which are harder to qualify for and from which they have been previously excluded.

Table 12 shows the vertical percentage breakdown for cumulative placements in Table 9 and is analagous to Table 11. These data indicate that more than 40 percent of all placements, since the inception of the outreach program, have been in the formerly exclusionary crafts. It is worthwhile to note that a substantial number of placements have been in the carpentry trade. The indenture of carpentry apprentices accounts for the majority of intermediate craft placements.

Additional interest rests in the effectiveness of a particular sponsor's placement of minorities in the more desirable and exclusionary crafts. This analysis was performed using August 1973 cumulative placement data.

The numerical breakdown of cumulative placements by sponsor in the three crafts categories as of August 1973, and sponsor placements as a percentage of the total are shown in Table 3. Table14 shows the vertical percentage breakdown over the craft categories for each Sponsor. As in the other tables providing these breakdowns, columns add up to 100 percent or unity.

The information in Table 14 indicates that the Urban League and the AFL-CIO programs have put greater portions of their placements in the intermediate crafts, whereas the Workers' Defense League and other local sponsors have placed most of their participants in the exclusionary

TABLE X-9. *Apprenticeship Outreach Program*
Cumulative Placements, December 1968-June 1973

Crafts	Time Intervals									
	12-68	6-69	12-69	6-70	12-70	6-71	12-71	6-72	12-72	6-73
Electro-pipe-mechanical trades:										
Electricians	294	437	599	746	892	1,053	1,464	1,906	2,647	3,057
Pipe trades	223	368	527	643	826	989	1,322	1,677	2,216	2,526
Iron workers	139	219	366	417	545	672	833	1,075	1,304	1,480
Sheetmetal workers	166	287	424	486	575	661	869	983	1,197	1,349
Subtotal	822	1,311	1,916	2,292	2,838	3,375	4,488	5,641	7,364	8,412
Intermediate trades:										
Carpenters	454	769	1,132	1,410	1,899	2.401	3,158	3,961	4,949	5,722
Glaziers	51	69	109	114	130	142	187	208	240	258
Painters	195	323	513	633	778	953	1,266	1,567	1,806	2,006
Roofers	195	316	411	450	531	599	700	751	959	1,080
Subtotal	895	1,477	2,165	2,607	3,338	4,095	5,311	6,487	7,954	9,066
Trowel trades:										
Brick-stone-tile masons	145	244	351	435	512	629	736	942	1,264	1,427
Cement masons	113	190	269	323	458	572	754	784	1,027	1,185
Lathers	2	23	44	90	115	155	190	213	263	300
Plasterers	47	85	100	122	141	192	278	303	334	368
Subtotal	307	542	764	970	1,226	1,548	1,958	2,242	2,888	3,280
Total	2,024	3,330	4,845	5,869	7,402	9,013	11,757	14,370	18,206	20,758

Source: U.S. Department of Labor, Bureau of Apprenticeship and Training.

TABLE X-10. *Apprenticeship Outreach Program Placements in Six-Month Intervals*

Crafts	12-68 to 6-69	6-69 to 12-69	12-69 to 6-70	6-70 to 12-70	12-70 to 6-71	6-71 to 12-71	12-71 to 6-72	6-72 to 12-72	12-72 to 6-73
Electro-pipe-mechanical trades:									
Electricians	143	162	147	146	161	411	442	741	410
Pipe trades	145	159	116	183	163	333	355	539	310
Iron workers	80	147	51	128	127	161	242	229	176
Sheetmetal workers	121	137	62	89	86	208	114	214	152
Subtotal	489	605	376	546	537	1,113	1,153	1,723	1,048
Intermediate trades:									
Carpenters	315	363	278	489	502	757	803	988	773
Glaziers	18	40	5	16	12	45	21	32	18
Painters	128	190	120	145	175	313	301	239	200
Roofers	121	95	39	81	68	101	51	208	121
Subtotal	582	688	442	731	757	1,216	1,176	1,467	1,112
Trowel trades:									
Brick-stone-tile masons	99	107	84	77	117	107	206	322	163
Cement masons	77	79	54	135	114	182	30	243	158
Lathers	21	21	46	25	40	35	23	50	37
Plasterers	38	15	22	19	51	86	25	31	34
Subtotal	235	222	206	256	322	410	284	646	392
Total	1,306	1,515	1,024	1,533	1,616	2,739	2,613	3,836	2,552

Source: U.S. Department of Labor, Bureau of Apprenticeship and Training.

TABLE X-11. *Apprenticeship Outreach Program Percent Distribution of Crafts in Six-Month Intervals*

Crafts	12-68 to 6-69	6-69 to 12-69	12-69 to 6-70	6-70 to 12-70	12-70 to 6-71	6-71 to 12-71	12-71 to 6-72	6-72 to 12-72	12-72 to 6-73
Electro-pipe-mechanical trades:									
Electricians	10.9	10.7	14.4	9.5	10.0	15.0	16.9	19.3	16.1
Pipe trades	11.1	10.5	11.3	11.9	10.1	12.1	13.6	14.0	12.1
Iron workers	6.1	9.7	5.0	8.4	7.8	5.9	9.2	6.0	6.9
Sheetmetal workers	9.3	9.0	6.0	5.8	5.3	7.6	4.4	5.6	6.0
Subtotal	37.4	39.9	36.7	35.6	33.2	40.6	44.1	44.9	41.1
Intermediate trades:									
Carpenters	24.1	24.0	27.2	31.9	31.1	27.6	30.7	25.8	30.3
Glaziers	1.4	2.6	0.5	1.0	0.8	1.7	0.8	0.8	0.7
Painters	9.8	12.5	11.7	9.5	10.8	11.4	11.5	6.2	7.8
Roofers	9.3	6.3	3.8	5.3	4.2	3.7	2.0	5.4	4.8
Subtotal	44.6	45.4	43.2	47.7	46.9	44.4	45.0	38.2	43.6
Trowel trades:									
Brick-stone-tile masons	7.6	7.1	8.2	5.0	7.2	3.9	7.9	8.4	6.4
Cement masons	5.9	5.2	5.3	8.8	7.0	6.7	1.1	6.4	6.2
Lathers	1.6	1.4	4.5	1.6	2.5	1.3	0.9	1.3	1.4
Plasterers	2.9	1.0	2.1	1.3	3.1	3.1	1.0	0.8	1.3
Subtotal	18.0	14.7	20.1	16.7	19.8	15.0	10.9	16.9	15.3
Total	100.0	100.0	100.0	100.0	100.0	100.0	100.0	100.0	100.0

Source: Calculated from Table 10.

Note: Percents may not add to 100.0 due to rounding.

TABLE X-12. *Apprenticeship Outreach Program Percent Distribution of Crafts by AOP Cumulative Placements*

Crafts	12-68	6-69	12-69	6-70	12-70	6-71	12-71	6-72	12-72	6-73
Electro-pipe-mechanical trades:										
Electricians	14.5	13.1	12.4	12.7	12.0	11.7	12.5	13.3	14.5	14.7
Pipe trades	11.0	11.0	10.8	11.0	11.1	11.0	11.2	11.7	12.2	12.2
Iron workers	6.9	6.6	7.6	7.1	7.4	7.4	7.1	7.5	7.2	7.1
Sheetmetal workers	8.2	8.6	8.7	8.3	7.8	7.3	7.4	6.8	6.6	6.5
Subtotal	40.6	39.3	39.5	39.1	38.3	37.4	38.2	39.3	40.5	40.5
Intermediate trades:										
Carpenters	22.5	23.1	23.4	24.0	25.6	26.6	26.9	27.6	27.2	27.6
Glaziers	2.5	2.1	2.2	1.9	1.8	1.6	1.6	1.4	1.3	1.2
Painters	9.6	9.7	10.6	10.8	10.5	10.6	10.8	10.9	9.9	9.7
Roofers	9.6	9.5	8.5	7.7	7.2	6.6	5.9	5.2	5.3	5.2
Subtotal	44.2	44.4	44.7	44.4	45.1	45.4	45.2	45.1	43.7	43.7
Trowel trades:										
Brick-stone-tile masons	7.2	7.3	7.2	7.4	6.9	7.0	6.2	6.5	6.9	6.9
Cement masons	5.6	5.7	5.6	5.5	6.2	6.4	6.4	5.5	5.6	5.7
Lathers	0.1	0.7	0.9	1.5	1.6	1.7	1.6	1.5	1.5	1.4
Plasterers	2.3	2.6	2.1	2.1	1.9	2.1	2.4	2.1	1.8	1.8
Subtotal	15.2	16.3	15.8	16.5	16.6	17.2	16.6	15.6	15.8	15.8
Total	100.0	100.0	100.0	100.0	100.0	100.0	100.0	100.0	100.0	100.0

Source: Calculated from Table 9.

TABLE X-13. *Apprenticeship Outreach Program Cumulative Placements by Sponsor August 1973*

Craft Category	Total	Sponsor			
		Urban League	Workers' Defense League	AFL-CIO	Others
Electro-pipe-mechanical trades	8,986	3,000	2,239	2,271	1,476
Intermediate trades	9,537	3,326	1,923	3,198	1,090
Trowel trades	3,484	1,254	606	1,178	436
Total for sponsor	22,007	7,590	4,768	6,647	3,002
Sponsor as percent	100.0	34.5	21.7	30.2	13.6

Source: U.S. Department of Labor, Bureau of Apprenticeship and Training.

TABLE X-14. *Apprenticeship Outreach Program*
Percent Distribution of Sponsor Placements by Classification
August 1973

Craft Category	Total	Sponsor: Urban League	Workers' Defense League	AFL-CIO	Other
Electro-pipe-mechanical trades	40.8	39.5	47.0	34.2	49.2
Intermediate trades	43.4	43.8	40.3	48.1	36.3
Trowel trades	15.8	16.7	12.7	17.7	14.5
Total	100.0	100.0	100.0	100.0	100.0

Source: Calculated from Table 13.

electrical, pipe, and mechanical crafts. This may not be a reflection of the sponsoring agency, however, but a function of other conditions, such as the locality of the program and local demands for apprentices and craftsmen, as well as level of local construction activity.

As previously noted in the review of evaluative literature, the Boise Cascade study examined the distribution of placements among the various crafts.[16] This analysis of program operating statistics confirms the conclusions of the Boise Cascade study in regard to the distribution of placements across craft group and by sponsor.

Retention. The third objective of the outreach program is to achieve retention rates comparable to the previous nationwide experience. Follow-up activities for the retention of AOP participants in apprenticeship programs are just as important as the initial placements of these individuals. Dropout and retention rates can be calculated using cumulative placements and dropout data from the outreach activity reports. Retention rates cannot be consistently analyzed after January 1972 because activity reports were not prepared between February and May of 1972, and since June of that year, only monthly dropped indentures were reported.

Table 15 is a display of the data from the activity reports for six-month intervals from January 1969 through January 1972. These data consist of cumulative placements and voluntary, dismissed, and total dropouts. Three dropout rates are calculated:

1. the voluntary dropout rate is the number of outreach participants who voluntarily leave the program per 100 indentures;
2. the dismissed dropout rate is the number of outreach participants dismissed from apprenticeship programs per 100 indentures; and
3. the overall dropout rate is the number of outreach placed dropouts per 100 indentures.

The number of indentures include those retained and those who dropped out. The retention rate is calculated as the number placed, minus the number dropped, divided by the number placed. This is interpreted as the number of outreach participants retained as indentures per 100 indentures.

The overall dropout rate for the life of the program, as of January 1972, is 15.39 drops per 100 indentures, indicating a retention rate in excess of 84 percent. It is noteworthy that over time, the voluntary dropout rate has decreased, but the dismissal rate has increased. However, the overall dropout rate has decreased which may indicate somewhat improved and effective follow-up activity. In summary, these calculations tend to indicate that the program has been effective in achieving an acceptable retention rate for minority group members.

16. Boise Cascade Center for Community Development. *op. cit.*, pp. 22-31.

TABLE X-15. *Apprenticeship Outreach Program*
Dropout and Retention Rates for Newly-Placed Indentured Apprentices
January 1969-January 1972

Date	Total Placements	Dropouts			Dropout Rate			Retention Rate
		Total	Voluntary	Dismissed	Voluntary	Dismissed	Average	
1-69	2,544	447	386	61	15.2	2.4	17.6	82.4
7-69	4,254	688	553	135	13.0	3.2	16.2	83.8
1-70	5,806	979	763	216	13.2	3.7	16.9	83.1
7-70	7,294	1,145	914	231	12.5	3.2	15.7	84.3
1-71	8,912	1,464	1,129	335	12.6	3.7	16.4	83.6
7-71	11,388	1,715	1,301	414	11.4	3.6	15.0	85.0
1-72	14,421	2,239	1,667	572	11.5	4.0	15.5	84.5

Source: U.S. Department of Labor, Bureau of Apprenticeship and Training.

SUMMARY AND CONCLUSIONS

This study examined the Apprenticeship Outreach Program, a job development manpower program, as a possible solution to the problem of the exclusion of minority group members from the building trades; it further examined the nature of the outreach program and its effectiveness as a solution to this minority issue. The background and history of the program were presented, as well as an explanation of the program structure and operation. The evaluations of the program were reviewed and assessed and program impact was summarized. The program operating statistics were utilized to provide additional information on the effectiveness of the program in meeting its objectives.

On the basis of the evaluations reviewed and program operating statistics analyzed, the Apprenticeship Outreach Program has been effective in fulfilling its stated objectives. It has provided assistance to minority youths in securing entrance to construction trades in more than token numbers, and it has helped minority youths gain entrance to the apprenticeship programs which are harder to qualify for and from which they had previously been excluded, such as those in the electrical and mechanical trades. The program has provided the necessary selection process and follow-up services to achieve retention rates for minority apprentices equivalent to that for all apprentices. Furthermore, there have been significant changes in the employment and earnings of the program participants.

CHAPTER XI

Public Employment Program

by
Michael E. Sparrough
Research Associate
Under the Direction of
Charles R. Perry

The Emergency Employment Act (EEA) of 1971 was designed to "address the problems of unemployment and the inadequacy of many vital public services curtailed by inadequate local and State revenues."[1] Specifically, the Public Employment Program (PEP) under EEA seeks:

1. To provide transitional employment in public service jobs for the jobless and underemployed when the national unemployment rate averages 4.5 percent for 3 consecutive months—section 5 funds, and special emergency assistance in areas with unemployment rates averaging 6 percent or more for 3 consecutive months—section 6 funds.

2. To provide job opportunities for significant segments of the unemployed characterized as:

   a. Veterans who served in the Indochina and Korean theaters on or after August 5, 1964.
   b. Persons 45 years of age and over, as well as young persons at least 18 years of age entering the labor force.
   c. Migrant and seasonal farmworkers.
   d. Persons whose native tongue is not English and whose ability to speak English is limited.
   e. Persons from families with incomes below the poverty level or welfare recipients.
   f. Persons who have become unemployed as a result of cutbacks in the defense, aerospace, or construction industries.
   g. Persons experiencing difficulty in finding work due to technological changes or shifts in the patterns of Federal expenditures.
   h. Persons from socioeconomic backgrounds usually associated with substantial unemployment and underemployment.

3. To provide funds for unmet public service needs.

4. To provide training and manpower services to persons employed under the act to enable them to move permanently into other public or private employment.

5. To encourage State and local governments to reexamine job qualifications for their employees in order to eliminate artificial barriers to employment.[2]

---

1. U.S. Department of Labor, *Public Employment Program, Annual Report to Congress* (Washington, D.C.: U.S. Department of Labor, 1973), p. 5.

2. *Ibid.*

To accomplish these goals, $1 billion was allocated for the first year and $1.25 billion for the second year of the act. The "lion's share" of these funds were authorized under section 5, which stipulated that not less than 80 percent of all appropriated funds were to be apportioned among the states. The residual was available to the Secretary of Labor as he deemed "appropriate to carry out the purposes of the act."[3] He chose to appropriate a substantial portion of the money for 25 "demonstration projects." A dozen cities and counties were funded "to test the economic impact of a concentrated public employment program which would absorb between 10 and 25 percent of the unemployed in each of these areas."[4] Another 13 "welfare demonstration projects" were funded "to assess the feasibility of using public sector jobs to hire welfare recipients."[5] Both of these types of demonstration projects" have broad implications on minorities and women. The latter population (welfare recipients) is usually comprised of a large proportion of minorities and women; the former relates to minorities and women in a more general way because they have disproportionate high unemployment rates.

In keeping with its mandate of helping localities cope with unmet public service needs, wide latitude was given to them in the usage of funds. However, safeguards were placed in the bill to help ensure a "balanced" occupational distribution. "The act contains only two restrictions: salaries paid from Federal funds cannot exceed $12,000 per year; and no more than one-third of the jobs, excluding teaching positions, can be in professional categories."[6] These safeguards, however, contained their own potential loopholes. As Sar A. Levitan and Robert Taggart point out, "[L]ocal funds can be used to supplement the EEA salary maximum and because teachers are not included among the professionals, [it is] possible to hire one-third professionals, two-thirds teachers, and no disadvanttaged."[7]

The funds allocated for training and supportive services in PEP are small in comparison with other manpower programs, but this was to be expected given the intent of EEA. Section 10 of the act states that training and supportive services costs are "not to exceed 15 per centum of the amounts appropriated under section 5." The PEP Handbook states "approximately 6.8 percent of the funds allocated under the Program

3. Section 9a.2, Public Law 92-54, 92nd Congress, S.31, July 12, 1971.

4. U.S. Congress, Senate, Committee on Labor and Public Welfare, Subcommittee on Employment, Poverty, and Migratory Labor *The Emergency Employment Act: An Interim Assessment* 92nd Cong., 2nd sess., 1972, p. 15.

5. *Ibid.*

6. U.S. Department of Labor, *Annual Report to Congress, op. cit.*, p. 31.

7. U.S. Congress, *op. cit.*, p. 11.

Agent's section 5 EEA grant is available to provide training and other supportive services."[8]

In the Public Employment Program:

> Training may take the form of basic or remedial education, classroom vocational instruction, or on-the-job training. It is permissible to use Section 5 funds for the training of PEP participants whose wages and benefits are paid from Section 6. Funds provided by the Act may also be used for supervisors who need training in order to supervise PEP employees. Further, the PEP supervisors' wages need not be paid from Federal funds in order to qualify for such training.[9]

The range of supportive services stated as available to PEP participants under EEA is somewhat broad. Included among the major categories of such services are:

1. Health care services necessary to make a potential participant available for employment. These may include initial physical examinations, preventive and clinical medical treatment, minor dental treatment, nutrition services, voluntary family planning services, inexpensive prostheses such as glasses, dentures, and hearing aids, and diagnostic psychological services where they are necessary to secure appropriate employment.

2. Transportation to and from the job site, or from the job site to authorized training institutions is a manpower service and can be charged as training and supportive services.

   Travel which is incidental to a participant's official duties is an allowable cost and is reportable as an administrative cost.

3. Child care services where needed to enable the participants to enter employment or training.

4. Vocational or educational counseling.[10]

Although the potential exists for extensive services, EEA appropriated little money to provide them. The *Public Employment Program Handbook* states that "[t]he small size of this amount [6.8 percent of Section 5 funds for both training and supportive services] makes it essential that supportive services be provided only where absolutely necessary to enable unemployed persons to obtain appropriate jobs."[11]

8. U.S. Department of Labor, *Public Employment Program Handbook* (Washington, D.C.: 1972), p. 35.

9. *Ibid.*, p. 36.

10. *Ibid.*

11. *Ibid.*, p. 35.

The Nixon administration's apparent desire for the decategorization of manpower programs through an integrated manpower effort was reflected in the PEP Handbook. Particular emphasis was placed on the development of effective linkages to other manpower programs. In this way PEP, which is essentially a job creation program, could utilize both the supportive services of WIN and CEP, and the Skill Centers of MDTA to prepare unemployed disadvantaged persons for PEP jobs they might otherwise not be able to obtain. At the same time, the jobs created through EEA would complement the placement function of specific manpower training programs.

Program History

The Emergency Employment Act of 1971, passed at a time of high inflation, rising unemployment, and approaching political elections, constitutes a major departure from the manpower policies and programs of the 1960's. The true extent of this departure is dramatically illustrated in the following comparison of the perception of needs expressed in the preambles to the Manpower Development and Training Act of 1962 and the Emergency Employment Act of 1971:

Manpower Development and Training Act of 1962.[12]	Emergency Employment Act of 1971.[13]
1. There is a critical need for more and *better trained personnel*;	1. There are *unmet public service needs* in the economy;
2. There is a shortage of *workers* even in periods of high employment;	2. There is a shortage of *jobs*, especially in periods of high employment;
3. It is in the national interest to *identify and train for these shortages*.	3. During periods of high employment, it is in the national interest to *create jobs to fill these unmet public service needs*.

Although EEA represented a new course for active manpower policy, the underpinnings of the Public Employment Program which it created were conceived almost four decades earlier. The concept of government as "employer of last resort" achieved considerable acceptance in the 1930's

12. Section 101, Public Law 87-415, Manpower Development and Training Act of 1962 (emphasis added).

13. Section 2, Public Law 92-54, Emergency Employment Act of 1971 (emphasis added).

and found expression in a number of New Deal programs, of which the WPA was the largest. With the advent of World War II, the economy expanded, and the "employer of last resort" concept, along with its related programs, quickly lost their public and legislative appeal.

The resurgence of the "employer of last resort" concept and the rebirth of a job creation program in the 1970's was the result of a series of economic and political developments which began in the mid-1960's. Senator Gaylord Nelson has been given credit for initiating reconsideration of a public employment manpower approach during the 1965 Senate hearings which produced amendments to the Economic Opportunity Act (EOA).[14] He proposed "a massive funding of public employment,"[15] but only a token $10 million program, known as Operation Mainstream, was adopted. The following year, an EOA amendment which would have established a major job creation program was proposed. However, the mounting Vietnam war costs and the political overtones of expanding public employment in a tight labor market prompted the Johnson administration to oppose the measure and the bill was never passed.

"Employment in state and local governments [had] increased by 60 percent . . . and was the source of one out of every three additional jobs during the decade. Even so, large unmet needs for public services . . . persisted. Communities with above average rates of unemployment, and consequently reduced tax revenues [had] particular need for help in providing essential public services and also for additional job creation in their local areas."[16] In 1969, the Nixon administration reopened the legislative controversy when it proposed reforms to the entire manpower system. Republican Congressman William Steiger and the Administration introduced similar bills in the House (H.R. 10908) and the Senate (S. 2838), emphasizing the decentralization and decategorization of manpower programs. In the other camp, the Democrats, through Congressman James G. O'Hara, offered a bill (H.R. 11620), "containing a 'work guarantee' which would authorize public employment on a large scale."[17] This clear dichotomy of philosophy spelled doom for both sets of proposals. But the stage had been set for a future compromise measure. An attempt was made in the following year toward this end, but it failed when a comprehensive manpower bill (S. 3867) was vetoed by the President. The Senate had passed the bill which contained a major public employment section; the House Republicans agreed to support it if the jobs would be designated as "transitional," and other manpower programs would be decentralized.

---

14. U.S. Congress, *op. cit.*, p. 9.

15. *Ibid.*

16. U.S. Department of Labor, *Manpower Report of the President* (Washington, D.C.: Government Printing Office, 1973), pp. 59-60.

17. U.S. Congress, *loc. cit.*

House-Senate conferees met and retained the Senate version of the bill, which President Nixon promptly vetoed. He stated that "transitional and short-term public service employment can be a useful component of the nation's manpower policies. . . . But public employment that is not linked with real jobs, or which does not try to equip the individual for changes in the labor market, is not a solution."[18] It thus seemed evident that proponents of the public employment manpower concept would have to soften their stance if any form of public employment legislation was to be passed.

Certain economic developments of the 1970-1971 period, such as increasing unemployment and inflation, returning Vietnam veterans, and defense cutbacks contributed to the view that more public employment might alleviate these problems. With broader based support, but with the taste of past vetoes still lingering, the Senate passed a somewhat watered down public employment bill on April 4, 1971 (S. 31). It closely resembled the Emergency Employment Act which finally emerged. The bill contained an unemployment trigger mechanism of 4.5 percent and a two-year authorization to pacify those fearing the permanency of such a program. It also specified numerous target groups in order to satisfy various pressure groups and interests. However, the Administration had also submitted its version of proposed legislation. The Administration had offered the Manpower Revenue Sharing Act of 1971 on March 11 (H.R. 6181). It placed emphasis on providing federal revenues to state and local governments, who in turn, were to be given broad discretion on the usage of such moneys. The bill also contained a two-year duration stipulation, a "trigger" mechanism and a "transitional" public employment feature. However, the backers of the Senate bill took exception to the Administration's version because, although it authorized public employment, it provided very few additional funds for this purpose. On May 4, 1971, the House Committee on Education and Labor submitted its own bill (H.R. 3613) in lieu of the Administration proposal, passed it on June 2, 1971, and asked for a conference with the Senate. During June, House-Senate conferees met and ironed out the differences in the two acts in a set of amendments to the Senate bill. Congress reports the results: "Having vetoed a comprehensive public works bill and being increasingly cognizant of the political liability of opposing job creation efforts in a 6 percent unemployment economy, the Administration agreed to accept this compromise public employment bill. It was signed into law on July 12, 1971 (Public Law 92-54)."[19]

18. *Congressional Quarterly*, December 18, 1970, p. 11.

19. U.S. Congress, *op. cit.*, p.11.

PROGRAM SCOPE

At the time this report was prepared, 305,209 persons had been employed under EEA.[20] Of this number, there were 190,241 terminations and 109,127 persons still employed. The zenith of PEP employment was reached in July 1972, when 184,829 persons were "on board." Since then, the number has dropped consistently as the program entered a "phase down" process.

However, the number of persons who have been served by PEP tends to be overshadowed by the number of persons who could have been served. PEP's potential clientele is so broad that the majority of the 5.3 million persons unemployed at the time of EEA's passage could easily have qualified for PEP under at least one of the eight broad target group criteria already mentioned. It has also been stated that, at best, PEP could have only a marginal impact upon the national unemployment rate.

> If everyone hired under the program had been out of work and would have otherwise remained idle, the number of unemployed would have been reduced by less than three percent from the 1971 level, or the aggregate unemployment rate would have fallen by only 0.2 percentage points.[21]

Thus, PEP attempted to serve a wide range of interests by targeting broad classes of the unemployed with limited resources. PEP was therefore faced with two choices—attempt to serve all groups with mediocrity or concentrate its efforts on certain groups at the expense of others. The intent of both Congress and the Administration appears to have dictated the latter approach. For example, the PEP Handbook states:

> For the FY 1973 program, all Program Agents, subagents, and employing agencies must have the goal of at least 40 percent on board participation by veterans of the Vietnam era. . . .[22]

The opportunity cost of targeting any specific group was rather high. Thus, the extent to which veterans were targeted necessarily meant that women would be overlooked. Similarly, by placing emphasis on the hiring of unemployed aerospace workers, program agents had to reduce their efforts to reach down the labor queue for the disadvantaged.

It is interesting, therefore, to consider the characteristics of PEP parti-

---

20. PEP program statistics for the period August 1971 through March 1973. The 109,127 figure is as of September 1973.

21. U.S. Congress, *op. cit.*, p. 6.

22. U.S. Department of Labor, *Public Employment Program Handbook, op. cit.*, p. 24.

cipants (Table 1). These figures show that only about one in every four PEP enrollees was a woman, and about one-third were minorities. Three

TABLE XI-1. *Public Employment Program*
Percent Distribution of Socio-Economic Characteristics
August 1971-February 1973

Characteristic	Percent	Characteristic[a]	Percent
Age:		Race:	
18 and under	7	White	71
19-21	16	Negro	26
22-44	63	Oriental	1
45-54	9	American Indian	2
55-64	4	Other	*
65 and over	1	Ethnicity:	
Sex:		White	60
Male	72	Negro	24
Female	28	Oriental	1
Military service status:		American Indian	2
Special veteran	11	Spanish American	13
Vietnam-era veteran	16	Other	*
Veteran	14	Disabled veteran	3
Non-veteran	59	Migrant farm worker	1
Disadvantaged	39	Former federal manpower training enrollee	9
Public assistance recipient	12	Pre-PEP average hourly wage	$2.77
Handicapped	4	PEP average hourly wage	$2.81
Highest school grade completed:			
0-7	4		
8-11	23		
12	43		
13-15	18		
16 or over	12		

Source: Data obtained from U.S. Department of Labor, Manpower Administration, in author's possession.

[a] These data are applicable from August 1972 to February 1973 only.

* Less than 1 percent.

of every four participants had at least four years of high school education, and almost two-thirds were between 22 and 44 years of age. Fewer than two in five PEP participants were disadvantaged, but 41 percent of participants were veterans. Therefore, inferences can be drawn that PEP "creamed" extensively for its enrollees. It is also evident that minorities are overrepresented in relation to their proportion of the overall population but underrepresented when compared with enrollments in other manpower programs, such as the Work Incentive Program (WIN) with 43.8 percent, Concentrated Employment Program (CEP) with 73.0 percent, and Job Opportunities in the Business Sector (JOBS) with 69.3 percent. Women, on the other hand, are underrepresented both in relation to their proportion of the overall population and in relation to many other manpower programs, such as WIN with 63.1 percent, CEP with 42.4 percent, and JOBS with 31.6 percent. The labor force status of enrollees provides additional insight into PEP's outreach efforts. These data are presented in Table 2, which indicates that nine out of every ten PEP participants were unemployed at the time they entered the program; the remaining were underemployed. As an ethnic group, Spanish Americans were disproportionately highly underemployed. In the previous twelve-month period before entrance into PEP, the median participant was unemployed between five and 26 weeks, and probably closer to the latter. Public assistance recipients, disadvantaged persons, and blacks, in that order, tended to be unemployed most frequently. The last spell of unemployment was also the most severe for these groups.

The PEP jobs created for these groups were in various public service areas. Table 3 shows that both the unemployed and underemployed were most often placed in public works and transportation. When looking at ethnic groupings, underemployed blacks were also employed in this area but unemployed blacks were rather evenly distributed over four broad categories (education, public works/transportation, parks/recreation, and social services). This pattern seems to hold for most of the participant classifications shown. If entering PEP can be considered to be an upgrading experience for the underemployed, then they helped themselves most often through employment in the public works/transportation area.

However, it is also important to look at salaries by public service area. Unfortunately, minority breakdowns were not available, but Table 4 does present information for all participants. The highest salaries were in fire protection and law enforcement, which are predominantly male, whereas the lowest tended to be in the health/hospital area, which is heavily female.

As previously mentioned, PEP allocated far less funds than other manpower programs for training and supportive services. PEP's effort in providing training can be judged either by the amount of money spent, or by the number of participants who received training.

The evaluative literature tends to indict PEP for its lack of training. Most of the criticism is based on an examination of the direct federal cost of training. This method, however, tends to be somewhat misleading. Table 5 presents PEP man-year cost estimates for the period August 1971

TABLE XI-2. *Public Employment Program*
Percent Distribution of Selected Measures of Employment for Enrollees Prior to Participation
July 1, 1972-February 28, 1973

Employment Measures	All Participants	Negro	Spanish Americans	American Indians	Disadvantaged	Public Assistance Recipients
Labor force status:						
Unemployed	92	95	88	91	94	95
Underemployed	8	5	12	9	6	5
Weeks Unemployed previous 12 months:						
4 or less	20	17	19	19	13	8
5 to 26	33	25	34	39	24	19
27 or more	47	58	48	42	63	73
Weeks unemployed 'current spell':						
4 or less	32	26	30	34	24	16
5 to 14	21	17	20	25	16	14
15 or more	47	58	50	41	60	70
Total for each measure	100	100	100	100	100	100

Source: U.S. Department of Labor, Manpower Administration.

Note: Percents may not add to 100.0 due to rounding.

TABLE XI-3. *Public Employment Program Employment by Public Service Area According to Pre-PEP Labor Force Status July 1, 1972 Entrants to February 28, 1973*

Public Service Area	All Participants		Negroes		Spanish Americans		American Indians		Disadvantaged		Public Assistance Recipients	
	Unem-ployed	Under-employed	Unem-ployed	Under-employed	Unem-ployed	Under-employed	Unem-ployed	Under-employed	Unem-ployed	Under-employed	Unem-ployed	Under-employed
Law enforcement	7	10	4	7	7	5	8	12	5	6	4	8
Education	15	16	12	12	17	15	15	12	12	15	14	15
Public works and transportation	23	22	19	30	13	20	18	31	21	34	17	27
Health and hospital	6	5	7	6	6	4	9	3	7	7	11	11
Environmental quality	4	3	4	3	3	2	3	3	3	2	3	1
Fire protection	1	2	—	—	2	2	—	3	1	2	1	6
Parks and recreation	13	8	16	10	15	8	8	5	15	9	14	9
Social services	11	6	18	10	21	6	14	5	17	8	17	9
Other	20	28	19	20	18	39	25	24	19	17	18	13
Total	100	100	100	100	100	100	100	100	100	100	100	100
Total participants	33,635	3,060	9.252	524	2,931	400	590	58	14,017	933	5,556	300

Source: U.S. Department of Labor, Manpower Administration.

Note: Percents may not add to 100 due to rounding.

TABLE XI-4. *Public Employment Program Expenditures by Public Service Area August 1971-March 1973*

Public Service Area	Percent Employment	Average Hourly Wage	Man-Year Cost
Law enforcement	10	$3.14	$7539
Education	20	2.89	6939
Public works and transportation	22	2.66	6387
Health and hospitals	9	2.62	6291
Environmental quality	4	2.95	7083
Fire protection	2	3.17	7611
Parks and recreation	10	2.68	6435
Social service	6	2.80	6723
Administrative and other	17	2.83	6795
Total	100	2.81	6747

Source: U.S. Department of Labor, Manpower Administration, data in author's possession.

TABLE XI-5. *Public Employment Program Estimated Costs per Participant August 1971-December 1972*

Costs	Total Cost	Direct Cost	
		Federal	Agent
Wages	$3,240	$3,211	$29
Fringe benefits	396	366	30
Training	74	15	59
Support services	53	7	46
Local administration	429	66	363
Federal administration	57	—	—
Total	4,249	3,665	527

Source: U.S. Department of Labor, Manpower Administration, *Public Employment Program, December. Data Book* (Washington, D.C.: 1972), p. 11.

through December 1972. It can be seen that direct federal training costs are only $15 per participant, while agent costs are almost four times this amount. The broad point to be made is that, although PEP does not provide large sums of money for training, it at least provides the impetus for program agents to train participants.

A program should be judged not only by the average amount spent on all participants, but also by the funds spent on those enrollees who actually received training. Between August 1971 and December 1972, some 44,500 persons, or 15 percent of the cumulative PEP participants, received training. The total cost per participant was $447, the federal cost was $84, and the agent cost was $363. This amounts to more than 10 percent of the total average participant cost presented in Table 5.

PEP supportive services can also be assessed by the total funds spent on supportive services and by the number of persons who received the services. Table 5 showed that a similar relationship existed between training costs and supportive services costs. The direct federal cost per PEP participant was only $7 and the agent cost was $46 on the average. Some 46,750 enrollees, or 16 percent of cumulative PEP participants through 1972, had received supportive services. The cost for these enrollees actually receiving these services was an average $307 or over 7 percent of total participant costs (Table 5). Of this, only $38 was a direct federal cost; the remaining cost of $269 was borne by program agents. Again, one must remain cognizant of the fact that PEP was not an antipoverty program. PEP "creamed" for its enrollees, and thus the need for supportive services may not have been as pressing as in other programs, such as WIN or CEP.

Finally, it is important to consider the post-program outcomes of PEP participants. The only available information on the subject was an "in-house" Department of Labor study of PEP's performance through June 30, 1972. The report contained limited information on about 67,000 program terminees and generally showed PEP's "transitional" employment effect. Table 6 presents data on the post-program experience of these terminees. Seventy-five percent improved their job position and 67 percent secured employment in unsubsidized jobs; one-half of these unsubsidized jobs were in the private sector, one-fourth were with other public agencies, and the remainder were with program agents. Of the 25 percent who had unfavorable outcomes, 11 percent were unemployed and 14 percent dropped from the labor force. On the basis of these data, PEP appeared to have had at least a marginally positive post-program impact. Unfortunately, these data were not classified by race and sex.

REVIEW OF EVALUATIVE LITERATURE

Because the primary emphasis of PEP is on job creation rather than manpower training, much of the conventional wisdom for program evalua-

TABLE XI-6. *Public Employment Program Outcomes of Terminees, Fiscal Year 1972*

Status	Percent
Positive outcomes:	
Employed unsubsidized jobs	
with agent	16
with other public agency	18
with private sector	33
Subtotal employed unsubsidized jobs	67
School or training	7
Armed forces	1
Total positive outcomes	75
Other outcomes:	
Unemployed	11
Not in labor force	14
Total other outcomes	25
Total	100

Source: U.S. Department of Labor, Manpower Administration, *Public Employment Program Annual Report to Congress* (Washington, D.C.: 1973), p. 40.

tion developed in the 1960's is only of marginal benefit in assessing PEP's impact. For example, one of the more generally accepted indicators of program success is retention, yet PEP's emphasis is on transition. The National Manpower Policy Task Force points out that:

> [I]t is difficult to measure the impact and effectiveness of PEP, or to assess its broader implications. The program was implemented at a breakneck pace, but operational data and analysis have not kept up with the progress of the program. . . . Information is not available about many critical aspects of the program, and there are some judgments which cannot be made until the program has been in operation for a longer time. These are not unusual or insurmountable difficulties, but they are complicated by the particular characteristics of the program. The Emergency Employment Act developed as a legislative compromise, designed to meet a number of problems at once with multiple goals and vague priorities. There are no simple, articulated standards for judging program effectiveness. Moreover, state and local governments were given a great deal of authority to adapt PEP to local conditions. The broadly stated purposes of the Act permitted them to move in a number of different directions, and this is exactly what they did. The variability of all aspects of EEA among and within states, cities, and counties is staggering. It is, therefore, difficult to gain perspective on the program.

> Aggregate data and analysis tend to wash out the variability, sometimes leading to erroneous conclusions. Case studies on the other hand, can provide a much better picture of reality in microcosm, but they are not necessarily representative of the universe....
>
> Aggregate data must be considered in light of institutional and programmatic variations in the field, and the findings of case studies must be considered in relation to overall developments.
>
> It is not easy to achieve this balanced perspective and to assess performance relative to a wide range of goals....[23]

The Task Force further elaborates on EEA evaluation problems by stating:

> It is extremely difficult to assess whether the program is successful in the aggregate or in any particular case. There are a variety of goals and an even wider variety of approaches among areas. Is a city which hires teachers and laid off skilled or professional workers operating more effectively than one which uses its funds to hire chiefly disadvantaged workers? The answer depends on one's standards, the employment situation, public service needs, and the institutional and political setting. In other words, there is often no answer.
>
> This is vastly different than under a program such as MDTA or the Job Corps, where gains are measured by following up enrollees and control groups and comparing their employment experience. The performance of enrollees in different projects can be compared with national norms, and differing approaches, institutional settings, and other factors can be considered. An analytical foundation exists for the evaluation of these efforts. But such analysis cannot be applied to a situation like EEA in which variability and adaptation to local conditions are emphasized.[24]

Extent of Evaluation

Between fiscal years 1963 and 1972, the total amount of money authorized by Congress for the nation's entire manpower effort was $6.8 billion. During EEA's short two-year tenure (fiscal years 1972 through 1974), some $2.25 billion was appropriated by Congress, an amount which, by itself, is equal to almost 40 percent of manpower program allocations for the previous ten-year period. Yet few evaluations of PEP have been completed, and those usually assess PEP's impact upon minorities and women in an ancillary manner. Data on race and sex are particularly scant, and differential impact is mentioned only randomly, often in the context of a "for example" to support some other statement. A brief description of the major PEP studies follows.

A major set of ongoing EEA evaluations is being conducted by the U. S. General Accounting Office (GAO) at the request of the Senate Subcommittee on Employment, Manpower and Poverty. For the most part, the GAO evaluations contain administrative judgments of program effective-

23. U.S. Congress, *op. cit.*, p. 4.

24. *Ibid.*, p. 69.

ness and do not address themselves to PEP's impact upon minorities and women. At the time this report was prepared, five GAO evaluations were available. These studies are listed below:

1. *Review of the Allocation of Funds for the Public Employment Program under the Emergency Employment Act of 1971*, submitted to Congress December 17, 1971;

2. *Delay in Hiring of Persons under the Public Employment Program*, submitted to Congress, February 16, 1972;

3. *Report on the Preparation and Approval of Plans to Supplement the Public Employment Program*, submitted to Congress, March 17, 1972;

4. *Selection and Enrollment of Participants in Programs under the Emergency Employment Act of 1971*, submitted to Congress, October 12, 1972;

5. *Types of Jobs Offered to Unemployed Persons under the Emergency Employment Act of 1971*, submitted to Congress in 1972.

In a National Urban Coalition (NUC) study, a sample of 5,690 Section 5 and 286 Section 6 PEP participants in 26 cities was drawn in early 1972.[25] The Coalition's conclusions were based on three data sources: the sample drawn, EEA legislation rules and regulations, and PEP program statistics cumulative through February 29, 1972.

The National Planning Association (NPA) presents data gathered in the first of three NPA interview waves in its report.[26] The study is a longitudinal survey of participants in the dozen *High Impact Demonstration Projects* of PEP. This first wave of 1,200 interviews in five states resulted in the accumulation of detailed information about program participants at the time they were hired. At present, the analyses of waves two and three have not been completed. Unfortunately, data pertaining to race and sex are scarce, with statements concerning minorities interjected only randomly throughout the report. In all fairness, however, it must be stated that the preliminary nature of the study itself precludes any harsh judgment about it, or the lack of information presented therein.

Like the NPA evaluation, a report by Auerbach Associates, of Arlington,

---

25. National Urban Coalition, *The Public Employment Program: An Evaluation* (Washington, D.C.: 1972).

26. National Planning Association, "A Preliminary Analysis of the Impact of the Public Employment Program on its Participants," report prepared for Manpower Administration, U.S. Department of Labor, 1972.

Virginia, presents data only for the first of three interview waves.[27] The population sample was comprised of 1,697 completed interviews for thirteen welfare demonstration projects in four states. The demographic characteristics of the program participants examined in this study lend themselves particularly to inferences about PEP's impact upon minorities and women. The sample was comprised of 91 percent minorities, 84 percent blacks, and 82 percent females. Therefore, subjective judgments about minority women could be made with relative confidence. The study also presented data on the role of supportive services and training, as well as information on changes in work attitudes and wage rates of participants.

An interim report by WESTAT Research is based on data gathered in the first of four interview waves which are being conducted at eight-month intervals.[28] Some 4,000 PEP participants were sampled nationwide. This long-range study is designed to ultimately assess the effect of PEP on the work careers of participants and pre-PEP, PEP, and post-PEP work experience will be studied.

Unfortunately, only partial information from the Wave I interviews was available. These preliminary data generally examine pre-PEP and some PEP work experiences of participants. The available WESTAT information will also be used in conjunction with the summary of an "in-house" PEP report appearing in *PEP Talk* for February 1973. Attempts were made to secure this "in-house" report, entitled "Women in the Public Employment Program," but the attempts were unsuccessful.

Three reports were prepared for the Committee on Labor and Public Policy, U.S. Senate: *The Emergency Employment Act: An Interim Assessment* and *Case Studies of the Emergency Employment Act in Operation*, sponsored by the National Manpower Policy Task Force (NMPTF),[29] and *Evaluation of the First 18 Months of the Public Employment Program*, carried out by Sar A. Levitan and Robert Taggart.[30] *An Interim Assessment* and *Evaluation of the First 18 Months* are interim evaluation reports of the same two-year PEP assessment. The first assesses virtually

27. Auerbach Associates, Inc., "The Participants: Wave I Interview Data, Sixth Special Report, Welfare Demonstration Evaluation Project," report prepared for Manpower Administration, U.S. Department of Labor, 1973.

28. WESTAT Research Inc., "Longitudinal Analysis of the Public Employment Program: Wave I Analysis," report prepared for Manpower Administration, U.S. Department of Labor, 1972.

29. U.S. Congress, Senate, Committee on Labor and Public Welfare, Subcommittee on Employment, Poverty, and Migratory Labor, *The Emergency Employment Act: An Interim Assessment* and *Case Studies of the Emergency Employment Act in operation* 92nd Cong., 2nd sess., 1972 and 93d Cong., 1st sess., 1973.

30. U.S. Congress, Senate, Committee on Labor and Public Welfare, Subcommittee on Employment, Poverty, and Migratory Labor, *Evaluation of the First 18 Months of the Public Employment Program* 93d Cong., 1st sess., 1973.

every aspect of PEP's performance. The eighteen-month report is somewhat briefer and tends to reconfirm the earlier findings of the NMPTF. In addition, the eighteen-month analysis draws data from the NPA, Auerbach, and WESTAT studies already described. Not surprisingly, the general findings tend to echo those of these other three reports. *Case Studies*, which is the final report, was completed in September 1973.

Although Marjorie S. Turner's study is not so all-encompassing as some previously described, it does present some very enlightening information.[31] A specific section of the report was devoted to PEP's impact upon minorities and women. The study also includes an analysis of worker attitudes toward their PEP jobs based on the likelihood of termination of program participants.

PROGRAM IMPACT

In the 1960's three widely accepted measures of program impact were developed: (1) employment impact; (2) wage rate impact; and (3) earnings impact, a composite measure of the previous two. Ideally, they are assessed in relation to a carefully constructed control group, or through a "pre/post analysis." Although this methodology works well for manpower training programs, its appropriateness as a methodological tool tends to decline when measuring the impact of a job creation program like PEP. Furthermore, post-program follow-up data on enrollees are virtually nonexistent, and there is also a similar dearth of information on their earnings. Thus, an assessment of PEP's impact upon minorities and women must, of necessity, rest on analysis of participant characteristics data and the use of proxy measures, upon which inferential judgment can be made.

Employment

Since PEP is a job creation program, it seems logical to evaluate it first on the basis of its employment impact. However, in order to do so, three broad questions need to be asked:

1. Who was hired by the program?
2. What happened to enrollees once in the program?
3. What is the long-run employment impact of PEP?

The evaluative literature rather explicitly discussed the service rendered to participants by PEP. A common theme, which seemed to be repeated throughout the studies, was that PEP "creamed" extensively for its enrollees. The National Urban Coalition found that the "individuals ac-

31. Marjorie S. Turner, *The First Year Experience with Public Emergency Employment: San Diego City and County* (San Diego: California State University, 1972).

tually employed by program agents . . . point to a pattern of employing relatively skilled, albeit unemployed, middle class persons (the majority male)—both black and white."[32] The GAO found:

> Applicants hired were usually those deemed best qualified by whatever standards the program agents applied. . . . It appears that program agents were able to fill the jobs provided through EEA without significantly changing their normal screening and hiring procedures. This may be attributed in part to the practice of hiring best qualified persons. As long as the program guidelines do not specify who is to be hired and as long as the number of jobs provided is small in relation to the number of unemployed, agents will probably continue to operate in a similar manner and fill available jobs with persons who best meet the established job requirements.[33]

Levitan and Taggart arrived at similar conclusions about PEP's hiring of minorities and women. They state:

> Without carefully spelled out preferences among the unemployed, the clients generally served by manpower programs will be shortchanged. Blacks and Spanish Americans were overrepresented in PEP, largely because political pressures in most central cities reinforced by federal guidelines insured them a fair share. Women are not well-organized and there has been little pressure anywhere to increase the very low proportion hired under PEP. Likewise, younger and older workers have been largely ignored. More critically, however, the educationally handicapped and the disadvantaged have been seriously underrepresented. The proportion reported as disadvantaged in PEP was more than twice as high as the actual level. Almost without fail, program agents have creamed from each client group to get the best educated and most skilled workers. There has been very little reaching back down the labor queue. If this is to be achieved, much more careful stipulations must be enforced.[34]

The extent to which PEP "creamed" for its participants naturally affected its outreach to minorities and women. The evaluative literature indicated that minorities were neither specifically targeted nor generally ignored by PEP. The GAO found:

> None of the agents [sampled] placed minority group members first on their list of hiring priorities. However, 14 program agents indicated special outreach efforts had been made to attract minority applicants. . . . [T]hese agents used minority or bilingual outreach workers to recruit Spanish-speaking persons, blacks, orientals, etc.; [they] advertised in minority newspapers or on minority radio stations; and a few agents held meetings with, or sent

32. National Urban Coalition, *op. cit.*, p. 42.

33. Comptroller General of the United States, *Selection and Enrollment of Participants in Programs Under the Emergency Employment Act of 1971* (Washington, D.C.: General Accounting Office, 1972), pp. 9, 10.

34. U.S. Congress, Senate, *Evaluation of the First 18 Months*, *op. cit.*, p. 40.

job listings to, minority organizations. The use of special outreach workers proved to be an effective means of attracting minority applicants.[35]

The Turner study tended to be somewhat more critical of PEP than the GAO study:

[T]here is no evidence that PEP's hiring of minorities significantly changed minority employment outlook. One can conclude, however, that without PEP, the . . . minority persons served would have been unemployed more often, and thus PEP avoided a worsening outlook. . . . Of the minorities served, blacks were more adequately served than Mexican Americans if you use the labor force as a base. . . . American Indians were more adequately served than any other minority, mainly because of the deliberate program on the reservations which committed $1 million of PEP money over two years to Indian purposes. In terms of unemployment rates (estimated sometimes as high as 40 percent), the Indians were not by any means overserved. . . . Oriental groups were not served particularly, and this may be because need has not been established locally. . . .[36]

In regard to women, Turner stated in the study:

PEP did not serve this group adequately, . . . the proportion of cumulative participants which are female is slightly less than their part in the labor force. Apparently, no allowance was made for their higher unemployment rate. More than anything else, this is probably accounted for by the fact that not a single top administrator was a woman. Typically many of the women who were working on PEP coordinating staffs had as high or higher educational preparation than their male bosses. So far as I could determine, the enormity of this situation never bothered anyone, including the females. . . . The only bright light in this dismal picture is the abnormally high placement of females in City regular jobs.[37]

Finally, National Planning Association stated, "PEP is not hiring women to the degree that they are represented among the unemployed and underemployed of the Demonstration areas. To hire women to this degree, it would be necessary for PEP to hire 60 to 70 percent more women."[38]

Once through the intake process, the enrollee must then perform in the workaday world. It can be argued that, in many instances, his potential for job performance can be measured by the amount of training he receives. To the extent that PEP "creamed" for its participants, the need for

35. Comptroller General of the United States, *op. cit.*, p. 6.

36. Turner, *op. cit.*, pp. 25-26.

37. Ibid., pp. 32-34.

38. National Planning Association, *op. cit.*, p. 12.

training necessarily declined. However, for the disadvantaged, for minorities, and less frequently for women, the need for training would appear to be significantly greater. Thus, PEP's impact upon minorities and women must be judged in relation to the training received by program participants.

Training, in the context of a job creation program, is a rather intriguing concept. One PEP evaluator commented:

> A really interesting possibility arises when one considers that it is certainly as reasonable for a person to go from job to training as from training to a job. Job creation programs would be extremely useful screening devices for determining what persons need training (either from among applicants or participants), and what persons who accept jobs could benefit from further training. In either case the connection between training and holding a job would be closer than in the past where the training program has all too often been a deadend.[39]

However, PEP's performance in this activity has been open to considerable scrutiny by evaluators. The National Manpower Policy Task Force reported that "If PEP is really to serve as a 'transitional' program, serving those who find it difficult to compete for employment, manpower and supportive services are crucial."[40] Levitan and Taggart stated:

> Transition Without Training Is A Revolving Door: The PEP experience suggests the difficulties of achieving transition to permanent employment. If workers are hired who qualify for their jobs, and are performing needed public services, it makes little sense to go through the motions of finding them a permanent job and refilling the slot. If those hired are not qualified, the states and localities are usually reluctant to hire them on a permanent basis. An individual without the needed credentials could demonstrate his capabilities on the PEP job or could improve them enough to be attractive to other employers; in other words, PEP could conceivably serve as a probationary employment. PEP was not well structured, however, to accomplish transition. Initial haste and later uncertainty created impediments and there were limited funds for training. Clearly PEP has almost no leverage on the regular employment system and it will have been less if it is completely absorbed into this system.
>
> The PEP experience does not support the claim that such a program will alleviate structural employment problems. Not only were few disadvantaged hired and even fewer moved into permanent jobs, but they were the least likely to get the meager training and education available through the program. States and localities complained that they lacked adequate training funds under PEP, but few spent the full authorized amounts. Though most positions paid more on the average than similar private sector jobs, they were dead-end for many.[41]

39. Turner, *op. cit.*, p. 101.

40. U.S. Congress, *An Interim Assessment*, *op. cit.*, p. 47.

41. U.S. Congress, *Evaluation of the First 18 Months, op. cit.*, pp. 40-41.

Three evaluations present data on the incidence and type of training received by PEP enrollees. National Planning Associates found that 36.9 percent of the PEP participants they surveyed had received training while in the program. Unfortunately, no race or sex data were provided.

Auerbach Associates devoted a section of its report to training and supportive services. Their treatment of this aspect of PEP is enlightening and raises some interesting definitional questions about training in general. The report explained:

> Participants state that little formal training is being received. Since entering the . . . [project] only 21 percent of the participants have received job training and only 12 percent have enrolled in educational training. . . . When the training question was broadened to include OJT, training rates went up. Sixty percent of the participants stated that they had received some type of training after starting to work and 84 percent of these participants indicated that they were receiving exclusively OJT training.[42]

Thus, it appears that training per se is a rather ambiguous term, and its incidence can be governed by the way it is defined and the way enrollees are questioned about it.

The WESTAT Research study provided some additional insights into the extent of PEP training. Table 7 presents data by race and sex for PEP participants receiving training. WESTAT found that 46.7 percent of the participants surveyed had received training for their jobs. There was virtually no difference between the amounts received by males and females, but whites tended to be trained more often than nonwhites. When asked if this training were formal, 34.8 percent answered "yes." Males and nonwhites were more often the beneficiaries of such training than females and whites. Seven of every eight persons receiving training stated that it was obtained during working hours. This proportion was rather stable over all race and sex groups. Therefore, it appears that the amount of training received, and PEP's performance in providing it, can only be judged by the way one is predisposed to define it.

The available PEP evaluations present some data on the incidence of supportive services among enrollees. Table 8 presents information derived from the Auerbach Associates, Inc., study which dealt exclusively with welfare recipients. These types of enrollees characteristically require more supportive services than the average program participant.

The most needed, but unavailable, supportive service for the persons in this survey was transportation aid, followed by medical and dental services, and child-care services. The incidence of persons actually receiving such services is somewhat high. For example, almost 60 percent received medical and dental services, over one-half received child-care services, and over one in four enrollees received transportation aid.

42. Auerbach Associates, Inc., *op. cit.*, pp. 5-10, 5-11.

TABLE XI-7. *Public Employment Program*
Percent Distribution of Participants Receiving Training for Jobs

Characteristics	Total	Did You Receive Any Training For Your PEP Job?		If Yes, Was This A Formal Training Program?			Percent Of Those Receiving Training Who Attended During:		
		Yes	No/Other	Yes	Partly Formal	No/Other	Working Hours	Own Time	Both
Sex:									
Male	100.0	46.8	53.2	37.8	16.6	45.6	88.0	6.8	5.2
Female	100.0	46.6	53.4	27.9	15.9	56.2	87.2	9.9	2.9
Race:									
White	100.0	48.6	51.4	32.3	16.2	51.5	87.3	7.4	5.3
All other races combined	100.0	43.1	56.9	39.9	16.7	43.4	88.8	8.3	2.9
Negro	100.0	44.2	55.8	39.9	19.4	40.7	89.1	7.1	3.8
Spanish American	100.0	47.0	53.0	38.4	13.3	48.3	87.5	9.8	2.7
All other	100.0	38.7	61.3	40.7	12.6	46.7	88.8	9.9	1.3
Total	100.0	46.7	53.3	34.8	16.4	48.8	87.7	7.7	4.5

Source: WESTAT Research, Inc., "Longitudinal Analysis of the Public Employment Program: Wave I Analysis," report prepared for Manpower Administration, U.S. Department of Labor 1972, p. 2-23.

Note: Percents may not add to 100 due to rounding.

TABLE XI-8. *Public Employment Program*
Percent of Welfare Demonstration Project Enrollees
Needing or Receiving Supportive Services

Type of Supportive Service	Persons Needing Supportive Service Which Was Unavailable	Persons Receiving Supportive Service
Child-care	8.0	50.8
Transportation aid	15.4	26.4
Medical and dental	9.8	57.7
Job counseling	3.5	14.8
Legal counseling	3.2	3.2
Family counseling	3.2	1.9

Source: Auerbach Associates, Inc., "The Participants: Wave I Interview Data, Sixth Special Report, Welfare Demonstration Evaluation Project" report prepared for Manpower Administration, U.S. Department of Labor, 1973, p. 4-15.

The WESTAT study, which covered a broader range of enrollees, also provided data on supportive services. Fortunately, there are race and sex breakdowns and Table 9 presents these data.

Unlike Auerbach Associates, WESTAT found the incidence of PEP supportive services to be remarkably low, with the exception of medical and dental services. Males and females availed themselves of these services at about the same rate. Among each group, Negroes and Spanish Americans were frequent users of medical and dental services. Negroes received transportation assistance more often than Spanish Americans or whites. Spanish Americans were more likely to receive financial counseling than any other group for which data were presented.

It appears, therefore, that the incidence of supportive services is dependent on which segment of the unemployed was targeted by a specific locality or project. The degree to which the group of persons served was disadvantaged, minority, or on public assistance, seems to determine the extent of supportive services provided.

PEP must also be assessed in relation to how enrollees were upgraded while in the program. In many respects, this is a very subjective area of evaluation. In addition, very little data on the subject exist. However, some preliminary information on promotions, transfers, and job title changes was available and was used as a proxy measure of PEP enrollee upgrading.

WESTAT Research gathered data on the above three items, and they are presented in Table 10. An analysis of the table reveals that women were transferred more frequently than men. However, the types of personnel actions which usually result in pay gains (promotions and job title changes) were experienced more often by males than females. Whites tended to be promoted more frequently than other races, but were transferred or had their job titles changed less often than other races. Thus, it appears that minorities and women were shifted, both physically and administratively, rather frequently, whereas whites and males were experiencing monetary gains through promotions.

One can theorize that EEA's success as a job creation program can in part be measured by the types of jobs it created. One testament to the quality of these jobs is the attitudes of workers toward them. This concept, taken in the context of transitional employment, has even greater implications of long-run worker impact. It can be hypothesized that if workers are placed in jobs they like, and gain experience in them, they will be able to use these job experience credentials toward similar post-program employment. Conversely, if enrollees are placed in jobs which are undesirable to them, the experience gained will be of little future value because it will not be utilized.

TABLE XI-9. *Public Employment Program*
Percent Distribution of Participants by Their Use of Special Services While in the Program

	Percent of Participants Receiving						
Characteristics	Medical or Dental Exam	Other Medical or Dental Care	Family or Personal Counseling	Child Care Assistance	Trans-portation Assistance	Financial Counseling	All Other Assistance
Sex:							
Male	41.2	5.0	0.9	0.2	3.1	1.2	0.5
Female	37.7	3.9	0.8	1.8	3.2	1.3	1.0
Race:							
White	38.4	4.5	0.8	0.5	2.5	1.3	0.7
All other races combined	43.1	4.9	1.1	1.0	4.3	1.2	0.6
Negro	50.3	4.0	0.7	1.4	4.6	0.8	0.6
Spanish American	49.5	3.3	1.7	—	1.4	2.2	—
All other	25.7	7.5	1.5	0.7	5.2	1.5	1.1
Total	40.1	4.7	0.9	0.7	3.1	1.2	0.7

Source: WESTAT Research, Inc., "Longitudinal Analysis of the Public Employment Program: Wave I Analysis," report prepared for Manpower Administration, U.S. Department of Labor (Bethesda: 1972), p. 3-18.

TABLE XI-10. *Public Employment Program*
Percent Distribution of Participants Still in the Program
By Changes in Job or Status of Job

Characteristics	Proportion[a] of Participants Who Have: Been Transferred	Been Promoted or Received Increase in Pay	Change in Job Title
Sex:			
Male	11.6	30.6	8.1
Female	12.7	25.7	6.3
Race:			
White	11.1	32.2	7.2
All other races combined	13.4	22.9	7.9
Negro	14.7	24.6	8.8
Spanish American	15.8	31.3	8.0
All other	9.0	14.3	5.8
Other Participant Characteristics:			
Disadvantaged	10.8	19.2	5.7
Not disadvantaged	12.1	30.8	7.8
Welfare recipient	15.6	31.8	7.2
Special or Vietnam veteran	14.4	33.2	10.4
Total	11.9	29.0	7.5

Sourcc: WESTAT Research, Inc., "Longitudinal Analysis of the Public Employment Program: Wave I Analysis," report prepared for Manpower Administration U.S. Department of Labor (Bethesda: 1972), p. 3-11.

[a] Percents given in the table are based upon an estimated 94,000 participants who are still in the PEP program.

Three of the major PEP evaluations specifically assess PEP's impact on workers' attitudes toward their jobs. In general, PEP participants were well satisfied with their positions. The NPA study reported:

> When asked how the PEP job compares with the characteristics sought in an ideal job, 23 percent of the respondents said their PEP job had them all, [and] 62 percent said their PEP job had some of them. . . . Finally, 83 percent . . . felt that their Public Employment Program job was useful rather than just a job or a make-work job.[43]

43. National Planning Association, *op. cit.*, pp. 37, 39.

The Auerbach Associates study, which employed a vastly different sample, disclosed similar findings:

> Eighty-one percent of the participants stated that they would like to continue in the line of work where they are currently employed. When asked how their WDP job compared with their "ideal job," 86 percent said their . . . job had some or all the characteristics.[44]

Program participants with previous work experience also seemed to have viewed PEP as somewhat of an upgrading experience and held their jobs in high esteem (Table 11). Concerning women, these findings tended to be corroborated by an "in-house" Labor Department study based on WESTAT data. The report stated that "in their PEP jobs, most women find at least as much, if not more, satisfaction as they did in their last jobs."[45]

The Turner study provided specific data about minorities and women. Job satisfaction was approximated by a proxy measure, the Likelihood of Termination (L.O.T.) from PEP. The L.O.T. is the ratio of the number of program terminees of a specific demographic category to the cumulative number of program participants for that same demographic category. The following is a symbolic example of the statistic:

$$\text{Black L.O.T.} = \frac{\text{Number of Black Terminees}}{\text{Number of Blacks in Program}}$$

TABLE XI-11. *Public Employment Program Comparison of PEP Job With Previous Job*

Qualities of PEP Job As Compared with Previous Job	Percent
More interesting	62.7
Less boring	64.0
More secure	53.0
More satisfying	62.3
More rspected	52.9

Source: National Planning Association, "A Preliminary Analysis of the Impact of the Public Employment Program on Its Participants," report prepared for Manpower Administration, 1972, p. 40.

44. Auerbach Associates, Inc., *op. cit.*, p. 6-6.

45. U.S. Department of Labor, *PEP Talk: A Technical Bulletin on the Public Employment Program* (Washington, D.C.: February 1973), p. 8.

The rationale for this measure was that those workers least satisfied with their PEP jobs would be more likely to leave PEP, and vice versa. Therefore, Turner hypothesized that an inverse relationship existed between L.O.T. and job satisfaction. Table 12 presents data which are either presented in or derived from the Turner study.

On the basis of their low likelihood of termination ratio, American Indians were judged to be the most satisfied PEP participants; they were followed by Mexican Americans, women, and all minorities, in that order. Comparing the proportion of total terminations to the proportion of cumulative participants, these same groups were again considered to be highly satisfied with their jobs. Thus, minorities and women, at least in San Diego, appear to have received job experience in occupations they enjoyed.

The Auerbach Associates study also provided a good base for judgments about PEP's impact upon minorities and women. The nature of the sample drawn (91 percent minorities, 84 percent blacks, and 82 percent females) also allows general statements about PEP's impact upon minority women. Of the PEP participants surveyed:

> 86 percent contend that their work is useful, 75 percent indicate they usually have work to do, and 71 percent hold that their jobs are not "make-work." Moreover, the majority . . . contend that negative aspects associated with work . . . are not usually present in their job situations. Of the items rated, the one pertaining to decision-making had the smallest percentage replying in a positive direction . . . since the participants are new employees and are in the process of gaining new skills, this result is not unexpected.[46] (See Table 13).

Thus, it seems that women in general, and particularly minority women, were happy with their PEP jobs. These positive attitudes may be reflected in future employment gains.

As previously stated, not all the effects of manpower programs are easily quantifiable, and thus, specific dollar and cents values cannot easily be assigned to them. The full impact of noneconomic benefits will typically not be realized in the short run. One such noneconomic benefit is the change in civil service requirements. These reforms clearly affect the intake process of future public service job seekers. Traditionally, these requirements have served to lock the door to employment for many persons, particularly minorities and women. The extent to which PEP is instrumental in bringing about a relaxation of these requirements can easily be judged to be a societal benefit of the program.

One of PEP's stated objectives is "[t]o encourage State and local governments to reexamine job qualifications for their employees in order to

46. Auerbach Associates, Inc., *op. cit.*, p. 6-6.

eliminate artificial barriers to employment."[47] This, of course, means revising civil service requirements. One study reported that to meet these changes:

> Program agents could pursue any of three courses of action: first, they might reform civil service rules and hiring generally; second, they might make special efforts on behalf of EEA participants to get them through the system into permanent jobs; or third, they might respond only nominally, with study and analysis but no changes or special efforts. Put another way, PEP might be a wedge to force general reform, a port-of-entry to get inside the existing system or merely the basis for another fact finding and research endeavor.[48]

The general tone of the evaluative literature concerning PEP's performance toward institutional change is that "in only a few cases has EEA led to comprehensive civil service reform."[49] However, there have been some significant changes instituted by individual program agents. The nature of these changes indicates that PEP played at least a catalytic role in reducing some of the civil service requirements which historically have separated minorities and women from meaningful job opportunities.

According to the available PEP evaluations, one of the most comprehensive sets of civil service reforms occurred in Los Angeles, California. Shortly after EEA's enactment, the mayor announced his desire to make the Los Angeles PEP "the showcase of the Nation." Recognizing PEP's crucial role in the intake process, an eight-member Advisory Recruiting and Selection Committee was set up. However, the committee's establishment was of minor importance when compared with the characteristics of its staff. It consisted of a black, Chicano, an Oriental, an American Indian, a veteran, and a representative of laid-off aerospace workers. Therefore, the interests of minorities were adequately represented and the Committee thus acted as a leader of reform. The relaxation of formal education requirements was a major modification in the city's selection standards. "Three quarters of the jobs which, on September 1, 1971, had a high school graduation requirement, no longer have such a requirement."[50] The city also "determined that requirements such as . . . height, weight, age, and sex can be dropped when not deemed relevant to job perform-

47. U.S. Department of Labor, *Annual Report to Congress*, *op. cit.*, p. 5.

48. U.S. Congress, *An Interim Assessment*, *op. cit.*, p. 48.

49. *Ibid.*

50. *Ibid.*, p. 199.

TABLE XI-12. *Public Employment Program*
Likelihood of Termination Ratios of San Diego PEP Participants
Cumulative Through July 31, 1972

Group	Likelihood of Termination Ratio (in percent)	Rank Order of Likelihood of Termination	Assignable Terminations[a] (Percent of Total)	Cumulative Participants[b] (Percent of Total)
Race:				
White	29.5	7	64.4	62.0
Minorities	26.6	11	35.6	38.0
Negroes	30.5	4	16.2	15.0
Mexican Americans	23.3	13	11.7	14.3
American Indians	20.7	14	4.2	5.8
Other	33.7	1	3.5	2.9
Sex:				
Male[c]	30.5	3	71.0	66.1
Female	24.3	12	29.0	33.9
Disadvantaged	29.2	8	34.7	33.7

TABLE XI-12 *continued*

Veterans:	29.7[c]	6[c]	47.6	45.5
Special	30.2	5	14.7	13.9
Vietnam	30.7	2	17.4	16.0
Other	28.2	10	15.5	15.6
All Employees	28.4	9	100.0	100.0

Source: Marjorie S. Turner, *The First Year Experience With Public Emergency Employment: San Diego City and County* (San Diego: California State University, 1972), p. 28.

[a]Total assignable terminations is N = 998.
[b]Total cumulative participants is N = 3,514.
[c]By Industrial Research Unit computation.

TABLE XI-13. *Public Employment Program*
Percent Distribution of Job Qualities by Welfare Demonstration Project Participants

Qualities	Number of Participants Sampled	Total	Almost Always	Often	Sometimes	Almost Never	Don't Know
Positive:							
Work useful	1,674	100.0	76.0	9.7	11.2	3.0	0.1
Work respected	1,672	100.0	68.2	10.5	14.2	6.8	0.3
Negative:							
Work too hard	1,674	100.0	1.1	1.9	17.7	79.2	0.1
Work boring	1,672	100.0	5.9	3.6	27.6	62.8	0.1
Don't like work	1,672	100.0	3.8	2.7	16.1	77.3	0.1
No work to do	1,672	100.0	11.4	3.1	16.7	68.7	0.1
Make-work job	1,664	100.0	12.8	4.2	16.1	65.2	1.7
Others make decisions	1,669	100.0	16.7	7.6	28.9	46.7	0.1

Source: Auerbach Associates, Inc., "The Participants: Wave I Interview Data, Sixth Special Report, Welfare Demonstration Evaluation Project", report prepared for Manpower Administration, U.S. Department of Labor, 1973, p. 6-14.

ance."[51] Like Los Angeles, San Diego also initiated modest changes "to provide PEP hires a port-of-entry into public employment. . . . [The city] relaxed weight and height requirements for policemen and firemen to hire minority group trainees."[52]

Various other localities have also revised these job requirements as a result of EEA programs. A partial victory in Los Angeles was gained over the use of arrest and conviction records in the selection process. Washington, D.C. also "accepted a number of applicants whose criminal records would have excluded them from regular jobs. . . . It was agreed to waive such barriers in the case of offenders who graduated from manpower programs, presumably on the basis that their successful experience in the manpower program had nullified any adverse experience with the law."[53] "[These types of changes] . . . will be important to all future applicants for city jobs, as well as PEP hires."[54] The employment opportunities of minorities will, of course, be greatly enhanced by such revisions.

In San Diego, a breakthrough was made on "selective certification." This revision allows selective certification of persons "on the basis of race or ethnicity if a city department has an 'unbalanced' race or sex mix."[55] Some jurisdictions revised their testing procedures to allow for greater flexibility in hiring. Replies to a U.S. Senate questionnaire sample by EEA program agents indicate at least moderate advances have been made toward the altering of "testing procedures to allow for greater flexibility in hiring."[56] For example, in many instances, oral or performance tests have been substituted for written tests in Pawtucket, Rhode Island. New Castle, Delaware, actually dropped written tests for all entry-level positions. The state of Missouri now ". . . provides on-the-job training for PEP participants and delays testing until they can meet the established performance requirements."[57]

These PEP-initiated civil service reforms, although not as all-encompassing or widespread as they could have been, still served to open the door to employment for minorities. It is somewhat difficult to assess the

51. Ellen Yaffa, "Replies to Questionnaires from Emergency Employment Act Program Agents," in U.S. Congress, Senate, Committee on Labor and Public Welfare, *Comprehensive Manpower Reform 1972*, Hearings before the Subcommittee on Employment Manpower and Poverty, 92nd Cong., 2d sess., April 26, 1972, p. 1851.

52. U.S. Congress, *An Interim Assessment*, *op. cit.*, p. 49.

53. *Ibid.*, pp. 48, 189.

54. *Ibid.*, p. 48.

55. Turner, *op. cit.*, pp. 95-96.

56. Yaffa, *op. cit.*, p. 1850.

57. *Ibid.*

TABLE XI-14. *Public Employment Program*
Percent Distribution of Average Hourly Earnings of Participants
Fiscal Year 1972 Entrants

Wage Rates	Total	Negroes	Spanish American	American Indian	Disadvantaged	Public Assistance	Male[a]	Female[a]
Pre-PEP average hourly wage rate (percent of total)								
Under $1.60	9	8	4	10	13	11	n.a.	n.a.
1.60 to 1.99	19	22	14	21	24	21	n.a.	n.a.
2.00 to 2.99	37	39	50	38	37	38	n.a.	n.a.
3.00 to 3.99	20	20	25	18	17	19	n.a.	n.a.
4.00 to 4.99	8	7	5	7	6	7	n.a.	n.a.
5.00 and over	7	4	2	7	4	5	n.a.	n.a.
Total	100	100	100	100	100	100	n.a.	n.a.
Average hourly wage rate (in dollars)	2.77	2.59	2.64	2.70	2.50	2.59	3.10	1.99
PEP average hourly wage rate (percent of total)								
Under $1.60	3	—	—	—	7	2	n.a.	n.a.
1.60 to 1.99	15	18	7	15	19	13	n.a.	n.a.
2.00 to 2.99	46	47	52	56	47	55	n.a.	n.a.

TABLE XI-14 *continued*

3.00 to 3.99	24	27	34	18	21	24	n.a.	n.a.
4.00 to 4.99	8	6	4	7	4	5	n.a.	n.a.
5.00 and over	4	2	3	3	2	1	n.a.	n.a.
Total	100	100	100	100	100	100	n.a.	n.a.
Average hourly wage rate (in dollars)	2.83	2.79	2.96	2.75	2.59	2.71	2.98	2.69
Change in average hourly wage rates (in cents)	+6	+20	+32	+5	+9	+12	-12	+70

Source: U.S. Department of Labor, Manpower Administration.

Note: Percents may not add to 100 due to rounding.

[a] These data are based on preliminary information contained in an "in-house" U.S. Department of Labor report, "Public Employment Program Performance as of June 30, 1972.

impact of these changes upon women. But, to the extent that tests were geared to males and job requirements were written to exclude females, women must necessarily have registered at least marginal gains in employment opportunities.

Wage Rate

A somewhat more quantifiable measure of PEP's performance is the wage rate impact. It was, therefore, not surprising to discover that these data were rather easy to obtain. Unfortunately, there is a severe lack of post-program wage rate information. Therefore, inferences must be drawn from limited data on pre-PEP and PEP trainee wage rates.

EEA program statistics provide wage rate data which can be used as a basis to gain a broader perspective of PEP's impact upon minorities and women. Table 14 presents wage rate data for fiscal year 1972 and Table 15 provides information on fiscal year 1973 entrants through February 28, 1973.[58] Unfortunately, neither year of data is strictly comparable with the other. The 1972 data provide a better base for analysis, but include no cross-tabulations by race and sex; the 1973 data are somewhat biased because of the large numbers of summer program participants who are included in the statistics and who had no pre-PEP employment. These persons were *excluded* from the pre-PEP, but *included* in the PEP average hourly wage rate calculation. These predominantly young persons with little or no job experience tended to be hired at the lowest rates of pay, and their low overall average wage rate pulled down the average for the rest of the participants. A cursory glance at the two tables shows that the average wage gain for PEP jobs over pre-PEP jobs in fiscal year 1972 was four cents per hour; the statistics for fiscal year 1973 entrants, however, show an average three cents per hour loss. In fact, all but one of the classifications shown for 1972 registered gains, whereas five of the same eight categories in 1973 showed a decline.

Considering the impact of wage rates upon individual segments of the fiscal year 1972 PEP population, the primary gainers appear to be Spanish Americans, followed by blacks and public assistance recipients. Comparing 1973 pre-PEP and PEP wage rates for individual categories is undesirable for reasons previously stated. However, a general review of Tables 14 and 15 reveals that, on the average, women appear to have gained more than men. It is also evident that, despite their gains, they were and still are paid less than their male counterparts. Most of this can be explained by the types of jobs in which the women were placed.

Although occupational breakdowns by race and sex were unavailable, an examination of participant characteristics by public service area allows

58. These data were the most current at the time this report was prepared.

TABLE XI-15. *Public Employment Program*
Percent Distribution of Average Hourly Earnings
July 1, 1972—February 28, 1973
Fiscal Year 1973 Entrants

Wage Rates	All PEP Participants						Male						Female					
	Total	Negro	Spanish American	American Indian	Disadvantaged	Public Assistance Recipient	Total	Negro	Spanish American	American Indian	Disadvantaged	Public Assistance Recipient	Total	Negro	Spanish American	American Indian	Disadvantaged	Public Assistance Recipient
Pre-PEP average hourly wage rate																		
Under $1.60	7	7	9	6	9	11	5	4	8	5	3	9	10	12	12	10	13	14
1.60 to 1.99	20	23	20	24	26	24	16	17	17	18	21	17	31	34	29	34	37	33
2.00 to 2.99	39	38	40	36	38	40	39	36	40	33	38	38	41	41	42	41	39	43
3.00 to 3.99	21	24	22	19	19	17	24	30	24	23	23	23	12	11	12	13	9	9
4.00 to 4.99	7	6	[illegible]	8	5	5	9	8	6	12	6	9	4	2	2	2	1	1
5.00 and over	6	3	[illegible]	6	4	3	7	4	4	9	4	5	2	1	2	1	1	—
Total	100	100	100	100	100	100	100	100	100	100	100	100	100	100	100	100	100	100
Average hourly wage rate (in dollars)	2.73	2.61	[illegible]	2.74	2.47	2.43	2.87	2.82	2.70	3.02	2.54	2.72	2.32	2.19	2.29	2.19	2.09	2.08
PEP average hourly wage rate																		
Under $1.60	—	—	—	—	—	—	—	—	—	—	—	—	—	—	1	—	—	—
1.60 to 1.99	25	38	37	7	36	31	21	32	31	5	32	32	35	47	53	10	44	31
2.00 to 2.99	42	33	32	56	40	45	40	28	31	48	38	34	47	40	34	71	44	57
3.00 to 3.99	24	24	34	24	19	20	29	32	30	30	24	28	12	10	9	14	10	11
4.00 to 4.99	6	4	5	8	3	3	8	6	6	12	5	5	3	1	2	2	1	1
5.00 and over	3	1	2	4	1	1	3	2	2	5	1	1	2	1	1	3	—	—
Total	100	100	100	100	100	100	100	100	100	100	100	100	100	100	100	100	100	100
Average hourly wage rate (in dollars)	2.70	2.56	2.56	2.91	2.45	2.50	2.81	2.71	2.69	3.05	2.56	2.61	2.44	2.27	2.22	2.62	2.25	2.39
Change in average hourly wage rates (in cents)	-3	-5	-5	+17	-2	+7	-6	-11	-1	+3	-3	-11	+12	+8	-7	+43	+16	+31

Source: U.S. Department of Labor, Manpower Administration.

Note: Percents may not add to 100 due to rounding.

TABLE XI-16. *Public Employment Program*
Percent Distribution and Average Hourly Earnings of Male and Female Participants by Public Service Area Cumulative Through January 31, 1973

Earnings and Participants	Total Enrollees	Total Percent	Law Enforcement	Education	Public Works and Transportation	Health and Hospital	Environmental Quality	Fire Protection	Parks and Recreation	Social Services	Other
Negroes:											
Male	67	100	9	16	26	8	6	2	15	5	13
Female	33	100	7	31	4	20	2	—	5	13	19
Average hourly earnings	$2.79		3.15	2.80	2.66	2.64	2.87	3.23	2.65	2.90	2.83
Spanish Americans:											
Male	73	100	7	12	26	11	3	1	14	12	14
Female	27	100	2	34	1	20	2	—	1	22	18
Average hourly earnings	$2.96		3.19	2.96	3.05	2.75	2.64	3.34	2.81	3.10	2.98
American Indians:											
Male	73	100	9	8	31	4	6	1	11	9	21
Female	27	100	7	23	8	9	1	—	3	20	29
Average hourly earnings	$2.75		2.81	2.83	2.66	2.65	2.88	3.18	2.46	2.78	2.84

TABLE XI-16 *continued*

Disadvantaged:											
Male	69	100	8	15	32	8	5	2	12	4	14
Female	31	100	6	32	5	20	1	—	4	12	21
Average hourly earnings	$2.59		2.90	2.57	2.45	2.45	2.79	2.95	2.60	2.71	2.66
Public assistance recipients:											
Male	62	100	7	16	33	7	5	2	12	4	13
Female	38	100	7	28	4	19	1	—	3	17	21
Average hourly earnings	$2.71		3.01	2.60	2.68	2.60	2.76	3.23	2.83	2.70	2.75
All participants:											
Male	72	100	12	15	29	6	5	3	11	4	14
Female	28	100	8	33	5	16	1	—	4	10	23
Average hourly earnings	$2.83		3.15	2.88	2.64	2.63	2.97	3.17	2.76	2.94	2.87

Source: U.S. Department of Labor, Manpower Administration.

Note: Percents may not add to 100 due to rounding.

TABLE XI-17. *Public Employment Program*
Percent Distribution and Average Hourly Earnings of Male and Female Participants by Public Service Area Cumulative Through February 28, 1973

Earnings and Participants	Total Enrollees	Total	Law Enforce-ment	Edu-cation	Public Works and Transpor-tation	Health and Hospital	Environ-mental Quality	Fire Pro-tection	Parks and Recre-ation	Social Services	Other
All participants:											
Male	71	100	8	12	30	4	4	2	14	7	19
Female	29	100	6	21	5	11	1	—	9	18	28
Average hourly earnings	$2.70		3.05	2.95	2.77	2.57	2.60	3.19	2.36	2.37	2.68
Negroes											
Male	65	100	5	11	29	4	5	1	17	13	16
Female	35	100	5	14	3	11	1	—	13	26	26
Average hourly earnings	$2.56		3.00	2.92	2.81	2.51	2.57	3.18	2.37	1.99	2.56
Spanish Americans:											
Male	71	100	7	16	18	5	3	2	15	14	20
Female	29	100	5	17	2	9	1	—	10	30	26
Average hourly earnings	$2.56		3.00	2.92	2.81	2.51	2.57	3.18	2.37	1.99	2.56

TABLE XI-17 *continued*

American Indians:											
Male	66	100	10	14	21	5	3	1	10	12	23
Female	34	100	5	17	15	14	3	—	4	14	29
Average hourly earnings	$2.91		2.89	2.91	3.14	2.87	2.88	3.65	2.69	2.77	2.86
Disadvantaged:											
Male	65	100	5	11	31	4	4	1	16	12	15
Female	35	100	5	16	4	13	1	—	11	24	26
Average hourly earnings	$2.45		2.82	2.69	2.70	2.53	2.66	2.76	2.21	2.02	2.40
Public assistance recipients:											
Male	53	100	4	11	32	4	5	2	17	12	13
Female	47	100	6	18	2	18	1	—	10	22	23
Average hourly earnings	$2.50		2.79	3.65	2.75	2.54	2.90	2.99	2.24	2.11	2.53

Source: U.S. Department of Labor, Manpower Administration.

Note: Percents may not add to 100 due to rounding.

some subjective judgments to be made. An "in-house" Labor Department study based on WESTAT data found that "females more often find EEA jobs in education and health, while men are commonly placed in positions in the areas of law enforcement and public works/transportation."[59] Tables 16 and 17 present detailed information of wage rates by public service area; it is interesting to compare average hourly pay scales. For example, in the fire protection area where virtually no women are employed, the average rate of pay is above the overall average. Conversely, in the heavily female health-hospital category, the average hourly earnings are substantially below the overall average. Similarly, with the exception of Spanish Americans, the average pay scales within a public service area tend to be below the overall average for those population segments which traditionally suffer greater labor market disadvantages (blacks, American Indians, disadvantaged persons, and public assistance recipients).

Unfortunately, Tables 16 and 17 are not strictly comparable, but aggregate data for PEP's tenure through March 1973 were available. Table 4 presented these data and can be used to verify the inferential judgments made from the analysis of the two previous tables. On the average, health and hospital occupations tend to trail the field, and fire protection and law enforcement jobs lead it. Education professions are only slightly above average, but it must be remembered that a substantial portion of those are teaching-related positions, where educational attainment is usually high. It can easily be hypothesized that average pay is not higher in this female-dominated profession precisely because it is a female-dominated profession. PEP, therefore, appears to have had little impact in changing this situation.

Additional insights and supportive data of EEA's impact upon minorities and women were gained from the PEP evaluation studies. Auerbach Associates found that "[t]here is a definite wage differential in terms of sex with males earning 50 cents more per hour, than females. . . . [but] There is little differentiation in terms of ethnic backgrounds."[60] This information is presented in Table 18.

Unfortunately, the evaluative literature, such as PEP program statistics, is particularly deficient in terms of post-program outcomes data. Only the NPA and WESTAT studies made attempts to gather such information. WESTAT data dealt exclusively with PEP work experiences but were presented in such a way as to show PEP's impact. In the NPA study, no race or sex data were provided. Thus, the NPA findings were only of marginal benefit when judging PEP's impact upon minorities and women. Specifically, NPA found:

59. U.S. Department of Labor, *PEP Talk, loc. cit.*

60. Auerbach Associates, Inc., *op. cit.*, p. 6-8.

TABLE XI-18. *Public Employment Program*
Percent Distribution of Welfare Demonstration Project Hourly Wages Before Deductions
By Sex and Race of Participants

Hourly Wage	Total	Sex		Race		
		Male	Female	White	Negro	Puerto Rican
1.25 and under	1.9	1.7	1.9	—	1.8	5.4
1.26 to 1.60	3.5	0.8	4.4	1.3	4.0	1.1
1.61 to 1.99	8.8	1.9	10.7	8.7	9.4	1.1
2.00 to 2.50	26.7	15.1	29.8	32.5	25.8	25.8
2.51 to 2.99	29.4	24.7	30.7	21.9	30.0	37.6
3.00 to 3.50	19.3	28.9	16.6	20.0	19.1	20.4
3.51 to 4.99	9.5	25.5	5.2	15.6	9.2	5.4
5.00 and over	0.7	1.1	0.6	—	0.6	3.2
Refused	0.2	0.3	0.1	—	0.1	—
Total	100.0	100.0	100.0	100.0	100.0	100.0
Total in sample	1,697	365	1,329	160	1,421	93
Average hourly wage	2.66	3.10	2.56	2.68	2.65	2.72

Source: Auerbach Associates, Inc., "The Participants: Wave I Interview Data, Sixth Special Report, Welfare Demonstration Evaluation Project," 1973, p. 6-18.

> Entrance into PEP significantly altered the distribution of hourly wages upward as can be seen by comparing columns 1 and 2 of Table [19]. Also, those that have left PEP and then found employment have a significantly higher income distribution than all participants prior to PEP, and have maintained the during-PEP hourly wage distribution. Before the credit for this shift can be assigned to PEP, however, it will be necessary to examine the pre-PEP hourly wage distribution for those . . . who found employment, to examine the stability of the employment, and to take explicit account of those who left PEP and are unemployed.[61]

WESTAT, however, found a different wage rate impact of PEP. Fortunately, this study contains the most representative sample of the national EEA population, and therefore statements of PEP's wage rate impact can be made with greater confidence. Table 20 reveals that PEP's wage

61. National Planning Association, *op. cit.*, p. 30.

TABLE XI-19. *Public Employment Program*
Percent Distribution of Hourly Wage Pre-, During, and Post-PEP

Hourly Wage	Pre-PEP	During PEP	Post-PEP
Less than 1.00	2.4	0.5	2.5
1.00 to 1.99	20.4	6.2	12.3
2.00 to 2.99	40.4	50.8	36.5
3.00 to 3.99	17.4	26.3	27.7
4.00 to 4.99	7.2	8.4	7.4
5.00 to 5.99	3.0	2.5	4.9
6.00 to 6.99	1.7	0.6	1.8
7.00 to 7.99	1.1	0.2	0.4
8.00 and over	0.8	0.5	1.1
Refused to answer	5.6	4.1	5.6
Total	100.0	100.0	100.0
Total sample	1,782	2,101	284

Source: National Planning Association, "A Preliminary Analysis of the Impact of the Public Employment Program on Its Participants," U.S. Department of Labor, 1972), p. 31.

Note: Percents may not add to 100.0 due to rounding.

ratc impact was rather neutral. The average enrollee was placed at $2.92 per hour and terminated at $2.89. Thus, tenure in PEP resulted in about a one percent decline in average hourly wage rates. However, minorities and women tend to have gained from their PEP job experience. Females were placed at an average rate of $2.60 and exited the program at $2.62 per hour, a gain of 0.8 percent. Conversely, the male outcome of PEP was a 3.9 percent decrease in average hourly wage rates. Commenting on the WESTAT data in an "in-house" report, the Labor Department stated that "as in private employment, the study discloses, female public employment participants both enter and leave the program at lower average hourly wage-rates than males. However, women increase their average earnings during their time in PEP, while men as a group do not."[62] It is also useful to look at the gains of those men and women who were promoted or transferred. Considering this aspect of PEP, males fared far better than women in both wage and percentage gain.

62. U.S. Department of Labor, *PEP Talk*, *loc. cit.*

Minorities generally benefited more from PEP than women and whites, according to the WESTAT study. Only blacks registered declines in wage rates. On the other hand, those blacks who were promoted or transferred got larger raises than women, but less than minorities as a group. The group which benefited most from its stay in PEP was Spanish Americans; they entered PEP at an average pay rate of $2.71 per hour and terminated at an average of $3.50 per hour, a gain of 29.2 percent.

CONCLUSIONS

Based on PEP program statistics and the available EEA evaluative literature, the following observations were made:

1. PEP "creamed" extensively for its participants.

2. When PEP concentrated its efforts on a particular segment of the unemployed, its opportunity costs were high. For example, by specifically targeting veterans, PEP's outreach effort for women, and, to a lesser extent, minorities had to be reduced.

3. Minorities were rather well served by PEP, although some such groups were better represented than others.

4. Women were consistently underrepresented in PEP, especially when their higher educational attainment and general unemployment rates are considered.

5. Women were well satisfied with their PEP jobs and held them in higher esteem than minorities, or any other group. Minority women were particularly happy with their jobs.

6. PEP's effort toward training and supportive services was small when compared with other manpower programs. However, this was to be expected given the monetary restrictions of EEA and the extent of "creaming" that occurred.

7. Female PEP participants increased their earnings more than males while in the program, even though men tended to be promoted more frequently.

8. Spanish Americans and American Indians were the minority groups who most often benefited from PEP in monetary gains.

TABLE XI-20. *Public Employment Program*
Comparison of Hourly Wage Rate Between First Job Assignment, After Transfer and/or Promotion, and at Time of Termination

Characteristics	Wage for First PEP Job Assignment	Following Transfer and/or Promotion[a]		At Time of Termination From Program[b]	
		Dollars	Percent Change	Dollars	Percent Change
Sex:					
Male	3.06	3.47	13.4	2.94	-3.9
Female	2.60	2.87	10.4	2.62	0.8
Race:					
White	3.07	3.37	9.8	2.94	-4.2
All other races combined	2.63	3.13	19.0	2.80	6.5
Negro	2.75	3.10	12.7	2.55	-7.3
Spanish American	2.71	3.08	13.6	3.50	29.2
All other	2.36	3.19	35.2	3.00	27.1

TABLE XI-20 *continued*

Other participant characteristics:					
Disadvantaged	2.35	2.92	24.2	2.55	8.5
Not disadvantaged	3.03	3.36	10.9	2.96	-2.3
Welfare recipient	2.67	3.10	16.1	2.81	5.2
Special or Vietnam veteran	3.04	3.40	11.8	2.96	-2.6
Total	2.92	3.31	13.4	2.89	-1.0

Source: WESTAT Research, Inc., "Longitudinal Analysis of the Public Employment Program: Wave I Analysis," report prepared for Manpower Administration, U.S. Department of Labor 1972, p. 3-12.

[a] Hourly rates are based upon an estimated 29,000 participants who were transferred and/or promoted.
[b] Hourly rates are based upon an estimated 4,000 terminees who responded to this question.

9. PEP served as a catalyst toward significant civil service reform, although many more changes could have been initiated.

The Public Employment Program under EEA has, therefore, resulted in some definite short- and long-run benefits for minorities and women. However, PEP is a relatively new program, and definitive statements concerning its impact upon these groups and society are somewhat difficult to make at this time. None of the major outside evaluations (National Manpower Policy Task Force, Auerbach Associates, National Planning Association, and WESTAT Research) were completed at the time this report was prepared, and consequently there are virtually no post-PEP data. With such a paucity of follow-up information, many of the necessary judgments concerning PEP's impact are particularly vulnerable to criticism. Thus, only the passage of time and the completion of more PEP evaluations will reveal the real impact of the Public Employment Program upon minorities and women.

CHAPTER XII

Opportunities Industrialization Centers, Inc.

by
Peter P. Amons
Research Associate
Under the Direction of
Bernard E. Anderson

The Opportunities Industrialization Centers, Inc. (OIC) is a private nonprofit manpower training program which provides both basic and prevocational skill training to the unemployed and underemployed. The program, founded in Philadelphia by the Reverend Leon H. Sullivan in 1964, operated initially with a federal government grant of about $50,000 in addition to almost $250,000 obtained from private sources. In 1972 total funding reached nearly $50 million, of which $32 million was allocated through the national prime contract with the federal government.[1] Another $18 million was obtained from other governmental agencies and from OIC's participation in CEP and in the WIN and NYC programs.[2]

Between 1964 and 1971, 162,708 persons participated in the OIC programs.[3] Of that number, 80,593 completed training and 48,043 were placed in jobs (Table1). The downward trend in placement between 1970 and 1971 was attributable, in large part, to the poor job market during those years. Another contributing factor was the decline in program expenditures made necessary by the reduction in the federal government's allocation of funds to OIC.

DEVELOPMENT AND ORGANIZATION OF OIC

The Opportunities Industrialization Centers program was born in the struggle for racial equality in Philadelphia and was a natural outgrowth of the civil rights movement of the 1960's.[4] Discrimination, joblessness, and alienation among youth during the middle 1950's and early 1960's

1. Opportunities Industrialization Centers of America, Inc., *Annual Report 1971-1972* (Philadelphia: 1972), p. 14.

2. *Ibid.*

3. *Ibid.*

4. The discussion of the origin and nature of the OIC is largely drawn from Leon H. Sullivan, *Build, Brother, Build* (Philadelphia: Macrae Smith Co., 1969).

TABLE XII-1. *Opportunities Industrialization Centers, Inc. Enrollment Statistics, 1964-1971*

Characteristics	Total[a]	1964-1969	1970	1971
Number completing training	80,593	48,231	17,314	15,048
Number placed in employment	48,043	28,518	12,210	7,315
Expenditures (dollars in thousands)	67,877	48,500	14,024	5,353
Total enrollees	162,708	101,876	25,424	35,408

Source: OIC, *Opportunities Industrialization Centers of America, Inc., Annual Report, 1971-72* (Philadelphia: 1972), p. 14.

[a]Total by Industrial Research Unit computation.

led to growing discontent among blacks. Black ministers frequently emerged as spokesmen for the black community as the civil rights movement progressed. One such minister, the Reverend Leon Sullivan, galvanized the support of Philadelphia's black community to organize active citizen groups whose main goal was to improve the plight of the city's black minority. In response to job discrimination, Sullivan spearheaded the Selective Patronage campaign—an economic boycott to pressure local firms into hiring more black workers.

The Selective Patronage program and the emergence of the civil rights movement stimulated Philadelphia firms to begin looking for blacks to fill jobs which in the past had never been open to minorities. As new jobs were opened, Sullivan's problem shifted from finding skilled jobs for blacks to that of finding skilled black workers. The need for job training among blacks prompted Sullivan to organize OIC. Local grass-roots fund raising campaigns, the Zion Baptist Church, and private donors provided the initial funds for the program. Since 1964, the program has grown to 105 centers located throughout the United States, Latin America, and Africa.

The distinguishing factors in the program's development are the grass-roots, community-based support of the centers' operations and its doctrine of self-help—a program designed and operated by blacks in response to the needs of blacks. Government manpower policy was undergoing a subtle change as the OIC was coming into existence. The policy during the 1960's began to emphasize the employment problems of minorities and youth. Simultaneously, Sullivan's accomplishments at the Philadelphia OIC and the start-up of other OICs began to receive more public attention. Legislators' increased awareness of social and economic inequality began to manifest itself in the funding of employability development programs such as OIC. Thus, the OIC has become an integral part of the government's national manpower policy scheme. The recent enactment of the $1.8 billion Comprehensive Employment and Training Act provides for the continuation of OIC as a locally administered categorical manpower program, and assures that OIC will retain its separate identity under manpower revenue sharing.[5]

Program Services

The OIC program attempts to coordinate the delivery of outreach, recruitment, intake, assessment, motivational training, skill training, referral, job development, job placement, and follow-up services. In its own words, it is meant to serve the "whole man." The Feeder component seeks to improve trainee attitudes and motivation, and provide a fundamental orientation to the world of work through classroom courses and personal counseling. These courses aim to instill pride and confidence in the enrollees who may be unfamiliar with the normal procedures of the workplace and with expectations of employers.

The skill training courses offered by the OICs vary among centers depending on local needs. Among the most common are: clerk-typing, stenography, keypunch, teletype, merchandising, office machine services and repairs, air conditioning and refrigeration, drafting, and food service. Females generally choose the clerical skills and males enroll in the mechanical courses. When trainees are judged proficient enough in a skill to function in an entry-level job, they are referred to prospective employers.

The training process is very flexible, allowing enrollees to spend as much or as little time as necessary in each of the components. The OIC recognizes that any manpower program created for the disadvantaged must remain flexible in its procedures to keep the enrollees interested in training and to ensure their motivation to enter employment. Also, OIC's goal is not to get a few enrollees into high paying positions, but to get a reasonable number into entry-level jobs. Once on the job, the primary responsibility for individual development lies with the worker and his employer.

5. Warren Brown, "Future of OIC Assured—President Signs Manpower Bill," *The Philadelphia Inquirer*, December 29, 1973, p. B-1.

CHARACTERISTICS OF ENROLLEES

Table 2 contains information on the demographic characteristics of enrollees and Table 3 contains race and sex figures for the 21 centers for which data were available. The proportion of minorities among all enrollees has remained at about 95 percent, 90 percent of whom are black. Table 3 aptly demonstrates that black enrollment varies substantially among centers. Certain communities have small black populations and a number of cities in the West, such as San Jose, have substantial proportions of Mexican Americans.

This same geographical disparity exists in the male-female enrollment proportions. The evaluative studies do not clarify the underlying causes of the varying percentages, but there is some evidence which suggests that a center's female enrollment may vary considerably over time. Data from other sources for different periods indicate that Menlo Park and Oakland are closer to the national norm of 70 percent female enrollment. The rather high percentage of females in OIC is often attributed to the emphasis of OIC in such courses as power sewing, clerk-typing, and keypunch operation which tend to be oriented toward female employees. In addition, OIC's policy of not providing trainee stipends undoubtedly reduces the attractiveness of the program to some men who may be eligible for other manpower programs which have financial support during training.

The median number of school years completed is approximately ten years for OIC trainees and 12.4 years for the civilian labor force.[6] Seventy-five percent of the enrollees are high school dropouts.[7] One study points out that the testing programs of various centers indicate the actual achievement performance levels of OIC enrollees to be at a fifth grade level in reading and a sixth grade level in math, despite the average stated attainment of ten years.[8]

Ninety percent of enrollees are under 45 years of age, compared to 73 percent of the total labor force.[9] Evaluators acknowledge that

6. U.S. Department of Labor, *Manpower Report of the President* (Washington, D.C.: Government Printing Office, 1973), p. 176.

7. Legal Resources, Inc., *A Synthesis and Analysis of Fifteen OIC Final Reports* (Washington, D.C.: 1969), p. 89.

8. *Ibid.*

9. U.S. Department of Labor, *op. cit.*, pp. 139-140.

TABLE XII-2. *Opportunities Industrialization Centers, Inc. Demographic Characteristics of Enrollees 1968-1970*

Characteristics	Percent	Characteristics	Average Percent
Race:		Source of income prior to training:	
Negro	90.0	Employment	31.0
Caucasian	5.0	Public welfare and	
Puerto Rican	3.5	unemployment compensation	56.3
Mexican American	1.0	Family	27.3
American Indian and		Other	5.4
Oriental	0.5		
Sex:		Employment status prior to training:	
Female		Employed or underemployed	41.0
January 1968	70.0	Unemployed	50.0
January 1969	75.0	Unknown	9.0
January 1970	68.0		
Educational attainment:			
8 grades or fewer	24.0		
9-11	51.0		
12 or more	25.0		
Age:			
18 and under	6.5		
19-21	26.4		
22-34	54.9		
45-54	9.9		
55-64	1.8		
65 and over	0.5		
Total	100.0		100.0

Sources: Race, sex age—OICNI, *Helping Others Help Themselves* (Washington, D.C.: 1970), pp. 30-32.

Employment status and educational attainment—Legal Resources, Inc., *A Synthesis and Analysis of Fifteen OIC Final Reports* (Washington, D.C.: 1969), p. 88.

Source of income—Francis D. Barry, *The Roxbury OIC: An Economic Case Study of Self-Help Job Training in the Ghetto* (Ithaca: Cornell University, 1970), p. 180.

Source of income—Marvin E. Lawrence, *Training the Hard-Core in an Urban Labor Market: The Case of the Bedford-Stuyvesant OIC* (Philadelphia: Industrial Research Unit, Wharton School of Finance and Commerce, University of Pennsylvania, 1970), p. 50.

Source of income—David A. Scott, *An Evaluation of the Washington Institute for Employment Training The OIC of Washington, D.C.* (Philadelphia: Industrial Research Unit, Wharton School of Finance and Commerce, University of Pennsylvania, 1969), p. 59.

Note: Numerical base differs for each demographic characteristic.

TABLE XII-3. *Opportunities Industrialization Centers, Inc. Percent Distribution of Enrollment by Race and Sex in Selected OICs 1969-1970*

City	Negro	White	Chicano, American Indian, Other	Female
Birmingham, Ala.	90.0	10.0	—	67
Camden, N. J.	79.0	1.0	20.0	68
Charleston, W. Va.	50.0	50.0	—	53
Cleveland, Ohio	100.0	—	—	94
Dallas, Tex.	93.0	1.0	6.0	84
Erie, Pa.	41.5	57.5	1.0	60
Harrisburg, Pa.	67.4	28.0	4.6	70
Jacksonville, Fla.	97.0	3.0	—	80
Little Rock, Ark.	82.0	18.0	—	70
Menlo Park, Calif.	53.0	15.0	32.0[a]	36
Milwaukee, Wis.	95.6	1.0	3.4	56
Minneapolis, Minn.	44.5	51.9	3.6	60
Oakland, Calif.	n.a.	n.a.	n.a.	35
Oklahoma City, Okla.	65.0	25.0	10.0	68
Omaha, Nebr.	94.0	5.0	1.0	75
Philadelphia, Pa.	93.5	6.2[b]	1.0[c]	64
Phoenix, Ariz.	38.0	58.0	4.0	64
Roanoke, Va.	66.0	33.0	1.0	61
San José, Calif.	20.0	10.0	70.0[d]	—
Seattle, Wash.	46.0	39.0	15.0	61
Washington, D.C.[e]	98.0	1.5	0.5	59

Sources: OICNI, *The New Institutes Bi-Monthly Progress Report No. 3* (Washington, D.C.: February-March 1969).

OICNI, *Helping Others to Help Themselves* (Washington, D.C.: 1970), p. 32.

OICNI, *Final Report Draft* (Washington, D.C.: August 1, 1968-July 31, 1969), p. 155.

David A. Scott, *An Evaluation of the Washington Institute for Employment Training: The OIC of Washington, D.C.* (Philadelphia: Industrial Research Unit, Wharton School of Finance and Commerce, University of Pennsylvania, 1969), pp. 58-59.

[a]Spanish surname.
[b]White and Puerto Rican.
[c]American Indian and Oriental.
[d]Mexican American.
[e]Data for November 1966-June 1968 only.

the OIC is reaching a relatively young target population. Age data by race were unavailable, but one evaluator found that female trainees were, on the average, four years older than males.[10]

According to the Social Security Administration, a family of four with an income of less than $3,531 in 1968 could be classified as "disadvantaged."[11] A sample of 3,000 OIC enrollees from fifteen centers as of March 1969 revealed that 75.8 percent could be classified as disadvantaged.[12] This figure may overstate the poverty status of the trainees because other evaluators found somewhat lower proportions for certain centers. The unavailability of time series data for poverty status also calls into question the reliability of this statistic.

REVIEW OF EVALUATIVE LITERATURE

There were eighteen studies available on OIC, only twelve of which were useful for purposes of program evaluation. Table 4 identifies the evaluating organization, date of reports, and frequency of study of the centers. Five of the studies were prepared by private consulting agencies and the remaining seven were completed by university-based evaluators. All were prepared under contract to the federal government, usually the Manpower Administration of the Department of Labor. Nine studies each examined one OIC center, and one report analyzed the annual reports of fifteen OIC programs.[13] The evaluative studies covered the period between 1967 and 1971.

The list of cities in Table 4 indicates the wide geographic distribution of the centers selected for study. Each of the twenty centers is located in an urban area (only one of the 105 OICs can be classified as rural). Seattle is included in three reports, thus making it the most frequently evaluated OIC.

The fact that only twenty of the 105 centers are represented does not significantly detract from the value of an analysis of the program's impact on minorities and women. Many of the OICs for which data were unavailable had small enrollments, offered limited services, or were just emerging from the planning stage. An evaluation of these centers would not fairly reflect the overall effectiveness of the program. In addition,

10. Francis D. Barry, *The Roxbury Opportunities Industrialization Center: An Economic Case Study of Self-Help Job Training in the Ghetto* (Ithaca: Cornell University, 1973), pp. 170-171.

11. U.S. Department of Labor, *Manpower Report of the President* (Washington, D.C.: Government Printing Office, 1970), p. 120.

12. OICNI, *The New Institutes Bi-Monthly Progress Report No. 3* (Washington, D.C.: February-March 1969).

13. Legal Resources, Inc., *loc. cit.*

TABLE XII-4 *Opportunities Industrialization Centers, Inc. Frequency and Selected Characteristics of Evaluation Studies*

City	Evaluative Organization			Dates of Evaluations
	University	Private Consultant	15 OIC Summary[a]	
Bedford-Stuyvesant	x			1970
Boston (Roxbury)	x	x		1970, 1971
Camden			x	1969
Charleston	x		x	1968, 1969
Cincinnati			x	1969
Dallas			x	1969
Denver		x		1971
East Palo Alto (Menlo Park)			x	1969
Erie	x		x	1968, 1969
Harrisburg			x	1969
Jacksonville	x		x	1969, 1970
Little Rock			x	1969
Milwaukee		x	x	1968, 1969
Oakland		x		1971
Oklahoma City		x	x	1968, 1969
Omaha			x	1969
Philadelphia		x		1967
Roanoke			x	1969
Seattle	x	x	x	1968, 1968, 1969
Washington, D.C.	x		x	1969, 1969

Source: These data are taken from studies of each specific city listed and are noted in the bibliography.

[a]This study by a private research firm examined the annual reports of fifteen OICs.

all of the evaluations occurred at least one year after the centers began operation and most after two years; consequently, the investigators were appraising ongoing operations. Although the evaluations fairly reflect the OIC during the 1967 to 1971 period, the studies have become dated and there may be additional economic impact on minorities and women which has not been examined.

Evaluative Methodology

The methodology of a typical evaluative study involved choosing one OIC center and examining all of its reports, files, and records. OIC administrators, trainees, and employers were interviewed and various field surveys were conducted. The only exception to this rule was a study summarizing fifteen OICs' annual reports. Some investigators attempted to study the post-placement aspects of the program, but insufficient OIC data, limited time, and budget constraints made most follow-up research inadequate for the formulation of valid conclusions concerning job retention and income benefits. Evaluators universally questioned the lack of follow-up data and the reliability and validity of OIC statistics. Still, they usually relied on OIC files for trainee characteristics, number of placements and occupations, and starting wage data. The few evaluators who conducted field surveys of trainees generated their estimates of post-training employment and wage impact largely independent of OIC statistics.

All the studies contained the number of placements for a given period, but only four reports contained surveys of OIC graduates which shed light on job retention.[14] Three of the twelve reports included an analysis of the pre- and post-training earnings of graduates and one study included a comparable analysis for its hard-core enrollees.[15] Very few statistics denoting job placement by race or sex were available and no evaluators used control groups.

14. Barry, *loc. cit.;* Greenleigh Associates, Inc., *A Pilot Study of the Opportunities Industrialization Center, Inc.—Philadelphia, Pennsylvania* (New York: 1967); Olympus Research Corporation, "The Total Impact of Manpower Programs: A Four-City Case Study," report prepared for Office of Policy, Evaluation and Research, Manpower Administration, U.S. Department of Labor, 1971; David A. Scott, *An Evaluation of the Washington Institute for Employment Training—The Opportunities Industrialization Center of Washington, D.C.* (Philadelphia: Industrial Research Unit, Wharton School of Finance and Commerce, University of Pennsylvania, 1969).

15. Marvin E. Lawrence, *Training the Hard-Core in an Urban Labor Market: The Case of the Bedford-Stuyvesant Opportunities Industrialization Center* (Philadelphia: Industrial Research Unit, Wharton School of Finance and Commerce, University of Pennsylvania, 1970); Olympus Research Corp., *loc. cit.*; Richard B. Peterson, *An Evaluation of the Seattle Opportunities Industrialization Center* (Seattle: University of Washington, 1968); Noah R. Robinson, *The Opportunities Industrialization Center: Jacksonville, Florida* (Philadelphia: Industrial Research Unit, Wharton School of Finance and Commerce, University of Pennsylvania, 1970).

The evaluative reports focused on two main topics: (1) critique of the OIC administration, management, and program components—recruitment, intake, counseling, orientation, Feeder, skill training, and job development and placement; and (2) examination of the OIC's economic (and occasionally noneconomic) impact on enrollees, employers, and the community. Appraisal of the program components, discussion of the operational problems, and formulation of recommendations overshadowed the analysis of economic impact.

An assessment of the OIC's impact on minorities and women is heavily influenced by the composition of enrollment. Any economic impact of the program is likely to benefit the black minority more than other ethnic groups because 90 percent of trainees are blacks. Therefore, one may assume that all evidence of general economic impact in this study is applicable primarily to blacks, unless otherwise noted. In this context, where the analysis is not a question of the differential impact by race, the focus of discussion shifts to the economic impact on women.

ECONOMIC IMPACT OF TRAINING

The length of time trainees spend in a manpower training program and the extent to which they receive its services help to determine the program's impact.

Participation in Program Components

Only one study provides statistics which bear directly upon the question.[16] Data for the Charleston OIC, where enrollment was 50 percent white, suggest that Negroes remained in the program longer than whites (see Table 5). White males remained in training (including both prevocational and vocational) longer than black males, and black females remained in the program longer than white females. Because there is no other evidence pertaining to the conclusions based on race, these observations may not be representative of other OICs. The Charleston case and other studies suggest that female tenure in the program is longer than that of males; most evaluators attributed this pattern to the no-stipend policy.

The skills courses of the Philadelphia OIC were examined to determine the length of time a trainee typically spent in skill training.[17] Philadelphia was representative since other centers' skills courses were pat-

16. Bernard E. Anderson and Harvey A. Young, *An Evaluation of the Opportunities Industrialization Center of Charleston, West Virginia* (Philadelphia: Industrial Research Unit, Wharton School of Finance and Commerce, University of Pennsylvania, 1968).

17. Greenleigh Associates, Inc., *op. cit.*, p. 7.

TABLE XII-5. *Opportunities Industrialization Centers, Inc. Length of Training by Race and Sex Charleston, West Virginia*

Length of Training	Total	Percent	White Male	White Female	Negro Male	Negro Female
Less than 1 month	36	33.6	6	16	2	12
2 months	33	30.8	11	6	2	14
3 months	13	12.1	—	5	1	7
4 months	9	8.3	3	2	—	4
4 months plus	16	14.0	—	2	—	14
Total	107	100.0	20	31	5	51

Source: Bernard E. Anderson and Harvey A. Young, *An Evaluation of the OIC of Charleston, West Virginia* (Philadelphia: Industrial Research Unit, Wharton School of Finance and Commerce, University of Pennslyvania, 1968), p. 47.

Note: Percents may not add to 100.0 due to rounding.

terned after those of the Philadelphia prototype. The courses most popular with women, such as power sewing, teletype, and IBM keypunch, required only eight to twelve weeks of training. Males usually enrolled in courses which required more training electronics (78 weeks), and brick masonry, plumbing, bowling machine repair, printing, and welding (each 50 weeks). Although this sex difference in tenure might suggest that males tended to remain in the program longer than females, the enrollment records show otherwise, primarily because of the high proportion of male dropouts. In addition, evaluators observed that females remained in the Feeder longer than males, and males remained in skill training longer than females.

Table 6 contains the course enrollment data for the Washington, D.C. OIC, whose enrollment was 98 percent black and 59 percent female.[18] The data are presented to illustrate the relative popularity of skill training courses among trainees. The enrollment pattern for Washington appeared to be representative of most OICs, with the exception of driver training which had a particularly large enrollment in Washington. Course offerings varied to some extent in response to different local needs, such as aerospace mechanics in Seattle or power sewing in Philadelphia.

18. Scott, *op. cit.*, pp. 58-59.

TABLE XII-6. *Opportunities Industrialization Centers, Inc. Course Enrollment Through June 1968 Washington, D.C.*

Course	Total Enrollees
Auto mechanics	40
Body and fender	40
Carpentry	40
Clerk-typing	350
Driver training	285
Keypunch	64
Merchandising-sales	100
Offset duplicating	80
Painting and paper hanging	40
Radio and television repair	15
Stenography	75
Teletype	60
Brick masonry	40

Source: David A. Scott, *An Evaluation of the Washington Institute for Employment Training: The OIC of Washington, D.C.* (Philadelphia: Industrial Research Unit, Wharton School of Finance and Commerce, University of Pennsylvania, 1969), p. 60.

To conclude, the evaluative literature contained little useful data to measure the distributional impact of trainee participation in program components on minorities and women. Yet, the available data suggest that women remained in training longer than men.

Job Development

The raison d'être of the OIC has been to train and to place the unemployed and underemployed, many of whom are disadvantaged. A sizable number of the OIC target population had not been able to compete for existing employment opportunities; consequently, the OICs have accepted the responsibility for finding and developing work opportunities for the enrollees.

Ideally, the job development function goes beyond the mere location of jobs. An effective job development department must be aware of the need to find entry-level jobs with the potential for upgrading. Changing the attitudes of employers toward disadvantaged minority workers through effective public relations and personal contacts is part of its function. Inducing firms to drop arbitrary job requirements, such as the passage of entrance tests or the possession of a high school diploma, which often bar minority members from employment, has been a prime concern. The essence of OIC job development efforts is opening up more job opportunities to the enrollees, most of whom are hard-to-employ minority workers.

The evaluative literature was replete with evidence that job placement overshadowed job development. The reports indicated the tight supply of labor (except in Charleston) led to a preoccupation with filling job orders. Investigators suggested OIC administrators looked upon job development as an unnecessary activity during periods of tight labor supply. In fact, job development efforts are more effective during periods of tight supply when trainees can be more selective in job choice. A few studies mentioned that insufficient job development efforts would not be detrimental to job placement. Whenever the supply of labor is tight, they warn that a less favorable labor market would require increased job development efforts to induce employers to hire minority workers.

The OIC's policy of providing stopgap employment to needy trainees was another area of concern. Some evaluators stated that the search for stopgap employment detracted significantly from the staffs' efforts to locate full-time, post-training work opportunities. They contended that stopgap employment induced trainees to leave the program, since some trainees valued immediate income more than the promise of higher income after training.

Another long-standing policy of the OIC, no stipends, was interpreted as an unintended "creaming" mechanism. It served to attract the more motivated members of the target population—those who were willing to undertake training without renumeration—but it served to discourage the individuals most in need of training—those who could not afford to forego present income to accept it. This policy worked to the detriment of male enrollment because males usually had family responsibilities whereas females were often supported by husbands or by some form of public assistance.

Within the job development function, the absence of close ties with local trade unions was a particularly weak point in OIC community relations. In all but two cases, the centers had not sought to establish good relations with unions or they had tried and failed to interest the groups in supporting OIC. Few union members sat on OIC Advisory

Boards. One evaluator stated a number of OICs reported that breaking the color line in unions has been far more difficult than convincing employers to hire the disadvantaged.[19]

On the other hand, a close rapport with employers has characterized the OIC movement. Local business leaders often sit on the OIC's Industrial and Technical Advisory Committees, which help to establish personal contacts useful in job development and placement efforts. It was noted that the courses for which local employers had supplied technical instruction and equipment were the most successful in leading trainees into employment. For instance, in Seattle, Boeing supplied course instruction and equipment which provided the OIC's aerospace mechanics graduates with direct and smooth entrance into jobs with Boeing. In Erie, Pennsylvania, Litton Industries donated welding equipment and instruction in anticipation of the opening of its new shipbuilding plant.

National industry support comes from the National OIC Industrial Advisory Council (NIAC), a group composed of the top executives from 33 major U.S. corporations. The NIAC offers the OIC a link to the industrial community and helps to expedite activities such as plant visitations, OIC visits, improved fund raising techniques, the loan of skilled volunteer instructors, and equipment solicitation.

The general consensus of the evaluative studies is that OIC is developing or locating suitable employment for its target population. Whether this success is attributable to job development efforts or a tight supply of labor is uncertain. In addition, some evaluators remarked that employers often hired minority workers for "do-good" reasons or for compliance with certain federal contract regulations, rather than hiring trainees on the basis of performance.

Placement Experience

The post-training employment experience of trainees is often used to measure the effectiveness of manpower training programs. OIC statistics indicate that 45,046 enrollees have been placed in jobs through 1971.[20] One study, however, warned that OIC placement statistics could be misleading because follow-up data were invariably absent from the final reports.[21] The literature discussed the difficulty of assessing the economic impact on trainees who underwent the Feeder and skill training vis-à-vis individuals who used the OIC merely as an employment service. The OIC's practice of placing enrollees whenever they are deemed "job ready"

19. Legal Resources, Inc., *op. cit.*, p. 105.

20. OIC, *op.cit.*, p. 15.

21. Legal Resources, Inc., *op. cit.*, p. 75.

enabled trainees to graduate at any stage in the program. One-fourth of the walk-ins to the Philadelphia center were placed immediately in jobs.[22] Some reports suggested the OIC was overstating its economic impact by combining all such placement figures. The data implied that all the enrollees underwent training and consequently were placed. On the other hand, the placement statistics may have been understated because they did not reflect the impact of graduates who found jobs on their own or who turned down jobs which did not meet their income requirements.

The percentage of training-related placements is frequently used as a measure of the effectiveness of a manpower program's skills instruction. A low proportion of such placements may imply little beneficial impact on graduates. Four evaluatve reports contained such percentages for their respective cities (Table 7). The average figure was 75 percent and the statistics indicated the centers' abilities to locate training-related jobs varied considerably. Some evaluators questioned the significance of training-related placement proportions by arguing that the Feeder imparted to enrollees motivational and attitudinal benefits which were not reflected in such figures.

A complete reliance on job placement statistics without regard to job retention rates can lead to an inflated view of the impact of a manpower training program. Three evaluators calculated the percentage of trainees who were placed and were still on the job after some interval of time. However, the reliability of the data is in doubt, because the post-placement time interval used to check job retention varied within each sample. Therefore, the post-placement time periods of the following job retention rates are not known (but there are indications they are no more than one year): (1) Washington, D.C.—84 percent of a sample of 100; (2) Philadelphia—56 percent of a sample of 116; and (3) Boston—72 percent of a sample of 92.[23] OIC data indicated that 84 percent of graduates in Washington, D.C. and 75 percent of those in Philadelphia were still on the job six months after placement.[24] Overall, the OIC claims a 79 percent rate of job retention after six months and a 76 percent rate after twelve months.[25] Their figures after six months ranged from 40 percent in Little Rock to 92 percent in Jacksonville and 94 percent in Erie. Unfortunately, job retention rates were not examined on the basis of race or sex.

22. Greenleigh Associates, Inc., *op. cit.*, p. 107.

23. Scott, *op. cit.*, p. 71; Greenleigh Associates, Inc., *op. cit.*, p. 110; Barry, *op. cit.*, p. 152.

24. OICNI, *Helping Others to Help Themselves* (Washington, D.C.: 1970), p. 21.

25. *Ibid.*

TABLE XII-7. *Opportunities Industrialization Centers, Inc. Percent of Training-Related Placements in Four Cities*

City	Percent Training-Related Placements	Sample Size
Boston	74	66
Philadelphia	80	116
Washington, D.C.	96	279
Jacksonville	50	326

Sources: Francis D. Barry, *The Roxbury OIC: An Economic Case Study of Self-Help Job Training in the Ghetto* (Ithaca: Cornell University, 1973), p. 154.

Greenleigh Associates, Inc., *A Pilot Study of the Opportunities Industrialization Center, Inc.: Philadelphia, Pennsylvania* (New York: 1967), p. 107.

David A. Scott, *An Evaluation of the Washington Institute for Employment Training: The OIC of Washington, D.C.* (Philadelphia: Industrial Research Unit, Wharton School of Finance and Commerce, University of Pennsylvania, 1969), p. 62.

Noah R. Robinson, *The Opportunities Industrialization Center—Jacksonville, Florida* (Philadelphia: Industrial Research Unit, Wharton School of Finance and Commerce, University of Pennslyvania, 1970), p. 59.

One study measured the average percentage of time a graduate was employed during a specified period for two OIC centers. Table 8 contains the employment stability of graduates at three time intervals at the Boston and Oakland centers. Both samples were 66 percent female. The following statistics, like those identifying job retention rates, do not include a specific post-placement time interval. The procedure of data collection, however, indicated that the post-placement period could have been no longer than fifteen months. As the table indicates, the training improved the employment stability of Boston's graduates, but did little to benefit the employment status of Oakland's graduates. The generalization of this limited evidence is questionable and the reader can draw his own conclusions from the data. Again, the data were not broken down by sex or race (although it is known that the Boston OIC was predominantly black).

TABLE XII-8. *Opportunities Industrialization Centers, Inc. Employment Stability, Boston and Oakland*

Time Employed	Boston	Oakland
Percent of time employed during 36 months before enrollment [a]	49.8	56.2
Percent of time employed during 12 months before enrollment [a]	62.0	53.5
Percent of time employed during 12 months before enrollment [b]	45.0	32.0
Percent of time employed during post-placement interval [c]	71.8	54.2
Percent of time employed during post-placement interval [b]	65.0	31.0
Number in sample	41	36

Source: Olympus Research Corp., "The Total Impact of Manpower Programs: a Four City Case Study," report prepared for Office of Policy, Evaluation, and Research, Manpower Administration, U.S. Department of Labor, 1971, pp. 13, 23.

[a] For trainees with at least one job prior to enrollment.
[b] For all trainees
[c] For trainees with at least one job during post-placement interval.

Post Training Earnings

The economic impact on enrollees measured by a comparison of pre- and post-training earnings depends on the data used for examination. No evaluative report contained such statistics on a national level; therefore, it is necessary to extrapolate from limited local OIC data to gain insight into the overall impact of the program.

One study, whose results appear to be representative, calculated the before and after training earnings for graduates. It was found that the average hourly wage rate was $1.89 before training and $2.23 after training in Boston, and $1.42 and $2.15 respectively in Oakland, thus suggesting a significant beneficial impact on enrollees.[26] The average change in income of 303 graduates from thirteen centers was calculated to gain further insight into earnings impact. This analysis included the usable before-after income data available for the February-March 1969

26. Olympus Research Corporation, *op. cit.*, pp. 13, 23.

period.[27] The average post-training annual increase was $2,089. This figure, considerably higher than most estimates, is influenced significantly by the fact that many OIC trainees had been previously unemployed. According to the OIC's own follow-up statistics, the average enrollee's earnings were boosted about $1,000 from $2,900 per year in 1969 as a result of OIC training.[28] There is no indication of the number of centers included in the estimate.

Post-Training Earnings by Race

The most comprehensive analysis of pre- and post-training earnings and the only analysis classified by race is the 33 percent sample of the Seattle OIC's graduates.[29] Table 9 contains the hourly wage changes of 111 graduates as of May 1968. The median change in income was $0.40 to $0.59, and 23.4 percent of the graduates experienced a decrease in income, whereas 15.3 percent experienced an increase of $1.00 or more. Evaluators attributed post-training declines in income to the costs of leaving a low-level job where seniority may have contributed to increased earnings and the cost of entering a better job with lower starting wages but more potential.

Table 10 contains the annual income of those graduates whose ethnic backgrounds are known. The data indicate that 14.3 percent of the whites and only 7.7 percent of the blacks had starting salaries of $3,000 or less. There were more blacks than whites with incomes over $5,000—46.1 percent versus 33.3 percent. The Peterson study suggested two reasons for the blacks' higher starting salaries—either the black sample was not a relatively disadvantaged group or the white group was a particularly disadvantaged group. The greater changes in post-training earnings for blacks suggested they benefit from training proportionately more than whites; however, no other studies presented data which could have validated the generalization of the Seattle results to a national level.

Post-Training Earnings by Sex

Two studies included data which shed light on trainees' incomes on the basis of sex. The average starting wage for Jacksonville graduates who were placed in jobs as of January 1969 was $1.77 per hour for males and $1.51 per hour for females.[30] These data were based on 78 male placements (65 Negro, 13 white) and 114 female placements (102 Negro,

27. OICNI, *Bi-Monthly Progress Report No. 3, op. cit.*

28. OICNI, *Helping Others to Help Themselves, op. cit.*, p. 31.

29. Peterson, *loc. cit.*

30. Robinson, *op. cit.*, pp.61-65.

TABLE XII-9. *Opportunities Industrialization Centers, Inc.*
Change in Hourly Wage Rates
Seattle Graduates, May 1968

Change After Completion of Training	Number	Percent
Decrease in income	26	23.4
Increase of 0 - .19	11	9.9
.20 - .39	11	9.9
.40 - .59	20	18.0
.60 - .79	15	13.5
.80 - .99	11	9.9
1.00 - 1.19	6	5.4
1.20 and over	11	9.9
Total	111	100.0

Source: Richard B. Peterson, *An Evaluation of the Seattle OIC* (Seattle: Graduate School of Business Administration, University of Washington, 1968), p. 24.

Note: Percents may not add to 100.0 due to rounding.

TABLE XII-10. *Opportunities Industrialization Centers, Inc. Post-Training Entry-Level Salary by Race Seattle Graduates, 1968*

Annual Starting Salary	White		Negro		Other	
	Number	Percent	Number	Percent	Number	Percent
$ 0-2,000	1	4.8	—	2.6	1	25.0
2,001-3,000	2	9.5	2	5.1	—	—
3,001-4,000	5	23.8	9	23.1	—	—
4,001-5,000	6	28.6	9	23.1	1	25.0
5,001-6,000	2	9.5	5	12.8	—	—
6,001-7,000	1	4.8	5	12.8	1	25.0
7,001 and over	4	19.0	8	20.5	1	25.0
Total	21	100.0	38	100.0	4	100.0

Source: Richard B. Peterson, *An Evaluation of the Seattle OIC* (Seattle: Graduate School of Business Administration, University of Washington, 1968), p. 20.

12 white). The experience of the Boston OIC (Table 11) also supports the conclusion that male graduates earn more than female graduates. Within Table 11, there are three male-female groups because trainees' records varied in their completeness. Females experienced greater increases in income after training, although their post-training incomes were lower than the males' pre-training incomes. Thus, OIC training appears to have a greater effect on women's incomes than men's. The study of fifteen OICs' final reports also concluded that females benefited from OIC training more than males, although supporting evidence was not provided.[31] The consensus is that females are more dependent on training to obtain jobs because of sex discrimination in the labor market and other factors.

Earnings in the Absence of Training

Ideally, a study of the economic impact of a manpower training program should include an analysis of the income gain attributable solely to training. The evaluative literature employed a number of different approaches to measure income in the absence of training. One team of evaluators examined the records of 660 Seattle enrollees placed between

31. Legal Resources, Inc., *op. cit.*, p. 79.

TABLE XII-11. *Opportunities Industrialization Centers, Inc.*
Total Annual Earnings Pre- and Post-Training by Sex
Boston

Income	Total		Persons with Pre-training Data Only		Persons with Complete Data Pre- and Post-Training		Persons with Post-training Data Only	
	Men	Women	Men	Women	Men	Women	Men	Women
Income before training	$2,900	$1,100	$2,400	$1,000	$3,200	$1,200	n.a.	n.a.
Income after training	$4,100	$2,400	n.a.	n.a.	$3,900	$2,500	$4,200	$2,300
Increase in income	$1,200	$1,300	n.a.	n.a.	$ 700	$1,300	n.a.	n.a.
Percent increase	41.4	118.2	n.a.	n.a.	21.9	108.3	n.a.	n.a.
Number in sample	46	108	13	27	18	63	15	18

Source: Francis D. Barry, *The Roxbury OIC: An Economic Case Study of Self-Help Job Training in the Ghetto* (Ithaca: Cornell University, 1970), p. 211.

Note: Sample includes graduates from October 1967 to May 1968.

February 1967 and August 1968. The median hourly starting wage was between $2.01 and $2.25 for 158 of these enrollees who were placed directly in jobs without Feeder or skill training.[32] The remaining 502 trainees who completed training experienced the same post-program wage rates.[33] Based on this evidence, the evaluator concluded that the training did little to boost income. It is quite likely, however, that those placed immediately were more employable than those who underwent training.

A study of the Boston OIC included an analysis which attempted to separate the increase in income specifically attributable to training. Table 12 contains the change in annual earnings by sex for Boston trainees. The evaluator estimated the projected natural wage inflation increase and subtracted it from the total wage increases to derive the increase attributable to training. The table indicates that training boosted the mean income only 2 percent for males and 9 percent for females. This

TABLE XII-12. *Opportunities Industrialization Centers, Inc. Weekly Wages in the Absence of Training by Sex Boston, 1967-1968*

Income	Mean		Median	
	Men	Women	Men	Women
Income before training	$87	$70	$82	$68
Income after training	$94	80	90	76
Total increase in income	$ 7	10	8	8
Estimated increase due to natural wage inflation	$ 5	4	5	4
Total increase minus wage inflation increase	$ 2	6	3	4
Percent increase unaccounted for by wage inflation	2.3	8.6	3.7	5.9
Number in sample	33	77	36	86

Source: Francis D. Barry, *The Roxbury OIC: An Economic Case Study of Self-Help Job Training in the Ghetto* (Ithaca: Cornell University, 1973), p. 244.

Note: Mean includes only persons who held at least one post-training job for 30 days or more.

32. A. L. Nellum and Associates, *An Evaluation of the Opportunities Industrialization Centers in Oklahoma City, Oklahoma and Seattle, Washington* (Washington, D.C.: 1968), pp. 95-96.

33. *Ibid.*

study concluded that OIC training had more impact on women's incomes than men's, but that the impact was small. In sum, there is simply not enough evidence to determine the impact solely attributable to training. No studies used control groups and the crude analyses examined above cannot isolate the unique effect of OIC training.

Earnings by Job Type

Much of the wage impact of the OIC program depended on the occupational career an enrollee chose to follow. Five of the twelve reports contained the starting salaries for graduates according to occupation—the Washington, D.C., data were typical. Table 13 does not contain the in-

TABLE XII-13. *Opportunities Industrialization Centers, Inc.*
Annual Salaries by Job Type
Washington, D.C. Graduates, January 1967—November 1968

Course	Total Placed	Annual Salary High	Annual Salary Average	Annual Salary Low	Average Increase
Auto mechanic	25	$6,500	$4,056	$2,912	$2,184
Body and fender	13	6,500	3,500	2,912	1,628
Bricklaying	18	6,240	4,659	3,432	2,787
Carpentry	6	4,680	4,030	3,640	2,158
Clerk-typing	180	6,822	3,609	1,955	1,737
Computer	8	5,100	4,586	4,108	2,714
Keypunch	70	5,600	4,560	3,609	2,688
Cashier	31	5,557	4,004	3,328	2,132
Offset duplicating	85	5,250	4,160	2,600	2,288
Plant maintenance	7	5,564	4,446	3,328	2,574
Radio and television	10	5,500	4,640	3,950	2,768
Tile setting	14	4,929	3,828	3,828	1,956
Ward clerk	17	5,649	4,438	3,328	2,566
Clerk-stenographer	12	5,200	4,360	3,494	2,488
Teletype	11	5,304	4,794	4,284	2,922

Source: David A. Scott, *An Evaluation of the Washington Institute for Employment Training: The Opportunities Industrialization Center of Washington, D.C.* (Philadelphia: Industrial Research Unit, Wharton School of Finance and Commerce, University of Pennsylvania, 1969), p. 64.

comes prior to training, but the pre-/post-training average increases were included. The length of time needed to complete a skills course and the starting salary in the resulting job are directly related. For example, the more lengthy courses, such as bricklaying, radio and television repair, and computers, led to higher starting salaries. Thus, the evidence suggests that OIC trainees' earnings were somewhat dependent on the skills courses they chose. It also appears that the courses which females tended to select led to slightly lower average starting salaries than those chosen by males.

Self-Sufficiency as a Result of Training

Examining the number of individuals whose incomes after training rose above the poverty level is an effective method of measuring the economic value of the program's training. Only one study included an analysis of the trainees who moved above the poverty level and the data are conveniently broken down by sex in Table 14 (these data by race were not available). The poverty level was based on the 1967 Social Security poverty criteria with a 5 percent revision upward to adjust for Boston's higher living expenses. The analysis indicates that training had little beneficial impact on males because the same number of men were below the poverty line before and after training. However, the study dismissed these results as unreliable because of the small male sample size. The results were vastly different for women, with 60 percent in poverty before training compared to only 30 percent afterwards. This supports other evidence which suggests females tended to benefit proportionately more from the program than males.

TABLE XII-14. *Opportunities Industrialization Centers, Inc. Number of Men and Women Who Became Self-Sufficient by Moving Above the Poverty Line Boston, January–June 1968*

Characteristics	Men	Women
Number in poverty before training	7	32
Number moved out of poverty	3	16
Number moved into poverty	3	2
Number in poverty after training	7	18
Number in sample	18	52

Source: Francis D. Barry, *The Roxbury OIC: An Economic Case Study of Self-Help Job Training in the Ghetto* (Ithaca: Cornell University, 1970), pp. 260-261.

Hard-Core Enrollment in Bedford-Stuyvesant

Only one study distinguished between its hard-core and non-hard-core enrollment in an analysis of the program's economic impact.[34] Its criteria for identifying members as disadvantaged were as follows: (1) those trainees listed as single with an annual income of less than $1,800; (2) those trainees listed as members of a household of four with an annual income of less than $3,600; (3) those trainees who were high school dropouts; and (4) those trainees who were mentally and physically handicapped. The following statistics classifying the hard-core and non-hard-core by race result from the above criteria (data by sex were not available):

	Negro	Puerto Rican	White	Other	Total
Hard-Core	1,054	163	24	9	1,250
Non-Hard-Core	230	41	7	4	282
Total	1,284	204	31	13	1,532

A sample of 79 of the hard-core enrollees' files were examined to measure the impact of training on the disadvantaged and hard-to-employ. An analysis of the incomes prior to and after training (Table 15) shows that of the 79 enrollees, 89 percent experienced an increase in income, 9 percent remained the same, and one percent suffered a decline in in-

TABLE XII-15. *Opportunities Industrialization Centers, Inc. Changes in Weekly Income Distribution of Hard-Core Trainees Prior to OIC Enrollment and Upon Placement After OIC Training*

Pre-Training Hard-Core Income		Post-Placement Income Distribution of Hard-Core			
Income	Total	$50-69	$70-89	$90-109	$110 and over
$0-29	9	—	8	1	—
30-49	23	—	16	7	—
50-69	32	1	26	5	—
70-89	14	1	6	5	2
90-109	1	—	—	—	1
Total	79	2	56	18	3

Source: Marvin E. Lawrence, *Training the Hard-Core in the Urban Labor Market: The Case of the Bedford-Stuyvesant OIC* (Philadelphia: Industrial Research Unit, Wharton School of Finance and Commerce, University of Pennsylvania, 1970), p. 69.

34. This discussion and data are based on the study by Lawrence, *op. cit.*, pp. 63-72.

come. This sample was 67 percent female; 53 percent listed their source of income as welfare, 19 percent as employment, and 15 percent as unemployment compensation. The Bedford-Stuyvesant case is presented because it is the only analysis to measure the impact on its hard-core enrollees as a group. The results demonstrate that the disadvantaged, most of whom were black or Puerto Rican, experienced significant income gains after training. A comparison of the economic impact on hard-core enrollees vis-à-vis non-hard-core enrollees was not possible because the study did not include an analysis of the latter group.

NONECONOMIC IMPACT

The OIC offers a wide variety of supportive services to its registrants, the extent of which varies from center to center. Most supportive referrals involved medical care or financial assistance. For example, during the third quarter of 1968, the Philadelphia prototype made 79 supportive referrals—37 to the Pennsylvania College of Optometry (47 percent), 13 to the Department of Public Assistance (16 percent), 9 to the Immigration Service (11 percent), and 20 to other agencies (25 percent).[35] The results for other OICs were comparable, whereas any differences were primarily due to the availability of each center's resources. For instance, the more developed centers had their own day care facilities, but the smaller OICs referred enrollees to local child-care programs sponsored by the YWCA, church groups, or other organizations. Virtually all OICs were in contact with local public assistance agencies because funds were available to welfare recipients for training allowances under the Economic Opportunity Act of 1964.

According to the evaluative reports, most OICs communicated frequently with state employment offices. The Wisconsin State Employment Service cooperated with the Greater Milwaukee OIC by sending it a weekly list of job openings. The Pennsylvania State Employment Service had an employee out-station at the North Philadelphia branch of OIC. In Omaha, such agencies as Alcoholics Anonymous, Planned Parenthood, Visiting Nurses Association, Omaha Urban League, Legal Aid Society, and the Senior Citizens Recreation Center have provided services. For the ultimate in supportive services, the Dallas Weight Watchers donated scholarships which enabled a number of trainees to attend meetings.

Table 16 contains the number of supportive referrals for which data were available during January and February 1969. Statistics providing a cumulative record of supportive referrals were not available; therefore,

35. OIC of Philadelphia, Pennsylvania, *Management Information System—Third Quarter 1968* (Philadelphia: 1968), p. 27.

TABLE XII-16. *Opportunities Industrialization Centers, Inc. Number of Supportive Referrals for Selected Centers January–February 1969*

Center	Number of Trainees Who Reported for OIC Intake Interview	Number Entering OIC Training	Number of Supportive Referrals	Number of Terminal Referrals
Harrisburg	160	83	—	—
Pittsburgh	29	29	20	n.a.
New York City	146	74	3	n.a.
Erie	187	130	23	—
Camden[a]	17	9	—	
Baltimore	12	1	4	—
Washington, D.C.	256	58	—	—
Oklahoma City	96	99	5	—
Little Rock	70	55	—	—
Charleston	92	58	24	15
Jacksonville	275	84	21	15
Dallas	480	234	n.a.	42
Birmingham	60	60	n.a.	—
Roanoke	134	105	n.a.	—
Boston (Roxbury)	152	49	8	14
Cincinnati	531	322	24	16
Cleveland	23	10	5	5
Milwaukee	189	180	22	1
Minneapolis	100	84	—	—
Omaha	106	68	5	—
Menlo Park	66	25	n.a.	12
Phoenix	2	2	32	—
Seattle	219	130	266	4

Source: OICNI, *The New Institutes Bi-Monthly Report No. 3* (Washington, D.C.: February-March 1969).

[a] Camden figures are for December 1968.

data from the OICNI *Progress Report No. 3* (February-March 1969) were used. The terminal referrals in Table 16 are referrals to other manpower training programs. The OICs did not always provide the type of training desired nor could they offer subsidies to needy trainees as could government manpower programs. Individuals were terminally referred in such cases. The other statistics in the table are presented merely to provide a background in which to view the supportive referrals. It was possible for more enrollees to enter training than to report for an intake interview because of the table's coverage of only a short period of time and the existence of waiting lists. The author found several cases where the OICs apparently confused supportive referrals with terminal referrals or they combined both types into either one of the categories. The unusual figures for Phoenix were the result of the lack of a functioning vocational component; Phoenix enrollees were sent to other programs for technical training after completion of the Feeder. The 266 supportive referrals for Seattle seemed rather high, but one evaluator found that 80 percent of the persons who visited that OIC were referred to receive other services.[36] A close examination of this list does not suggest a relationship between the compostion of enrollment (by race or sex) and the use of supportive services.

The evaluative studies frequently alluded to supportive services and referrals and occasionally described them, but numbers did not accompany the descriptions. In short, the impact of the OIC's supportive services on minorities and women (or any enrollees) is in doubt. Investigators simply did not address themselves to that question.

Trainees' and Employers' Views of OIC

There are inherent difficulties in measuring the noneconomic or social benefits of manpower training programs. Most of the studies briefly discussed trainees' and employers' opinions of the program, but few investigators were able to specify precisely the extent of noneconomic benefits which accrued to trainees as a result of program participation. Table 17 contains the opinions of 100 Washington, D.C., graduates concerning OIC training. It is evident that trainees' responses were very favorable to OIC efforts, and when this same group was asked to evaluate OIC training, 44 percent judged the quality of the training as excellent, 52 percent as good, and 4 percent as fair. The trainees of the Erie and Charleston centers felt the OIC teaching philosophy and methods were vastly superior to those of public schools.[37] Also, most evaluators re-

36. A. L. Nellum and Associates, *op. cit.*, p. 79.

37. Anderson and Young, *op. cit.*, p. 15; and *An Evaluation of the Opportunities Industrialization Center, Inc,: Erie, Pennsylvania* (Philadelphia: Industrial Research Unit, Wharton School of Finance and Commerce, University of Pennsylvania, 1968), p. 10.

TABLE XII-17. *Opportunities Industrialization Centers, Inc. Opinions of 100 Trainees on the Effects of Training Washington D. C.*

Results of Training	Number	Significance Rank
Better job	24	2
Better pay	22	3
Higher skill level	11	4
Better job-seeking and retention ability	3	7
Greater sense of pride and self-worth	26	1
Better ability to support family	8	5
Better attitude and motivation	4	6
More confidence and poise	2	8
OIC did little or nothing	—	—

Source: David A. Scott, *An Evaluation of the Washington Institute for Employment Training: The Opportunities Industrialization Center of Washington, D.C.* (Philadelphia: Industrial Research Unit, Wharton School of Finance and Commerce, University of Pennsylvania, 1969), p. 69.

ceived the general impression that OIC graduates were satisfied with their jobs. The only complaint expressed was that the trainees sometimes experienced "snobbery" or "social frigidity" in their new jobs.[38] The lack of data made trainees' opinions impossible to compare by race or sex.

Most evaluators briefly mentioned their general impressions of employers' opinions, but none conducted comprehensive field interviews. Apparently, employers were satisfied with their OIC workers. They were occasionally critical of OIC skill training but were pleased with the trainees' motivation and attitude toward work.[39] The motivational and attitudinal qualities of the OIC employees were believed to be the result of the "grooming" aspects of the Feeder.[40] There were more examples of employer satisfaction than dissatisfaction concerning the value of OIC skill training, but the evidence suggests a need for improvement in the skill component. The percentages of training-related placement (75 percent average) discussed earlier support this conclusion.

38. Robinson, *op. cit.*, p. 80.

39. A. L. Nellum and Associates, *op cit.*, p. 46.

40. *Ibid.*

The Dropout Problem

Dropping out has been a significant problem for OIC; therefore, virtually all investigators discussed the enrollees' reasons. The list contains the Oklahoma City dropouts' reasons for discontinuance which appear to be representative:[41] economic reasons, 34 percent; dissatisfaction with program, 1 percent; child care, 24 percent; transportation, 33 percent; moved, 2 percent; and employed, 6 percent. Financial reasons accounted for the overwhelming majority of discontinuances, and the consensus reached in the literature was that stipends would have enabled more trainees, especially males, to remain in the program.

On the basis of sex, it appears that males were more likely to drop out of the program than females. Dropout data by sex were available for only three cities (Table 18). These data indicate that the percentage of females who dropped out was consistently lower than their proportion

TABLE XII-18. *Opportunities Industrialization Centers, Inc. Trainee Enrollment and Dropout Data by Sex for Three Centers*

Centers	Percent of Total Enrollment		Percent of Dropouts		Sample Size of Dropouts
	Male	Female	Male	Female	
Bedford-Stuyvesant	29	71	53	47	1,152
Philadelphia [a]	36	64	47	52	350
Washington, D.C.	45	55	59	41	725

Sources: Enrollment data—OICNI, *Final Report Draft* (Washington, D.C.: August 1, 1968—July 31, 1969), p. 155.

Percent of dropouts by sex—Marvin E. Lawrence, *Training the Hard-Core in an Urban Labor Market: The Case of the Bedford-Stuyvesant OIC* (Philadelphia: Industrial Research Unit, Wharton School of Finance and Commerce, University of Pennsylvania, 1970), p. 60.

Greenleigh Associates, Inc., *A Pilot Study of the OIC of Philadelphia, Pennsylvania* (New York: 1967), p. 34.

David A. Scott, *An Evaluation of the Washington Institute for Employment Training: The OIC of Washington, D.C.* (Philadelphia: Industrial Research Unit, Wharton School of Finance and Commerce, University of Pennsylvania, 1969), p. 65.

[a] This city's data include 40 of the 350 trainees who were placed by the OIC before completing training.

41. Legal Resources, Inc., *op. cit.*, p. 92.

of the total enrollment. One investigator noted that OIC dropouts sometimes enrolled in local government training programs which provided stipends.[42] The evaluative literature contained few statistics which would indicate how many enrollees typically dropped out of OIC training. The available data were based on questionable OIC records and limited spans of time, thus making most dropout figures highly unreliable.

CONCLUSIONS

The economic impact of OIC on its enrollees is difficult to estimate from the evaluative literature on the program. No evaluative data provide the post-training labor market experience of a national sample of OIC enrollees. There are, however, follow-up studies for small groups of trainees in a few centers throughout the nation. Thus, general conclusions regarding the impact of OIC nationally must be extrapolated from the limited local samples to the nation at large. Because the evaluative studies focused on the larger and more established centers, the measurement of post-training outcomes may not be fully representative of the experience of all OIC enrollees.

Despite such limitations, an examination of the literature leads to several conclusions. First, the overwhelming share of the OIC's impact benefits Negroes, who comprise 90 percent of the enrollment. Other minorities such as American Indians, Mexican Americans, Puerto Ricans, and Orientals were poorly represented in the total enrollment, although such groups are significant in the enrollment of a few centers in the West and Midwest. Because women made up 70 percent of the enrollment, it is reasonable to assume that a good share of the economic benefits were also allocated to women—primarily black women.

The evaluative studies show a wide range of post-training wage and employment experience among OIC enrollees. OIC data and evaluative reports for Boston and Washington, D.C., suggest an average increase in post-training earnings between $1,000 and $1,300 per year for trainees who complete the program.[43] Estimates of the change in hourly wages earned by OIC completers vary widely across centers for which data are available. Improved employment stability, higher real wages, and natural wage inflation have all been suggested as causes of the increase. Whatever the case, the evaluators generally agree that OIC has had a beneficial economic and noneconomic impact on enrollees, most of whom are minorities and women.

---

42. Robinson, *op. cit.*, p. 79.

43. OICNI, *Helping Others to Help Themselves, op. cit.*, p. 31; Barry, *loc cit.;* Scott, *loc. cit.*

CHAPTER XIII

Concentrated Employment Program

by

Bernard E. Anderson

The Concentrated Employment Program (CEP), created in April 1967, is a manpower service delivery system directed specifically toward the disadvantaged population in areas with a high concentration of unemployment, underemployment, and poverty. The program was funded originally at $100 million drawn jointly from federal obligations, authorized under the Manpower Development and Training Act of 1962, and the Economic Opportunity Act of 1964. The first contract for the establishment of a CEP was awarded to Cleveland, Ohio, but by the end of 1967, contracts had been awarded to nineteen urban and two rural areas. Together, the first round of CEPs were expected to serve about 60,000 disadvantaged persons.[1] By 1972, CEPs had expanded into eighty areas and had served at least 384,000 persons.

NATURE AND STRUCTURE OF CEP

CEP was designed to be a coordinated manpower service delivery system within a designated geographic area characterized by a high rate of poverty and unemployment. The program was expected to coordinate outreach, intake, counseling, prevocational training, job development, and job placement activities in a systematic delivery process directed toward preparing the disadvantaged person for jobs in either the private or the public sector. Prior to the establishment of CEP, manpower services, if available in the local labor market, were offered by separate government and nonprofit community agencies. The advantage of CEP was its potential for bringing the available services together in a concerted effort to help to relieve the employment difficulties of the urban and rural poor.

CEP is limited to a specific "target area." According to U.S. Department of Labor guidelines for the establishment of CEPs, the target area should have a high concentration of poor residents, but must be small enough to enable CEP to exercise "adequate control, measurable impact, and high visibility." The application of the target area criteria usually led to the selection of a major part of the low-income section of the inner-city as the operating jurisdiction for urban CEPs. In many

1. U.S. Department of Labor, *Manpower Report of the President* (Washington, D.C.: Government Printing Office, 1968), p. 195.

cases, the geographic boundary of CEP is roughly contiguous with the Model Cities target area. The geographic scope of operations for rural CEPs is much wider, naturally reflecting the less concentrated location of the rural poor. The large geographic area covered by most rural CEPs was identified by one evaluator as a major factor contributing to the inability of rural CEPs to satisfy the control, impact, or visibility criteria noted in the guidelines on the selection of target areas.[2]

Within the target area, CEP is administered by a "sponsor organization." The sponsor is responsible for program planning and administration, including the submission of a contract proposal to the U.S. Department of Labor and the receipt of operating funds from the funding agency. The sponsor organization is also responsible for monitoring program operations in order to ensure that enrollment and job placement targets are met.

In most cases, the local community action agency (CAA) was designated the sponsor for CEP. The rationale behind the selection of CAAs was their closeness to the disadvantaged population and their credibility within the community which were necessary to attract members of the target pupulation. When special circumstances surrounding the operation of community action agencies suggested that they would not be the best sponsors of CEP, new organizations were created specifically to undertake the role of sponsorship. In Philadelphia, for example, a new organization called the "Philadelphia Employment Development Corporation" (PEDC) was created in 1968 to administer the local CEP.[3] At the time it was created, PEDC was an independent, nonprofit agency with a board of directors drawn from prominent individuals in business, labor, civil rights, government, and civic affairs. Similar organizations were formed in Tennessee and Arkansas as sponsors for the rural CEPs in those states. It is important to note that according to Labor Department guidelines, at least 50 percent of the CEP sponsor's staff must be drawn from the target area. This requirement, together with the racial composition of most urban poverty areas, helps to explain why CEP has a higher proportion of minorities among its staff than MDTA and several other major manpower programs.

Although the sponsor organization has overall responsibility for program administration, manpower services offered by CEP are typically delivered by various agencies in the community acting under contract to CEP. Among the more prominent subcontractors are the state Employment Service (ES), Opportunities Industrialization Centers (OIC),

2. Urban Systems Research & Engineering, Inc., "The Impact of Five Rural CEPs," report prepared for Office of Policy, Evaluation and Research, Manpower Administration, U.S. Department of Labor, 1971, pp. 33-35.

3. Richard D. Leone *et al., Employability Development Teams and Federal Manpower Programs: A Critical Assessment of the Philadelphia CEP's Experience* (Philadelphia: Temple University, 1972), pp. 11-12.

Urban League (U.L.), and Manpower Development and Training program skills centers (MDTA). Additional services for CEP clients are often provided under subcontracts awarded to local public school systems, government agencies, and state and local welfare and rehabilitation organizations.

When CEP was first organized, the prime sponsor was responsible for obtaining the services of the subcontractors, awarding contracts to the organizations, coordinating the flow of CEP clients through the multiple services available, and monitoring the performance of the subcontractors to ensure that CEP objectives were being met. Administrators of the sponsor organization were subject to policy and program guidelines established by the U.S. Department of Labor, and they communicated to local CEP's through regional manpower administrators. The rather cumbersome administrative structure of CEP created innumerable problems in operating the programs on the local level.[4] Among the most difficult problems facing CEP was the coordination of manpower service delivery through diverse and often competing subcontractors. As a result, the CEP structure was reorganized in 1969. The major policy instruments which reorganized CEP were the Human Resource Development (HRD) model and Manpower Order 14-69.

Human Resource Development Model

The HRD model consists of procedural and staffing guidelines designed to improve the manpower service delivery system.[5] The model largely consists of: (1) limited, defined, and controlled caseload; (2) defined team staffing pattern; (3) planned continuity in all services and program phases; (4) carefully planned feedback and reassessment; and (5) constant client support and encouragement.

The "employability development team" (EDT) is central to the operation of the HRD model. Counseling in CEP formerly had been viewed as a relatively passive process through which a client could attain levels of adjustment and job performance according to his desires and ability. The HRD concept gives an active and assertive role to a team of professionals and paraprofessionals consisting of a counselor, job development specialist, work and training specialist, coach, and clerk stenographer.

In effect, the HRD model placed primary responsibility for trainee progress toward employment upon the employability development team; before, the responsibility had been widely dispersed among the various

4. U.S. Department of Labor, *Manpower Report of the President* (Washington, D.C.: Government Printing Office, 1971), p. 67.

5. U.S. Department of Labor, Division of Counseling and Test Development, "The Human Resource Employability Development Model," Manpower Administration, U.S. Department of Labor, n.d., pp. 3-4.

subcontracting organizations which delivered manpower services to CEP clients. The reorganization of CEP under the HRD model influenced significantly the relationship between the sponsor and the subcontracting organizations and helped to rationalize the manpower delivery system.

Manpower Administration Order 14-69

Although the inauguration of EDTs greatly affected the operation of CEPs, the major modification of program goals and structure was generated by Manpower Order 14-69, issued in July 1969.[6] The order was written in response to numerous CEP administrative problems, focusing mainly on sponsor-subcontractor relations. Manpower Administration reviews of CEP operations suggested that of all the problems adversely affecting the performance of CEPs through 1968, the sponsor-subcontractor problems were the most vexing and the most difficult to solve under the existing administrative structure. As a result, Order 14-69 mandated substantial changes in the program affecting: (1) standards for client assignment after intake; (2) use of job banks; (3) use of employability development teams; (4) standardization of CEP success measures; and (5) grouping of manpower tasks in a single package to be subcontracted to the local employment service.

The major effect of the reorganization was to limit the CEP sponsor's direct control over most operational components. The Employment Service acquired control over the employability development teams and all manpower services from outreach to follow-up. Although the ES did not have to provide all manpower services itself, it controlled the subcontracting of such services to local organizations that would participate in CEP.

Among the major operational changes generated by Order 14-69 were the new guidelines on trainee eligibility for CEP. Originally, an individual was eligible to participate in CEP if he was a member of a poor family (i.e., annual income less than $4,000 for a family of four), unemployed or underemployed, handicapped, a high school dropout, or a member of a minority group. The focus of CEP, as originally planned, was toward the hard-core unemployed and disadvantaged who experienced the most difficulty in the job market because of personal limitations. Under Order 14-69, the focus shifted toward emphasis on only those individuals who had a reasonable chance of becoming employable through the services offered directly by CEP. The new guidelines specifically excluded from eligibility these individuals: alcoholics, drug addicts, and the physically and mentally handicapped. Moreover, under the limited caseload system, only the number of persons who could be served in a reasonable period of

6. U.S. Department of Labor, Manpower Administration, Order 14-69 (July 19, 1969).

time were to be accepted into CEP. The purpose of this policy was to reduce significantly the number of persons waiting to enroll in CEP.

The changes in CEP structure and operation generated by the HRD model and the implementation of Order 14-69 are important for a clear understanding of the results of CEP evaluations conducted after 1970. As discussed more fully below, the data on program enrollees, placement, and follow-up vary according to the time of the evaluation. Differences in enrollee composition, placement success, and overall operation of CEPs reflect in part the operational changes generated by the use of employability teams and the increased role of the Employment Service after 1969.

CEP Enrollment Characteristics

In fiscal year 1972, CEP was funded at almost $155 million and served 84,700 persons as first-time enrollees. The program expanded rapidly during the first two years of its existence. After beginning in nineteen urban and two rural areas, CEP had spread to sixty-three urban and thirteen rural areas by 1969. During this time, program enrollment more than doubled from 53,000 to 127,000 and federal expenditures for the program rose from $93 million to almost $188 million.

After 1970, the rate of growth in CEPs declined, and both federal obligations and enrollment have shown a steady downward trend (see Table 1). Between fiscal years 1970 and 1972, for example, first-time enrollment declined by 23.1 percent as program appropriations fell by $33 million. The declining level of CEP operations since 1970 probably reflects the changes in the administrative guidelines inaugurated in late 1969. In addition, increased competition from NAB-JOBS and WIN, two manpower programs also beamed toward the CEP target population, probably contributed to the lower enrollment levels of 1971 and 1972.

Throughout its existence, CEP has been characterized by a high proportion of Negro participants. The heavy concentration of black enrollees is largely a product of the racial composition of urban poverty areas where most CEPs are located. Although black participants have always represented more than a majority of CEP enrollees, their proportion relative to other enrollees has dropped significantly from the levels observed during the early development of the program. Since fiscal year 1971, black participation in CEP has leveled off to about six out of ten enrollees, down from eight out of ten enrollees at the inception of the program. At the same time, the relative proportion of poor whites and of nonwhite minorities other than Negro has doubled in CEP's enrollment since 1968. It is likely that this trend is also the product of the administrative changes affecting urban CEPs since 1969, as well as the expansion of program operations into the rural areas of states where the poor are predominately white, American Indian or Mexican American.

TABLE XIII-1. *Concentrated Employment Program*
Federal Obligations, First-Time Enrollments, and Race-Sex Composition
Fiscal Years 1967-1972

Characteristics	1967	1968	1969	1970	1971	1972
Federal obligations (millions of dollars)	78.4	89.7	114.2	187.3	166.8	154.6
First-time enrollments (thousands)	n.a.	53.0	127.0	110.1	93.7	84.7
Race (percent):						
White	n.a.	15.0	28.0	26.1	31.2	29.0
Negro	n.a.	81.0	65.0	67.4	60.2	61.2
Other	n.a.	4.0	7.0	6.5	8.6	9.8
Sex (percent):						
Male	n.a.	48.0	58.0	58.5	59.7	58.6
Female	n.a.	52.0	42.0	41.5	40.3	41.4

Source: U.S. Department of Labor, *Manpower Report of the President* (Washington, D.C.: Government Printing Office)
1969, Table F-11, p. 247;
1970, Table F-3, p. 306;
1971, Table F-12, p. 310;
1972, Table F-8, p. 268;
1973, Table F-3, p. 229;
1973, Table F-8, p. 234.

Over time, the sex composition of CEP enrollees has shifted away from a female majority and toward a dominant enrollment of men. The trend toward increasing male participation was observed as early as fiscal year 1969 and has steadily increased in each subsequent year. The expansion of the WIN program may partly explain this trend, although other factors not fully discussed in the evaluative literature might also be responsible.

Trend data on other characteristics of CEP enrollees are not as complete as those on race and sex, but useful information on the enrollees may be obtained from the analysis of CEP termination data conducted by Analytic Systems, Inc., in 1970.[7] The analysis covered 18.6 percent of the 220,000 estimated terminations from CEP between 1969 and April 1970. A review of the demographic characteristics of trainees showed the following:

1. 60 percent were male;
2. 38 percent were less than 21 years old;
3. 63 percent were Negro;
4. 50 percent had no dependents;
5. 28 percent were high school graduates;
6. 77 percent had not participated in any other manpower program;
7. 97 percent of the men and 98 percent of the women received no public assistance.

REVIEW OF EVALUATIVE LITERATURE

Twelve evaluative studies of CEP were available for review. With the exception of the General Accounting Office studies of the programs in Detroit, Chicago, and Los Angeles, each of the evaluations was conducted by a private consulting agency. One study, the investigation of employability development teams in the Philadelphia CEP, was conducted by a group of university-based evaluators.

The twelve evaluative studies covered CEP operations in 37 separate cities and 5 rural areas. The cities selected for study were mainly located outside the South, but cities of widely different size were well represented. In terms of frequency of evaluation, Chicago was the most prominent selection with its CEP included in the evaluations conducted by three separate investigators. The next most frequent choices for evaluation were Los Angeles, Springfield (Massachusetts), and Trenton (New Jersey). CEPs in each of these cities were evaluated at various times by two separate investigators.

7. Analytic Systems, Inc., "Analysis of CEP Automated Termination Data," report prepared for Office of Policy, Evaluation and Research, Manpower Administration, U.S. Department of Labor, 1970, pp. 36-67.

Five of the twelve evaluations were conducted during or after 1970. Each of the rural CEPs and 26 of the urban CEPs were included in the post-1970 evaluations. The remaining eleven urban CEPs were evaluated during or before 1969. It should be noted that the evaluations undertaken during 1969 occurred at the time when the CEP administrative structure and program form were undergoing substantial change. Because the administrative changes undoubtedly affected program performance and operation, the conclusions based upon the early studies should be accepted cautiously.

The major issues discussed in the evaluation reports included interorganizational relations in the administration of CEP, job development and job placement experience, and the impact of CEP on enrollees, employers, and the community. The reports emphasized these issues differently, but a review of the evidence and conclusions in the reports revealed the following broad results.

Interorganizational Conflict

The raison d'être for CEP was that a single coordinating organization in a local target area could orchestrate the services provided by various local manpower and social service agencies in an effort to improve the labor market experience of disadvantaged workers. Six of the eight evaluation reports challenged this rationale for CEP and offered documented evidence of the interorganizational conflict and lack of cooperation which adversely affected CEP's potential for achieving its objectives. The most systematic examination of this issue was found in the study of the Philadelphia CEP.[8] The investigators found that prior to 1970, the CEP sponsor was very weak in relation to the loose confederation of subcontracting agencies which served as the principal deliverers of manpower services to CEP enrollees. As a result, interorganizational conflict, rather than cooperation, characterized the operation of the manpower delivery system; as a result, trainees were not served efficiently or effectively. Among the adverse effects of the system were: (1) enrollees were not assigned to the various component services in accordance with their individual needs; instead, subcontracting agencies tried to justify their funding by meeting quotas stipulated in their contracts without regard to trainee needs; (2) subtle antagonisms existed between the professionals from one agency and paraprofessionals from another agency; (3) no agency accepted major responsibility for the efficient operation of the manpower delivery system; and (4) the CEP director was unable to deal adequately with program planning and development; instead, he spent much of his time mediating internal disputes. Many of these problems were corrected only through the application of program guide-

8. Leone *et al., op cit.*

lines and functional responsibility assignments contained in Manpower Administration Order 14-69.

The study of CEP in rural areas also focused on the problem of interorganizational dissonance, but attributed the problem to the large geographic scope of coverage of the rural CEPs.[9] There was also some evidence that lack of communication between CEP administrators and powerful minority group organizations adversely affected minority group enrollment in the rural CEPs. In Minnesota, for example, the failure of the CEP director to seek the counsel of Indian tribal leaders led to a boycott of CEP by the Indian disadvantaged populations.

In other cases, the coordination of services offered by subcontractors in rural areas was made difficult because of conflicting responsibilities of state and federally funded organizations already active in the community. The rural CAAs had a mandate to assist the poor, but other organizations, such as local representatives of the Area Redevelopment Agency and representatives of the Bureau of Indian Affairs, resented the intrusion of CAA-sponsored CEPs into an area of activity considered within the jurisdiction of the older organizations. The result was a somewhat restricted role for rural CEPs even in areas where manpower services were limited or nonexistent.

One of the major factors contributing to the interorganizational problems was the lack of a clear understanding of CEP's mission by many subcontracting organizations. Moreover, there were no clear guidelines for organizational linkages to implement the program prior to Order 14-69. In the absence of a clear set of operational procedures, the CEPs were left to work out their relationship with subcontractors on an *ad hoc* and program-specific basis. The result was that cooperation among disparate organizations varied significantly across cities and rural areas served by CEPs. The variation was most clearly marked in the role of the Employment Service in CEP from 1967 through 1969. In a few cities and rural areas, ES enjoyed a close relationship with CEP, but in far more areas, the ES-CEP relationship varied from restrained cooperation to open hostility. The evaluators generally attributed the ES-CEP difficulties to the conflict between Employment Service professionalism and CAA aspirations for black self-determination. The Employment Service traditionally had served the non-disadvantaged work force and had acquired a distinct orientation toward meeting employer needs for manpower. The CAAs, on the other hand, were vocal advocates of the poor, who often viewed employer hiring standards as the major obstacle to

9. Urban Systems Research & Engineering, Inc., *op. cit.*, pp. 50-90.

increased employment opportunities for the disadvantaged.[10] The evaluative reports also noted the CEP staff-Employment Service friction arising out of the predominantly white composition of ES management personnel compared with the predominately black CAA and CEP personnel. The racial overtones were clearly evident in the evaluative reports of CEP in Philadelphia, Atlanta, Chicago, and five Northeast cities.[11]

The role of the Employment Service and the rationalization of the manpower delivery system were modified by MA Order 14-69, but the impact of the Order on interorganizational cooperation was mixed. The Order apparently had little effect upon improving the relationship between CEP and ES in manpower regions I and II, and it tended to exacerbate interorganization tension in several of the seventeen CEPs evaluated by the System Development Corporation in June 1971.[12] On the other hand, there was evidence in the Philadelphia CEP evaluation, and in some cities studied by SDC, that the implementation of employability development teams helped to improve the CEP-ES relationship, as well as the interaction among other subcontractors. In general, the improvement of interorganizational relations after 1969 seemed to occur in CEPs where either the employability development teams were implemented successfully or where informal linkages were worked out independently between the Employment Service and the manpower service agencies.

Job Development

CEP evaluations devoted a considerable amount of attention to job development and job placement activities. Much of the interest in these topics stems from the special mission of CEP to be a system designed to open new job opportunities for the disadvantaged. Part of the rationale behind the establishment of CEP was the existence of jobs in private industry and in government that disadvantaged workers might fill if they could overcome their personal problems and if employers could be made aware of the employment potential of the disadvantaged population.

10. A. L. Nellum and Associates, "Final Report for an Evaluation of the Concentrated Employment Program in Atlanta, Georgia: Baltimore, Maryland; and Chicago, Illinois," report prepared for the Office of Policy, Evaluation and Research, Manpower Administration, U.S. Department of Labor, 1969, p. 11; Kirschner Associates Inc., "Evaluation of Five Concentrated Employment Programs in Manpower Regions I and II," report prepared for Manpower Administration, U.S. Department of Labor, 1969, p. 41; and System Development Corporation, "Evaluation of the Impact of Selected Urban Concentrated Employment Programs," report prepared for the Office of Policy, Evaluation and Research, Manpower Administration, U.S. Department of Labor, 1970, pp. 10-11.

11. Nellum and Associates, *op. cit.*, pp. 28-31.

12. System Development Corporation, "Analysis of the Concentrated Employment Program Subsequent to MA 14-69," report prepared for Office of Policy, Evaluation and Research, Manpower Administration, U.S. Department of Labor, 1971, p. 52.

Job development was considered the key to new job opportunities for the disadvantaged. The term "job development" meant not only locating job vacancies, but also encouraging employers to modify their hiring standards and pre-selection practices in order to increase the probability that disadvantaged workers might be hired. In short, job development was expected to make employers willing to take a chance on CEP enrollees who might have a police record, an inadequate level of basic education, few marketable job skills, and such personal problems as alcoholism, drug addiction, or mental or physical disabilities. Ideally, CEP was expected to mitigate many of the serious problems of the disadvantaged prior to referring them to jobs, but once CEP declared an individual "job ready," it was expected that an employer would hire him into a job offering reasonable stability and some opportunity for upgrading.

The evaluative studies call into question both the underlying assumptions of job development for CEP and the effectiveness of procedures through which job development was attempted. An assessment of the urban CEPs showed that employers were generally unenthusiastic about hiring employees with personal characteristics similar to those of the hard-core unemployed and disadvantaged population. As a result, there was little evidence that employers had modified their hiring standards or redesigned entry-level semiskilled jobs in an effort to expand employment opportunities for CEP enrollees.

Overall, the jobs offered to CEP enrollees had limited training content, little upgrading potential, and low socioeconomic status.[13] Because such jobs had always been available to the disadvantaged, many CEP enrollees failed to perceive any change in their employment experience following participation in the program. According to evidence presented in the evaluation studies, the failure to develop "good jobs" in significant numbers for CEP enrollees produced two major results: (1) persons placed in jobs after leaving CEP often showed a high quitting rate together with much tardiness and absenteeism; and (2) employer complaints about the lack of motivation of CEP hires were numerous and widespread.[14] Yet, although employers often had an unfavorable image of CEP and its trainees, many employers stated that persons hired from CEP were, on the average, no worse in job performance than other employees holding similar jobs in the firm. This conclusion implies that CEP did not make disadvantaged workers better acclimated to low-level jobs. Such workers would have been equally acclimated to low-level jobs in the absence of CEP.

13. Nellum and Associates, *op. cit.*, pp. 101-106, and Kirschner Associates Inc., *op. cit.*, pp. 131-132.

14. Kirschner Associates Inc., *op. cit.*, p. 107, and System Development Corp., "Impact of Selected Urban CEPs," *op. cit.*, pp. 89-91.

The lack of success in developing "good jobs" for CEP enrollees was in part attributable to the job development procedures used by many CEPs. In most cases, the job development function was widely dispersed among the subcontractors with no central guidance and direction. Moreover, job development specialists did not always understand the nature of their responsibility. Instead of working closely with employers to consider ways to redesign jobs and adjust hiring criteria in the interest of increasing the number of jobs available to the disadvantaged, CEP administrators and the job development staff often engaged in general public relations efforts intended merely to inform employers about the special employment problems of ghetto residents.[15] Job development efforts often were not organized systematically or were not based upon a strategy that would produce measurable results. All too often, appeals to the employer community focused on the "social obligation" of private enterprise and the potential for civil disruption if the disadvantaged were not hired. Such approaches failed to capture the interest of employers or to persuade them to open attractive jobs to CEP enrollees.

In rural areas, job development consisted mainly of identifying local job vacancies. Little effort was expended to ensure that the vacancies were suitable to CEP enrollees or that CEP enrollees were being prepared for the vacancies which existed. Indeed, one of the major themes, in the evaluation of both rural and urban CEPs, was the lack of coordination between job development and other components of the manpower delivery system.

Following Order 14-69, there were mixed results in the success of job development activities. The Order gave all responsibility for job development to the Employment Service. In addition, a new element—the Job Bank—was introduced into the system. Evaluation studies showed that in Philadelphia the job development process became more effective as a result of the use of employability development teams. In several other cities, however, no positive change occurred. In fact, there was some evidence that activity declined as CEP staff members relied more heavily on the Job Bank and reduced their direct contacts with employers.

Job Placement

The prime contract for each CEP contained a projected goal for the placement of enrollees after training. The programs were expected to emphasize enrollee placement in private industry, but administrative procedures permitted CEPs to take credit for placement in other program components including Public Service Careers and Work-Experience. Thus, the CEP placement records do not fully reflect the impact

15. Nellum and Associates, *op. cit.*, pp. 106-108.

of the program in getting the disadvantaged into useful industrial employment.

The evaluative studies were replete with evidence showing the failure of CEP to meet its placement goals. In almost every study, it was noted that performance fell short of placement goals, but the problem was given special prominence in the Nellum and Associates' evaluation of CEPs in Atlanta, Baltimore, and Chicago. In each of these CEPs studied in 1969, placement rates were 50 percent below the projected goal. A steady decline in placement success was noted in a study of 40,000 CEP terminations between 1969 and 1970.[16]

During this period, the proportion of placement among all CEP terminations declined from 78 percent in the first quarter of 1969 to 44 percent in the third quarter of 1970. The declining rate of placement in 1970 was undoubtedly related to the worsening economic conditions which reduced the number of job opportunities. In rural areas, however, the low placement record was in part related to a conscious CEP strategy to concentrate on placement in "good jobs." The limited number of such jobs in rural areas constricted placement success. In addition to the failure to meet placement goals, CEPs in Philadelphia and in several other Northeast cities showed a disproportionate number of enrollees placed in Public Service jobs, New Careers, and Work-Experience.[17] Placement of this type was relatively easy because the components were part of the program itself. Although wages in the program component jobs were often higher than those in private industry, the low private sector placement was viewed as a mark of failure for CEP. Indeed, CEP's poor record of getting its trainees into private industry was cited by a *Wall Street Journal* reporter as evidence that the newly organized NAB-JOBS program might face difficulties in 1969.[18]

Despite the relatively low rate of placement, several patterns were evident in the evaluative studies. The study of CEP termination data showed that placement rates were highest for those with the highest educational attainment.[19] Another study of CEP placement in Chicago, Atlanta, and Baltimore showed a clear trend toward equal success in placing men and women as CEP matured in 1968 and 1969.[20] Still another study showed that the use of employability teams increased the rate at which job-ready enrollees, referred by CEP to employers, were hired.[21]

16. Analytic Systems, Inc., *op. cit.*, p. 26.

17. Leone *et al., op. cit.*, p. 114.

18. James P. Gannon, "LBJ's Job Plan: Failure Warmed Over," *Wall Street Journal*, January 22, 1968.

19. Analytic Systems, Inc., *op. cit.*, p. 54.

20. Nellum and Associates, *op. cit.*, pp. 101-102.

21. Leone *et al., op. cit.*, pp. 113-114.

Similar evidence on the impact of administrative procedures on CEP placement patterns was found in the seventeen-city evaluation of the impact of Order 14-69. The study showed that before 1969, 46 percent of those hired stayed on the job 30 days or more. After the administrative changes generated by Order 14-69, 21 percent of the trainees entered unsubsidized jobs, and 60 percent of the hires stayed 30 days or more. The evaluators interpreted this placement pattern as evidence that after Order 14-69 was issued, relatively more CEP enrollees were placed in jobs which offered on-the-job training.

One study, conducted in 1972, revealed a favorable attitude among CEP enrollees regarding the jobs obtained through the program.[22] Of the 53 former enrollees interviewed, about 68 percent were in training-related jobs, and 43 percent indicated that the jobs provided by CEP offered great potential for advancement. Moreover, almost 68 percent felt that the job into which CEP had placed them was better than one they might have located on their own. Still, almost 42 percent of the respondents indicated that their jobs offered limited potential for advancement, and 11 percent reported that their jobs offered no potential for advancement. This evidence, perhaps unrepresentative because of the small sample size, is inconclusive in regard to the quality of CEP placement since 1969. A more definitive picture is not available, however, because few evaluations conducted after 1969 contained detailed data on the quality of job placement for CEP enrollees.

Participation in Program Components

Two of the most important factors that might affect the impact of CEP on enrollees are the length of time enrollees spent in the program and the range of manpower services obtained by enrollees while in the program. Few of the evaluative reports provided statistical evidence on these aspects of program operation, but the limited information available suggests that the CEPs varied significantly in the mix of services offered to enrollees.

The most comprehensive data available were found in a study of 41,000 enrollees who terminated their experiences in CEP between April 1969 and April 1970.[23] The study included an analysis of the length of time spent by enrollees in the various component service sectors of CEP. Less than one-half of the enrollees had orientation, and most enrollees spent less than one month in that program component. As shown in table 2, the enrollees spent most of their time in the training sectors of

22. Booz Allen, Public Administration Services, Inc., "Evaluation of Job Development in Standard Metropolitan Statistical Areas," report prepared for Office of Policy, Evaluation and Research, Manpower Administration, U.S. Department of Labor, 1972. This is a general study of job development not confined to CEP.

23. Analytic Systems, Inc., *op. cit.*, p. A-15.

TABLE XIII-2. *Concentrated Employment Program Average Weeks in Program by Program Termination Status 1969-1970*

Characteristics	Total Average	Placed in Jobs	Dropouts
Male:			
Orientation	3.1	2.9	3.5
Training	14.3	15.2	13.3
Holding	10.2	6.3	14.5
Female:			
Orientation	3.3	3.2	3.6
Training	16.9	18.4	15.9
Holding	11.5	6.6	17.0

Source: Analytic Systems, Inc., "Analysis of CEP Termination Data," report prepared for Office of Policy, Evaluation and Research, Manpower Administration, U.S. Department of Labor, 1970, p. 30.

CEP; female enrollees, on the average, stayed in training longer than males. The evidence on enrollee exposure to training may be deceptive, however, because the records on enrollee participation in program components include thirteen different categories of "training" ranging from basic education to special work projects. Thus, although male CEP enrollees spent almost seventeen weeks in the program, and female enrollees spent almost twenty weeks in the program as of mid-1970, it is difficult to determine in general how much the program contributed to the investment in human capital associated with increasing the marketable skills of CEP enrollees.

Somewhat more evidence on program component use is available in the evaluation of the rural CEPs and of selected urban CEPs. The study of rural programs revealed that orientation was widely used, with the focus placed upon informing rural workers about the nature of industrial employment.[24] Orientation was also used as a device for helping enrollees deal with various aspects of their personal lives, including household budgeting, consumer education, and civil rights.

Basic education in rural CEPs was rarely used for its intended purpose of increasing the enrollee's capability to receive skill training. Instead, the basic education component was often viewed as a place where trainees could be held temporarily while waiting to be assigned to another program component.

24. Urban Systems Research & Engineering, Inc., *op. cit.*, pp. 194-196.

Institutional training and on-the-job training were stressed by three of the five rural CEPs, but the use of these program components was constricted because of the nature of the job market in rural areas and the level of skills training offered by CEP. Employers willing to hire skilled workers in the rural areas demanded more sophisticated vocational training and experience than those that were available to enrollees participating in the MDTA components of the rural CEPs. As a result, enrollees sent to MDTA courses often became frustrated because the jobs obtained at the end of training usually did not require the skills learned in CEP. There was evidence that, in many cases, area demand for labor was not carefully surveyed before decisions on course offerings were made. On the whole, the evidence emerging from the evaluation of rural CEPs suggests that the program components were used as devices to keep enrollees in the program until an industrial job could be found. While in CEP, with the exception of orientation, the enrollee experience in program components bore little relation to the job training enrollees would need before entering the labor market.

The most complete evidence on program component use in urban CEPs was provided in the evaluation of the Philadelphia CEP.[25] The study showed that between 1969 and 1970 the proportion of enrollees assigned to orientation and assessment increased from 49.0 percent to 69.3 percent. At the same time, enrollees in the least-used component, Basic Education, increased from 0.7 percent to 3.3 percent. A reverse trend was observed among those assigned to skill training, with the proportion falling to 11.0 percent in 1970 compared to 12.3 percent in 1969. This evidence on differences in component usage during the two years was attributed to the use of employability development teams, as well as the decline in the proportion of enrollees coming into the program classified as "job ready" and thus in need of few CEP services.

The only other urban CEPs with detailed and available component use data were Chicago, Atlanta, and Baltimore; each was evaluated in 1969.[26] The evidence for these cities showed that skill training was not used very frequently. CEPs emphasized orientation, assessment, and OJT, buttressed by job development efforts to generate employment opportunities for the enrollees. In these cities, as in Philadelphia, a disproportionate number of enrollees were not placed in private industry, but in various types of subsidized jobs in the government sector. Because

25. Leone *et al., op. cit.*, pp. 29-64.

26. Nellum and Associates, *op. cit.*, pp. 54-105. See also Human Interaction Research Institute, "A Clinical, Dynamic and Statistical Assessment of the CEP in Oakland, California," report prepared for Office of Policy, Evaluation and Research, Manpower Administration, U.S. Department of Labor, pp. 2-3.

so few enrollees were placed in private sector jobs, perhaps CEP administrators saw little need to assign program participants to such components as basic education and skill training.

In summary, the limited evidence in the evaluative reports dealing with program component use showed that CEP served more as a dispenser of supplementary job information and an employment referral system than as a system directed toward upgrading the marketable skills of the disadvantaged in preparation for better jobs. The evaluative reports, although limited in number and scope of coverage, suggest that because most CEP enrollees did not receive a significant amount of skill training, the program might be expected to exert little impact on the occupational and income position of the disadvantaged. The extent to which the evidence confirms this expectation will be discussed in the assessment of the economic impact of CEP.

ECONOMIC IMPACT OF CEP

The economic impact of a job training program depends upon two factors—post-training placement and post-training earnings. Participants in a job training program will experience a positive economic outcome from training to the extent that they obtain employment in occupations paying higher wages and having greater job stability than jobs they would have obtained in the absence of training. Ideally, the contribution of the job training program to positive economic gains for its participants should be measured by comparing the post-program labor market experience with that of a comparison group which did not participate in the program. In addition, in making judgments about the magnitude of wage and employment gains following participation in the training program, some adjustment should be made for the nature of enrollee pre-program employment experience. Variations among members of population groups with different pre-program employment experiences may generate significant variations in post-program earnings and employment, aside from whatever change in economic status may be attributable to participation in the program.

Only three of the evaluative reports included in this study contained data that permit an assessment of the post-program economic gains of CEP enrollees. The reports are the System Development Corporation (SDC) study of fourteen urban CEPs, the Urban Systems Research report of CEP in five rural areas, and the Temple University study of CEP in Philadelphia.

The most comprehensive post-program data are contained in the SDC study in which 702 former CEP participants were interviewed between July 1969 and July 1970. The study focused on the effect of CEP training upon the employability status and the earning power of the CEP trainee. The total population interviewed were employed 17 percent of the time prior to entering the program compared to 37 percent of the time after leaving CEP. Participants with work experience prior to entering the program showed an average of 48 percent of their time in employment prior to entering CEP; this figure increased to 55 percent after they left the program. Of the 253 former enrollees who had work experience, 189 (75 percent) went into jobs upon leaving CEP. In comparison, 291 (65 percent) of those with no pre-program work experience were placed in jobs upon terminating involvement in the program.

A comparison of relative wage gains before and after CEP participation is shown in Table 3. These data exclude all persons who had no pre- or post-CEP work history. Because of this exclusion, the data may tend to bias the wage gains for CEP enrollees as a whole, depending upon the extent of unemployment and labor force participation of CEP enrollees before entering and after leaving the program. The evidence shows that the number of jobs held after CEP which paid less than $1.60 per hour was significantly less than the number of such jobs held prior to CEP, and the number of jobs held subsequent to CEP paying between $2.00 and $2.50 more than doubled in comparison with the number in this wage category held prior to participation in the program. A comparison of relative wage gains by sex is shown in Table 4. The data show that gains in hourly earnings were greater for women than men in all wage rate categories. The largest relative gains for women were re-

TABLE XIII-3 *Concentrated Employment Program Average Starting Wages for Jobs Pre- and Post-CEP 14 Urban CEPs*

Hourly Wage	Pre-CEP		Post-CEP	
	Percent	Number	Percent	Number
$0-1.24	22	221	5	73
1.25-1.59	29	284	13	177
1.60-1.69	17	166	23	309
1.70-1.99	11	112	19	252
2.00-2.49	9	92	22	298
2.50 plus	11	109	18	240
Total	100	984	100	1,349

Source: System Development Corporation, "Evaluation of the Impact of Selected Urban Concentrated Employment Programs," report prepared for Office of Policy, Evaluation, and Research, Manpower Administration, U.S. Department of Labor, 1970, p. 128.

Note: Percents may not add to 100 due to rounding.

TABLE XIII-4. *Concentrated Employment Program*
Average Starting Wages for Jobs Pre- and Post-CEP

	Pre-CEP				Post-CEP			
	Male		Female		Male		Female	
Hourly Wage	Total	Percent	Total	Percent	Total	Percent	Total	Percent
$0-1.24	79	15	137	30	28	4	45	7
1.25-1.59	128	25	155	34	84	12	86	14
1.60-1.69	85	16	81	18	122	17	190	30
1.70-1.99	63	12	48	10	100	14	152	24
2.00-2.49	70	14	22	5	195	28	105	17
2.50 plus	92	18	13	3	180	25	51	8
Total	517	100	456	100	709	100	629	100

Source: System Development Corporation, "Evaluation of the Impact of Selected Urban Concentrated Employment Programs," report prepared for Manpower Administration, U.S. Department of Labor, 1970, p. 131.

gistered in jobs paying $2.00 or more. Still, even after training, there were only one-third as many women as men in jobs paying more than $2.00 per hour; the wage rate distribution shows men concentrated in jobs paying above $2.00 whereas women are concentrated in the lower wage categories.

A comparison of relative wage gains by sex is shown in Table 4. The SDC study does not attribute all the post-CEP gains in wages to the effects of the program. Several contributing factors, including the increase in the federal minimum wage from $1.40 to $1.60 per hour, help to explain the decline in the proportion of persons in the lowest wage rate categories. In addition, the years between 1965 and 1970 witnessed an overall increase in average hourly earnings in private employment of 29.4 percent. This increase would undoubtedly affect the wages earned by former CEP enrollees in the fourteen cities studied, although it would be difficult to ascertain the full effect of general wage increases. Unfortunately, for purposes of this review, the SDC study did not report data separately by minority group identity.

Impact in Rural Areas

In 1970 Urban Systems Research & Engineering conducted a study of almost 1,000 participants in five rural areas to determine what impact participation in rural CEP had upon their patterns of employment. The five rural areas studied were in Arkansas, New Mexico, Tennessee, Minnesota, and Maine. These areas included a cross-section of minority group participants, and the study provides some evidence of relative economic impact across members of different population groups.

The investigation used a "before-after" method to measure the gains of CEP enrollees. This technique eliminates individual variation and assumes that, apart from exogenously determined wage rate changes, an individual's employment pattern will not change over the period of comparison. In order to gauge more fully the impact of the program, the data were separated according to whether the enrollees did or did not complete the program. Tables 5, 6, and 7 report the more interesting findings of the rural CEP study.

Estimated hourly wage rates are obtained by dividing reported earnings from employment by hours worked. The increase in money wage rates for both completers and noncompleters is clearly measurable. Although the noncompleters do not do as well as the completers in absolute terms, their relative improvement is greater (Table 5).

Quite simply, the evidence in Table 6, which is based upon an estimate of annual earnings before and after training, show that average gains from the program are greater for male than female completers, but are less for male than female dropouts. It should be noted, however, that when a standard "t" test was applied, neither of the sex differences was

TABLE XIII-5. *Concentrated Employment Program Means of Estimated Wage Rates and Changes in Wages for Rural CEPs*

Characteristics	Number in Sample	Before	After	Change
Completers	784	$1.44	$1.74	$0.30
Noncompleters	215	1.21	1.68	.47

Source: Urban Systems Research & Engineering, Inc., "The Impact of Five Rural Concentrated Employment Programs," report prepared for Office of Policy, Evaluation and Research, Manpower Administration, U.S. Department of Labor, 1971, p. 106.

TABLE XIII-6. *Concentrated Employment Program Estimated Yearly Benefits by Sex for Rural CEPs*

Characteristics	Male		Female	
	Total	Benefits	Total	Benefits
Completers	500	$602	273	$538
Noncompleters	134	761	80	$903

Source: Urban Systems Research & Engineering, Inc., "The Impact of Five Rural Concentrated Employment Programs," report prepared for Office of Policy, Evaluation, and Research Manpower Administration, U.S. Department of Labor, 1971, p. 109.

found to be statistically significant. When inspecting the racial classifications, whites appear to do somewhat better than nonwhites in terms of their increased capacity to earn. (Table 7) A notable difference, however, is evident in the comparison of blacks and other minorities. Both completers and noncompleters within the black group gain less, on the average, than do Chicanos or American Indians. Moreover, when differences between the gains of completers and noncompleters within each

TABLE XIII-7. *Concentrated Employment Program Estimated Yearly Benefits by Race for Rural CEPs*

Characteristics	White		Negro		American Indian		Chicano	
	Total	Benefits	Total	Benefits	Total	Benefits	Total	Benefits
Completers	442	$724	149	$197	103	$565	64	$341
Noncompleters	115	997	49	368	23	706	24	1,127

Source: Urban Systems Research & Engineering, Inc., "The Impact of Five Rural Concentrated Employment Programs," U.S. Department of Labor, 1971, p. 110.

group are calculated, the racial rank order of benefits from completing the program are as follows: (1) Chicanos ($786); (2) whites ($273); (3) blacks ($171); and (4) American Indian ($141). Of course, inter-race comparisons are highly influenced by local labor market conditions and the different groups tend to be concentrated in different rural areas. Blacks, for example, were concentrated in the rural CEPs in Arkansas and Tennessee, whereas American Indians were concentrated in Minnesota and Chicanos in New Mexico. Because of these sampling characteristics, no general conclusions can be drawn from the evidence concerning the relative impact of CEP on the different ethnic groups at large, unless the data are corrected for variations in local labor market conditions.

Impact in Philadelphia

A group of 535 former enrollees in the Philadelphia CEP were interviewed during 1971 to determine the impact of the program upon their economic status. The sample included 261 persons who had been enrolled in the program during 1969 and 274 who were enrolled during 1970. One major object of the study was to compare the success of those who participated in CEP before and after employability development teams were activated. Thus, the evidence presented below shows pre- and post-program economic values for each group separately, depending upon whether the enrollee was in the program in 1969 or 1970.

TABLE XIII-8. *Concentrated Employment Program Summary of Economic Success of Completers Philadelphia, 1969 and 1970*

Success Measure	Status of Completers 1969	1970
Weeks worked:		
Pre-	25.4	22.1
Post-	30.3	32.5
Difference	+4.9	+10.4
Average weekly wages:		
Pre-	$79.87	$81.60
Post-	$91.20	$89.88
Difference	+$11.33	+8.28 [a]

Source: Richard D. Leone *et al.*, *Employability Teams and Federal Manpower Programs: A Critical Assessment of the Philadelphia CEP's Experience* (Philadelphia: Temple University Press, 1972), p. 116.

[a] By Industrial Research Unit computation.

Table 8 presents the comparison of weekly wage and number of weeks worked for enrollees who participated in 1969 or 1970. On the average, those who were in the program in 1970 and who stayed long enough to complete their training registered a 47.1 percent gain in number of weeks worked compared to a gain of only 19.3 percent in weeks worked by completers who were enrolled in 1969. In regard to wages, however, the 1969 enrollees showed a greater gain (14.2 percent) compared with those who had gone through CEP in 1970 (10.0 percent).

A closer look at the comparative post-program experience of enrollees can be obtained from the data according to sex.

For weeks worked, male enrollees in 1970 showed markedly better post-program job experience, whereas 1970 female enrollees did somewhat worse. The success measured in weekly wage gains showed little percentage change for either men or women who had been in CEP in either year. The absolute level of wage changes, however, revealed smaller upward adjustments in average weekly wages among both male and female enrollees who participated in CEP in 1970 compared to those who went through the program in 1969.

TABLE XIII-9. *Concentrated Employment Program Summary of Economic Success of Enrollees by Sex Philadelphia, 1969 and 1970*

Success Measure	1969		1970	
	Male	Female	Male	Female
Weeks worked:				
Pre-	25.1	25.1	20.6	25.0
Post-	27.7	24.6	33.0	19.0
Difference	+2.6	-0.5	+12.4	-6.0[a]
Change ratio[b]	1.10	0.98	1.60	0.76
Average weekly wages:				
Pre-	$86.92	$72.25	$84.71	$73.20
Post-	$97.59	$81.30	$94.33	$78.86
Difference	+$10.67	+9.05	+9.62	+5.66
Change ratio[b]	1.12	1.13	1.11	1.08

Source: Richard D. Leone *et al.*, *Employability Development Teams and Federal Manpower Programs: A Critical Assessment of the Philadelphia CEP's Experience* (Philadelphia: Temple University Press, 1972), p. 126.

[a] By Industrial Research Unit computation.

[b] Calculated by dividing post-program enrollee figures by the respective pre-program figure.

TABLE XIII-10. *Concentrated Employment Program*
Summary of Economic Success of Negro and Puerto Rican Enrollees
Philadelphia, 1969 and 1970

Success Measure	1969 Negro	1969 Puerto Rican	1970 Negro	1970 Puerto Rican
Weeks worked:				
Pre-	27.5	13.7	23.3	20.0
Post-	27.2	23.0	27.9	26.1
Difference	-0.3	+9.3	+4.6	+6.1
Change ratio [b]	0.99	1.68	1.20	1.31
Average weekly wage:				
Pre-	$82.11	82.24	81.69	81.50
Post-	$91.01	95.32	90.48	91.19
Difference	+$ 8.90	+13.08	+8.79 [a]	+9.69
Change ratio [b]	1.11	1.16	1.11	1.12

Source: Richard D. Leone *et al., Employability Teams and Federal Manpower Programs: A Critical Assessment of the Philadelphia CEP's Experience* (Philadelphia: Temple University Press, 1972), p. 122.

[a] By Industrial Research Unit computation.
[b] Calculated by dividing post-program enrollee figures by the respective pre-program figure.

Because over 90 percent of all CEP program participants in Philadelphia were black, no statistically meaningful comparison based on racial identity can be drawn from the data. It is useful, however, to compare the gains made by black and by Puerto Rican enrollees. The comparison is shown in Table 10. The data suggest that in 1969, CEP attracted Puerto Ricans whose employment regularity was markedly lower than that of blacks, although the pre-program earnings of the two groups were similar. In 1970, the black and Puerto Rican enrollees were more nearly comparable in their labor force status prior to entering the program. In regard to post-program gains, however, the Puerto Rican enrollees in both 1969 and 1970 had a slight edge over the blacks in their relative gain in weeks worked. Neither group showed significant gains in weekly wages between the two years.

Summary

The major conclusion to be drawn from the reports is that there is little evidence upon which to base firm judgments regarding the economic impact of CEP. Few studies devoted attention to this question, and among those that did, only small samples of former enrollees were interviewed for purposes of assessing post-program economic success.

Moreover, measures of success varied widely across evaluative reports, although each study included variables pertaining to some measure of stability. In short, the evidence is limited and the conclusion regarding economic impact must be accepted cautiously.

Still, several observations based on the evaluative literature might be made. It appears that whatever economic success was registered, the gains were highly sensitive to local conditions. The structure of CEP operations in a given location and the conditions in the area labor market seem to be dominant factors determining enrollee success.

On the whole, the evidence suggests that rural CEPs had less impact upon the enrollees than did urban CEPs. This is not to say there were no gains among participants in rural CEPs; instead, it is merely an observation that the evaluation of rural CEPs revealed a generally lower range of economic outcomes than was evident in the limited evaluations of urban CEPs.

Concerning the nature of economic gains, the evaluative reports suggest that improvement in employment experience, measured by regularity of work, is more significant than improvement in wages for CEP enrollees. Where meaningful wage gains were registered, the data were affected by the effects of changes in the federal minimum wage and the trend in wages for the economy at large—two factors that would contribute to upward wage adjustments for the CEP target population in the absence of the program.

Except in Philadelphia, the evidence suggests that female CEP enrollees in urban areas experience slightly greater relative gains than men. Also, except for rural areas, program completers show gains which exceed those of noncompleters. Again, however, these conclusions are based on very limited evidence and may require modification in the light of more comprehensive data.

Finally, the evaluative reports reviewed for this summary contain little data that permit an assessment of the distributional impact of CEP on minorities and other enrollees. It is important to note here that CEP is now, and has been from its inception, a predominantly black manpower program. Whatever positive economic effects the program at large might have had probably helped black workers more than others simply because of the racial composition of enrollment. In the study of rural CEPs which offered a cross-racial comparison, blacks were found to benefit less from CEP than whites and Chicanos. This evidence, however, is highly influenced by the geographic location of rural CEPs and should not be taken as a reliable indicator of the relative impact of CEP on blacks and other enrollees.

NONECONOMIC IMPACT

Because CEP focuses upon the highly disadvantaged population, the program would be expected to produce positive outcomes other than increases in earnings and employment stability. Such outcomes, identified as the so-called "noneconomic" impact of training, might contribute significantly to the improvement of the post-program labor market experience of CEP participants. Despite the importance of such outcomes, however, only three studies of CEP provided information useful in measuring the noneconomic benefits of program participation. The available evidence documents the prevalence of three types of noneconomic impact: (1) use of supportive services; (2) changes in trainee attitudes toward work; and (3) nature of trainee attitudes toward the program. In almost no case are data available on noneconomic impact by race and sex.

Supportive Services

The Urban Systems Research & Engineering study of five rural CEPs revealed a significant distribution of supportive services, mainly medical care, among trainees (Table 11). Slightly more than three of every four trainees in all centers combined received a medical examination, but the incidence of this service ranged from 50 percent to 97 percent within different areas. The evidence also reveals the prevalence of dental and eye examinations provided under the auspices of CEP.

TABLE XIII-11. *Concentrated Employment Program Percent of Respondents Receiving Supportive Services in Five Rural CEPs, 1970*

Service	Average Percent	CEP I	CEP II	CEP III	CEP IV	CEP V
Medical exam	77	97	88	50	69	93
Dental exam	25	49	37	10	16	22
Eye exam	48	80	65	19	27	67
Medical treatment	7	7	9	3	7	13
Dental treatment	7	3	21	4	3	9
Glasses	11	11	19	6	7	15
Legal aid	4	2	11	4	2	1
Day care	5	3	—	3	10	7

Source: Urban Systems Research & Engineering, Inc., "The Impact of Five Rural CEPs," report prepared for Office of Policy, Evaluation, and Research, Manpower Administration, U.S. Department of Labor, 1971, p. 124.

Although trainees undoubtedly benefited from the medical examinations, the improvement in health care associated with CEP was probably limited by the low treatment rates reflected in the evidence of supportive services. Overall, only 7 percent of all trainees were treated for medical and dental problems after such health needs were identified in the medical examinations. In spite of the highly publicized health needs of the rural poor, only one percent of rural CEP funds was devoted to supportive services compared to 4 percent for urban CEPs.[27]

Further evidence of the receipt of supportive services may be drawn from a study of the Columbus, Ohio, CEP.[28] In contrast to the rural CEPs, however, only a minority of enrollees in the Columbus program reported receiving supportive services (Table 12). Of the 295 program completers, only 20 percent reported receiving any type of supportive services, and of that number, almost one-half received health care. A similar distribution of supportive services was evident among program dropouts, although the number of such persons was less than one-half of the number of completers. In view of the often repeated lament that many disadvantaged workers have difficulty finding and keeping jobs because of child-care problems, it may seem odd that so few trainees in either the urban or rural CEPs received day care assistance. In the case of Columbus, the paradox might be explained by the disproportionately large number of young men enrolled in the program. It is more difficult to provide an explanation for the limited use of day care facilities in rural CEPs, except that in such areas the long distance typically traveled by trainees to the program might necessitate the use of a family member for child-care responsibilities.

TABLE XIII-12. *Concentrated Employment Program*
Percent of Enrollees Receiving Supportive Services
Columbus, Ohio, 1970

Enrollees	Completers	Dropouts
Received supportive services:	20	10
Health care	9	5
Day care	8	1
Legal aid	4	4
Did not receive services	74	70
Number in sample	295	93

Source: Morgan V. Lewis *et al., Recruiting, Placing, and Retaining the Hard-to-Employ* (University Park: Institute of Research on Human Resources, Pennsylvania State University, 1971), p. 148.

27. Urban Systems Research & Engineering, Inc., *op. cit.*, p. 124.

28. Morgan V. Lewis *et al., Recruiting, Placing, and Retaining the Hard-to-Employ* (University Park: Institute of Research on Human Resources, Pennsylvania State University, 1971), p. 148.

Evidence on Trainee Attitudes

One of the most important noneconomic effects is the impact of CEP on trainee attitudes toward work. Positive and strongly held work attitudes are considered essential for improving the quality of the labor market experience of the disadvantaged. The study of CEP in Columbus, Ohio, produced measures of work attitudes among 232 trainees interviewed between January and June 1969.[29] Both completers and dropouts scored high on several tests used to measure positive work attitudes. The strength of work attitudes, however, depended heavily upon the nature of the post-CEP employment experience. Trainees who acquired and kept a job after leaving the program had more positive attitudes than those who did not find jobs. In addition, although the post-CEP work attitudes were positive, the investigators found evidence that such attitudes were less positive than pre-CEP attitudes as a result of participating in the program. Most of the apparent negative effects were concentrated among program dropouts and seemed strongly influenced by job prospects.

Similar mixed effects of CEP upon work attitudes were observed among rural participants. Of the program completers, 43 percent reported an increase in job satisfaction, and 20 percent noted a decline in satisfaction after leaving the program. Among dropouts, 37 percent experienced an increase, and 18 percent reported a decline in post-program job satisfaction. Such differences might, on balance, affect the prospects for job retention among former program participants.

Finally, only one study estimated the degree of impact upon trainee attitudes toward the program itself.[30] The evidence revealed that one-half of all trainees had positive attitudes toward their training experience, whereas one-fifth were negative toward the program. These attitudes seemed to be determined largely by the quality of the interaction between CEP staff members and the trainees. The willingness of staff members to help trainees find jobs proved very important in conditioning enrollee attitudes toward CEP. In cases where staff assistance was less than enthusiastic or where the jobs obtained were less than that desired by the enrollees, negative attitudes toward the program were generated.

---

29. *Ibid.*, pp. 122-128.

30. System Development Corporation, "Impact of Selected Urban CEPs," *op. cit.*, p. 71.

CHAPTER XIV

Work Incentive Program

by
Peter P. Amons
Research Associate
Under the Direction of
Herbert R. Northrup

The 1967 amendments to the Social Security Act authorized the creation of the Work Incentive Program (WIN) to serve exclusively the recipients of Aid to Families with Dependent Children (AFDC).[1] It was hoped that training would provide the target population—welfare recipients—with the necessary skills and attitudes to become employable. The primary goal of WIN was to train and place enrollees in jobs, thereby reducing both an individual's dependency on welfare and the number of families receiving public assistance. As one would expect, WIN has had a special significance to women, many of whom were minorities, because AFDC recipients were the target population.

NATURE OF THE PROGRAM

The original enabling legislation provided that "appropriate" persons receiving welfare be referred to WIN by the local public assistance agencies. Unemployed fathers were to be referred within 30 days of the receipt of assistance. Requirements for women were much less rigorous and the program, at that time, was considered to have an "essentially voluntary nature."[2] In 1971, the original enabling legislation was amended by the Social Security Act (Talmadge amendments) to refer welfare people directly to jobs and to make referral to WIN mandatory for most AFDC recipients; continuing welfare support was contingent upon referral to WIN.

The Talmadge amendments reaffirmed the primary goal of the WIN program—to reduce welfare rolls by increasing recipients' earned income. Therefore, the most appropriate measures of WIN's performance (and those attempted by most evaluators) were post-training earnings and placement experience and observable reductions in welfare dependency. The Talmadge amendments introduced basic changes in the WIN program which will certainly have an impact upon its minority and female

1. The basis for the discussion of the background of the WIN program is from J. David Roessner, *Employment Contexts and Disadvantaged Workers* (Washington, D.C.: Bureau of Social Science Research, Inc., 1971), pp. 1-6.

2. U.S. Department of Labor, *Manpower Report of the President* (Washington, D.C.: Government Printing Office, 1973), p. 37.

enrollees. Unfortunately, there was only one study available for review which was recent enough to focus on post-Talmadge WIN (WIN II). A few of the most recent evaluative studies contain discussions of or references to the potential impact of the new policies, but none are able to support their predictions with data on earnings, placements, or reduction in welfare dependency. Consequently, this chapter analyzes WIN's impact prior to the 1971 amendments. The effect of the amendments is mentioned wherever possible, and their potential is discussed in a final section; however, any comparisons between WIN pre-amendments and WIN post-amendments must be subjective because of the lack of WIN II data.

Program Services

WIN has attempted to provide a full range of services to enrollees: orientation, supportive services, remedial education, vocational training (classroom and on-the-job), placement, and follow-up. With the implementation of the directives under Talmadge, the program has re-emphasized relevant labor market experience through increased on-the-job training. More OJT assignments in private industry (for which employers receive the 20 percent tax credit) and subsidized jobs in public and private nonprofit agencies have been made available. The program's prevocational training, which had been severely criticized by evaluators as being ineffective, has since been used more selectively.

WIN Enrollment

The Work Incentive program served 406,100 persons (first-time enrollments) and cost the federal government over $427 million through 1972.[3] Table 1 contains the WIN enrollment opportunities, first-time enrollments, and federal obligations associated with WIN for fiscal years 1968 through 1972. It was possible for first-time opportunities (number of new enrollees) to exceed enrollment opportunities (number of slots in the program) because more than one trainee may have filled a slot during the year. The 1972 data indicate a significant expansion in both enrollment opportunities and federal obligations; WIN has been one of the largest and fastest growing manpower training programs in terms of enrollment and expenditures. The more stringent referral requirements of the Talmadge amendments, coupled with the projected increases in the program's 1974 budget, suggest that WIN will continue to play an important role in the government's overall manpower training effort.

3. U.S. Department of Labor, *op. cit.*, p. 227.

TABLE XIV-1. *Work Incentive Program Enrollment Opportunities, First-Time Opportunities, and Federal Obligations Fiscal Years 1968-1972* (in thousands)

Fiscal Year	Enrollment Opportunities	First-Time Opportunities	Federal Obligations
1968	9.9	—	$9,000
1969	99.0	80.6	100,817
1970	65.7	92.7	78,780
1971	60.7	112.2	64,085
1972	149.5	120.6	174,788
Total	384.8	406.1	427,470

Source: U.S. Department of Labor, *Manpower Report of the President* (Washington, D.C.: Government Printing Office, 1973), Table F-1, p. 227.

CHARACTERISTICS OF TRAINEES

National policy of the WIN program has given WIN the responsibility for serving AFDC recipients. The demographic data of the WIN population should, therefore, have reflected the AFDC population. Table 2 contains race, sex, age, and education data of the WIN population for fiscal years 1969-1972. At the end of the four-year period, the participants were 60 percent female and 39 percent black. Black enrollment has been declining in proportion to white enrollment, and the reason for this was unclear; yet the 39.6 percent black enrollment (1971) was still well above the proportion of blacks in the total population. The 39.6 percent figure is slightly low when compared to the percentage of Negro AFDC recipients—43.3 percent (1971).[4] Spanish-speaking enrollees and Spanish-speaking AFDC recipients were both at the 16 percent level in 1971.[5]

Eighty-one percent of the AFDC population and 62 percent of WIN participants were female (1971). The disparity appeared to result from WIN's policy that only men were required to register for WIN training. The 1971 amendments' provisions for mandatory referral for women (with some exceptions) may in the future lessen the male-female disparity.

4. Auerbach Associates, Inc., "An Impact Evaluation of the Work Incentive Program, Final Report," report prepared for Office of Policy, Evaluation and Research, Manpower Administration, U.S. Department of Labor, 1972, Vol. I, p. 3-3.

5. *Ibid.*

TABLE XIV-2. *Work Incentive Program*
Percent Distribution of Enrollee Characteristics
Fiscal Years 1969-1972

Characteristics	1969	1970	1971	1972
Sex:				
Male	40.0	29.2	38.3	39.8
Female	60.0	70.8	61.7	60.2
Race:				
White	56.0	51.9	55.8	60.2
Negro	40.0	42.7	39.6	36.2
Other	4.0	5.4	4.6	3.6
Spanish surname	18.0	19.9	16.0	19.0
Age:				
Under 22	16.0	22.7	27.4	27.8
22-44	74.0	71.1	67.5	67.5
45 and older	10.0	6.3	5.1	4.8
Years of school completed:				
8 or less	31.0	23.7	19.8	16.9
9-11	41.0	44.0	42.6	41.1
12 and over	28.0	32.3	37.6	41.9
Total percent	100.0	100.0	100.0	-100.0
Total (In thousands)	80.6	92.7	112.2	120.6

Source: U.S. Department of Labor, *Manpower Report of the President* (Washington, D.C.: Government Printing Office). 1972, Table F-8, p. 268, 1973, Table F-8, p. 234; Table F-12, p. 310.

Note: Percents may not add to 100.0 due to rounding.

On the basis of age, the WIN program has been serving an increasingly younger target group. One evaluator found that the trainees 16 to 18 years of age were only one-third as likely to be placed as trainees 45 years of age and over.[6] Table 2 also suggests that the most recent participants have had higher levels of educational achievement than their predecessors. It was forecast that the Talmadge amendments' emphasis on "potential employability as a criterion for WIN participation" would result in a

6. J.David Roessner, *Youth in the WIN Program, Phase I Final Report* (Washington, D.C.: Bureau of Social Science Research, Inc., 1972), p. 5.

more employable WIN population, i.e., younger, better educated, having more work experience, etc. [7] Table 3 contains income, unemployment, and poverty-status data for the WIN population in the 1969-1972 period.

Overall, the data do not indicate a more employable group of WIN participants; however, it is too soon to evaluate the Talmadge amendments' impact upon program enrollment, as reflected by the evaluative literature. To conclude, the data suggest that the WIN program is reaching its AFDC target group with a fair representation to minorities and women.

REVIEW OF EVALUATIVE LITERATURE

The WIN program has not suffered from evaluative neglect. There were 35 studies and a host of supplementary material available for review. Fourteen reports contained post-training earnings or placement data and three contained statistics concerning reduction in welfare dependency. Table 4 lists these fourteen reports by author (see bibliography for complete listing). It also includes their dates, whether they contained post-training data on minorities or women or on observable reductions in welfare dependency, and whether or not they used control groups. The data of the reports indicate the studies evaluated WIN I and not WIN II. Even the latest study, dated April 1973, used 1970 data.[8] The only WIN II evaluation available did not contain post-program data on enrollees; it discussed the problems of implementing the WIN II changes at several program locations.[9] On the basis of geographic location, the evaluations primarily covered urban programs located throughout the United States. A few of the studies centered on rural programs and a few others used national WIN data (these latter studies proved to be the most useful).

Methodology

The majority of the evaluative studies, which attempted to measure the impact of the program, focused on the labor market experience of enrollees, i.e. post-program earnings and placement rates. A major problem encountered by evaluators who used this procedure was the

7. Auerbach Associates, Inc., *op. cit.*, Vol. I, p. 2-7.

8. Eugene Inman, *Characteristics and Components Study of Work Incentive Program Enrollees Who Terminated in 1970* (Sacramento: State of California—Department of Human Resources Development, 1973), p. 1.

9. Martin Lowenthal *et al., WIN II Initial Impact Study—Final Report* (Boston: Social Welfare Regional Research Institute, Institute of Human Sciences, Boston College, 1972), pp. 6-7.

TABLE XIV-3. *Work Incentive Program*
Percent Distribution of Economic Status of Participants
Fiscal Years 1969-1972

Characteristics	1969	1970	1971	1972
Family income:				
Below $1,000	n.a.	12.1	12.1	14.2
1,000-1,999	n.a.	23.4	21.2	19.1
2,000-2,999	n.a.	27.7	24.9	25.6
3,000-3,999	n.a.	18.7	19.2	18.4
4,000 and over	n.a.	18.1	22.6	22.8
Duration of unemployment:				
Under 5 weeks	n.a.	8.0	10.8	4.5
5-14 weeks	n.a.	15.3	15.4	10.5
15-26 weeks	n.a.	14.8	16.6	15.5
27 weeks and over	n.a.	61.8	57.3	69.4
Disadvantaged	88.0	92.6	91.8	89.9
Poverty status	89.0	95.9	94.6	90.9
Public assistance recipient	n.a.	100.0	98.3	98.6
Unemployment insurance claimant	n.a.	2.1	2.7	1.9
Handicapped	n.a.	7.5	7.9	6.2
Eligible for allowance	n.a.	67.1	57.8	95.0
Total	100.0	100.0	100.0	100.0
Total (In thousands)	80.6	92.7	112.2	120.6

Source: U.S. Department of Labor, *Manpower Report of the President* (Washington, D.C.: Government Printing Office) 1971, Table F-12, p. 310; 1972, Table F-8, p. 268; 1973, Table F-8, p. 234.

Note: Percents may not add to 100.0 due to rounding.

TABLE XIV-4. *Work Incentive Program*
Background of Data Included in Evaluative Reports[a]

Author of Evaluation Data	Contained Post-Training Data			Evaluators Using Control Groups
	Minorities	Women	Welfare Reduction	
Analytic Systems, Inc. (November 1970)	x	x		
Analytic Systems, Inc. (May 1971)	x	x	x	
Auerbach Associates, Inc. (September 1972)	x	x		
Diamond, Daniel E. (December 1971)				
Fine, Ronald E. (June 1972)		x	x	x
Franklin, David S. (April 1972)	x	x		
Inman, Eugene (April 1973)		x		
Klausner, Samuel (1972)				
Opton, Edward M. (1971)			x	
Roessner, J. David (November 1971)		x		
Roessner, J. David (November 1972)				
Schiller, Bradley (May 1970)				
Smith, Georgina (March 1972)		x		
Youmans, Rita L. (June 1971)		x		x

Source: The fourteen individual reports are cited by author in the bibliography.

Note: Studies for which no categories are checked indicate that placement or earnings data were not broken down by race or sex.

[a] These fourteen were all the studies containing post-training labor market experience data.

lack of pre-training earnings and employment history. Frequently, trainees either were unemployed for long periods of time before WIN or had never worked before. In such cases where there were no pre-WIN data, any post-training earnings then suggested significant impact. For this reason, a number of other evaluators used control groups or attempted to evaluate earnings and placement rates as a function of program participation. These latter investigators focused on the value of participating in the various program components.

ECONOMIC IMPACT

The length of time an enrollee spends in a training program and the range of services he receives, help to determine the economic and non-economic impact of that program. Most of the relevant WIN evaluations contained discussions of the trainee participation in program components, but only a few provided such statistics by sex, and none by race. Investigators often centered their discussions around the comparative value of one component over another from a social perspective rather than from an economic perspective. Nevertheless, a few studies focused on the economic value of certain components, and these results are the basis of this discussion.

The training component of WIN, including both basic education and vocational training, has long been the major one. Table 5 presents the breakdown of enrollment's component use for 1970 and 1971. The number of slots available in the basic education and vocational training components far exceeded the on-the-job training and job experience categories. In addition, 22,149 individuals were being detained in some form of holding. Evaluators were somewhat critical of the heavy use of training (especially basic education) and the under-utilization of on-the-job training and job experience. According to one evaluator, "OJT positions are not a guarantee of enrollee success, although the training is considerably more job oriented and therefore more likely to result in successful enrollee termination."[10]

The literature was generally critical of the program structure, but the evaluators recognized that they were examining WIN I and not WIN II. The few investigators who discussed the potential effects of the Talmadge amendments suggested there would be a reemphasis on actual work experience:

> It is our understanding that the Talmadge Amendments to WIN will create about 8,000 Public Service Employment (PSE) jobs and 24,000 OJT slots in the first year. Moreover, the local Labor Advisor Unit established by the amendments may bring attention to more job oriented and indi-

10. Auerbach Associates, Inc., *op. cit.*, Vol. I, p. 2-8.

TABLE XIV-5. *Work Incentive Program Enrollment Data by Component Use for April 1970 and April 1971*

Component	April 1970	April 1971	Percent Change
Orientation and assessment	6,517	8,697	+33.5
Training:			
Basic education	19,450	22,714	+16.8
Vocational training	18,901	25,860	+36.8
Other training	3,986	2,172	-45.5
On-the-job training	661	1,416	+114.2
Subtotal	42,998	52,162	+21.3
Job experience:			
Special work projects	976[a]	1,149	+17.7
Other types of work experiences	n.a.	3,503	—
Subtotal	n.a.	4,652	n.a.
Holding:			
Component holding:			
Program related (holding between components)	n.a.	7,318	—
Job ready (awaiting job placement)	n.a.	7,445	—
Holding due to problems not related to WIN program	n.a.	7,821	—
Component subtotal	15,053	22,584	+50.0
Intake phase holding	7,096	5,240	-26.2
Subtotal	22,149	27,824	+25.6
Follow-up	12,282	12,879	+4.9
In other Manpower programs	4,523	6,122	+35.4
Total	89,445	112,336	+25.6

Source: U.S. Department of Labor, "Second Annual Report of the Department of Labor to Congress on Training and Employment Under Title IV of the Social Security Act," June 1971, Table 3, p. 15.

[a] Included in total.

vidualized training as well as current labor market information specific to the WIN enrollee population. . . .With the emphasis on OJT and PSE slots, it is more likely that the proportion of successful WIN enrollee attributable to WIN would increase.[11]

The Talmadge amendments also provided for direct placement into jobs when referrals did not need training or other services. Evaluators believed this practice could have a significant impact in reducing the number of enrollees in the holding categories.

The length of time a trainee spent in WIN varied from none (immediate referral into a job) to well over 52 weeks. One evaluation, which analyzed WIN data collected by the Office of Manpower Management Data Systems (Department of Labor), found that in 1970, males stayed an average of 35 weeks in the program and females an average of 33 weeks.[12] These data are summarized in Table 6.

This was an increase of seven weeks for males and six weeks for females from 1969. It is worthy to note that placed males and placed females spent more time in training than all males and all females. This fact may be an indication of the benefit of WIN training, especially in the case of females where the difference (44.1 weeks vs. 32.6 weeks) was most significant.

A breakdown of the length of time an enrollee spent in the four major components is presented in Table 7. The mean time spent in training was 20.4 weeks for males and 19.3 weeks for females. Additional data from this report indicated that placed females spent 22 weeks in the program compared to 18 weeks for placed males. These data were supported by other evaluations, which led most investigators to conclude that females, as a group, were more dependent on training in order to obtain jobs than males.

The reasons given for females' greater dependence on training were their well-known barriers to employment: lack of employment experience, sex discrimination, and family responsibilities. These barriers were especially great for AFDC mothers.[13] The job-entry period was meant to last from 13 to 25 weeks, during which the trainees were employed (full-time usually), but were still receiving follow-up and supportive services from WIN. For both males and females, the period was about twenty weeks. The holding category meant "non-participating," which included waiting for entry into the first or any component, waiting for

11. *Ibid.*

12. Analytic Systems, Inc., "Analysis of WIN Program Termination Data—Fiscal Year 1970," report prepared for Office of Policy, Evaluation and Research, Manpower Administration, U.S. Department of Labor, 1971, p. 40.

13. Georgina M. Smith, *Job Training for Welfare Mothers—The WIN Program* (New Brunswick: Institute of Management and Labor Relations, Rutgers University, 1972), pp. 20-26.

TABLE XIV-6. *Work Incentive Program*
Data Related to Number of Weeks in Program by Sex
Fiscal Year 1970

Characteristics	Placed Males	All Males	Placed Females	All Females
Mean	39.1	35.1	44.1	32.6
Median	38.4	35.2	43.7	31.9
Number responding	2,110	8,965	2,293	12,517
Response rate	99.6	99.0	98.3	95.7
Success rate	23.5	—	18.3	—

Source: Analytic Systems, Inc., "Analysis of WIN Program Termination Data—Fiscal Year 1970," report prepared for Office of Policy, Evaluation and Research, Manpower Administration, U.S. Department of Labor, 1971, p. 41.

TABLE XIV-7. *Work Incentive Program*
Length of Time in Weeks in Components by Sex
Fiscal Year 1970

Characteristics	Male	Female
Orientation:		
Mean	3.4	3.2
Median	2.3	2.3
Training:		
Mean	20.4	19.3
Median	17.9	17.0
Job entry:		
Mean	20.5	20.6
Median	17.7	18.2
Holding:		
Mean	17.3	14.9
Median	14.3	11.7

Source: Analytic Systems, Inc., "Analysis of WIN Program Termination Data—Fiscal Year 1970," report prepared for Office of Policy, Evaluation and Research, Manpower Administration, U.S. Department of Labor, 1971, pp. 43, 44, 46, 47.

employment with training completed, or simply not participating for any reason. The evaluative literature did not make clear why the mean holding period for men (17.3 weeks) was longer than for women (14.9 weeks).

The Analytic Systems study summarized in Table 8 was the only report which contained statistics directly relating to component participation and placement rates. The term "percent participating" referred to the percent of enrollees who had participated in that component for any length of time. In the training category, it is significant that 20.6 percent of females who underwent training were placed compared to only 12.7 percent for females not participating in training. This was further evidence of the greater relative value of training to women than men. The difference in placement rates for the two groups in the job-entry category was not surprising in view of the definition of job entry. Differences in placement rates were significant in the holding component since they showed that successful terminees spent more time in holding than unsuccessful terminees.

Another evaluation which contained an analysis of the relationship among components and program completion reached the same conclusion.[14] Whether holding was the cause or effect of the different placement rates could not be determined on the basis of these data. An examination of individual cases would have been necessary for such interpretation. Unfortunately, program participation data on the basis of race were not contained in the evaluative literature, thereby making racial comparisons impossible.

Program Dropouts

An analysis of program dropouts shed light on what benefits trainees needed and proved useful for comparisons with successful enrollees. Table 9 contains dropout rates by race and sex for WIN enrollees, based on data through March 1970. The definition of a dropout was one who terminated for one of three reasons: (1) refused to participate; (2) could not be located; or (3) was denied participation by administrators because of conduct. The data indicated that the dropout rate of black males (28 percent) was significantly higher than that of the other races (19-20 percent). Turning to the females, there appeared to be no difference between blacks and whites (18 percent), although the rate for Puerto Rican women was considerably lower (10 percent). Overall, it seemed that females were less likely to drop out than males. It was not clear why black males were more apt to leave WIN than males of other races. The evaluative literature clearly indicated, however, that female dropout rates were lower than male because women were more dependent

14. Inman, *op. cit.*, p. iv.

TABLE XIV-8. *Work Incentive Program*
Placement Rate by Participation and Components by Sex
Fiscal Year 1970

Characteristics	Orientation		Training		Job Entry		Holding	
	Male	Female	Male	Female	Male	Female	Male	Female
Percent participating	46	54	55	65	33	23	87	80
Placement rate of those participating	21.3	15.4	23.1	20.6	66.0	71.5	22.0	15.8
Percent not participating	54	46	45	35	67	77	13	20
Placement rate of those not participating	25.1	20.6	23.8	12.7	2.2	1.9	32.5	25.8

Source: Analytic Systems, Inc., "Analysis of WIN Program Termination Data—Fiscal Year 1970," report prepared for Office of Policy, Evaluation and Research, Manpower Administration, U.S. Department of Labor, 1971, pp. 43, 45, 46, 47.

TABLE XIV-9. *Work Incentive Program Percent Dropouts by Race and Sex Cumulative Through March 1970*

Dropouts	White	Negro	Puerto Rican	Mexican American
Males:				
Percent dropout	19	28	20	20
Total sample	4,671	1,570	270	1,150
Females:				
Percent dropout	18	18	10	22
Total sample	4,039	3,770	425	552

Source: Analytic Systems, Inc., "Analysis of WIN Program Automated Termination Data," report prepared for U.S. Department of Labor, 1970, pp. 49, 52.

on training to secure employment; consequently, they were more reluctant to leave WIN.

Post-Program Earnings

Pre- and post-training earnings were the most frequently used measure of economic impact in the reports. Tables 10 through 13 contain the before and after earnings of WIN trainees.

The Analytic Systems study was the only report which contained data by both race and sex. Using the data from Table 10, the net increase in hourly earnings for urban males was 10 percent; rural males, 9 percent; urban females, 45 percent; and rural females, 41 percent. It is important to note that these data reflected only those trainees who were placed in jobs. Also, Negroes appeared to have larger increases in earnings after training than whites. Since no other evaluative study contained such data on an urban-rural basis, conclusions concerning impact, as related to location, cannot be based on this limited evidence.

Table 11 data are from the report by Auerbach Associates, a three-year impact evaluation study of WIN which collected data on a nationally representative sample of approximately 4,000 enrollees. The evidence indicates that completers of WIN training enjoyed greater post-training gains in hourly wages and higher absolute wages than noncompleters. The most significant increase occurred among female completers, who averaged a $0.53 per hour increase in income.

Table 12 suggests that both sexes, but especially women, had higher incomes after WIN training. These data, however, probably overestimated the gain, since the post-training statistics included the assumption that the entire sample remained employed for the full year.

TABLE XIV-10. *Work Incentive Program Pre- and Post-Training Hourly Wage Rates By Race and Sex*

Race & Sex	Urban Pre-Training Hourly Wage Rates	Urban Post-Training Hourly Wage Rates	Rural Pre-Training Hourly Wage Rates	Rural Post-Training Hourly Wage Rates
Sex:				
Male	$2.49	$2.76	$2.18	$2.38
Female	1.46	2.12	1.50	2.11
Race:				
White	1.91	2.35	1.82	2.20
Negro	1.55	2.17	1.79	2.27

Source: Analytic Systems, Inc., "Incomplete Study Prepared for the Manpower Administration" (1972), VI, pp. 21-24.

TABLE XIV-11. *Work Incentive Program Pre- and Post-Training Mean Hourly Wages For Completers and Noncompleters*

Wages	Completers Male	Completers Female	Noncompleters Male	Noncompleters Female
Pre-WIN Wages	$2.28	$1.45	$2.07	$1.41
Post-WIN Wages	2.43	1.98	2.11	1.45

Source: Auerbach Associates, Inc., "An Impact Evaluation of the Work Incentive Program, Final Report," report prepared for Office of Policy, Evaluation and Research, Manpower Administration, U.S. Department of Labor, 1972, Vol. I, Table 4-4, p. 4-28.

TABLE XIV-12. *Work Incentive Program Average Estimated Annual Income by Sex Pre- and Post-Participation*

Sex	Total Number in Sample	Average Estimated Income Year Prior to WIN: Earned	Average Estimated Income Year Prior to WIN: Received by Family	Average Estimated Annual Income [a]
Total sample	75	$1,785	3,635	5,091
Men	48	$2,526	4,214	5,501
Women	27	$505[b]	2,813[b]	4,712

Source: Rita L. Youmans *et al.*, *A Study of the Relationship of Overindebtedness and Garnishment to Employability Among Milwaukee WIN Families* (Milwaukee: Center for Consumer Affairs, University of Wisconsin, 1971), p. 37.

[a] Calculated at the rate of pay in first full-time post-WIN job.
[b] Two women had no previous work history.

One study shown in Table 13 examined the earnings of welfare mothers in two different labor markets in New Jersey—Paterson, a relatively stable and prosperous area, and Asbury Park, a seasonal one. The distributions of earnings of the first job after WIN were more concentrated in the higher hourly rates than were those of the last jobs after WIN. It is worth noting that the more seasonal area, Asbury Park, had lower before and after earnings than Paterson. This is additional evidence that the nature of the labor markets has had a direct impact upon WIN females' employment.

Placement Experience

The New Jersey study concluded that there were small gains in income for WIN graduates, but that the real value of the program was its ability to upgrade the trainees' job status.[15] All evaluators admitted that graduates were placed in low-level jobs, but the evidence suggested that the post-WIN jobs offered more potential for advancement than previous ones.

One evaluation, which did not purport to judge the program's performance in light of the stated program goals, examined the "interrelation of work, welfare, child rearing, and homemaking in the lives

15. Smith, *op. cit.*, pp. 17-18.

TABLE XIV-13. *Work Incentive Program Percent Distribution of Hourly Wages Pre- and Post-Training New Jersey Welfare Mothers*

Hourly Wage Rate	Asbury Park Last Job Pre-WIN	Asbury Park First Job Post-WIN	Paterson Last Job Pre-WIN	Paterson First Job Post-WIN
$1.30 or less	28.0	2.4	6.8	2.7
1.31-1.50	18.7	21.4	16.2	9.3
1.51-1.70	25.3	19.0	39.2	9.3
1.71-1.90	16.0	14.3	17.6	17.3
1.91-2.10	4.0	23.8	8.1	25.3
2.11-2.30	4.0	7.1	6.8	14.7
2.31-2.50	1.3	11.9	2.7	10.7
2.51 or more	2.7	—	2.7	10.7
Total	100.0	100.0	100.0	100.0
Total number in sample	75	42	74	75

Source: Georgina M. Smith, *Job Training for Welfare Mothers—The WIN Program* (New Brunswick: Institute of Management and Labor Relations, Rutgers University, 1972), p. 136.

Note: Percents may not add to 100.0 due to rounding.

of low income mothers who are heads of households."[16] Table 14 contains the occupational self-classification of these Camden welfare-WIN mothers who were deferred from entering WIN, nominated to enter WIN, and actually participated in WIN. "Among those deferred, there is little change in occupational self-classification between 1969 and 1970."[17] Among the participants, the proportions in personal service and business service dropped and the proportion in the manual and manufacturing category increased. "This shift from service to industrial labor is an upgrading of skill and wage level and, most significantly, in chances for advancement."[18]

One can, however, question whether manufacturing jobs are automatically of a higher skill or always represent significant improvements in advancement potential. A stronger case for job enhancement as a

16. Samuel Z. Klausner *et al., The Work Incentive Program: Making Adults Economically Independent* (Philadelphia: University of Pennsylvania, 1972), Vol. I, p. 1-5.

17. *Ibid.*, p. 4-31.

18. *Ibid.*

TABLE XIV-14. *Work Incentive Program Percent Distribution of Occupational Self-Classification Among Females in Each WIN Status 1969 and 1970*

	WIN Status					
	Deferred		Nominees		Participants	
Highest Skill	1969	1970	1969	1970	1969	1970
Personal service	26	27	21	29	21	9
Business service	20	21	32	24	35	25
Manual and manufacturing	27	24	24	25	26	43
Other	27	28	23	22	18	23
Total percent	100	100	100	100	100	100
Total number in sample	220	229	81	84	43	45

Source: Samuel Z. Klausner *et al., The Work Incentive Program: Making Adults Economically Independent* (Philadelphia: University of Pennsylvania, 1972), Vol. I, p. 4-31.

result of WIN training was found in the study of the New Jersey AFDC mothers. It contained data which indicated that a considerably higher proportion of post-WIN jobs were in the technical and managerial occupations than were the pre-WIN jobs.[19]

The placement rate is another frequently used measure of a manpower training program's effectiveness. One study which measured the placement rate of 32 urban WIN programs arrived at a placement rate of 76 percent.[20] The 76 percent included those who dropped out of training to accept employment. Whether it was fair to include these dropouts in the placement statistics was disputed. Some evaluators argued that because noncompleters who accepted employment did not receive the full benefits of the program, WIN administrators should not have counted them as part of the placement record. The broader view taken by other evaluators was that many noncompleters left WIN as soon as they felt skilled enough to function on a job, and therefore, they should be classified as placements. The Schiller study

19. Smith, *op. cit.*, p. 136.

20. Bradley Schiller, *The Impact of Urban WIN Programs—Phase II Final Report* (Washington, D.C.: Pacific Training and Technical Assistance Corporation, 1972), p. 17.

also noted that only 39 percent of trainees completed training and only 29 percent were placed in jobs by WIN. Again, the 29 percent terminal rate did not include dropouts who located employment on their own.

Table 15 data indicate that there were no significant differences in placement rates between blacks and whites. On the other hand, the females' rate of 18 percent was considerably lower than the 24 percent for males, apparently the result of females' traditional barriers to employment. The placement rates of the other minorities categories differ significantly from the norm, but the investigator mentioned that the sample sizes in these groups were too small from which to draw conclusions.

The two Analytic Systems studies separated the Spanish surnamed terminees to discover whether Puerto Ricans and Mexican Americans

TABLE XIV-15. *Work Incentive Program Placement Rates by Race and Sex 1970*

Race & Sex	1970 Placement Rate (Percent)	Overall Sample[a] (1970)	Placement Rate As of March 1970 (Percent)	Overall Sample[a] (as of 3/70)
Male:				
White	25	5,989	24	4,671
Negro	22	2,257	25	1,570
Other	17	434	18	285
Total	24	8,680[b]	24	6,526
Female:				
White	18	5,751	17	4,039
Negro	19	6,119	19	3,770
Other	14	367	14	340
Total	18	12,237[b]	17	8,149

Source: Analytic Systems, Inc., "Analysis of WIN Program Termination Data—Fiscal Year 1970," report prepared for Office of Policy, Evaluation, and Research, Manpower Administration, U.S. Department of Labor, 1971, p. 49 and "Analysis of WIN Program Automated Termination Data," report prepared for U.S. Department of Labor, 1970, p. 49.

[a] Samples include both placed and unplaced individuals.
[b] Samples exclude Spanish surnamed.

had placement rates comparable to blacks and whites. Their data indicated a 10 percent placement rate for Puerto Rican males and an 18 percent rate for Chicano males. A 6 percent rate for Puerto Ricans and a 15 percent rate for Mexican Americans were found for women.[21] The investigators concluded that the differences among the races were significant and that Puerto Ricans were less likely to be placed than any other minority.[22] These results were qualified, however, by the evaluators' observation that two-thirds of the Puerto Rican sample pertained to the WIN program in Puerto Rico, not in the continental United States. They believed the very low placement rate of WIN enrollees in Puerto Rico lowered the results for the entire Spanish surnamed group.

Reduction in Welfare Dependency

The Work Incentive program was "designed to move an estimated 1.1 million adults on welfare rolls to economic self-sufficiency through job training and employment."[23] Therefore, an observable reduction in welfare dependency or a decrease in the number of AFDC recipients were two important measures of WIN's economic effectiveness. The more common measures of a manpower training program's economic impact, pre- and post-training earnings and placement rates, were not sufficient to assess WIN's impact. These measures alone did not indicate whether a trainee's new job and earnings were enough to remove him from welfare, or at least to reduce his welfare dependency.

According to the Department of Health, Education and Welfare, public welfare agencies closed approximately 14,800 cases, following participation in WIN, which resulted in an estimated savings in welfare benefits of $38 million.[24] Reportedly, payments have been reduced in additional cases, but the amount of resulting savings is not known.[25] A later source indicated that for all cases closed through December 1970, the total annual savings were $50 million.[26]

21. Analytic Systems, Inc., "Analysis of WIN Program Termination Data," *op. cit.*, p. 50; and "Analysis of WIN Program Automated Termination Data," *op. cit.*, p. 52.

22. Analytic Systems, Inc., "Analysis of WIN Program Automated Termination Data," pp. 52-53.

23. U.S. Department of Labor, *Manpower Report of the President* (Washington, D.C.: Government Printing Office, 1971), p. 52.

24. *Ibid.*, p. 53.

25. *Ibid.*

26. U.S. Department of Labor, "Second Annual Report of the Department of Labor to the Congress on Training and Employment Under Title IV of the Social Security Act," June 1971, p. 25.

For a case to be closed, earnings would have had to at least equal the assistance payments, work expenses, and the mandatory disregarding of certain earned income (the incentives to participate in WIN). In sum, government statistics indicated considerable savings in welfare costs attributable to trainees' participation in WIN. Few of the evaluation reports included discussions of welfare reduction and still fewer presented hard data to support their conclusions.

Among those including such data was an investigator of the WIN program of certain counties in California. He found that the number of cases closed after participation in WIN was "miniscule."[27] The data summarized in Table 16 indicated that of the total number of welfare caseloads in WIN counties as of December 1970, only 5,943 cases, or 1.4 percent of the total caseload, were closed. The data also show that the results for males were considerably better than for females, which supported the generally accepted view that it was easier for males to become self-sufficient than females. A flaw in Opton's analysis, however, appears to be the lack of additional data concerning reductions in welfare dependency. There may have been a significant number of persons who had higher earnings after WIN and less welfare income, yet not enough to leave the welfare rolls entirely.

Another evaluator obtained statistics concerning post-WIN welfare participation for a national sample of 1,715 enrollees from October 1969 to September 1971.[28] It was found that 74 percent of the enrollees would continue to receive some amount of public assistance throughout the first year after termination.[29] Of the 74 percent still receiving welfare, 51 percent would be working during that time.[30]

The evaluator also stated that ". . . by 12 months after termination, 15 percent of the total enrollee population will be off welfare by virtue of being employed at a sufficient wage."[31]

On the basis of sex, 80 percent of the women compared to 59 percent of the men remained on welfare for 12 months after WIN.[32] It was suggested the difference resulted from the females' right to disregard the first $30 and the following one-third of earnings; also there was a lower percentage of females than males who obtained stable employ-

27. Edward M. Opton, Jr., *Factors Associated with Employment Among Welfare Mothers* (Berkeley: The Wright Institute, 1971), p. 165.

28. Auerbach Associates, Inc., *op. cit.*, Vol. I, p. 1-4.

29. *Ibid.*, p. 4-17.

30. *Ibid.*

31. *Ibid.*

32. *Ibid.*, p. 4-20.

TABLE XIV-16. *Work Incentive Program*
Welfare Cases Closed as a Result of Program Participation in California
Cumulative from September 1, 1968—December 31, 1970

Area	AFDC Families in 12/70	Individuals Assessed for WIN	Individuals Referred to WIN or HRD	Cases Closed After WIN or HRD Referrals		
				Total AFDC	AFDC Females	AFDC Males
WIN counties only	433,852	403,903	129,864	5,943	1,725	4,218
Contra Costa county only	13,696	5,659	5,235	280	118	162
Non-WIN counties only	22,610	—	26,014	2,730	1,149	1,581
All California counties	456,662	403,903	155,878	8,673	5,799	2,874

Source: Edward M. Opton, Jr., *Factors Associated with Employment Among Welfare Mothers* (Berkeley: The Wright Institute, 1971), p. 166.

ment (27 percent and 39 percent, respectively).[33] Unfortunately, the report did not contain such data by race nor did it attempt to measure the actual dollar savings of the reduction in welfare dependency. The Auerbach Associates study concluded that "WIN participation does not result in post-WIN removal from welfare for most enrollees."[34] One of the better evaluations used a regression model to measure the impact of race, age, education, employment history, and other variables on earnings and employment of WIN-welfare mothers from nine counties in Michigan, Minnesota, and Florida. The report stated that "very few clients in our samples, either receiving or not receiving WIN services, earned enough to become ineligible for welfare. . . ."[35] This empirically based longitudinal study also produced the finding that "[p]olicies allowing clients to retain more of their earnings appear to result in increased welfare employment, at least, when favorable labor market conditions also exist."[36] The Talmadge amendments supported this belief by continuing the income disregarding incentives of females on AFDC.

The evaluator of the Asbury Park and Camden, New Jersey, welfare mothers observed that, despite higher earnings for females after participation in WIN, the earnings were still too low for self-sufficiency and family support.[37] Only 11 percent of the mothers in Paterson and none in Asbury Park were earning over $2.50 per hour; the head of a family of four would have required a 40-hour work week with earnings of $2.50 per hour to achieve the same level of living as that provided by welfare in New Jersey.[38] The evaluator did not regard the low earnings as an indictment of WIN, but rather as the result of sex discrimination in the labor market. The evidence for this view was "data indicated that one-half of the fully employed women in the United States—representing all levels of training, experience and skill—were earning less than $2.50 per hour."[39] This is, of course, an opinion based on a rather crude statistical measure. Overall, the evaluative literature was highly critical of WIN's ability to lessen welfare dependency. The survey of the available literature indicated that WIN has had almost no impact on AFDC dependency. Males were more apt to become less dependent on welfare

33. *Ibid.*

34. *Ibid.*, p. 1-16.

35. Ronald E. Fine *et al.*, *Final Report: AFDC Employment and Referral Guidelines* (Minneapolis: Institute for Interdisciplinary Studies, 1972), p. 29.

36. *Ibid.*, p. 31.

37. Smith, *op. cit.*, p. 25.

38. *Ibid.*

39. *Ibid.*, p. 26.

as a result of WIN training than females (if any reduction were observed at all). However, these conclusions were somewhat questionable because so few studies presented pertinent data. It also appeared that much of the criticism was unwarranted in view of the lack of evidence supporting or refuting such conclusions.

NONECONOMIC IMPACT

The discussion, thus far, has focused on the quantifiable economic impact of WIN on minorities and women. There were, however, noneconomic benefits of manpower training which could not be so easily quantified. The evaluative literature contained brief discussions of enrollees' perceptions of WIN and their life aspirations, employers' opinions of WIN graduates, the extent and effectiveness of supportive services, trainee characteristics associated with program success, and other noneconomic factors. The brief discussions of the noneconomic aspects of WIN were seldom accompanied by data, and the little available data were virtually never categorized by race or sex; therefore, one may assume that a fair proportion of such benefits accrued to minorities and women in view of the composition of enrollment (approximately 40 percent minority and 60 percent female).

Participants' Views of WIN

The concept of noneconomic impact remained largely undefined in the evaluative literature. This appeared to result from the unlimited number of meanings that could be attached to the word noneconomic and from the difficulty in separating economic from noneconomic factors. There was little question among evaluators, however, that an examination of trainees' life aspirations and perceptions of WIN was the first step in measuring the noneconomic effectiveness of the program. Quite a few evaluations contained the results of polls which attempted to identify the attitudes, life aspirations, and opinions of WIN enrollees. One evaluator polled both enrollees and dropouts to discover what the two groups liked most and least about WIN.[40]

Tables 17 and 18 show that the most frequently chosen benefits of WIN were the chance to advance and to train and the good content of training. The sources of dislike were more evenly divided and there were not one or two faults which could be singled out. This study also contained two polls which measured the enrollees' and dropouts' attitudes

40. David S. Franklin, *A Longitudinal Study of WIN Dropouts: Program and Policy Implications* (Los Angeles: School of Social Work, University of Southern California, 1972), pp. 154, 158.

TABLE XIV-17. *Work Incentive Program*
What Enrollees and Dropouts Liked Best About Their Experience

Characteristics	In WIN Total	In WIN Percent	Dropouts Total	Dropouts Percent
Chance to advance and train	85	37.8	13	20.3
Supportive WIN climate	32	14.2	3	4.7
Clear employability plan	3	1.3	1	1.6
Good content in training	32	14.2	13	20.3
Incentive payments	7	3.1	2	3.1
Other	49	21.8	11	17.2
No positive comment	17	7.6	21	32.8
Total	225	100.0	64[a]	100.0

Source: David S. Franklin, *A Longitudinal Study of WIN Dropouts: Program and Policy Implications* (Los Angeles: School of Social Work, University of Southern California, 1972), p. 154.

[a] Three observations are missing.

TABLE XIV-18. *Work Incentive Program*
What Enrollees and Dropouts Liked Least About Their Experience

Characteristics	In WIN Total	In WIN Percent	Dropouts Total	Dropouts Percent
Little chance to advance	10	4.5	6	9.2
Unsupportive WIN climate	22	9.8	6	9.2
Aimless employability plan	1	0.4	—	—
Unorganized and time-wasting	21	9.3	7	10.8
Useless training content	5	2.2	6	9.2
Incentive payments insufficient	23	10.2	6	9.2
Other particular comment	49	21.8	19	29.3
No negative comment	94	41.8	15	23.1
Total	225	100.0	65[a]	100.0

Source: David S. Franklin, *A Longitudinal Study of WIN Dropouts: Program and Policy Implications* (Los Angeles: School of Social Work, University of Southern California, 1972), p. 158.

[a] Two observations are missing.

toward the education and training components. Eighty-two percent of enrollees believed the education component was "very important" to obtaining employment and 82 percent preferred that it not be changed or eliminated. Forty-three percent of the dropouts believed the education component was "very important" to obtaining employment and 43 percent preferred that it not be changed or eliminated.[41] Sixty-one percent of the dropouts believed the education component was "very important-somewhat important"; however, 57 percent said they would "prefer something else" in place of it.[42] Eighty-three percent of the tainees believed the training component was "very important" to getting employment and 87 percent preferred it not be changed.[43] Seventy-two percent of the dropouts felt the training component was "very important-somewhat important" to obtaining employment and 70 percent did not prefer "something else."[44] With minor exceptions, the evaluative literature suggested that the trainees had a high regard for the WIN program and that their levels of achievement were being raised by participation in WIN. This was obviously more true for successful graduates and enrollees than dropouts, as the preceding statistics suggested.

Although the evaluative reports did not contain any significant evidence of noneconomic benefits broken down by race, the evaluators noted a number of such benefits accruing especially to females. One exhaustive study of the resocialization process of AFDC-WIN mothers and their decisions to become economically independent found that "WIN trained mothers are modernized, activistic and socially mobile than are other low income working mothers."[45] Klausner's study states:

> Low income women workers, projected into the job market through the usual economic mechanisms, tend to occupy traditional service occupations. WIN participants move from welfare to work through a politically based agency—and are more likely to become "politicized," that is, actively oriented to shaping their environment and advancing themselves socially in the process.[46]
>
> WIN participants aspire to social mobility for themselves and for their children, are active and extroverted personalities and are oriented positively

41. *Ibid.*, p. 165.
42. *Ibid.*
43. *Ibid.*, p. 167.
44. *Ibid.*
45. Klausner, *op. cit.*, Vol. I, p. xi.
46. *Ibid.*, pp. xi-xii.

> to the world of work. These indices of modernizing are more significant than purely economic considerations in motivating WIN participants. Modernizing mothers self select for the WIN program.[47]

The investigator of the New Jersey welfare mothers found that 60 percent of the mothers reported that the program had had some positive effect on their general outlooks or hopes. The change was usually described as "an improvement in their self-esteem or as a personal revitalization."[48]

Work Aspirations

A large segment of the evaluative literature provided some insight into the noneconomic effects of WIN by examining the work aspirations of WIN trainees, AFDC recipients, and the poor as a group. They also evaluated the impact of employment on the trainee (working mother usually) and her family, with the implication that if there were additional nonfinancial benefits to employment, these benefits accrued to the WIN program which provided the employment.

A central question in the work aspiration area which had a direct significance to the design of the WIN program was, "Do the poor want to work?" There was substantial evidence that the poor identified their self-respect with work to the same extent as did the nonpoor.[49] Interviews with low income mothers reinforced this conclusion.[50] It was suggested, therefore, that any time spent in the work orientation component, trying to motivate people to work, was superfluous. Evaluators cited the public's belief that the poor would rather accept welfare than work as a long-standing misconception which has been manifested in WIN's mandatory referral policies. Turning to the second category of evaluators who examined the costs and benefits of AFDC mothers' working, it was found that there were additional nonmonetary benefits of employment (and therefore of participation in WIN) for welfare mothers. They were:

---

47. *Ibid.*, p. x.

48. Smith, *op. cit.*, p. 20.

49. Leonard Goodwin, *A Study of the Work Orientations of Welfare Recipients Participating in the Work Incentive Program* (Washington, D.C.: The Brookings Institution, 1971), pp. 2-5.

50. Harold Feldman and Margaret Feldman, "A Study of the Effects on the Family Due to Employment of the Welfare Mother," report prepared for Office of Research and Development, Manpower Administration, U.S. Department of Labor, 1972, Vol. I, pp. 60-70.

1. Working mothers felt their children had more respect for them since they were working.
2. Their children were doing as well in school as those of the nonemployed women, were in more school activities, and were looking forward to more education.
3. The women had a higher level of self-esteem and did not lose their feminine qualities when they became more active in the work world.
4. They were interested in getting even more education and training.
5. Working mothers reported fewer physical illnesses.[51]

On the other hand, the AFDC mothers reported that working would have been difficult when their children were sick and they would have had less time to cook good meals and less time for their families. Another cost may have resulted—the data indicated that marriage was less of a source of satisfaction for working mothers than for nonworking mothers.[52]

Factors Associated with Success in WIN

One evaluator, who sampled nationwide 704 white and 212 black female WIN enrollees, attempted to identify characteristics of WIN enrollees that affected their success in the program.[53] Success was defined as program completion and placement in a job. It was found that younger females were not as successful as older females and that education and prior work experience were directly related to program completion and employment. These conclusions were also supported by other evaluators.[54]

The North Star study found that measures of self-confidence were related to success for white females, but that no such relationship existed for black women. It concluded that, on the whole, attitudes toward work, welfare, and WIN were not good predictors of enrollee completion and placement. Data indicated that the work aspirations of WIN enrollees who found jobs were not different from those enrollees who were not able to obtain jobs. It was believed that placement should be reflected in terms of increased feeling of self-worth, beneficial effects on the children, and improvement in family stability. Such improvements did occur, but the report concluded that the improvement was not related to whether enrollees got jobs and that "the findings of this study suggest that the WIN program is not effective in bringing about positive changes in en-

51. *Ibid.*, p. v.

52. *Ibid.*

53. Guy H. Miles and David L. Thompson, *The Characteristics of the AFDC Population That Affect Their Success in WIN* (Minneapolis: North Star Research and Development Institute, 1972), p. 1.

54. Inman *et al.*, *op. cit.*, pp. iii-iv.

rollees' attitudes toward work."[55] First, as Goodwin and others indicated, there was no difference between the poor and nonpoor's work ethic; consequently, the alleged failing was meaningless. Second, the subjects were all interviewed after entering WIN, so it is possible that any change in attitude associated with employment would have already occurred primarily in anticipation of that employment. The statement, "there appears to be no support within our findings for the assumption that a move from welfare to a job will result in these secondary gains," leads only to inaccurate implications.[56]

Employers' Views of WIN Trainees

Only one evaluator expressly studied the attitudes of employers toward disadvantaged workers, in general, and WIN graduates, specifically.[57] He found that one-half of the employers interviewed thought it was a "good idea" to change the hours or rules for disadvantaged workers so they could hold down jobs. Another 12 percent said that it depended on the circumstances.[58]

Despite such apparent willingness to accommodate, there was little evidence that employers actually made many accommodations for WIN employees (or needed to make them). Only 5 percent of the employer respondents actually created jobs for WIN workers, 9 percent modified jobs for WIN employees, 12 percent changed hours or rules for WIN workers, and 11 percent made exceptions to stated job qualifications to hire their WIN employees.[59] The apparent reason for the actual lack of accommodation is the result of the belief of most employers (68 percent) that WIN workers were no different from most of their other workers. "Rarely did the supervisor know the employee as a 'WIN worker' . . ."; they were most often considered ". . . just like everyone else."[60] Thus, the evaluator concluded that WIN workers were not singled out by their managers because of below-average performance, nor did they manifest unusually serious problems on the job that threatened their continued employment.

55. Miles and Thompson, *op. cit.*, p. 62.

56. *Ibid.*, p. 3.

57. Roessner, *Employment Contexts, op. cit.*

58. *Ibid.*, p. 88.

59. *Ibid.*, p. 91.

60. *Ibid.*, p. 95.

Supportive Services

The guidelines by the Department of Health, Education and Welfare for WIN required certain services to be provided for participants by social service agencies. Included were child care, family planning, health-related services, homemaker services, housing improvement services, and transportation needed to make the other services accessible.[61] The lack of child care, medical services, and transportation were often cited as major obstacles to successful program completion. However, one evaluator found that "projects with more adequate supportive service components do not demonstrate higher completion rates and evidence only slightly higher placement rates."[62] It was suggested that if a program did not offer the needed services, a welfare recipient who valued WIN highly would search for those services elsewhere. The evaluator also noted that the most commonly needed service, child care, was provided by welfare and the availability of such care was assumed at WIN intake. Consequently, ". . . the availability of child care is more likely to determine who gets into the WIN program rather than who completes it."[63] Following this train of thought, supportive services would then have had an indirect impact on program completion, because they had an effect on program entrance. Most evaluators concluded that ". . . the usage of welfare-financed child care was very closely related to increased employment and earnings for AFDC female household heads. . . ."[64]

The evaluative literature contained discussions concerning what supportive services were offered by WIN, the effectiveness of those services, and the failings of those services, but no significant data were presented to demonstrate exactly how many enrollees were receiving which services. We must continue to assume that minorities and females received their fair share of supportive service benefits by virtue of the composition of enrollment.

Child care, as provided by day care centers, appeared to be the most important and needed service available to AFDC mothers. WIN trainees made greater use of day care facilities than enrollees of other man-

61. Camil Associates, Inc., "Evaluation of Supportive Services Provided for Participants of Manpower Programs—Final Report," report prepared for Office of Policy, Evaluation and Research, Manpower Administration, U.S. Department of Labor, 1972, p. 34.

62. Schiller, *op. cit.*, p. 66.

63. *Ibid.*, p. 67.

64. Fine, *op. cit.*, p. 22.

power training programs.[65] This was not attributable to WIN, however, because the services actually provided by the manpower agency were transportation allowances, medical examinations needed to determine whether a recipient was required to register for manpower services and employment, and purchase and repair of work-related equipment.[66] The child-care services were accorded them primarily because of their AFDC status; these services were provided by the local social service agencies and were available to non-WIN mothers also.[67]

Evaluators reached several important conclusions regarding child care. First, the AFDC mothers tended to prefer the more informal "in-home" child care over the closely supervised day care centers.[68] "Mothers who were more satisfied with their child-care were more likely to feel that their children were helped, or at least not harmed, by their WIN participation."[69] Another study indicated that proportionately more females than males cited child-care problems associated with WIN participation; this finding leads to the generally accepted conclusion that child care was important to females' participation in WIN and that they benefited from the child-care services.[70]

Federal regulations required that all individuals referred to WIN have medical examinations, but the medical care provided to family members was derived from their AFDC status. One evaluator contended that health-related problems were a major cause of the designation of 35,000 potential WIN enrollees as inappropriate for WIN referral.[71] He also indicated that present medical services were insufficient and that the availability of such services varied significantly among states.

A study of the health and nutritional status of 469 low income women in upstate New York indicated that tiredness, insomnia, headaches, nervousness, and obesity were more common among nonworking women.[72] Most of these cases were considered to be chronic ailments

65. Camil Associates, Inc., *op. cit.*, pp. 55-57.

66. *Ibid.*, p. 35.

67. *Ibid.*

68. William J. Reid, *Decision-Making in the WIN Program* (Chicago: School of Social Services Administration, University of Chicago, 1972).

69. *Ibid.*, p. 151.

70. Charles D. Garvin, *Incentives and Disincentives to Participation in the Work Incentive Program* (Ann Arbor: School of Social Work, University of Michigan, 1973), p. 220.

71. Auerbach Corporation, "WIN Systems Analysis: Final Report and WIN Model," report prepared for Office of Policy, Evaluation and Research, Manpower Administration, U.S. Department of Labor, 1971, p. 19.

72. Daphne A. Roe and Kathleen R. Eichwort, *Health and Nutritional Status of Working and Non-Working Mothers in Poverty Groups* (Ithaca: Cornell University, n.d.), pp. 1-2.

which could have been prevented. The implication of this and other studies was that increased medical expenditures might have provided significant benefits to enrollees.

Transportation allowances, which were specifically covered under WIN, also varied geographically. Some states provided adequate funds to cover most forms of transportation, whereas others paid for round-trip bus tickets to the program with no allowance for the extra trip the mother had to make to the day care facility for her child.[73] A study of rural WIN programs stated, ". . . [M]ore than any other problem facing rural WIN programs, lack of transportation impedes the functioning of WIN."[74] This evaluator believed that staff transportation and bus transportation had not been used enough and that the best solution appeared to be providing trainees with reliable automobiles for their own use. This seemed a drastic view even without the energy crisis.

Evaluators acknowledged the need for more extensive supportive services for WIN enrollees; yet, it was found that WIN trainees received more such services than members of other manpower programs. "The WIN 'fringe benefits,' then, appear rather generous when compared with those of some other training programs."[75] Again, these accrued to WIN individuals because of their AFDC status. Hence, many of these services continued after the trainee left the program. The evaluators also indicated that the Talmadge amendments should have a beneficial impact upon the number and quality of supportive services offered. The federal government, under WIN II, assumes 90 percent of the costs of supportive services compared to the 75 percent in the past.[76]

Discrimination in WIN

Minorities and women constituted a significant proportion of WIN enrollment, which leads to the conclusion that any racial or sex discrimination in WIN would have affected these groups. One evaluator who studied 29 urban WIN sites during the summer and fall of 1971 concluded:

> . . . no evidence of racial discrimination in WIN training allocations is observable, i.e., blacks and whites are referred to WIN training opportunities on an equal basis.

73. Auerbach Corporation, "An Appraisal of the Work Incentive Program," prepared for Office of Evaluation, Manpower Administration, U.S. Department of Labor, 1970, p. B-16.

74. William F. Henry and Guy H. Miles, *Alternatives to the Current WIN Approach in Rural Areas* (Minneapolis: North Star Research and Development Institute, 1972), p. 32.

75. Camil Associates, Inc., *op. cit.*, p. 35.

76. U.S. Department of Labor, *Manpower Report of the President, op. cit.*, 1973, p. 37.

> . . . substantial evidence exists that women are not being referred to WIN training slots on the same basis as men, even after taking account of previous background.[77]

Two explanations for the apparent sex discrimination were offered. First, female WIN enrollees were subject to the same socialization pressures as all women and may, therefore, have been conditioned to constrained occupational goals. This socialization was manifested in the training preferences the women selected. Second, this socialization pressure was reinforced by the views of the WIN staff and counselors; indeed, "the WIN staff play a significant role in guiding the training decisions made by WIN clients. . . ."[78] The sex discrimination charge stemmed from the labor market, and Schiller admitted ". . . our observations provide little guidance to a WIN program administrator who must choose between a discriminatory training curriculum which leads to employer discrimination and no job."[79] Thus, WIN may not have been introducing discrimination, but rather responding to the discriminatory realities of the labor market.

It is important to note that this study examined WIN I and that the new referral guidelines under WIN II could affect these conclusions. It is also pertinent to ask whether WIN enrollees desired jobs ordinarily held by men, were qualified to hold them, or preferred to seek more traditional employment. Given the latter case, Schiller would appear to define discrimination subjectively.

THE POTENTIAL IMPACT OF THE TALMADGE AMENDMENTS

Because of the youth of the WIN II program and the length of time necessary to prepare a thorough evaluation study of a new program, this survey of WIN literature necessarily pertained to WIN I. The more recent studies, however, occasionally contained references to the potential impact of the Talmadge amendments, and these references were cited in this report wherever pertinent. Still, there is a need to highlight evaluators' conclusions and projections concerning WIN II.

Only one investigator examined the operation of WIN II specifically, and the study evaluated the change-over process from WIN I to WIN II at several program centers.[80] It was not an evaluation of economic or

77. Only one evaluation report thoroughly examined discrimination in WIN, therefore, it is the basis of the discussion. Bradley R. Schiller, *Discrimination in the WIN Training Programs* (College Park: University of Maryland, 1973), p. 1.

78. *Ibid.*, p. 15.

79. *Ibid.*, p. 2.

80. Lowenthal, *loc. cit.*

noneconomic effectiveness. Consequently, it must be assumed that any potential impact of WIN II will accrue to minorities and women in relation to this composition in total WIN enrollment, unless evidence suggests otherwise.

Government data for the first year achievements of WIN under Talmadge are impressive. Table 19 contains the operating statistics for the first year of WIN II, ending June 30, 1973. The results show that 142,000 placements were made in jobs in one year under WIN II compared to only 85,000 placements in the preceding four years under WIN I. It is these results which suggest that the shift from a training orientation to an employment orientation has been somewhat successful.

TABLE XIV-19. *Work Incentive Program (II) Cumulative Operating Statistics as of June 30, 1973*

Characteristics	Total
Registration	1,280,000
Appraisals	526,000
Certifications	380,000
Participants	359,000
Participants placed in jobs	174,000
Unsubsidized	142,000
Subsidized	32,000
Completed job entry	67,000
Individuals terminated	282,000

Source: U.S. Department of Labor, "The Work Incentive Program and National Manpower Policy— A Working Paper for the 37th Meeting of the National Manpower Advisory Committee," prepared in the Manpower Administration, U.S. Department of Labor, 1973, p. 9.

Referral Under WIN II

The Talmadge amendments mean that a substantial portion of the female enrollment will be mandatory participants. One evaluator who measured the work aspiration and motivation levels of WIN I and WIN II females found that the aspiration levels of trainees had fallen.[81] Indeed, a number of evaluators charged that the WIN I referral process involved "creaming." The most motivated AFDC mothers volunteered for training; consequently, the results of the program did not validly reflect the

81. Garvin, *op. cit.*, pp. 41-43.

AFDC population. With mandatory referral for females in effect, it is expected that the WIN participants will be less employable than in the past, adding to the costs of the program. One evaluator concluded that since persons whose participation in WIN is self-motivated tend to value WIN training, ". . . self-selection should be the primary basis for deciding which AFDC mothers should be referred to and accepted by WIN."[82] A study which examined the legal aspects of the work and training requirement suggested, "The potential for conflict and for grievance and hearing procedures will definitely increase."[83] More litigation is expected as precedents are set and as trainees learn about their alternatives.

Work Experience and Placement

The Talmadge amendments required that at least one-third of all WIN expenditures from each year's appropriation be made available for Public Service Employment (PSE) and on-the-job training. This requirement appeared to be in response to evaluation of WIN I which indicated that classroom training was less effective than actual work experience in preparing trainees for permanent employment. PSE employment has proved to be very costly and is, therefore, used only when an unsubsidized job or on-the-job training slot is not available. In 1973 only 3,797 PSE slots were filled, although 9,000 slots were authorized.[84] Two apparent reasons for this were: (1) employers did not want to promise they would convert WIN hires to permanent status after six to twelve months; and (2) female participants disliked PSE, since they were not allowed the WIN income disregard which would be available if they took a regular job.[85]

The PSE salary ceiling has been lifted from $7,500 to $12,000 per year in response to the latter problem. Improvements in the PSE and on-the-job training components were needed and welcome, but they did not appear to be the primary cause of WIN II's impressive placement figures. The new policy of referring registrants immediately to employment, if they are judged job-ready, seems to have had greater impact.

Supportive Services Under WIN II

It has been mentioned that under the Talmadge amendment the federal government assumes 90 percent of the cost of supportive services com-

82. Reid, *op. cit.*, p. 5.

83. Associate Control, Research and Analysis, Inc., *A Legal Analysis of Work and Training Requirement Under the Work Incentive Program* (Washington, D.C.: National Technical Information Service, 1973), p. 47.

84. U.S. Department of Labor, *Manpower Technical Exchange*, Vol. V, no. 19 (October 19, 1973).

85. *Ibid.*

pared to 75 percent during WIN I. State welfare agencies are not required to establish separate administrative units (SAUs) to provide trainees with the needed supportive services at all stages of the program. A new restriction in child care has also been added by the 1971 amendments: "When more than one kind of child-care is available, the mother may choose the type, but she may not refuse to accept child-care services if they are available."[86] This was interpreted as a step in the wrong direction, since it initiated a source of conflict between mothers and WIN.[87] Another evaluator mentioned that the voucher system for child-care (in force in some WIN II sites) is ineffective since payment to babysitters is slow (over one month) and the system's procedures are somewhat complicated.[88] However, conclusions should not be based on the latter study because it included only a small sample of trainees, for a narrow span of time, from only six sites. Thus, the impact of the supportive services under WIN II (and even before WIN II) has not yet been satisfactorily determined.

Tax Incentives

WIN II provides tax credits to employers as an inducement to develop more opportunities for employable welfare recipients. Government statistics show there were 24,583 tax credit hires during the first year of WIN II.[89] In June 1973 the tax incentive was extended from participants placed by WIN to include all WIN registrants who find employment on their own. It is not yet clear who benefits from the tax credit employers or employees. If the tax credit hires are in low-level service and clerical positions, where the jobs have high turnover rates, these jobs would be a source of employment for the unskilled without the tax credit. In that instance, the tax incentive's goal of expanding employment opportunities would be unrealized.

One evaluator examined the tax credit from the employer's viewpoint, but did not address himself to the preceding issue.[90] He found, however, that only one-half of the employers in his sample had ever heard of the tax credit. Only 4 percent of the companies definitely intended

86. Associate Control, Research and Analysis, Inc., *op. cit.*, p. 49.

87. *Ibid.*, p. 48.

88. Lowenthal, *op. cit.*, p. 10.

89. U.S. Department of Labor, "The Work Incentive Program and National Manpower Policy—A Working Paper for the 37th Meeting of The National Manpower Advisory Committee," prepared in the Manpower Administration, U.S. Department of Labor, 1973, p. 18.

90. John V. Schappi, *Tax Credit for Wages Paid to Workers Hired from WIN or Welfare Rolls* (Washington, D.C.: Bureau of National Affairs, n.d.).

to hire WIN workers, and over one-half of the respondents indicated that financial assistance with on-the-job training would increase utilization of the program significantly, but an increase in the tax credit would have little impact.[91] The most frequent reasons given for nonuse of the credit were: too much bureaucratic red tape, union contract restrictions, need for skilled employees, no local WIN program, and ongoing reduction of the work force. To conclude, there has been so little research concerning the tax credit that it is impossible to determine its ultimate impact upon minorities and women.

CONCLUSIONS

The economic impact of the WIN program upon minorities and women was measured in terms of earnings, employment, and reduction in welfare dependency. Pre- and post-training earnings and employment data indicated that WIN participation had a beneficial impact upon enrollees, approximately 40 percent of whom were black and 60 percent were female. It was clear that females benefited from WIN more than males, but no such conclusions could be made concerning the differential impact by race. The evaluative literature rarely addressed itself to the question of welfare savings, but what limited evidence exists suggested that WIN resulted in little or no reduction in welfare dependency. Essentially, the success or failure of WIN depends upon which criterion is used.

WIN's noneconomic impact has not been satisfactorily quantified to determine what benefits accrued to minorities and women. Still, there was a fair amount of descriptive material available which strongly suggested that there were significant noneconomic benefits to enrollees in terms of their work aspirations and use of supportive services.

Operating statistics for WIN II in its first full year of operation indicate considerable improvement over WIN I in terms of the number of placements. The impact of WIN II upon minorities and women cannot be determined until the evaluative literature catches up to the changes in the program; however, evaluators' brief discussions of WIN II's potential impact suggest there will be significant economic and noneconomic benefits to enrollees.

---

91. *Ibid*

CHAPTER XV

Job Corps

by
Harriet Goldberg
Research Associate
Under the Direction of
Richard L. Rowan

In response to the high incidence of teenage unemployment despite a tight labor market, Title I-A of the Economic Opportunity Act of 1964 authorized the establishment of the Job Corps program for low-income and disadvantaged youth. The purpose of the program is "to assist young persons who need and can benefit from an unusually intensive program, operated in a group setting, to become more responsible, employable, and productive citizens."[1] More explicit objectives of the Job Corps include helping youth to "secure and hold meaningful employment, participate successfully in regular schoolwork, qualify for other training programs suitable to his needs, or satisfy Armed Forces requirements."[2] The participants in Job Corps are largely black males. The Job Corps attempts to reduce the handicaps faced by its enrollees in attaining and maintaining employment through intensive programs of education, vocational training, work experience, and counseling.

Eligibility for the Job Corps is based on the following criteria:

1. permanent United States residency;
2. 14 to 22 years of age at time of enrollment;
3. low income status or member of a low income family.

In addition, the applicant must be living in an environment characterized by cultural deprivation, disruptive homelife, or other disorienting conditions which impair prospects for successful participation in any other program providing needed training, education, or assistance.[3] A minimum age of 16 has been an applied standard and the government poverty level determines the guideline for income requirements.

Changes in the Job Corps Program

The Job Corps program has undergone some major alterations since its establishment. In part, modifications in the operation of the program reflect changes in the basic assumptions of the program. At the same time, there has been a movement to give all eligible individuals an equal chance to join any given program component.

1. 42 U.S.C. 2701.
2. 42 U.S.C. 2713.
3. *Ibid.*

At first, the Job Corps made a conscious effort to place youths in centers away from their homes to preclude weekend visits on the assumption that frequent contacts with their impoverished home environments would act as a restraint in their training program. High dropout rates, attributed to homesickness and the cost of transportation have been cited as reasons for changing this policy. An enrollee is now assigned to the appropriate center closest to his or her home. Nonresidential participants are now trained at some centers.

Five types of residential Job Corps centers have been established: (1) civilian conservation centers for men; (2) large centers for men; (3) centers for women; (4) residential manpower centers for men and women; and (5) residential support centers. Centers have been operated by both government agencies and private industry. The emphasis placed on different types of manpower services varies by center.

Initially, few women were sought to work in the Job Corps centers because of the difficulties associated with setting up different programs. The 1967 amendment of the Economic Opportunity Act required that women enrollees constitute 25 percent of the total enrollment by June 1968. This led to a search for potential female participants.

The Job Corps program has undergone a major change in management. In 1969, President Nixon directed the Department of Labor to assume the responsibility of the Job Corps from the Office of Economic Opportunity (OEO). Following this shift in management, the Department of Labor created residential manpower centers and residential support centers with enrollees drawn from communities in which they are located. The year 1969 also marked the closing of 59 of the 82 centers (of which 50 were civilian conservation centers), which may be attributed to pressure from surrounding communities.

Characteristics of Enrollees

Unlike most manpower programs, aggregate enrollment data along pertinent demographic variables are not presented in the *Manpower Report of the President* from the time of the establishment of Job Corps through the current fiscal year. The 1966 *Manpower Report* provides data on enrollee characteristics in the program in December 1965, but does not indicate the sex and ethnic distribution of the participants.[4] No Job Corps statistics are cited in the 1967 edition. A sample of over 3,000 enrollees serves as the basis for determining the demographic characteristics of enrollees in October 1966 by type of center.[5] The

4. U.S. Department of Labor, *Manpower Report of the President* (Washington, D.C.: Government Printing Office, 1966), Table F-5, p. 222.

5. U.S. Department of Labor, *Manpower Report of the President* (Washington, D.C.: Government Printing Office, 1968), Table F-10, p. 317.

1969 *Manpower Report* indicates that 194,215 individuals participated in the program from January 1965 through June 1968, and it provides tables of enrollee characteristics, June 1968.[6] Characteristics of enrollees for the 1968 calendar year and a total of participants for fiscal year 1969 are noted in the 1970 report.[7] The shift in responsibility of the Job Corps program from OEO to the Department of Labor is marked with the reporting of enrollee characteristics and total enrollment statistics by fiscal year. By totaling the 247,700 reported total enrollees from January 1965 through the 1969 fiscal year[8] and the total first-time enrollees in fiscal years 1970, 1971, 1972, the total enrollment in Job Corps through fiscal year 1972 is calculated as 389,000.[9]

Table 1 indicates selected characteristics of Job Corps enrollees for fiscal years 1970, 1971, and 1972, for those participating in the program in the 1968 calendar year, and for those in Job Corps in June 1968. Women have consistently comprised less than 30 percent of the Job Corps participants. Minority groups are well represented in the program; approximately 60 percent of the enrollees are black. The typical enrollee is seventeen years of age or younger and has entered but not completed high school. Thus, although a small percentage of enrollees are female, the large number of blacks and other minority group members indicates that the program is concerned with the target group reviewed in this study.

REVIEW OF EVALUATIVE LITERATURE

Most of the studies assessing the impact of the Job Corps program are based on surveys conducted by Louis Harris and Associates that provide data on employment, earnings, and noneconomic impacts.[10] This information is classified by type of center, ethnic group, and three categories of termination. The Louis Harris and Associates statistics are

6. U.S. Department of Labor, *Manpower Report of the President* (Washington, D.C.: Government Printing Office, 1969), Tables F-15 and F-16, p. 252.

7. U.S. Department of Labor, *Manpower Report of the President* (Washington, D.C.: Government Printing Office, 1970), Tables F-19 and F-20, p. 321.

8. *Ibid.*

9. U.S. Department of Labor, *Manpower Report of the President* (Washington, D.C.: Government Printing Office, 1973), Table F-1, p. 227.

10. Louis Harris and Associates, "A Study of Job Corps Non-Graduate Terminations," January 1967; "A Study of Job Corps 'No-Shows,' Accepted Applicants Who Did Not Go To A Training Center," February 1967; "A Study of August 1966 Terminations From The Job Corps," March 1967; and "A Continuing Study of Job Corps Terminations: Wave II—Initial Interview with Terminations from August 15, 1966 to December 15, 1966," May 1967; all in *Hearings on the Economic Opportunity Amendments of 1967,* 90th Cong., 1st sess., Committee on Education and Labor (Washington, D.C.: Government Printing Office, 1967), Part 1.

TABLE XV-1. *Job Corps*
Percent Distribution of Selected Characteristics of Enrollees

Characteristics	June 1968[a]	1968[b]	1970[c]	1971[c]	1972[c]
Sex:					
Male	71.0	72.0	74.0	73.8	74.1
Female	29.0	28.0	26.0	26.2	25.9
Age:					
Under 17	n.a.	n.a.	39.8	35.0	34.0
17	n.a.	n.a.	26.1	27.0	26.0
18	n.a.	n.a.	15.2	17.0	17.0
19	n.a.	n.a.	10.0	11.0	12.0
20 and 21	n.a.	n.a.	8.9	10.0	11.0
Race:					
White	32.0	31.0	26.2	26.6	34.2
Negro	59.0	58.0	60.8	60.2	62.3
Other	9.0	11.0	13.0	13.2	3.5
Spanish-speaking	n.a.	n.a.	n.a.	n.a.	10.3
Years of school completed:					
8 or less	38.0	n.a.	37.4	32.5	29.7
9-11	51.0	n.a.	56.0	58.9	61.1
12 and over	12.0	n.a.	6.6	8.6	9.1
Total	100.0	100.0	100.0	100.0	100.0
Total number In thousands	33.0	58.8	42.6	49.8	49.0

TABLE XV-1 *continued*

Source: U. S. Department of Labor, *Manpower Report of the President* (Washington, D. C.: Government Printing Office)
June 1968 data: January 1969, Table F-15, p. 252;
1968 data: March 1970, Table F-19, p. 321;
1970 data: April 1971, Table F-14, p. 311;
1971 data: March 1972, Table F-8, p. 268;
1972 data: March 1973, Table F-8, p. 234.

Note: Figures may not add to 100.0 due to rounding.

[a] Includes only those in the program June, 1968.
[b] Includes only enrollees for 1968 calendar year.
[c] Includes only enrollees for specific fiscal year.

widely used in computing cost-benefits and assessing cost-effectiveness. Enrollees participating in Job Corps, since the Department of Labor assumed responsibility, have not been the subject of comparable studies.

Methodologies Used in Studies Assessed

Louis Harris and Associates conducted a series of polls of sample Job Corps terminees at different intervals after they left the program and interviewed a sample of no-shows for comparison. These surveys were conducted because of the difficulty in acquiring enrollee data on the early Job Corps program. Charles E. Goodell notes in the *Hearings on the Economic Opportunity Amendments of 1967* that "after 2 years, to get information on Job Corps enrollees who had left, the OEO was forced to resort to polls."[11] The findings of these surveys indicating the pre- and post-Job Corps experience of terminees (both graduate and dropouts) and another survey of pre- and post-application activities of no-shows (accepted applicants who did not go to a training center) are presented in tables by race and sex. Little if any analysis or conclusions are included in the presentation.

Follow-up studies were conducted of the August and November 1966 terminees six, twelve, and eighteen months after they left the program. Smaller samples of ex-corpsmembers were interviewed in each subsequent poll. In the later surveys, those who remained in the program less than three months act as a control. Early terminees are a better comparative group than no-shows, since 39 percent of those who did not enter the program did so because they were offered a job.[12]

The Louis Harris and Associates studies provide data on the labor market experience of Job Corps participants and attempt to develop measurements of better citizenship. The data obtained in these interviews provide the most comprehensive information available on the program.

Glen G. Cain used the Louis Harris and Associates data on Job Corps terminees six months after separation from the program in calculating benefit/cost estimates.[13] Cain was only interested in increases in earnings, not in general improvements in civic behavior. Two alternative measures of improved earnings were used—based on educational gains and comparisons of wages earned by ex-corpsmembers and no-shows as reported in the Harris polls. Earnings attributable to educational advancement

11. U.S. Congress, *Hearings on the Economic Opportunity Amendments of 1967*, 90th Cong., 1st sess., House Committee on Education and Labor (Washington, D.C.: Government Printing Office, 1967), Part 1, p. 774.

12. Louis Harris and Associates, "A Study of Job Corps 'No-Shows,' " *op. cit.*, p. 284.

13. Glen G. Cain, "Benefit/Cost Estimates for Job Corps," Institute for Research on Poverty, University of Wisconsin, 1968.

made in the Job Corps were based on a study of four region/color groups (whites and nonwhites living in the North and South).

In his doctoral dissertation, Stephen R. Engleman uses multiple regression analysis to determine the impact of the program.[14] He considers the relationship of educational gains and length of stay in the program and how these improvements are related to increases in earnings. Separate regressions were estimated for whites and nonwhites. The independent variables in the regression used to explain past Job Corps earnings included age, race, region, years of schooling, size of city, and Job Corps center attended. Data obtained from the Louis Harris and Associates surveys served as the basis for analysis; the control group consisted of corpsmen who stayed in the program less than three months.

Earnings gains were estimated by the Resource Management Corporation based on the Louis Harris and Associates sample data for eighteen months after termination.[15] In an attempt to compare the impact of the Job Corps with another youth program, the Neighborhood Youth Corps, the RMC analysis computed net program effects on hourly wages for both white and black Job Corps participants.

A series of "in-house" reports are some of the few studies that are not based on the findings by Louis Harris and Associates. Data were collected in October 1966 and January 1967 from a sample of more than 2,000 corpsmembers. *A & R Reports #5* dealt with educational gains measured in the difference in achievement levels of tests administered at two points in time.[16] *A & R Reports #11,* a Job Corps cost-benefit study, computed net lifetime benefits by discounting wage compensation gains compounded over a working lifetime of 47 years (18 to 65).[17]

Other reports on the Job Corps are primarily descriptions of service. Unco evaluated the effectiveness of pre- and post-enrollment services based on interviews with ex-corpsmembers and administrative, support, and volunteer personnel.[18] The General Accounting Office conducted

14. Stephen R. Engleman, "An Economic Analysis of the Job Corps," Ph. D. dissertation, University of California at Berkeley, 1971.

15. Harry R. Woltman and William W. Walton, "Evaluations of the War on Poverty—The Feasibility of Benefit-Cost Analysis for Manpower Programs," Resource Management Corporation, report prepared for the General Accounting Office, Bethesda, 1968.

16. Office of Economic Opportunity, *A & R Reports #5* (Washington, D.C.: Evaluation and Research Branch, Plans and Evaluation Division, Plans and Programs Directorate, Job Corps, Office of Economic Opportunity, 1967).

17. Office of Economic Opportunity, *A &R Reports #11* (Washington, D.C.: Evaluation and Research Branch, Plans and Evaluation Division, Plans and Programs Directorate, Job Corps, Office of Economic Opportunity, n.d.). pp. 7-8.

18. Unco, Inc., "Evaluation of the Effectiveness of Pre- and Post-Enrollment Services to Job Corps Enrollees," final report prepared for Office of Policy, Evaluation and Research, Manpower Administration, U.S. Department of Labor, Washington, D.C., 1972.

a separate analysis of some Job Corps centers with the major focus of the GAO studies on the efficiency of operation of the program and not on ascertaining differential impacts.

Differential impacts have been assessed for whites and nonwhites. Determining the relative impact by sex is limited by the extent to which separate analysis is provided on women's centers. The literature on the Job Corps is basically restricted to studies of the early programs.

ECONOMIC IMPACT

The major objective of the Job Corps is to reduce the psychological, environmental, educational, and institutional barriers to full labor market participation of Job Corps enrollees. The program's impact on employment and earnings has been discussed in the literature. Differential impacts by race and, to a limited degree, by sex (when evaluating different types of centers) have been ascertained. In comparing the labor market experience of Job Corps enrollees and control groups, initial positive gains were found to be attributable to the program. These gains, however, were not found to be of lasting duration.

Wages

The Harris polls provide the data used in most of the analyses of improvements in wage rates. Changes in wages are calculated by subtracting the median hourly wage received prior to enrollment from the median wage after termination from Job Corps. A comparison of the net differences in median wage rates of Job Corps completers and control groups (for the same period) indicate gains in hourly earnings attributable to Job Corps participation.

Table 2 indicates the changes in hourly wages of no-shows. The sample group of 517 potential Job Corps enrollees, whose application screening interviews were conducted in 1965 and 1966, was 87 percent male and 60.5 percent black. The no-shows serve as a comparison or control group when analyzing the results of Job Corps enrollees. It is important to remember, however, that many of these individuals did not join the program because they had obtained a job while waiting to hear about placement in a center.

Interviews were conducted in February and May of 1967 with excorpsmen who had left centers six months earlier (August and November 1966, respectively). Some of the polls were conducted by telephone in an attempt to overcome an urban bias. Potential interviewees were telegraphed and asked to call New York collect to answer some questions on their Job Corps experience. Of the 1,254 completed interviews, 91

TABLE XV-2. *Job Corps*
Median Hourly Wage Rate of "No-Shows" by Race and Sex

Race and Sex	Median Wage of No-Shows Prior to Application[a]	Median Wage Rate of No-Shows at Time of Interview[b]	Net Difference
Men	$1.17	$1.44	+0.27
Women	1.14	1.25	+.11
Negro	1.14	1.39	+.25
White	1.19	1.50	+.31
Total	1.17	1.42	+.25

Source: Louis Harris and Associates, "A Study of Job Corps 'No-Shows,'" in *Hearings on the Economic Opportunity Amendments of 1967*, 90th Cong., 1st sess., Committee on Education and Labor (Washington, D. C.: Government Printing Office, 1967), Part I, pp. 259, 301.

[a] Base 30 percent employed.
[b] Base 60 percent employed.

percent were male and more than one-half were black.[19] Table 3 shows the median wage of Job Corps enrollees before they entered the program and six months after they left.

In comparing the net differences in earnings of no-shows (Table 2) and six-month terminees (Table 3), there seems to be little change in hourly earnings that can be attributed to Job Corps. The gains in median wages for both blacks and whites in the no-show group were higher than for Job Corps participants. This may reflect, however, the longer time that no-shows were in the labor force. The few women Job Corps enrollees that participated in the sample seem to have made some positive gains compared to women who did not join the program.

Job Corps graduates made greater gains in wage rates than dropouts and discharges, thus reflecting a possible relationship between length of stay in the program and gains in wages. Black dropouts and enrollees discharged by program administrators before completion made the smallest improvement in hourly earnings six months after leaving Job Corps.

Harris conducted polls of August and November 1966 terminees, twelve and eighteen months after they left the program.[20] Table 4 indi-

19. Discrepancies exist in the total number in the sample and the sum of the component parts.

20. Louis Harris and Associates, Inc., "A Study of the Status of August 1966 Job Corps Terminees 18 Months After Termination," report prepared for Job Corps, 1968.

TABLE XV-3. *Job Corps Median Hourly Earnings Of August and November 1966 Terminees*

	Median Hourly Earnings of Enrollees Employed Prior to Enrollment	Median Hourly Earnings of Enrollees Employed 6 months after Termination	Net Difference
Graduates:	$1.18	$1.48	+0.30
Negro	1.20	1.49	+.29
White	1.14	1.46	+.32
Dropouts:	1.18	1.39	+.21
Negro	1.17	1.36	+.19
White	1.18	1.40	+.22
Discharges	1.18	1.34	+.16
Sex/type of center:			
Men	1.19	1.42	+.23
Urban	1.21	1.46	+.25
Conservation	1.17	1.37	+.20
Women	1.06	1.27	+.21
Race:			
Negro	1.18	1.41	+.23
White	1.17	1.41	+.24
Total	1.18	1.41	+.23

Source: Louis Harris and Associates, "A Continuing Study of Job Corps Terminations: Wave II—Initial Interviews with Terminations From August 15, 1966 to December 15, 1966," in *Hearings on the Economic Opportunity Amendments of 1967*, 90th Cong., 1st sess., Committee on Education and Labor (Washington, D. C.: Government Printing Office, 1967), pp. 484, 500.

[a] Base 44 percent August and 49 percent November Terminees employed.

[b] Base 58 percent August and November Terminees employed.

cates the average hourly wage of 668 individuals who had been interviewed at the twelve-month point and 430 who participated in the last survey.

In assessing the relative impact of the program on the participants, it is important to note that men continue to earn more per hour than women and that whites generally do better than blacks. It is questionable that increases in hourly earnings can be attributed to participation in the program; among male terminees for which data is provided, the relationship of length of time spent in the program and wage rates is not maintained over the eighteen-month period after termination.

TABLE XV-4. *Job Corps Average Hourly Wage Pre-and Post-Training*

		After Termination			Net Increase
	Pre-Job Corps	6 Months	12 Months	18 Months	from Pre-Job Corps
Men:	$1.23	$1.56	$1.80	$1.90	+0.67
Graduates	1.24	1.63	1.92	2.12	+.88
Dropouts (in Job Corps over 3 months)	1.24	1.54	1.78	1.76	+.52
Dropouts (in Job Corps less than 3 months)	1.21	1.44	1.69	1.80	+.59
Discharges	1.19	1.43	1.79	1.84	+.65
Negro	1.23	1.51	1.82	1.85	+.62
White	1.23	1.60	1.82	1.98	+.75
Women:	1.14	1.40	1.37	1.67	+.53

Source: Louis Harris and Associates, "A Study of the Status of August 1966 Terminees 18 Months After Termination," report prepared for Job Corps, 1968, p. 3.

Employment

The change in employment is the difference in the number of Job Corps enrollees (or no-shows) working at the time of their interview and the number employed prior to applying to the program. The Louis Harris and Associates surveys show the activities of no-shows and three categories of Job Corps terminees both before enrollment and at the time the individuals were polled. Adding the percentage working to the percentage unemployed indicates the proportion of those questioned in the labor force. A comparison of the percentage of Job Corps completers and control groups who are employed or seeking work indicates the impact of the program on labor market activities.

Table 5 indicates the activities of the no-shows when they signed up for the program and when they were interviewed. More no-shows tend to be working or in school at the time of their interview than when they signed up for Job Corps. The increase in school attendance was particularly notable among women and blacks. At the same time, men and whites shifted from the unemployed to the working category. Of those working before signing up, one-third were in the service industry before they applied for Job Corps and at the time of their interview.[21] The median

21. Louis Harris and Associates, "A Study of Job Corps 'No-Shows,' " *op. cit.*, pp. 257, 298.

TABLE XV-5. *Job Corps*
Percent Distribution of No-Show Activities

Race & Sex	At Time of Application[a]				At Time of Interview[b]				Net Difference Working Now—Working Pre-Job Corps
	In School	Working	Unemployed	Other	In School	Working	Unemployed	Other	
Sex:									
Men	12	31	57	2	14	63	27	3	+32
Women	4	26	69	1	10	40	29	24[c]	+14[d]
Race:									
Negro	10	32	57	2	15	61	28	4	+29[d]
White	12	25	64	1	10	59	26	11	+34[d]
Total	11	30	58	2	14	60	27	6	+30

Source: Louis Harris Associates, "A Study of Job Corps 'No-Shows,'" in *Hearings on the Economic Opportunity Amendments of 1967*, 90th Cong., 1st sess., House Committee on Education and Labor (Washington, D.C.: Government Printing Office, 1967), pp. 256, 296.

[a] Figures add to more than 100 percent as some respondents gave more than one answer.
[b] Figures add to more than 100 percent because 7 percent were both working and in school.
[c] 17 percent keeping house.
[d] Figures have been corrected due to apparent computation error.

hours worked per week was 36.2 for the total sample of no-shows, with women working a median of 23.8 hours compared to 36.9 hours for men. Males tended to work significantly longer hours.[22] This differentiation by sex is not maintained when the no-shows were interviewed; both men and women worked about 36.5 hours per week.[23]

Table 6 summarizes the activities of Job Corps participants before and six months after they enrolled in the program. An increase in employment is indicated, especially for white graduates and women. There is a notable decrease in employment of black dropouts. The service industry still provides the bulk of employment opportunities; there is, however, a sizable increase of workers in the machine trades and structural work.[24] In assessing the labor market impact, it should be noted that Job Corps terminees also experienced a decrease (though small) in the number of hours worked per week. There is no sizable difference, however, in hours worked per week by sex.[25]

The activities of eighteen-month terminees are indicated in Table 7. A larger percentage of white than black males were employed and a correspondingly smaller percentage were unemployed. Men, however, continue to do better in the labor market than women. A comparison with Table 6 shows that gains attributable to length of time spent in the program are not maintained over the year.

Sar A. Levitan and Garth L. Mangum attempted to draw conclusions from the data provided in the Harris polls. They found that employment status of the August 1966 terminations appears to be positively correlated with the time spent in the program and not retained over an extended period of eighteen months. Women showed greater employment gains than men but this relationship was only temporary because women left the labor force for reasons of pregnancy or marriage. The employment record of blacks is not as good as whites; whereas the proportion of blacks working decreased after eighteen months, the proportion of whites increased.[26]

The initial increase in employment among Job Corps terminees reflects the job placement ability of the agencies responsible for getting partici-

22. *Ibid.*, p. 258.

23. *Ibid.*, p. 299.

24. Louis Harris and Associates, "A Continuing Study of Job Corps Terminations," *op. cit.*, pp. 482, 495.

25. *Ibid.*, pp. 483, 497.

26. Sar A. Levitan and Garth L. Mangum, "Job Corps," in *Federal Work Training Programs in the Sixties* (Ann Arbor: Institute of Labor and Industrial Relations, University of Michigan and Wayne State University, 1969), pp. 201-204.

TABLE XV-6. *Job Corps*
Percent Distribution of Pre- and Post-Job Corps Activities
August and November Terminees

Characteristics	Activities Before Entering Job Corps				Activities 6 Months After Job Corps				Net Difference	
	Working	In School	Unemployed	Other	Working	In School	Unemployed	Other	Working Now—Working Before Job Corps	In School Now—In School Before Job Corps
Graduates:	53	10	36	1	65	8	27	2	+12	-2
Negro	58	10	32	—	68	9	24	2	+10	-1
White	45	9	45	1	62	7	32	3	+17	-2
Dropouts:	48	9	41	2	53	10	39	1	+5	+1
Negro	53	11	35	1	52	10	41	1	-1	-1
White	43	8	48	1	54	10	39	2	+11	+2
Discharges	49	12	38	1	55	10	37	1	+6	-2
Current status:										
Working	58	7	34	1	n.a.	n.a.	n.a.	n.a.	n.a.	n.a.
In school	39	25	34	2	n.a.	n.a.	n.a.	n.a.	n.a.	n.a.
Unemployed	40	9	50	1	n.a.	n.a.	n.a.	n.a.	n.a.	n.a.
Sex:										
Men	51	10	38	1	58	9	35	1	+7	-1
Women	30	13	56	1	48	12	39	6	+18	-1
Race:										
Negro	54	11	34	1	58	9	34	1	+4	-2
White	44	8	47	1	57	9	36	2	+13	+1
Total	49	10	40	1	58	9	35	2	+9	-1

Source: Louis Harris and Associates, "A Continuing Study of Job Corps Terminations: Wave II—Initial Interview with Terminations from August 15, 1966 to December 15, 1966," in *Hearings on the Economic Opportunity Amendments of 1967,* 90th Cong., 1st sess., House Committee on Education and Labor (Washington,D.C.: Government Printing Office, 1967), pp. 481, 493.

Note: Figures may not add to 100 due to rounding.

TABLE XV-7. *Job Corps*
Percent Distribution of Terminee Activities
18 Months After Termination

Terminees	Excludes Military			Married— Not Working	Includes Military			
	Employed	In School	Unemployed		Employed	In School	Military	Unemployed
Graduates	62	4	35	—	48	3	22	27
Dropouts (in program 3 months or more)	59	5	38	—	n.a.	n.a.	n.a.	n.a.
Dropouts (in program less than 3 months)	59	3	39	—	n.a.	n.a.	n.a.	n.a.
Discharges	60	9	34	—	55	8	9	31
Negro	54	6	41	—	n.a.	n.a.	n.a.	n.a.
White	68	2	31	—	n.a.	n.a.	n.a.	n.a.
Total male	60	4	37	—	49	3	19	30
Total female	47	6	39	8	—	—	—	—

Source: Louis Harris and Associates, "A Study of the Status of August 1966 Job Corps Terminees 18 Months After Termination," report prepared for Job Corps, 1968, pp. 7-9.

Note: Percents may not add to 100 due to rounding.

pants jobs. The lack of sustained labor market performance can be attributed to the type and value of the training that enrollees received while in the program.

In evaluating the effectiveness of the civilian conservation center programs, the General Accounting Office found that a major deterrent to the centers' accomplishment of the primary Job Corps goal—training of underprivileged youth—was the policy of carrying out vocational training primarily within the context of conservation work projects, with little emphasis upon developing a skill training program. Many projects appeared to have limited utility toward producing skills for marketable trades.[27] In its evaluation of men and women urban centers, GAO found that graduating corpsmembers did not necessarily have the skills necessary for employment in the area of their vocational training.[28] Increases in employment were attributed to age and other factors.

In its evaluation of pre- and post-enrollment services to Job Corps enrollees, Unco found that 41 percent of the 433 ex-corpsmembers were employed (full- or part-time), 23 percent were unsuccessfully looking for work, 13 percent were doing "nothing," and the remaining 23 percent were in other activities.[29] Only 26 percent of those interviewed who were holding jobs said that they had been trained for that type of employment while in the program. At the same time, 62 percent of these participants felt it had been important to get jobs in the area of their Job Corps training.[30]

Earnings

Cain used two alternative measures of earnings improvements. One is based on educational gains achieved while in the program in conjunction with the relationship between education and lifetime earnings. The second measure of earnings gains is based on a comparison of wages earned by ex-corpsmembers with wages of a comparable group of youth with no Job Corps experience. Using data from the Louis Harris and Associates surveys of August 1966 terminees, Cain found an annual earnings differential

27. Comptroller General of the United States, *Effectiveness and Administration of the Acadia Job Corps Civilian Conservation Center Under the Economic Opportunity Act of 1964—Bar Harbor, Maine,* Department of the Interior, Office of Economic Opportunity (Washington, D.C.: Government Printing Office, 1969), p. 22.

28. Comptroller General of the United States, *Effectiveness and Administration of the Kilmer Job Corps Center for Men Under the Economic Opportunity Act of 1964—Edison, N.J.,* Office of Economic Opportunity (Washington, D.C.: Government Printing Office 1969); and *Effectiveness and Administration of the Albuquerque Job Corps Center for Women Under the Economic Opportunity Act of 1964—Albuquerque, New Mexico,* Office of Economic Opportunity (Washington, D.C.: Government Printing Office, 1969).

29. Unco, Inc., *op. cit.,* p. 3-68.

30. *Ibid.,* p. 3-67.

ranging from $187.20 to $259.60,[31] based on $0.12 an hour increase in wage rates.[32]

The Resource Management Corporation analyzed the Louis Harris and Associates data, including the eighteen months after terminations statistics. Although estimates for gains in hourly wages were calculated, a low level of confidence in the reliability of these findings was attributed to the statistical uncertainties in the data from which they were derived. Similarly, estimates of increased hours of work were subject to a high degree of uncertainty; thus, gains in earnings could not be assumed to occur as a result of working more hours.[33] The RMC Incorporated study concurs with the general finding that earnings gains are not significant after eighteen months.

In his economic analysis of the Job Corps, Engleman also used data taken from computer tapes containing personal interviews with ex-corpsmembers by Louis Harris and Associates. Separate regressions were estimated for whites and nonwhites. Included among the independent variables in the regressions to explain post-Job Corps earnings are age, race, region, years of schooling, size of city, and Job Corps center attended. The dependent variable used in the multiple regression analysis was the average monthly earnings for Job Corps terminations.

Engleman found that whites earned more than nonwhites, even holding constant such factors as years of education, region, and Job Corps experience if they stay in the program for more than one year.[34] Unfortunately, the Job Corps program has a problem of a high dropout rate among its participants. As Table 8 indicates, there is a reported drop in monthly earnings by white enrollees who stay in the program seven to twelve months, while the earnings of nonwhites are closely correlated to length of stay in the program. However, Engleman does not show how long these high wage gains are maintained after termination from the program.

In summary, it has not been shown that participation in the Job Corps program has a long-term effect on the labor market experience of its enrollees. It is questionable that increases in hourly earnings can be attributed to participation in the program; among male terminees for whom data is provided, the relationship of length of time spent in the program and wage rates is not maintained over the eighteen-month period after termination. Similarly, the increase in employment cited for six-month terminees is not maintained for the following year.

A short-term positive effect on employment and earnings is indicated for those interviewed by Louis Harris and Associates. Perhaps the

31. Cain, *op. cit.*, p. 45.

32. *Ibid.*

33. Woltman and Walton, *op. cit.*, pp. 87-120.

34. Engleman, *op. cit.*, p. 62.

TABLE XV-8. *Job Corps*
Difference in Monthly Earnings of Enrollees and Controls By Number of Months in Program [a]

Enrollees	4-6 Months	7-12 Months	13-25 Months
Whites	86.50	50.00	115.30
Nonwhites	15.40	52.90	67.10

Source: Stephen R. Engleman, "An Economic Analysis of the Job Corps," Ph.D. dissertation, University of California at Berkeley, 1971, pp. 92.93.

[a] Control group—those in program less than 3 months.

labor market impact of the Job Corps program has its role in helping young men and women obtain employment when they are too young to compete for jobs. Eighteen months after leaving the program, both those who participated in Job Corps and those who did not may have overcome the age barrier.

It is difficult to discern a differential impact by sex because few women participated in the Louis Harris and Associates surveys. The analyses used in determining relative impact of male Job Corps enrollees cannot be conducted for females because data on women's centers are not provided by length of time in the program. Findings on the labor market impact of the program are generally restricted to males. When the data were categorized by race, it was found that the employment history of blacks is not as good as that of whites.

NONECONOMIC IMPACT

Changes in work attitudes, personal self-esteem, educational gains, and reduced crime rates may be the most significant impacts of some manpower training programs. The literature, however, does not focus on the noneconomic aspects of the Job Corps. Some recent reports have noted this absence. Dave M. O'Neill, in an examination of the MDTA institutional and Job Corps programs states, "Unfortunately, we have not been able to uncover any attempt at systematic analysis of the many possible noneconomic benefits."[35] Citing the difficulty of analyzing noneconomic issues and recognizing the need to include such gains where they exist,

35. Dave M. O'Neill, *The Federal Government and Manpower ; A Critical Look at the MDTA-Institutional and Job Corps Programs* (Washington, D.C.: American Enterprise Institute for Public Policy Research, 1973), p. 34.

some cost-benefit studies have used direct economic gains as a reflection of social growth. Harry R. Woltman and William W. Walton report:

> To date, it does not appear that anyone has been able to measure the effects of the Job Corps and similar programs on their participants' social responsibility. Because the evidence that is available is contradictory and the Job Corps data available to us did not shed additional light on the question, we have elected to . . . measure program benefits in terms of increased earnings. This measure includes both program objectives of increased employability and productivity.[36]

Thus, changes in labor market activities have been used as proxies for noneconomic impacts in discerning program benefits.

In an attempt to acquire additional information concerning what evidence exists of noneconomic benefits, individuals involved in the administration of the Job Corps were contacted. Unfortunately, no definitive data were offered, although several facets of possible gains were discussed. Statistics are available concerning the number of Job Corps enrollees who received medical care, but the data are insufficient for forming definitive conclusions. Letters written by former participants and case histories provide anecdotal testimony about possible gains, but the need still exists for careful analysis using a well-defined comparison group.

In the following discussion, noneconomic impacts are defined as activities which result in the removal of employment obstacles for women and members of minority groups. Of particular interest will be evidence of real or perceived changes in and impact upon:

1. job satisfaction and work attitudes;
2. educational attainment;
3. reduction in antisocial behavior;
4. measurements of responsible citizenship;
5. need and provisions for supportive services.

Ex-Corpsmembers' Feelings Concerning the Program and Changes in Work Attitudes

Louis Harris and Associates asked former participants to evaluate their Job Corps experience. When questioned six months after they left their program, more than one-half of the August 1966 terminees felt that they were better off than before enrollment. Significantly more graduates than dropouts shared this feeling; the value placed on participation was

36. Woltman and Walton, *op. cit.*, p. 81.

related to the category of termination. Approximately 25 percent felt that their situation was "about the same" as before their Job Corps enlistment, and the remainder felt they were "worse off."[37]

When questioned about the helpfulness of Job Corps training, 75 percent of the female and 64 percent of the male participants responded positively. More graduates than dropouts found their training helpful; urban centers received higher ratings than the conservation centers. Generally, a larger percentage of blacks than whites, and women than men, found the job training helpful.[38] Two-thirds of the corpsmembers thought their training was helpful, whereas only one-quarter felt that they were given enough training to get a job.[39]

In its evaluation of pre- and post-enrollment services, Unco questioned 433 ex-corpsmembers on their feelings about their present situation. Those that answered "yes, they were satisfied" comprised 43 percent of the sample; 25 percent replied "no" and that they were unemployed. The remaining 32 percent were dissatisfied and cited such factors as lack of education, want of a better job, and a need for additional skill training experience as the reasons for their displeasure.[40]

Educational Gains

Educational achievement is not a direct labor market impact of manpower programs. Yet such gains are reflected in the working life of participants. Changes in reading and arithmetic skills have been measured; records could be maintained concerning enrollees who acquire a high school equivalency diploma or return to school. Thus, the impact of basic education and programs geared toward helping Job Corps members obtain a high school diploma could be quantified.

In its evaluation of the civilian conservation centers, the General Accounting Office noted that various required educational programs were being made available to corpsmen, and participants were achieving a reasonable rate of progress in the reading program. In light of the short time that corpsmen are in the program and their general low academic level at the time of entry, few could have been expected to meet the academic program minimum goal of a seventh grade reading level.[41]

---

37. Louis Harris and Associates, "A Study of August 1966 Terminations," *op. cit.*, p. 434.

38. *Ibid.*, p. 387.

39. *Ibid.*, p. 389.

40. Unco, Inc., *op. cit.*, p. 3-69.

41. Comptroller General of the United States, *Effectiveness and Administration of the Acadia Job Corps Civilian Conservation Center, op. cit.*, p. 29.

A general lack of emphasis on the academic training program reduced the opportunity for corpsmen to achieve their maximum potential. Enrollees were often assigned to projects without regard to their vocational needs and were excused from educational classes to ensure completion of their projects. GAO found that excessive class absences by both corpsmen and their instructors existed at some centers;[42] however, neither specific examples nor data are provided to support this statement.

The Harris polls questioned terminees on their school attendance and the helpfulness of the program in preparation for school. There was little difference in the percentage of enrollees in school before and six months after participation in Job Corps (see Table 6). Of those in school at the time of their first interview, 71 percent replied that Job Corps helped them prepare for their return; of those who graduated and were continuing their education, 70 percent indicated that Job Corps "helped a lot."[43]

Educational gains was the subject of an "in-house" report based on a sample of 2,000 corpsmembers for whom achievement levels were determined in both October 1966 and January 1967. Participants were administered the Paragraph Meaning and Arithmetic Computation subtests of the Stanford Achievement Test. *A & R Reports #5* concluded that once enrollees had entered the Job Corps program, they demonstrated a faster rate of achievement than the norm of school students.[44] It was also found that education programs varied by type of center. For example, men in urban centers made the most progress, followed by men in conservation centers; women made the least achievement.[45] No data were provided on gains by racial group.

Engleman, while noting possible biases in the tests, also based his analysis of educational achievement on these exams. The data he used consisted of test scores for 712 corpsmen from six urban centers. The initial test was given to the corpsmen within the first 30 days of their arrival; the terminal test was administered during the final 60 days.[46]

In assessing the relationship between length of stay in the program and educational achievement, Engleman carefully notes that the time spent in Job Corps is not necessarily synonymous with time spent in the general education program. Formal academic classes did not necessarily begin within the first thirty days, nor did the corpsmen necessarily attend these classes until the time of the terminal test. For example, it is possible that

42. *Ibid.*

43. Louis Harris and Associates, "A Study of August 1966 Terminations," *op. cit.*, p. 428.

44. Office of Economic Opportunity, *A&R Reports #5, op. cit.*, p. 4.

45. *Ibid.*

46. Engleman, *op. cit.*, pp. 44-45.

a corpsman was in the academic program for only four months, but in Job Corps for one year. The educational gains, however, were considered in the context of a one-year study.[47]

Engleman's results, however, were consistent with the A & R study which found that the program was more successful with those who entered with achievement levels below sixth grade than with those who entered with higher achievement levels. The length of stay coefficient is both small and insignificant.[48]

While findings on the rate of increase in the academic skills of Job Corps enrollees may be interesting, the significance of the education program lies in determining how many leave the program with the reading and arithmetic skills necessary to obtain and maintain a job. The following crucial questions should be asked: (1) how valuable are these achievements to the participants; (2) do these programs aid them in acquiring a high school diploma; and (3) how are academic gains reflected in the labor market?

Activities and Involvements with the Community

One of the goals of the Job Corps program is to assist young people to become better citizens. Among the factors that have been used in ascertaining the impact of the program on the citizenship of its participants are the following: contact with police, religious attendance (i.e., church attendance), membership in a social club, and voter registration. Harris polled ex-corpsmembers on these matters six months after they left the program.

Of those polled, 15 percent of the August 1966 terminees answered that they had contact with the police. Black graduates and women comprised the smallest groups (8 percent each), while approximately 15 percent each of the discharges, dropouts, and white graduates cited this difficulty. Six months after termination from the program 19 percent of the whites and 12 percent of the blacks were involved in a crime-related matter.[49]

Harris asked ex-corpsmembers to categorize their religious attendance, both before and after their Job Corps experience, as regular, occasional, or never. All groups indicated a decrease in such activities.[50] Only 12 percent of those polled stated that they belonged to a club or social group; more males than females, and more graduates answered that this was the case.[51]

47. *Ibid.*

48. *Ibid.*, p. 48.

49. Louis Harris and Associates, "A Study of August 1966 Terminations," *op. cit.*, p. 453.

50. *Ibid.*, p. 443.

51. *Ibid.*, p. 445.

Of the 20 percent interviewed who were eligible to vote, only 29 percent were registered. Blacks comprised 32 percent of this total, whites only 19 percent; more men than women were involved in the electoral process. Category of termination was also a major factor; dropouts and discharges were more likely to be registered voters than graduates (35, 34, and 24 percents, respectively).[52]

Statistical tests have not been conducted to determine if the program has had a significant impact upon the level of responsible citizenship of Job Corps enrollees as a whole, or to show differential impact by ethnic group. Analysis is further hampered when control data are absent. Conclusions should not be drawn based on these insufficient findings. To do so would involve value judgments on the relative worth of these measurements; for example, should decreased religious activities be considered as a negative or positive result of participation in the program? Difficulties also arise in discerning to what extent the act of leaving home for the first time has on these activities. Thus, findings in the impact of participation in Job Corps on the citizenship of former enrollees are inconclusive.

Supportive Services

There is a great deal of difficulty in measuring the impact of supportive services. Questions arise concerning whether participants in the program would receive such services without enrolling in a manpower program. Since referring individuals to the proper agency for help is one of the major means through which supportive services are provided, determining what impact Job Corps has had in the delivery of these services is not obvious.

The supportive services provided include medical and dental care, child care, and legal aid. A physical examination is included in the screening procedure used to determine eligibility for Job Corps. Help is offered in providing for the care of children so that Job Corps women can participate in the program. In its evaluation of supportive activities, Unco notes that pre-enrollment services include referrals to other agencies or individuals for legal or medical assistance.[53] A U.S. Department of Labor report explains:

> The major health goal of Job Corps is to minimize health conditions which are impediments to an enrollee's reaching and sustaining a level of sound health, including the realization of maximum psychosocial potential. To help enrollees achieve this level of health and well-being, Job Corps (1) provides appropriate care for acute and episodic illness, (2) provides

52. *Ibid.*, p. 447.

53. Unco, Inc., *op. cit.*, p. 3-40.

continuing care for chronic health conditions that do not preclude successful participation in the training program, (3) identifies remediable health defects and corrects them within budgeting constraints, and (4) provides information essential for enrollees to make their own health decisions.[54]

Every Job Corps enrollee receives a cursory medical check-up for signs of communicable or other disease within 24 hours of entry, followed within two weeks by a comprehensive examination.[55] Dental disease is the most common health problem among entering enrollees.[56] In a random sample of over 950 Job Corps participants, about 70 percent had never been to a dentist or had not seen one regularly.[57] Many Job Corps participants were not properly immunized; in the 1973 fiscal year, there were 46,625 visits for immunization against polio, diptheria, etc.[58]

The Job Corps health program includes an attempt to educate all Job Corps enrollees and staff about sickle cell anemia. Voluntary testing of 38,925 Job Corps participants between May 1972 and May 1973 found 27 with sickle cell anemia, 29 with hemoglobin sickle cell disease, and 61 with other unusual hemoglobin.[59] Additional special health programs include gonorrhea screening and detection and drug abuse prevention projects.[60]

In the 1973 fiscal year, Job Corps provided 38,000 inpatient days, 55,000 complete medical and dental examinations, 76,000 dental visits, 46,000 immunization visits, and 555,000 other outpatient visits.[61] Although data are available pertaining to the number of Job Corps participants receiving medical care, no attempt has been made to determine if the Job Corps program is the best vehicle for administering a health program.

An Atlanta Residential Manpower Center was the site of an experimental child development and day care program. In addition to participating in the regular center program, mothers with children received training in child psychology.[62] An evaluation of enrollees with children re-

54. U.S. Department of Labor, Manpower Administration, Job Corps, "The Job Corps Health Program 1973-1974," p. 2.

55. *Ibid.*, p. 3.

56. *Ibid.*

57. Ellen Sehgal, "Information on Job Corps," memorandum to Howard Rosen, Manpower Administration, U.S. Department of Labor, October 9, 1973, p. 1.

58. *Ibid.*

59. *Ibid.*

60. U.S. Department of Labor, Manpower Administration, Job Corps, *op. cit.*, pp. 6-10.

61. *Ibid.*, p. 4.

62. Howard Vincent, "A Cost Effectiveness Analysis of the Job Corps, " internal report, Manpower Administration, U.S. Department of Labor, 1972, p. 36.

ceiving child care, compared to mothers who were not provided child care, indicated that those in the child-care program stayed in Job Corps longer and had a significantly higher completion rate.[63]

In summary, the supportive services received by Job Corps enrollees varied by center and requirements of the individual. Many have noted the need for supportive services. Little emphasis, however, has been placed on such aid or on evaluating the best means of providing it. In the long run, these factors may have the most positive impact on helping ex-enrollees achieve gainful employment and participate as productive citizens.

CONCLUSIONS

Although the Job Corps has been modified since it was first established, evaluative studies of the program's impact on enrollees have concentrated on the program as it existed in the mid-1960's. The primary source of data was the information obtained from interviews conducted with participants who left the Job Corps in August and November 1966. Approximately 60 percent of those polled were black; less than 10 percent were enrolled in urban centers for women. Data on the demographic characteristics of corpsmembers are available only from 1968; women comprised about 25 percent of the enrollees and minority group members accounted for over 60 percent.

Data obtained from the Louis Harris and Associates surveys show that participation in the program had a positive effect on the labor market experience of Job Corps enrollees six months after they left the program. This conclusion is based on a comparison of the reported employment and earnings of male enrollees who stayed in the program less than three months with those who graduated or remained in the program for a greater length of time. It has not been shown, however, that enrollment in Job Corps has a long-term impact on the employment and wages of its enrollees. The Louis Harris and Associates data suggest that the positive relationship between time spent in Job Corps and labor market experience is not maintained eighteen months after termination. This can be attributed to the increased employment of early dropouts and not to a change in the status of those who stayed in the program. Perhaps the labor market impact of Job Corps lies in its role in helping young men obtain a job when age is a barrier to their employment.

The analyses used in determining the impact on male Job Corps enrollees cannot be duplicated for females because the data on women's centers are not provided by length of training or type of termination. When labor market status was classified by race, the data revealed less favorable employment histories among black ex-corpsmembers compared to whites.

63. *Ibid.*

Whites continued to earn more than nonwhites, even when such factors as years of education, region, and Job Corps experience were held constant.

The focus of the literature has not been placed on determining the noneconomic impact of the Job Corps. Information is presented on the educational gains made by participants while in the program and their activities six months after termination. Some statistics are available on the scope of medical and dental care received by enrollees while they were in the program.

The evaluative literature concluded that the Job Corps program was more successful in upgrading the educational skills of enrollees who entered the program with achievement levels below sixth grade than those with higher achievement levels. The length of time spent in the program, however, was found to be insignificant in the attainment of academic gains. The literature does not focus on an analysis of the relative impact of the educational program on minorities and women.

Among the factors that have been used in measuring the impact of the program on the citizenship of its participants are the following: contact with police, religious attendance, membership in a social club, and voter registration. Statistical tests have not been conducted to determine if the program has had a significant impact upon the activities of Job Corps enrollees as a whole, or to show differential impact by race or sex. Firm conclusions should not be drawn from these insufficient findings, since analysis is hampered by the absence of control data.

It is evident that the low-income and disadvantaged youth enrolled in Job Corps require a variety of supportive services. The aid provided varies by the center and the needs of the individual. All enrollees receive some medical care. Little emphasis has been placed in evaluating the services provided, or determining if the Job Corps is the best means of providing this aid. In the long run, the supportive services received while enrolled in the Job Corps may have the most positive impact in helping participants achieve gainful employment and participate as productive citizens.

CHAPTER XVI

Neighborhood Youth Corps

by
Harriet Goldberg
Research Associate
Under the Direction of
Richard L. Rowan

The Neighborhood Youth Corps (NYC), established under Title I-B of the Economic Opportunity Act of 1964, was created to provide part-time work experience, remedial education, and limited job training for disadvantaged youth who either did not complete high school or were potential high school dropouts. NYC consists of three distinct but related programs: a full-time program for high school dropouts, a part-time job-school program for youths, and a summer employment program. The goals of NYC, whether explicitly or implicitly stated, can be summarized as follows:

1. to increase the employment of youth;
2. to increase the lifetime earnings of enrollees through training, work experience, and incentives to stay in school and work;
3. to reduce teenage crime; and
4. to redistribute income to the poor.

The in-school program attempts to motivate and equip youths to stay in school, to perform better academically, and to make sound career and educational choices. Enrollees are provided with part-time employment while they are attending classes and, in many cases, summer jobs are made available.

The NYC out-of-school program provides work experience with the objectives of providing earning opportunities, improving self-discipline, and developing sound work-oriented attitudes. In 1970 the Department of Labor restructured the program to place greater emphasis on skill training. The revised NYC-2, operating in about one-half of the projects when the 1973 *Manpower Report* went to press, focuses upon skill training, supportive services, and remedial education, rather than upon work experience. Although both occur at the worksite, NYC-2 stresses learning through instruction pursuant to a curriculum, rather than learning through work experience.

The change from a work experience orientation recognizes that, if the target youth are to succeed in the labor market, they need job training as well as educational skills and improved attitudes toward work. Nevertheless, the ultimate objective of the program, to prevent the participants of NYC from maintaining a position of social and economic dependence, has not changed.

PROGRAM ENROLLMENT CHARACTERISTICS

From the time of its establishment through the 1972 fiscal year, 4,321,700 youths from low-income families enrolled in NYC (see Table 1). The percentage distribution of participation in NYC by component is indicated in Table 2. The out-of-school program has consistently enrolled the smallest percentage of participants. The proportion of enrollees in the summer component has increased significantly from 34.5 percent in 1965 to 75.2 percent in 1972.

The NYC out-of-school program was instituted to aid youths who are at least sixteen years of age. Recently, greater emphasis has been placed upon the younger group; 90 percent of the new entrants are supposed to be sixteen or seventeen years old at the time of enrollment. The in-school and summer programs are open to youths who are only fourteen years old. The number of participants in the program is determined by the monetary appropriations allotted for NYC; however, attempts have been made to reduce the number of hours each participant is employed rather than to reduce enrollment in the program.[1] The emphasis has been to increase the enrollment of younger individuals in the hope that they will remain in or return to school and have fewer discouraging contacts with the labor market. Older individuals are generally placed in other manpower programs.

As shown in Tables 3 and 4, the percentage of female participants has increased significantly from the first year of the program, rising from 36.6 percent in the 1965 fiscal year to 43.4 percent in the 1972 fiscal year for the in-school and summer components and from 39.8 to 49.9 percent in the same years for the out-of-school group. The ratio of black to white participants has also increased in the in-school and summer programs while the out-of-school segment maintained a racial composition of approximately 50 percent black and 50 percent white. The *Manpower Reports of the President* do not indicate the number of males and females by race.

An overwhelming percentage of NYC enrollees are in the ninth to eleventh grades. The out-of-school component has involved increasing proportions of those who had some high school education but who did not complete the twelfth grade. The in-school program has focused increasingly on those with at least an eighth grade education.

1. Interview, U.S. Department of Labor, Division of Work Experience, Washington, D.C., January, 1973.

TABLE XVI-1. *Neighborhood Youth Corps Enrollment by Program, Fiscal Years 1965-1972*
(In thousands)

Program	Total	1965	1966	1967	1968	1969	1970	1971	1972
In-school	965.3	54.7	160.8	166.8	118.3	84.3	74.4	120.0	186.0
Out-of-school	696.6	35.6	166.9	161.6	93.8	74.5	46.2	53.0	65.0
Summer	2,659.8	47.6	95.2	227.9	255.2	345.3	361.5	567.2	759.9
Total enrollment	4,321.7	137.9	422.9	556.3	467.3	504.1	482.1	740.2	1,010.9

Source: U. S. Department of Labor, *Manpower Report of the President* (Washington, D. C.: Government Printing Office, March 1973), Table F-1, p. 227.

TABLE XVI-2. *Neighborhood Youth Corps Percent Distribution of Enrollment by Program Fiscal Years 1965-1972*

Program	Total	1965	1966	1967	1968	1969	1970	1971	1972
In-school	22.3	39.7	38.0	30.0	25.3	16.7	15.4	16.2	18.4
Out-of-school	16.1	25.8	39.5	29.0	20.1	14.8	9.6	7.2	6.4
Summer	61.6	34.5	22.5	41.0	54.6	68.5	75.0	76.6	75.2
Total	100.0	100.0	100.0	100.0	100.0	100.0	100.0	100.0	100.0

Source: Derived from Table 1.

TABLE XVI-3. *Neighborhood Youth Corps*
Percent Distribution of Demographic Characteristics of Out-of-School Participants
1965-1972

Characteristics	January 1965 to August 1965	September 1965 to August 1966	September 1966 to August 1967	September 1967 to August 1968	September 1968 to August 1969	September 1969 to August 1970	Fiscal Year 1971	Fiscal Year 1972
Sex:								
Male	60.2	57.0	51.6	49.1	46.0	47.5	50.7	50.1
Female	39.8	43.0	48.4	50.9	54.0	52.5	49.3	49.9
Race:								
White	51.4	48.2	47.0	50.2	48.2	50.3	53.1	48.0
Negro	45.1	45.2	49.4	45.6	47.5	44.2	41.3	42.6
Other	3.5	6.6	3.6	4.2	4.4	5.5	5.6	9.4
Spanish surname	n.a.	n.a.	n.a.	n.a.	n.a.	n.a.	16.5	15.7
Age:								
Under 19	58.3	56.7	68.6	61.9	64.1	90.8	89.5	89.0
19-21	41.7	43.3	31.5	36.7	32.8	6.7	4.5	4.8
22 and over	—	—	—	1.5	3.1	2.4	6.0	6.2
Years of school completed:								
8 or less	18.4	24.9	27.2	27.6	26.8	32.3	28.6	25.1
9-11	43.6	55.9	63.4	65.6	69.0	65.5	68.7	72.3
12 and over [a]	38.0	19.2	9.4	6.8	4.2	2.3	2.7	2.6
Family income:								
Below $1,000	n.a.	17.8	7.4	0.3	—	—	0.1	4.1
1,000-1,999	n.a.	27.0	40.6	49.8	62.6	37.4	35.3	25.2
2,000-2,999	n.a.	25.0	23.8	19.0	4.3	24.1	23.2	22.3
3,000-3,999	n.a.	16.7	16.0	13.5	4.2	21.1	20.3	22.0
Over 4,000	n.a.	13.5	12.3	17.4	28.9	17.4	21.1	26.4
Total	100.0	100.0	100.0	100.0	100.0	100.0	100.0	100.0

Source: U. S. Department of Labor, *Manpower Report of the President* (Washington, D. C.: Government Printing Office)
1970, Table F-9, p. 312;
1971, Table F-10, p. 308;
1972, Table F-8, p. 268;
1973, Table F-8, p. 234.

Note: Percents may not add to 100.0 due to rounding.

[a] Not necessarily high school graduates.

TABLE XVI-4. *Neighborhood Youth Corps*
Percent Distribution of Demographic Characteristics of In-School and Summer Participants
1965-1972

Characteristics	January 1965 to August 1965	September 1965 to August 1966	September 1966 to August 1967	September 1967 to August 1968	September 1968 to August 1969	September 1969 to August 1970	Fiscal Year 1971	Fiscal Year 1972
Sex:								
Male	63.4	54.8	54.8	54.2	53.4	50.0	54.9	56.6
Female	36.6	45.2	45.2	45.8	46.5	50.0	45.1	43.4
Race:								
White	67.3	55.8	52.4	47.3	46.3	53.7	38.1	40.0
Negro	28.7	39.0	43.3	48.0	47.4	42.5	56.5	53.4
Other	4.0	5.2	4.3	4.7	6.2	3.9	5.4	6.6
Spanish surname	n.a.	n.a.	n.a.	n.a.	n.a	n.a.	12.1	11.8
Age:								
Under 19	89.7	92.0	95.6	95.1	96.1	93.5	96.5	97.1
19-21	10.3	8.0	4.4	4.9	3.9	6.5	3.5	2.9
22 and over	—	—	—	—	—	—	—	—
Years of school completed:								
8 or less	5.0	8.6	9.9	15.1	20.2	17.2	20.2	19.3
9-11	81.1	85.5	85.5	83.6	78.6	82.0	75.6	77.2
12 and over [a]	13.9	2.9	1.5	1.4	1.2	0.8	4.2	3.6
Family income:								
Below $1,000	n.a.	10.4	5.9	0.1	—	—	7.0	8.0
1,000-1,999	n.a.	24.6	28.9	62.8	48.2	31.1	14.0	16.8
2,000-2,999	n.a.	28.3	25.8	13.9	15.5	27.0	20.8	22.5
3,000-3,999	n.a.	20.2	21.4	11.8	17.5	22.8	26.1	24.2
Over 4,000	n.a.	16.5	18.0	11.3	18.8	19.0	32.1	28.5
Total	100.0	100.0	100.0	100.0	100.0	100.0	100.0	100.0

Source: U. S. Department of Labor, *Manpower Report of the President* (Washington, D. C.: Government Printing Office)
1970, Table F-9, p. 312;
1971, Table F-10, p. 308;
1972, Table F-8, p. 268;
1973, Table F-8, p. 234.

Note: Percents may not add to 100.0 due to rounding

[a] Not necessarily high school graduates.

PROGRAM OPERATION

NYC projects are administered by state and local governments and by private non-profit agencies. The training that can be associated with any job title differs with each NYC work site. In addition, programs vary in the degree and type of remedial education and supportive services offered. Training and services provided by NYC for its participants differ by site and sex: for the most part, females are placed in clerical and nursing positions, while males are assigned to custodial and janitorial slots. Thus, it cannot be said that there is one NYC program model that is followed by each of the participants. NYC has undergone major revisions since 1970; what effect this has upon the impact of the program has yet to be indicated in the literature. With the recent passage of the Comprehensive Employment and Training Act, NYC may be terminated unless the local prime sponsors continue the program.

REVIEW OF EVALUATIVE LITERATURE

The voluminous literature on the Neighborhood Youth Corps can be grouped into three categories:

1. descriptive reviews of who is in a particular project and what the program entails, but providing no follow-up or analysis;
2. assessments of the NYC program at particular sites or cities, most of which compare NYC participants with control groups; and
3. cost-benefit analyses which attempt to quantify the value of the program and thus measure its relative success.

Classification of a study is determined by the number of individuals identified, the extent and scope of follow-up subjects, and the existence and reliability of a control group.

Reports vary concerning the time period covered by their reviews; in light of the changes in the emphasis of NYC, many different programs have been described. For the most part, each of the NYC components—in-school, out-of-school, and summer programs—have been considered as separate units. Studies that discuss more than one program segment generally do not do so in a comparative sense.

Studies of Program Impact

Analysis of the Neighborhood Youth Corps is based primarily upon the cost-benefit analyses and assessments of NYC programs at particular sites. The literature also includes descriptive and/or anecdotal narratives which do not offer any substantive data, other than a statement of how NYC helped a limited number of individuals. No attempt shall be made to draw conclusions pertinent to the impact of NYC on minorities and women that would be based upon accounts that are descriptive in nature and lack control group information.

Studies of programs at particular sites generally describe NYC projects with large female and minority (primarily black) populations. Thus, any impact conclusions that can be drawn from these reports can be associated with these target groups. The major questions investigated by the studies, which attempt to do more than delineate the number of participants and services provided, involve an assessment of the educational and employment effects of the program, and the effectiveness of supportive services. These studies will be used to the extent that they provide some insight into the impact of the program.

Although some reports of small projects did not attempt to select a control group, the basic methodology employed in the literature was the use of a comparative group to determine if changes among NYC enrollees were a function of participation in the program. These accounts indicated that groups were matched by age, race, sex, educational background, and other demographic characteristics; but in many reports, the extent to which this is true cannot be confirmed.

Three studies of NYC use multiple regression and cost-benefit analysis. One cost-effectiveness study, based upon a nationwide sample, assesses the in-school component.[2] Two reports on the out-of-school component employ these techniques; one is based on a sample of participants in the Indiana program,[3] and the other uses data collected in an earlier report of the impact on participants enrolled in 1966-68.[4] Control groups are utilized in determining impact attributable to enrollment in NYC.

The basic framework for ascertaining the impact of participation in NYC on the labor market position of trainees (minorities and women), and for evaluating noneconomic gains that may have accrued to participants while they were in the program and upon termination, involves asking some of the following questions:

1. What are the effects of the out-of-school, in-school and summer programs on the employment and earnings of their enrollees?
2. What types of jobs did the participants obtain?

---

2. Gerald G. Somers and Ernst W. Stromsdorfer, *A Cost-Effectiveness Study of the In-School and Summer Neighborhood Youth Corps* (Madison: Industrial Relations Research Institute, University of Wisconsin, 1970).

3. Michael E. Borus, John P. Brennan, and Sidney Rosen, "A Benefit-Cost Analysis of the Neighborhood Youth Corps," *Journal of Human Resources,* Vol. V, no. 2(Spring, 1970), pp. 139-159.

4. Harry R. Woltman and William W. Walton, "Evaluations of the War on Poverty—The Feasibility of Benefit-Cost Analysis for Manpower Programs," Resource Management Corporation, prepared for General Accounting Office 1968.

3. How effective was the program in decreasing the high school dropout rate?
4. How effective were the supportive services in providing improved health and education?
5. How effective was the program in reducing the juvenile crime rate?
6. What effect did enrollment in the program have on the attitudes and motivation of the participants?
7. Was NYC basically a system of providing transfer payments to youth rather than a job-training or educational experience?
8. Did the program provide improved services to the public?

In-School Program Studies

Two studies of the in-school component provide a well-conceived methodological framework for evaluating the impact of the program. Gerald D. Robin assessed the behavioral changes that could be derived from participation in the NYC program in Cincinnati and Detroit.[5] Gerald G. Somers and Ernst W. Stromsdorfer conducted a cost-effectiveness study based upon a nationwide sample of in-school and summer participants. Other reports about the in-school program are generally poor in quality; few substantive conclusions can be based upon studies which do not use control groups.

The Robin study employs extensive data categorized by sex and summarized within the body of the report. Evaluation of the effectiveness of NYC participation is based upon data obtained from selected groups of NYC youths in personal interviews conducted at three points in time over a one-year period. supplemented by information collected from school files and police records, and interviews with a subsample of the mothers of the interviewed youths. Four distinct empirical and analytic groups—year-round enrollees, summer-only enrollees, program dropouts, and control subjects—were selected as samples for study. The number of white youths interviewed during the initial phase of the investigation was too small for meaningful statistical treatment; therefore, the evaluation was restricted to a study of black youths.

There was a real attempt to use a valid control group in the Robin evaluation. The controls were not self-selecting. In the Cincinnati study, a list of youths who had applied for admission to NYC and had been screened and found eligible for the program were arranged alphabetically and then randomly assigned to the program or control group. Since there were not enough slots for all these youths to take part in the

5. Gerald D. Robin, *An Assessment of the In-Public School Neighborhood Youth Corps Projects in Cincinnati and Detroit, with Special Reference to Summer-Only and Year-Round Enrollees* (Philadelphia: National Analysts, Inc., 1969).

program, an experimentally created control was formed without reducing total participation. Since a sample of financially eligible applicants not admitted to NYC was not available in Detroit, applicants, who prior to the date of sample selection had been rejected because they were over the income ceiling, were utilized as the control subjects. The smallest possible over-income cut-off point that would identify an adequate size of controls was chosen. This served to minimize serious poverty status differences between the control group and the enrollees, who had met the eligibility criteria.

The extensive study by Somers and Stromsdorfer of a nationwide sample of NYC participants employed multiple regression and cost-effectiveness analyses to investigate the costs and benefits of the program. Social, governmental, and private benefits were measured. Based upon information gathered about participants enrolled in sixty in-school and summer NYC programs sometime between July 1, 1965 and June 30, 1967, the labor market and educational performances of both the sample NYC group and controls were ascertained. Data are provided by race and sex.

As with the samples used in the Robin study, the two groups studied by Somers and Stromsdorfer are quite similar in regard to basic socio-demographic variables. Statistical tests, however, indicate that the NYC and control samples are not from the same population. The control group, therefore, is a comparison group; thus, assertions of a definitive cause and effect relationship between participation in the program and the measurements of performance cannot be made.

Few substantive conclusions can be based upon the remaining reports of specific NYC in-school projects which do not use control groups. The lack of a well-conceived methodological framework for evaluating these programs mirrors the misunderstanding of what is expected of a manpower program on the part of the administrators of these projects. An example of an in-school project of the type mentioned above was a program in communication, film making, and advertising.[6] The program was conceived as a means of providing opportunities for entrance to a professional career for talented minority high school students. Enrollees, however, lacked realistic information about the knowledge, skills, and attitudes needed for their positions, and they were not directed so that they could gain access to such information. In addition, professional workers, with whom the NYC participants worked, did not understand their lack of motivation. The program provided meaningless work experience and little or nothing in the way of counseling; it did nothing to motivate the students to better themselves through a career or con-

6. Hudson Guild, *Teenage Opportunity Program: An Experimental and Demonstration Project Linking Professional/Technical Employers to the NYC In-School Program—A Final Report* (New York: The Hudson Guild, 1972).

tinued education. Thus, the descriptive account of the Hudson Guild project indicates that the basic program was one of misunderstanding both on the part of the NYC participants and of the administrators of the project.

In-School Rural Programs

Most of the accounts of the in-school program dealt with projects in urban sites. The rural program, however, has been described extensively, but not evaluated. NYC programs in rural areas differ considerably from their urban counterparts. For the most part, NYC rural projects are limited to the in-school component because of difficulties in filling their out-of-school slots. The difference between rural and other youth programs is that rural ones are meant to serve not only youths from low-income families but also any nonurban youth who, by reason of growing up in a sparsely settled region, has been socially, culturally, and geographically isolated from the type of community in which he is most likely to live as an adult. Although the program does not encourage rural youth to migrate to the city, it is a significant attempt to prepare youth for urban life. The effectiveness of this program has not been substantiated, but in view of the prevailing migration patterns, there may be a definite need for some program of this type.[7]

The Summer Program

Analysis of the summer program is generally limited to a few paragraphs in accounts of the in-school program, because both the summer and in-school components basically aim at the same target group. No attempt is made to determine the long-run employment effect of the program. In addition, no evaluation of the effect of the summer component upon the education of enrollees is considered. The emphasis has been upon possible attitudinal changes, measured in police contacts, thus reflecting the intent of the program to serve as a deterrent to civil unrest.

Studies of Out-of-School Programs

Studies of the out-of-school component of NYC concentrate on the employment effects of the program upon the enrollees and place secondary emphasis upon their educational attainment. This reflects the priority of the goals of the out-of-school segment which tries to enhance the labor market status of those who have already quit school. The em-

7. Guy H. Miles, *Optimizing the Benefits of Neighborhood Youth Corps Projects for Rural Youth: Final Report* (Minneapolis: North Star Research and Development Institute, n.d.):

ployment effect is measured by comparing the number of NYC participants and a control group made up of people who have jobs, are looking for work, are in the armed forces, or are in other manpower programs. The assessment of the educational gains is based upon a similar comparison of these groups measured in terms of the number who return to school or attain a high school diploma or its equivalent.

Control groups, such as the ones used both by Robin and by Somers and Stromsdorfer, are more difficult to pick out in an out-of-school program. The school system provides a means of identifying those who are not admitted to the in-school program and those who are rejected for lack of space. It was found, however, that individuals who were rejected by the out-of-school program by one administrative agency were admitted by another which had an open slot.

Evaluations of the out-of-school segment were restricted to studies of urban sites or to programs of the inner city. An early study by Dunlap and Associates did, however, attempt to compare the rural and urban impact. This report attempts to measure the impact of the program upon the education and employment experience of participants enrolled in NYC in 1966-1967 and 1967-1968.[8] Using control groups, this evaluation compares the impact of the program upon males and females, whites and nonwhites, and urban and rural groups.

The data collected by Dunlap and Associates were applied in a cost-benefit study conducted by the Resource Management Corporation.[9] The control group used in this analysis consisted of NYC dropouts (those in the program less than five weeks) and a proxy control (changes in the wage rates in a group of representative industries during the time of interest).

Another cost-benefit study, by Michael E. Borus, John P. Brennan, and Sidney Rosen, included an analysis of the earnings of 604 participants in the out-of-school programs in five urban areas of Indiana.[10] The control group consisted of 166 individuals eligible for the programs, but who did not enroll because (1) they were placed on a waiting list and never called; (2) could not be reached for a job assignment; or (3) did not report when assigned a job. The experimental group of NYC participants in each area was selected from all those youth who were eligible for the program, reported to work at least one day, and left the program by December 31, 1966.[11] Earnings information was ob-

8. Dunlap and Associates, Inc., "Final Report—Survey of Terminees From Out-of-School Neighborhood Youth Corps Projects, Vol. I—Summary of Findings," report prepared for Office of Policy, Evaluation, and Research, Manpower Administration, U.S. Department of Labor.

9. Woltman and Walton, *op. cit.*

10. Borus, Brennan, and Rosen, *op. cit.*

11. *Ibid.*, pp. 142-144.

tained from the Indiana Employment Security Division. Extensive use was made of basic NYC forms in the collection of demographic, termination, and cost information about the enrollees. In age, education, marital status, race, family size, and language spoken at home, the averages for the participants and the control group were almost identical. Sizable differences were found, however, in the sex compositions of the samples: 51.2 percent of the participants were female, yet 57.8 percent of the control group were female.[12]

In the series of reports comparing the NYC programs of various inner-city areas, Regis H. Walther examines the impact of NYC at different points in time.[13] Using control groups, these studies try to measure the effect of the program on the educational attainment, employment, and attitudinal changes of the enrollees. The impact upon education is measured on the basis of returns to school, participation in remedial education programs, school attendance records, and educational achievement tests. Changes in labor market status are evaluated on the employment activities of participants at various time intervals after leaving NYC; this includes an analysis of the number of job changes incurred by NYC participants. The nature of termination from NYC was also investigated. Terminees were classified as leaving the program for one of four reasons: (1) planned terminations (employment, training, school, or military reasons); (2) administrative reasons (expiration of agreement, completion of standard term, or ineligibility); (3) premature, NYC initiative (poor attendance, fired, misconduct); and (4) premature, other (quit, could not adjust, lost interest, moved, married, family problems, pregnancy, committed to an institution). The basic format used was the same in all of the Walther studies; thus, this series of reports might be considered one analysis of NYC.

At least a majority of the participants in the demonstration and control groups of studies of NYC-1 sites were black women; the second largest group consisted of black men. A large proportion of women were in the program because they left school as a result of pregnancy or for other health reasons. Since unwed motherhood has major social implications, NYC is a major attempt to bring these unmarried mothers back into society after they have been rejected by their families and friends because of their condition.

Disciplinary problems were most often cited as reasons for males leaving school. For the most part, female enrollees tended to be some-

---

12. *Ibid.*, p. 144.

13. Regis Walther, Margaret L. Magnusson, and Shirley E. Cherkasky, *A Study of the Effectiveness of Selected Out-of-School Neighborhood Youth Corps Programs Implications for Program Operations and Research, A Study of Selected NYC-1 Projects* (Washington, D.C.: Social Research Group, George Washington University 1971).

what older than their male counterparts and to have completed more years of schooling. In many studies, the percentage of white males in the program was too small to be statistically meaningful.

In addition to the Walther studies, there are two reports which review attitudinal changes that could be attributed to participation in the program. The objective of an investigation of NYC enrollees in North Carolina was to examine the problems, characteristics, and potential of participants.[14] Melvin Herman and Stanley Sadofsky attempted to assess changes in self-esteem and work attitudes six months after enrollment in NYC.[15] This study was based upon attrition rates, respondents' views of NYC, and the impact of NYC assignments upon the nonworking life of the respondents.

Summary

Despite the large number of reports on the Neighborhood Youth Corps, few attempt to assess the impact of the program. Evidence of differential impact by race and sex is limited. Some studies, however, discuss the effect of the program upon the labor market performance, educational achievement, and delinquent behavior of NYC participants.

ECONOMIC EFFECTS

The NYC program is evaluated in terms of the educational, employment, and social gains of the participants. NYC components differ over which factors are asserted as the primary objective of the program; the in-school component places greater emphasis upon educational impact, and the out-of-school segment stresses employment gains.

The Out-of-School Program

As noted earlier, the NYC out-of-school program has been revised, but the remodeled programs have not been evaluated. Completed studies of the restructured NYC-2 programs, which stress skill training instead of work experience, have been restricted to longitudinal reports providing demographic data and descriptions of the program. Analysis of the difference between NYC-2 and NYC-1 must await the completion

14. William C. Eckerman, Eva K. Gerstel, and Richard B. Williams, "A Comprehensive Assessment of the Problems and Characteristics of the Neighborhood Youth Corps Enrollees: A Pilot Investigation" report prepared for Office of Policy, Evaluation, and Research, Manpower Administration, U.S. Department of Labor, Research Triangle Institute, 1969.

15. Melvin Herman and Stanley Sadofsky, "Study of the Meaning, Experience, and Effects of the Neighborhood Youth Corps on Negro Youth Who Are Seeking Work. Part V," mimeographed report, Center for Study of the Unemployed. Graduate School of Social Work, New York University, 1968.

of evaluative reports. The results described below apply primarily to minorities and females who comprise the bulk of NYC-1 enrollees studied.

The Dunlap and Associates' report defined employment to include full-time work, part-time work, and enrollment in the Armed Forces, Job Corps, MDTA institutional or on-the-job training, a registered Apprenticeship program or Community Action Agency Work Training program.[16] Given this definition, this early study of NYC found that after termination from the program, males were employed more frequently than females. Dunlap and Associates findings indicate that more whites than nonwhites and more urban than rural participants were involved in employment activities.[17] Table 5 compares the activities of NYC enrollees and a control group. The changes in activities reported by the control group appear more significant than the comparison of the pursuits of those who did and did not participate in NYC.

A study conducted by the Resource Management Corporation used the Dunlap and Associates data to determine the feasibility of applying benefit-cost analysis to antipoverty programs. In assessing the impact of NYC enrollment upon the labor market performance of participants, the control group consisted of dropouts (those in the program less than five weeks) and a proxy control (changes in wage rates in a group of representative industries during the time of interest). A 2 percent increase in employment was calculated (from 58 to 60 percent); however, the lack of data on employment rates at entry, needed to serve as a baseline, was noted.[18] The net program effect in hourly wages was computed at seven cents an hour for males and four cents an hour for females.[19] A low level of confidence in the reliability of these estimates was indicated, because of the inherent statistical uncertainties in the data from which they were derived.

The Walther group's final evaluation of selected NYC-1 projects found that the major component of the NYC experience—work training—characteristically involved few specific occupational skills.[20] Two-thirds of the first work assignments, for example, either required no tool skills or the ability to handle hand tools such as rakes, mops, and shovels. The level of responsibility and interpersonal skills required also tended to be

16. Dunlap and Associates, *op. cit.*, p. 47.

17. *Ibid.*, p. 64.

18. Woltman and Walton, *op. cit.*, p. 13.

19. *Ibid.*, p. 20.

20. Walther, Magnusson, and Cherkasky, *op. cit.*

TABLE XVI-5. *Neighborhood Youth Corps Percent Distribution of Man-Weeks Spent in Various NYC Related Activities*

Activities	During NYC	After NYC	
	Control	Control	NYC Enrollees[a]
Employment	44.5	49.9	46.2
Schooling	2.4	6.4	11.4
Looking for work	14.8	12.2	18.7
Not working or looking for work	18.1	12.3	9.6
Housewife or pregnant	13.0	12.7	19.7
Other activities	7.2	6.5	3.4
Total	100.0	100.0	100.0

Source: Dunlap and Associates, Inc., "Survey of Terminees From Out-of-School Neighborhood Youth Corps Projects, Vol. I, Summary of Findings," report prepared for Office of Policy, Evaluation, and Research, Manpower Administration, U.S. Department of Labor.

Note: Percents may not add to 100.0 due to rounding.

[a]Sample enrolled in NYC, 1966-1967 and 1967-1968.

low. Successful performance in generally undemanding work situations tends to involve work habits and social skills and little job-related skill training.

In comparing the labor market status of the control group to NYC participants, Table 6 indicates that attempts to improve work habits without providing skill training are not sufficient to increase the employability of NYC participants. Former enrollees in the program did not do as well in the labor market as their control groups. In this final study of NYC-1, Walther concluded that the primary hypothesis of their research—that the NYC programs helped enrollees achieve satisfactory adjustment to life and to the world of work—was not confirmed.[21]

Although NYC-1 was not generally effective in improving the employability of its participants, components which involved some type of skill training had better results. One such program was the Cincinnati Clerical

21. *Ibid.*, p. 34.

TABLE XVI-6. *Neighborhood Youth Corps*
Percent Distribution of Activities at Time of Follow-Up
January 1968 and January 1969

Activities	Male Subjects				Female Subjects			
	NYC		Controls		NYC		Controls	
	1968	1969	1968	1969	1968	1969	1968	1969
In NYC	21	6	—	—	31	16	—	—
Employed full-time	37	47	54	61	21	31	36	42
Employed part-time	8	6	13	6	2	1	4	7
Not working, laid off, etc.	2	2	—	—	1	2	1	1
Not working, looking for work	11	13	12	9	17	18	19	13
In school vocational training	5	—	10	10	7	7	14	10
In military service	14	14	4	3	—	—	—	—
Housewife not wanting employment	—	—	—	—	7	9	12	13
Idle, not looking for work	2	5	7	6	10	11	11	12
In jail	2	5	—	6	n.a.	n.a.	n.a.	n.a.
Other	—	3	—	—	5	4	4	1
Total	100	100	100	100	100	100	100	100

Source: Regis H. Walther, Margaret L. Magnusson, and Shirley E. Cherkasky, *A Study of the Effectiveness of Selected Out-of-School Neighborhood Youth Corps Programs: A Study of Selected NYC-1 Projects* (Washington, D. C.: Social Research Group, George Washington University, 1971), Tables 7.7 and 7.8, pp. 298-299.

Note: Percents may not add to 100 due to rounding.

Co-Op,[22] a formal skill training program designed to enhance the clerical employability of its enrollees. At the time of the follow-up, 86 percent of the participants, virtually all of whom were black females, were in the labor force and over 50 percent of these were employed full-time. The excellent results of this particular program could be considered a function of the characteristics of the participants. As originally planned, participation was to be limited to NYC enrollees who had completed at least ten years of school, had at least minimal clerical skills, possessed the ability to handle basic mathematics, and had at least an eighth grade reading ability. For the most part, the enrollees were unwed mothers who dropped out of school because of their physical condition. Since the length of time in which the enrollees had been out of the program before the follow-up interview was not specified, the results of this study might be questioned as an indication of a long-term effect. The initial increase in employment potential, however, is highly significant even if not maintained.

The question of "creaming" arises in reviewing the Clerical Co-Op study. The "creaming" phenomenon exists when enrollees are chosen for participation, although they would probably succeed without this help. It seems reasonable that manpower programs should first focus on those lacking some skills and then work with individuals in need of more help. Successful NYC enrollees—both male and female—averaged higher educational attainment and greater rated improvement in employability by their counselors. Many of these successful enrollees reported NYC help in getting a job. The Clerical Co-Op was an attempt to aid at least some individuals sufficiently to have a real effect on their employment potential.

Borus, Brennan, and Rosen investigated the impact of NYC enrollment on participants of NYC programs in five urban areas of Indiana. They reported:

> Using simple averages, we found that the NYC participants earned $278 more in 1967 than did members of our control group.[23]

When earnings were regressed on the demographic variables of sex, education, and age, they were found to be statistically significant. Men earned more than women, and the effects of further education upon earnings declined until about ninth grade and then increased. Until

22. Regis H. Walther, "A Retrospective Study of the Effectiveness of the Cincinnati Out-of-School Neighborhood Youth Corps Program," mimeographed report Social Research Group, George Washington University, July 1967.

23. Borus, Brennan, and Rosen, *op. cit.*, p. 147.

approximately nineteen years of age, earnings increased and then declined slightly.[24] According to Borus, Brennan, and Rosen:

> The other variables had the expected signs but were all clearly not statistically significant, i.e. $p>.10$. The coefficient of the variable for enrollment indicated that the average NYC participant in the sample earned $136 more than did the average control group member, but this was only significant at $p=.33$. Thus we were forced to conclude that on the average the NYC out-of-school program did not have a demonstrably significant effect on the earnings of the program participants.[25]

In-School Programs

The Somers and Stromsdorfer study is the most extensive attempt to determine the earnings and employment effects of participation in the in-school and summer Neighborhood Youth Corps. The unweighted data of the labor market performance, since leaving high school, show that the NYC group was unemployed slightly more months than the control group and experienced somewhat lower before-tax earnings. The NYC group, however, was out of the labor force a somewhat shorter time after leaving high school.[26]

Regression analysis showed that the NYC program has a significant positive impact upon post-high school gross earnings. There is, however, no statistically significant difference in the number of months unemployed nor in the average hourly wage rates of the NYC and control groups. The earnings difference is attributed to the smaller number of months of labor force withdrawal on the part of NYC participants.[27]

Males earn more than females and have less voluntary labor force withdrawal. There is, however, no difference in unemployment. A comparison of male and female NYC participants, and their respective controls, indicates that males who enrolled in the program earn more than their controls, while females do not. Although NYC males tend to be unemployed more than their control counterparts, they work more hours per week. NYC females are unemployed more, have fewer months of non-labor force participation, and work less hours per week on the average than their controls.[28]

Black NYC participants earn more than their controls and are unemployed less. The white NYC participant earns more than his control; this is attributed to fewer labor force withdrawals on the part of white

24. *Ibid.*

25. *Ibid.*

26. Somers and Stromsdorfer, *op. cit.*, p. 64.

27. *Ibid.*, p. 151.

28. *Ibid.*, pp. 157-165.

NYC enrollees. Although white males earn $2,069 more than white females, black males earn only $1,020 more than black females.[29]

In summary, the empirical findings of Somers and Stromsdorfer show that, in comparison with their control group, NYC in-school enrollees had higher earnings. The difference in earnings is attributed to more employment rather than higher wages. The study demonstrates that blacks benefit more than whites from NYC, with positive gains evident among both males and females. The benefits attained by the black females account for much of the overall gains of the total sample.[30] In response to criticisms of the cost-benefit estimation function chosen, Stromsdorfer has advised the authors that the original formulation using a dummy variable was replaced with a time in program and time squared variable. This resulted in a reduction in the original benefit estimate. Even though these findings have not been published, Stromsdorfer correctly indicates that they should be considered by those interested in future evaluations.

Summary—Labor Market Impact

A comprehensive study of the impact of NYC on the employment of teenagers should investigate the effect of the demand for teenage labor. Two important questions are: (1) to what extent is the overall demand for teenage labor increased; and (2) to what extent are nonwhite teenagers substituted for white youths.[31] The differential impact of NYC upon blacks and whites is dependent upon its ability to create jobs. Since a majority of NYC slots are filled by blacks—who represent only 9 percent of employed teenagers—the absolute and relative gains of increased demand for teenage labor will be larger for blacks. If NYC slots merely replace jobs which otherwise would have been filled by teenagers, the absolute and relative gains of blacks depend on the racial composition of the replaced employees.[32] Unfortunately, empirical evidence of NYC's impact upon increased labor market demand for youths has not been investigated.

Evaluation of the labor market impact of the out-of-school component has as yet been limited to assessments of the NYC-1 program. The restructured NYC-2 programs, which stress skill training instead of work experience, have not been subject to careful evaluations. There is some evidence, however, that participants in programs emphasizing skill

29. *Ibid.*, pp. 168-183.

30. *Ibid.*, p. 183.

31. Robert S. Smith and Hugh M. Pitcher, "The Neighborhood Youth Corps: An Impact Evaluation," Preliminary Working Draft Technical Analyses Paper No. 9, Office of Evaluation, Office of Assistant Secretary for Policy, Evaluation and Research, U.S. Department of Labor, 1973, p. 15.

32. *Ibid.*, p. 21.

training experience increased initial employment potential. A low level of confidence in the reliability of estimated hourly wage gains was indicated, by the Resource Management Corporation, because of statistical uncertainties in the data. A cost-benefit study of the employment impact of the Indiana program concluded that NYC did not have a demonstrably significant effect upon enrollees' earnings.

The empirical findings of Somers and Stromsdorfer indicate that NYC in-school enrollees earned more than their controls. The gains of black females account for much of the overall benefit to the total sample.

NONECONOMIC EFFECTS

Noneconomic effects are less tangible and more difficult to quantify than labor market impacts. In the following discussion, noneconomic impacts are defined as activities, other than skill training, which tend to reduce the employment obstacles of women and members of minority groups. Of particular interest will be evidence of real or perceived changes in and impact upon: (1) work attitudes; (2) educational attainment; and (3) reductions in antisocial behavior. Citing the difficulty of handling noneconomic issues, and recognizing the need to include such gains where they exist, some studies have used direct economic gains as a reflection of the processes of social growth. Woltman and Walton comment:

> Each of these issues are difficult to handle analytically. We have taken the position that youth programs cannot be evaluated merely as diversions, but rather, must be appraised in economic terms that to some extent also reflect the processes of social maturation.[33]

Despite the fact that economic gains have been used as proxies for noneconomic benefits, some evidence exists on the impact of NYC on work attitudes, performance, and delinquent behavior.

Impact on Work Attitudes

The Neighborhood Youth Corps is aimed at helping youth overcome barriers to effective labor market participation. Poor work attitudes and the lack of self-esteem can present major handicaps for increased employment.

In a study directed by Walther, enrollees rated the NYC out-of-school program in four cities on a five-point scale ranging from (1) "not at all useful" to (5) "very useful." The mean rating of overall usefulness was

33. Woltman and Walton, *op. cit.*, p. 25.

generally over "4," with female respondents indicating more positive replies to this question.[34] Enrollee estimates of their chances of achieving their ten-year occupational goals were also noted. Most of the enrollees included in the study had employment objectives that were perhaps beyond their capacities to achieve in that they required new job and training experience. About three-fourths of the respondents, however, rated their chances of goal achievement as "very good" or "fairly good."[35]

William C. Eckerman, Eva K. Gerstel, and Richard B. Williams studied the characteristics of NYC enrollees in North Carolina, and found a realtionship between academic achievement and work attitudes:

> . . . [E]nrollees who have proceeded further in formal education and score more highly on aptitude and achievement tests also seem to subscribe to a philosophy of life which may be highly instrumental to upward mobility in our society.[36]

Another review of NYC participants, six months after enrollment, concluded that there was an initial shift in self-esteem and work attitudes which thereafter tend to remain rather stable.[37]

Robin attempted to ascertain what impact NYC had upon participants' attitudes toward work. It was concluded that the in-school program:

> . . . had no discernible impact on the youths' conception of work, their willingness to relinquish the security of steady employment for training that would prepare them for better jobs, their perception of conditions which may interfere with obtaining suitable employment, their professed job characteristic preferences, or their occupational expectations.[38]

Impact on Education

The extent to which participation in NYC has resulted in improved educational experience is measured by: (1) improvements in basic education, generally measured by increased reading ability and arithmetic skills; (2) the number of in-school participants who continue to attend classes; (3) the number of dropouts who return to school; and (4) the number of enrollees who receive a high school diploma or its equivalent. Difficulties have been documented in testing the school achievement of

34. Walther, Magnusson, and Cherkasky, *op. cit.*, p. 229.

35. *Ibid.*, p. 325.

36. Eckerman, Gerstel, and Williams, *op. cit.*, p. 134.

37. Herman and Sadofsky, *op. cit.*

38. Robin, *op. cit.*, p. 90.

disadvantaged youth. In addition, comparisons of groups in terms of educational attainment are inconclusive because in many cases the act of withdrawing from school may have occurred years after the individual had lost interest in schooling.

The effect that the in-school component could have upon the dropout rate appears to be limited by the manner in which youths are selected for enrollment. Because of the lack of evaluative data, the General Accounting Office (GAO) was unable to determine the extent to which the NYC program may have influenced the high school dropout rate.[39] The GAO found that there were no significant efforts made by project sponsors to select youths who were potential dropouts and who were likely to be dissuaded from this course by what the NYC programs had to offer.

There was a real attempt to use a control group in Robin's assessment of the in-school Neighborhood Youth Corps projects. This study was restricted to black youths because too few white youths were interviewed in the initial phase of the investigation to provide statistically meaningful information. Based upon data collected through school files, the general findings of this methodical study of the in-school program revealed no evidence that the program had a favorable effect upon the scholastic achievement of its enrollees. In fact, because enrollees spent time working instead of at their studies, participation in NYC actually impaired grades of enrollees who had previously performed adequately in their studies (at least a C average). ". . . [A]nalysis of NYC participation and school performance reveals no evidence that being in the program, either during exposure or after termination from it, had a favorable effect upon the scholastic achievement of its enrollees."[40]

Somers and Stromsdorfer analyzed the educational benefits of the in-school and summer components of NYC. For the total sample, it was concluded that the NYC program had no statistically significant impact upon the probability of high school graduation or the number of years of school completed.[41] Somers and Stromsdorfer ascertained:

> . . . [F]or males, participation in the NYC leads to a decreased probability of high school graduation. . . .There is no difference between the male NYC and control group on the basis of years of high school completed. . . .
>
> There is no difference in the probability of high school graduation between NYC females and their control group counterparts.[42]

39. Comptroller General of the United States, *Effectiveness and Administrative Efficiency of the Neighborhood Youth Corps Under Title I-B of the Economic Opportunity Act of 1964* (Washington, D. C.: Government Printing Office, 1969).

40. Robin, *op. cit.*, p. 161.

41. Somers and Stromsdorfer, *op. cit.*, p. 213.

42. *Ibid.*, p. 227.

White NYC in-school participants are no more likely to graduate from high school than their controls, but black NYC participants are 8.2 percent more likely to graduate than their control group. American Indian participants are about 14.6 percent more likely to graduate, whereas Mexican American enrollees are about 21.2 percent less likely to graduate than their controls. The positive effect of the NYC program upon blacks is attributable to the 12.5 percent greater likelihood of graduation of black female NYC participants than their control counterparts.[43]

At least one study found that participation in the NYC out-of-school program did not significantly affect the high school dropout problem (Table 7). Compared to male subjects, females in both the control and NYC groups were more apt to return to school after dropping out, and they were more likely to complete high school when they did return.[44] In comparison, a greater percentage of the control group than NYC enrollees returned to school.

TABLE XVI-7. *Neighborhood Youth Corps Percent Distribution of Post-Training Educational Status by Sex*

	Males		Females	
Variables	NYC	Control	NYC	Control
Never returned to full-time school	88	84	78	68
Returned to full-time school:				
Completed high school or more	2	6	7	12
Did not complete high school	11	10	14	20
Total	100	100	100	100

Source: Regis H. Walther, Margaret L. Magnusson, and Shirley E. Cherkasky, *A Study of the Effectiveness of Selected Out-of-School Neighborhood Youth Corps Programs: A Study of Selected NYC-1 Projects* (Washington, D.C.: Social Research Group, George Washington University, 1971), p. 254.

Note: Percents may not add to 100 due to rounding.

43. *Ibid.*, p. 228.

44. Walther, Magnusson, and Cherkasky, *op. cit.*, p. 254.

Out-of-school enrollees—even those who graduated from high school—are usually deficient in reading and arithmetic skills. Some evidence is supplied by the Accelerated Learning Experiment (ALE) of programmed instruction. These classes were conducted near work sites in St. Louis, Cincinnati, and Pittsburgh. Of the males who left the original ALE groups, 44 percent left the experiment and NYC for activities that were consistent with program objectives—most were employed by the military, others were engaged in employment and preparation for employment activities. An additional 5 percent left because they received a high school diploma or an equivalent.[45]

It was concluded that ALE achieved significantly better results than conventional programs, especially with male enrollees; attendance records were considered the major criterion for the conclusion. Progress in reading and arithmetic, as measured by the California Achievement Tests, however, showed that a sizable percentage of subjects' scores six months afterwards were lower than their initial scores.[46]

A New Education Program (NEP) was designed to provide more effective education for the revised NYC-2 program. Of the NEP student body, males averaged significantly lower than females in interest ratings and initial academic test scores. Chi square comparisons of all students by race indicated some association between race and interest ratings, and test scores and schooling.[47]

A Walther study compares ALE and NEP:

> In general, the ALE students participated about the same length of time as NEP students, but ALE students showed far less gain on measures of academic achievement. In the ALE, 36 percent of the initial students were in the program at least six months while the comparable NEP proportion was 31 percent; but, only about 55 percent of ALE students tested after six-months' participation showed academic improvement as compared with 90 percent of the comparable NEP students.[48]

It was thus concluded that NEP is a more effective program than ALE. Eight percent of the participants in NEP returned to school, 5 percent passed the GED or got a diploma, 72 percent experienced improved

45. Regis H. Walther, Margaret L. Magnusson, and Shirley E. Cherkasky, "The A-celerated Learning Experiment: An Approach to the Remedial Education of Out-of-School Youth," final report Social Research Group, George Washington University, 1969, p. 19.

46. *Ibid.*, pp. 23-27.

47. Regis H. Walther, Margaret L. Magnusson, and Shirley E. Cherkasky, *A Study of the Effectiveness of the Graham Associates' Demonstration Project on NYC-2 Education Programming* (Washington, D.C.: Manpower Research Projects, George Washington University, 1973), pp. 30-31.

48. *Ibid*, p. 56.

subject skills, 2 percent showed other improvements, whereas only 13 percent indicated no progress.[49] Because many trainees were in the programs for only a few months, there is some question about how much of their gains in schooling should be attributed to participation in ALE or NEP.

Studies do not indicate that minority or female participants in the out-of-school program either return to school or make other educational gains that can be associated with participation in the program. There is no attempt to document how many of the in-school enrollees were potential dropouts, and there is some evidence that participation in the program has hindered the scholastic performance of its participants. Given the overwhelming minority and female participation rate in NYC, this conclusion would apply to male minorities and to females.

Impact on Antisocial Behavior

The impact of NYC upon teenage crime rates has been discussed in the literature about the in-school and summer components. Studies about the out-of-school program have not focused on this issue.

Over one-half of the participants in NYC have been enrolled in the summer component. The enrollment of such a large number of youths for a short period of time does not seem to be consistent with the stated objectives of NYC. Employment of short duration cannot realistically involve much skill training or work experience. Even though the drop-out rates are far higher during the school year than in the summer, NYC resources have been allocated to finance large summer projects. Some have argued that the disproportionately large allocation to summer NYC has been made to minimize anticipated civil unrest. To the extent NYC is a vehicle of providing transfer payments and keeping urban (overwhelmingly minority) youths occupied, the program may have dampened potential disturbances.

The objective of the Robin study of the in-school program was to ascertain what behavioral changes could be attributed to participation in NYC projects. Both subjective criteria—evaluations of the program by the enrollees themselves—and more objective criteria—effects on school performance and number of police contacts—were examined. The program appeared relatively successful when judged by subjective criteria. The enrollees were satisfied with the program and there was a relatively high degree of satisfaction with work assignments. However, the program was not effective when assessed by a number of objective attitudinal, behavioral, and performance criteria. The delinquency profile for the experimental youths was delineated for the periods before they enrolled in NYC, while they were working in the program, and from

49. *Ibid.*, p. 45.

the point of enrollment to the date of offense-check. Robin concluded that ". . . NYC participation, among both males and females, is unrelated to delinquency prevention or reduction."[50]

One analysis of the NYC summer project in Washington, D.C., found an inverse relationship between the number of NYC slots and the incidence of crime. This study concluded that NYC had an impact upon aggregate juvenile delinquency statistics.[51] This alleged relationship does not appear to be statistically conclusive. The Center for Naval Analysis (CNA) used an index of reported crimes in Washington, D.C., along with information on the size of the summer and in-school NYC programs in a regression analysis of the impact of changes in program size on crime. The dependent variables are changes in summer NYC slots, changes in in-school NYC slots, time, and changes in the unemployment rate.[52] A number of additional variables, however, should be included in the model. Moreover, the positive coefficient for the in-school program is not explained, and the unemployment coefficient is extremely negative. Thus, CNA's findings that the NYC summer program has had a negative impact upon the number of reported offenses can be considered highly tentative.

NYC—An Income Transfer Program

The legislation does not dictate a specific hourly wage to be paid participants in NYC; the "appropriate" wage is to be determined on the bases of the education and training of the enrollee, the size of the family, the geographic location, and the nature of the job assignment. Administratively, this has been interpreted to mean that the in-school enrollees are paid the highest of the federal, state, and local minimum wages. Although in-school participants are supposed to work a maximum of 15 hours a week, fiscal appropriation difficulties have necessitated a policy whereby the regional office restricts enrollees to 10 to 12 hours of employment. Similarly, summer programs have cut back the number of hours a participant may work rather than reduce the number of youths in the program. The out-of-school NYC-1 program (basically the rural component at this time) pays its enrollees whichever is the highest of the federal, state, and local minimum wages. NYC-2 enrollees receive three-fourths of the MDTA allowance of the state; however, if one is the head

---

50. Robin, *op. cit.*, p. 151.

51. U.S. Department of Labor, "Analysis of the Neighborhood Youth Corps Summer Program," mimeographed, 1972, p. 34.

52. George P. Brown, Jr. *et al.*, "Analysis of the Neighborhood Youth Corps Program," memorandum, Center for Naval Analysis, December 19, 1972, pp. 19-20.

of the household, he or she is paid the total MDTA allowance and an additional five dollars per dependent.[53]

Evaluating NYC as a system of transfer payments raises the question of whether it is the most effective way of providing such funds. NYC involves more than a distribution of funds; it is an attempt to aid youths so that they will eventually not need public assistance. In any case, the evaluation studies do not squarely meet the social issues and the question of alternatives.

CONCLUSIONS

Based more upon observations of the content of Neighborhood Youth Corps programs than upon the stated purpose, NYC seems to function as a combination income maintenance and maturation device to help youths stay out of trouble until they are old enough to get a sustaining job or to enroll in a training program.

Evaluation of the labor market impact of the out-of-school component has up to now been limited to assessments of the NYC-1 program. The restructured NYC-2 programs, which place greater emphasis upon skill training instead of work experience, have not been subject to careful evaluation. A low level of confidence in the reliability of estimated hourly wage gains was indicated by the Resource Management Corporation, because of statistical uncertainties in the data. A cost-benefit study of the employment impact of the Indiana program concluded that NYC did not have a demonstrably significant impact upon enrollees' earnings.

The findings of an investigation of the economic impact of the in-school programs are more positive than those of the out-of-school component. Somers and Stromsdorfer concluded that NYC in-school enrollees earned more than their controls. The gains of black females account for much of the overall benefit to the entire sample.

Given the shortness of the summer program, it is not surprising that enrollees appear to gain little in the way of work experience. There is some inconclusive evidence that the summer component may reduce the number of crimes committed by youth during the summer months. One methodical study of the in-school program in Detroit and Cincinnati, however, concluded that NYC participation, among both males and females, is not related to delinquency prevention or reduction. One goal of NYC is to reduce crime in the inner city by employing teenagers

53. Interview, U.S. Department of Labor, Division of Work Experience, Washington, D.C., January, 1973.

living in poverty. Theoretically, employment and criminal activities are substitutes. Empirically, however, the relationship between participation in NYC and crime is not well established.

The most that can be said about the impact of NYC upon the education of minorities and women is that the findings are inconclusive. In regard to the summer program, there is no attempt to ascertain its academic value. Assessment of the educational impact of NYC is hindered by the characteristics of the program including: (1) the attitudes of the participants toward test-taking; (2) the attempts to determine which of the possible enrollees in the in-school component are seriously considering dropping out of school; and (3) the short length of time out-of-school participants attend classes.

CHAPTER XVII

Operation Mainstream

by
Larry R. Matlack
Research Associate
Under the Direction of
Bernard E. Anderson

One approach to meeting the diverse needs of disadvantaged groups is through work experience programs. These programs are designed to provide meaningful work experiences for members of the labor force having serious difficulty finding employment in the competitive labor market. Operation Mainstream is one of several work training programs developed during the 1960's to alleviate the competitive disadvantage of the hard-to-employ.

The purpose of this report is to examine the Operation Mainstream program with specific reference to its impact on minorities and women. This examination will include a review of the general nature of the program, including its history, program structure, and operation. These and other aspects of Operation Mainstream will be explored through a review of the evaluative studies of the program.

Program Purpose

When Congress enacted the legislation creating Operation Mainstream, the scope of existing manpower programs was not broad enough to meet the needs of all geographic areas and all groups within the work force. In particular, Operation Mainstream was organized to meet the special needs of rural communities and workers over 55 years of age.

The employment problems of the elderly are complex. The elderly are retiring earlier because of the increased Social Security funds and the marginal financial utility of working longer. However, a large proportion of elderly families are poor. Paradoxically, this poverty is largely attributable to low Social Security benefits, as well as restrictions on work activity. In addition, age is a major barrier to employment; in our youth-oriented society, a person of 45 may have difficulty finding work. Even the Federal Age Discrimination in Employment Act protects people only 40 through 65 years of age. In the absence of efforts specifically directed toward increasing the employment and income of the elderly, these problems could get worse.

If employment opportunities for the elderly are scarce in industrialized urban areas, the job market in rural communities is even less favorable. Because much of the black population is concentrated in the rural South, the elderly black worker is worse off than others. Additional factors contributing to poverty among the black elderly are: (1) less eligibility for Social Security pensions; (2) lower family income and lifetime earnings; (3) previous restrictions in the job market to low level service and laboring occupations; and (4) race and age discrimination in hiring.

Employment problems are even more acute for the older woman, particularly those who are widows or heads of households. Because of their lower mortality rates, many older women find themselves without husbands and thus without adequate income at a period in life when age imposes severe restrictions on employment opportunities.

Operation Mainstream was created to be the major federally supported program to provide needed manpower resources in public service agencies in rural communities. Funding for the program is authorized under the Economic Opportunity Act (EOA) of 1964 (Title I-B), as amended in 1965. Under this legislation, financial assistance is available to public or private nonprofit agencies that sponsor programs providing unemployed adults with jobs and low-income workers with improved career opportunities. The Operation Mainstream program is designed to provide counseling and basic education services to enrollees, but emphasis is placed on providing work experience for chronically unemployed poor adults in newly created jobs in community improvement, beautification, and services. Enrollees are, typically, displaced farm workers or older rural poor who lack formal training or nonfarm experience and have little education.

In general, Operation Mainstream enrolls individuals who are from low-income families and have no substantial prospects for unsubsidized full-time employment. In addition, such individuals must be ineligible for other manpower training programs for any of the following reasons: (1) advanced age; (2) physical condition; (3) obsolete or inadequate skills; (4) declining economic conditions; and (5) lack of job availability.

NATURE AND DEVELOPMENT OF THE PROGRAM

In 1965, an amendment (known as the Nelson Amendment) was appended to the Economic Opportunity Act. Included under Title II, the new Section 205(d) provided for meeting the needs of "chronically unemployed and poor adults who are not being, or cannot be, reached under existing programs."[1] However, other than the requirements that the enrollee be poor, unemployed, and an adult, no specific eligibility guidelines were included.

In December 1965, the first contract for an Operation Mainstream program was signed. This contract, awarded by the Office of Economic

1. U.S. Senate, Labor and Public Welfare Committee, *Senate Report No. 599*. August 13, 1965.

Opportunity (OEO), was with Green Thumb, Inc., a nonprofit organization for rural workers that is affiliated with the National Farmers' Union. Enrollees in this program were involved mainly in rural conservation and beautification projects.[2]

In 1967, a congressional review of the OEO legislation resulted in two modifications of the Mainstream program. First, the program was shifted to Title I-B of the EOA and administrative responsibility for the program was shifted to the Department of Labor. Second, enrollee eligibility was modified. The most significant addition to enrollment criteria was a "lack of employment opportunity" clause under which program enrollees were protected from displacement from Operation Mainstream as long as no other jobs were available in the competitive labor market.[3] At the time this clause was added to the Mainstream legislation, 60 percent of the program enrollees were over 45 years old. In essence, then, a significant portion of the Operation Mainstream program became an income maintenance program as well as a work experience program. By the end of fiscal year 1967, the Department of Labor had signed 145 agreements (most of them renewals of OEO projects) which opened approximately 8,000 job opportunities for out-of-work adults.[4]

During 1968, the Department of Labor established nationally contracted Mainstream programs with the National Council on the Aging (NCOA) and the National Council of Senior Citizens (NCSC). By mid-1969, there were more than 200 active Operation Mainstream programs. During fiscal years 1967 and 1968, an estimated 24,000 disadvantaged adults were enrolled at a cost of $45.9 million.[5]

In 1969 programs operated under national contract by the National Retired Teachers Association (NRTA) and by Virginia State College (VSC), were started, and the Green Thumb program was expanded through the addition of the Green Light component of the project. The development of the nationally contracted programs signaled a slight shift in the focus of Operation Mainstream. The previous programs had involved community beautification and conservation projects, but the new programs were designed to aid the elderly by placing them in sub-

2. U.S. Department of Labor, *Manpower Report of the President* (Washington, D.C.: Government Printing Office, 1968), p. 203.

3. Dale W. Berry *et al.*, "National Evaluation of Operation Mainstream, A Public Service Employment Program—Phase IV: Comparative Analysis" Kirschner Associates, Inc., 1971, p. 40.

4. U.S. Department of Labor, *loc. cit.*

5. U.S. Department of Labor, *Manpower Report of the President* (Washington, D. C.: Government Printing Office, 1969), p. 104.

professional positions as aides in social service agencies. In addition, these programs were required to enroll only persons who had reached the age of 55.

In 1969 a new Title I-E was added to the existing Mainstream legislation. This section broadened the "lack of employment opportunity" clause to include persons who were unable to obtain employment or training because of age, physical condition, obsolete skills, or declining economic conditions. Work opportunities available to Mainstream programs were also expanded to include housing rehabilitation and the expansion of health and day care services.[6]

The I-E programs were designed to aid economically depressed areas during a period of declining aggregate demand. Subsequent to the transfer of administrative authority for I-E programs from OEO to the Department of Labor, more than 100 of these programs were established.[7]

Enrollment levels in April 1972 (21,600) were more than double those in April 1968 (9,000). In addition, as a reflection of the administration's commitment to the elderly in the 1972 White House Conference on the Aging, recent Mainstream growth has resulted from a doubling of funding for the older worker program component to $26 million in fiscal 1972, to support an additional 5,000 subsidized jobs in public and private nonprofit agencies.[8]

Goals

Although individual Mainstream projects have slightly different objectives, three explicit goals seem to be common to all programs: (1) supplementing income of low-income adults through work activity in the program; (2) improving enrollee competitiveness in the open job market; and (3) providing communities with a new manpower resource for beautifying public properties, improving public facilities, and providing social services to needy citizens.[9] Implicit in these three objectives is an attempt to reduce the number of older people dependent on public assistance and living in poverty.

Also underlying the above goals are the secondary effects of the program, which are important to the health and well-being of the enrollees. Among these important secondary effects are the sense of dignity and usefulness gained by the elderly through work activity, and the in-

6. Berry *et al.*, *op. cit.*, p. 45.

7. *Ibid.*

8. U.S. Department of Labor, *Manpower Report of the President* (Washington, D.C.: Government Printing Office, 1973), p. 53.

9. Berry *et al.*, *op. cit.*, pp. 6-7.

creased supply of productive labor available to employers who might otherwise ignore the elderly worker.

Program Structure

Operation Mainstream is a heterogeneous program consisting of a variety of projects that have some elements in common and some that differ sharply. Although the programs within Operation Mainstream vary in enrollee characteristics and program activities, they are most sharply distinguished by their administrative organization.

Administratively, Operation Mainstream operates on a contract basis. The programs within Mainstream may be divided into two groups classified by the administrative organization which executes the contracts (see Table 1). First, there are the nationally contracted programs which are operated by a few private organizations under contracts monitored and enforced by the United States Training and Employment Service (USTES) of the Department of Labor. In 1971 there were 54 projects of this type with a total enrollment of 4,595.[10] Included among the nationally contracted programs are Green Thumb-Green Light, the Senior AIDES Program, the Senior Community Service Project, the Senior Community Service Aides Project, and the Senior Community Service Program.[11] These programs focus directly on the older rural worker and provide income maintenance for work in community service projects.

The second type of Mainstream program is that administered by the Manpower Administration regional offices through contracts with local nonprofit organizations. In 1971 there were 352 such programs with a total enrollment of 10,542.[12] These programs are either funded under Title I-B or Title I-E of the EOA or are operated as components of the Concentrated Employment Program. Emphasis in the regionally administered programs is on training and permanent job placement outside the program. There are fewer older workers in these projects because the goal of job placement is less likely if enrollees are predominantly in the older age groups. For the most part, program participants in the regionally administered projects are assigned to agencies to gain work experience as sub-professional aides, community workers, or clerical workers. In general, Mainstream enrollees supplement the work of their agency staff, often freeing professional members from routine duties.

10. Berry *et al., op. cit.*, Table 1, p. 27 and Table E-3, p. 200.

11. The title Senior Aides is commonly applied to all nationally contracted programs except Green Thumb-Green Light.

12. Berry *et al., op. cit.*, Table 1, p. 27 and Table E-1, p. 187.

TABLE XVII-1. *Operation Mainstream*
Nationally Contracted and Regionally Administered Programs
1971

Program	Contractor	Number of Program Sites
Nationally contracted programs:[a]		
Green Thumb Program (and Green Light, a component program)	National Farmers Union	17
Senior AIDES Program	National Council of Senior Citizens (subcontracts with local nonprofit organizations)	19
Senior Community Service Project	National Council on the Aging (subcontracts with local nonprofit organizations)	11
Senior Community Service Aides Project	National Retired Teachers Association	6
Senior Community Service Program	Virginia State College	1
Regionally administered programs:[b]		
Operation Mainstream programs funded under Title I-B of EOA	Local nonprofit organizations	197
Operation Mainstream programs funded under Title I-E of EOA	Local nonprofit organizations	113
Operation Mainstream programs operated as components of Concentrated Employment Programs	Local nonprofit organizations	42
Total number of program sites		406

Source: Dale W. Berry *et al.*, "National Evaluation of Operation Mainstream, A Public Service Employment Program—Phase IV: Comparative Analysis" Kirschner Associates, Inc., 1971, p. 27.

[a] Programs administered by U. S. Department of Labor, Manpower Administration, Mainstream Project Office.

[b] Programs administered by U. S. Department of Labor, Manpower Administration Regional Offices.

REVIEW OF EVALUATIVE LITERATURE

The only comprehensive evaluation of the Operation Mainstream program is a five-volume, four-part report compiled in 1971 by Kirschner Associates of Albuquerque, New Mexico. This study, *National Evaluation of Operation Mainstream*, is national in scope and includes each type of Operation Mainstream program. In total, 53 projects (13 percent of nationwide projects) were sampled and 3,286 formal interviews were conducted from August 1970 to June 1971.[13]

The Kirschner Associates study had two major objectives: (1) to provide the Department of Labor with information about the impact of Operation Mainstream on the participants and program communities; and (2) to assess the validity of Mainstream programs as a means of assisting the elderly poor.

In most cases, manpower program effectiveness is measured by the change in employment, wage rate, and earnings of enrollees. As mentioned above, program goals for Operation Mainstream are very subjective. As a result, Mainstream's utility may not be measured by standards usually applied to other manpower programs. Although the Kirschner Associates study includes a discussion of the change in earnings, job placement rate, improvements in health and increase in general social satisfaction, the authors did not analyze program effectiveness on a cost-benefit basis. Because much of the Operation Mainstream program performs an income maintenance function and enrolls people over 55, it may be more appropriate to judge the outcome of the projects by the social benefits that income maintenance have on the lives of the program participants. Therefore, the Kirschner Associates study relies heavily on subjective criteria to measure program impact. Particular attention is paid to the enrollee evaluations of their program experiences in terms of improved outlook on life or improved self-image.

The study concludes that Operation Mainstream has been successful in providing work activity for the elderly and has demonstrated that the older worker is productive and capable of providing necessary community services. The program has also improved the economic condition of the target population. This is particularly true of the nationally contracted programs where there is often an unlimited enrollment period. In comparison, improvements in enrollee income in the regionally administered programs are generally temporary, except for those enrollees who obtain other jobs after their participation in Mainstream.[14] In terms of impact on enrollees, according to the study,

13. *Ibid.*, pp. 32-33.

14. *Ibid.*, pp. 14-16.

the program has been a success. Ninety-six percent of the enrollees sampled indicated that the program had helped them financially, and 58.2 percent felt the program had a positive influence on their outlook on life.[15]

The study does not analyze the differential impact of Mainstream on minorities or women. The nationally contracted programs enroll a majority of women and a higher proportion of blacks than the regionally administered programs. Since the nationally contracted programs have done the most to improve the economic condition of their target group, the program has been beneficial to minorities and particularly to women.

A study conducted by the Olympus Research Corporation, "The Total Impact of Manpower Programs: A Four-City Case Study,"[16] includes an assessment of the Operation Mainstream programs in Boston and Denver. The study concludes that, although the programs have had mixed success, their achievements have been better than should have been expected given the nature of the target population. Both programs are components of the local CEP organizations.

The Boston program's 100 slots are filled entirely by males, with priority given to older workers. Typically, the enrollees are drifters, alcoholics, or drug users and often have police records. Despite the enrollees' general unsuitability for employment in the private sector, the program managed to place about 220 enrollees (or about one quarter of total enrollment) in permanent jobs between 1967 and and 1969.[17] Until 1970 the program activities tended to be menial and were performed by work crews. However, the program has upgraded its work experience to include participation as sub-professionals in public agencies. No records were kept on the program's success with minority groups.

The Denver Operation Mainstream program provides work experience through an effort to physically restore the city's blighted areas. The majority of enrollees were either black or Spanish-speaking males with a history of alcoholism. Again, despite the drawbacks of the enrollees' work history, the Denver program was able to place about one-third of its participants in jobs outside of the Mainstream agency.[18] Although the average enrollee showed a wage increase of only three cents per hour after program completion, the black enrollees benefited the

15. *Ibid.*, Table E-3, p. 201.

16. Olympus Research Corporation, "The Total Impact of Manpower Programs: A Four-City Case Study" 1971.

17. Olympus Research Corporation, "The Total Impact of Manpower Programs: A Four-City Case Study—Volume II: Final Report" 1971, p. 6-14.

18. Olympus Research Corporation, "The Total Impact of Manpower Programs: A Four-City Case Study—Volume I: Summary of the Final Report" 1971, p. 46.

most by gaining an average of $0.52 an hour. Conversely, white enrollees showed a drop in earning power of $0.36 an hour.[19] The program, then, appears to have had a substantial impact on the black enrollee who completed the program.

TARGET GROUP

Nationwide in 1972, Operation Mainstream had 31,400 enrollees (see Table 2). Of these enrollees, 69.1 percent were male and 30.9 percent were female; two-thirds were white and one-third were members of minority groups. Forty-four percent of all enrollees were over 45. These statistics seem to indicate that Operation Mainstream is not precisely meeting the guidelines originally established for the program.

Prior to the legislation instituting the program, federally sponsored manpower programs were serving primarily the urban areas and those workers under 55. Although it is clear that for Operation Mainstream the Congressional intent was to place emphasis on enrolling those people over 55, this guideline is only adhered to in the nationally contracted programs. In the Kirschner Associates study cited earlier, more than 97 percent of the enrollees sampled in the nationally contracted programs were over 55 and about 53 percent were between the ages of 65 and 74. The regionally administered programs, on the other hand, had about one-third of their enrollees in the 22 to 34 years of age range.

The results of the Kirschner Associates study are tabulated in Table 3. These data, obtained through interviews of about 5 percent of program enrollees, represent the broad patterns of participation across the nation at large.

According to the data, the Green Thumb-Green Light programs are predominantly serving the elderly white worker. Of the participants Kirschner Associates surveyed, 84.7 percent were white, 88.8 percent were male, and the average age of participants was 68. The Green Light component of this program is composed almost entirely of females over 55 and one quarter of its enrollees are members of minority groups.

The Senior Aides programs are also meeting the target group identified in the initial Mainstream legislation. Almost three-quarters of the Senior Aides surveyed by Kirschner Associates were women and one-third were from minority groups. The average age was 66 years.

The average age of enrollees in the regionally administered programs is about 43 years. The target group varies from individual project to individual project and it appears that local administrators take the liberty of modifying enrollment criteria according to their perceptions of the needs of the local target group. As a result, about 70 percent of

19. Olympus Research Corporation, "Volume II-Final Report," *op. cit.*, p. 12-21.

TABLE XVII-2. *Operation Mainstream*
Percent Distribution of Enrolled Trainee Characteristics
Fiscal Years 1968-1972

Characteristics	1968	1969	1970	1971	1972
Sex:					
Male	84.3	82.2	70.8	73.3	69.1
Female	15.7	17.8	29.2	26.7	30.9
Age:					
Under 22	3.7	1.9	3.7	4.8	3.8
22-44	51.7	40.3	45.8	55.4	52.2
45 and over	44.6	57.8	50.6	39.8	44.1
Race: [a]					
White	59.5	67.5	61.6	64.1	66.7
Negro	25.4	20.8	24.6	24.4	18.6
Other	15.1	11.7	13.8	11.5	14.7
Years of school completed:					
8 or less	57.2	59.9	51.6	45.4	42.0
9-11	25.5	24.0	28.1	30.0	28.8
12 or more	17.4	16.1	20.3	24.6	29.1
Estimated annual family income:					
Below $1,999	—	—	—	0.2	8.0
1,000-1,999	69.9	31.4	69.7	61.9	48.0
2,000-2,999	19.7	3.3	18.9	22.1	23.8
3,000-3,999	6.8	1.4	7.3	10.1	12.6
4,000-4,999	2.6	57.1	2.9	4.3	4.8
5,000 plus	1.1	6.8	1.3	1.4	2.8
Total	100.0	100.0	100.0	100.0	100.0
Total number enrolled	12,600	11,300	12,500	21,900	31,400

Source: U. S. Department of Labor, *Manpower Report of the President* (Washington, D. C.: Government Printing Office), 1969, Table F-12, p. 249;
1970, Table F-10, p. 313;
1971, Table F-11, p. 309;
1972, Table F-8, p. 268;
1973, Table F-8, p. 234.

Note: Percents may not add to 100.0 due to rounding.
[a]1968 statistics include 10.4 percent American Indian and 1.6 Oriental enrollees;
1969 statistics include 8.7 percent American Indian and 0.6 percent Oriental enrollees;
1970 statistics include 12.2 percent enrollees with Spanish surnames;
1971 statistics include 28.1 percent Spanish-American enrollees;
1972 statistics include 10.2 percent Spanish-speaking enrollees.

the interviewees sampled in the regionally administered programs were under the federally mandated age of 55.

The percentage of women enrolled in Mainstream programs has almost doubled from 15.7 percent in fiscal 1968 to 30.9 percent in fiscal 1972. This upward trend in enrollment reached this level in fiscal year 1970, the time when the nationally contracted programs discussed earlier were operating at full capacity. The addition of these components to Operation Mainstream broadened the program's scope. This increase in female enrollment does not indicate a disincentive for elderly males to participate, but it does indicate that Congress recognized the need to develop programs addressing the needs of women, a long ignored group.

PROGRAM IMPACT

The Kirschner Associates study provides little evidence on Operation Mainstream impact measured according to cost-benefit analysis. In general, the study considers Operation Mainstream to be an effective program for meeting the work activity and financial needs of its enrollees. In addition, the program has been successful in providing needed social services to the program communities.[20] The report concludes that nationally contracted programs have been more effective than regionally administered programs in meeting the needs of the enrollees and the communities. Although no objective evidence is presented to substantiate the conclusion, Kirschner Associates suggests that the difference in impact is due to the different objectives of the two programs.[21] The regionally administered programs appear to have complicated their objectives by emphasizing training and placement for a diverse group of enrollees, people under 35 as well as those over 55, who have vastly different needs. In this situation, the goal of serving older workers is apt to be subordinated to other objectives in these programs. On the other hand, the nationally contracted programs have continued to focus on the elderly worker and on the services he can render to the community.

In view of the goals of the Mainstream program—providing work experience for chronically unemployed adults in newly created jobs in community improvement—the impact of the program can be measured in two areas: impact on the worker and impact on the community.

One goal of the Mainstream program is to raise the income of the worker above the poverty level, thereby reducing his dependence on family or other government support agencies and helping him to meet his immediate financial needs. One measure of program effectiveness

20. Berry *et al.*, *op. cit.*, p. 151.

21. *Ibid.*, p. 152.

TABLE XVII-3. *Operation Mainstream*
Selected Characteristics of Active Enrollees
By Total and Selected Program Units
1971

Characteristics	Total		Green Thumb-Green Light		Senior Aides		Regionally Administered	
	Total	Percent	Total	Percent	Total	Percent	Total	Percent
Age:								
Under 55	189	48.8	5	2.3	2	0.6	182	69.4
55-64	252	21.3	51	25.6	162	37.0	39	17.1
65-74	330	24.1	99	53.6	205	52.0	26	11.6
75 plus	70	4.3	32	18.3	38	9.4	—	—
No response	9	1.5	—	—	3	1.0	6	1.8
Mean [a]	50.0		68.0		66.2		42.7	
Race:								
White	537	58.4	160	84.7	242	66.0	135	50.8
Mexican-American	26	7.9	—	—	2	0.6	24	11.3
Negro	221	36.2	16	9.0	153	30.2	52	25.5
American Indian	25	4.4	1	0.6	—	—	24	6.1
Oriental	13	2.5	—	—	1	0.2	12	3.6
Other	9	0.3	—	—	9	2.2	—	—
No response	19	2.8	10	5.7	3	0.7	6	2.6
Head of household:								
Yes	682	79.7	149	80.9	330	83.1	203	78.7
No	125	16.4	18	7.0	63	13.7	44	19.0
No response	43	4.0	20	12.1	17	3.2	6	2.3

TABLE XVII-3 *continued*

Monthly unemployed: (Average)	25.4		34.3		60.0		16.1	
Sex:								
Male	409	60.5	147	88.8	114	25.5	148	61.2
Female	438	39.4	40	11.2	293	73.6	105	38.8
No response	3	0.1	—	—	3	0.9	—	—
Educational level	8.5		7.2		10.5		8.3	
Total monthly income excluding OM wages	$89.46		$113.46		$127.73		$76.04	
Hourly wages as OM worker	$1.71		$1.61		$2.06		$1.66	
Total enrolled nationally	15,137		2,407		2,188		10,542	
Total interviewed	850	100.0	187	100.0	410	100.0	253	100.0

Source: Dale W. Berry *et al.*, "National Evaluation of Operation Mainstream, A Public Service Employment Program—Phase IV: Comparative Analysis" Kirschner Associates, Inc., 1971, Table E-1, pp. 187-193.

Note: Percents may not add to 100.0 due to rounding.

[a] Weighted values, 1971.

would be to determine the proportion of program costs which are allocated to enrollees. The data in Table 4 indicate that each man-year of service provided by a Mainstream enrollee costs the federal government

TABLE XVII-4. *Operation Mainstream Federal Cost Data*

Program	Cost per Man Year of Service	Percent Total Costs Allocated to Enrollees
Nationally contracted:		
Green Thumb	$3,550	82
NCSC	5,258	91
NCOA	5,704	86
NRTA	5,478	80
VSC	5,142	80
Regionally administered	4,760	81
Weighted average, all programs	4,631	83

Source: Dale W. Berry *et al.*, "National Evaluation of Operation Mainstream, A Public Service Employment Program—Phase IV: Comparative Analysis," Kirschner Associates, Inc., 1971, p. 151.

about $4,630. Of this amount 83 percent, or about $3,840, goes to the enrollee in the form of wages and other fringe benefits. Although many enrollees in all programs have sources of income other than their wages, few would be above the poverty level without program assistance. The mean family extra-program income amounts to slightly less than $1,000 per year. Average annual extra-program income in the nationally contracted programs ranges from a low of $1,022 in the Virginia State College program, virtually an all-black program, to a high of $1,743 in the National Council on the Aging project. The regionally administered programs generally have lower supplemental incomes of about $912 per year.[22] Many Mainstream projects limit enrollees to twenty working hours per week. Therefore, if we assume an average employee receives only one-half of the cost per man-year of service calculated above, the wages will in many cases double his income.

This income maintenance is particularly significant since the majority of enrollees in the nationally contracted programs are women. The economic consequences of being an elderly female and black are illustrated by the low extra-program income of enrollees in the Virginia

22. *Ibid.*, p. 92.

State College project. Slightly more than $4,000 is allocated to project enrollees, 80 percent of whom are black and 55 percent of whom are women, in the form of income, transportation subsidies, or other program expenses. This amount is still less than the amount allocated to nationally contracted enrollees in any other project except Green Thumb.

An indirect financial impact results when an enrollee is placed in regular employment because of his program experience. Unfortunately, this is Mainstream's weakest area, specifically because its target group is difficult to employ and because the program does not have skill training as its primary goal. Of the nationally contracted programs, only the National Retired Teachers Association has had any success placing enrollees in jobs outside Operation Mainstream, and even then only 15.6 percent have found permanent positions with program assistance.[23] In general, age and poor health have made it difficult for the participants in the Senior Aides programs and Green Light-Green Thumb projects to find employment.

As would be expected, the younger terminees from the regionally administered programs are much more likely to obtain jobs after leaving. However, only the CEP-affiliated programs have had any success in placing their enrollees. In fact, only 46.3 percent of their enrollees found jobs through Operation Mainstream. The other regionally administered programs were able to place only about 20 percent of their enrollees.[24]

The CEP-affiliated programs in Boston and Denver studied in the Olympus Research Corporation report highlight the difficulties Mainstream projects face in placing enrollees. Generally used as drying-out places for alcoholics and drug addicts, the projects experienced high turnover and had little time to develop skills in the participants. Despite this, the Boston program was able to place one-fourth, and Denver one-third, of their eligible enrollees. Due to inadequate record keeping in both programs, the study could make little follow-up analysis of these enrollees.

An alternative approach to evaluating the impact of the program is to estimate the opportunity costs of the services supplied by Mainstream. If the host agency could have the same service performed at less cost through other means, then Operation Mainstream could not be considered to have a favorable cost-effectiveness ratio. Based only on their observations during the survey period, Kirschner Associates hypothesized that older workers are more productive than younger workers in performing certain tasks, specifically providing services to other poor and elderly persons or working on tedious tasks that prove boring or un-

23. *Ibid.*, p. 98.

24. *Ibid.*

TABLE XVII-5. *Operation Mainstream Perception of Program and Program Services By Active Enrollees in Selected Programs (Values weighted by 1971)*

Attitudes	Total		Green Thumb Green Light		Senior Aides		Regionally Administered	
	Total	Percent	Total	Percent	Total	Percent	Total	Percent
How satisfied are you with your Operation Mainstream job?								
Very satisfied	700	74.6	161	86.6	364	88.2	175	69.1
Somewhat satisfied	135	22.4	26	13.4	43	11.3	66	26.7
Somewhat dissatisfied	11	2.1	—	—	3	0.6	8	2.8
Very dissatisfied	4	1.1	—	—	—	—	4	1.6
What do you like most about your job? (more than one response allowed)								
Specific work	358	44.8	64	34.5	170	44.2	124	47.4
Other enrollees	205	21.0	35	16.6	121	27.9	49	20.5
Financial	94	11.6	37	19.7	28	6.7	29	10.7
Serving community	130	8.8	12	6.6	105	28.8	13	5.2
Activity	108	8.3	31	17.1	62	16.7	15	4.5
Everything	68	8.0	17	8.7	32	7.4	19	8.1
Other	110	18.1	27	16.0	25	5.1	58	21.2

TABLE XVII-5 *continued*

What do you like least about your job? (more than one response allowed)								
Likes everything	565	63.1	109	57.7	301	69.8	155	63.0
Financial	53	10.3	9	5.4	14	4.2	30	12.8
Other	241	27.3	68	36.2	202	27.4	72	21.8
Would you recommend Operation Mainstream to others?								
Yes	809	93.9	180	95.7	396	96.8	233	93.0
No	18	2.5	1	0.6	8	1.6	9	3.1
Do not know	23	3.6	6	3.6	6	1.6	11	4.1
Has working in Operation Mainstream improved your health?								
Yes	553	66.6	140	76.2	285	71.0	128	49.2
No	191	22.6	21	10.4	65	13.2	105	41.7
Other	106	10.8	26	13.5	60	15.9	20	9.1
Has working in Operation Mainstream helped you financially?								
Yes	821	96.0	184	98.8	399	97.4	238	95.2
No	24	3.7	1	0.6	9	1.9	14	4.5
Other	5	0.3	2	0.6	2	0.8	1	0.3
Has working in Operation Mainstream changed your outlook on life?								
Yes-Positive	510	58.2	129	69.2	253	68.3	128	53.5
Yes-Negative	1	0.1	1	0.6	—	—	—	—
Yes-no explanation	59	6.8	—	—	32	4.7	27	8.7
No	262	33.1	48	25.5	120	26.1	94	36.3
Other	18	2.1	9	4.8	5	1.0	4	1.6

TABLE XVII-5 *continued*

Attitudes	Total		Green Thumb Green Light		Senior Aides		Regionally Administered	
	Total	Percent	Total	Percent	Total	Percent	Total	Percent
Has Operation Mainstream helped you learn new skills?								
Yes	472	60.7	86	44.5	224	55.7	162	65.4
No	365	36.5	101	55.5	181	43.3	83	30.7
No, but helped improve others	8	2.0	—	—	4	0.8	4	2.7
Other	5	0.9	—	—	1	0.2	4	1.2
Total interviewed	850	100.0	187	100.0	410	100.0	253	100.0

Source: Dale W. Berry *et al.*, "National Evaluation of Operation Mainstream, A Public Service Employment Program—Phase IV: Comparative Analysis" Kirschner Associates, Inc., 1971, Tables E-2 and E-3, pp. 194-202.

Note: Percents may not add to 100.0 due to rounding.

interesting to younger workers. Also, because the average hourly wage of older workers in all the Mainstream programs was less than $2.00, Mainstream tasks are performed with less cost to employers than if another system were used.[25]

The primary impact of the Operation Mainstream program has been to supplement the income of enrollees. However, the work activity involved in the program has had remarkable secondary impact, particularly in the nationally contracted programs.

Kirschner Associates interviewed 850 active Operation Mainstream enrollees to determine their perceptions of the program's impact on their lives (see Table 5). Ninety-seven percent of the enrollees interviewed were satisfied with their Operation Mainstream jobs. Significantly, 86.6 percent of the enrollees in the nationally contracted programs were very satisfied with their jobs, and about 69 percent in the regionally administered programs expressed the same enthusiasm. When asked which aspect of their jobs they enjoyed the most, the enrollees responded most frequently that they either liked the work they were doing or enjoyed associating with the other enrollees. Financial gain achieved through program work was the third most frequently cited enjoyable aspect of the job; it was noted only 11.6 percent of the time. Overall, 63 percent said there was nothing they disliked about the program.

The program's significant secondary impact, principally in improved health and outlook on life, is most likely related to the enrollee's age (average of 50) and station in society. These responses are not unexpected from a group of people who have been outside the mainstreams of society and who have been given, at last, the opportunity to serve their communities and to work with others. Different attitudes on the part of minorities and women were not detected by the Kirschner Associates study.

About one-half (49.2 percent) of the enrollees in the regionally administered programs and almost three-quarters (71.2 percent) of those in the nationally contracted programs felt that their participation in Operation Mainstream improved their health. The greater percentage of nationally contracted enrollees who felt they had improved health through program participation may be seeing the result of new work activity in their lives and heightened self-esteem. Significantly, more than 50 percent of all enrollees surveyed felt that they had developed an improved outlook on life through their association with Mainstream.[26]

The program's primary impact has been to enable the enrollees to meet their immediate needs, economic and otherwise. The program

25. *Ibid.*, Table E-1, p. 193.

26. *Ibid.*, p. 94.

sustains them and seems to improve their self-concept and health.[27] As originally conceived, Operation Mainstream was a program whose primary objective was work experience and income support for enrollees, not immediate job placement. However, the expansion of the program in the 1970's has placed more emphasis on training and placement. Unfortunately, with the exception of the regionally administered CEP-affiliated programs, Operation Mainstream has generally been unable to find employment for enrollees outside the program. This indicates that the program may have failed to change employer attitudes about hiring the elderly worker. This failure is compounded by economic conditions of less than full employment and other institutional barriers, such as agency and union policies and regulations regarding the hiring and retention of people over a certain age. These barriers cannot reasonably be expected to be changed perceptibly by the intervention of a small limited program such as Operation Mainstream.

Minorities and Women

Although Operation Mainstream is designed to serve a unique minority (the aged—as opposed to the racial and language minorities of other manpower programs), it does serve women and blacks as well. With the exception of a few local projects that enroll a majority of females, the regionally administered programs are dominated by men.[28] Only in the nationally contracted programs were women in the majority.

In 1970 the Green Light program had an authorized enrollment of 270 (virtually all female), one-fifth of whom were black.[29] The primary impact of this program has been to enrich the enrollees' lives with much needed work activity and income. However, even the addition of program wages could not raise the average family income of $3,000 per year.

The National Council of Senior Citizens (NCSC) Senior AIDES program had an authorized enrollment of 1,148 in nineteen communities in 1971.[30] More than three-quarters (77.1 percent) of the enrollees surveyed were female and 29 percent were from minority groups.[31] The Senior AIDES program stresses income maintenance and psychological

27. *Ibid.*, p. 100.

28. *Ibid.*, p. 86.

29. Dale W. Berry, Nancy Sandusky, and Steven Van Dresser, "National Evaluation of Operation Mainstream—Phase I: The Green Thumb-Green Light Program Kirschner Associates, Inc., 1971, p. 83.

30. Dale W. Berry et al., "National Evaluation of Operation Mainstream—Phase II: The Senior AIDES Program" Kirschner Associates, Inc., 1971, p. 135.

31. *Ibid.*, p. 143.

benefits for its enrollees through community service. Other than these benefits, the program has not been successful in placing its enrollees in jobs after program participation.[32]

The Senior Community Service Project of the National Council on the Aging has an authorized national enrollment of more than 550. Sixty-six percent are women and 26 percent are from minority groups.[33] The focus of the program is to demonstrate to the community that older people are productive workers. Although the program has been a success in this area, enrollee age and other factors have limited job placement outside the program.

The fourth nationally contracted program, the Senior Community Service AIDES Project, sponsored by the National Retired Teachers Association (NRTA), has a national authorized enrollment of 353. Of these enrollees, almost three-quarters are women and almost one-half (47 percent) are black.[34] Of all the nationally contracted programs, the NRTA has the best placement record. Through fiscal 1971, it had managed to place 242 of its first 1,100 enrollees (plus 287 nonenrollee placements).[35] This 22 percent placement rate is a marked improvement over the placement rates of the other programs.

The Virginia State College (VSC) program started in August 1969 and enrolled 125 persons from the Petersburg, Virginia, area. Of the enrollees, 55 percent are women and 80 percent are black.[36] The most profound impact of the VSC program has been on the income of enrollees, increasing it about two and one-half times. Although two-thirds of the enrollees sampled said the program helped them to learn new skills, analysis of those skills indicates that they are not the type that would prepare them for a new occupation.[37]

The experience of minorities and women has been consistent throughout all the nationally contracted programs. Enrollees in general have benefited through income supplements and work activity but, in keeping with the original intent of Mainstream legislation, have received little training to make them competitive in the open job market. The reality is that it is very difficult to find any jobs for people over 65, the average age of the Senior Aides enrollees.[38]

32. *Ibid.*, p. 152.

33. *Ibid.*, p. 171.

34. *Ibid.*, p. 200.

35. Emil Michael Aun, "Senior Aides: Fighting Stereotypes," *Manpower,* Vol. IV no. 2 (February 1972), p. 10.

36. Berry *et al.*, "Phase II," *op. cit.*, p. 230.

37. *Ibid.*, p. 233.

38. *Ibid.*, p. 234.

The two CEP-affiliated projects studied in the Olympus Research Corporation survey have had mixed success with minority groups. Both projects have a different client group and face different placement problems from the programs discussed above. The Boston and Denver projects enroll hard-core unemployed with histories of alcoholism or drug abuse. In these projects, placement is not difficult because of age but because of poor work history. Despite these handicaps, both projects have been more successful than might have been expected.

The Boston project, the Adult Work Crew, has managed to place about 25 percent of the approximately 800 persons who had contact with the project from 1967 to 1969.[39] Because of inadequate record keeping, however, there were few follow-up statistics on the characteristics and job retention of those who were placed by the program. The available statistics indicated that 37 percent of those placed were black and 2 percent were Spanish-speaking.[40]

Statistics for the Denver project were more complete. Through 1970, 112 enrollees had terminated their participation in the project and about one-third of these were placed in permanent jobs. Of the placements, 10.3 percent were black and 79.4 percent were Spanish American.[41] Although all placements showed only a three cents per hour improvement in wage rates, the gain made by blacks was a substantial $0.52 cents per hour. Spanish American placements gained an insignificant one cent per hour in wages. The study concludes that the "success of the program must be looked for in light of placement and job stability rather than in immediate wage rate improvements."[42] Despite this general conclusion, the Denver project has had a positive impact on the black enrollees who have completed the program.

CONCLUSIONS

Operation Mainstream was designed by Congress to meet the employment and income needs of rural unemployed workers with an emphasis on the elderly. Prior to the establishment of Mainstream, these groups were not served well by existing manpower programs.

In general, the Operation Mainstream program has not provided skill training which enables the enrollee over 55 to compete in the open labor market, nor has it markedly improved the employment status of minorities and women. The program's major impact has been to enable

39. Olympus Research Corporation, "Volume II—Final Report," *op. cit.*, p. 6-14.

40. *Ibid.*, p. 6-15.

41. *Ibid.*, p. 12-21.

42. *Ibid.*

the elderly worker to meet day-to-day financial needs through wages obtained from work activity under the program.

Projects operating under the national contracts section of Mainstream have a larger proportion of women and minorities than the regionally administered programs. The major impact on minorities and women has been to enable them to meet their immediate economic and social needs through program participation. However, most of the programs do not stress skill training or job placement, and as a result, the benefits of the program are lost once an enrollee terminates.

The Operation Mainstream program has had a significant secondary impact on its enrollees. Almost all of the elderly enrollees stated that participation in the program improved their mental and physical health and their self-image.

Social bias and institutional regulations against the older worker have often contributed to the program's failure to find jobs for enrollees. In spite of these labor market realities, however, Operation Mainstream has proved to be a viable concept. It has supplemented the income of the elderly worker and provided needed community services in exchange. A by-product of the program is an improved self-image by the Mainstream worker, less worker dependence on other federal aid programs, and an improved community concept of the older worker as a potential labor source.

Bibliography

BACKGROUND AND MULTIPROGRAM STUDIES

Published Works

American Indian Consultants. *An Evaluation of Manpower Services and Supportive Services to American Indians on Reservations*. Scottsdale, Arizona: American Indian Consultants, Inc., 1972. NTISPB 213030.

Backer, Thomas E. *Methods of Assessing the Disadvantaged in Manpower Programs: A Review and Analysis*. Los Angeles: Human Interaction Research Institute, 1972. NTISPB 213167.

Ball, Joseph H. *The Implementation of Federal Manpower Policy, 1961-1971: A Study in Bureaucratic Competition and Intergovernmental Relations*. Report prepared for Office of Policy, Evaluation, and Research, Manpower Administration, U. S. Department of Labor, 1972. NTISPB 210656.

Barbash, Jack. "Union Interests in Apprenticeship and Other Training Forms." *Journal of Human Resources* 3 (Winter, 1968): 75-85.

Barsby, Steve L. *Cost-Benefit Analysis and Manpower Programs*. Lexington Massachusetts: D. C. Heath and Company, 1972.

Barth, Michael C.; and Gramlich, Edward M. *The Inflation-Unemployment Tradeoff and Public Employment*. Washington, D. C.: Office of Economic Opportunity, 1971.

Bluestone, Barry. "The Tripartite Economy, Labor Markets and the Working Poor." *Poverty and Human Resources*. Cambridge: Harvard University, 1970.

———; and Hardman, Anna. *Women, Welfare, and Work*. Boston: Social Welfare Regional Research Institute, Boston College, 1972.

———; Murphy, William M.; and Stevenson, Mary. *Low Wages and the Working Poor*. Ann Arbor: Institute of Labor and Industrial Relations, University of Michigan and Wayne State University, 1971. NTISPB 206095.

Board, Delores. "Pointing Enrollees Toward the Mainstream." *Manpower* 5 (October 1973): 10-12.

Booz, Allen Public Administration Services, Inc. *Evaluation Study of Job Development in Standard Metropolitan Statistical Areas,* Vol. 1, 11. Washington, D. C.: Allen Booz Public Administration Services, Inc., 1972.

Borus, Michael E. *Evaluating the Impact of Manpower Programs.* Lexington, Massachusetts: D. C. Heath and Company, 1972.

Bracey, John H.; Meir, August; and Rudwick, Elliot. *Black Workers and Organized Labor.* Belmont, California: Wadsworth Publishing Company, Inc., 1970.

Brecher, Charles. *The Impact of Federal Anti-Poverty Policies.* New York: Praeger Publishers, 1973.

Briscoe, Alden I. *The WPA: What is to be Learned?* Washington, D. C.: Center for Governmental Studies, 1971.

Brookings Institution. *Summary of Findings and Discussion of the Conference on Manpower Services for the Welfare Poor, November 14-16, 1971.* Washington, D. C.: Brookings Institution, n.d. NTISPB 210334.

Decker, Floyd A. *et al. Municipal Government Efforts to Provide Career Employment Opportunities for the Disadvantaged.* Washington, D. C.: National League of Cities, Department of Urban Studies, 1969. NTISPB 189912.

Doeringer, Peter B. ed. *Program to Employ the Disadvantaged.* Englewood Cliffs, New Jersey: Prentice-Hall, Inc., 1969.

; Piore, Michael J. *Internal Labor Markets and Manpower Analysis.* Lexington, Massachusetts: D. C. Heath and Company, 1971.

Ferman, Louis A. *Job Development for the Hard-to-Employ.* Ann Arbor: University of Michigan and Wayne State University, 1969.

Fine, Sidney A. *Guidelines for the Design of New Careers.* Kalamazoo: W. E. Upjohn Institute, 1967.

Foster, Howard G. "Nonapprenticeship Sources of Training in Construction." *Monthly Labor Review* 93 (February 1970): 380-393.

Goldstein, William. *Work and Welfare: A Legal Perspective on the Rights of Women on Welfare.* Boston: Social Welfare Regional Research Institute, Boston College, 1971.

Gould, William B. "Racial Discrimination, The Courts, and Construction." *Industrial Relations* 2 (October 1963): 380-393.

Harrison, Bennett. "Education and Underemployment in the Urban Ghetto." *American Economic Review* 62 (December 1972): 796-812.

———. *Public Employment and Urban Poverty.* Washington, D. C.: The Urban Institute, 1971.

———. "Public Service Jobs for Urban Ghetto Residents." *Good Government.* Washington, D. C.: National Civil Service League, 1969.

Henry, William F.; Miles, Guy H. *The Social Ecology of the Rural Poor.* Minneapolis: North Star Research and Development Institute, 1972.

Hill, Herbert. "The New Judicial Perception of Employment Discrimination Litigation Under Title VII of the Civil Rights Act of 1964." *University of Colorado Law Review* 43 (March 1972): 243-268.

Honig, Marjorie Hanson. "The Impact of the Welfare System on Labor Supply and Family Stability: A Study of Female Heads of Families." Master's thesis, Columbia University, 1971. NTISPB 201127.

Kursh, Harry. *Apprenticeship in America*. New York: W. W. Norton and Company, Inc., 1965.

Levitan, Sar A. *Federal Aid to Depressed Areas*. Baltimore: Johns Hopkins Press, 1964.

———. *Antipoverty Work and Training Efforts: Goals and Reality*. Ann Arbor: Institute of Labor and Industrial Relations, University of Michigan and Wayne State University, 1967.

———; Mangum, Garth L. *Federal Training and Work Programs in the 1960's*. Ann Arbor: Institute of Labor and Industrial Relations, University of Michigan. 1969.

Levy, Frank; Wiseman, Michael. *An Expanded Public Service Employment Program: Some Supply and Demand Considerations*. Berkeley: Institute of Industrial Relations, University of California, 1971.

Lowenthal, Martin. *Work and Welfare: An Overview*. Boston: Social Welfare Regional Research Institute, Boston College, 1971.

Mangum, Garth L. "Manpower Research and Manpower Policy." *A Review of Industrial Relations Research* Vol. II. Madison: Industrial Relations Research Association, 1972.

Marcus, Philip M. *Undergraduate Social Work Education and the Needs of the Work Incentive Program*. East Lansing: Michigan State University, 1972.

Miller, Jay. *Unemployment, Youth and Welfare*. Boston: Social Welfare Regional Research Institute, Boston College, 1972.

Miller, Joe A.; Ferman, Louis A. *Welfare Careers and Low Wage Employment*. Ann Arbor: University of Michigan and Wayne State University, 1972. NTISPB 221197.

Mills, Daniel Quinn. *Industrial Relations and Manpower in Construction*. Cambridge: MIT Press, 1972.

Myers, Charles A. *The Role of the Private Sector in Manpower Development*. Baltimore: Johns Hopkins Press, 1971.

National Analysts Inc., *Effects of the Earnings Exemption Provision Upon the Work Response of AFDC Recipients*. Philadelphia: National Analysts Inc., 1972.

National Industrial Conference Board. *Employing the Disadvantaged: A Company Perspective*. New York: National Industrial Conference Board Inc., 1972.

Northrup, Herbert R. *Organized Labor and the Negro*. New York: Kraus Reprint Edition, 1971.

O'Neill, David M. *The Federal Government and Manpower: A Critical Look at the MDTA and Job Corps Programs*. Washington, D. C.: American Enterprise Institute for Public Policy Research, 1973.

Rein, Mildred. *Influences on the Work Behavior of AFDC Mothers*. Boston: Social Welfare Regional Research Institute, Boston College, 1973.

——; Wishnov, Barbara. *Patterns of Work and Welfare in AFDC.* Boston: Social Welfare Regional Research Institute, Boston College, 1971.

Roe, Daphne A.; Eickwort, Kathleen R. *Health and Nutrition Status of Working and Non-Working Mothers in Poverty Groups.* Ithaca: Cornell University, n.d.

Rowan, Richard L. "Discrimination and Apprenticeship Regualtions in the Building Trades." *Journal of Business* 40 (October 1967): 435-447.

——; Rubin, Lester. *Opening the Skilled Construction Trades to Blacks: A Study of the Washington and Indianapolis Plans for Minority Employment.* Philadelphia: Industrial Research Unit, The Wharton School, University of Pennsylvania, 1972.

Slichter, Sumner; Healy, James J.; and Livernash, E. Robert. *The Impact of Collective Bargaining on Management.* Washington, D.C.: The Brookings Institution, 1960.

Somers, Gerald G. *Innovations in Apprenticeship: The Feasibility of Establishing Demonstration Centers for Apprenticeship and Other Industrial Training.* Madison: Manpower and Training Research Unit, University of Wisconsin, 1972. NTISPB 213555.

——; Wood, W. D. eds. *Cost-Benefit Analysis of Manpower Policies.* Kingston, Ontario: Industrial Relations Centre, Queen's University, 1969.

Sovern, Michael I. *Legal Restraints on Racial Discrimination in Employment.* New York: The Twentieth Century Fund, 1966.

Strauss, George. "Minorities and Apprenticeship." Neil W. Chamberlain. ed. *Business and the Cities.* New York: Basic Books Inc.,1970.

Thompson, David L.; Miles, Guy H. *Factors Affecting the Stability of the Low-Income Family.* Minneapolis: North Star Research and Development Institute, 1972. NTISPB 211704.

——. *Self-Actuated Work Behavior Among Low-Income People.* Minneapolis: North Star Research and Development Institute, 1972. NTISPB 211703.

——. *A Study of Low-Income Families: Methodology.* Minneapolis: North Star Research and Development Institute, 1972. NTISPB 211705.

U. S. Congress. Joint Economic Committee. Subcommittee on Fiscal Policy. *Hearings, Parts 1 and 3*; and *The Effectiveness of Manpower Training Programs: A Review of Research on the Impact of the Poor.* 92d Cong. 2d sess., 1972.

——. Joint Economic Committee. Subcommittee on Fiscal Policy. *How Public Welfare Benefits are Distributed in Low-Income Areas*; *Income-Tested Social Benefits in New York: Adequacy, Incentives, and Equity;* and *The Family, Poverty, and Welfare Programs: Factors Influencing Family Instability.* 93d Cong. 1st sess., 1973.

——. Joint Economic Committee. Subcommittee on Fiscal Policy. *State and Local Public Facility Needs and Financing, Vol. I: Public Facility Needs.* 89th Cong. 2d sess., 1966.

——. Senate. Committee on Education and Labor. *Hearings on the Economic Opportunity Amendments of 1967, Part 1.* 90th Cong. 1st sess., 1967.

U. S. Department of Labor. *A Sharper Look at Unemployment in U. S. Cities and Slums.* Washington, D. C.: U. S. Department of Labor, 1966.

———. *Federal Manpower Policy in Transition—National Manpower Advisory Committee Letters to the Secretaries of Labor and of Health, Education and Welfare,* 1972-1973. U. S. Department of Labor, 1974.

———. *Low-Income Labor Markets and Urban Manpower Programs: A Critical Assessment*. Washington, D. C.: Government Printing Office, 1972.

———. Manpower Administration. "Manpower Program Job Placements." *Manpower* 4 (December 1972): 21.

———. "Minority Enrollment in Manpower Programs." *Manpower* 5 (September 1973): 27.

———. Manpower Administration. *Career Mobility for Paraprofessionals In Human Service Agencies*. Washington, D. C.: Manpower Administration, 1969.

———. "Manpower Program Job Placements." *Manpower* 4 (December 1972): 21.

———. "Manpower Programs in 4 Cities." *Manpower* 4 (January 1972): 8-12.

———. *Manpower Report of the President*. Washington D. C.: Government Printing Office. 1968, 1969, 1970, 1971, 1972, 1973.

———. *Statistical Reporting Requirements for the Economic Opportunity Act Work and Training Programs, Neighborhood Youth Corps, Operation Mainstream, New Careers*. Washington, D. C.: U. S. Department of Labor, 1971.

———. *Toward the Ideal Journeyman—Vol. I. An Optimin Training System in Apprenticeable Occupations*. 1970; *Vol. 2. The Training System in the Pipe Trades*. 1971; *Vol. 3. Apprenticeship Training in the Machinist and Tool and Die Makers Trades*. 1971; *Vol. 4. The Training System in the Printing Trades*. 1971. Manpower Research Monograph, No. 20. Washington D. C.: Government Printing Office.

Walther, Regis H.; Magnusson, Margaret L.; and Cherkasky, Shirley E. *A Study of Negro Male High School Dropouts Who Are Not Reached by the Federal Work-Training Programs*. Washington, D. C.: Social Research Group, George Washington University, 1970. NTISPB 202110.

Weber, Arnold R. "Role and Limits of Manpower Policy." *Proceedings of the Eighteenth Annual Meeting: IRRA*. Madison: Industrial Relations Research Association, 1965.

———; Cassell, Frank.; and Ginsburg, Woodrow L. eds. *Public-Private Manpower Policies*. Madison: Industrial Relations Research Association, 1969.

Wilson, Michael. *Job Development in the Federal Service*. Washington, D. C.: Social Development Corporation, 1971.

Wishnov, Barbara. *Determinants of the Work-Welfare Choice—A Study of AFDC Women*. Boston: Social Welfare Regional Research Institute, Boston College, 1973.

Wolfbein, Seymour L. ed. *Manpower Policy: Perspectives and Prospects*. Philadelphia: School of Business Administration, Temple University, 1973.

Unpublished Studies

Baldwin, Stephen Edward. "The Impact of Government Programs on the Employability of Youth in the Seattle Labor Market." Ph.D. dissertation, University of Washington, 1968.

Camil Associates, Inc. "Evaluation of Supportive Services Provided for Participants of Manpower Programs—Final Report." Report prepared for Manpower Administration, U. S. Department of Labor, 1972.

Center of Naval Analysis. "The Impact of Manpower Programs: A Summary and Evaluation of the Findings of Existing Studies." Memorandum for the Director of Evaluation, ASPER, January 31, 1972.

Crowell, Elizabeth. "An Analysis of Discrimination Against the Negro in the Building Trades Unions." Ph.D. dissertation, Indiana University, 1971.

J. A. Reves, Associates. "An Evaluation of Manpower Systems Services to Mexican Americans in Four Southwestern States." Report prepared for Office of Policy, Evaluation, and Research, Manpower Administration, U. S. Department of Labor, 1972.

Ketron, Inc. "Employability of AFDC Recipients: Survey of Relevant Literature." Report prepared for Office of Evaluation, U. S. Department of Health, Education and Welfare, 1972.

———. "The Employability Model Data Base: A Discussion of its Structure and Parameters." Report prepared for Office of Policy, Evaluation and Research, Manpower Administration, U. S. Department of Labor, 1972.

———. "Estimates of Annual Natural Turnover Rates from 1969 and 1971 AFDC National Surveys." Report prepared for Office of Program Planning and Evaluation, U. S. Department of Health, Education and Welfare, and Office of Evaluation, Manpower Administration, U. S. Department of Labor, 1972.

———. "Multivariate Regression Analysis of Annual Natural Turnover Rates Using the 1969 and 1971 AFDC National Surveys." Report prepared for U. S. Department of Health, Education, and Welfare, 1973.

Olympus Research Corporation. "The Total Impact of Manpower Programs: A Four-City Case Study." Vols. I and II. Report prepared for Office of Policy, Evaluation and Research, Manpower Administration, U. S. Department of Labor, 1971.

Oriel, Arthur E. "A Performance Based Individualized Training System for Technical and Apprenticeship Training—A Pilot Study." Development Systems Corporation. Report prepared for Manpower Administration, U. S. Department of Labor, 1973.

Sam Harris Associates, Ltd. "An Evaluation of the Utilization of Manpower and Social Services by Negroes in Eight Southern Cities." Report Prepared for Office of Policy, Evaluation and Research, Manpower Administration, U. S. Department of Labor, 1972.

———. "A Manpower Program Evaluation Project of All Federally Supported Manpower Programs in the City of Newark, N. J." Report prepared for Manpower Administration, U. S. Department of Labor, 1970.

Smith, Ralph E. "An Analysis of Efficiency and Equity in Manpower Programs." Ph.D. dissertation, Georgetown University, 1971.

Summerfield, Donald A. "Summary of Job Training Programs in Detroit: A Comparative Study." Report prepared for Office of Policy, Evaluation and Research, Manpower Administration, U. S. Department of Labor, n.d.

Unco, Inc. "Methodology for Measuring the Cost-Effectiveness of Manpower Programs Development and Application." Report prepared for the Office of Policy, Evaluation, and Research, Manpower Administration, U.S. Department of Labor, 1972.

U.S. Department of Labor. "The Role of Manpower Programs in Assisting Negroes and Puerto Ricans in Springfield, Massachusetts: A Pilot Evaluation Study." 1967.

Woltman, Harry R.; and Walton, William W. "Evaluation of the War on Poverty: The Feasibility of Benefit-Cost Analysis for Manpower Programs." Report prepared for General Accounting Office, 1968.

APPRENTICESHIP OUTREACH PROGRAM

Published Studies

Center for Studies in Vocational and Technical Education. *Research in Apprenticeship Training*. Proceedings of a conference, September 8-9, 1966. Madison: University of Wisconsin, 1967.

The Greater Washington Central Labor Council, AFL-CIO. *Project Build, A Manpower Demonstration Program*. Washington, D. C.: The Greater Washington Central Labor Council, 1969, 1970.

Marshall, F. Ray; Briggs, Vernon M. *Equal Apprenticeship Opportunities—The Nature of the Problem and the New York Experience*. Ann Arbor: Institute of Labor and Industrial Relations, University of Michigan, 1968.

———; Briggs, Vernon M. *The Negro and Apprenticeship*. Baltimore: Johns Hopkins Press, 1967.

———; Glover, Robert W.; and Franklin, William S. *A Comparison of Construction Workers Who Have Achieved Journeymen Status Through Apprenticeship and Other Means*. Austin: Center for the Study of Human Resources, University of Texas, 1973.

Roomkin, Myron. *Improving Apprenticeship: Employer and Union Reactions to Foreign Training*. Chicago: Graduate School of Business, University of Chicago, 1973. NTISPB 222830.

Roberts, Markley. "Labor-Sponsored Pre-apprenticeship Training: What is the Payoff?" *Labor Law Journal* 21 (October 1970): 663-667.

Roussel, Norman. *Apprenticeship Outreach in New Orleans*. Washington, D. C.: U. S. Department of Labor, 1971.

Shapiro, Theresa R. *Negro Craftsmen in a Southern Labor Market*. New Orleans: Louisiana State University, 1972. NTISPB 212233.

U. S. Congress. Senate. Committee on Labor and Public Welfare. Subcommittee on Employment Manpower and Poverty. *The Role of Apprenticeship in Manpower Development: United States and Western Europe*. 88th Cong. 2d sess., 1964.

U. S. Department of Labor. *Proceedings: Working Conference on Apprenticeship Research and Development, October 5-6, 1971.* Washington, D. C.: 1971.

Unpublished Studies

Boise Cascade Center for Community Development. "Report on an Evaluation of the Apprenticeship Outreach Program." Report prepared for Office of Policy, Evaluation, and Research, Manpower Administration, U. S. Department of Labor, 1970.

Derryck, Dennis A. "Improving the Retention Rate of Indentured Apprentices in the Apprenticeship Outreach Program." Report prepared for Office of Policy, Evaluation, and Research, Manpower Administration, U. S. Department of Labor, 1973.

———. "Retention of Minorities in Apprenticeship." Paper presented at a conference on Apprenticeship Research and Development, Manpower Administration, U. S. Department of Labor, May 30, 1973.

Roberts, Markley. "Pre-Apprenticeship Training for Disadvantaged Youth: A Cost-Benefit Study of Training by Project Build in Washington, D. C." Report prepared for Office of Policy, Evaluation, and Research, Manpower Administration, U. S. Department of Labor, 1970.

Swanson, S. M.; Herrnstadt, I. L.; and Horowitz, M.A. "The Role of Related Instruction in Apprenticeship Training." Report prepared for Office of Policy, Evaluation, and Research, Manpower Administration, U. S. Department of Labor, 1973.

U. S. Department of Labor, Bureau of Apprenticeship and Training. "Ethnic Composition of Registered Apprentices in Training by Major Industry, Fiscal Years 1967-1972 (Federally Serviced Workload only)."

———. "Outreach Program Activity Summary Charts." June 1968 through August 1973.

———. "Training Program Development and Review, Apprentices in Federally Serviced Workload, Selected Trades, January 1, 1968—June 30, 1972."

CONCENTRATED EMPLOYMENT PROGRAM

Published Studies

Ferman, Louis. *Job Development for the Hard-to-Employ.* Washington, D. C.: Manpower Administration, U. S. Department of Labor, 1968.

Kirschner Associates, Inc. *Evaluation of Five Concentrated Employment Programs in Regions I and II.* New York: Kirschner Associates. Inc., 1969.

Leone, Richard D. *et al.* *Employability Development Teams and Federal Manpower Programs: A Critical Assessment of the Philadelphia CEP's Experience.* Philadelphia: Temple University, 1972. NTISPB 213790.

Lewis, Morgan V.; Cohn, Elchanan; and Hughes, David H. *Recruiting, Placing, and Retraining the Hard-to-Employ.* University Park, Pennsylvania: Institute for Research on Human Resources, Pennsylvania State University, 1971. NTISPB 204600.

System Development Corporation. *Cost-Effectiveness Evaluation of the Urban Concentrated Employment Program—Final Report.* Falls Church, Virginia: System Development Corporation, 1973. NTISPB 222852.

———. *Evaluation of the Impact of Selected Urban Concentrated Employment Programs.* Falls Church, Virginia: System Development Corporation, 1970. NTISPB 197330.

U. S. Department of Labor, Office of Manpower Management Data Systems. *Concentrated Employment Program (CEP)—Information System Manual.* Washington, D. C.: U. S. Department of Labor, 1970.

Unpublished Studies

Analytic Systems, Inc. "Analysis of CEP Automated Termination Data." Report prepared for Office of Policy, Evaluation and Research, Manpower Administration, U. S. Department of Labor, 1970.

A. L. Nellum and Associates. "Final Report of Evaluation of the Concentrated Employment Program in Atlanta, Georgia; Baltimore, Maryland; and Chicago, Illinois." Report prepared for Office of Policy, Evaluation, and Research, Manpower Administration U. S. Department of Labor, 1969.

Revzan, L. H. *et al.* "Quantitative Analysis of the Concentrated Employment Program." Report prepared for Division of Planning, Manpower Administration, U. S. Department of Labor. Management Systems Group, Leasco Systems and Research Corporation, 1969.

System Development Corporation. "Analysis of the Concentrated Employment Program Subsequent to Manpower Administration Order 14-69." Report prepared for Office of Policy, Evaluation and Research, Manpower Administration, U. S. Department of Labor, 1971.

Urban Systems Research and Engineering, Inc., "The Impact of Five Rural Concentrated Employment Programs." Report prepared for Office of Policy, Evaluation and Research, Manpower Administration, U. S. Department of Labor, 1971.

JOB CORPS

Published Studies

Comptroller General of the United States. *Effectiveness and Administration of the Acadia Job Corps Civilian Conservation Center Under the Economic Opportunity Act of 1964—Bar Harbor, Maine.* Washington, D. C.: Department of the Interior, Office of Economic Opportunity, 1969.

———. *Effectiveness and Administration of the Albuquerque Job Corps Center for Women Under the Economic Opportunity Act of 1964—Albuquerque, New Mexico*. Washington, D. C.: Office of Economic Opportunity, 1969.

———. *Effectiveness and Administration of the Atterbury Job Corps Center For Men under the Economic Opportunity Act of 1964—Edinburg, Indiana.* Washington, D. C.: Office of Economic Opportunity, 1969.

———. *Effectiveness and Administration of the Aspus Job Corps Civilian Conservation Center Under the Economic Opportunity Act of 1964—Randle, Washington.* Washington, D. C.: Department of Agriculture, Office of Economic Opportunity, 1969.

———. *Effectiveness and Administration of the Collbran Job Corps Civilian Conservation Center under the Economic Opportunity Act of 1964—Collbran, Colorado.* Washington, D. C.: Department of the Interior Office of Economic Opportunity, 1969.

———. *Effectiveness and Administration of the Eight Canyon Job Corps Civilian Conservation Center under the Economic Opportunity Act of 1964—Mescalero, New Mexico.* Washington, D. C.: Department of the Interior, Office of Economic Opportunity, 1969.

———. *Effectiveness and Administration of the Keystone Job Corps Center for Women Under the Economic Opportunity Act of 1964—Drums, Pennsylvania.* Washington, D. C.: Office of Economic Opportunity, 1969.

———. *Effectiveness and Administration of the Kilmer Job Corps Center for Men Under the Economic Opportunity Act of 1964—Edison, New Jersey.* Washington, D. C.: Office of Economic Opportunity, 1969.

———. *Effectiveness and Administration of the Wellfleet Job Corps Civilian Conservation Center Under the Economic Opportunity Act of 1964—South Wellfleet, Massachusetts.* Washington, D. C.: Department of the Interior, Office of Economic Opportunity, 1969.

———. *Selected Aspects of Payments and Charges to Job Corps Members.* Washington, D. C.: Department of Defense, Office of Economic Opportunity, 1969.

Engleman, Stephen Robert. "An Economic Analysis of the Job Corps." Ph.D. dissertation, University of California at Berkeley, 1971. NTISPB 202891.

"How Unions are Breathing New Life into Job Corps." *U. S. News and World Report* 65 (August 1968): 61-62.

Lang, Duaine C. *et al. The AACTE-Job Corps Teacher Education Project: A Final Examination.* Washington, D. C.: American Association of Colleges for Teacher Education, 1972.

Levitan, Sar A. "An Antipoverty Experiment: The Job Corps." *Nineteenth Annual Industrial Relations Research Association Proceedings—Winter 1966.* Edited by Gerald Somers. Madison: Industrial Relations Research Association, 1967.

Louis Harris and Associates. "A Continuing Study of Job Corps Terminations: Wave II—Initial Interview with Termination From August 15, 1966 to December 15, 1966." *Hearings on the Economic Opportunity Amendments of 1967.* Part I. 90th Cong. 1st sess. Committee on Education and Labor. Washington, D. C.: Government Printing Office, 1967.

———. "A Study of Job Corps Nongraduate Terminations." *Hearings on the Economic Opportunity Amendments of 1967.* Part I. 90th Cong. 1st sess. Committee on Education and Labor. Washington, D. C.: Government Printing Office, 1967.

———. "A Study of Job Corps 'No-Shows' Accepted Applicants Who Did Not Go to a Training Center." *Hearings on the Economic Opportunity Amendments of 1967.* Part I. 90th Cong. 1st sess. Committee on Education and Labor. Washington, D. C.: Government Printing Office, 1967.

Office of Economic Opportunity. *A & R Reports #2.* Washington, D. C.: Evaluation and Research Center Assessment Branches, Job Corps, Office of Economic Opportunity, 1967.

———. *A & R Reports #3.* Washington, D. C.: Evaluation and Research Center Assessment Branches, Job Corps, Office of Economic Opportunity, 1967.

———. *A & R Reports #5.* Washington, D. C.: Evaluation and Research Branch, Plans and Evaluation Division, Plans and Programs Directorate, Job Corps, Office of Economic Opportunity, 1967.

———. *A & R Reports #6.* Washington, D. C.: Evaluation and Research Branch, Plans and Evaluation Division, Plans and Programs Directorate, Jobs Corps. Office of Economic Opportunity, 1967.

———. *A & R Reports #11.* Washington, D. C.: Evaluation and Research Branch, Plans and Evaluation Division, Plans and Programs Directorate, Job Corps, Office of Economic Opportunity, n.d.

U. S. Department of Labor, Manpower Administration. *Job Corps: Bilingual/Multicultural Program.* Washington, D. C.: Job Corps, Manpower Administration, U. S. Department of Labor, 1973.

———. *Job Corps: Center Developed Training Program.* Washington, D. C.: Job Corps, Manpower Administration, U. S. Department of Labor, 1972.

———. *Job Corps Residential Living Manual.* Washington, D. C.: Job Corps, Manpower Administration, U. S. Department of Labor, 1972.

———. *You make the Difference—In Job Corps Every Staff Member Helps.* Washington, D. C.: Manpower Administration, U. S. Department of Labor, 1972.

Unpublished Studies

Cain, Glen G. "Benefit/Cost Estimates for Job Corps." Institute for Research on Poverty, University of Wisconsin, 1968.

Center for Naval Analysis. "The Job Corps: A Program Analysis and Evaluation." Final Draft Report. Memorandum. April 4, 1972.

Chafkin, Sol H. *et al.* "An Evaluation of Project Threshold: A Job Corps Transition Program." Report prepared for Office of Economic Opportunity. Washington, D. C.: American Technical Assistance Corporation, 1968.

Daniel Yankelovich, Inc. "Qualitative Assessment of Factors Affecting Retention Rate in Job Corps." Report prepared for Job Corps, 1967.

Earle, Ralph. *et al.* "A Diagnostic and Developmental Project to Identify Job Corps Retention Factors." Report prepared for Job Corps, Abt Associates, Inc.,1973.

Hoyte, Stephney Keyset. "The Women's Job Corps—Patterns of Behavior Relating to Success or Failure." Ph.D. dissertation, Catholic University, 1969.

Institute for Resource Management. "Cost-Effectiveness Evaluation of Terminated Job Corps Centers." Report prepared for Office of Plans and Programs, Job Corps, 1968.

Louis Harris and Associates. "A Continuing Study of Job Corps Terminations: Wave III, Initial Interview with Terminations from January 15, 1967 to March 15, 1967." An interim report prepared for Job Corps, August 1967.

———. "A Study of the Status of August 1966 Job Corps Terminees 12 Months After Termination." Report prepared for Job Corps, 1967.

———. "A Study of the Status of August 1966 Job Corps Terminees 18 Months After Termination." Report prepared for Job Corps, 1968.

———. "A Study of the Staus of November 1966 Job Corps Terminees 12 Months After Termination." Report prepared for Job Corps, 1968.

———. "A Study of the Status of November 1966 Job Corps Terminees 18 Months After Termination." Report prepared for Job Corps, 1968.

———. "A Survey of Ex-Job Corpsmen." Report prepared for Job Corps, 1969.

Regelson, Lillian. *et al.* "Characteristics of Urban Enrollees Entering the Job Corps." Report prepared for Office of Planning. Research and Evaluation, Office of Economic Opportunity, n.d.

Schertler, Leon. "Study of the Universe of Need." Internal report prepared in Job Corps, Manpower Administration, U. S. Department of Labor, 1969.

Software Systems, Inc. "A Job Corps Study of Relative Cost Benefits." Report prepared for Office of Plans and Programs, Job Corps, 1969.

Unco, Inc. "Evaluation of the Effectiveness of Pre and Post-Enrollment Services To Job Corps Enrollees." Final Report prepared for Office of Policy Evaluation and Research, Manpower Administration, U. S. Department of Labor, 1972.

———. "Louis Harris Job Corps Follow-Up Questionnaire Analysis: Final Report." Report prepared for Job Corps, Manpower Administration, U. S. Department of Labor, n.d.

U. S. Department of Labor, Manpower Administration. "A Working Paper for the 37th Meeting of the National Manpower Advisory Committee, September 21, 1973—Job Corps: The Current Issues and Outcomes." Internal report, Manpower Administration, U. S. Department of Labor 1973.

———. "The Job Corps Health Program 1973-1974." Report of Jobs Corps, U. S. Department of Labor, Manpower Administration, n.d.

———. "Job Corps Placement Performance Fiscal Year 1970." Mimeographed. Report of Job Corps, U. S. Department of Labor, Manpower Administration, n.d.

———. Women's Bureau. "Women in Poverty." Report prepared at the request of the Women's Sector, The President's Task Force on the "War Against Poverty." 1964.

Vincent, Howard. "A Cost Effectiveness Analysis of the Job Corps." Internal Report of Manpower Administration, U. S. Department of Labor, 1972.

JOB OPPORTUNITIES IN THE BUSINESS SECTOR

Published Studies

Baum, John Franklin. *An Evaluation of a NAB-JOBS Training Program for Disadvantaged Workers*. Madison: Industrial Relations Research Institute, University of Wisconsin, 1973.

Comptroller General of the United States. *Evaluation of Results and Administration of the Job Opportunities in the Business Sector (JOBS) Program in Five Cities.* Washington, D. C.: U. S. General Accounting Office, 1971.

U. S. Congress. Senate. Committee on Labor and Public Welfare. Subcommittee on Employment, Manpower, and Poverty. *The JOBS Program: Background Information*. 91st Cong. 2nd sess., 1970.

U. S. Department of Labor. *Manpower Technical Exchange, Vol. V.* No. 19. Washington D. C.: Government Printing Office, 1973.

Unpublished Studies

Farber, David J. "Highlights—Annual Follow-Up: 1968, JOBS Contract and Non-Contract Programs." Report prepared for Office of Policy, Evaluation, and Research, Manpower Administration, U. S. Department of Labor, 1971.

Greenleigh Associates, Inc. "The Job Opportunities in the Business Sector Program—An Evaluation of Impact in Ten Standard Metropolitan Statistical Areas." Report prepared for Office of Policy, Evaluation and Research, Manpower Administration, U. S. Department of Labor, 1970.

Schlensky, Bertram C. "Determinants of Turnover in NAB-JOBS Program to Employ the Disadvantaged." Ph.D. dissertation, Massachusetts Institute of Technology, 1970.

System Development Corporation. "Evaluation of the JOBS Program in Nine Cities." Report prepared for Office of Policy, Evaluation, and Research, Manpower Administration, U. S. Department of Labor, 1970.

MANPOWER DEVELOPMENT AND TRAINING ACT

Published Studies

Azzi, Corry F. *Equity and Efficiency Effects from Manpower Programs*. Lexington, Massachusetts: D. C. Heath and Company, 1973.

Borus, Michael E. "The Effects of Retraining the Unemployed in Connecticut." In Gerald Somers, ed., *Retraining the Unemployed.* Madison: University of Wisconsin Press, 1968.

———. "Time Trends in the Benefits from Retraining in Connecticut." *Proceedings of the Twentieth Annual Winter Meeting, IRRA.* Madison: Industrial Relations Research Association, 1967.

Cain, Glen G; Stromsdorfer, Ernst W. "An Economic Evaluation of Government Retraining Programs in West Virginia." In Gerald Somers, ed., *Retraining the Unemployed.* Madison: University of Wisconsin Press, 1968.

Chernick, Jack; Indik, Bernard P; and Craig, Roger. *The Selection of Trainees Under MDTA.* New Brunswick, New Jersey: Rutgers University, 1965. ERIC ED 015255.

Cohen, Malcolm. "The Direct Effects of Federal Manpower Programs in Reducing Unemployment." *Journal of Human Resources* 4 (Fall 1969):491-507.

Dratning, John F. *Jobs, Education and Training: Research on a Project Combining Literacy and On-the-Job Training for the Disadvantaged.* Buffalo, New York: Research Foundation of the State University of New York, n.d. NTISPB 211181.

Ferman, Louis A.; Harvey, Scott. "Job Retraining in Michigan." In Gerald Somers, ed. *Retraining the Unemployed.* Madison: University of Wisconsin Press, 1968.

Gibbard, Harold A.; and Somers, Gerald G. "Government Retraining of the Unemployed in West Virginia." In Gerald Somers, ed. *Retraining the Unemployed.* Madison: University of Wisconsin Press, 1953.

Goldfarb, Robert S. "The Evaluation of Government Programs: The Case of New Haven's Manpower Training Activities." *Yale Economic Essays* 9 (Fall 1969): 59-104.

Gurin, Gerald. *A National Attitude Study of Trainees in MDTA Institutional Programs,* Ann Arbor: Survey Research Center, Institute for Social Research, University of Michigan, 1970. NTISPB 193723.

Hardin, Einar; Borus, Michael. *Economic Benefits and Cost of Retraining.* Lexington, Massachusetts: D. C. Heath and Company, 1971.

Indik, Bernard P. *The Motivation to Work.* New Brunswick, New Jersey: Rutgers University, 1965. ERIC ED 015255.

London, H. H. *How Fare MDTA Trainees.* Columbia, Missouri: University of Missouri, 1967. NTISPB 177626.

Mangum, Garth L. *MDTA: Foundation of Federal Manpower Policy.* Baltimore: Johns Hopkins Press, 1968.

Page, David A. "Retraining Under the Manpower Development Act: A Cost-Benefit Analysis." In John D. Montgomery, Arthur Smithies, eds. *Public Policy.* Vol. 13. Cambridge: Harvard University Press, 1964.

Prescott, Edward C.; Tash, William; and Usdane, William. "Training and Employability: The Effects of MDTA on AFDC Recipients." *Welfare in Review.* (January 1971).

Roomkin, Myron. *An Evaluation of Adult Basic Education Under the Development and Training Act in Milwaukee, Wisconsin.* Milwaukee: University of Wisconsin, 1970. NTISPB 196743.

Sewell, David O. *Training the Poor: A Benefit-Cost Analysis of Manpower Programs in the U. S. Anti-Poverty Program.* Kingston, Ontario: Industrial Relations Centre, Queen's University, 1971.

Solie, Richard J. "An Evaluation of the Effects of Retraining in Tennessee." In Gerald Somers, ed. *Retraining the Unemployed.* Madison: University of Wisconsin, 1968.

———. "Employment Effects of Retraining the Unemployed." *Industrial and Labor Relations Review* 22 (January 1968): 210-225.

Stromsdorfer, Ernst W. "Determinants of Economic Success in Retraining the Unemployed." *Journal of Human Resources* 3 (Spring 1968): 139-158.

Trumble, Robert R. "*Prediction Models for Institutional Training Programs Under the Manpower Development and Training Act.*" Ph.D. dissertation, University of Minnesota, 1971. NTISPB 220453.

U. S. Department of Labor. "Earnings Mobility of MDTA Trainees." *Manpower Evaluation Report, No. 7.* Washington, D. C.: Manpower Administration, U. S. Department of Labor, 1969.

———. "The Influence of MDTA Training on Earnings." *Manpower Evaluation Report, No. 8.* Washington, D. C.: Manpower Administration, U. S. Department of Labor, 1970.

———. "Inner-City Youth in a Job Training Project." *MDTA Experimental and Demonstration Findings, No. 7.* Washington, D. C.: Manpower Administration, U. S. Department of Labor, 1971.

———. "Manpower Development and Training on Correctional Programs." *MDTA Experimental and Demonstration Findings, No. 3.* Washington, D. C.: Manpower Administration, U. S. Department of Labor, 1968.

———. "MDTA Training Program: Comparison of 1963 and 1964." *Manpower Evaluation Report, No. 4.* Washington, D. C.: Manpower Administration, U. S. Department of Labor, 1964.

———. "Occupational Mobility Through MDTA Training." *Manpower Evaluation Report, No. 3.* Washington, D. C.: Manpower Administration, U. S. Department of Labor, 1964.

———. "Orientation, Counseling, and Assessment in Manpower Programs." *MDTA Experimental and Demonstration Findings, No. 5.* Washington, D. C.: Manpower Administration, U. S. Department of Labor, 1969.

———. "Training Disadvantaged Groups Under the Manpower Development and Training Act." *Manpower Evaluation Report, No. 1.* Washington, D. C.: Manpower Administration, U. S. Department of Labor, 1963.

———. "Training of Public Assistance Recipients under MDTA." *Manpower Evaluation Report No. 6.* Washington, D. C.: Manpower Administration, U. S. Department of Labor, 1966.

Unpublished Studies

Abt Associates. "An Evaluation of the Training Provided in Correctional Institutions Under the Manpower Development and Training Act, Section 251." Report prepared for Office of Policy, Evaluation and Research, Manpower Administration, U. S. Department of Labor, 1971.

Buenaventura, Agnes. "Follow-Up Study of MDTA Prospects Conducted by the Michigan Catholic Conference, Lansing." Report prepared for Office of Policy, Evaluation and Research, Manpower Administration, U. S. Department of Labor, 1967.

Carlson, Norma W.; Mallory, Patricia L. "Federally Funded Manpower Development Programs in Philadelphia: A Critical Evaluation." Economic Development Unit, Department of Finance, City of Philadelphia, 1967.

Decision Making Information. "MDTA Outcomes Study." Report prepared for Office of Policy, Evaluation and Research, Manpower Administration, U. S. Department of Labor, 1971.

Farber, David J. "Methods of Calculating Measures Used in Manpower Training Follow-up Systems." Memorandum, U. S. Department of Labor, n.d.

———. "A Reply to the Miller Critique of the M.A. Method of Evaluating Gains in Earnings of MDTA Trainees." Memorandum, U. S. Department of Labor, n.d.

———. "Changes in the Duration of the Post-Training Period and in Relative Earnings Credits of Trainees: The 1965-69 Experience of MDTA Institutional and OJT Trainees, Class of 1964." U. S. Department of Labor, 1971.

———. "Highlights: Some Findings from a Follow-up Study of Pre- and Post-Training Earnings Histories of 215,000 Trainees Participating in Two 1964 and Four 1968 Training Programs." U. S. Department of Labor, 1971.

Greenleigh Associates, Inc. "Opening the Doors: Job Training Programs." Report to the Committee on Administration of Training Programs, U. S. Department of Labor, 1968.

Hardman, William E.; Munn, Norton N. "A Study of Accelerated On-the-job Training for the First Year of On-the-job Training for the Precision Machinist Apprentice." Report prepared for Manpower Administration, U. S. Department of Labor, 1973.

Jones, Darrell G. "An Evaluation of the Socio-Psychological and Socio-Economic Effects of MDTA Training on Trainees in Selected Michigan Programs." Ph.D. dissertation, Michigan State University, 1966.

Miller, Herman P. "Critique of David Farber's Method of Evaluating the Gains in Earnings of MDTA Trainees." Memorandum, U. S. Department of Labor, n.d.

Muir, Allan H. *et al.* "Cost/Effectiveness Analysis of On-the-job and Institutional Training Courses." Report prepared for Office of Policy, Evaluation, and Research, Manpower Administration, U. S. Department of Labor, 1967.

National Analysts, Inc. "The Effectiveness of the Training Program Under MDTA." Report prepared for Office of Policy, Evaluation, and Research, Manpower Administration, U. S. Department of Labor, 1965.

Olympus Research Corporation, "Evaluation of the Effectiveness of Institutional Manpower Training in Meeting Employers' Needs in Skill Shortage Occupations." Report prepared for Office of Policy, Evaluation, and Research, Manpower Administration, U. S. Department of Labor, 1972.

———. "Evaluation of the MDTA Institutional Individual Referral Program." Report prepared for Office of Policy, Evaluation, and Research, Manpower Administration, U. S. Department of Labor, 1972.

Prescott, Edward C. "Analysis of MDTA Institutional and OJT Data Tapes for 1968." Report prepared for Office of Policy, Evaluation and Research, Manpower Administration, U. S. Department of Labor, 1971.

———; Cooley, Thomas F. "Evaluating the Impact of MDTA Training Programs on Earnings Under Varying Labor Market Conditions." Report prepared for Office of Policy, Evaluation, and Research, Manpower Administration, U. S. Department of Labor, 1972.

NEIGHBORHOOD YOUTH CORPS

Published Studies

Borus, Michael E.; Brennan, John P.; and Rosen, Sidney. "A Benefit-Cost Analysis of the Neighborhood Youth Corps." *The Journal of Human Resources* 5 (Spring 1970): 139-150.

Broughton, Frank.; Reinish, Hal. *Fulfilling the Potential of NYC-2—The Pre-Program Orientation Towards Enhancing Success in NYC-2 Job Training.* Manpower Monograph Series on Disadvantaged Youth, no. 13. New York: Experimental Manpower Laboratory, Mobilization for Youth, Inc., 1972. NTISPB 213897.

Comptroller General of the United States. *Effectiveness and Administrative Efficiency of the Neighborhood Youth Corps Program Under Title I-B of the Economic Opportunity Act of 1964: Carroll, Chanton, Lafayette, Ray, and Saline Counties, Missouri.* Washington, D. C.: General Accounting Office, 1969.

———. *Effectiveness and Administrative Efficiency of the Neighborhood Youth Corps Program Under Title I-B of the Economic Opportunity Act of 1964: Chicago, Illinois.* Washington, D. C.: General Accounting Office, 1969.

———. *Effectiveness and Administrative Efficiency of the Neighborhood Youth Corps Program Under Title I-B of the Economic Opportunity Act of 1964: Detroit, Michigan.* Washington, D. C.: General Accounting Office, 1969.

———. *Effectiveness and Administrative Efficiency of the Neighborhood Youth Corps Program Under Title I-B of the Economic Opportunity Act of 1964: Gary, Indiana.* Washington, D. C.: General Accounting Office, 1969.

———. *Effectiveness and Administrative Efficiency of the Neighborhood Youth Corps Program Under Title I-B of the Economic Opportunity Act of 1964: Gila River Indian Reservation and Pinal Country, Arizona.* Washington, D. C.: General Accounting Office, 1969.

———. *Effectiveness and Administrative Efficiency of the Neighborhood Youth Corps Program Under Title I-B of the Economic Opportunity Act of 1964: Grand Rapids, Michigan.* Washington, D. C.: General Accounting Office, 1969.

———. *Effectiveness and Administrative Efficiency of the Neighborhood Youth Corps Program Under Title I-B of the Economic Opportunity Act of 1964: Kansas City, Missouri.* Washington, D. C.: General Accounting Office, 1969.

———. *Effectiveness and Administrative Efficiency of the Neighborhood Youth Corps Program Under Title I-B of the Economic Opportunity Act of 1964: Los Angeles County, California.* Washington, D. C.: General Accounting Office, 1969.

———. *Effectiveness and Administrative Efficiency of the Neighborhood Youth Corps Program Under Title I-B of the Economic Opportunity Act of 1964: Maricopa County with Emphasis on the City of Phoenix, Arizona.* Washington, D. C.: General Accounting Office, 1969.

———. *Effectiveness and Administrative Efficiency of the Neighborhood Youth Corps Program Under Title I-B of the Economic Opportunity Act of 1964: Selected Rural Areas of Minnesota.* Washington, D. C.: General Accounting Office, 1969.

———. *Effectiveness and Administrative Efficiency of the Neighborhood Youth Corps Program Under Title I-B of the Economic Opportunity Act of 1964: St. Louis and St. Louis County, Missouri.* Washington, D. C.: General Accounting Office, 1969.

Daane, Calvin. *et al. Final Report on Developing Group Counseling Models for the Neighborhood Youth Corps.* Tempe, Arizona: Arizona State University, January 1969. NTISPB 182512.

Eckman, Bruce, and Simons, Judith. *Field Experiments In Manpower Issues: The Reward Preferences of NYC Trainees: II Program Tenure Correlates of Differential Preferences.* New York: Mobilization for Youth, Inc., 1972. NTISPB 214062.

Egloff, Marjorie. *The Neighborhood Youth Corps: A Review of Research.* Manpower Research Monograph, No. 13. Washington, D. C.: Manpower Administration, U. S. Department of Labor, 1970.

Freeberg, Norman E.; Reilly, Richard R. *Development of Assessment Measures for Use With Youth Training Program Enrollees—Phase II: Longitudinal Validation. Princeton: Educational Testing Service, 1973.*

———. *Development of Guidance Measures for Youth-Work Training Program Enrollees—Phase I: Measurement of Program Objectives and the Development of Criteria.* Princeton: Educational Testing Service, 1971. NTISPB 202807.

Goodman, Leonard H.; Myint, Thelma D. *The Economic Needs of Neighborhood Youth Corps Enrollees.* New York: Bureau of Social Science Research, Inc., 1969. NTISPB 202812.

Hudson Guild. *Teenage Opportunity Program: An Experimental and Demonstration Project Linking Professional/Technical Employers to the NYC In-School Program—A Final Report,* New York: The Hudson Guild, 1972.

Josman, Karyl F.; Sexton, Virginia Staudt. *Final Report—The American Scholarship Association Westchester Programs/ A Learning Center: Work Experience Design (Neighborhood Youth Corps Students Choose College Careers in the Allied Health Professions).* New York: American Scholarship Association, Inc., 1972.

Lorber, Fred. *Fulfilling the Potential of NYC-2-Criteria for the Selection and Training of Neighborhood Youth Corps Work Supervisors.* Manpower Monograph Series on Disadvantaged Youth, No. 2, New York: Experimental Manpower Laboratory, Mobilization for Youth, Inc., 1970. NTISPB 199437.

———; Feifer, Irwin. *Fulfilling the Potential of NYC-2: Linking the Neighborhood Youth Corps and MA-JOBS Program into a Sequential Training Employment Model.* Manpower Monograph Series on Disadvantaged Youth, No. 11. New York: Experimental Manpower Laboratory, Mobilization for Youth, Inc., 1972. NTISPB 213898.

Mandell, Wallace; Blackman, Sheldon; and Sullivan, Clyde E. *Disadvantaged Youth Approaching the World of Work: A Study of NYC Enrollees in New York City.* New York: Wakoff Research Center, 1969. NTISPB 189015.

Miles, Guy H. *Developing Model NYC Programs for Rural Youth—Phase I.* Minneapolis: North Star Research and Development Institute, 1971. NTISPB 202826.

———. *Phase I—Optimizing the Benefits of Neighborhood Youth Corps Projects For Rural Youth.* Final report. Minneapolis: North Star Research and Development Institute, n.d. NTISPB 212407.

———. Henry, William F.; Taylor, Ronald N. *Final Report on Optimizing the Benefits of Neighborhood Youth Corps Projects for Rural Youth—Phase II: A Follow-Up Study of 1144 Young Adults.* Minneapolis: North Star Research and Development Institute, n.d.

National Commission on Resources for Youth, Inc. *The Youth Tutoring Youth Model for In-School Neighborhood Youth Corps: An Evaluation—Final Report.* New York: National Commission on Resources for Youth, Inc., 1972.

Orth, Charles D.; and Jacobs, Frederick. *Demonstration Project to Design, Develop, and Teach a Model Health Care Program for the Neighborhood Youth Corps.* Weston, Massachusetts: Career Development International, 1973. NTISPB 221456.

Paolitto, Ralph A., Jr. *Final Report: In-School Neighborhood Youth Corps Project in the Area of Action Research.* New Haven: Education and Training Association, Inc., 1972. NTISPB 219641.

Reinish, Harold. *Fulfilling the Potential of NYC-2: Combining Professional Roles to Optimize Program Delivery.* Manpower Monograph Series on Disadvantaged Youth, No. 19. New York: Experimental Manpower Laboratory, Mobilization for Youth, Inc., 1972. NTISPB 213988.

———. *Fulfilling the Potential of NYC-2: Guidelines for Effective Placement and Follow-Up on Outstationed NYC-2 Job Training Sites.* Manpower Monograph Series on Disadvantaged Youth, No. 16. New York: Experimental Manpower Laboratory, Mobilization for Youth, Inc., 1972. NTISPB 213987.

Robin, Gerald D. *An Assessment of the In-Public School Neighborhood Youth Corps Projects Projects in Cincinnati and Detroit, with Special Reference to Summer-Only and Year-Round Enrollees.* Final report. Philadelphia: National Analysts, Inc., 1969.

Rodriguez, Emily, Schenkman, Jerome G. *Fulfilling the Potetntial of NYC-2: Using Government Agencies for Training the Disadvantaged for Employment in the Public and Private Sectors—II. The Consortium Model.* Manpower Monograph Series on Disadvantaged Youth, No. 12. New York: Experimental Manpower Laboratory, Mobilization for Youth, Inc., 1972. NTISPB 213896.

Schenkman, Jerome G. *Fulfilling the Potential of NYC-2: Integrating Remedial Education into Neighborhood Youth Corps Training Programs.* Manpower Monograph Series on Disadvantaged Youth, No. 1. New York: Experimental Manpower Laboratory, Mobilization for Youth, Inc., 1970. NTISPB199437.

Seldin, Joel R. *Fulfilling the Potential of NYC-2: Dropout Prevention—A Proposed Model for Utilizing NYC-2 to Facilitate Career Education.* Manpower Monograph Series on Disadvantaged Youth, No. 15. New York: Experimental Manpower Laboratory, Mobilization for Youth, Inc., 1972. NTISPB 213986.

———. *Fulfilling the Potential of NYC-2: Refining NYC-2 Guidelines Toward an Expanded Definition of Assessment.* Manpower Monograph Series on Disadvantaged Youth, No. 14. New York: Experimental Manpower Laboratory, Mobilization for Youth, Inc., 1972. NTISPB 213985.

———. *Fulfilling the Potential of NYC-2: Toward An Expanded Definition of Assessment—I. The Determination of Viable Job Training Areas.* Manpower Monograph Series on Disadvantaged Youth, No. 17. New York: Experimental Manpower Laboratory, Mobilization for Youth, Inc., 1972. NTISPB 213989.

Somers, Gerald G.; Stromsdorfer, Ernst W. *A Cost-Effectiveness Study of the In-School and Summer Neighborhood Youth Corps.* Madison: Industrial Relations Research Institute, University of Wisconsin, 1970.

Tobias, Richard. *Fulfilling the Potential of NYC-2: New Directions in the Vocational Counseling of Neighborhood Youth Corps Trainees.* Manpower Monography Series on Disadvantaged Youth, No. 3. New York: Experimental Manpower Laboratory. Mobilization for Youth, Inc., 1970.

Walther, Regis H. *A Longitudinal Study of Selected Out-of-School NYC-2 Programs in Four Cities: Report of Phase I (Site Selection and Data Forms).* Washington, D. C.: Manpower Research Projects, George Washington University, 1970. NTISPB 210176.

———; Magnusson, Margaret L; and Cherkasky, Shirley E. *A Longitudinal Study of Out-of-School NYC-2 Programs in Four Cities: Report on Phase II (Research Sites and Enrollee Characteristics).* Washington, D. C.: Manpower Research Projects, George Washington University, 1972. NTISPB 210177.

———. *A Study of the Effectiveness of the Graham Associates' Demonstration Project on NYC-2 Education Programming—Final Report*. Washington, D. C.: Manpower Research Projects, George Washington University, 1973.

———. *A Study of the Effectiveness of Selected Out-of-School Neighborhood Youth Corps Programs (A Study of Selected NYC-1 Projects).* Washington, D. C.: Social Research Group. George Washington University, 1971. NTIS PB 187933.

———. *A Study of the Effectiveness of Selected Out-of-School Neighborhood Youth Corps Programs—Implications for Program Operations and Research* Washington, D. C.: Social Research Group, George Washington University, 1969. NTISPB 187963.

Unpublished Studies

Brown, George P., Jr. *et al.* "Analysis of the Neighborhood Youth Corps Program." Memorandum. Center for Naval Analysis, December 19, 1972.

Computer Application Incorporated. "Preliminary Design of Comprehensive Evaluation System for the Neighborhood Youth Corps." Prepared by Social Science Research Department, Education and Training Departments, Computer Application. Inc., report prepared for Office of Policy, Evaluation and Research, Manpower Administration, U. S. Department of Labor, 1969.

Dunlap and Associates, Inc. "Final Report—Survey of Terminees from Out-of-School Neighborhood Youth Corps Projects, Vol. I: Summary of Findings." Report prepared for Office of Policy, Evaluation, and Research, Manpower Administration, U. S. Department of Labor, 1968.

Eckerman, William C.; Gerstel, Eva K.; and Williams, Richard B. "A Comprehensive Assessment of the Problems and Characteristics of the Neighborhood Youth Corps Enrollees: A Pilot Investigation." Report prepared for Office of Policy, Evaluation, and Research, Manpower Administration, U. S. Department of Labor, 1969.

Harwood, Edwin; Olasov, Robert. "Houston's Out-of-School Neighborhood Youth Corps: A Comparative Observational Study of NYC's Impact on Work Attitudes and Job Futures of Poverty Youth." Rice University, Department of Anthropology and Sociology, 1968.

Herman, Melvin; Sadofsky, Stanley. "Study of the Meaning, Experience, and Effects of the Neighborhood Youth Corp on Negro Youth Who are Seeking Work. Part V: Neighborhood Youth Corps Six Months after Enrollment—A Follow-up Study." Center for Study of the Unemployed, Graduate School of Social Work, New York University, 1968.

Miles,Guy H. "Report on Survey of Recent Literature Relevant to Optimizing the Benefits of Neighborhood Youth Corps Projects for Rural Youth." North Star Research and Development Institute, 1968.

Mobilization for Youth, Inc. "An Experiment to Test Three Major Issues of Work Program Methodology Within Mobilization for Youth's Integrated Services to Out-of-School Unemployed Youth." Twenty-month report prepared for Office of Policy, Evaluation and Research, Manpower Administration, U. S. Department of Labor. Mobilization for Youth, Inc., 1967.

Smith, Robert S.; Pitcher, Hugh H. "The Neighborhood Youth Corps: An Impact Evaluation." Preliminary working draft, Technical Analysis Paper No. 9. Office of Evaluation, Office of the Assistant Secretary of Policy, Evaluation and Research, Manpower Administration, U. S. Department of Labor, 1973.

Sykes, Richard E. *et al.* "A Pilot Study in Observational Measurement of Behavioral Factors Associated with Increased Employability of Out-of-School Neighborhood Youth Corps Enrollees." Final Report. University of Minnesota, 1969.

Training, Research and Development, Inc. "Evaluation of the 1971 Neighborhood Youth Corps Summer Recreation Support Program." Final Report prepared for Manpower Administration, U. S. Department of Labor, 1972.

U. S. Department of Labor. "Report of an Evaluation Study of the NYC Out-of-School Program." Report prepared for Office of Policy, Evaluation, and Research, Manpower Administration, U. S. Department of Labor, 1966.

Walther, Regis H. "A Retrospective Study of the Effectiveness of the Cincinnati Out-of-School Neighborhood Youth Corps Program." Social Research Group, George Washington University, 1967.

———. "A Study of the Effectiveness of Selected Out-of-School Neighborhood Youth Corps Program: The Measurement of Work-Relevant Attitudes—A Progress Report on the Development of a Measuring Instrument." Social Research Group, George Washington University, 1969.

———; Magnusson, Margaret L. "A Retrospective Study of the Effectiveness of the Out-of-School Neighborhood Youth Corps Programs in Four Urban Sites." Social Research Group, George Washington University, 1967.

———. "A Study of the Effectiveness of Selected Out-of-School Neighborhood Youth Corps Programs: The Cincinnati Clerical Co-Op: A Formal Skill Training Program." Social Research Group, George Washington University, 1969.

———. "A Study of the Effectiveness of Selected Out-of-School Neighborhood Youth Corps Programs: A Study of Terminated Enrollees in Three Urban Out-of-School Neighborhood Youth Corps Programs." Social Research Group. George Washington University, 1969.

———; Cherkasky, Shirley E. "The Accelerated Learning Experiment: An Approach to the Remedial Education of Out-of-School Youth." Final report. Social Research Group, George Washington University, 1969.

———. "A Study of the Effectiveness of Selected Out-of-School Neighborhood Youth Corps Programs: Implications for Program Operations and Research." Social Research Group, George Washington University, 1969.

OPERATION MAINSTREAM

Published Studies

Aun, Emil Michael. "Senior Aides: Fighting Stereotypes." *Manpower* 4 (February 1972): 7-12.

BWTP Research Contracts Group. *Research Issues and Priorities in the Operation Mainstream Program.* Washington, D. C.: Office of Manpower Research, Manpower Administration, U. S. Department of Labor, 1968.

Somers, Gerald G. *The Training and Placement of Older Workers: An Evaluation of Four Community Projects.* Madison: Center for Studies in Technical and Vocational Education, University of Wisconsin, 1967.

U. S. Congress. Senate. Committee on Labor and Public Welfare. *Report No. 599.* 89th Cong. 1st sess., 1965.

U. S. Department of Labor. "Crosstides in Mainstream." *Manpower* 4 (July 1972): 29-32.

Unpublished Studies

Berry, Dale W.; Sandusky, Nancy; and Dresser, Steven Van. "National Evaluation of Operation Mainstream—Phase I: The Green Thumb-Green Light Program; Phase II: The Senior Aides Program; Phase III (Part I): Regionally Administered I-B Programs; Phase III (Part II): Regionally Administered I-F Programs; Phase IV: Comparative Analysis." Kirschner Associates, Inc. Report prepared for Office of Policy, Evaluation, and Research, Manpower Administration, U. S. Department of Labor, 1971.

OPPORTUNITIES INDUSTRIALIZATION CENTERS

Published Studies

Anderson, Bernard E.; Young, Harvey A. *An Evaluation of the Opportunities Industrialization Center, Inc.—Charleston, W. Va.* Philadelphia: Industrial Research Unit, The Wharton School, University of Philadelphia, 1968.

———. *An Evaluation of the Opportunities Industrialization Center, Inc.—Erie, Pennsylvania.* Philadelphia: Industrial Research Unit, The Wharton School, University of Pennsylvania, 1968.

Lawrence, Marvin E. *Training the Hard-Core in an Urban Labor Market—The Case of the Bedford-Stuyvesant Opportunities Industrialization Center.* Philadelphia: Industrial Research Unit, The Wharton School, University of Pennsylvania, 1970.

Legal Resources, Inc. *Opportunities Industrialization Centers*: A *Synthesis and Analysis of Fifteen OIC Final Reports.* Washington, D. C.: Legal Resources, Inc., 1969. NTISPB 199551.

OIC National Institute. *The New Institute's Bi-Monthly Progress Report—No. 3.* Philadelphia: OIC National Institute. February-March 1969.

———. *Final Report Draft.* Philadelphia: OIC National Institute, 1969.

———. *Helping Others to Help Themselves—Final Report.* Philadelphia: OIC National Institute, 1970.

———. *Opportunities Industrialization Centers, Inc.—Annual Report*: 1971-1972. Philadelphia: OIC National Institute, 1972.

———. *OIC Program Source Book*. Philadelphia: OIC National Institute, 1969.

———. *OIC:The Way Out*. 8th Annual Convention, February 13-16, 1972. Philadelphia: OIC National Institute, 1972.

Peterson, Richard B. *An Evaluation of the Seattle Opportunities Industrialization Center*. Seattle: Graduate School of Business Administration, University of Washington, 1968.

Robinson, Noah. *The Opportunities Industrialization Center—Jacksonville, Florida.* Philadelphia: Industrial Research Unit, The Wharton School, University of Pennsylvania, 1970.

Scott, David A. *An Evaluation of the Washington Institute for Employment Training—The Opportunities Industrialization Center of Washington, D. C.* Philadelphia: Industrial Research Unit, The Wharton School, University of Pennsylvania, 1969.

Sullivan, Leon. *Build, Brother, Build.* Philadelphia: Macrae Smith Co, 1969.

Unpublished Studies

A. L. Nellum and Associates. "An Evaluation of the Opportunities Industrialization Center of Greater Milwaukee." Report prepared for Office of Policy, Evaluation and Research, Manpower Administration, U. S. Department of Labor, 1968.

Barry, Francis D. "The Roxbury Opportunities Industrialization Center—An Economic Case Study of Self-Help Job Training in the Ghetto." Master's Thesis, Cornell University, 1973.

Greenleigh Associates, Inc. "A Pilot Study of the Opportunities Industrialization Center—Philadelphia, Pennsylvania." Report prepared for Ford Foundation and Office of Economic Opportunity, 1967.

———. "An Overall Review Report—The Opportunities Industrialization Center for Greater Milwaukee." Report prepared for Office of Policy, Evaluation and Research, Manpower Administration, U. S. Department of Labor, 1968.

Jahina, Gool; Anderson, Bernard E. "Summary Report on Opportunities Industrialization Centers Training Program." Report prepared for the Department of Records Management and Evaluation of the Philadelphia OIC, 1967.

Newsome, Moses. "A Self-Help Prevocational Demonstration Program." Report formed a request for federal funds for the Charleston, West Virginia, OIC. February 5, 1968-January 31, 1969.

Philadelphia OIC, Office of Research and Evaluation. "A Survey of Hard-Core Unemployed OIC Trainees." Report prepared for Philadelphia OIC, 1968.

PUBLIC EMPLOYMENT PROGRAM

Published Studies

Comptroller General of the United States. *Review of the Allocation of Funds for the Public Employment Program Under the Emergency Employment Act of 1971*. Washington, D. C.: General Accounting Office, 1971.

Greenleigh Associates, Inc. *A Public Employment Program for the Unemployed Poor*. New York: Greenleigh Associates, Inc., 1965.

Johnson, Deborah; Moser, Collette. *Essays on the Public Employment Program in Rural Areas*. East Lansing: Center for Rural Manpower and Public Affairs, Michigan State University, 1973.

Lowenburg, J. Joseph. *et al. The Impact of Employee Unions on the Public Employment Program*. Philadelphia: Temple University, 1973.

National Urban Coalition. *The Public Employment Program: An Evaluation*. Washington, D. C.: National Urban Coalition, 1972.

National Civil Service League. *Public Employment and the Disadvantaged*. Washington, D. C.: National Civil Service League, 1971. NTISPB 203450.

Sheppard, Harold L. *The Nature of the Job Problem and the Role of New Public Service Employment, Kalamazoo*: W. F. Upjohn Institute, 1969.

Turner, Marjorie S. *The First Year Experience with Public Emergency Employment: San Diego City and County*. San Diego: California State University, 1972.

U. S. Congress. Senate. Committee on Labor and Public Welfare. Subcommittee on Employment, Poverty, and Migratory Labor. *Case studies of the Emergency Employment Act in Operation; Evaluation of the First 18 Months of the Public Employment Program*. 93d Cong. 1st sess., 1973.

———. Senate. Committee on Labor and Public Welfare. Subcommittee on Employment, Poverty, and Migratory Labor. *The Emergency Employment Act: An Interim Assessment*. 92d Cong. 1st sess., 1972.

———. Senate. Committee on Labor and Public Welfare. Subcommittee on Employment, Manpower, and Poverty. *Delay in Hiring of Persons under the Public Employment Program; Report on the Preparation and Approval of Plans to Implement the Public Employment Program; Selection and Enrollment of Participants in Programs Under the Emergency Employment Act of 1971;* and *Types of Jobs Offered to Unemployed Persons Under the Emergency Employment Act of 1971*. 92d Cong. 1st sess., 1972.

U. S. Department of Labor. *PEP Talk: A Technical Bulletin of the Public Employment Program*. Washington, D. C.: U. S. Department of Labor. February 1972 through March 1973.

———, Manpower Administration. *Public Employment Program—Annual Report to Congress*. Washington, D. C.: U. S. Department of Labor, 1973.

———. *Public Employment Program Handbook*. Washington, D. C.: U. S. Department of Labor, 1972.

Yaffa, Ellen. "Replies to Questionnaire from Emergency Employment Act Program Agents." in U. S. Congress. Senate. Committee on Labor and Public Welfare. Subcommittee on Employment, Manpower, and Poverty. *Comprehensive Manpower Reform, 1972*. 92d Cong. sess., 1972.

Unpublished Studies

Auerbach Associates, Inc. "The Participants: Wave I Interview Data, Sixth Special Report, Welfare Demonstration Evaluation Project." Report prepared for Manpower Administration, U. S. Department of Labor, 1973.

National Planning Association. "A Preliminary Analysis of the Impact of the Public Employment Program on its Participants." Report prepared for Manpower Administration, U. S. Department of Labor, 1972.

WESTAT Research, Inc. "Longitudinal Analysis of the Public Employment Program: Wave I Analysis." Report prepared for Office of Policy, Evaluation, and Research, Manpower Administration, U. S. Department of Labor, 1972.

PUBLIC SERVICE CAREERS AND NEW CAREERS

Published Studies

Falk, Frank R. *The Frontier of Action: New Careers for the Poor—A Viable Concept*. Minneapolis: General College and Minnesota Center for Sociological Research, n.d.

Rutstein, Jacob J. *Emergency Action Plan for Public Service Employment* Washington, D. C.: National Civil Service League, 1971. NTISPB 202818.

———; Schick, Richard. *Manpower Planning Strategies for Emergency Public Employment*. Washington, D. C.: National Civil Service League, 1972. NTISPB 213686.

Thompson, Margaret. "The New Careerist: A Description." In Frank R. Falk, *The Frontier of Action: New Careers for the Poor—A Viable Concept*. Minneapolis: General College and Minnesota Center for Sociological Research, n.d.

U. S. Department of Labor. *Clerical Procedures—Manpower Automated Reporting System (MARS), Project Status System, PSC*. Washington, D. C.: Government Printing Office, 1971.

———. *Public Service Careers Program Plan "A" and Plan "B" Handbook*. Washington, D. C.: U. S. Department of Labor, 1970.

———. *New Careers in State Employment Security Agencies (NCES)—Program Reporting Requirements*. Washington, D. C.: U. S. Department of Labor, 1971.

Unpublished Studies

RMC Incorporated. "Evaluation of the PSC Program—Final Report, Vol. 1: Findings and Conclusions; Vol. 2: Second Round Site Visit Results; Vol. 3: Second Round Interview Results". Report prepared for Office of Policy, Evaluation, and Research, Manpower Administration, U. S. Department of Labor, 1972.

WORK INCENTIVE PROGRAM

Published Studies

Associate Control, Research, and Analysis, Inc. *A Legal Analysis of Work and Training Requirements Under the Work Incentive Program.* Washington, D. C., 1973. NTISPB 220568.

Auerback Corporation. *An Impact Evaluation of the Work Incentive Program.* Philadelphia: Auerback Corporation, 1972.

———. *An Appraisal of the Work Incentive Program.* Philadelphia: Auerback Corporation, 1970.

———. *Special Report on Unable-to-Locate Respondents in the WIN Longitudinal Study.* Philadelphia: Auerback Corporation, 1970.

———. *WIN Systems Analysis: Final Report and WIN Model.* Philadelphia: Auerback Corporation, 1971.

Diamond, David E.; Bedrosian, Hrach. *The Impact of Manpower Placement and Training Programs on Low Wage Industries and Occupations.* New York: College of Business and Public Administration, New York University, 1971.

Feldman, Harold; Feldman, Margaret. *A Study of the Effects on the Family Due to Employment of the Welfare Mother. Vol. I-II.* Ithaca: College of Human Ecology, Cornell University, 1972. NTISPB 209019.

Fine, Ronald A. *et al. Final Report—AFDC Employment and Referral Guidelines.* Minneapolis: Institute for Interdisciplinary Studies, 1972.

Franklin, Davis S. *A Longitudinal Study of WIN Dropouts: Program and Policy Implications.* Los Angeles: Regional Research Institute in Social Welfare, University of Southern California, 1972. NTISPB 212033.

Gold, Stephen F. "The Failure of the WIN Program." *University of Pennsylvania Law Review* 119. (January 1971): 485-501.

Goodwin, Leonard. *A Study of the Work Orientations of Welfare Recipients Participating in the Work Incentive Program.* Washington, D. C.: The Brookings Institutions, 1971. NTISPB 202812.

Henry, William F.; Miles, Guy H. *Alternatives to the Current WIN Approach in Rural Areas—Final Report.* Minneapolis: North Star Research and Development Institute, 1972.

———. *The Present Status of the WIN Program in Rural Areas.* Minneapolis: North Star Research and Development Institute, 1972.

———. *Rural Counties not Currently Served by WIN.* Minneapolis: North Star Research and Development Institute, 1972.

———; Reid, Joseph M.; and Miles, Guy H. *The WIN Program in Rural Areas: Recommendations.* Minneapolis: North Star Research and Development Institute, 1973.

Innman, Eugene. *Characteristics and Components Study of Work Incentive Program Enrollees Who Terminated in 1970.* Sacramento: Department of Human Resources, State of California, 1973.

Kern, Richard P.; Caylor, John S. *Analysis of WIN Team Functioning and Job Requirements—Phase I: Duties and Tasks Performed by Teams and Team Members*. Alexandria: Human Resources Research Organization, 1971. NTISPB 202811.

Klausner, Samuel. *et al. The Work Incentive Program: Making Adults Economically Independent*. Philadelphia: University of Pennsylvania, 1972. NTISPB 220204, 220205.

Lowenthal, Martin. *et al. Final Report—WIN II Initial Impact Study*. Boston: Social Welfare Regional Research Institute, Boston College, 1972.

Macek, Albert J.; Thompson, David L.; and Miles, Guy H. *A Study of Low-Income Families: Implications for the Win Program*. Minneapolis: North Star Research and Development Institute, 1972. NTISPB 211702.

Miles, Guy H.; Thompson, David L. *The Characteristics of the AFDC Population that Affect Their Success in WIN—Final Report*. Minneapolis: North Star Research and Development Institute, 1972. NTISPB 219391.

Munger, Paul F. *et al. Employability Team Interaction Analysis: An Exploratory Study, Stage III*. Bloomington: Indiana University Foundation, 1971. NTISPB 222074.

Opton, Edward M. *Factors Associated with Employment Among Welfare Mothers*. Berkeley: The Wright Institute, 1971. NTISPB 201109.

Osborn, William C. *Development of a Program of Instruction for WIN Employability Orientation*. Alexandria: Human Resources Research Organization, 1972. NTISPB 210090.

Parvis, Richard J.; Carroll, Nancy K. *An Exploratory Study of Some Major Impediments to Success in the WIN Program*. St. Louis: George Warren Brown School of Social Work. Washington University, 1971.

Reid, William J.; Smith, Audrey, D. *Decision-Making in the WIN Program*. Chicago: School of Social Services Administration, University of Chicago, 1972.

Roessner, J. David.; Hamilton, Gloria Shaw. *Employment Contexts and Disadvantaged Workers*. Washington, D. C.: Bureau of Social Science Research, Inc.,1971. NTISPB 206492.

———. *Youth in the WIN Program—Final Report Draft*. Report prepared for Office of Policy, Evaluation, and Research, Manpower Administration, U. S. Department of Labor, 1972.

Schappi, John V. *Tax Credit for Wages Paid to Workers Hired from WIN of Welfare Rolls*. Special Personnel Policies Forum Survey. Washington, D. C.: Bureau of National Affairs. n.d.

Schiller, Bradley R. *The Impact of Urban WIN Programs—Phase II: Final Report*. Washington, D. C.: Pacific Training and Technical Assistance Corporation, 1972. NTISPB 210469.

Smith Georgina M. *The WIN Program—Job Training for Welfare Mothers*. New Brunswick, New Jersey: Institute of Management and Labor Relations, Rutgers University, 1972.

U. S. Congress. House. Committee on Ways and Means. *Work Incentive Program—Survey of Selected Welfare and Employment Service Agencies.* 91st Cong. 1st sess., 1970.

U. S. Department of Labor. *The WIN Information System Manual.* Washington, D. C.: U. S. Department of Labor, 1970.

Youmans, Rita L.; Miller, Arlene. *A Study of the Relationship of Overindebtedness and Garnishment to Employability Among Milwaukee WIN Families.* Milwaukee: Center for Consumer Affairs, University of Wisconsin, 1971. NTISPB 208335.

Unpublished Studies

Analytic Systems, Inc. "Analysis of WIN Programs Automated Termination Data, 1969." Report prepared for Office of Policy, Evaluation, and Research, Manpower Administration, U. S. Department of Labor, 1970.

———. "Analysis of WIN Program Termination Data, Fiscal Year 1970." Report prepared for Office of Policy, Evaluation, and Research, Manpower Administration, U. S. Department of Labor, 1971.

Camil Associates, Inc. "Abstracts of Studies Relevant to the Understanding of WIN or WIN Components." A bibliography prepared for Manpower Administration, U. S. Department of Labor, n.d.

———. "Welfare Dependency, Termination, and Employment: An AFDC Case Review." Report prepared for Department of Health, Education and Welfare, 1972.

Gavin, Charles D. "Incentives and Disincentives to Participation in the Work Incentive Program, First Draft Report, August 1973." Report prepared for Research and Development, Manpower Administration, U. S. Department of Labor, 1973.

Schiller, Bradley R. "Discrimination in WIN Training Programs." Report prepared for Office of Policy, Evaluation, and Research, Manpower Administration, U. S. Department of Labor, 1973.

———. "Welfare Reform: A Synthesis of Research on the WIN Programs." Report prepared for Office of Research and Development, Manpower Administration, U. S. Department of Labor, n.d.

U. S. Department of Labor, "The Work Incentive Program: Second Annual Report of the Department of Labor to the Congress on Training and Employment Under Title IV of the Social Security Act, June 1971."

———. Manpower Administration. "The Work Incentive Program and National Manpower Policy—A Working Paper for the 37th Meeting of the National Manpower Advisory Committee." 1973.

Index

D0518456